Managing Knowledge for Global and Collaborative Innovations

Series on Innovation and Knowledge Management

Series Editor: Suliman Hawamdeh *(University of Oklahoma)* **ISSN: 1793-1533**

Vol. 1 Managing Strategic Enterprise Systems and e-Goverment Initiatives in Asia: A Casebook
edited by Pan Shan-Ling *(National University of Singapore)*

Vol. 2 Knowledge Management: Through the Technology Glass
by Meliha Handzic *(University of New South Wales)*

Vol. 3 Governing and Managing Knowledge in Asia
edited by Thomas Menkhoff *(Singapore Management University)*, Hans-Dieter Evers *(Bonn University)* and Yue Wah Chay *(Nanyang Technological University)*

Vol. 4 Managing Emerging Technologies and Organizational Transformation in Asia: A Casebook
edited by Pan Shan-Ling *(National University of Singapore)*

Vol. 5 Creating Collaborative Advantage Through Knowledge and Innovation
edited by Suliman Hawamdeh *(University of Oklahoma)*

Vol. 6 Knowledge Management: Innovation, Technology and Cultures
edited by Christian Stary *(Johannes Kepler University, Austria)*, Franz Barachini *(Vienna University of Technology, Austria)* and Suliman Hawamdeh *(University of Oklahoma, USA)*

Vol. 7 Knowledge Management: Competencies and Professionalism
edited by Suliman Hawamdeh *(University of Oklahoma, USA)*, Kimberly Stauss *(University of Arkansas, USA)* and Franz Barachini *(Vienna University of Technology, Austria)*

Vol. 8 Managing Knowledge for Global and Collaborative Innovations
edited by Samuel Chu *(The University of Hong Kong)*, Waltraut Ritter *(Knowledge Dialogues, Hong Kong)* and Suliman Hawamdeh *(University of Oklahoma, USA)*

Series on Innovation and Knowledge Management – Vol. 8

Managing Knowledge for Global and Collaborative Innovations

Editors

Samuel Chu

The University of Hong Kong, Hong Kong

Waltraut Ritter

Knowledge Dialogues, Hong Kong

Suliman Hawamdeh

University of Oklahoma, USA

World Scientific

NEW JERSEY • LONDON • SINGAPORE • BEIJING • SHANGHAI • HONG KONG • TAIPEI • CHENNAI

Published by

World Scientific Publishing Co. Pte. Ltd.
5 Toh Tuck Link, Singapore 596224
USA office: 27 Warren Street, Suite 401-402, Hackensack, NJ 07601
UK office: 57 Shelton Street, Covent Garden, London WC2H 9HE

British Library Cataloguing-in-Publication Data
A catalogue record for this book is available from the British Library.

MANAGING KNOWLEDGE FOR GLOBAL AND COLLABORATIVE INNOVATIONS
Series on Innovation and Knowledge Management — Vol. 8

ISBN-13 978-981-4299-85-5
ISBN-10 981-4299-85-5

Printed in Singapore by World Scientific Printers

CONTENTS

PREFACE

Collaboration continues to be one of the difficult challenges for individuals and organizations. This year's ICKM coincides with the world's largest collaboration exercise, the UN Global Climate Summit in Copenhagen, where collaboration capabilities between stakeholders from government, business, science, and civil society determine our future. While our collaboration infrastructure has advanced significantly over the last few years with the development of social computing tools and models, we still need to rethink our strategies and business models to become more adaptive and responsive, focusing less on formal structure and hierarchies. Social collaboration and network tools allow us to "prepare the mind" for partnerships and different forms of thinking. Many of our traditional business models, public organizational structures, and educational systems are not yet ready for new forms of decision-making, problem-solving and collaboration that go beyond organizational boundaries. Concepts like "open innovation", "value networks", "wisdom of crowds" are some of the ideas that influence our thinking on collaboration and information sharing.

The move to open innovation and value networks can be attributed to advances in information and communication technology. We are now living in a knowledge-based society, where value is created through complex dynamic exchanges between individuals and organizations. Drawing upon intellectual capital theory, collaboration can be regarded as relationship capital which creates tangible and intangible value.

Our new understanding of the value of collaboration also takes us back to the roots of Knowledge Management as a social and human discipline. Social aspects of collaboration provide most of the value, while the networks, tools and enabling technologies are only part of the taken-for-granted basic communication infrastructure. Collaboration requires more than the ability to publish, display or aggregate information but rather requires the ability to leverage the know-how of many individuals.

The Internet and the Web are facilitating the dissemination of information and communication exchanges, empowering us to engage in new forms of collaboration, like in the way we gather and create new ideas. Open innovation is a paradigm that assumes organizations should use external as well as internal ideas to sustain their growth.

Many of the knowledge processes such as knowledge creation, utilization and transfer depend on the frequency and density of interaction as well as openness and willingness to adapt to the changes in the business environment. The ability to innovate and create new knowledge has become a major source of competitive advantage in the knowledge society. Today, most innovations are brought into the market by a network of organizations that realized the importance of collaboration and knowledge sharing. This realization is characterized by the complexity associated with the new products and services, the distribution of skills and competency in different regions of the world. The knowledge economy has opened the door for organizations to tap expertise and skills remotely without the need to physically bring such skills into one geographical location as it was in the industrial era.

Managing collaboration goes beyond merely managing technologies necessary for people to communicate. It involves leveraging partner's capabilities as well as gaining access to the knowledge and relationship that partners possess. Successful organizations focused on knowledge transfer between teams and building collaborative capabilities with the objective of maintaining competitive advantage. We are moving from the decade of personal and organizational productivity to the decade of inter-personal productivity where value is created through relationships and networks.

Samuel Chu
Waltraut Ritter
Suliman Hawamdeh

TECHNOLOGICAL AND KNOWLEDGE DIFFUSION THROUGH INNOVATION NETWORKS

BEATRIZ HELENA NETO

COPPE/UFRJ, Federal University of Rio de Janeiro (UFRJ), Mailbox 68.511
Rio de Janeiro, RJ, ZIP: 21941-972, Brazil
beatrizneto@cos.ufrj.br

JANO MOREIRA† DE SOUZA and JONICE DE OLIVEIRA

†COPPE/UFRJ, Federal University of Rio de Janeiro (UFRJ), Mailbox 68.511
DCC/IM/UFRJ, Federal University of Rio de Janeiro (UFRJ)
Rio de Janeiro, RJ, ZIP: 21941-972, Brazil
{jano†, jonice}@cos.ufrj.br

This paper is a study about innovation and its role in transforming society. Currently, organizations need to be more competitive to keep itself in a dynamic and globalized market. Innovation emerges as a strategy for survival, as well as a competitive advantage for organization. Innovation and knowledge management creates new business opportunities and acquisition of assets. Organizations meet to development of an innovation, forming networks of innovation in order to reduce the innovative process' risks and improve their technology knowledge.

1. Introduction

Currently, the life cycle of products decreases, while the need of organizations to improve their products and services increases. R&D activities costs grow in an attempt to supply needs inherent dynamism of the capitalist market. The organizations endeavor to remain in the market and monitor their competitors - competitors are willing innovating their products, services or management processes to gain market - in order to overcome them.

Many organizations value the stability, protecting old ideas and techniques in place of renewal and creation of new ideas. Consequently, they do not become sufficiently competitive to survive or to remain in a satisfactory position in the market. According to Porter (1990), organizations that have the ability to deal with pressures and challenges get greater progress in relation to theirs competitors and become more competitive and profitable. Another advantage is the capacity to understand and predict changes in the market, in order that identify and feed beforehand new opportunities for innovation.

The organization uses their knowledge and gets a product, service or process throughout process of innovation. Usually after a certain time, the result of the previous process of innovation suffers a process of incremental innovation. Result of this new process is adapted to meet new needs of the market. Thus, the organizational knowledge generates new knowledge to be reused and recombined in the process of incremental innovation, which may suffer the same process. It illustrates cyclical nature of knowledge in the innovation process.

The organizational knowledge is a determining factor for development of innovation. When an organization decides to innovate, it takes risks. There are risks normally derived from the changes. Innovation requires an appropriate management of process. Therefore, the ability of evaluation and selection of projects is an important dimension of the activities of R&D. Knowledge management allied R&D activities can optimize the process, increasing the innovative capacity of organization.

Innovation comes through extremely complex processes. These processes are related to the emergence, dissemination and combination of knowledge, beyond the transformation of knowledge into new products, services or processes. During the transformation of knowledge, the activities are not necessarily linear, have feedback mechanisms and relations of cooperation between various bodies such as government, university and industry, as observed in the Triple Helix model and between different areas of knowledge such as industry, science and technology, politics and economy.

This paper is a study on role of knowledge management and technological innovation, both combined under forms of cooperation for organizational potential improvement. In section 2, there is a review of the literature about innovation. In section 3, it highlighted the importance of knowledge management for innovation. In section 4, innovation and technological diffusion are discussed. In section 5, there is analysis about networks of innovation. In section 6, innovation analysis models are studied. Section 7 concludes paper and presents suggestions for future works related to this topic of research.

2. Revision about Innovation

According to Marx (1890), innovation is way to get temporary monopoly on superior technique or differentiated product. One of the principles of evolutionary theory is dynamic economy, following Marx and Schumpeter. Dynamic economy is based on innovations in products, processes and forms of organizing production (Tigre, 2006). In doing so, innovations are not necessarily gradual. They may take a radical character that results in instability in the economic system, alternating periods of crisis and prosperity.

Schumpeter made an important distinction between invention and innovation. Invention relates to an idea, sketch or model for improvement or creation of product, while innovation occurs with the effective implementation of invention (Freeman and Soete, 1997). Consequently, it is possible to realize the coexistence of the invention and innovation.

According to Oslo Manual (Finep, 2004), developed by Organization for Economic Cooperation and Development (OECD), all innovation must contain some degree of novelty. Four types of innovations are defined: product innovation, process innovation, organizational innovation and marketing innovation. These innovation types contain a wide range of changes in the company activities.

Product innovation is technological upgrading of existing product or developing a new product technology. Developed product must have different characteristics from other products previously developed by the organization. Products which have only aesthetic changes or which are only sold by the organization and developed by another one are not considered innovations.

Innovation process is the usage of new or improved production technology, as well as methods for handling and delivery new or improved products. Results obtained with this type of innovation change quality and production and product delivery costs.

Organizational innovation is a change in the organization management structure. It can occur in the form of links between its different areas, expertise of employees, relationships with customers and suppliers and business processes.

Innovation marketing implements new methods of marketing, including changes in design of product or package, promotion or placement of product and methods of establishing prices for goods and services.

Initially, innovation is result of interaction between scientific discovery, spreading economic and political power. Innovation systems are designed to develop more than simple changes - transformations that challenge analytical understanding, in the same way that change *status quo*. Concepts are being reshaped. This way, interest on past good performance is replaced by interest in importance knowledge gained has for the future. Nowadays, the problem is how to recombine existing knowledge in improved and new ways in order to supply future demands (Etzkowitz, 2002).

3. Knowledge Role in Innovation Process

According to Penrose (1959), firm is a collection of resources. Creation of new productive services depends on capacity to internalize knowledge needed to develop them and produce them efficiently. The services, generated from new knowledge, depend on training of workers involved in its use. Development of this training is defined in part by resources available for the workers.

Consequently, survival and success of an organization are linked not only with external factors, but also how the organization uses and incorporates knowledge. This method depends on individual and collective capacity of organization. According to Nonaka (1996), knowledge is contextualized in tacit and explicit. Tacit knowledge is personal, difficult to communicate and formalize and belongs to a context specific. While explicit knowledge is transmitted in a formal and systematic language. They are not entirely separate, but complementary, since no experience is not possible to obtain a real understanding of something.

Many innovations are improvements of products, services or processes - incremental innovations. These innovations are based on past experiences and knowledge, i.e. explicit and tacit knowledge. This knowledge generates personal knowledge, which its turn results in organizational knowledge. Experiences and organizational knowledge used in productive activities are important inputs to innovation process.

Efficient dissemination of information and communications technologies permits an increasing transfer of explicit knowledge. However, the transfer of tacit knowledge remains extremely difficult (Lastres, 2004). It impedes development of innovation due to its importance in this process. In an effort to overcome these difficulties, it is necessary to understand systems and local productive arrangements in order to investigate relationships between organizations sets and other participants with their flow of knowledge.

Knowledge in organizations is a competitive advantage and a decisive factor for innovation. Dissemination and sharing of knowledge in the organization, through Knowledge Management should be widely encouraged. Social and cultural barriers imposed and that ultimately hinder acquisition of knowledge must be overcome in order to allow for transformation of personal knowledge into organizational knowledge.

Knowledge, in all its forms, plays a crucial role in current economic processes. Nations have a performance better than other when develop and effectively manage their assets of knowledge (OECD, 1996). And, innovation seems to play a central role in a economy based knowledge.

4. Innovation and Technological Diffusion

According to Edquist and Johnson (1997), technological innovation is introduction of new knowledge or a new combination of existing knowledge in the economy. That is, innovation is result of a process of interactive learning. It is possible to obtain new knowledge or a new combination from different parts of knowledge through interactions in the economy.

Adam Smith (1999) was the first to recognize relationship between technological change and economic growth. He identified two innovations that promote growth of productivity, when following structural changes occurred in England in the eighteenth century: division of labor and development of machinery.

In reference to Tiger (2006), the major technological changes are accompanied by economic, social and institutional changes, since technology doesn't spread in vacuum. In other words, innovation requires legal systems, economic motivation and political and institutional conditions appropriate to develop.

Technological change results of innovative activities, such as R&D investments, besides create opportunities for greater investments in productive capacity (Finep, 2004). Generation of new jobs and additional income are long-term results through technological changes.

According Maculan (2002), technological change follows a trajectory and its result is innovation. This trajectory is constructed based on dominant paradigm and contemporary change. Innovation is a selective activity and has an exact purpose. The technological trajectory is a mechanism that selects the technological alternatives available to achieve this purpose.

Freeman and Soete (1997) classify innovation according to their impact on technology, i.e. which intensity of technological change caused by innovation. This classification consists of four types of technological change: incremental, radical, new technological system and new paradigm technological and economic, as shown in table 1.

Users and consumers' needs (demand-pull), opportunities offered by advances in science and technology (technology push) and costs of production factors induce innovation (Tigre, 2006). According Tidd (2006), adoption of an innovation will depend on interaction between two factors: demand and supply. By contrast in less developed countries, main induction factors are consumers' demands and costs of production factors.

Table 1. Taxonomy of technological change (Freeman and Soete, 1997).

Change Type	Characteristics
Incremental	Continuous improvements and modifications. Its source is not necessarily from R&D activities. Usually, it is result of accumulated learning and internal training.
Radical	Discontinuous changes in technology products and services. It creates a new technological route. Usually, it is a R&D result.
New Technological System	Changes that affect more than one sector and giving rise to new economic activities.
New techno-economic paradigm	Changes that affect the entire economy.

Organization can develop and implement a technological innovation or acquire it from the other organization through process of technological diffusion. In doing so, innovations broadcast and reach different consumers, countries, regions or markets through diffusion (Finep, 2004). Diffusion process is extremely important, because without it there is not how an innovation generates an economic impact on society.

According to Rogers (2003), diffusion of innovation is a process in which an innovation is spread through certain channels over time among members of a social system. It is possible identify four main elements in this definition: innovation, communication channels, time and social system. Innovation itself is defined as an idea, practice or object used by other individuals or segments. Communication channels are means by which information is disseminated. Time is development of innovation, adoption of an innovation by individual or group and rate of adoption. And finally, social system is group of individuals with a common goal - adoption of innovation.

Following innovation characteristics influence the rate and extent of its spread: (i) relative advantage towards rival, compatibility with target consumers' values, experiences and needs, complexity to be understood and used, test capability with pre-defined parameters and level of visibility of innovation (Rogers, 2003 and Tidd, 2006).

Technological diffusion process can be analyzed from four dimensions (Tigre, 2006). Firstly, direction or technology strategy involves decisions in various aspects for creation of a new technology and its adaptation to demand. Besides, it affects the future of innovation.

Second is rate of diffusion. It is speed which society adopts innovation adopted. It can be represented by a logistic function of growth known as "Law of Pearl". Increase companies adopt a new technology depends increase companies already assimilate technology and have potential to assimilate in model analyzed by function.

Third dimension is conditional factors. They act not only positively in order to stimulate adoption of innovation, but also negatively so as discourage adoption. Factors' nature may be: (i) technical, usability determines it; (ii) economic, cost of acquisition and deployment of new technology, such as risks and expectations for return on investment, determine it and (iii) institutional, available incentive tax for innovation, favorable investment climate, trade and investment international agreements, intellectual property system, existence of human capital investment and support institutions, social stratification, culture and religion and political system determine it.

Economic, social and environmental impacts compose fourth dimension. Technological innovation diffusion sources theses impacts. Diffusion can generate economic impacts, affect industrial structure, destroy or create markets, sectors and companies, change economic growth pace and competitiveness between companies and countries. Diffusion of innovation generates social impact, such as change volume of jobs and source or elimination skills, and environmental impacts.

Generally innovation activities need to interact with several innovation system components. Among these components are government laboratories, universities, policy departments, regulators, competitors, suppliers and consumers. Innovation process interactions are internal and external.

Internal interactions play an important role for innovation. Internal information supply of innovation process can be improved through mapping relevant organizational knowledge to innovation and identifying which organization parts are important source of information for innovation activities.

External interactions were classified into three types: open sources of information, cooperative innovation knowledge and technology acquisition (Finep, 2004). Cooperative innovation occurs as active cooperation with other companies or research institutions. It results creation of innovation networks, which will be addressed further in the next section.

5. Innovation Networks

According to Porter (1990), organization can be part of a cluster of large national customers, suppliers and industries have a major competitive advantage, because it has a better vision about future needs of market and technology. Another way to organization obtain a competitive advantage is identify its major rivals in the market, use this information to compare its performance and use results of this comparison as a stimulus for growth and innovation.

In agreement Piori e Sabel (1984), Ford's crisis and fall in global demand resulted in new cooperative arrangements based on flexible specialization. These new forms of production seek to reduce costs, stimulating innovation and greater flexibility in volume and diversity of production.

It is interesting to note that development of new cooperative arrangements occurred mainly in industrial districts and groups with cultural, social and institutional ties favored cooperation and trust. These links are important factors for cooperative arrangements development. Thus, members of the network condemned opportunistic behavior.

According to Tigre (2006), firm networks emerge in organizations because they abandon peripheral activities and transfer them to other organizations. These activities are essential to profitability and safety organizational. Relationship between participants of networks is guided by long-term agreements, mutual commitment with investments in specific assets, logistics integration and unified quality management.

Virtual networks expand organizational reach. They transpose economic limits of industrial district going beyond geographical boundaries. As time goes by, new users join network, its size increases and possibilities of communication between members appear with creation of new connections. So network grows, it becomes more useful to its members and more attractive to new members.

According Lastres (2004), local production and innovative systems (SPILs - Sistemas Produtivos e Inovativos Locais) are sets of economic, political and social agents. Each set is located in same territory and developing economic activities related. These activities are production, interaction, cooperation and learning activities. SPILs keep organizations that work in the area of education and training, information, R&D, engineering, promotion and funding. SPIL is a network of innovation, because of its potential in the area of R&D and cooperation.

Collaboration networks between organizations and public institutions of R&D are widely recognized as an important form of organizational innovation. Innovation *locus* is present in inter-organizational relationship networks so they can support the scientific and technical knowledge flow and improvements (Nesta and Mangematin, 2004).

Interaction and collaboration are important external technological expertise sources. They result in an increase in productivity and competitiveness of organizations through innovation (Freeman, 1991). Thus, a network improves innovation and provides a differential to organization.

Innovation networks structure is related to holding policy industry development about a specific set of knowledge and technologies. According to Freeman (1991), there are 10 subdivisions to innovation networks, as shown in table 2. These subdivisions are not exclusive, that is, organizations may be part of different categories simultaneously.

Organizations can expand to international market. For this, they use theirs national advantages in other nations through alliances or coalitions. These alliances can take different forms among the innovation networks subdivisions.

According to Tidd (2006), purpose for creation of a network may be development of new product or process through combination of different skills that each participant has or meeting of stakeholders interested in adopting and combining innovative ideas.

Participants join due to having interest in same geographical area (cluster) or to being part of a supply chain that tries to develop new ideas for improving system. Participants know that networks provide stimulus necessary to obtain solutions through innovation.

Table 2. Categories of innovation systems.

Subdivisions of Innovation Networks
Joint ventures and research corporations.
Cooperation in research agreements.
Technology transference agreements.
Direct investment driven by technological factors.
Licensing and agreements of outsourcing.
Sub-contracting, production sharing and supplier networks.
Research associations
Research programs sponsored by Government.
Databases and networks of aggregated value used exchange information technical and scientific.
Other networks, including informal networks.

According Oslo Manual (Finep, 2004), cooperative innovation is a type of external interaction or knowledge flow and technologies businesses. It is defined as an "active cooperation with other companies or research institutions for innovation activities (which may include purchases of knowledge and technology)."

There is active involvement of several organizations in the design of innovation in cooperative innovation. Thus, organization has access to information and technologies that could not achieve in isolation. Besides, cooperation has potential for synergies, which participants learn from each other.

Network is heterogeneous. As a result of its various participants often play distinct roles. It is possible to establish relations between participating organizations through four elements: objective of network, dependency between participants to reach goal, implementation of connections between participants and sharing of costs, profits and risks (Lastres, 2004).

It is important for adoption an innovation that it is inedited to all nodes of network and market. Consequently, motivation and encouragement during R&D phases will be equal and all participants will be interested in development, acquisition and use of innovative results.

Organization provides a hierarchical coordination of its process through direct control of main steps of production chain. This way, transaction costs of relations between independent enterprises are minimized. Currently, institutional and technological changes and relations with market have been demanding greater production specialization and more structured forms of cooperation between enterprises (Tigre, 2006). Gradually, networks of firms have replaced verticalization model, in order to address these needs. Companies specialize in their core competencies in networks of firms, while maintaining its scope in the market that it operates.

Several factors stimulate formation of networks: fusion technology, globalization of markets, information and communication technologies and flexible specialization (Tigre, 2006). Fusion technology occurs when technology becomes so complex that no company can develop necessary skills to act at all stages of production chain.

Market globalization happens through open trade and growing competition. It encourages alliances between companies, seeking to obtain forms of empowerment, to resolve problems of more competitive environment. Information and communication technology facilitate cooperation and communication between different organizations and allow information exchange and knowledge management. Flexible specialization is a characteristic of networks to respond market and technology changes. In doing so, network participating adapt to change better than isolation.

Participating organization of a network should define its goals and assess its role and mobility in production chain. That's why it can identify profitable cores and prevent competitive cores. Profitable cores are composed many nodes that aggregate value to organization while competitive cores are composed many nodes which price competition is more stimulated.

Organizations don't choose its network position freely. Unfortunately there are inequalities between network participants. Therefore, organizations need to evaluate network before join it, to create appropriate strategies and to identify profitable core for their participation results in qualitative and quantitative benefits.

6. Innovation Analysis Model

6.1. *Innovation Zones*

Tidd (2006) mapped different types of innovation networks to identify their specific needs and improve network management. Diagram has four zones. Areas are positioned on coordinate axis according to similarity of participating organizations. Areas of abscissa axis are positioned according to radicalism that innovation has developed in comparison to current innovative activities known, as shown in Figure 1.

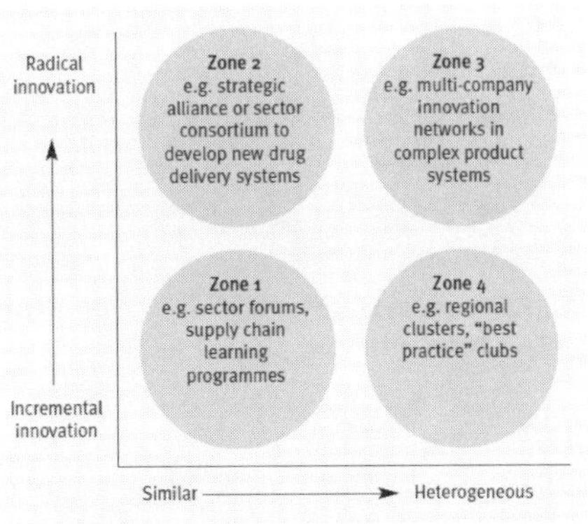

Fig. 1. Types of innovation networks.

Area 1 has companies with a similar orientation. They work with issues of tactical innovation. Usually they are clusters linked adoption and modeling of "best practice" in production. In this type of area, issues to be addressed involve training of networks for sharing experiences, disclose information, build trust and transparency and implement a system that shares goal related to innovation.

Area 2 involves participants with similar orientation, besides industry that creates and explores new concepts of products and services, such as biotechnology and pharmaceuticals networks. In this case, main interest is to explore and challenge existing limits. Information and risks are shared, usually as joint ventures and strategic alliances.

In zones 3 and 4, participants are very heterogeneous and bring different parts of knowledge to network. In order to mitigate risks of knowledge revelation, it is necessary to ensure a careful management of IP and establishment of basic security rules. Source of this type of innovation involves many risks, which makes critical investments in risky environments and encouraging cooperation.

6.2. *Innovation Radar*

Sawhney, Wolcott e Arroniz (2006) proposed a framework called Innovation Radar, shown in Figure 2. This model shows all dimensions in which an organization may search opportunities for innovation. Innovation Radar is divided into four main dimensions: offers created by company, customers attended, processes employed and opportunities used to take their offerings to market.

Besides these four main areas, there are eight dimensions of business system. These subdivisions orient organization. Thus Radar Innovation contains 12 dimensions in total, which are in figure 2.

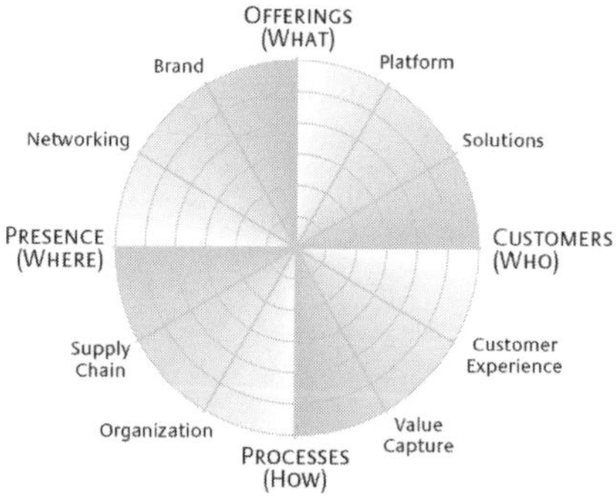

Fig. 2. Innovation Radar and its 12 dimensions.

6.3. *Potter's National Diamond*

According to Potter (1990), innovation creates pressures and challenges. It also arises when certain challenges are identified by organization. Organization leader plays an important role in creating an environment conducive to innovation. One of its key tasks is to create conditions necessary for innovation. National Diamond or Diamond in Potter helps organizational decision make towards this goal. It describes competition in the industry and becomes a useful tool.

Diamond of Potter is a proposed model to help understand competitive advantage of nations. It has 4 factors that are linked between companies: strategy, structure and rivalry of firms, demand conditions, relationship between industry and conditionals factors. Government acts as a catalyst, encouraging companies to achieve high levels of competitiveness. This model can be seen in figure 3.

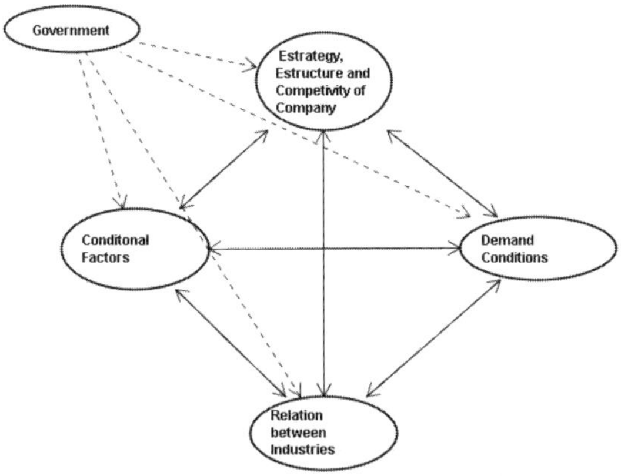

Fig. 3. Potter's National Diamond.

6.4. *Triple Helix Model*

Triple Helix is a model for transformation processes that involve relationship between government, industry and university. Leydesdorff and Etzkowitz (1998) identify 3 main forms of Triple Helix model.

Triple Helix I model is institutionally defined following spheres: university, industry and government. Organizations such as coalitions industrial, technology disseminators and contractors mediate interaction and boundaries between each level.

Propellers of Triple Helix II are defined as communication systems, formed by operations of markets, technological innovations and control interfaces. Interface between these systems operates in a distributed way, producing new forms of communication.

Institutional spheres of Triple Helix III are university, industry and government. Spheres perform their typical functions. In addition to that they act role of other spheres. Interfaces between these different functions work in a distributed function that generates new forms of communication.

According to Etzkowitz (2002), Triple Helix is a spiral innovation model. It captures multiple and reciprocal relationships between different points in knowledge capitalization process. First dimension of model is internal transformation in each helix. Second is influence of a propeller on other. Third dimension is creation of a new aggregation of trilateral networks and organizations from interaction of 3 propellers. Aggregation aims to create new ideas and formats for development of new technologies.

Dynamism of society has changed from a system based on rigid boundaries separating institutional spheres and organizations, for more flexible system of rotation. Each sphere plays the role of the other in this new system. University becomes a company founded by stimulating incubators. Industry becomes an educator through corporative universities. Finally, government a bold venture capitalist through programs of research.

These new models are different from model in which institutional spheres are separated from each other, i.e., there is not cooperation or one dominates other spheres, as shown in Figure 4a and 4b, respectively. Currently, there is a migration to model in which spheres alternate in each role and work together, as shown in Figure 4c.

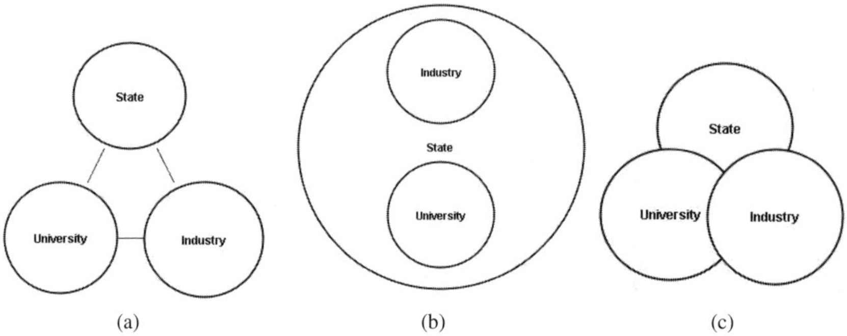

Fig. 4. Triple Helix Models.

7. Conclusion

Greater awareness of innovation importance has made it to be included in agenda of most developed countries. Innovation politics results primarily from science and technology policy, but also significant aspects of industrial policies. Substantial changes in development of policies related to innovation have been achieved. It happens due to innovation understand improvement.

High level of competition requires redefinitions of organizational strategies in order to incorporate more cooperation in theirs activities. Technologies change constantly, for this way access to innovation external sources remains critical to continued technological progress. Innovation and networks alignment has great potential for transforming society, besides offering equilibrium to organizations. In doing so, they can build a stability zone in the market.

In Knowledge Age, innovation and knowledge are main factors for nations development. Competitive and dynamics power construction is a way to combat predatory methods of competition, such as low salaries and exploitation of natural resources. For this, it is necessary organizational knowledge growth and innovation process stimulus.

Challenges of organizations to obtain competitive advantages are participation in new markets; enjoy new technological opportunities; improvement skills of its employees and its collection of knowledge and to overcome inertia to seize new opportunities.

Innovations incessantly transform society. In due this dynamism, it is difficult choices an innovation development model to be followed. Cultural, economic and social characteristics of each region are also factors should be considered. Because they indicate paths and appropriate strategies are not necessarily similar to each region.

Study on innovation networks will be addressed in future work. Studies will aim to identify and assess efficient networks management ways. Survey on use of IT tools to provide support networks innovation. Investigations will specific characteristics of hierarchical and non-hierarchical innovation networks, as well as search improvement ways of management innovation networks. In accordance with this information will propose a model of autonomic innovation networks.

References

Edquist, C. & Johnson, B. (1997). System of innovation: overview and basic concepts. In C. Edquist (Ed). *Systems of innovation: technologies, institutions and organizations*. Abigdon, OX: Routledge Press from http://books.google.com/books?hl=ptR&lr=&id=Sf0POR0ffWEC&oi=fnd&pg=PT8&dq=innovation+edquist&ots=7oklC3f6v8&sig=hcHSQ8WaFoN8Yie_cOmBbUkzZ00#v=onepage&q=&f=false.

Etzkowitz, H. (2002). The triple helix of university – industry – government implications for policy and evaluation. [Working paper 2002·11]. *Institutet för Studier av Utbildning och Forskning. Stockholm*, SE from http://www.sister.nu/pdf/wp_11.pdf.

Financiadora de Estudos e Projetos – Finep. (2004). *Manual de Oslo: proposta de diretrizes para coleta e interpretação de dados sobre inovação tecnológica* [Manual]. FINEP and Organisation for Economic Co-operation for Development – OECD from http://www.finep.gov.br/imprensa/sala_imprensa/manual_de_oslo.pdf.

Freeman, C. (1991). Network of innovators: a synthesis of research issues. Research. Policy n° 20, pp. 499-514.

Freeman, C. & Soete, L. (1997). *The economics of industrial innovation* (3rd ed). Cambridge, MA: MIT Press.

Lastres, M. H. (2004). *Política para inovação de arranjos produtivos e inovativos locais de micro e pequenas empresas: vantagens e restrições do conceito e equívocos usuais* (Report of activities) Rio de Janeiro, RJ, Federal University of Rio de Janeiro from http://www.redesist.ie.ufrj.br/nt_count.php?projeto=ar1&cod=1.

Leydesdorff, L. & Etzkowitz, H. (1998). *The triple helix as a model for innovation studies* (Conference Report/1998), Science & Public Policy, Vol. 25(3), pp. 195-203 from http://users.fmg.uva.nl/lleydesdorff/th2/spp.htm.

Maculan, A.M. (2002). Tecnologia, conhecimento e gestão das inovações (educational note). Rio de Janeiro: Federal University of Rio de Janeiro.

Marx, K. (1890). *O capital: crítica da economia política* (3rd ed.). Rio de Janeiro: Editora Civilização Brasileira.

Nesta, L. & Mangematin, V. (2004). The dynamics of innovation networks [Working Paper Series 114]. *University of Sussex, SPRU - Science and Technology Policy Research*, East Sussex from http://ideas.repec.org/p/sru/ssewps/114.html.

Nonaka I. (1996). Knowledge has to do with truth, goodness, and beauty. [Conversation with Professor Ikujiro Nonaka]. Tokyo: MIT Center for Organizational Learning from http://www.dialogonleadership.org/docs/Nonaka-1996.pdf.

Organisation for Economic Co-operation for Development – OECD. (1996). *The OECD jobs strategy: technology, productivity and job creation*. Paris: OECD from http://www.oecd.org/dataoecd/57/7/1868601.pdf.

Piori, M. & Sabel, C. (1984). *The second divide: possibilities for prosperity*. New York: Basic Books.

Porter, M. (1990). New global Strategies for competitive advantage. *Strategy & Leadership*, 18(suppl.), 4-14.

Rogers, E.M. (2003). *Diffusion of innovations* (5th ed.). New York: Free Press.

Smith, D. (1999). *The wealth of nations*. 1999. London: Penguin Books.

Tidd, J. (2006). *A review of innovation models* (discussion paper, nr.1). London: Imperial College London, Tanaka Business School from http://emotools.com/archivo/innovation_models.pdf.

Tigre, P.B. (2006). *Gestão da inovação: a economia da tecnologia no Brasil* (3rd ed.). Rio de Janeiro: Elsevier.

KNOWLEDGE FLOW NETWORKS AND COMMUNITIES OF PRACTICE FOR KNOWLEDGE MANAGEMENT

RAJIV KHOSLA & MEI-TAI CHU

Research Centre for Computers, Communication and Social Innovation
School of Management, La Trobe University, Melbourne, Vic 3086, Australia
E-mail: r.khosla@latrobe.eud.au

K. G. YAMADA, S. DOI, K. KUNEIDA & S. OGA

C&C Innovation Res. Labs, NEC Corporation
8916-47 Takayama-cho, Ikoma-Shi, Nara, 630-0101, Japan
E-mail: kg-yamada@cp.jp.nec.com

This research discusses KFNs in the context of Communities of Practice (CoPs) and Knowledge Management (KM). KFNs unlike workflow can often transcend organizational boundaries and are distinct and different than workflow models. CoPs involve both personal and organizational aspects, and are an iteration of the transmission between explicit and tacit knowledge. This research develops, implements, and analyzes a CoPs Centered KFNs model in a multinational organization. The CoPs Centered KFNs model is underpinned in a CoPs model built around four organization performance evaluation dimensions and sixteen criteria. Many criteria and comprehensive segments should be taken into consideration while establishing CoPs model, this explains why this research employs fuzzy multi-criteria decision making. The cluster analysis techniques are used for evaluation of the CoPs Centered KFN model. The result of attribute analysis via KFNs model has been designed to determine the characteristic of each cluster and identify suggestions for effective linkage among knowledge workers.

1. Introduction

KFNs not only fall within the scope of managers, information technologists and knowledge workers but involve CoPs in organization learning (Lesser, 2001). Most of the existing work on knowledge flow networks has centered around linking people based on organization structure, tasks, and knowledge compatibility (Zhuge, 2006). This research proposes to enhance in design of KFN by modeling them based on CoPs in organization learning. In CoPs, like in KFNs, people with a common goal come together to create, learn, process and share knowledge and learning based on best practices. A CoPs model has been defined in this study, which constitutes 16 criteria along four performance measurement dimensions. These criteria and dimensions are used to identify common interaction factors (beliefs and attitudes) which link and facilitate effective knowledge sharing and learning between knowledge workers in KFNs. These factors and the CoPs model have been validated using a large multinational organization as a case study.

The research is organized as follows. Section 2 covers the theoretical considerations underpinning the definition and construction of KFNs model. Section 3 describes implementation and Techniques of KFNs model based on survey of R&D personnel in a multinational organization to enhance organization learning. Section 4 concludes the research.

2. KFNs Model

In this section KFNs model based on CoPs is constructed. The assumptions are made that design of KFNs is driven by the need to develop effective knowledge sharing and knowledge management (KM) mechanisms in order to enable organizations to compete in a knowledge based economy. In this context, firstly, defining a CoPs model, the criteria and dimensions it is based and the business strategies or benefits which can be evaluated using the model. The work is followed with definition of CoPs centered KFNs model which is used for implementation and analysis in this case study.

2.1. *CoPs Context and its Benefits*

Despite the rise of technology-based Knowledge Management tools, implementations often fail to realize their stated objectives (Ambrosio 2000). It is envisaged that 70% of existing knowledge management tools have failed to achieve the anticipated business performance outcomes they had been designed for (Malhotra 2004). One of the primary reasons identified for the failure of existing KM tools has been that existing Knowledge Management tools and research have primarily been designed around technology-push models as against strategy-pull models (Malhotra 2004). The technology-push model which is based on application of information technologies on historical data largely produce pre-specified meanings/knowledge and pre-specified outcomes which are useful in predictable and stable business environments. On the other hand, strategy-pull model turns the technology-push model on its head and drive the construction and creation of knowledge and related actions based on business strategy and performance driven outcome rather than somehow find a business strategy fit for the pre-specified knowledge and outcomes produced by technology-push models.

In an era where organizations are undergoing rapid, discontinuous and turbulent change it is imperative that KM systems and organizational entities like CoPs which facilitate KM and organizational transformation are more closely aligned with business strategies and goals of an organization. This would enable organizations to respond more quickly to changing business environments and business process and corresponding change in their KM needs from time to time.

Wenger (1998) first proposed CoPs in the Harvard Business Review, who believes CoPs is an informal group sharing knowledge, points out CoPs is composed by three critical elements (mutual engagement, joint enterprise, shared repository). Allee (2000) thought knowledge should include and utilize CoPs to create organizational knowledge. Besides, CoPs are distinguishing from other organizational groups such as formal divisions, project teams and informal network (Cohendet & Meyer-Krahmer, 2001; Allee, 2000; Wenger et al., 2002). CoPs can enable member interaction, knowledge sharing, organization learning, and open innovation simultaneously; it emphasizes more on facilitating, extracting and sharing tacit knowledge to maximize KM value. Many world class companies have taken CoPs as a new central role in the value chain (Chu et al, 2007).

Acknowledging that CoPs can link with organizational performance very well, CoPs are essential to overcome the inherent problems of a slow-moving traditional hierarchy in a fast-moving knowledge economy. Therefore, this research uses the four CoPs benefits or business strategies Induce Innovation Learning, Promote Responsiveness, Increase Core Competency, and Enhance Working Efficiency to develop the CoPs model as shown in Figure 1. These four CoPs business strategies need to be well defined and then pursued, because they will influence the KM achievements and the community's resources allocation direction.

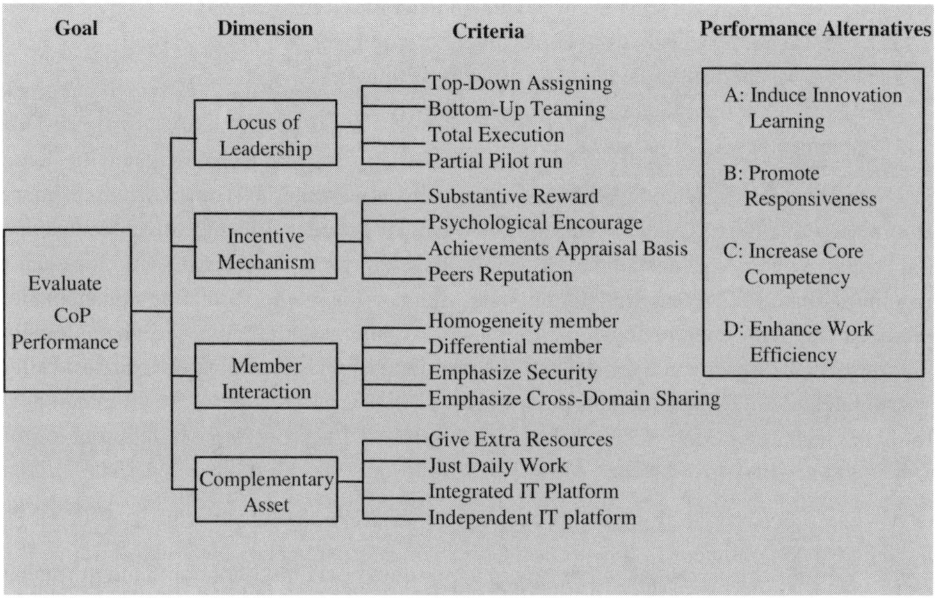

Figure 1: CoPs Centered Evaluation Hierarchy Model

The first benefit is to Induce Innovation Learning. The specific characteristics include cross-domain sharing to support new idea and creation according to common interests through group learning. The CoPs under this strategy often provide a safe or low-cost infrastructure for try and error attempts freely to facilitate new thinking and innovation.

The second benefit is to Promote Responsiveness by collecting and classifying knowledge objects. CoPs can directly obtain the problem-oriented solution, because the colleagues with similar working experiences are easy to find. They can help other members who are facing same questions based on the common language and shared foundations which lead to promote responsiveness.

The third benefit is to Increase Core Competency. Members can promote skill by shifting the best knowledge practices. It will be efficient to figure out who are domain-experts, how to enable insight exchange between senior and junior members. The organization principals can be established and increase core competency.

The fourth benefit is to Enhance Working Efficiency. CoPs members can reuse existing intellectual property invented by others in a well structured database easily, access related documents and authors' information quickly. The entire productivity will be improved and working efficiency will be enhanced in a disciplined way.

2.2. *CoPs Model and its Components*

In order to realize the four business benefits or strategies the CoPs model is defined and evaluated along four performance dimensions and sixteen criteria as outlined in Chu et al, (2007). The four dimensions are explained as follows respectively:

- Locus of Leadership: relates to enforcement or volunteer, wholly or partially adoption
- Incentive Mechanism: relates to award or punishment
- Member Interaction: relates to sharing or security
- Complementary Asset: relates to infrastructure and resource

The Locus of Leadership dimension contains four criteria: Top-Down Assigning, Bottom-Up Teaming, Total Execution, and Partial Pilot run. The Incentive Mechanism dimension contains: Substantive Reward, Psychological Encourage, Achievements Appraisal Basis, and Peers Reputation. The Member Interaction contains: Homogeneity of members, Differential members, Emphasize security, and Emphasize cross-domain Sharing. The Complementary Asset dimension contains: Give Extra Resources, Just Daily Work, Integrated IT Platform, and Independent IT platform.

2.3. *CoPs Centered Knowledge Flow Network Model*

In the preceding section the ground related to definition and construction of CoPs model has been outlined. In this section CoPs cantered parameters are used to define the components and terminologies of the knowledge flow network model. The KFN includes quantitative implications of the human and social factors like beliefs and attitudes for interaction between knowledge workers derived from the CoPs model (Thomas et al., 2001). These interaction beliefs and attitudes for knowledge sharing are based on the sixteen criteria used by the CoPs model. KFN can also be considered as CoPs in an organization where people with a common goal come together to create, learn, process and share knowledge based on best practices. Organizations and research teams are held together by CoPs or KFNs.

The purpose for designing a KFN model in this research is to develop actual human networks which can then be used for creation, learning, processing and sharing of knowledge (Davenport et al., 2004; Malhotra, 2004; Ratcliffe et al., 2000; Nissen, 2002; Nonaka, 1994; Thomas et al., 2001; Zhuge, 2003; Desouza, 2003). Knowledge especially that resulting from innovation needs, is regarded as an organizational transformation issue. It involves transmission of explicit, tacit and embodied knowledge in an iterative manner through KFN.

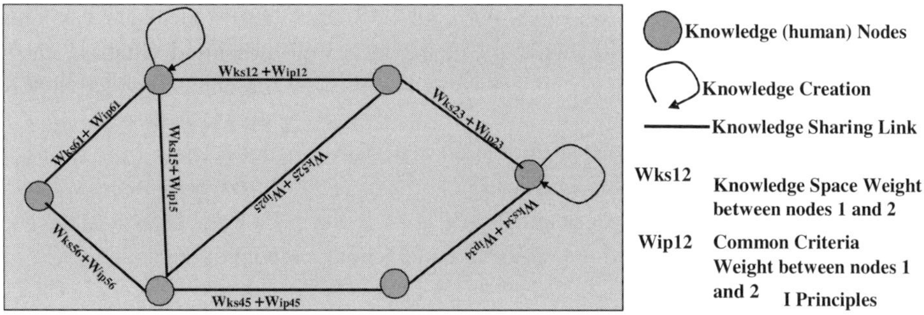

Figure 2: Knowledge Flow Network Model

A KFNs model as shown in Figure 2 consists of knowledge nodes (human or knowledge portal or process), knowledge links and weight which help to specify the strength of the knowledge link. With the definition of CoPs and existing research, knowledge workers share knowledge based knowledge compatibility as well as a set of interaction principles and beliefs which define their underlying knowledge sharing philosophy (Thomas et al., 2001). Although these interaction principles are not a determining factor for knowledge sharing they do influence the effectiveness and efficiency of knowledge sharing between two knowledge workers. These interaction principles and beliefs are defined based on the 16 criteria defined in CoPs model.

To draw an analogy, consider a situation for recruitment of sales person for selling computers. On one hand the recruitment panel will determine the knowledge compatibility of the sales person in the domain of computers. On the other hand, they will also study or analyze (based on range of criteria) how this sales person will interact with a customer in an actual selling situation. Similarly, knowledge level and space of a knowledge worker or a researcher can be determined based on their experience, CV, etc. However, to what extent they actually engage in knowledge sharing (especially, tacit knowledge) may be influenced by the 16 criteria for knowledge sharing and management. Other factors which can influence knowledge sharing can be trust and psychological profiles of the cooperating knowledge workers. However, the latter factors can be extended based on this research.

Therefore in Figure 2 we consider two types of weights, knowledge space weight and interaction principles weight. The knowledge space weight can vary between 0-1 and can be specified by the group or network leader based on knowledge and experience of the two knowledge workers, between discussions and consensus to calculate the impact of interaction principles on the overall effectiveness and efficiency of the knowledge link between two human nodes.

Thus knowledge link weight between two human nodes is calculated as follows:

$$KLWmn = KSWmn + \sum i{=}16i{=}1\ CCWmni$$

Where KLWmn is the knowledge link weight between nodes m and n, KSWmn is the knowledge space weight between nodes m and n, and CCWmni is the common criteria weight of criteria i between nodes m and n. The criteria weight is normalized between 0-1. The criteria with weight 0.1 or above may be added to determine CCWmn. However, the knowledge flow pattern is different than work flow and may or may not follow the same pattern or path as the work flow.

KFNs model can also assist in formation and growth of knowledge flow teams for R&D organizations as well as identification of high and low knowledge energy nodes. The human node with the highest number of links is the node with highest knowledge energy as it represents knowledge sharing and interaction potential of the node.

3. Techniques and Implementation of CoPs Centered KFN Model

In this section the authors describe the techniques used for construction of CoPs Centered knowledge flow network model in a large multinational organization. These techniques include a CoPs questionnaire based survey of knowledge workers. The survey is used to evaluate the importance attributed by knowledge workers to 16 CoPs criteria of knowledge workers along four business performance evaluation dimensions. Fuzzy MCDM (Multi-Criteria Decision-Making) techniques are used to calculate the importance attributed to each dimension and each criterion by the knowledge worker participating in the survey. Finally clustering technique is used to connect knowledge workers with common criteria (attitudes and beliefs) in CoPs centered KFNs model. Intuitively, common attitudes and beliefs between two knowledge workers imply that knowledge sharing among them is likely to be more effective than between knowledge workers with dissimilar attitudes and beliefs. The common criteria between two knowledge workers in KFNs are also used to determine strength of CCWmn link between knowledge workers in a KFN. The implementation was conducted in one large R&D organization, and the questionnaire was distributed to a broad sampling of researchers, to seek their views and calculate their final values. The aim is to provide a valuable reference when choosing suitable CoPs business strategies. Thirty nine valid questionnaires out of seventy were collected with a response rate at 55.7%.

The attribute analyses of KFN Model for CoPs designs can determine the characteristic of each cluster and identify suggestions for effective linkage. This KFN model adopted cluster analysis to be the basis of attribute analysis. Based on the differences of each participant, a hierarchical cluster diagram is generated. The similarity degree increased gradually from top down; the lower the knowledge workers are on the hierarchy, the more unique they appear to be (Pellitteri, 2002; Akamatsu et al., 1998; OECD, 1996).

The cluster analysis contains several steps. First, we input the factor scores to the model of cluster analysis. Second, we divided five clusters among all the participants. Third, we calculated the mean value and variable number of score of factor for each knowledge worker so as to explain their differences and characteristics. This research divided into five groups after the analysis results and actual discussions about the features towards CoPs beliefs. Table 1 demonstrates the participant distribution of five clusters.

Table 1: Participants in each Knowledge Flow Network

Knowledge Flow Network Number	No. of People
1	9
2	7
3	5
4	9
5	9

4. Results

In order to illustrate the application of knowledge link weight, the KFNs of the case study is shown in Figure 3. The knowledge flow network has been constructed using the CoPs Centred model designed in previous section. The CoPs model is used to design a questionnaire involving four dimensions, sixteen criteria, and four business strategies or performance preferences. The sixteen criteria represent among other aspects, represent beliefs and interaction principles of knowledge workers for knowledge sharing and management.

The feedback from 39 participants is used to compute the weight or relative importance assigned to each criterion by a participant. The weight values were than used to cluster the weighted responses from 39 participants. The purpose of clustering is to determine the similarities in relative importance of sixteen criteria among 39 participants. The clustering technique was derived from SPSS software (Zadeh, 1981). Five clusters or groups of researchers are identified. Each group or cluster in this research is considered to be eligible to form a knowledge flow network.

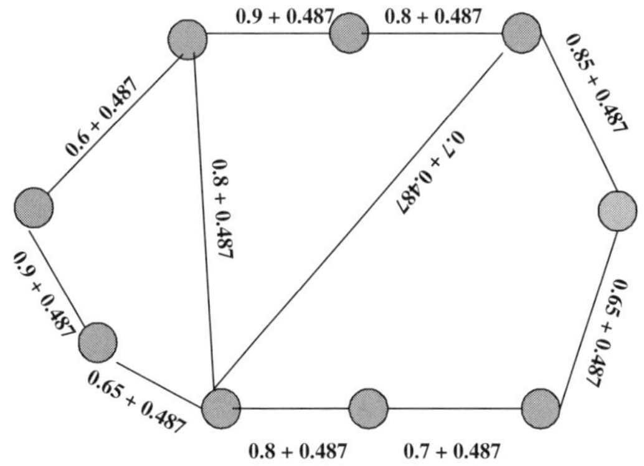

Figure 3: Sample Knowledge Flow Network for Number 5

Table 2 shows similar weight values for various criteria allocated by members of 5 KFNs. The weight values above 0.1 are highlighted in bold. These are used to calculate the Common Criteria Weight (CCW) between two members in KFNs. The criteria weights for criteria differential member and cross-domain sharing are added up. The values based on experience of members/researchers in a related knowledge domain have been used for illustration purpose only.

Table 2: Common Criteria Weight and Knowledge Flow Network Number

Variables	Cluster Group				
	1	2	3	4	5
Top-Down Assigning	**0.156**	0.060	0.022	0.052	0.043
Bottom-Up Teaming	**0.101**	**0.132**	0.063	0.044	0.066
Total Execution	0.085	0.043	0.021	0.038	0.020
Partial Pilot Run	**0.126**	0.076	0.025	0.038	0.060
Substantive Reward	0.044	0.083	0.062	0.036	0.019
Psychological Encourage	0.059	0.077	**0.214**	0.039	0.071
Achievement Apprasial Basis	0.051	**0.122**	0.094	0.045	0.038
Peers Reputation	0.048	0.079	**0.182**	0.035	0.043
Homogeneity Member	0.031	0.054	0.027	0.047	0.062
Differential Member	0.053	0.077	**0.121**	**0.142**	**0.207**
Empahasize Security	0.028	0.034	0.023	0.049	0.035
Emphasize Cross-Domain Sharing	0.080	0.068	0.087	**0.126**	**0.280**
Give Extra Resources	0.041	0.024	0.019	**0.101**	0.014
Just Daily Work	0.031	0.024	0.012	0.077	0.023
Integrated IT Platform	0.034	0.019	0.013	0.092	0.011
Independent IT Platform	0.031	0.030	0.014	0.040	0.009

5. Conclusion

Organizations in this research are viewed as KFNs involved in knowledge creation, knowledge sharing and innovation. This is in contrast to the traditional view that organizations consist primarily of workflow networks. KFNs consist of knowledge nodes, knowledge links and knowledge link weight respectively. The knowledge nodes are primarily human nodes but also can be resource nodes (e.g., robot, knowledge portals, databases, WWW).

The significant goal of this research is to study how CoPs can help to synergize the existing collaboration and construction of KFN in an open innovation infrastructure. The KFN are constructed based on actual study of CoPs in one large multinational R&D organization. The knowledge link weight between two human nodes consists of Knowledge Space (or compatibility) Weight (KSW) and Common Criteria Weight (CCW). KSW between two human nodes is determined by a manger or group leader based on CV, experience of the two human nodes and their knowledge compatibility. The 16 criteria along four Performance evaluation dimensions (Locus of leadership, Member interaction, Incentive mechanism and Complementary asset) in the CoPs questionnaire, among other aspects, can be considered to provide information on the interaction attitude and beliefs of researchers for cooperation and knowledge sharing. These interaction principles although, not a determining factor for knowledge sharing, can improve or enhance the effectiveness of knowledge sharing, creation and innovation. The feedback on the CoPs questionnaire, among other aspects, is used for clustering the researchers in knowledge flow network group. In this research 39 participants have been clustered into five KFNs. Organization can implement CoPs as a major approach to outline the future roadmap by frequent member interaction. Thus findings of this research can promote performance and can facilitate allocation of organizational resources for knowledge sharing and innovation among the participants.

References

Allee, Verna. (2000), *Knowledge Networks and Communities of Practice*, OD Practitioner Online, 32(4)

Ambrosio, J. (2000), *Knowledge Management Mistakes*, http://www.computerworld.com/industrytopics/energy/story/0,10801,46693,00.html

Buckley, J. J. (1985), Ranking Alternatives Using Fuzzy Number, *Fuzzy Sets and Systems*, 15(1), 21-31.

Chu M. T., Shyu J. Z., Tzeng G. H. & Khosla R. (2007), Comparison among Three Analytical Methods for Knowledge Communities Group-Decision Analysis, *Expert Systems with Applications*, 33(4), 1011-1024.

Chu M. T., Shyu J. Z., Tzeng G. H. & Khosla R. (2007), Using Non-Additive Fuzzy Integral to Assess Performance of Organization Transformation via Communities of Practice, *IEEE Transactions on Engineering Management*, 54(2), 1-13.

Clatworthy, J., Buick, D., Hankins, M., Weinman, J., & Horne, R. (2005), The use and reporting of cluster analysis in health psychology: A review, *British Journal of Health Psychology* 10: 329-358.

Cohendet P. & Meyer-Krahmer F. (2001), The Theoretical and Policy Implications of Knowledge Codification, *Research Policy*, 30, 1563-1591.

Davenport, T. H., Jarvenpaa, S. I., Beer, M.C. (2004), Improving Knowledge Work Process, *Sloan Management Review*, 34 (4), 53-65.

Desouza, K.C. (2003), *Facilitating Tacit Knowledge Exchange*, CACM, 46(6), 85-86.

Fowlkes E. B. & Mallows C. L. (1983), A Method for Comparing Two Hierarchical Clusterings, Journal of the American Statistical Association, **78** (383): 553–584.

Genrich, A. & Lautenbach, K. (1981), System Modelling with High Level Petri Nets, *Theoretical Computer Science*, 35, 1-41.

Huang, Z. (1998), Extensions to the K-means Algorithm for Clustering Large Datasets with Categorical Values, *Data Mining and Knowledge Discovery*, 2, 283-304.

Hwang, C. L. & Yoon, K. (1981), *Multiple Attribute Decision Making: Methods and Applications*, A State-of-Art Survey, Springer-Verlag, New York.

Jensen, K. (1981), Colored Petri Nets and the Invariant Method, *Theoretical Computer Science*, 14, 317-336.

Kerzner, H. (1989), *A System Approach to Planning Scheduling and Controlling*, Project Management, New York, 759-764

Lesser E. L. & Storck J. (2001), Communities of Practice and Organizational Performance, *IBM Systems Journal*, 40(4)

MacKay, David J.C. (2003), *Information Theory, Inference, and Learning Algorithms*, Cambridge University Press

Malhotra, Y. (2004), Why Knowledge Management Systems Fail? Enablers and Constraints of Knowledge Management in Human Enterprises, *American Society for Information Science and Technology Monograph Series*, 87-112.

Michael J. Lyons, Shigeru Akamatsu, Miyuki Kamachi & Jiro, (1998), *Coding facial expressions with Gabor wavelets Automatic Face and Gesture Recognition*, Third IEEE International Conference, 200-205, 4-16 April.

Mon, D. L., Cheng, C. H. & Lin, J. C. (1994), Evaluating Weapon System Using Fuzzy Analytic Hierarchy Process Based on Entropy Weigh, *Fuzzy Sets and Systems*, 61, 1-8.

Nissen, M. E. (2002), *An Extended Model of Knowledge Flow Dynamics*, CACM, 8, 251-266.

Nonaka, I. (1994), A Dynamic Theory of Organizational Knowledge Creation, *Organizational Science*, 5(1), 14-37.

OECD 1996: *The Knowledge Based Economy*. Science, Technology and Industry Outlook, Paris.

OECD 1999: *Measuring Knowledge in Learning Economies and Societies*. Draft Report on Washington Forum.

Pellitteri, J. (2002), The Relationship between Emotional Intelligence and Ego Defence Mechanisms, *The Journal of Psychology*, 136, 182-194, March.

Petri, C. (1966), *Communication in Automata*, in Technical Report RADC-TR-65-377, 1, Rome Air Development Center, Griffths Air Base, USA, January.

Ratcliffe-Martin V., Coakes E., & Sugden G., (2000), Knowledge Management Issues in Universities, *Vine Journal*, Dec 121, 14-19, ISSN: 0305-5728.

Saaty, T. L. (1977), A Scaling Method for Priorities in Hierarchical Structures, *Journal of Mathematical Psychology*, 15(2), 234-281.

Saaty, T. L. (1980), *The Analytic Hierarchy Process*, New York, McGraw-Hill.

Tang, M. T. & Tzeng, G. H. (1999), A Hierarchy Fuzzy MCDM Method for Studying Electronic Marketing Strategies in the Information Service Industry, *Journal of International Information Management*, 8(1), 1-22.

Thomas, J.C., Kellog, W.A., & Erickson, T. (2001), The Knowledge Management Puzzle: Human and Social factors in Knowledge Management, *IBM Systems Journal*, 40 (4), 863-884.

Tsaur, S. H., Tzeng, G. H. & Wang, K. C. (1997), Evaluating Tourist Risks From Fuzzy Perspectives, *Annals of Tourism Research*, 24(4), 796-812.

Tzeng, G. H. & Shiau, T. A. (1987), Energy Conservation Strategies in Urban Transportation: Application of Multiple Criteria Decision-Making, *Energy Systems and Policy*, 11(1), 1-19.

Tzeng, G. H. & Teng, J. Y. (1994), Multicriteria Evaluation for Strategies of Improving and Controlling Air-Quality in the Super City: A case of Taipei city, *Journal of Environmental Management*, 40(3), 213-229.

Tzeng, G. H. (1977), A Study on the PATTERN Method for the Decision Process in the Public System, *Japan Journal of Behavior Metrics*, 4(2), 29-44.

Tzeng, G. H., Shian, T. A. & Lin, C. Y. (1992), Application of Multicriteria Decision Making to the Evaluation of New Energy-System Development in Taiwan, *Energy*, 17(10), 983-992.

U.S. Department of Commerce (1965), *National Technical Information Service*, NASA, PATTERN Relevance Guide, 3.

Wenger, E. (1998), *Communities of Practice*, Cambridge University Press.

Wenger, E., McDermott R. A., & Snyder W. (2002), *Cultivating Communities of Practice*, Boston: Harvard Business School Press.

Zadeh, L. A. (1981), *A Definition Of Soft Computing*, http://www.soft-computing.de/def.html.

Zhuge, H. (2003), Component-based Workflow Systems Design, *Decision Support Systems*, 35 (4), 517-536

Zhuge, Hai. (2006), Knowledge Flow Network Planning and Simulation, *Decision Support Systems*, 42, 571-592

A CASE STUDY OF KNOWLEDGE SHARING IN FINNISH LAUREA LAB AS A KNOWLEDGE INTENSIVE ORGANISATION

ABEL USORO & GRZEGORZ MAJEWSKI
School of Computing, University of the West of Scotland
Paisley, PA1 2BE, UK
abel.usoro@uws.ac.uk
grzegorz.majewski@uws.ac.uk

Virtual communities of practice (VCoP) are one of the most important tools for knowledge sharing in both business and academia. Roused interest in on-line knowledge sharing resulted in research into the most influential factors affecting the behavior of the participants of VCoPs. Existing research in this area are non-comprehensive of the influential factors – some concentrate on the technological while others on the non-technical aspects. After examining key current research and identifying the most critical factors, this paper proposes a conceptual model for the purposes of knowledge sharing in knowledge intensive organizations using VCoPs. This model combines the important factors, the notion of reciprocity and social ties between the VCoP participants. Hypotheses are formulated between the constructs of the model. An attempt is made to validate the model. This statistical validation and drawing of conclusions are to be continued but meanwhile, a brief presentation of qualitative part of the research is presented to prove that effective VCoPs in knowledge intensive organizations need a good sense of community and active knowledge exchange. For the case study, this paper used Laurea Labs, which is a member of the European Network of Living Labs.

1. Background

Successful knowledge sharing can result in the increase of organizational effectiveness (Gupta and Govindarajan, 2000) because, unlike other resources, knowledge tends to increase with use or when shared as expressed by Davenport and Prusak (1998) that "ideas breed new ideas and shared knowledge stays with the giver while it enriches the receiver" (pp. 16, 17).

Communities of practice (CoPs) have become one of the most important tools of knowledge sharing. Lave and Wenger (1991) described it as an activity system with individuals sharing common values, interests, and experiences and trying to extend their knowledge by sharing it with each other. They normally cut across traditional organisational and geographical boundaries, are informal and therefore easier to share both explicit and implicit knowledge after locating the right subject expert (Brown and Grey, 1995; Lesser and Everest 2001).

Members of CoPs use ICT tools ranging from email to virtual conferences to "extend the boundaries of traditional face-to-face communities by creating virtual communities that enable global asynchronous and real-time collaboration" (Usoro et al., 2007, p. 200). Their reliance on computer mediation adds virtuality to their name hence "virtual communities of practice" (VCoPs).

VCoPs are socio-technological and extensive studies into its influential factors have revealed one of the general factors to be "an active participation of a substantial part (ideally, all) of its members" (Ardichvili et al., 2003, pp. 65-66). The knowledge provider perspective rather than the knowledge receiver perspective is emphasized in most studies on knowledge sharing and knowledge management (e.g.: Chow & Chan, 2008; Lin et al., 2009; Yang & Farn, 2009; Willem & Buelens, 2009; Van den Hooff & Huysman, 2009). Some studies though endeavour to tackle the receiver perspective (e.g. Bock et al, 2006). However, only a few studies have both perspectives coexisting together, but the coexistence is implicit in the research background rather than explicitly examined. The two roles may be intermingled and hard to separate in real life, but for research analytical purposes, it is necessary to identify and separate the roles so as to study them and the possible influencing factors that may be unique to each role.

The rest of this paper presents the research model, methodology, quantitative findings, qualitative findings, conclusions and areas for further studies, and managerial implications.

2. Research Model

Antecedents of on-line knowledge sharing identified in existing research range from trust (and its components: integrity, competence and benevolence) (Chiu et al. 2006, Usoro et al. 2007) to reciprocity (norm of reciprocity, perceived reciprocity) (Bock et al., 2006; Chiu et al. 2006; Lin et al., 2009). Eventually however it is necessary to consider the whole picture and synthesise these factors into a logical model. An example of search for such a generic model was the reason behind the proposal of a conceptual model based on the Prisoner's Dilemma (PD) (Usoro and Majewski 2008).

For this research we begin with the conclusion reached from earlier discussion that it is necessary to take into account two roles - knowledge giving and knowledge receiving - that VCoP participants can play. Consequently it is necessary to perceive these two perspectives as antecedents to on-line knowledge sharing in VCoPs as expressed in these two hypotheses:

- H_1: Knowledge *provision* is positively associated with online knowledge sharing.
- H_2: Knowledge *reception* is positively associated with online knowledge sharing.

Chiu et al. (2006) focus on the knowledge provision perspective (although it is not mentioned explicitly) and investigate the influence of social relationships on knowledge sharing (quantity of knowledge sharing and knowledge quality). They go further to put trust, the norm of reciprocity and identification as antecedents of knowledge sharing. They argue that "people who come to a virtual community … also treat it as a place to meet other people, to seek support, friendship and a sense of belonging" (Chiu et al 2009, p. 1874). Kankanhalli et al. (2005a) concluded that reciprocity is positively related to knowledge sharing. Chiu et al. (2006) assign the factors to three distinct dimensions: structural, relational and cognitive. The structural dimension is mostly related to social ties and social capital and for the purposes of our research it will be the social dimension, while the factors assigned to this dimension will be social factors. The term that will be used to describe the social interaction, ties and relationships for the purposes of this research will be the "perception of community". The hypotheses that can be derived are that:

- H_3: The perception of a community is positively associated with knowledge provision in VCoP.
- H_4: The norm of reciprocity is positively associated with the perception of community while providing knowledge in VCoP.

Hypothesis H_3 states that the way an individual perceives the community as a whole (and also how he or she identifies with the community) influences their eagerness to provide knowledge. Hypothesis H_4 states that the expectation of reciprocity (i.e. of being helped in the future by other members) influences the way the community is perceived.

The perception of community also influences the way knowledge is received. Participants are more eager to receive knowledge from a community with an established reputation than from a new one they do not yet know, and consequently the reputation and perception of the community determines the way its members treat each other as expressed in this hypothesis:

- H_5: The perception of community is positively associated with knowledge reception in VCoP.

H_5 is also supported by the view expressed by Kankanhalli et al (2005b) that "the exchange of intellectual capital can be facilitated by norms of collaboration and sharing" (p. 1158).

Kankanhalli et al. (2005b) indicate also that the availability of incentives or benefits is positively associated with knowledge seeking. With the knowledge receiver, the incentive may be the knowledge itself (Kankanhalli et al., 2005b; Nebus, 2004). To the knowledge provider the reward may be economic for instance "increased salary ... [and] greater job security" (Kankanhalli et al, 2005b, p. 1159). Others associated with knowledge contribution are: appraisal, respect, being seen as skilled and of higher status in the community (Butler et al., 2002), as well as networking opportunity (Zhang & Hiltz, 2003). Besides, "karma points" for "thank you" from stackover.com virtual community or some "social reward" e.g. friendship may be the benefit (Chiu et al., 2006). Thus it is possible to formulate the following hypotheses:

- H_6: Perceived benefits are positively associated to VCoP usage for knowledge provision.
- H_7: Perceived benefits are positively associated to VCoP usage for knowledge reception.

Another important factor is trust which distinguishable components are: competence (expertise), benevolence and integrity (Usoro et al., 2007; Willem & Buelens, 2009). Usoro et al. (2007) confirmed a positive association been these components and knowledge provision in VCoP. Trust may also facilitate social ties (Chow & Chan, 2008) and thus positively impact on knowledge sharing. On the other hand social ties positively influence mutual trust (Van den Hooff & Huysman, 2009). Hence, it seems that trust is highly associated with the social aspect of VCoP. Lin et al. (2009) indicate that norms of reciprocity influence trust, which in turn affect knowledge sharing self-efficacy, perceived relative advantage, perceived compatibility and knowledge sharing behaviour. Usoro et al. (2007) link some trust components with reciprocity, while indicating that it further influences the sense of community: "Where the sense of community is strong and benevolence is high, community members are more likely to perceive knowledge as a public good, owned and maintained by the community. Conversely, if one's sense of community's benevolence is low, expectations of future reciprocity may likewise be low, and knowledge sharing is unlikely to be fostered" (Usoro et al., 2007, p. 203).

Trust also affects knowledge reception whether online or not. It is trust in the credibility, expertise and reputation of the contributor (knowledge source) "and the contributor's willingness to help" that matters (Bock et al., 2006). If a community is perceived as competent in answering queries it is expected that a knowledge seeker will keep posting his or her questions. Other trust components count as well, because a knowledge receiver needs to be able to rely on the knowledge provided by the community. Thus benevolence and integrity are also important. It is possible to formulate the following hypotheses based on these facts:

- H_8: Trust is positively associated with the perception of community while providing knowledge in VCoP.
- H_9: Trust is positively associated with the perception of community while receiving knowledge in VCoP.
- H_{10}: The Norm of reciprocity is positively associated with trust while providing knowledge in VCoP.
- H_{11}: The Norm of reciprocity is positively associated with trust while receiving knowledge in VCoP.

Apart from positive influence of on-line knowledge sharing, it is possible to also identify barriers, risks and fears such as that of losing face or being laughed at (Ardichvili et al., 2003). In the case of knowledge provision it may also be the fear of taking additional responsibility and, even more important, losing competitive advantage over others. Kankanhalli et al. (2005b) notes that "incentives may be needed to encourage knowledge reuse to counteract the inertia to seek knowledge and the propensity of employees to "reinvent the wheel" (p. 1159). These perceived costs can also be in terms of time and money (Bock et al., 2006, p 358). Contribution to VCoP often takes significant amount of time which is a very scarce resource in the busy business environment.

These perceived costs can be related to the competence, benevolence and integrity of other participants of VCoP as indicated by Usoro et al., 2007: "This facet of trust can be related to the fear of losing face that Ardichvili et al. (2003) identified as one of the main barriers to knowledge sharing in online communities of practice" (p. 202). They also influence the way participants perceive the community as a whole and whether they in turn will be eager to provide and receive knowledge from this particular VCoP. Based on these facts it is possible to formulate the following hypotheses:

- H_{12}: Perceived costs are negatively associated with trust while providing knowledge in VCoP.

These hypotheses are utilized in the construction of a conceptual model that will embrace both roles that can be played by the participants of VCoP. A simplified version of such research model is presented on Figure 1 below:

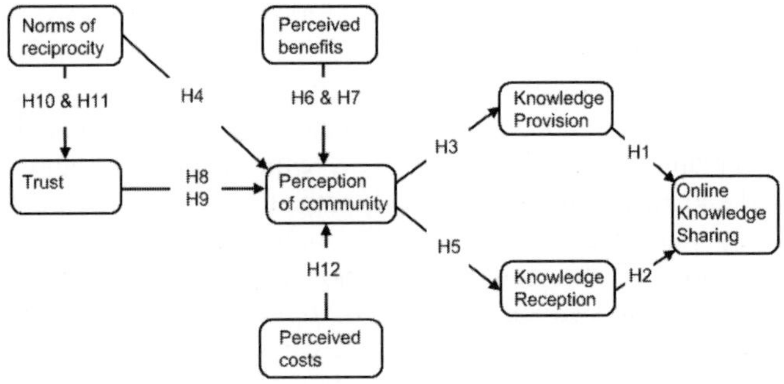

Figure 1 Conceptual model of factors influencing knowledge sharing in VCoP (both knowledge provision and knowledge reception perspectives as well as corresponding factors are displayed)

This figure presents two perspectives of knowledge sharing. Appropriate hypotheses indicate the way antecedents of knowledge sharing influence each other. As a result we have a given participant behavior (as knowledge receptor or knowledge provider).

3. Methodology

The hypotheses were tested with qualitative and quantitative research with Laurea Labs in Finland. The paragraphs below describe the development of the survey instrument, data collection procedures, and the validation of the measures.

The proposed conceptual model was operationalised into a questionnaire (see Appendix I). The questionnaire was distributed to the members of the Laurea Labs and Laurea University of Applied Technology in Finland. The Labs constituted a convenient sample of VCoP because of their use of information technology to complement face to face knowledge sharing among members and clients who possess common interests. It has to be acknowledged though that some communities of practice such as Open Source communities may have unique characteristics that may not be reflected in the selected sample but the scope of this paper may not sufficiently take care of them. The members of the selected community of practice come from diverse backgrounds and all walks-of-life, thus making the sample representative. In the first attempt a hard copy of the questionnaire was distributed. Some of the participants indicated that an on-line version would simplify the process. Therefore an on-line version of the questionnaire was designed and its Internet link was distributed. Additionally an interview with the coordinator of Internationalization of R&D at the Laurea Living Lab was conducted.

4. Data Analysis

There were a total of 121 responses. After excluding 11 invalid responses, 110 valid responses were used for data analysis. Nearly all the measurement items were derived from literature. A seven point Likert scale was used to measure the relative importance of each item. Additionally participants were able to select factors that they thought to be most important ones in the last section of the questionnaire. There was also an option for respondents to type in their own factors – i.e. ones that were not listed. The questionnaire items were pilot tested with experts from the IS (information system) area as well as cognitive sciences (psychology and sociology). Feedback provided by them as well as by ordinary respondents (during the pilot study) was very important and helped to increase the quality of the questionnaire.

4.1. *Reliability and validity of measures*

Data gathered from respondents had to first undergo reliability test which is a very important tool in positivist research because it indicates stability and the fact that the research is replicable (Golafshani 2003, p 599). For this analysis, internal consistency reliability, using Cronbach's coefficient alpha, was considered most appropriate because of the elimination of the necessity to ask the same respondents to retake the same questionnaire (test-retest) or take a changed questionnaire (alternate-form) (Litwin, 1995, p 6). Cronbach's coefficient alpha values of 0.70 and above are generally accepted as representing good reliability (Litwin 1995, pp 24-31). In the case of short scales (e.g. fewer than ten items) low Cronbach values may occur.

This statistics when performed on the questionnaire returns high value of above 0.869, which indicates a very good reliability. In other words, the questionnaire items measure the same variable or concept – in this case this concept could be the knowledge sharing. The same reliability statistics when performed for the items measuring knowledge reception (15 items) and knowledge provision (22 items) return slightly lower values (0.692 and 0.742). It may thus be claimed that they measure the two given sides of knowledge sharing. Exact statistics are shown in figures 2 and 3 below.

Cronbach's Alpha	Cronbach's Alpha Based on Standardized Items	N of Items
.692	.824	15

Figure 2 Reliability of the knowledge reception items

Cronbach's Alpha	Cronbach's Alpha Based on Standardized Items	N of Items
.742	.800	22

Figure 3 Reliability of the knowledge provision items

Besides measuring the reliability of the scales it is also necessary to examine their validity. Validity is a term which describes how well a questionnaire or survey measures what it is meant to measure. For example an item that is supposed to measure pain should measure pain and not some related variable (e.g. anxiety) (Litwin, 1995, p 33). Factorial validity with the most common technique, such as principal components analysis or confirmatory factor analysis, has been identified as one of the most appropriate in IS research (Straub *et al,* 2004, p 10).

A principal components analysis (PCA) was conducted. Nine factors were extracted using oblique rotation (Pallant, 2005). Results are provided in Appendix II. It was hypothesized that knowledge sharing (in two perspectives) is influenced by perception of community, which in turn is influenced by a range of factors (trust, norms of reciprocity, perceived benefits and perceived costs). PCA seems to support the theory. Together the factors explain almost 76% of the total variance, which is a very good outcome and an indication of the fitness of the factors. The first factor is very highly related with the two perspectives of knowledge sharing: knowledge reception (KRecFreq – variable measuring frequency of knowledge reception activities and KRecQua – variable measuring quality of knowledge stored in the community) and knowledge provision (KProvFreq - variable measuring frequency of knowledge provision activities and KStatus – variable measuring whether those who provide knowledge achieve higher status in the community). This factor will be termed as knowledge sharing frequency - KShaFreq. The second factor is highly related with the social side of knowledge provision (KProSoc1 and KProSoc2) and also one variable measuring the social side of knowledge reception (KRecSoc1). It seems that although our model distinguishes these two perspectives (i.e. knowledge provision and knowledge reception) in reality they very often intermingle with each other. This factor will be termed as perception of community – PoC.

The third factor is highly related with knowledge provision reciprocity and benefits. It will be termed as knowledge provision benefits – KPB. The fourth factor seems to cover knowledge provision duration and knowledge reception duration. These two variables were measuring how long a given participant was engaged in these activities in the community. It seems that high correlation between these two variables may implicitly support first two hypotheses that knowledge provision and knowledge reception are crucial activities for the knowledge sharing to exist. This factor will be termed as knowledge sharing duration – KSD. The fifth factor is highly related to knowledge provision quality, reciprocity and cost. It will be termed as knowledge provision reciprocity – KPR. The sixth factor is highly related with variables: K_App (measuring knowledge applicability) and KRecRecip2 (measuring knowledge reciprocity). Both of these variables are on the knowledge reception side. This factor will be termed as knowledge reception reciprocity – KRR. The seventh factor measures whether social ties (acquaintance) are important while providing (Kpro_Acq) and receiving knowledge (Krec_Acq). There is also variable measuring knowledge reception reciprocity. Therefore it is possible to say that it implicitly supports the fourth hypothesis. It will be termed as knowledge reception reciprocity – KRR.

The eighth factor covers variables associated with knowledge provision (K_Innova – measuring whether new solutions are welcomed in the community and Kpro_cost – measuring costs of providing new knowledge). The variable measuring knowledge innovation also reflects the potential fears of coming up with new ways of dealing with problems. A person usually takes some responsibility and risks of being laughed at when the new solution is not very good. This factor will be termed as knowledge provision costs – KPC. The last factor seems to cover the social side of knowledge provision (KProSoc2) as well as knowledge reception (KRecSoc2) and trust (KProTrust). It could be an implicit indication that hypotheses H_5 and H_9 are valid. It will be termed as knowledge sharing trust – KST.

There are only nine factors as compared with eleven hypotheses mentioned in the research model. These factors however seem to cover in some cases more than one hypothesis. Variables that were supposed to measure given hypothesis in reality often combine with each other and it is difficult to distinguish one from another. Therefore factors proposed should be perceived as an amalgam of the underlying variables. Some of our hypotheses seem however not to reflect the reality.

5. Quantitative Findings

Hypothesis testing was performed in two steps. In the first step, multiple regressions analysis was performed on the original variables to evaluate whether any of the hypotheses could be supported. Appendix II presents some of the results[1]. Hypothesis H_{11} was very strongly supported, while some of the other hypotheses gained a moderate to weak support. The value of R Square is very high in the case of H_{11} (above 0.9) and is a very good indication of the relationship between the variable measuring trust when receiving knowledge with those measuring reciprocity also on knowledge reception side. Therefore hypothesis H_{11} is strongly supported. Other hypothesized relationships have much lower values of R Square (below 0.2)

[1,2] Full results of data analysis can be provided by email if requested.

and can offer only moderate or weak support of the hypotheses from the research model. This is the case with hypotheses H_1, H_2, H_6 and H_7. Hypothesis H_1 was tested with multiple regression between dependent variable KProFreq (measuring frequency of knowledge provision) and three independent variables (KProAcq – measuring familiarity, KProSoc1 – measuring social ties, and KStatus – measuring status in society given knowledge provision). At one point variable KProSoc2 was included as an independent variable as well. However it was highly correlated with variable KProSoc1 and was excluded to avoid multicollinearity. In this case tolerance values were well above 0.10, while VIF are well below 10. Therefore multicollinearity should not be suspected in this case (Pallant, p. 156). The value of R Square is however not that high with 0.198. That means the three independent variables explain about 20 percent of KProFreq.

On knowledge reception side, hypothesis H_2 was tested using multiple regressions between the dependent variable KRecFreq (measuring frequency of knowledge provision) and two independent variables (KRecAcq – measuring familiarity and KRecSoc2 – measuring social ties). At one point variable KProSoc1 was included as an independent variable as well. However, it was highly correlated with variable KProSoc2 and was excluded to avoid multicollinearity. R Square in this case however was slightly lower and equated to 0.18.

In the second step Pearson bivariate correlations analysis was conducted in order to evaluate whether there are any significant relationships between the factors extracted in the Principal Components Analysis[2]. These factors combine the underlying original variables into new factors. Based on this fact this analysis tries to "translate" these new factors into relationships between the underlying variables. Given the strong support some of the hypotheses gained in the first step, authors did not want to completely remove them or replace them with new hypotheses based on PCA factors, but instead use PCA as another way of proving whether hypotheses of the research model are significant. It is possible to identify significant correlations, which could indicate the relationships between the given factors. This in turn may be an indication of the significant relationships between the underlying original constructs. The first factor has a significant relationship with factors five and eight. These relationships are in support of hypothesis H_1 and it also indirectly supports hypotheses H_2, H_4 and H_{12}. It is with the assumption that the norms of reciprocity influence knowledge provision and that some factors were intermingled. In the case of the second factor there are significant relationships with factors five and nine. This fact is in support of hypotheses: H_3, H_4 and H_8. The seventh factor (measuring social ties while providing and receiving knowledge) is in significant relationship to the fifth factor (measuring knowledge provision reciprocity). Therefore it supports hypothesis H_4.

6. Qualitative Findings

The pure data analysis may not be enough to prove whether the hypotheses of the proposed research model are right or wrong. As it was described previously there are some hypotheses that have very strong support, some that gained moderate support and some only with weak support. The qualitative analysis will serve as another mean of verifying and validating the research model proposed. For the qualitative analysis we present the outcome of an interview with the coordinator of the internationalization of Laurea Leppävaara's R&D environment SIDLabs. SIDLabs is an organization (according to the definition provided by the Cambridge Online dictionary[3]) whose members engage in knowledge-intensive tasks (e.g. development, design) therefore it meets the criteria for being the subject of this research. The interview was carried out on the 4th of May, 2009[4]. Given the geographical distance it was in a form of a written interview with questions and the response was sent back by email. Some of the details were also discussed by phone. Besides measuring collaboration it was also evaluated how the knowledge sharing activities may result in increased innovation. The questions of the interview were measuring the constructs indirectly by rephrasing the pure scientific constructs in a more natural and better understandable fashion.

The SIDLabs, like other VCoPs, use ICT to exchange information, collaborative work and maintain their community. They use different platforms depending on the projects. Skype is an example of communication tool that they commonly use between researchers and representatives from working life and video conferencing for international projects. Sometimes they develop in-house "specific platforms [and systems]", added the coordinator.

It is clear that with the Labs the giver and the receiver roles exist. Sometimes knowledge sharers exchange these roles. The lab's handful of permanent staffs is involved in research and publications. The bulk of workers are students most of which are from abroad. For instance between 2008 and 2009, the School of Computing of the University of the West of Scotland provided 4 Erasmus internship students.

It is evident that some knowledge comes from the user community. The users here are the companies who have the projects such as the Finish Nokia Company. The Labs coordinator stated on the interview that 60% to 70% of the projects were executed in cooperation with external organisations. At the same time, the Living Lab itself develops some models and techniques from its experience as well as R&D to complement the user community knowledge. Also contributing to the knowledge base is the network knowledge passing from various communities of practice to which staff and internship students belong.

Perception of community exists in the form of social ties. The coordinator considered the social ties as mandatory if they were to involve the different actors. He added that "Laurea's learning model 'Learning by Developing' requires important social ties to be able to create 'real life' projects for the students."

A general threat that came from the qualitative primary research is that besides technology, a sense of community or social ties in addition to active share of knowledge are the life-blood of a healthy VCoP. Table 1 presents the summary of the findings. Based on the score achieved during each face the outcome for each hypothesis is calculated (with "Weak" adding one point, "Moderate" adding two points and "Strong" adding three points). Positive outcome is achieved with at least five points in total; indecisive outcome is with three or four points. Any points below three result in negative outcome.

---

[3] http://dictionary.cambridge.org/define.asp?key=55930&dict=CALD (retrieved 17.09.2009)

[4] Full text of interview may be provided by email on request.

	Quantitative Analysis		Qualitative Analysis	Outcome
Hypothesis	**First Step**	**Second Step**	**Interview**	
H_1	Weak	Moderate	Strong	Positive
H_2	Weak	Weak	Strong	Indecisive
H_3	Moderate	Moderate	Strong	Positive
H_4	Moderate	Moderate	Strong	Positive
H_5	Moderate	Weak	Strong	Positive
H_6	Weak	Weak	Strong	Indecisive
H_7	Weak	Weak	Strong	Indecisive
H_8	Weak	Moderate	Moderate	Indecisive
H_9	Weak	Weak	Moderate	Negative
H_{10}	Weak	Weak	Moderate	Negative
H_{11}	Strong	N/A	Moderate	Positive
H_{12}	Moderate	Weak	Weak	Negative

Table 1 Summary of the findings

7. Conclusions and Area for Further Studies

Knowledge sharing in virtual communities of practice requires the existence of some factors like reciprocity, trust and a sense of community. This research has endeavored to build a research model with these factors as constructs with hypotheses to relate them to each other. The analyses of the questionnaire responses received from SIDLabs indicate the necessity to revisit the model to reflect the changes in the constructs as revealed by the statistical factor analysis. The revisit of the model plus the re-working of the hypotheses is the subject for further research. Meanwhile, this paper has presented a brief report of the qualitative research at the same VCoP. The research shows that the existence of a sense of community and active participation of community members are essential to the working of a VCoP.

8. Managerial Implications

To leverage the knowledge sharing potential of VCoPs, managers should be conscious to provide not only technology to connect members of these communities but also a sense of community and the building of social ties as these factors came out strong from the findings of both quantitative and qualitative data analysis. There is a variety of methods, such as arranging social events, which they can use to stimulate the non-technical aspects of VCoPs. Explanation of these methods is beyond the scope of this research.

However given the factors that were selected and investigated it is possible to reason out what a given VCoP may need in order to achieve high volume and quality of knowledge sharing. As an example let us consider norms of reciprocity (in both the knowledge provision and the knowledge reception perspective). This factor can be utilised and enhanced by assuring the VCoP members of the existence of future opportunities for collaboration and knowledge sharing. This assurance would motivate community members and make them more cooperative since they are confident of the continuity of their relationships.

Another implication for managers and knowledge management professionals is the distinction of the two important knowledge sharing perspectives – knowledge provision and knowledge reception. By distinguishing these two perspectives in the analysis of the functioning of a given VCoP it is possible to diagnose problems much faster and adjust the policy to improve the situation in a much more efficient way. For instance, the weakness of VCoP may lie in the small number of givers to a large number of receivers. The recognition of this weakness should prompt managers to stimulate more "giving" attitude to knowledge sharing.

References

Ardichvili, A., Page, V. and Wentling, T. (2003), Motivation and barriers to participation in virtual knowledge-sharing communities of practice, *Journal of Knowledge Management* 7(1), 64-77.

Bock, G-W., Kankanhalli, S. S. & Sharma, S., (2006), Are norms enough? The role of collaborative norms in promoting organizational knowledge seeking, *European Journal of Information Systems*, Vol. 15, 357 – 367.

Brown, J. S., & Gray, E. S., (1995), The people are the company. Fast Company, p. 78, Available online: http://www.fastcompany.com/magazine/01/people.html [January 2009]

Butler, B., Sproull, L., Kiesler, S. & Kraut, R., (2002), Community effort in online groups: who does the work and why, in: S. Weisband, L. Atwater (Eds.), Leadership at a Distance, Lawrence Erlbaum Publishers, Mahwah, NJ, 2002

Chiu, C-M., Hsu, M-H., Wang, E. T. G., (2006), Understanding knowledge sharing in virtual communities: An integration of social capital and social cognitive theories, *Decision Support Systems*, Vol. 42, 1872 - 1888

Chow, W. S. & Chan, L. S., (2008), Social network, social trust and shared goals in organizational knowledge sharing, *Information & Management*, Vol. 45, 458-465

Davenport, T. H. & Prusak, L (1998), *Working Knowledge*, Harvard Business School Press, Boston, MA.

Gannon-Leary P. and Fontainha E., (2007), Communities of Practice and virtual learning communities: benefits, barriers and success factors. *eLearning Papers*, no. 5. ISSN 1887-1542.

Golafshani, N., (2003), Understanding Reliability and Validity in Questionnaire Research, *The Qualitative Report*, Vol 8, No, 4 December, 597-607.

Gupta, A.K. & Govindarajan, V. (2000), Knowledge management's social dimension: lessons from Nucor steel, *Sloan Management Review*, 42 No. 1, 71-80.

Hooff van den, B. & Huysman, M., (2009), Managing knowledge sharing: Emergent and engineering approaches, *Information & Management*, Vol. 46, 1-8

Kankanhalli, A., Tan, B. C. Y. & Wei, K-K., (2005a), Contributing knowledge to electronic knowledge repositories: an empirical investigation, MIS Quarterly 29 (1), 113- 143.

Kankanhalli, A., Tan, B. C. Y. & Wei, K-K., (2005b), Understanding seeking from electronic knowledge repositories an empirical study, *Journal of the American Society for Information*, Science and Technology, Vol. 56 (11), 1156-1166.

Lesser, E. & Everest, K. (2001), Communities of practice: making the most of intellectual capital, *Ivey Business Journal*, 65(4), 37-41.

Lin, M-J., J., Hung, S-W., Chen, C-J., (2009), Fostering the determinants of knowledge sharing in professional virtual communities, *Computers in Human Behaviour*, 25, 929-939

Litwin, M. S., (1995), How to Measure Survey Reliability and Validity, London: Sage Publications.

Nebus, J., (2004), Learning by networking: knowledge search and sharing in multinational organizations, Proceedings of the 46th Academy of International Business, Bridging with the Other: The Importance of Dialogue in International Business, Stockholm, Sweden.

Pallant, J., (2005), *SPSS Survival Manual*, Maidenhead: Open University Press.

Straub, D.; Boudreau, M. & Gefen, D., (2004), Validation guidelines for IS positivist research, *Communications of the Association for Information Systems*, Vol. 13, 380-427.

Usoro, A., Sharratt, M. W., Tsui, E. & Shekhar S. (2007) Trust as an antecedent to knowledge sharing in virtual communities of practice. *Knowledge Management Research & Practice*, 5, 199-212.

Usoro, A. & Majewski, G. (2008), *Trust and Risk as Critical Factors of Knowledge Sharing in Virtual Communities of Practice: A Conceptual View*, Proceedings of the 9th European Conference on Knowledge Management, 443-452.

Wenger, E. (1998), *Communities of Practice: Learning, Meaning and Identity*, Cambridge University Press, Cambridge.

Wenger, E., McDermott, R. & Snyder, W. (2002), Cultivating Communities of Practice: A Guide to Managing Knowledge, Harvard Business School Press, Boston.

Willem, A. & Buelens, M., (2009), Knowledge sharing in inter-unit cooperative episodes: The impact of organizational structure dimensions, *International Journal of Information Management*, Vol. 29, 151-160.

Yang, S-C. & Farn, C-K., (2009), Social capital, behavioural control, and tacit knowledge sharing – A multi-informant design, *International Journal of Information Management*, Vol. 29, 210 – 218.

Zhang, Y. & Hiltz, S. R., (2003), *Factors that influence online relationship development in a knowledge sharing community*, Proceedings of the Ninth American Conference on Information Systems, 410 – 417.

Appendix I (Operationalisation)

No	Construct	Operationalisation	Source	Questionnaire Item
1	Knowledge provision (KP)	KP Duration		A08
		KP Frequency	Usoro et al., 2007	B03
		KP Environment	Chiu et al. (2006) p. 1874	B06 & B07
2	Knowledge reception (KR)	KR Duration		A07
		KR Frequency	(based on) Usoro et al., 2007	B01
		KR Environment	Chiu et al. (2006) p. 1874, Kankanhalli et al., 2005b, p. 1161	B05 & B09
		KR Applicability		B08
3	Norms of reciprocity (NRKP)	Reciprocity (KP)	Chiu et al. (2006) p. 1874, Kankanhalli et al. (2005a), Lin et al. (2009), p. 932, Usoro et al., 2007, p. 203, Gannon-Leary & Fontainha E, 2007, p. 6,	B15 B20
		NRKP Past Experiences		B21 & B22
		NRKP Affiliation	Chow & Chan, 2008, p. 459-460	C02
4	Norms of reciprocity (NRKR)	Reciprocity (KR)	Kankanhalli et al. (2005a), Kankanhalli et al., 2005b, p. 1158, Lin et al. (2009), p. 932, Gannon-Leary & Fontainha E, 2007, p. 6,	B14 C01
		NRKR Affiliation	Bock et al., 2006, p. 359, Chow & Chan, 2008, p. 459-460	C01
5	Perception of community (PCKP)	PCKP Affiliation	Chiu et al. (2006) p. 1874, Chiu et al 2009, p. 1874	B13
		PCKP Social	Kankanhalli et al. (2005a), Chiu et al. (2006) p. 1874, Chiu et al 2009, p. 1874, Zhang & Hiltz, 2003, Usoro et al., 2007, p. 203, Butler et al., 2002 p. 5, Gannon-Leary & Fontainha E, 2007, p. 6,	C02
		PCKP Competence	Usoro et al., 2007; Willem & Buelens, 2009, Bock et al., 2006,	C02
6	Perception of community (PCKR)	PCKR Affiliation	Bock et al., 2006, p. 359, Chow & Chan, 2008, p. 459-460	B12
		PCKR Social	Bock et al., 2006, 2005b p. 359, Butler et al., 2002 p. 5, Gannon-Leary & Fontainha E, 2007, p. 6, Kankanhalli et al., 2005b, p. 1158, Usoro et al., 2007,	C01
7	Perceived benefits (PBKP)	PBKP Status	Chiu et al. (2006) p. 1874	B11
		PBKP Incentives	Ardichvili et al. (2003), Chiu et al. (2006) p. 1874, Kankanhalli et al. (2005a), Butler et al., 2002, Butler et al., 2002 p. 9, Gannon-Leary & Fontainha E, 2007, p. 6	B16 B18
8	Perceived benefits (PBKR)	PBKR Incentives	Kankanhalli et al. (2005a), Bock et al., 2006, p. 357-359, p. 1158, Nebus (2004), Butler et al., 2002 p. 9, Gannon-Leary & Fontainha E, 2007, p. 6, Kankanhalli et al., 2005b, p. 1159	C01
9	Perceived costs (PCKP)	PCKP Conformism/ Peripherial Participation	Usoro et al., 2007, Wenger (1998)	B10
		PCKP Barriers	Davenport and Prusak 1998, Ardichvili et al. (2003), Bock et al., 2006, p 358, Kankanhalli et al. (2005a), Bock et al., 2006, p. 357-358, Gannon-Leary & Fontainha E, 2007, p. 3	B17 B19
		Integrity	Kankanhalli et al. (2005a), Chiu et al. (2006) p. 1877, Usoro et al., 2007; Willem & Buelens, 2009	C02
10	Perceived costs (PCKR)	PCKP Barriers	Ardichvili et al. (2003), Bock et al., 2006, p. 357-358, Gannon-Leary & Fontainha E, 2007, p. 3, Nebus (2004),	C01
11	Trust (KP)		Kankanhalli et al. (2005a), Chiu et al. (2006) p. 1874, Usoro et al., 2007; Willem & Buelens, 2009, Chow & Chan, 2008, Van den Hooff & Huysman, 2009, Lin et al. (2009), p. 932, Bock et al., 2006, Gannon-Leary & Fontainha E, 2007, p. 6,	C02
12	Trust (KR)		Bock et al., 2006, p. 358, Chow & Chan, 2008, Van den Hooff & Huysman, 2009, Lin et al. (2009), p. 932, Gannon-Leary & Fontainha E, 2007, p. 6,	C01

Appendix II (Principal Component Analysis)

	Component								
	1	2	3	4	5	6	7	8	9
KRecFreq	.772								
KProvFreq	.768								
KRecQua	.576								
K_Status	.537								
Kpro_Recip									
KProv1									
KProRecip2									
KProSoc		-.925							
KRecSoc1		-.832							
KProSoc1		-.500							
KPRecipNeg			-.630						
Kpro_ben			-.590						
KrecDur				.909					
KProvDur				.904					
KproQ					-.713				
Kpro_Recip1					-.707				
Kpro_cost2					.682				
Kpro_ben2									
K_App						.836			
KRecRecip2						.503			
KProRecip3									
Krec_Acq							.905		
Kpro_Acq							.746		
KRecRecip							.507		
K_Innova								.768	
Kpro_cost								.701	
KProSoc2									.852
KRecSoc2									.845
KProTrust									.540
KRecTrust									

Extraction Method: Principal Component Analysis. Rotation Method: Oblimin with Kaiser Normalization.
a) Rotation converged in 26 iterations.

Appendix III (Multiple regression analysis – original variables)

Hypothesis H_{11}.

(A) Model Summary

Model	R	R Square	Adjusted R Square	Std. Error of the Estimate
1	.984(a)	.968	.967	.468

a) Predictors: (Constant), KRecRecip2, KrecRecip b) Dependent Variable: KRecTrust

(B) Coefficients

Model	Unstandardized Coefficients		Standardized Coefficients	T	Sig.	Correlations			Collinearity Statistics	
	B	Std. Error	Beta	Lower Bound	Upper Bound	Part	Tolerance	VIF	B	Std. Error
1 (Constant)	-.737	.177		-4.162	.000					
KRecRecip	.200	.046	.078	4.373	.000	.288	.389	.076	.952	1.050
KRecRecip2	1.178	.022	.964	54.094	.000	.981	.982	.941	.952	1.050

a Dependent Variable: KRecTrust

THE ROLE OF "BRIDGE" SE IN KNOWLEDGE SHARING: A CASE STUDY OF SOFTWARE OFFSHORING FROM JAPAN TO VIETNAM

NGUYEN THU HUONG
School of Knowledge Science, Japan Advanced Institute of Science and Technology
1-1 Asahidai, Nomi, Ishikawa 923-1211, Japan
E-mail: thuhuong@jaist.ac.jp

UMEMOTO KATSUHIRO
School of Knowledge Science, Japan Advanced Institute of Science and Technology
1-1 Asahidai, Nomi, Ishikawa 923-1211, Japan
E-mail: ume@jaist.ac.jp

This paper examines the impact of the nature of software offshoring on knowledge sharing. A case study of software offshoring from Japan to Vietnam has been conducted. We focus on analyzing some features such as cross-cultural context, the high security and Intellectual Property Right issues, the one-way knowledge sharing process. Findings indicate that these factors slow down knowledge sharing process. We also recognized that utilizing Bridge SE (System Engineer) is an effective way to cope with these challenges. We finally concluded that the term Bridge SE should be studied more by both academics and practitioners.

1. Introduction

An increasing number of organizations choose offshore outsourcing as a strategic decision. According to statistics from Ventoro Institute with 5,231 executives in North America and Europe, 19% of all companies in their polls have current Offshoring strategy. And among Fortune 1000 firms, the number of firms using Offshore Strategy is 95%.[a] The reasons why companies choose to outsource include cost savings, improved performance, and access to wider labor markets (Krishna et al., 2004).

While the traditional focus is on manufacturing offshoring, success in high technology, especially, is of more recent interest (Carmel, 2003). In the context of the global knowledge economy, major corporations are more involved with knowledge intensive work such as software development. And in fact, the successful software export nations (China, India, and Ireland) also raise concerns about software development. Many developing nations now promote and consider Software development for their own economic strategy.

As software offshoring is "knowledge intensive work", both client (service receivers) and vendor (service providers) realize that knowledge management (KM) is an important contributor to the success of their organizations (Balaji and Ahuja, 2005; Lee, 2001; Oshri, 2007). One of the most important topics discussed among KM issues in offshoring is knowledge sharing between clients and vendors. Other issues are knowledge transfer, knowledge retention or knowledge integration. However, most of the research hasn't

1. [a] Ventoro, Offshore 2005 Research, Preliminary Findings and Conclusions.

mentioned the impact of the nature of software offshoring on KM practice, although software offshoring complicated KM.

Our study focuses on the impact of the nature of software offshoring on Knowledge sharing, and explores the relationship between coordinator and knowledge sharing in software offshoring in the cross-cultural context. The term "cross-cultural context" refers to an environment in which a business is operated by members of different organizations with different capacities and professional levels of working, cultural norms of social behavior, attitudes to authority, and language issues. Among many KM issues, we choose to study knowledge sharing because has been proved to be important for successful software offshoring projects, by supporting the communication process in a cross-cultural context.

In this paper, we adopt case study as research strategy. In detail, the case analysis is based on our ongoing research with an offshore software service provider in Vietnam with their Japanese customers. We selected software offshoring from Japan to Vietnam as our case study because:

- Vietnam is an emerging software exporting nation which made significant gains this year as the quality and availability of their labor forces improved and ranked 10th in the Global Service Local Index 2009's top 10[b].
- Vietnamese government promotes software outsourcing industry development, and considers Japan as the most important strategic destination for software service export.
- Japanese software developers have recently had strong interest in offshoring to Vietnam as a "China plus One" because of the increase of labor costs and competition in China, as well as some attractive features of Vietnam such as: near shore location, cultural compatibility, political stability, governmental incentives, time zone and travel time.

Our paper is organized as follows: we first give a comprehensive review of knowledge sharing and the concept of "coordinator" in the offshore outsourcing field. The next section describes the research methodology and data collection since August 2008. We then present our case analysis with FPT Software. Finally we describe the conclusion of our research.

2. Literature Review

2.1. *Knowledge Sharing in Offshore Outsourcing*

"Offshore outsourcing" and "offshoring" are often used interchangeably and incorrectly for the term "outsourcing." However, "outsourcing is the act of transferring the work to an external party" [Power et al., 2006, p.3] while "offshore outsourcing" is, in fact, a small but important subset of outsourcing, wherein, a company outsource work to a

---

2. [b] http://www.atkearney.com/index.php/News-media/geography-of-offshoring-is-shifting.html

third party in a country other than the one in which the client company is based, primarily to take advantage of lower labor costs (Nguyen et al., 2008).

Among many KM issues, knowledge sharing has been discussed extensively, due to a typical characteristic of offshore projects: the business transactions happen among partners in different countries. At its most basic level, knowledge sharing is defined as involving the ***processes*** through which knowledge is channeled between a source and a recipient (Cummings, 2003). There are many criteria for knowledge sharing. In the case of offshore outsourcing, we understand that it can be divided into two types based on geographical distance: knowledge sharing inside borders and knowledge sharing across-borders. In the scope of this research, we focus on studying knowledge sharing across-borders, or cross-cultural knowledge sharing in offshore outsourcing.

According to him, there are five key relational factors that affect successful knowledge sharing implementations: the organizational distance, physical distance, institutional distance, knowledge distance and relationship distance. When we link these factors to the practices of offshore outsourcing, we recognize that the cross-cultural context of offshore outsourcing makes it challenge with all five factors, which create barriers for effective communication among partners across borders.

The importance of knowledge sharing in offshore outsourcing has been discussed much in recent research. Some studies emphasized the relationship between knowledge sharing and outsourcing success, such as Lee (2001) or Kotlarsky and Oshri (2005). According to Lee (2001), knowledge sharing is one of the major predictors of outsourcing success, and organizational capability to learn or acquire the needed knowledge from other organizations is a key source of successful knowledge sharing. Also, partnership quality is a significant factor in knowledge sharing and outsourcing success. By an in-depth ethnographic study of globally distributed software development projects, Kotlarsky and Oshri (2005) argued that human related issues in the form of social ties and knowledge sharing contribute to successful collaboration in distributed IS development teams, and they emphasize the importance of "rapport" and "transactive memory". Rapport is defined as 'the quality of the relation or connection between interactants, marked by harmony, conformity, accord, and affinity' while transactive memory is defined as the set of knowledge possessed by group members, coupled with an awareness of who knows what.

Differing from the above research, Prikladnicki et al. (2003) identified problems that organizations have faced when going global in software development. Their research showed that one of the most difficult problems is information sharing between teams across geographic and cultural boundaries. The interviews conducted with two software units indicated that investment in Knowledge Management (tools or activities that stimulate information sharing) minimized many obstacles to global software development. This research topic has also been discussed by Nicholson and Sahay through a case study of British software developers working with their counterparts in India. They used three types of knowledge proposed by Blacker (1995), encoded, encultured and embedded knowledge, to analyze knowledge sharing in communities of practice in the international context. According to Blacker, encoded knowledge is conveyed by signs and symbols within manuals, notations, and standards and codes of practice that need to be encoded and transmitted electronically using various ICTs. Encoded knowledge is recorded and can be accessible. It can either be structured or unstructured. Some examples are Internet, intranet, email, newsletter, etc. Encultured knowledge reflects more broadly the structures, policies, norms, traditions, rituals and values of an organization or society (Smircich, 1983). Embedded knowledge is that which resides in routines, best practices, policies, programs, technologies, roles, formal procedures and methods. The study of Nicholson and Sahay concluded that these 3 types of knowledge are useful for identifying some of the barriers which may exist to the legitimacy of community learning in the international context. A key contribution of their study is showing the importance of encultured knowledge, and the means by which this can affect the legitimacy of participation in the community.

By a game theory analysis, Bandyopadhyay and Pathak (2007) argued knowledge sharing to be a strategic interaction between employees of the "host" firm and the outsourcing firm who have to share knowledge and skill sets in order to work effectively as a team, but might be naturally antagonistic toward each other. They concluded that when the degree of complementary knowledge between the employees is high, better payoffs can be achieved if the top management enforces cooperation between the employees.

In short, there are many research studies on the relationship between knowledge sharing and offshore outsourcing, and some studies of which focus on offshore software development. However, most of the research hasn't mentioned the impact of the nature of offshore software development on knowledge sharing practice, which complicated knowledge sharing.

2.2. *Coordinator in Offshore Outsourcing*

For the case of offshore outsourcing, we understand a coordinator can be staff of client's company or vendor company and work as a middle man between two partners in cross-cultural context (as in Fig.1). The concept "coordinator" has also been named by several terms, such as Onsite Coordinator, Straddler, Envoys, Customer's Representatives, Offshore Intermediaries, or Bridge SE.

Explaining the roles and responsibilities of participants in offshore activities, Braun (2007) emphasized the important role of ***Onsite Coordinator***. The Onsite Coordinator is explained as the Single Point of Contact for the offshore team leaders. They coordinate all requests from the offshore staff and track the status of assignments and work packages on a daily basis. He argued that the most important role regarding communication between the onshore (project) and the offshore domain is the Single Point of Contact or the Onsite Coordinator.

Rost (2006) mentioned in his research that a major challenge for offshore software projects is the unavoidable long-distance communication. If this problem is not solved, the communication costs are likely to take up most of the potential cost savings. Following this line of argument, he proposed some tactical approaches that can help reduce the cost of communication as well as cultural distance. The ***Straddler*** (also known as ***Liaison***) is a staff member on the vendor side, who works either for a certain time or periodically at the client's site, and travels back and forth between client and vendor. He concluded that the Straddler significantly reduces the cultural distance between the client's business culture and the industrialized country's culture. The concepts of ***Envoy*** and ***Customer's Representatives*** have also been discussed. Envoys are staff of client companies who travel between client and vendor's country. During the periods of time when the Envoy comes is in the vendor company's country, the envoy is usually embedded into the vendor's team. Meanwhile, the Customer Representative can be staff of the client company or of an independent company that runs an office geographically close to the vendor. The duties of representatives are to take on surveillance tasks and make decisions on the customer's behalf.

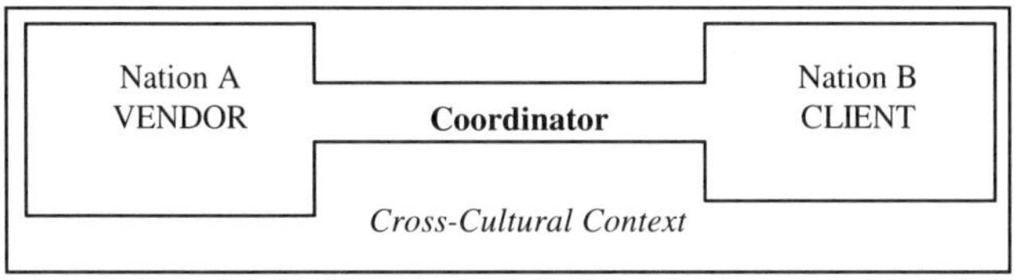

Fig. 1: Coordinator in Offshore Outsourcing

In addition to some concepts of Rost, Krishna et al. (2004) use the term ***'Cultural Bridging Staff'*** to describe the role of coordinator in offshore outsourcing projects. They stated that cultural bridging staff are people who are rooted in both cultures and can "bridge" cultures. For example, people originally from India, but with higher education and long-term residence in North America, have been reposted to India as expatriate managers for offshore outsourcing projects. Research of Mahnke et al. (2008) mentioned the term ***"Offshore Intermediary"***, a new breed of offshore 'broker' or 'middleman' providing offshore intermediation capabilities. He argued that there is a need for boundary spanning capabilities in offshore systems development partnerships - a need that can be fulfilled by offshore intermediaries. The capabilities of a 'middleman' include moderating disparities in expertise, culture, and communication styles that often reduce performance in offshore relationships. The author explained that one key task of the offshore intermediary is to develop inter-firm social and intellectual capital to create interfaces allowing for inter-firm knowledge identification, knowledge sharing, and knowledge combination across company and cultural boundaries.

The term ***"Bridge SE"*** has recently been used by some Japanese scholars. According to Honda et al. (2004), Bridge SE is a system engineer, who is in charge of bridging between client and vendor company's staff in the project. It's popular that Bridge SE is from the staff of vendor side, can speak Japanese and understand Japanese business culture to get over the communication gap. They explained also that "Bridge SE" is similar to the concept "Onsite Coordinator". However, while the main task of the Onsite Coordinator is to connect with people offsite, the Bridge SE's role is to bridge between vendor's national culture and Japanese culture.

Despite some minor differences regarding the function and duty in Offshore Projects, we found that the terms: Onsite Coordinator, Straddler, Envoys, Customer's Representatives, Offshore Intermediaries, or Bridge SE share the same characteristic: they work as a coordinator who bridges two sides across a border. Therefore they can be called "Cross-cultural Coordinator". The term cross-cultural coordinator started to appear in some studies, but a definition of cross-cultural coordinator has not been adopted yet. Based on these above terms, cross-cultural coordinator can be understood as a coordinator who masters both languages, understands two cultures and works as a bridge to harmonize the cross-border relationship. In this research, we propose a hypothesis that there is a relationship between cross-cultural coordinator and knowledge sharing. In order to test this hypothesis, we conduct a case study of a software offshore project from Japan to Vietnam.

3. Research Methodology

In this paper, we chose case study as the research strategy. We chose FPT Software, one of the fastest growing companies in Vietnam's software development outsourcing industry for our case study. Our study focuses on the software outsourcing relationship between FPT Software and their Japanese customers such as Cannon IT Solutions, Hitachi, TIS and so on. This analysis is based on our ongoing research with operation group leaders in Hanoi headquarters and project managers in the Tokyo subsidiary. In detail, we study the impact of the nature of offshore outsourcing on knowledge sharing, and then explore the role of cross-cultural coordinator in the offshore project.

FPT Software is a member of FPT Corporation, the biggest IT Company in Vietnam. FPT Software now has 21 operating groups which are located in 3 biggest cities of Vietnam (Ha Noi, Da Nang, Ho Chi Minh). Also, they have branches in Japan (Tokyo, Osaka), Southeast Asia (Singapore, Malaysia, Thailand, the Philippine), Europe (France), the United States and Australia.

The data collection was composed of primary and secondary sources. The primary data analysis is based on our ongoing research where we have conducted 15 interviews with group leaders, and project managers (10 in Hanoi and 5 in Tokyo). We chose the offshore project with Japan as our case study because Japan is the biggest customer of FPT Software, with 61% of the market by revenue. The primary data collection includes two phases with two questionnaires; the first is on the current state of software offshoring relationship, and the knowledge sharing practices between FPT software operation groups and Japanese partners, through face to face semi-structured interviews. The second is on the role of coordinator in offshore projects through email interviews. We also visited their offices and joined some remote seminars. Secondary sources are also used: document reviews on organizational structure, business field and their business strategy, beyond access to the home pages and company brochure.

4. Findings and Analysis

4.1. *Case Background*

FPT Software Joint Stock Company (homepage: www.fpt-soft.com) is a subsidiary of FPT Corporation, the biggest IT Company in Vietnam. During the past 20 years FPT Software has been one of the fastest growing companies in Vietnam's software development outsourcing industry, with over 42 million USD in 2008 revenues. FPT Software employed 2,700 young and dynamic staff as of 2008. Their development centers have been certified with CMMi level 5, BS 7799-2: 2002 (ISO 27001:2005) and ISO 9001: 2000.

FPT Software has business mainly in the domains of Banking and Financial services, Utilities, Telecom, Manufacturing, Insurance, Government and Public Services, IT Services, Retail, and Infrastructure. They provide Software services such as: Software development, Maintenance, ERP Implementation, Quality Assurance Testing, Migration Services, Business Process Outsourcing, Embedded Systems Development.

Their business segmentation focuses mainly on the overseas market. The country that has most customers is Japan which, with 19 clients, occupies 61% of the market by revenue. Others are Asia Pacific (13%), EU (10%), US (10%) and domestic market with only 6%.

The main competences includes: Large pool of young staff, Multi-Languages and International Presence. FPT Software is among the 50 VN Best Employers[c], said to be the largest pool of software engineers in Vietnam with competitive turnover rate (8% in 2006)[d] and comprehensive training process. FPT Software recognized human capital is a core feature in developing and executing organizational strategy, as an available resource for large scale projects with high motivation and fast learning. By providing opportunities to the entire staff to develop their work-related knowledge and skills, they expect to increase effectiveness and also make a richer contribution to the work of FPT Software. As a software development firm, FPT Software strives to be a learning organization, with its responsibility to encourage and support learning throughout its constituent departments. Most staff in FPT Software can speak English. Although the levels are various, English is the most widely-used language at FPT Software. In addition, the company provides its staff with a number of English training courses, as well as an English club to encourage English communication within the company. The third value core contributing to success for FPT Software is International Presence, which has been created basing on these above 2 core values. Communications between FPT Software staff and customers are conducted in English, French, or Japanese. This includes all project documentation, e-mails, phone

---

3. [c] Ranking by Navigos Group, AC Nielsen, April, 2007.
4. [d] FPT Software Overview, Company Profile, 2007.

conversations, and Net meetings. There were only 350 staff in FPT Software in 2003, but this number increased nearly 3 times every 2 years up to 1000 members in 2005, and 2700 members in 2009. With this number, FPT Software is really a large pool of young, talented, IT professionals. 90% of these employees graduated from the three most well known IT universities in Vietnam, the remaining 10% graduated from a series of FPT Aptech IT Professional training centers.

FPT Software has 21 operation groups (OG) which are located in the 3 main cities of Vietnam: Hanoi, Danang and Ho Chi Minh City. In this research, we present our data collection from 3 OGs, which mainly supply software offshore services for the Japanese market, and 3 project managers who are working in FPT Japan, a subsidiary of FPT Software in Tokyo. And Japanese customers include Cannon IT Solutions, Hitachi, TIS, Nippon Steel, Toshiba, and Fujitsu Software.

4.2. *The Impact of Offshore Outsourcing on Knowledge Sharing*

Knowledge which has been shared between offshore teams of FPT Software and Japanese customers includes:

- Explicit knowledge: requirements, technical documents, specification information, and test reports. This knowledge is easy to share by using advanced ICTs, one of the strengths of software development field.
- Tacit knowledge: Question and Answer (Q&A) regarding requirement and proposal, common rules, cultural match, post-mortem analysis results, and the new ideas of engineers, project managers, Bridge SEs and other members from both FPT Software side and Japanese customers' companies. This tacit knowledge is said to be difficult to share and manage.

Our data collection focuses mainly on the tacit knowledge sharing between two partners. First, although Vietnamese and Japanese culture have similarities basing on Eastern culture root, there still remains some cultural differences that is obstacles in the relationship. We found that there are many factors challenging the knowledge sharing between offshore teams of FPT Software and their Japanese customers that we call "cross-cultural" factors, such as: the language differences, cultural differences, or differences in the capacity and professional levels of staff. These are the main challenges preventing the communication process between two partners, which also is the key indicator of a successful offshore relationship. For instance, the Japanese clients tend to be relatively clear about separation between work and home. When a Japanese developer came in to work, he would not respond to a personal phone call or run out for private errands during working hours. Japanese people are encouraged to work overtime or even on weekends when the work is required. The situation is different in Vietnamese offshore development teams where work and home lives were more tightly integrated. Some developers made private phone calls even using the company's telephone, or went out for lunch with friends until late. Also they aren't accustomed to overtime culture, and they refuse overtime work on evenings or weekends, and instead go out with their friends.

Second, the data collection indicates that the high security and Intellectual Property Right issues in offshore software development make knowledge sharing become very complicated. If the client company (service receiver) isn't concerned about management decisions on what knowledge may be shared and what may not, their staff will have no orientation on what they are allowed to share and what not, and will become stuck. This prevents the knowledge sharing process among staff at the two partners, and proves that the management of knowledge is very important and should be a major concern of offshore project managers.

Third, the knowledge sharing in software offshoring from Japan to Vietnam is almost one-way relationship due to limitations in capacity of Vietnamese IT engineers such as limited IT skills, communication skills, group working skills, misunderstanding of Japanese working way. These limitations slow down the knowledge sharing process. And the Japanese customers take a lot of time to educate and train Vietnamese engineers from the starting point. Vietnamese project managers see this factor as strength as well as limitation. They high appreciate the cooperation and patience of Japanese customers to educate Vietnamese IT engineer at the beginning of project. Also they mentioned that this factor make the progress of knowledge sharing between two partners slower.

We recognized that the cross-cultural factors, the high security and IPR issues, the one-way knowledge sharing slow down the knowledge sharing process. Although Japanese customers are very constructive to shorten the communication gap or the knowledge sharing limitation, it takes time for both sides to get acquaintance of each other. And in order to deal with these challenges, some coordinators have been utilized to enforce the relationship.

4.3. *The Role of Coordinator and its Relationship to Knowledge Sharing*

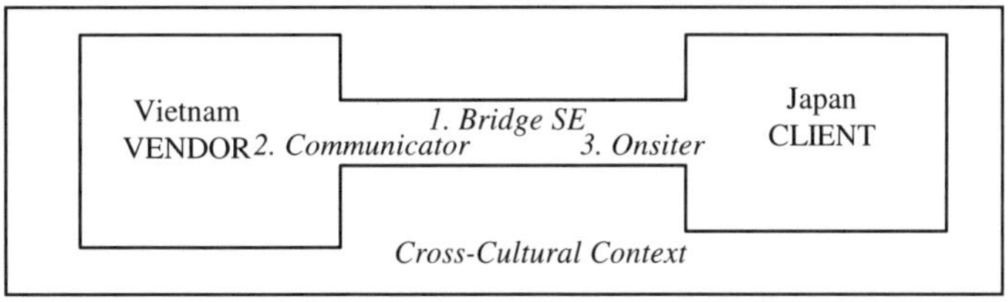

Fig. 2: Coordinators in Offshore Outsourcing from Japan to Vietnam

Two types of coordinators that are popular in Offshore Projects with Japanese customers are "Bridge SE" and "Communicator". These roles are explained in Table 1.

In addition to Bridge SE and Communicator, an ***Onsiter*** is also used to support Bridge SE in the technical design phase. The Onsiter is an engineer of FPT Software, who is sent to Japan and works with the Bridge SE. However, onsiter is not used as often as other coordinators, just in cases when the Bridge SE does not have good IT skills, or on complicated and large-scale projects. Fig. 2 shows the positions of 3 types of coordinators in offshore projects from Japan to Vietnam:

Table 1: Coordinators in Offshore Software Project

	Communicator	***Bridge SE***
Main duties	- translate technical requirements and others documents from Japanese to Vietnamese - work as an interpreter in meetings with customers	- get requirements from customers and deliver to offshore team - manage project such as Q&A, progress report, review detailed design, review test case
Requirements	Japanese skill	- Japanese skill - IT skills - Communication skill - Project management skill - 3-5 years experience as a system engineer
Other	- work with offshore project teams in Vietnam - often is a staff member of FPT Software	- work independent of offshore project teams, travel back and forth between Japan and Vietnam - often is a staff member of FPT Software

All managers agreed that among 3 types of coordinators, Bridge SE is the most useful actor due to their involvement in the project. In fact, many Bridge SEs work as project managers. Fig. 3 shows the working process of a Bridge SE. Our data collection showed that all projects need the presence of Bridge SE. This is explained by the fact that most IT engineers in projects can't speak Japanese and don't speak English very well, while Japanese customers don't want to speak English. There are no other ways except using coordinators who can speak Japanese. With IT skills, communication skills and other capacities, Bridge SE (System Engineer) works as not only a general coordinator but also a member involved in the offshore project and improves the quality of projects. Therefore, the role of Bridge SE in the project is very important and influences the success of the project, especially in this context: Japan is the biggest customer of FPT Software (with 65% market share). However, there are not many System Engineers able to become Bridge SEs due to the many requirements for a Bridge SE. Our data show that there is a serious lack of Bridge SEs, both regarding quality and quantity. And educating Bridge SEs is one of the important missions of FPT Software.

As in our analysis in the previous part, the main knowledge sharing challenge includes cross-cultural factors such as language differences, cultural differences, or differences in the capacity and professional level of staff. Overcoming these challenges improves the communication within the offshore project, which is the main success indicator of the project. By using their IT skill, Japanese skill, and understanding of Japanese culture as well as Japanese business customs, Bridge SEs can fill this communication gap.

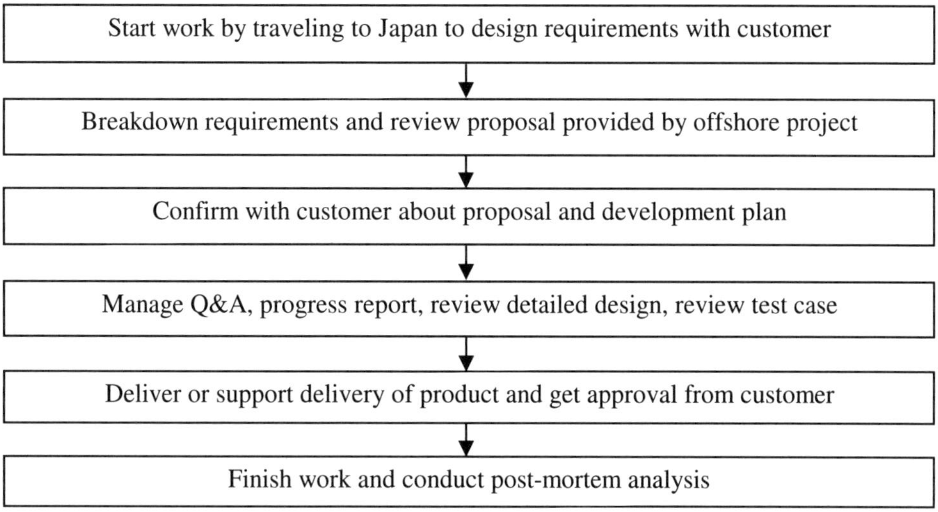

Fig. 3: Working process of a Bridge SE

5. Conclusion

In this research, we gave a review of knowledge sharing and the concept of "Coordinator" in the offshore outsourcing field. A case study of an offshore software project from Japan to Vietnam has been conducted through 3 Operation Groups of FPT Software, with two main topics: the impact of the nature of software offshoring on knowledge sharing; the role of cross-cultural coordinator and their relationship with knowledge sharing between a Vietnamese service provider and Japanese clients.

We recognized that the cross-cultural factors, the high security and the Intellectual Property Right issues, the one-way knowledge sharing slow down the knowledge sharing process. Our data analysis shows that the Bridge SE (System Engineer) has been utilized to fill communication gaps, and thereby, to cope with knowledge sharing challenges. The next step of this research is to study how cross-cultural factors – the main challenge of software offshoring - are managed from a Knowledge Management point of view, which has yet to receive adequate research attention.

References

Balaji S. and Ahuja M.K. (2005) "Critical Team-Level Success Factors of Offshoring Outsourced Projects: A Knowledge Integration Perspective", *Proceedings of Hawaii International Conference on Systems Science, HICSS 2005,* (2): 52-60.

Bandyopadhyay, S. and Pathak, Praveen (2006) "Knowledge sharing and cooperation in outsourcing projects - A game theoretic analysis", *Decision Support Systems,* 43: 349-358.

Blacker, F. (1995) "Knowledge, Knowledge Work and Organizations: An Overview and Interpretation", *Organization Studies,* 16(6): 1047-75.

Braun, A. (2007) "A framework to enable Offshore Outsourcing", *International Conference on Global Software Engineering, ICGSE 2007.*

Carmel, E. (2003) "The new software exporting nations: success factors", *The Electric Journal of Information Systems in Developing Countries*, 13(4): 1-12.

Cummings, J. (2003) *Knowledge Sharing: A Literature Review*, The World Bank Washington, D.C

Honda N. et al, (2004) "The successful conditions of Offshore Software Development", In: Higuchi T. (edited) *Perfect Guide for Offshore Software Development*, S-open Offshore Software Development Research Association (in Japanese)

Huong, T.N., Umemoto K., Dam H.C (2008) "Offshore Software Development: A Knowledge Management Perspective", *The Proceedings of The 3rd International Conference on Knowledge, Information and Creativity Support Systems, KICSS2008*, Dec. 22-23, Hanoi, Vietnam, pp 9-13.

Kotlarsky, J. and Orhri, I. (2005) "Social ties, knowledge sharing and successful collaboration in globally distributed system development projects", *European Journal of Information Systems,* 14: 37-48.

Krishna, S., Sahay, S., and Walsham, G. (2004) "Managing cross-cultural issues in global software outsourcing", *Communications of the ACM*, 47(4): 62-66.

Lee J.N. (2001) "The impact of knowledge sharing, organizational capability and partnership quality on IS outsourcing success", *Information and Management*, 38: 323-335.

Nicholson B. and Sahay S. (2006) "Knowledge Management in Offshore Software Development", In: Hirschheim R. et al. (eds). *Information Systems Outsourcing*, Springer: 659-686.

Oshri, I. et al. (2007) "Managing Dispersed Expertise in IT Offshore Outsourcing: Lessons from TATA Consultancy Services", *MIS Quarterly Executive*, 6(2): 53-65.

Power, M. J. et al. (2006) *The Outsourcing Handbook: How to implement a Successful Outsourcing Process*, Kogan Page Limited.

Prikladnicki, R., Audy, J.L.N. and Evaristo, R. (2003) "Global Software Development in Practice: Lessons Learned", *Software Process Improvement and Practice,* 8: 267-281.

Rost, J. (2006) *The Insider's Guide to Outsourcing Risks and Rewards*, Auerbach Publications.

Smircich, L. (1983) "Concepts of culture and organizational analysis", *Administrative Science Quarterly,* 28(3): 393-58.

FACTORS INFLUENCING KNOWLEDGE SHARING IN IMMERSIVE VIRTUAL WORLDS: AN EMPIRICAL STUDY WITH A SECOND LIFE GROUP

GRZEGORZ MAJEWSKI and ABEL USORO
School of Computing, University of the West of Scotland
Paisley, PA1 2BE, UK
grzegorz.majewski@uws.ac.uk, abel.usoro@uws.ac.uk

Immersive virtual worlds such as Second Life have recently gained much attention from education and business because of its adaptability to address real world challenges such as: on-line presentations, meetings, collaboration, 3D data visualization and on-line knowledge sharing. It is also possible to use immersive virtual worlds for the purpose of facilitating knowledge sharing in Virtual communities of practice (VCoP). Varieties of such communities exist in Second Life and help their members to achieve their goals. There is however not enough research into knowledge sharing in immersive virtual worlds. Therefore the purpose of this research is to fill this gap in knowledge. The conceptual model proposed by Usoro and Majewski (2008) will be applied to knowledge sharing in immersive virtual world environment. It will be investigated what factors are the most influential while residents of immersive virtual worlds share their knowledge. As a first attempt to validate the research model, quantitative and qualitative research was carried out with participants of Second Life group.

1. Introduction

Knowledge sharing is valued by modern organisations because they view their success to be highly dependent not only on their employees' possession of knowledge but more importantly on the dynamic flow of this knowledge between the employees. Research so far indicates that Collaborative Virtual Environments (CVE) may be effective ways of capturing and sharing knowledge (Tomek, 2001). CVE is a "software environment that emulates some of the features of the real world" (Tomek 2001, pp 458-459). The characteristics of the real world that are usually emulated are: the concept of space, the representation of an object, the representation of a human (in a form of avatar), and various tools that can be used to interact with other objects.

A CVE "channels" knowledge sharing activities through software medium. However instead of a knowledge giver having to type into the system explanations of some accomplished task, he or she can easily perform the task in a CVE using his or her electronic surrogate (avatar). The playing out of activities or knowledge is very useful especially in the case of sharing tacit knowledge which may not be fully realized by even their owners. A CVE, such as Second Life (SL) essentially captures relevant parts of the work process, organizes it and provides data retrieval and data mining functions. It may motivate employees to share their knowledge by combining work and entertainment-like functions (Tomek 2001, p 459). The 3D environment can also "help develop a common understanding in a collaborative mind set and engage people through appealing and memorable experiences" (Schmeil & Eppler 2008, p 667). Apart from encouraging creativity at a high scale, the opportunity to interact with the 3D world via a virtual self – avatar - helps participants to develop much stronger social ties as compared with a static web discussion board or forum.

While employing SL in knowledge management and collaboration related activities it is necessary to consider the following characteristics of this environment (Tomek 2001, Ondrejka 2008, Schmeil & Eppler 2008):

- As a prerequisite for a successful groupware, physical topology is emulated as a common metaphor to give a natural perception of the environment.
- People, information and knowledge can be organized spatially.
- Awareness of co-workers, usage policies for tools and objects is enhanced.
- Content is produced by residents of the world; developers provide powerful tools designed to be used by everyone.
- Group and private chat functionality, as well as object sharing provide inherent collaboration possibilities are provided (additionally all communication can be logged instantly).
- Social/collaborative aspect – inherent collaboration between avatars – is facilitated.
- Constructivist aspect – playing or creating objects and so creating correlations and knowledge from current structures is inherent in SL (Antonacci, 2005).
- Collaborative problem solving engaging several avatars is supported.

Second Life and other environments based on Virtual Reality resemble the physical reality and thus it is easier for the participants to engage with them and usually such engagement is to a higher degree. It comes however at a price – 3D models are more difficult to use (require more manipulation of the user's avatar) and may distract from the communication (Tomek 2001, p 461). In comparison to a "flat" graphical CVE a truly 3D environment makes it possible to interact with information that is dynamic and interactive.

2. Theoretical Background

As it was discussed before through the use of virtual immersive worlds it is possible to engage employees to a much higher level as compared with traditional means. Edirisingha et al. indicate that 3D environments such as Second Life promote socialisation among participants (learners) and that is a "key stage for learning in online environments" (p. 459). Learning may be perceived as reception of knowledge provided by other participants. Immersive virtual worlds have the potential to generate much greater sense of presence and belonging to a given community or subculture. These in turn may result in increased levels of knowledge sharing. The feeling of presence helps reduce the emotional and psychological distance between geographically dispersed participants. Collaboration is successful when the "learners feel comfortable with each other and when they are provided with opportunities for socialisation" (p. 460). Online socialisation is more than just getting to know each other. It extends to participants establishing their online identities, finding others with whom to interact online, developing trust and mutual respect, and working on common tasks online.

In some cases a shared 3D virtual environment may enable the creation of a virtual community of practice, and in fact extend into real-life collaboration (Jarmon & Sanchez, 2008). It is necessary to understand that usually in virtual worlds such as Second Life, the main experience of the user is the experience of a variety of social networks with different goals (e.g.: building, playing, buy, selling, working). Second Life in this view is more of a social experience than a simple game. It may be perceived as both a social and a technical system. Jarmon & Sanchez (2008) describe the community grounded in the framework of Communities of Practice (Wenger 1998) – The Educators Coop Island. The technical system was based on the *spiral of knowledge* by Nonaka and Takeuchi (1995), where participants have opportunities to participate in a spiral of sharing explicit and tacit knowledge. The research found out that "through their experiential learning, the residents are building on their part knowledge and expertise and are improvising a new community of practice in Second Life." (p. 70). Authors conclude the virtual world environment creates opportunities to experience and understand issues that may be difficult to comprehend without actually "living" through them in the real life. Moreover participants began to rapidly expand their networking activity by using other networks outside Second Life (Google social software – joint documents and calendars).

3. Research Model

Knowledge sharing in immersive virtual worlds is a complex phenomenon. As it was discussed previously social perspective is one of the most important ones. The perception of a given community a person (in a form of avatar) participates in is central to knowledge sharing processes. For the purposes of this research it will be investigated how the perception of community affects two most common knowledge sharing activities: knowledge provision and knowledge seeking. The importance of social ties in knowledge sharing is also emphasized by Chiu et al. (2006). It can be argued that people coming to a community in Second Life "are not just seeking information or knowledge to solve problems but they also treat it as a place to meet other people, to seek support, friendship and a sense of belonging." (Chiu et al 2009, p. 1874). Kankanhalli et al. (2005a) agree. These ideas are put into the following hypotheses:

- H_1: Perception of community is positively associated with knowledge *provision*.
- H_2: Perception of community is positively associated with knowledge *reception*.

Perception of community is itself influenced by such factors as trust and norm of reciprocity. Kankanhalli et al. (2005a) concluded that reciprocity is positively related to knowledge sharing. The hypotheses that can be derived are that:

- H_3: The norm of reciprocity is positively associated with the perception of community while providing knowledge.
- H_4: The norm of reciprocity is positively associated with the perception of community while seeking knowledge.

Hypothesis H_3 states that the expectation of reciprocity (i.e. of being helped in the future by other members) influences the way the community is perceived. Participants are also more eager to receive knowledge from a community with an established reputation than from a new one they do not know yet, and consequently the reputation and perception of the community determines the way its members treat one another. In the case of H_4 it is also supported by the view that "the exchange of intellectual capital can be facilitated by norms of collaboration and sharing". The opinions of superiors and peers affect human decisions to use a given technology and to seek knowledge (Kankanhalli et al., 2005b, p. 1158).

Another important factor influencing knowledge sharing in VCoP is trust. It is possible to distinguish the following components of trust: competence (expertise), benevolence and integrity (Usoro et al., 2007; Willem & Buelens, 2009). The study by Usoro et al. (2007) investigates how these components affect knowledge provision in VCoP and conclude that there is a positive association. Trust may also be seen as a facilitator of social ties (Chow & Chan, 2008) and thus has a positive impact on knowledge sharing. "The level of social trust influences expectations of a colleague's intention and behaviour. Organizational members are thus more likely to expect those who are trustworthy to share their knowledge" (Chow & Chan 2008, p. 460). On the other hand social ties positively influence mutual trust (Van den Hooff & Huysman, 2009). In other words it seems that trust is highly associated with the social aspect of VCoP. A study by Lin et al. (2009) indicates that norms of reciprocity influence trust, which in turn affect knowledge sharing self-efficacy, perceived relative advantage, perceived compatibility and knowledge sharing behaviour. Usoro et al. (2007) link some trust components with reciprocity, while indicating that it further influences the sense of community: "Where the sense of community is strong and benevolence is high, community members are more likely to perceive knowledge as a public good, owned and maintained by the community. Conversely, if one's sense of community's benevolence is low, expectations of future reciprocity may likewise be low, and knowledge sharing is unlikely to be fostered" (Usoro et al., 2007, p. 203).

Trust also affects knowledge reception. It is trust in the credibility, expertise and reputation of the contributor (knowledge source) that matters. "Perceived value from knowledge seeking depends on the contributor's (source's) expertise and credibility, while perceived expectation of value is determined by trust, obligation, and the contributor's willingness to help" (Bock et al., 2006). It is possible to say that trust in on-line community affects the perception of the community on the knowledge receiver side. If the community is perceived as competent in answering queries it is expected that a knowledge seeker will keep posting his or her questions. Other trust components count as well, because a knowledge receiver needs to be able to rely on the knowledge provided by the community. Thus benevolence and integrity are also important. It is possible to formulate the following hypotheses based on these facts:

- H_5: Trust is positively associated with the perception of community while providing knowledge.
- H_6: Trust is positively associated with the perception of community while receiving knowledge.
- H_7: The Norm of reciprocity is positively associated with trust while providing knowledge.
- H_8: The Norm of reciprocity is positively associated with trust while receiving knowledge.

These hypotheses are utilized in the construction of a conceptual model that will embrace both roles that can be played by the participants of VCoP. A simplified version of such research model is presented on Figure 1:

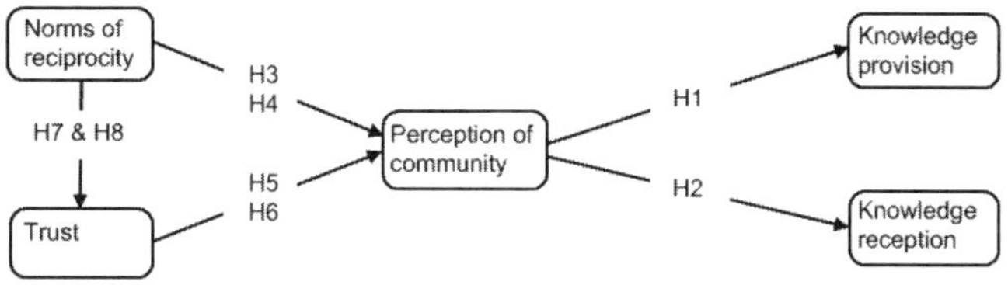

Figure 1 Conceptual model of factors influencing knowledge sharing in VCoP in immersive virtual environment.

4. Research Methodology

The hypotheses were tested by way of qualitative and quantitative research with the Lucky Tribe group in Second Life. The group was carefully selected to reflect the Second Life environment. This huge 3-D immersive virtual world embraces profit-oriented organisations as well as people that seek different sorts of entertainment. The idea behind the group was to promote various vendors across the grid as well as generate traffic on their lands. It is however achieved through the activities that are very often entertaining in their nature. The economic analysis of the whole venture is beyond the scope of this paper; however it is possible to say that in this case knowledge sharing between participants has some economic aspects in the background. By participating in the community and sharing knowledge participants may be rewarded in a variety of ways.

Lucky Tribe group at the time of the distribution of the questionnaire had more than 1,480 members. Participants of this group perform a variety of functions in Second Life for which they are awarded the group own "currency" – kudos points. Furthermore there are tools and practices that enhance the strength of the social ties: dedicated Heads Up Display (HUD) showing achievements of the given member and also ability to check status (by showing the number of kudos points a given person has). The practices that enhance the social ties are special events or quests where members have to gather together to collaboratively do a given task. This community actually expands to other technologies (such as flicker and blogs). For successfully accomplishing a given activity members are rewarded kudos points and a special badge that is visible in their HUD. The proposed hypotheses were operationalised into a set of questions measuring each of the hypotheses (see Appendix I). Additionally a special set of interviews were developed to further validate the model.[1] The group owner was contacted and asked for permission to do the research. This is a different approach to the Second Life social research as compared to Messinger et al. (2009) who distributed the questionnaire directly to the participants. After permission had been granted by the group owner a few members of the community were asked to evaluate the questionnaire. Nearly all the measurement items were based on literature or were operationalised from the conceptual model. A seven point Likert scale was used to measure the relative importance of each item. The feedback of the community members was the basis for the improvement of the questionnaire items which were thus pilot-tested.

[1] Full interview data is available on email request.

An online version of the questionnaire was designed and a link to it distributed by way of group notices (special group mechanism available in Second Life), so that all of the members had the opportunity to access it. Additionally, after some time, a reminder was sent through a group notice and a group instant message announcement. These additional steps were taken due to technical problems with the delivery of group notices experienced by Second Life at that time. Participants of the on-line questionnaire were awarded kudos points, they received a specially designed "Research Assistant" badge visible on their HUD and the first 150 of them were paid 100 Linden Dollars (Second Life currency equivalent to about $0.40)[2].

The questionnaire required 15 to 20 minutes to complete. It is important to note that this approach provided very good results (good quality and number of responses). One of the important implications for the future researchers is that when carrying out such a study in Second Life it is best to combine two kinds of incentives. The first incentive should be the one that can be used by the participants within immersive virtual environment (in the case of this research it was the badge and the kudos points), while the other one may be an incentive that "translates" to real world gains (linden dollars in our case). Such configuration is important as it motivates both the participants that engage in immersive virtual environment for its own sake as well as those who aim to achieve real world benefits. The members of the group are truly global and come from a variety of countries and backgrounds. The interviews were distributed to the group owner, top members (with top 20 kudos points) and random members of the community.

5. Data Analysis

Questionnaires were distributed on the 13th of September 2009. At the time of writing a total of 161 responses were received. Incomplete surveys were removed and after data cleaning there was a total of 152 responses. In terms of demographic data the participants of the survey were mainly from the U.S.A. (63%), followed by U.K. 10% (some of them selected England - 2% and Scotland - 1%), Netherlands (6%), Germany (6%), Canada (6%), Australia (4%) and some other countries. It is worth to note that there were no participants from Asian countries, which is quite surprising given their huge population. Participants were mainly female (71%) with some fraction of males (24%) and 5% did not specify their gender. These results provide insight that immersive virtual worlds are quite popular with women as compared with the game-based industry where males dominate. This may also indicate that the social part of immersive virtual worlds plays an important part in attracting women.

As far as age of participants is concerned the leading group are people below 20 and 29 (more than 50 participants), followed by those in their thirties (almost 40 participants). It is worth to mention that these two groups are usually associated with the most active consumers. Therefore Second Life may be perceived as a good platform for marketing products and services from real world. The number of participants decreases with the age. It is also surprising that the people below 20 were not that well represented. A possible explanation is that there is a separate grid (Teen Grid) for people below 18 years old. Most of the

[2] Questionnaire data is available on email request.

questionnaire participants held College Certificate (33%), followed by BSc (21%) and Secondary School Certificate (19%), MSc (10%) and PhD (1%). These results are not very surprising given the high percentage of the participants from the U.S.A. where education usually finishes with college training. As far as profession is concerned 22% of the participants were engage in the Science, followed by Social Sciences (16%) and Arts (15%). Some of the participants (e.g. one working as an accountant) indicated in the comments that the scale did not provide enough choices. It may be necessary to adjust the scale in future studies. The results indicate that the participants where active across many professions with little dominance of Science[3].

6.1 Reliability and validity of measures

Data gathered from respondents were first assessed with reliability test which is a very important tool in positivist research because it indicates stability and the fact that the research is repeatable (Golafshani 2003, p 599). Reliability is a "statistical measure of how reproducible the survey instrument's data are" (Litwin, 1995, p 6). The most common forms of reliability are: test-retest, alternate-form and internal consistency. For the purposes of this research internal consistency is the most appropriate form as the other two would involve asking the same respondents to retake the same questionnaire (test-retest) or take a changed questionnaire (alternate-form).

Internal consistency reliability applies to groups of items that are perceived to measure different aspects of the same concept. Internal consistency may be measured by determining the value of Cronbach's coefficient alpha. It measures internal consistency reliability among a group of items combined to form a single scale. It examines the degree to which the items measure the same underlying concept (Pallant 2005, p 95). In other words it is possible to state that it mirrors the homogeneity of the scale – reflects how well various items harmonize with each other to measure different aspects of the same variable. It is usually expressed as a correlation coefficient and values of 0.70 and above are generally accepted as representing good reliability (Litwin 1995, pp 24-31). In the case of short scales (e.g. fewer than ten items) low Cronbach values may occur. This statistics when performed on the whole questionnaire returns value of 0.686 (0.708), which is slightly less than the goal of 0.7. It still may be considered as a good reliability. In other words the questionnaire items measure a very similar concept – in this case it could be the knowledge sharing in immersive virtual worlds. Figure 2 presents the reliability statistics.

Cronbach's Alpha	Cronbach's Alpha Based on Standardized Items	N of Items
.686	.708	21

Figure 2 Reliability statistics for the whole scale.

Besides measuring the reliability of the scales it is also necessary to examine their validity. Validity is a term which describes how well a questionnaire or survey measures what it is meant to measure. For example an item that is supposed to measure pain should measure

[3] Full demographic data is available on email request.

pain and not some related variable (e.g. anxiety) (Litwin, 1995, p 33). It gives the researchers, their peers and the scientific society the assurance that the methods chosen are appropriate for searching the truth (Usoro *et al,* 2007). There are different types of validity that are usually measured when evaluating the performance of a questionnaire: face, content, criterion and construct (Litwin, 1995, p 33).

Construct validity is the most valuable and most difficult way of evaluating a questionnaire. This is due to the fact that it measures how meaningful the scale or questionnaire is when in practical use. It thus requires years of experience (Litwin, 1995, p 33-43). It was not possible to employ this validity technique to the full given the limited time scope of the study. Instead a substitutive method of factorial validity was used. This is a different approach where statistical techniques are employed to explain the construct validity instead of a long lasting research. Factorial validity with the most common technique, such as principal components analysis or confirmatory factor analysis, has been identified as one of the most appropriate in IS research (Straub *et al,* 2004, p 10). The results of the principal components analysis are provided in Appendix II in supplementary files. Five factors were extracted. From the analysis it appears that the first factor is highly correlated with positive aspect of the constructs discussed before. It is an indirect indication that there is a significant relationship between the items. The second factor is highly correlated with questions that were added to balance the scale and avoid positive slant (except the questions that could have been misunderstood by the participants). These two factors explain almost 50% of the total variance. The other three factors are scattered among different constructs and therefore explanation of what they could mean is much more difficult. The principal components analysis provides rather moderate support of the hypotheses. Therefore in the next step the hypothesis testing will be based on the original variables and constructs.

6.2 Hypothesis testing

In order to test the hypotheses mentioned bivariate correlation analysis was performed. The results are grouped into two perspectives: knowledge provision and knowledge seeking[4].

Results for the knowledge provision indicated that there is a variety of significant correlations. Items that are measuring reciprocity (first three questions) are significantly correlated with those that are measuring trust. Only one out of nine possible correlation turns to be insignificant (NR1 and TR2). They are also correlated with the variables measuring perception of community. NR3 was added to balance the scale and avoid the positive slant of the scale; and it is clearly negatively correlated with the other variables measuring reciprocity (NR1 and NR2) and with most of the items measuring trust (TR1 and TR3) and perception of community (PC1 and PC3). It is also significantly and positively correlated with items TR2 and PC2 that were supposed to measure the distrust and negative sides of the community (in a similar fashion to avoid the positive slant). The items TR2 and PC2 behave in a similar fashion (significant negative correlation within the scale and with those variables that measure

[4] Full results are available on email request.

the given phenomenon from a positive point of view). The data is therefore a strong evidence of the hypotheses H_3 and H_7.

The questions measuring trust indicate high correlation with the variables measuring perception of community. Only TR2 and PC3 seem not to have a significant correlation. Additionally questions that were added to balance the scale behave in a similar fashion to the ones presented previously. They have significant positive correlations with each other and highly negative correlations with those that measure the advantages of trust and perception of community. This is a strong evidence in support of hypothesis H_5.

There is also a strong correlation between items measuring perception of community and questions on knowledge provision. All of the correlations are significant except PC2 and two variables - KP2 and KP3. Additionally, variables PC1 and PC3 measuring positive aspects of the community are strongly negatively correlated with question KP1 that was added to the knowledge provision scale to balance it and avoid a positive slant. Although the correlation is not as strong as in the previous cases it is still in strong support of hypothesis H_1.

Norms of reciprocity play an important role in the knowledge seeking behaviour as well. Each question on reciprocity is highly positively correlated with those measuring trust in knowledge seeker perspective. However the items that were added to both scales in order to balance the scales and avoid a positive slant do not match that well with each other and with those measuring positive aspects. The first question on trust, although formulized in a negative way, seems to be positively correlated with the items measuring reciprocity from the positive perspective. It is still possible that there is a strong relationship between reciprocity and trust in knowledge reception perspective. However the exact nature of this relationship needs to be further studied. The relationship between reciprocity and perception of community is much clearer than that. It is even clearer than in the knowledge provision perspective. All the reciprocity items are significantly correlated with those measuring perception of community. Moreover the items that were added to avoid a positive slant (NR3 and PCKR3) are only positively correlated with each other, while highly negatively correlated with those measuring a positive perspective. Therefore hypotheses H_4 and H_8 are valid. Hypothesis H_8 which addresses norms of reciprocity, trust and knowledge sharing needs further elaboration and investigation into the questions themselves.

Hypothesis H_6 which is about the relationship between Trust and Perception of Community in knowledge seeker perspective has similar problem with Hypothesis H_8 that refers to the norms of reciprocity and trust. All the items are significantly correlated; however the question measuring the negative aspect of trust (TKR1) seems to have a positive relationship with questions measuring positive aspects of the community. On the other hand the variable that was supposed to measure the positive aspects of trust (TKR3) is negatively correlated with the questions measuring the positive aspects of the community and positively correlated with PCKR3 that was measuring the negative aspects of the community. In this case it is necessary to get back to the questions and from the quick analysis it appears that questions 13 and 15 (TKR1 and TKR3) are very similar to each other and use similar words ("afraid" and "not afraid"). This could be the reason and could mislead the participants of the survey. It is advised that these questions should be reformulated in any future studies. It is still possible to claim that the hypothesis itself was correct.

There is no doubt that the data provided is in strong support of hypothesis H_2. All the variables measuring perception of community are in significant relationship with the items measuring knowledge reception. Additionally questions added to balance the scale and avoid a positive slant (PCKR3 of perception of the community scale and KR3 of the knowledge reception scale) are positively correlated only with each other, while they maintain significant negative correlation with the rest.

6.3 Interviews

Qualitative research was done in parallel with the distribution of the questionnaire. Out of ten planned interviews only three took place. Respondents were from the top 20 list of participants with most kudos points. It may be an indication that they associated themselves with the community to a much higher degree and therefore were more eager to share their experiences. Answers to question one were in favour of the lucky tribe group. It was termed as being friendly and polite. It turned out that although these three persons were high achievers they were also eager to help other members. Two of them try to treat all the members the same. One of the interviewees indicated that it is normal that friends are closer to them than other members are. Two of them find their own ways to do things in most cases before the rest (thus their high scores). One interviewee tests the knowledge provided by others and based on it reasons on future occasions. It would be an indication that on average they play knowledge provision role to other group members as indicated by the words of one of them: "I tend to figure things out before most others in the group".

They seem to share the same view and see the group as friendly companion with friendly competition. One of the interviewees said very clearly that the way the community functions (very well) "translates" from the contributions made to it. The difference was in the way the participants responded to the fifth questions. While one of them answered positively another one argued that it does not matter. The third one provided an insight into what happens when the group owner does not provide a central repository. In this case members themselves archive, store and share necessary information. They all have agreed that trust plays a very important role in the community life. The first interviewee indicated that trust is absolutely important and that reciprocity plays an important role in it as well. Another one extended this view to all other communities in Second Life. While answering the last question first, the interviewee indicated the problem that newcomers to the community may have difficulty locating whom to ask. Another participant answered that the group owner did a "great job with the 'mentor tiki', which encourages one member to help another". Mentor tiki is a special ritual that establishes a somewhat formal relationship between two participants (one as a mentor and one as a student – similar to knowledge provider and knowledge seeker) and helps share knowledge within the community.

7. Findings

Both quantitative and qualitative data analyses indicate that the hypotheses tested were valid. An interesting point was that although Second Life was envisioned as a primarily entertainment platform it evolved (due to the effort of its participants) to provide environment where knowledge sharing activities do take place as well.

The 3D environments also provide opportunities for interaction and socialization unseen in any other environments. These in turn can result in higher levels of knowledge sharing among avatar which are electronic surrogates of real world individuals.

Table 1 summarizes the results and findings of both quantitative as well as qualitative study. The final outcome is based on the results of the quantitative and qualitative analysis. It is positive in all of the hypotheses tested, because there is a strong quantitative support in nearly every case (except H_6 and H_8). Additionally interviews are in strong support of the hypotheses mentioned.

	Quantitative Analysis	Qualitative Analysis	Outcome
Hypothesis	**First Step**	**Interview**	
H_1	Strong	Strong	Positive
H_2	Strong	Strong	Positive
H_3	Strong	Strong	Positive
H_4	Strong	Strong	Positive
H_5	Strong	Strong	Positive
H_6	Moderate	Strong	Positive
H_7	Strong	Strong	Positive
H_8	Moderate	Strong	Positive

Table 1 Summary of findings.

8. Conclusions and Areas for Further Studies

Knowledge sharing in immersive virtual worlds may take much richer form than in a "flat" static web environment. It however still requires very similar set of factors to exist. Norms of reciprocity, trust and perception of community are among the most prominent ones. This research has endeavoured to build a research model with these factors as constructs with hypotheses to relate them to each other. The analysis of the questionnaire responses from the Second Life group as well as interviews indicate that majority of them were valid. The obvious next step is the testing of the model with a larger sample as well as with other groups in Second Life, which share knowledge in a different way (virtual universities, campuses, laboratories, etc).

The findings of this research may be important for the organizations involved in the knowledge sharing in Second Life or other immersive virtual worlds or for those that plan to engage in this activity. It seems that such environments greatly enhance the most important factors of knowledge sharing as presented previously. It is however important to have clear goals of such knowledge sharing. While it may be expected that the engagement of users is much greater, the environment itself and increased socialisation level should not pose distraction for the participants. Therefore Second Life may find very good uses in the case of knowledge sharing where social part (e.g. perception of community, trust, social network) plays the crucial role. However in other cases it should be considered in advance whether or not to apply the pure flat 2D web instead or a combination of both so as to avoid the distraction of social activities.

An additional general implication for the people thinking of carrying out, in Second Life, research that includes questionnaires and interviews is that if any incentives are provided it is good to combine the incentives that can be utilized inside the virtual world with those that can yield real world profit for the participants. By doing so it is easier to a cover wider spectrum of participants - those that are involved in immersive activities for their own sake only and those who also try to gain profit from these activities in order to enjoy the profits in real world.

Areas for further research emerging from this study are the analysis of the impact of economic aspects on knowledge sharing in immersive virtual worlds and further analysis of the factors mentioned (with reworking of some of the questionnaire items). In the first case economic impact may play an important role. It could be analyzed how a variety of incentives could encourage members to provide and seek knowledge. In the second case some of the factors could be further elaborated. For example different aspects of trust (as indicated by Usoro et. al., 2007) could be analyzed.

References

Antonacci, D. & Moderass, N., (2005), *Second Life: The educational possibilities of a massively multiplayer virtual world (MMVW)*, Retrieved July 14 2009, from http://connect.educause.edu/library/abstract/SecondLifeTheEducati/43821

Bock, G-W., Kankanhalli, S. S. & Sharma, S., (2006), Are norms enough? The role of collaborative norms in promoting organizational knowledge seeking, *European Journal of Information Systems*, Vol. 15, 357 – 367.

Chiu, C-M., Hsu, M-H., Wang, E. T. G., (2006), Understanding knowledge sharing in virtual communities: An integration of social capital and social cognitive theories, *Decision Support Systems*, Vol. 42, 1872 – 1888

Chow, W. S. & Chan, L. S., (2008), Social network, social trust and shared goals in organizational knowledge sharing, *Information & Management*, Vol. 45, 458-465

Davenport, T. H. & Prusak, L., (1998), Working knowledge: How organizations manage what they know, Boston: Harvard Business School Press.

Edirisingha, P., Nie, M., Pluciennik, M. & Young, R., (2009), Socialisation for learning at a distance in a 3-D multi-user virtual environment, *British Journal of Educational Technology*, Vol. 40, No. 3, 458-479.

Golafshani, N., (2003), Understanding Reliability and Validity in Questionnaire Research, *The Qualitative Report*, Vol 8, No, 4 December, 597-607.

Hooff van den, B. & Huysman, M., (2009), Managing knowledge sharing: Emergent and engineering approaches, *Information & Management*, Vol. 46, 1-8

Jamaludin, A., Chee, Y. S. & Ho, C. M. L., (2009), Fostering argumentative knowledge construction through enactive role play in Second Life, *Computers & Education*, Vol. 53, 317-329

Jarmon, L. & Sanchez, J., (2008), The Educators Coop Experience in Second Life: A Model for Collaboration, *Journal of the research centre for educational technology*, Vol. 4, No. 2, 66-83.

Kankanhalli, A., Tan, B. C. Y. & Wei, K-K., (2005a), Contributing knowledge to electronic knowledge repositories: an empirical investigation, *MIS Quarterly* 29 (1), 113-143.

Kankanhalli, A., Tan, B. C. Y. & Wei, K-K., (2005b), Understanding seeking from electronic knowledge repositories an empirical study, *Journal of the American Society for Information*, Science and Technology, Vol. 56 (11), 1156-1166.

Lin, M-J. J., Hung, S-W. & Chen, C-J., (2009), Fostering the determinants of knowledge sharing in professional virtual communities, *Computers in Human Behavior*, Vol. 25, 929-939.

Litwin, M. S., (1995), How to Measure Survey Reliability and Validity, London: Sage Publications.

Messinger, P. R., Stroulia, E., Lyons, K., Bone, M., Niu, R. H., Smirnov, K. & Perelgut, S., (2009), Virtual worlds – past, present, and future: New directions in social computing, *Decision Support Systems,* Vol. 47, 204-228.

Nonaka, I. & Takeuchi, H., (1995), *The knowledge-creating company: How Japanese companies create the dynamics of innovation*. New York: Oxford University Press.

Oliver, M. & Carr, D., (2009), Learning in virtual worlds: Using communities of practice to explain how people learn from play, *British Journal of Educational Technology*, Vol. 40, No. 3, 444-457

Ondrejka, C., (2008), *Education Unleashed: Participatory Culture, Education, and Innovation in Second Life*, The Ecology of Games: Connecting Youth, Games, and Learning – Digital Media and Learning, Cambridge, MA, The MIT Press

Pallant, J., (2005), *SPSS Survival Manual*, Maidenhead: Open University Press.

Schmeil, A. & Eppler, M. J., (2008), Knowledge sharing and collaborative learning in Second Life: A Classification of Virtual 3D Group Interaction Scripts, *Journal of Universal Computer Science*, Vol. 14, No. 3, 665-677.

Straub, D.; Boudreau, M. & Gefen, D., (2004), Validation guidelines for IS positivist research, *Communications of the Association for Information Systems*, Vol. 13, 380-427.

Tomek, J., (2001), Knowledge Management and Collaborative Virtual Environments, *Journal of Universal Computer Science*, Vol. 7, No. 6, 458-471.

Usoro, A., Sharratt, M. W., Tsui, E. & Shekhar S. (2007) Trust as an antecedent to knowledge sharing in virtual communities of practice. *Knowledge Management Research & Practice*, 5, 199-212.

Usoro, A. & Majewski, G. (2008), *Trust and Risk as Critical Factors of Knowledge Sharing in Virtual Communities of Practice*: A Conceptual View, Proceedings of the 9th European Conference on Knowledge Management, 443-452.

Wenger, E., (1998), *Communities of Practice: Learning, Meaning and Identity*, Cambridge. UK: Cambridge University Press.

Willem, A. & Buelens, M., (2009), Knowledge sharing in inter-unit cooperative episodes: The impact of organizational structure dimensions, *International Journal of Information Management*, Vol. 29, 151-160.

Appendix I (Operationalisation)

No	Construct	Operationalisation	Source	Questionaire item
1	Norms of reciprocity (NR)	Reciprocity (KP)	Chiu et al. (2006) p. 1874, Kankanhalli et al. (2005a), Lin et al. (2009), p. 932, Kankanhalli et al., 2005b, p. 1158, Usoro et al., 2007, p. 203, Gannon-Leary & Fontainha E, 2007, p. 6, Bock et al., 2006, p. 359, Chow & Chan, 2008, p. 459-460	Question 1 Question 2
		Negative Aspect		Question 3
2	Trust (KP)		Kankanhalli et al. (2005a), Chiu et al. (2006) p. 1874, Usoro et al., 2007; Willem & Buelens, 2009, Chow & Chan, 2008, Van den Hooff & Huysman, 2009, Lin et al. (2009), p. 932, Bock et al., 2006, Gannon-Leary & Fontainha E, 2007, p. 6,	Question 1 Question 3
		Negative Aspect		Question 2
3	Trust (KR)		Bock et al., 2006, p. 358, Chow & Chan, 2008, Van den Hooff & Huysman, 2009, Lin et al. (2009), p. 932, Gannon-Leary & Fontainha E, 2007, p. 6,	Question 2 Question 3
		Negative Aspect	(based on) Usoro et al., 2007	Question 1
4	Perception of community (PCKP)		Kankanhalli et al. (2005a), Chiu et al. (2006) p. 1874, Chiu et al 2009, p. 1874, Zhang & Hiltz, 2003, Usoro et al., 2007, p. 203, Butler et al., 2002 p. 5, Gannon-Leary & Fontainha E, 2007, p. 6,	Question 1 Question 3
		Negative Aspect		Question 2
5	Perception of community (PCKR)		Bock et al., 2006, 2005b p. 359, Butler et al., 2002 p. 5, Gannon-Leary & Fontainha E, 2007, p. 6, Kankanhalli et al., 2005b, p. 1158, Usoro et al., 2007,	Question 1 Question 2
		Negative Aspect		Question 3
6	Knowledge provision (KP)	KP Frequency	(based on) Usoro et al., 2007	Question 2 Question 3
		Negative Aspect	Chiu et al. (2006) p. 1874	Question 1
7	Knowledge reception (KR)	KR Evaluation	(based on) Usoro et al., 2007	Question 1 Question 2
		Negative Aspect		Question 3

Appendix II (Principal Component Analysis)

	Component							Component				
	1	2	3	4	5			1	2	3	4	5
NR1	.525						KP3	.332		-.675		
NR2	.729						TKR1	.483				
NR3		.775					TKR2	.760				
TRP1	.789				.302		TKR3				-.682	.431
TRP2		.436		-.661			PCKR1	.424	-.364			
TRP3	.727						PCKR2	.800				
PCP1	.570						PCKR3		.377			.405
PCP2		.665					KR1	.646				
PCP3	.545			-.363			KR2	.833				
KP1		.810					KR3					.847
KP2			-.867									

Extraction Method: Principal Component Analysis.
Rotation Method: Oblimin with Kaiser Normalization.
a Rotation converged in 19 iterations.

RE-ESTABLISHING GRASSROOTS INVENTORS IN NATIONAL INNOVATION SYSTEM IN LESS INNOVATIVE ASIAN COUNTRIES

C. N. WICKRAMASINGHE
Faculty of Commerce and Management Studies,
University of Kelaniya, 11600, Sri Lanka
nalakacw@yahoo.com

NOBAYA AHMAD*, S.N.S.A. RASHID** and Z. EMBY***
Faculty of Human Ecology
University Putra Malaysia, 43400, Serdang, Selangor, Malaysia
**nobaya@putra.upm.edu.my, **sharifah@putra.upm.edu.my*
****zahid@putra.upm.edu.my*

This paper conceptualizes novel segmental development strategy through Niche Empowerment on the prioritized area of "innovations." It argues the importance of a mechanism to improve the utilization and adaptation of available information and local knowledge to create valued activities that generate localized innovations. To do that, without thinking what they do not have, they must try to make use what they have at fullest capacity. More focused mechanism to identify and empower grassroots inventors as supply side community to invent what country needs, moreover help them to commercialize their inventions, would give opportunity to overcome lack of inventions and bridging the cognitive divide of stagnating countries in digital age.
Key words: Grassroots Innovations, community development, Digital Divide, Developing countries, empowerment, Knowledge Economy

1. Introduction

The Knowledge Management (KM) has contributed to the acceleration of the knowledge diffusion and technology innovations in the world. However, present KM practice has focused towards the formal organizational structures and it has over looked the importance of Grassroots level social knowledge (Alavi & Laidner, 2001). Owing to the inherent limitations in defining the appropriate KM approach in the stagnating developing countries, they have not received equal benefits. Continuous improvements of information and communication technologies (ICT) has influenced the expansion of innovations and technology transfer from developed to developing countries. However, due to the disparity in the access and utilization of ICT for technological development, developing countries have been segmented as newly industrial countries, middle-of-the-road and less dynamic or stagnating countries (Wickramasinghe & Ahmad, 2009). With the emergence of the concepts of Community Informatics (CI) and local innovations, community- based initiatives are growing rapidly in less dynamic and stagnating countries. Community knowledge centre, community technology centre, community access programs, Internet, and cybercafés have allowed the community members to improve the social knowledge by interacting more locally and globally (Simpson, 2005). However, the existing digital divide is continuously creating limitations for stagnating countries' communities to gain the required knowledge level to be competitive and sustained in a digital age. The digital divide is more serious than the binary concept of "have" and "have not" the access to ICT; what matters is its impact on the knowledge creation and diffusion in less innovative countries.

Even though the importance of local innovations for the developing countries highlighted in the literature, the level of technical innovations in the developing countries has been inherently lower (Zachariassen, 1977). As per the patent data, the Sub Saharan African, Caribbean, and Asian countries generally have lower level of residence patent applications (WIPO, 2007). In general, Sub-Saharan Africa, South Asia, Caribbean region, and Latin American regions have comparatively marginalized in technological development, and lacks of innovations are becoming the cause for further marginalization (Arunachalam, 1999; Chantasasawat, Fung, Lizaka, & Siu, 2004). The ICT revolution increases the level of competitive inventions in some of the Asian developing countries, but still there is significant disparity among the Asian countries (Wickramasinghe & Ahmad, 2009).

The aim of this paper is to emphasize the seriousness of the cognitive divide that will arise due to the continuously widening digital divide in stagnating countries in the digital age. It also intends to describe the importance of the amalgamation between ICT, patent systems, and community development movements to improve the grassroots level inventors, and then in conclusion, the paper suggests a community level solution for the economically stagnating countries to narrow down the innovation gap that they are having due to the cognitive divide.

Starting with a discussion of the digital divide, reasons for it and the possible seriousness of the consequences of it especially to developing countries, the paper proceeds to the construction of a relationship between ICT, innovations and modern economic development. Then it discusses the changing nature of the innovation systems in the world by giving focus to patent systems in Third World countries. Furthermore, it points to the importance of grassroots inventions and indigenous knowledge in modern societies. Finally, this paper discusses the grassroots inventors as a supply-side community within the context of demand-driven community development practices. In conclusion, the paper creates a new framework for the local innovation system to empower grassroots inventions in developing countries by combining the elements of bridging the digital divide, building up the supply-side community capacity, and empowering grassroots inventors with a flexible patent system.

2. Background of the Issue

Emergence of Digital technologies, Internet and mobile phones is connecting geographically dispersed regions through information more than during any other era of mankind. It has made the pathway to globalization and turned countries into 'Information Societies'. In an Information Society, citizens are expected to access available information and strengthen their social and economic life better than earlier. Information is expected to empower the citizens to increase their knowledge and rational behaviors as employees, consumers and citizens. Even though the expectation was high, level of participation for the Information Society did not achieve the expected limits. The majority of the average population is excluded from technology access for various reasons (Husing & Selhofer, 2002). This exclusion is not only for the modern digital ICT such as computers, the Internet, mobile phones or satellite communication, but also for the analog media such as radio, television and fixed phones. Even though the world is excited about mobile and satellite phones, some parts of the world are still having very few fixed-line phone connections. Therefore, the saying that "half the world is yet to make a phone call" is still pertinent to highlight the significance of the disparity in access to communication (BBC, 2003).

Owing to this debate on partial inclusion of the population to access the ICT, the term 'Digital Divide' has established in the world. The Digital Divide marks "the gap between individuals, households, businesses and geographical areas at different socio economic levels with regard to their opportunity to access information and communication technologies and their use of the Internet for a wide variety of activities" (OECD, 2001). According to this definition, it is clear that there are at least four layers of the digital divide. The digital divide can be at individual level, entity level, national level and international level. Despite the fact that the layers are separated conceptually, they are actually interconnected. A digital divide in one layer can be either an effect or a cause of a digital divide in another layer.

The main reasons for the digital divide are identified as lack of economic resources and infrastructural capabilities required to use technologies (Husing & Selhofer, 2002). This argument is applicable for all the layers identified from individual to international level of access to ICT. Even though the economic reasons are highlighted, the current digital divide is multi-dimensional. The International and national level disparities happens to be explained by economic reasons, but most of the inner-layers of the digital divide, entity and individual layers, are influenced by the attitudes, capabilities and the knowledge of handling the technology (Wills & Tranter, 2006). Digital literacy and computer literacy are playing major roles to expand or narrow the gap of the digital divide. Some researchers have revealed that "lack of interest on computers and internet" is also contributing to the digital divide (Lenhart, 2001).

According to the literature, the symptoms of a possible "knowledge gap" due to an information divide were identified even before the computer and internet revolution (Tichenor, Olien, & Donohue, 1970; Goldmark, Kraig, & Eginton, 1977). "Segments of the population with higher socio economic status tend to acquire information at faster rate than the lower segments, so that the gap in knowledge between these segments tends to increase rather than decrease" (Tichenor, Olien, & Donohue, 1970). Therefore, the countries that went up the development ladder with the first generation information revolution of printing machines are already experiencing a higher socio-economic standard. It laid the knowledge foundation to create, absorb and adapt modern ICT as a knowledge disseminator. Countries that failed to see the benefits of the first revolution showed very slow progress in their socio-economic development until the second and third revolutions in ICT. China, India, Korea, Thailand, Hong Kong and Taiwan are becoming modern day innovative countries with the knowledge created and disseminated by the expansion of digital technologies. Unfortunately, at present some of the countries that affected by the existing knowledge gap are desperate to move ahead with the knowledge revolution created by modern digital technologies.

It seems that the digital divide is not the outcome of low economic standard, but it is becoming the cause of it (BBC, 2003). However, the less-developed countries have not considered the consequences of the Digital Divide. The digital divide would exclude citizens from up-to-date information on events, technologies, inventions and possible problems. The segments that do not have access to information will gain lesser knowledge and be trapped by deep marginalization. Most of the Sub-Saharan African and South Asian countries are showing very marginal improvements in utilizing ICT in a wide variety of socio-economic activities in order to gain better economic standards. Existing marginalization leads them not to be involved in ICT revolution, and they believe they have other priorities. The argument that providing access to information for the people is as important as providing food for the hungry, health facilities for ill people and employment to unemployed youth is not yet justified in most of the developing nations (BBC, 2003).

3. ICT, Innovations and Development

Modern ICT has drastically increased the diffusion of knowledge around the world. Not only the direct impact of the Internet as the knowledge depository, but also electronic versions of newspapers, podcasts and online video streaming of television channels are becoming popular. The traditional mass media are also indirectly influenced by the Internet and digital technologies, and becoming efficient and more effective in information delivery that affects everyday life of citizens (Tracy & Anderson, 2001). Therefore, modern-day citizens who are equipped with information and exposed to dynamic environments appear to be more rational and creative. By utilizing ICT smartly, societies can transfer technological knowledge among citizens and rouse their innovative capabilities to localize those technologies. However, the problem is, it would not happen automatically in stagnating countries and calculated effort is needed to cultivate it.

According to the "Knowledge Gap" theory even though the same information is available to all, receivers absorb it differently. The absorption capacity is based on their communication skills, existing knowledge of the phenomenon, relevant social context, selective exposure, acceptance and retention (Tichenor, Olien, & Donohue, 1970). A famous example of this difference is the "falling apple story" behind Isaac Newton's theory of gravity. Before he thought about why an apple falls down rather than going up, millions of people saw apples falling down rather than going up. Isaac Newton absorbed this everyday phenomenon speculatively and discovered one of the most important theories of mankind. Therefore, not only the access, but also the cognitive level of the individual plays a significant role in the continuity and growth of knowledge. Knowledge is more complex than information and it includes tacit elements (Polanyi, 1966). Development of ICT to bridge the digital divide is not just about increasing the access and affordability of citizens, it is also about the increasing awareness and utilization of information to create knowledge.

A higher level of ICT capital stock allows a typical economy to achieve higher growth with the given level of labor and capital inputs (Tseng, 2008; United Nations, 2007). Improvement of ICT has its impact on world innovation in two ways. With the improvements of ICT, information availability has been raised multiple times; hence, innovators have been able to innovate more inventions rapidly. Secondly, ICT itself has grown as an industry with a significant number of innovations for software and ICT related products since early 1980 (Commission on Interlectual Property Rights, 2002). Drastic developments of global telecommunication itself occurred mainly due to the continuous research and development effort by companies, research institutes, as well as individual inventors who enthusiastic on innovations and patents (Trainer, 2007). However, learning and adaptation of new technologies does not transfer inventive skills and know-how knowledge from one country to another, unless it is embodied in social and cultural practices in that country. The Least Development Countries Report, 2007, published by the United Nations stated that, "unless less developed countries adopt policies to stimulate technological catch-up with the rest of the world, they will continue to behind over the other countries technologically and face deepening marginalization in global economy" (United Nations, 2007). Therefore, the importance of developing ICT and utilizing ICT to develop internationally competitive inventions is explicated in a modern day development agenda.

4. Conditions Demand for Innovations in Less Innovative Countries

Innovation is an attractive tool, which enables less developed countries with creative skills to gain economic advantages (Wu, Xu, & Zheng, 2004), but one still needs to remember that the process of innovation is not the same thing as creativity (Minagawa, Trott, & Hoecht, 2007). That process needs to be stimulated by providing the incentives and opportunities. Anyone could have a good idea, but it is only an idea; creativity cannot be considered as part of innovation, if it does not offer real value to those who might use it (Cullen, 2007). The offering of real value relates with the expansion of capabilities to do valued activities. Output of the activity can be either a tangible product or an intangible product. Even though the valued activities include the activities that generate income for the economy, the whole range of public activities that contribute to physical, psychological, and social well-being of the citizens should also be considered as valued activities.

At the international level, developed and newly industrialized countries are claiming 95% of the patents in the world (Noorbakhsh & Paloni, 2001). Apart from the traditional determinants such as natural resources, access to market and low-cost labor, current technological capabilities, an educated labor force to carry out R&D activities, and efficient intellectual property systems are becoming factors of production that are more demanding (Shefer & Frenkel, 2005). Most of the governments of developing countries are continuously changing their infrastructures, investment policies, tax policies and intellectual property rules and regulations to encourage foreign investors to invest their countries without having much effect. The developing countries with a sound combination of all the determinants are becoming dominators in attracting foreign direct investments (FDI). Especially in Asia, technologically stabilized countries led by China and India attracted 2/3 of the world FDI inflow. Remaining portions of the FDI are largely shared by countries like Taiwan, Korea, Singapore, Thailand, Malaysia and Indonesia. Therefore, the competitiveness to attract FDI to the developing countries in South Asia, Latin America, Africa and Caribbean regions are diminishing rapidly (Chantasasawat, Fung, Lizaka, & Siu, 2004; Noorbakhsh & Paloni, 2001). This has created a situation where 5% of the population in the world creates the majority of technologies and next 95% are forced to accept and adapt to these technologies. This technological dependency is inappropriate and costly practice for majority of the countries (Fabayo, 1996).

The current understanding and discussion of the disadvantage of less innovative countries is incomplete. The low level of technological development does not merely a problem of policy and infrastructure; it is a problem of craft utilization of available resources. The developing countries might not have natural resources, but most of them have ignored human and traditional intellectual resources. Without thinking what they do not have, they must think about what they have and make them use at the fullest capacity in technological development. Even though they are late, this lateness still can be converted to an opportunity. According to Wu, Xu and Zheng, 2004, there are at least five advantages of lagging behind the first movers. Less time is needed to grope in the darkness of technology, mature technology and skills can be acquired from first movers, leapfrogging can be achieved when a technology trajectory is clear, the success of pioneers sets a good example, and assistance is available from the first movers. In order to gain the economic and social well being of the citizens, stagnating countries need to encourage the use of digital content and patent system as incentive tools to motivate the 'inventors' to creative 'local innovations'.

The strengthening of property rights, investing money on ICT infrastructure development and relaxing the import policies to satisfy the requirements of other countries or multinational companies (MNCs) to gain FDI flow has discriminated the local inventions in stagnating countries and hence, the practice is counter-productive (Fabayo, 1996; Gupta, 2009). Even though there is discussion on harmonizing the patent process by implementing a standardized universal patent process, economically and technologically marginalized countries need to give serious attention to decide the best-suited patent system for their countries, specifically addressing local issues (Commission on Intellectual Property Rights, 2002). In order to convert the digital content available in the Internet to local innovations, a certain level of cognitive process needs to be executed by individuals (Nonaka, Toyama, & Konna, 2000). Hitherto stagnating countries lack the capacity to generate inventions that are new to the world. The creative imitation and reverse engineering of existing technologies would be a better solution to gain the advantages of secondary innovations (United nations, 2007; Wu, Xu, & Zheng, 2004). Therefore, modern-day patent systems in stagnating countries need to address the development of the local technologies rather than serious protection of the invention or the inventor of the west (Kingston, 2001).

5. Re-establishing Grassroots Level Inventors in Innovation System

In an innovation system, either formal organizations (companies, universities, and research institutes) or independent inventors invent all the innovations. Independent inventors invent their inventions without having any obligation to third party and they are group of ordinary people who utilize their knowledge and resources to solve existing technical problems of the society. Owing to the fact that developing countries do not have multinational companies, FDI and resources to invest in formal research and development activities, the contribution of independent inventors in the technological development in developing countries is expected to be high (Weick & Eakin, 2005). Even at the worst conditions, that discourage inventions, independent inventors develop the majority of available inventions that are coming to the patent system in the developing countries (IFIA, 2006). Hence, the developing countries need to identify independent inventors as the key intellectual resource that completes the local innovation system (figure 01).

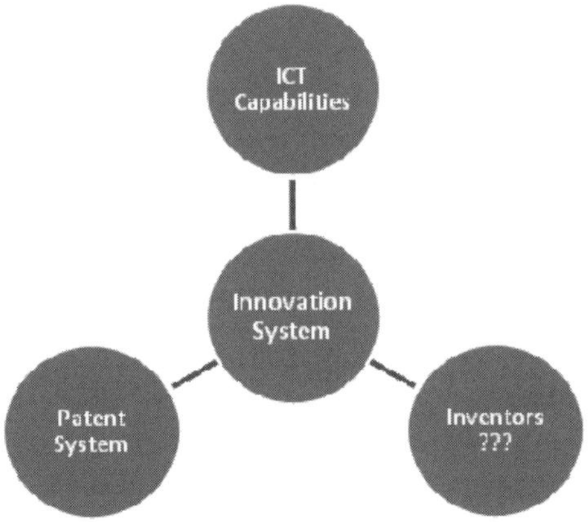

Figure 01: Triangular relationship of ICT, Patent system and Inventors

Because of the independent inventors are common people of the society, they are defined as the grassroots inventors (Gupta, 2000). In the rest of the paper, grassroots level is defined as "ordinary people" and any person who invents anything outside the formal organization structure is considered as "grassroots inventor". In most of the developing countries, private sector organizations are given permission as a driving force of the modern- economic development. However, private sector neglects the importance of R&D activities and continuous innovations as strategy to gain competitive advantages. Therefore, grassroots inventors' community is needed to be identified special economic niche that would help to overcome the lack of innovations in stagnating countries.

Grassroots level inventions can be modern as well as traditional. Modern inventions are defined as the products or processes that invented to facilitate current-day requirements with the assistance of relatively new technologies, products and processes (Franke & Shah, 2003). The traditional innovations, more relate to the traditional practices available within the communities. The Asian countries with a very long history have well established traditional knowledge that indigenous people have brought down with them from earlier times via oral tradition (Sen, 2005). According to Sen., Indigenous Knowledge (IK) is embedded in community practices, institutes, relationships, and rituals. IK can be technical or non-technical, rational or non-rational, tacit in nature, transmitted orally or through imitation and demonstration. In order to make use the IK for development of other communities, IK needs to be identified, validated, recorded, stored, disseminated, tranfered and exchanged in a accpetable manner. It gives opportunities for further value additions and modernization of the traditional local knowledge. Modern ICT, such as vedio recorders, tape recorders, databases and Internet can be used in various stages.

Recent discussions on promoting appropriate technologies in the developing countries have highlighted the importance of local innovations. Human development report, 2001, acknowledged the relationship between technology and development in developing countries. It concluded that poor people need more innovations and access to technology (UNDP, 2001). The Local innovations have played a crucial role in the evolution of knowledge and practice in rural development (Vinanchiarachi, 2006, p. 2). Owing to these discussions, there is an emerging trend towards promoting social and community level local innovations in the developing countries (Deka, Qutub, Barbaruah, Omore, Staal, & Grace, 2009; Wettansinha, Wongtschowski, & Waters-Bayers, 2008; Prolinnova, 2009; IFAD, 2009).The Rural communities in developing countries are observing, adapting, experimenting, and innovating as part of their daily work. In order to overcome the social problems in rural and poor agrarian communities in developing countries, organizations like UNDP, UNIDO, IFAD, World Bank and NGOs have initiated grassroots innovation development projects (Hansen & Egelyng, 2006). However, these community development movements are top-down and demand driven projects that are trying to satisfy the social needs of the pre-defined marginalizeed communities. The social and community innovation promotions have focused on rural communities and the concentration has given more to the problem oriented community innovations. It focussed on the "social innovations in communities" rather than "community of technical innovations". The current practice of promoting community and social innovations neglects the patent applied grassroots inventors from their attention. The practitioners think the existing patent system as an obstacle for the grassroots innovation (Gupta, 2009). How to address issue of the grassroots inventor invented something with the expectation of getting a patent and commercial exploitation is remain unanswered.

Industrial boom, that started soon after the World War II created a question of grassroots inventors' future in western countries. Schumpeter (1942) started the technological expansion debate by saying; formal institutes will replace individual inventors (Schumpeter, 1942). Nevertheless, after 15 years later in 1957, Schmookler pointed out "Most of us believe the independent inventor is dead and buried. Most of us believe too, that invention today has become the exclusive stamping ground of the Ph.D. working in the laboratories of large corporations, surrounded by mysterious instrument panels, electronic brains, but they are still exists." (Schmookler,1957). In his study, he highlighted the importance of identify those who are engaging in inventive activities. At that period in USA, more than 35% of domestic patents were issued to independent inventors. Scotchmer has expected the end of the grassroots inventors in emerging digital revolution by saying, "the technological imperative put innovation beyond the reach of basement tinkerers" (Scotchmer, 2004). However still there are significant number of independent patent applicants in industrial countries like Norway, Ireland, Belgium, Austria, Finland, France, UK, USA, Canada, Australia, Italy, and Denmark (Amesse & Desranleau, 1991; Sirilli, 1987; Sorenson & Vidal, 2004; Wills & Tranter, 2006; Moussa, 2001). In the developing countries the contribution of grassroots inventors is much higher than the industrial countries, but they are been ignored and under studied (Weick & Eakin, 2005).

This problem is significant in the countries with high proportion of independent patent to applications. Sri Lanka is a South Asian country with high ranked proportion of independent inventions in the national innovation system (Sri Lanka National Intelectual Property Office (NIPO), 2008). Even though the commercialization levels are not very promising, during 2000-2008 the independent inventors forwarded 77 percent of the patent applications in Sri Lanka and in the year 2007 and 2008 the proportions raised to 80 percent and 85 percent respectively. However, their inventions not capture the attention of either formal innovation promotion or the grassroots level innovation promotion practices. In order to avoid this scope limitation and the ignorance, the Grassroots inventors that defined in this paper comprise the independent inventors who are involving in technical inventions with the intention of intellectual property protection and commercialization of the inventions.

6. Grassroots Inventors (GRI) as a Supply Side Knowledge Community

The products, processes, or practices developed by the Grassroots inventors can be direct solution or tentative solutions (that need some modifications) for other communities. By allowing Grassroots inventors to communicate, interact, and transact between each other as a network, they can develop novel solutions and modify available product and processes (Franke & Shah, 2003). In an environment, which patent system and stakeholders of the innovation system encourage grassroots inventions, realization of bottom up solutions for the problems faced by the marginalized communities would be able to achieve at a grater pace than earlier years (Chung, 2002). By identifying, assessing, and empowering grassroots inventive community, they can be encouraged to invent the technical solutions to the requirements of the communities, societies, and countries. Therefore, Grassroots inventive communities of the society are actually provide solutions to the existing social and technical problems of the communities. As far as they supply solutions, tools and techniques to the society, they needed to be identified as

"Supply side community". The Capacity building and empowerment of supply side communities will not only give the chance to solve their problems by their own, but would solve macro level socio-economic problem of the general society as well. The Grassroots inventors have the capabilities to provide technical innovations to industrial problems of a country. Therefore, they need to be identified as important innovation niche of the less innovative economies.

As far as cooperate visions, missions and formal objectives of the formal organizations and life threatening social issues of their communities not create the boundaries on their innovations, they are "seamless inventors" who can invent the products and processors to satisfy the bottom of the pyramid needs and national level requirements while improving the technological innovations of the country.

7. Conclusion and Discussion

ICT is a powerful tool that increases the knowledge revolution and diffusion of technology. However, not all the nations are getting the benefits of it. The Digital divide is recognized as one of the major hindrance of marginalized sections of the world to be involved in knowledge revolution taking place in other parts of the world. However it is more complex than the binary concept of 'have' and have not'. It is a matter of how to utilize ICT to do value activities. The value activities include the innovations and knowledge creation. The disability to engage in the innovation and knowledge creation in knowledge era has given serious disadvantage for some of the developing countries. The lack of basic competencies in current era, majority of the countries in South Asia, Sub-Saharan Africa, Latin America and Caribbean regions have been unable to attract FDI and improve the large-scale R&D investments to be competitive innovative nations. The less innovative countries do not have slack resources to working on it and the fulfillment of basic human needs has given a higher priority. In order to avoid the existing stagnation to be a permanent scenario, concentrated narrow scoped initiatives at the identified segments of the national innovation system would be an effective strategy within the boundaries of all the negative conditions of these countries. Without thinking what the less innovative countries do not have, they must try to make use what they have at full capacity.

Even if the scenario is unfavorable to independent inventors in the digital age, still there are large number of garage tinkerers in Asia, who convert their ideas into powerful inventions and demanding for patents. Hence, the local innovation systems need to have provisions to motivate these rare heroes. In the setting of Inventions are becoming vital important aspect of the economic development, independent inventors in less inventive countries need to be identified and considered as supply side community niche. Specific mechanism need to empower them to invent what community needs and help them to commercialize their inventions. Instead of trying to provide solutions to the problems and issues created by unfavorable economic environment, national innovation system should be changed according to the real problems and issues of the inventive community. Implementing niche empowerment strategy, countries can narrow down the focus towards requirements of limited number of inventors that can be more manageable within their available capacity. This would give opportunity to overcome the competency mismatch and bridging the cognitive divide of less innovative countries in coming ages.

The Grassroots inventors, community development, ICT, and patent systems are the major players in proposed niche innovation system for the developing countries (Figure 02). The success of proposed strategy depends on the holistic transformation of the key elements of the innovation system. The community development needs to have more holistic scope than the current practice. It should not narrow down to the demand side issues of rural villages and specific capacity building and empowerment effort in rural communities. The Patent system needs to be more flexible, affordable and encouraging the local requirements and the independent inventors. ICT policy of the country needs to bridge the digital divide of grassroots inventors. It should include the ICT infrastructure and knowledge required to utilize the resources for their innovation activities.

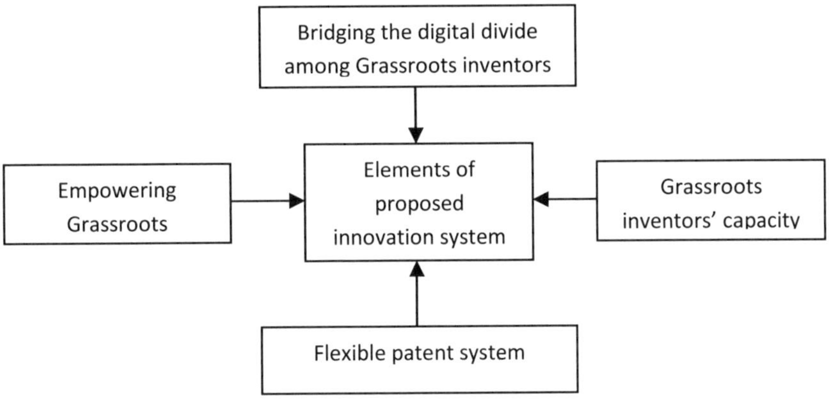

Figure 02: Key elements of proposed hybrid innovation system

All four elements of proposed innovation system are inter-related and achievement of individual element does not guarantee the achievement of desired objective or any other element. Therefore, the entire system needs to be identified holistically rather than in isolation. More focused mechanism needs to identify and empower grassroots inventors to invent what community needs and help them to commercialize their inventions. It would give opportunity to the less innovative countries to overcome lack of inventions and bridge the cognitive divide in the digital age. This would be the appropriate macro level Knowledge Management practice that give benefits to the less innovative countries to re-established the social and technical knowledge of grassroots inventors in national innovation system to interrupt the continuity of the deepen in the marginalization.

References

Alavi, M., & Laidner, D. E. (2001). Reveiw: Knowledge Management and Knowledge Management Systems: Conceptual foundations and research issues. *MIS quarterly*, *25* (1), 107-136.

Amesse, F., & Desranleau, C. (1991). The independent inventor and the role of entreprenurship: A survey of the Canadian evidence. *Research Policy*, 13-27.

Arunachalam, S. (1999). Information and knowledge in the age of electronic communication: a developing country perspective. *Journal of Information Science*, *25* (6), 465-476.

BBC. (2003). The Digital Divide debate ; The Earth Report. Geneva.

Chantasasawat, B., Fung, K. C., Lizaka, H., & Siu, A. (2004). Foreign direct Investment in East Asia and Latin America: Is there People's Republic of China effect? *LAEBA ANNUAL CONFERENCE.* Beging: Latin America/Caribbean and Asia/Pacific.

Chung, S. (2002). Building a national innovation system through regional innovation systems. *Technovation* (22), 485-491.

Commission on Intellectual Property Rights. (2002). *Integrating Intellectual Property rights and Development policy.* London.

Cullen, J. (2007). Information work and the oppertunity of innovation: from corporate to social product development. *Business information review*, *24* (3), 156-160.

Deka, R., Qutub, A., Barbaruah, M. I., Omore, A., Staal, S., & Grace, D. (2009, May 4-7). Mission Imposible? Pro-poor innovation that is socially equitable, gender fair, and environment friendly. *Innovation Asia Pacific Symposium* . Kathmandu, Nepal: Prolinnova Partners.

Fabayo, J. A. (1996). Technological Depenes in Africa: its nature, causes, consequences and policy derivatives. *Technovation*, *16* (7), 357-370.

Frank, F., & Smith, A. (1999). *The Community Development Handbook: A tool to build Community capacity.* Quebec, Canada: Human Development Canada.

Franke, N., & Shah, S. (2003). How communities support innovative activities: an exploration of assistance and sharing among end-users. *Research Policy* (32), 157-178.

Goldmark, P. C., Kraig, B., & Eginton, A. (1977). Communication for Survival: Perspective and Proposed programs. *Habitat: An international Journal*, *2* (1/2), 13-35.

Gupta, A. (2000, May 20). Rewarding Traditional Knowledge and Contemporary Grassroots Creativity; the Role of intellectual property protection. *Paper Presentation seminar at Kennedy School, Harward University* . Boston: Harward University.

Gupta, A. (2009, July o2). Bottom up inventors. (B. Sones, Interviewer) http://sms.cam.ac.uk/media/644435.

Hansen, E. F., & Egelyng, H. (2006). *Supporting Local innovation for support Rural Development.* Danish Institute for International Studies.

Husing, T., & Selhofer, H. (2002). The Digital Divide Index-A measure of Social Inequalities in the Adoption of ICT. *ECIS 2002* (pp. 1273-1286). Gdansk: ECIS.

IFAD. (2009). *Community driven Development Decision tools: for rural development programmes.* Rome, Italy: Internatinal Found for Acgriculture Development.

IFIA. (2006, May 16). *Independent Inventor's statistics.* Retrieved August 16, 2009, from www.invention-ifia.ch: http://www.invention-ifia.ch/independent_inventors_statistics.htm

Kingston, W. (2001). Innovation needs patents reform. *Research policy* (30), 403-423.

Lenhart, A. (2001). *Who's not online.* Washington,DC: Pew Internet & American life Project.

Minagawa, T. J., Trott, P., & Hoecht, A. (2007). Conterfeit, imitation, reverse engineering and learning: reflections from Chinese manufacturing firms. *R&D Management , 37* (5), 455-467.

Moussa, F. (2001, November 6). The role of innovation. *Key not address: XIIth World Productivity Congresss* . Hong Kong: International Federation of Inventors' Association (IFIA).

Mowbray, M. (2005). Community capacity building or state opportunism. *Community development Journal , 40* (3), 255-264.

Nonaka, I., Toyama, R., & Konna, N. (2000). SECI, Ba and Leadership: a unified Model of Dynamic Knowledge Creation. *Longrange Planning* , 5-34.

Noorbakhsh, F., & Paloni, A. (2001). Human capital and FDI inflows to developing countries: New emperical evidence. *World Development , 29* (9), 1593-1610.

OECD. (2001). *Understanding the Digital Divide.* Paris: OECD Publications.

Polanyi, M. (1966). The Tacit Dimention. In P. L., *Knowledge in Organization* (pp. 135-147). Boston: Butterworth-Heinemann.

Prolinnova. (2009). Notes on Local innovation and Participatory Innovation Development. *Notes on LI and PID Workshop* (pp. 1-6). Leusden: Prolinnova Secretariat.

Schmookler, J. (1957, Aug.). Inventors Past and Present. *the Review of Economic and Statistics , 39* (3), pp. 321-333.

Schumpeter, J. M. (1942). *Capitalism, socialism and Democracy.* New York: Harper & Row.

Scotchmer, S. (2004). *Innovation and Incentives.* London: The MIT press.

Sen, B. (2005). Indigenious knowledge for development: Briging research and practice together. *The International Information & Library Review* (37), pp. 375-382.

Shefer, D., & Frenkel, A. (2005). R&D, Firm size and innovation: an empirical analysis. *Technovation* (25), 25-32.

Simpson, L. (2005). Community Informatics and Sustainability: Why social capital matters. *The Journal of Community Informatics , 1* (2), 102-119.

Sirilli, G. (1987). Patents and inventors: An empirical Study. *Research policy* , pp. 157-174.

Sorenson, L., & Vidal, R. V. (2004). Grass-roots community innovation & action in Denmark: the development Centre in Odsherred. *Community Network Analysis Conference.* Brighton.

Sri Lanka National Intelectual Property Office (NIPO). (2008). *Patent Information Database.* Colombo: NIPO.

Tichenor, P. J., Olien, C. N., & Donohue, G. A. (1970). Mass media flow and differential growth in knowledge. *Public Opinion Quarterly* , 159-170.

Tracy, K., & Anderson, B. (2001). Digital living: the impact(or otherwise) of the Internet on Everyday Life. *American Behavioral scientist , 45* (3), 456-475.

Trainer, M. (2007). The role of patents in establishing global telecommunications. *World Patent Information* (29), 352-362.

Tseng, C. Y. (2008). Technolo innovation and knowledge network in Asia: Evidence from comparison of information and communication technologies among six countries. *Technological Forcasting & Socail Change , 2008.03.07.*

UNDP. (2001). *Human Development Report 2001: Making new technologies works for human development.* New York: Oxford University Press.

United Nations. (2007). *The Least Developed Countries Report 2007.* United Nations.

Vinanchiarachi, J. (2006, May 22-26). Grassroots Innovations serving as Rural Growth Impulses. *IAMOT 2006* . Bejing, China: 15th International Conference on Management of Technology.

Weick, C., & Eakin, C. F. (2005). Independent Inventors and innovation: An empirical study. *Entrepreneurship and innovation* , 5-15.

Wettansinha, C., Wongtschowski, M., & Waters-Bayers, A. (2008). *Recognising Local innovations: Experiences of Prolinnova partners* (Revised Edition ed.). Leusden, Philippines: Porlinnova International Secretariat.

Wickramasinghe, C. N., & Ahmad, N. (2009). Revolution of Digital communication and Asian Competitive Creativity Chasm. *Asian Journal of Technology innovation , 17* (1), 13-29.

Wills, S., & Tranter, B. (2006). Beyond the Digital divide: Internet diffusion and Inequality in Australia. *Journal of Sociology , 42* (1), pp. 43-59.

WIPO. (2007). *The WIPO Patent Report 2007 Edition.* Geneva: WIPO.

World Bank Organization. (1999). *World Development Report 1998/99.* World Bank Org.

Wu, X. B., Xu, G. N., & Zheng, S. L. (2004). Acquiring late mover advantage through secondary innovation. *International Engineering Management Conference* (pp. 417-421). China: IEEE.

Zachariassen, J. (1977, February 21-24). Encouragement of Inventiveness and Innovation in Developing Countries. *Paper Presentation* . Colombo, Sri Lanka: The World Intellectual Property Organization (WIPO).

KNOWLEDGE MANAGEMENT & COLLABORATION IN STEEL INDUSTRY: A CASE STUDY

CHAGARI SASIKALA
Dept of Library & Information Science, Andhra University, Visakhapatnam-530003, India
E-mail: prof.csasikala@gmail.com

In a globalized economy, business excellence can be achieved only with a strong foundation in knowledge. For this, organizations have to find effective ways to translate their ongoing experience into knowledge and disseminate the same. Further they have to collaborate with other companies in the industry for giving better products to the customers. This paper is based on a study of Knowledge Management practices in a large integrated steel company- Vizag Steel, a Govt. of India Enterprise. It emphasizes the need for reengineering KM practices in manufacturing sector to meet the challenges arising out of economic liberalization and globalization.

1.0 Introduction

"Knowledge has become the key economic resource and the dominant and perhaps even the only resource of competitive advantage."

- Peter Drucker

In a globalized economy, knowledge is becoming the greatest asset of organizations. Organizations are recognizing that business excellence can be achieved only with a strong foundation in knowledge. Many times people do not distinguish between data, information and knowledge. Knowledge can be described as the information subjected to judgment and context, while information is nothing but the processed data and data is the unorganized and unprocessed facts and figures. Events generate data, processed data becomes information, information subjected to judgment and experimentation becomes knowledge and this experience again generates newer events. In India acquiring `*Gnana*' (which in Sanskrit language means knowledge) is the ultimate and the Upanishads talk of the knowledge in various terms. Kalam (2004), former President of India, observed that a knowledge society is one of the basic foundations for the development of any nation.

Knowledge Management can be defined as "a systematic process of identifying, capturing and transferring information and knowledge to help make best decision, exploit business opportunities and innovate". It basically aims to bridge the gap between 'what an individual knows and what he/ she needs to know' and 'what an organization knows and what it needs to know'.

2.0 Need for Knowledge Management (KM)

It is a well-known fact that knowledge of many is always better than individual excellence. Prusak (1996) listed the following factors which lead to the recognition and growing importance of KM:

i) The globalization of the economy, which is putting terrific pressure on firms for increased adaptability, innovation and process speed.
ii) The awareness of value of specialized knowledge as embedded in organizational process and routines, in coping with the above pressures.
iii) The awareness of knowledge as a distinct factor of production.
iv) Networked computing which enables us to work and learn with each other.

Corrall (1998) observed that the primary objective of KM is to convert human capital (individual learning/ team capabilities) to structural capital (organizational knowledge such as documented processes and knowledge bases) and thereby move from tacit to explicit knowledge and reduce the risk of losing valuable knowledge if people leave the organization.

3.0 Knowledge Management in Industry

Knowledge management had enabled many reputed companies to comprehensively change their approach and service capability both internally (towards their employees) and externally (share holders). Using vivid examples from leading Japanese companies like Honda, Canon, Matsushita and Mazda, Nonaka (1991) emphasized that making personal knowledge available to others is the central activity of the knowledge- creating company.

Buckman Laboratories, Memphis, USA based manufacturer of specialty chemicals for aqueous industrial systems can be described as the pioneer in knowledge sharing in industry. Robert (Bob) Buckman, Chairman& CEO of the company is the key architect of its successful knowledge sharing system. In March, 1992 he established the Knowledge Transfer Department with focus on 'creating information that has value for action'. The company had received the Arthur Andersen Enterprise Award for knowledge sharing. Fullmer (1999), highlighted that K'Netix, the Buckman Knowledge Network played a key role in the company's sales crossing $300 million by 1999 and in '90% culture change'.

In the oil and gas industry, Chevron emphasized the concept of 'the learning organization' by sharing and managing knowledge throughout the company. According to Derr (1999), former Chairman of Chevron, finding and applying new knowledge makes everyone's work more interesting and more challenging. In 1998 the company created Global Information Link creating a single desktop and operating environment worldwide. Innovative Knowledge Management was one of the key factors in reducing the company's operating costs by more than $2 billion per year.

Hansen and Oetinger (2001) while introducing the concept of T-shaped Managers- Knowledge Management's Next Generation, stress that companies should utilize their intellectual resources to enable them to face an array of challenges. They also gave the following examples of KM across the world in three different sectors- Petroleum, Engineering and Steel.

Energy giant British Petroleum (BP), a company with more than one lakh employees and operations across 100 countries is well known for its knowledge-sharing practices. In 1990's Graham Hunt was the Head of a BP petro-chemical business unit, responsible for the design and construction of a giant acetic acid plant in China. Due to the complexity of bringing such a plant on stream in 30 months time, 75 employees of BP from different parts of the world flew to China. They gave advice on technical, safety, legal, accounting and financial issues. This peer assistance enabled the project commissioning on time and within budget.

Siemens, the German MNC launched a training programme that brings high potential managers of different divisions together in small teams to solve a problem facing one of the business units. Team members work together for about a year, which includes attending several weeklong meetings at an off-site corporate campus. They then make recommendations to the business unit manager involved, who serves as the team coach during the project. Through the programme, team members develop their business skills, build informal relationships across the units and saved the company millions of dollars by solving real business problems.

Arcelor Mittal Steel, the London based world's number one steel maker has institutionalized several simple mechanisms for sharing knowledge across their far flung units (in Europe and North / Central American, Africa, CIS countries) that could easily be implemented in companies from many other industries. One is the company's policy on directorships, which requires the General Manager of every operating unit to sit on the board of at least one other unit. The CEOs of Germany and Trinidad plants sit on each other's boards because they both produce long steel products - bars, rods and other structural products. This enables Arcelor Mittal's Steel plants to adopt best practices from other plants. Managing Directors of each operating unit also have a phone meeting lasting nearly two hours. Executives report exceptions and things that in company parlance `keeps them awake at night'. In one of such tele-conferences, the Managing Director in Trinidad mentions problems he was having with a transformer that repeatedly failed. Managers in Mexico and Canada plants also had similar problems with similar transformers. The three plants ended up cooperating on trouble shooting and getting the expertise to perform repairs.

3.1 *Knowledge Management in Indian Industry*

In the post-independence economic history of India, 1991 was a watershed year in which wide ranging economic reforms were introduced. India has recently emerged as a vibrant free-market democracy after the economic reforms in 1991, and it began to flex its muscles in the global information economy (Das, 2002). In order to meet the challenges arising out of globalization of Indian economy, KM assumes great importance. Consequently a number of enterprises, both in private sector and public sector in India have initiated KM practices.

Larsen & Toubro, the diversified engineering giant has established a world class Technology Innovation Centre at Baroda, Gujarat state to develop new/improved processes in hydrocarbon, fertilizer, cement, power and other core industries through the use of modern technologies and sophisticated instrumentation. The Centre has linkages with Indian Institutes of Technology and research institutions like National Chemical Laboratory, Pune.

At Infosys, the Bangalore based global IT giant uses an integrated KM Strategy covering people, content and technology architecture (Kochikar, 2000). Since its inception, Infosys gave importance to learning in the organization. Its efforts to assimilate and distribute knowledge within the company began with the establishment of Education and Research Department in the year 1991. The department began gathering content and knowledge that was available within the organization and the scope of the department grew with the launch of Intranet.

A fully fledged KM programme began in 1999 with the launch of K-shop. Through K-shop, knowledge generated in each project across the global operations of Infosys was captured. Infosys was inducted into the global Most Admired Knowledge Enterprise (MAKE) Hall of Fame in the year 2005 due to its innovative KM initiatives.

Tata Steel, which has a 5 million tonne per annum capacity plant at Jamshedpur in Jharkhand state can be described as the pioneer in Knowledge Management practice in Indian steel industry. Tata Steel embarked on KM initiative in the year 1999 to systematically share and transfer learning concepts, best practices and other implicit knowledge (Mishra and Arora, 2001).

The KM system of Tata Steel underwent a lot of improvements and changes and in the process, it passed through many learning phases to reach the current state. In its latest phase, Knowledge Management has been identified as one of the key enablers to make Tata Steel self reliant in technology and will enable the company to become a truly global player.

In his pioneering study on the state of organizational culture for KM in Indian industry, Pillania (2006) emphasized the need for proper organizational culture for knowledge creation, sharing and dissemination which has serious implications for competitiveness of the firms, industry and the country.

4.0 Knowledge Management in Vizag Steel

Visakhapatnam Steel Plant (VSP) popularly known as 'Vizag Steel' is India's first shore based integrated steel plant with a capacity of 3 million tonne of liquid steel per annum. The plant which became operational in 1990 is located at Visakhapatnam in the state of Andhra Pradesh, India. After a decade of turbulent times and losses, the plant got stabilized and made net profit for the first time during 2002. The company's products enjoy market premium due to high quality and its sales turnover during 2008-09 was Rs.10,400 crores (US $ 2166 million).

4.1 *Phases of Knowledge Management*

Vizag Steel decided to embark on Knowledge Management (KM) initiative in the year 2001. The beginning was made in the Steel Melting Shop of the plant. Steel Melting Shop (SMS) is a core operational department of VSP, where iron (hot metal) is converted into liquid steel through LD process. Liquid steel is then made into blooms through the continuous casting process. Blooms are made as billets which are later converted as wire rods, bars, angles, channels etc. in Rolling Mills. The Steel Melt Shop has three LD converters of 150 tonne capacity each and 6 numbers of continuous bloom casters.

VSP was deep in troubled waters for almost a decade after its commissioning in 1991 and the Steel Melting Shop was the sick child of the plant, wherein Continuous Casting Department (CCD) was considered the most unreliable one. The technology was new (at that time in India only Bhilai Steel Plant was having a commissioned continuous casting shop). The employees were new with barely few experienced hands. The major problems faced by CCD were: Slide -gates, high number of breakouts, choked tundishes and bending blooms.

In its struggle to success the following changes/modifications/innovations have been done in the Steel Melting Shop.

- Russian technology on which the shop was operated was supplemented with Voest Alpine (Austria) technology, which resulted in continuous casting at higher speeds.
- For de-oxidation, Aluminum wire feeding (in place of Aluminum bars) greatly reduced running stoppers.
- Elimination of secondary oxidation and modification of tundish nozzle lead to large reduction in break-outs.
- Strict adherence of Standard Operating and Maintenance practices.
- Increased crane reliability
- Upgradation of Electrical and Instrumentation controls.
- Change in the mindset of the people on the shop-floor through a series of communication exercises and HRD programme for shop-floor employees.

The results of the above measures were extremely good as productivity has vastly improved. The average heats per day have gone up from 20 in 1992 to 62 in 2002.The Steel Melt Shop achieved the rated capacity of 3 million tonnes of liquid steel for the year ending March 31, 2002. This is the saga of `Struggle to Success' of Steel Melting Shop of VSP. The Steel Melting Shop thus played a major role in the turn around of Vizag Steel Plant.

The phases of Knowledge Management initiative at Vizag Steel are as follows:

Phase-I 2001-02	Phase-II 2002-06	Phase-III 2006-09
• Establishment of KM cell in SMS • Process design • System design	• Awareness • C o P • Gnana Puraskar	• Launch of KM portal – *Gnana* • Expansion to other departments

Fig. Various phases of KM at Vizag Steel

The key drivers behind different phases of KM movement in Vizag Steel are:

• Not to reinvent the wheel	- Phase-I
• Promote learning and Innovation	- Phase-II
• Inventing Technology for Leadership	- Phase-III

4.2 *KM Strategies*

Vizag Steel follows two strategies for Knowledge Management. Knowledge may be contributed by an employee (Codification) or a group of employees (Personalization). The other strategy – Knowledge distribution, derives the benefit of following the best practices identified and thus eliminating the process of 're-inventing the wheel'.

- Codification
- Personalization
- Knowledge Distribution

One of the objectives of Vizag Steel is to become a low cost steel producer. The company believes that this can be achieved through operational excellence besides other management strategies. The company therefore provides a platform to the employees to collaborate and contribute by each other's experience and to innovate to achieve business excellence.

4.3 *KM Processes*

Vizag Steel's Knowledge Management initiatives are now coordinated by the KM group in Corporate Strategic Management Department, which facilitates knowledge generation and sharing within and outside the Company. The main processes are:

- Day to day operation
- New lessons learnt
- Cross-functional teams
- Quality Improvement Projects
- Knowledge sharing across the Division / Deptt.
- Follow-up actions for improvement

4.4 *Domains of Knowledge Management*

Domain knowledge can be defined as the name given to the purpose of knowledge bit (K-Bit). Each of the K-Bits given by a K-Source should have a purpose and should fit into any one of the following domains:

i. Procedures
ii. Practices
iii. Learning
iv. Root causes
v. Planning & Scheduling
vi. Success stories
vii. Systems improvement
viii. Savings

4.5 *'GNANA' – KM Portal of Vizag Steel*

Gnana, the web based KM program at Vizag Steel is an expert evaluation based system. The knowledge piece called as K-Chip submitted by an employee is automatically sent to the K-Veteran (knowledge expert) for evaluation of its quality depending on the category / sub-category chosen. After evaluation, if the K-Veteran approves the same it gets accumulated in the database as K-Asset and if it is not approved it will be turned as I-Piece. Facility is given to the K-Author for editing the I-Piece and resubmitting the same as per the guidance / comments of K-Veteran. The K-Veteran gives the rating on a 10 point scale depending on common guidelines whether the knowledge is tacit or explicit.

To recognize and reward the quality contributors to GNANA, a reward scheme "Gnana Puraskar Yojana" was launched in April 2005. So far 6000 K-chips and more than 4500 K-assets have been generated in Vizag Steel.

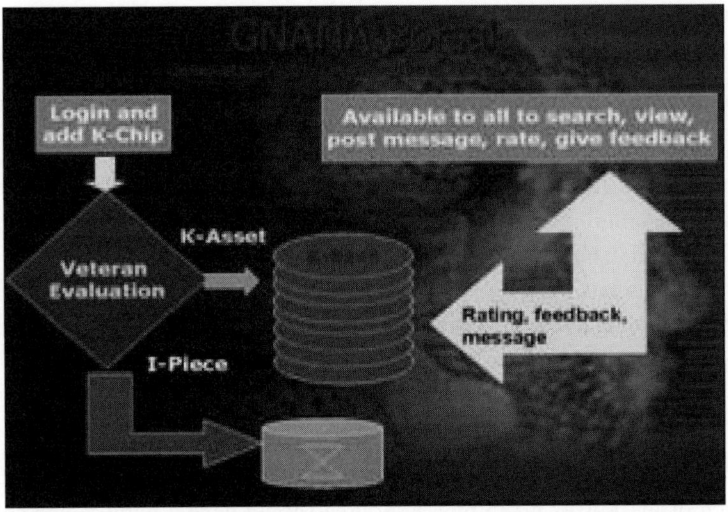

4.6 *Community of Practice & Collaboration*

Communities of Practice (CoP) are groups of people who share a passion for something that know how to do and who interact regularly to learn how to do it better .Such groups are called as “K-Groups” (Knowledge Groups) in Vizag Steel.

It is voluntary effort of people driven by the passion to excel in their work and people with similar interest and concern come together with the support of the management/superiors to enrich their knowledge through face-to-face interaction, conversations and communication. This helps the organization to create business value by breaking the silo of individual knowledge and developing group knowledge. This helps in establishing a network of people and knowledge. Ardichivili (2003) was apt in stating that when employees view knowledge as a public good belonging to the whole organization, it shows easily and trust increases knowledge sharing.

All CoP Coordinators are provided with access to update the time and venue details in the knowledge Management portal. After completion of the CoP session, the coordinator fills a standard form about the topic discussed, level of participating and future plans. They upload the presentations given at the session and add the details about the members present. This over a time became a digital library and helps others who are not able to attend a particular session to view the details and download the presentations. The attendance feed and other details available to the KM team are helpful in analyzing the progress and learning of the Communities.

As CoPs provide a platform to share experiences, learning and failures, this has helped in bringing process improvements. Some of the outcomes of CoPs in Vizag Steel are:

improvement in specific energy consumption in Light and Medium Merchant Mill furnace; reduction in crane-rail consumption of Wire Rod Mill; reduction in drives' failures etc.

Collaboration in Knowledge Management has become the *sine qua non* for growth and development of any industry. Collaboration can be within the organization and between organizations. According to Anklam (2002), within most companies, collaboration- co-laboring, sharing, creating something new together is the focus of several distinct type of communities, communities of learning, CoPs and communities of purpose. *In situ* repair of Turbo Generator-2 in Thermal Power Plant of Vizag Steel can be cited as an example of collaboration within the organization. The repair job done in 2001 was the first of its kind in steel industry in India and was accomplished with collaboration between various departments of the plant- Thermal Power Plant, Electrical Repair Shop, Central Maintenance (Electrical), Engineering Shops and Instrumentation. The total repair cost worked out to Rs.62 lakhs (US $128,000) in place of core replacement cost of Rs. 4 crore (US $ 830,000) and repair time was restricted to 4 months at plant site in place of 8 months at the Turbo generator manufacturer's plant at BHEL- Hyderabad.

As regards collaboration between organizations, developing new knowledge along with competing partners is increasingly adopted in industry in order to gain a competitive advantage. Lanza (2005) stated that prior to entering knowledge based collaboration; companies should identify their coopetitors, choosing one of the following as the main goal:

- Acquiring and co-developing knowledge for a non-immediate new product development which mainly relies in knowledge exchange and sharing, whose main outcome is future technology development
- Acquiring and co-developing knowledge for a rapid market launch, aiming at knowledge creation, whose main result is a fast market entry with new products

Learning from Each Other (LEO) workshops conducted by Management Training Institute of Steel Authority of India Ltd. (SAIL) is a unique model of collaboration in KM between different organizations in steel industry in India. The Ranchi based Institute conducts the 3 day LEO workshops for shop- floor personnel of SAIL, Vizag Steel and Tata Steel. The areas covered include Coke Ovens, Blast Furnaces, Steel Melt Shop, Rolling Mills, Mechanical and Electrical Maintenance. Presentations are made by different Plants of the innovations/ modifications made and knowledge shared in respect of problems solved and benefits derived. Time bound plans are drawn up for bringing similar changes in other plants. For example, based on knowledge sharing in a LEO workshop on Reduction of failure rate of castings in the Continuous Casting Shop of Durgapur Steel Plant, a time-bound action plan was drawn up for reduction in failure rate of castings in the Continuous Casting Shop of Bokaro Steel Plant (MTI, SAIL, 2008). Though the above three steel manufacturing companies are competitors, collaboration in knowledge sharing is enabling them in technology optimization.

In order to face the challenges of globalization, growth, competitiveness and increasing knowledge content of products and services etc. Vizag Steel is striving to be a learning organization by collaboration in knowledge management. Zhujiang Iron and Steel Company (ZISCo), a Chinese state-owned enterprise encountered various challenges in 2007 particularly in the areas of Knowledge Management and development of organizational competence and learning capability (Huang, 2007). Vizag Steel, also a state owned enterprise, faced several challenges before its turnaround during 2001.These two companies with similar background may do well to collaborate for mutual benefit in Knowledge Management and organizational development.

5.0 Conclusion

Knowledge Management is a growing field in Indian industry. Thus there exist many opportunities and challenges for Indian companies in the field of KM. Creation of proper organizational culture and top management support are essential for knowledge dissemination and collaboration. Besides production and R&D, collaboration in KM, based on LEO model, can be expanded to other areas like materials and human resource management. In the technology driven global economy, effective knowledge management is the key for business excellence. As the focus is on learning organizations across the globe, there is a need for steel companies in India to reengineer their KM strategies based on the experiences of global giants like Arcelor Mittal Steel, Chevron and Siemens.

The learning from this experience of KM practices and collaboration in steel industry in India could be extended to enterprises in other core sectors of the economy - Power, Infrastructure, Heavy Engineering and Mining.

Acknowledgment

The author gratefully acknowledges the valuable inputs and suggestions from Mr. Subhendu Mohapatra, Asst.General Manager (Projects), Vizag Steel Plant in the preparation of this case study.

References

Anklam, P. (2002) "Knowledge Management : the Collaboration Thread", *Bulletin of the American Society for Information Science and Technology,* 28(6): 1-8

Ardichvili, Alexander; Page, Vaughn and Wentlinge, Tim (2003) "Motivation and barriers to participation in virtual Knowledge–sharing communities of practice", *Journal of Knowledge Management,* Kemptsan, 7(1):64-77

Corral, Sheila (2008) "Knowledge Management: Are we in the Knowledge Management Business?" Ariandne,18.

Das, Gurcharan (2002) *India Unbound,* New Delhi, Penguin Books India.

Derr, Kenneth T. (1999) "Managing Knowledge: The Chevron Way", speech delivered at the Knowledge Management World Summit, San Francisco, CA (URL: www.chevron.com)

Fullmer, William E. (1999) "Buckman Laboratories (A)", Harvard Business School, Boston, MA

Hansen, Morten T. and Oetinger, Bolko von (2001) "Introducing T-Shaped Managers: Knowledge Management's Next Generation", *Harvard Business Review*, March :107-116.

Huang, Xueli (2007) "Strategic Management at Zhujiang Iron and Steel Company", Hong Kong, Asia Case Research Center, University of Hong Kong

Kalam, APJ. (2004) "Challenges for Knowledge Society", Convocation address at Bundelkhand University, Jhansi, India.

Kochikar, VP. (2000) "Knowledge – The currency of the New Millennium", URL: www.infosys.com

Lanza, A. (2005) "Managing heterogeneity, allocative balance and technology concerns in competitive and cooperative inter-firm relationships", In Arturo Capasso *et al.* (Ed) *Strategic Capabilities and Knowledge Transfer within and between organizations*, 12-18, Cheltenham, UK: Edward Edgar Publishing

Management Training Institute, Steel Authority of India Ltd. Ranchi, (2008)

Mishra R. and Ravi Arora (2001) "Knowledge Management Initiatives in Tata Steel" *Tata Search*

Nonaka, Ikujiro (1998) "The Knowledge Creating Company", In *Knowledge Management:* 21-46, Boston, MA : Harvard Business School Press.

Pillania, Rajesh K. (2006) "State of Organizational Culture for Knowledge Management in Indian Industry", *Global Business Review* 7(1): 119-136

Prusak, Laurence (1996) "Why Knowledge? Why Now? ", In: Meyers, Paul S (Ed) *Knowledge Management and Organizational Design:* ix-x, Newton, MA: Butterworth-Heinemann.

CONTINGENCY BETWEEN KNOWLEDGE CHARACTERISTICS AND KNOWLEDGE TRANSFER MECHANISM: AN INTEGRATIVE FRAMEWORK

ZIYE LI*

School of Management, Xi'an Jiaotong University, 28 Xianning West Road, Xi'an, 710049, China
E-mail: zyli@xjtu.edu.cn

YOUMIN XI

Xi'an Jiaotong-Liverpool University
Suzhou, 215123, China y
E-mail: ymxi@xjtu.edu.cn

Drawing on the knowledge-based view of the firm, this paper investigates the effectiveness of different organizational mechanisms on knowledge transfer. In this study, we propose a paradigm for managing the complex process of knowledge transfer. Its central theme is that the effectiveness of knowledge transfer depends on the fit between knowledge characteristics and transfer mechanism. It is argued that different knowledge requires different organizational mechanisms to support its transfer. A theoretical framework is developed to provide an analytical perspective on this issue. Two categories of organizational mechanism for knowledge transfer are identified (i.e., formal and informal mechanism), the types, dimensions, and characteristics of knowledge are discussed, and the nature of this fit is examined.

1. Introduction

It is argued that in a fast-moving and increasingly competitive world, a firm's only enduring source of advantage is its knowledge—individual employees' knowledge and the knowledge embedded in its structures and systems (Birkinshaw, 2001). As noted by Grant (1996a), "knowledge has emerged as the most strategically-significant resource of the firm". "To put it somewhat more dramatically, there is evidence suggesting that the winners in tomorrow's market place will be the masters of knowledge management" (Bresman et al., 1999).

The increasing importance of knowledge has prompted the issue of managing knowledge to the organization's benefit — identifying and leveraging the collective knowledge in an organization to help it compete (von Krogh 1998). One of the most cited reasons for the importance of knowledge management is the increasing speed of competition (e.g. Hedlund, 1994; Nonaka and Takeuchi, 1995). "Reinventing the wheel, it is argued, is a serious waste of time when the requisite knowledge is already contained in other parts of the organization (Bresman et al., 1999)". In terms of this logic, the ability to transfer existing knowledge, not only between firms, but even more critically, within the firm (Grant, 1996b), is one of the most strategic capabilities which organization possesses, and a principal source of sustainable competitive advantage (Dixon, 2000;

* Work supported by National Nature Science Foundation of China (70121001 and 50539130)

Galbraith, 1990; Teece et al., 1997). Knowledge transfer is defined here as the transfer of either expertise (skills and capabilities e.g., purchasing skills, product, process, and packaging designs, marketing know-how, and distribution expertise) or external market data of strategic value (e.g., key customers, competitors, or suppliers) (Gupta and Govindarajan, 1991), among individuals, groups, units, and departments. Kogut and Zander (1992) take the argument even further when they insist that a firm's ability to transfer knowledge is a reason for its very existence (Bresman et al., 1999).

2. Knowledge Characteristics and Transfer Mechanism: A Conceptual Model

If it is accepted that the interdependence between knowledge characteristics and organizational mechanism of knowledge transfer is one of the cornerstones of knowledge management and organizational theory, then clearly the explicit reconciliation of these two bodies of work is a valuable contribution. Giving the dimensions of knowledge being transferred and the multiple, complementary types of knowledge involved, it becomes clear that it is necessary to use multiple knowledge transfer mechanisms flexibly and simultaneously, offering the richness and diversity of organizational mechanisms that are available within firms, because different knowledge will require different corporate settings and approaches to transfer. The implication being that certain organizational arrangements may be more appropriate to specific knowledge types than others. Figure 1 shows a summary of these constricts in detail with an eye toward identifying the potential implications for the management of knowledge transfer.

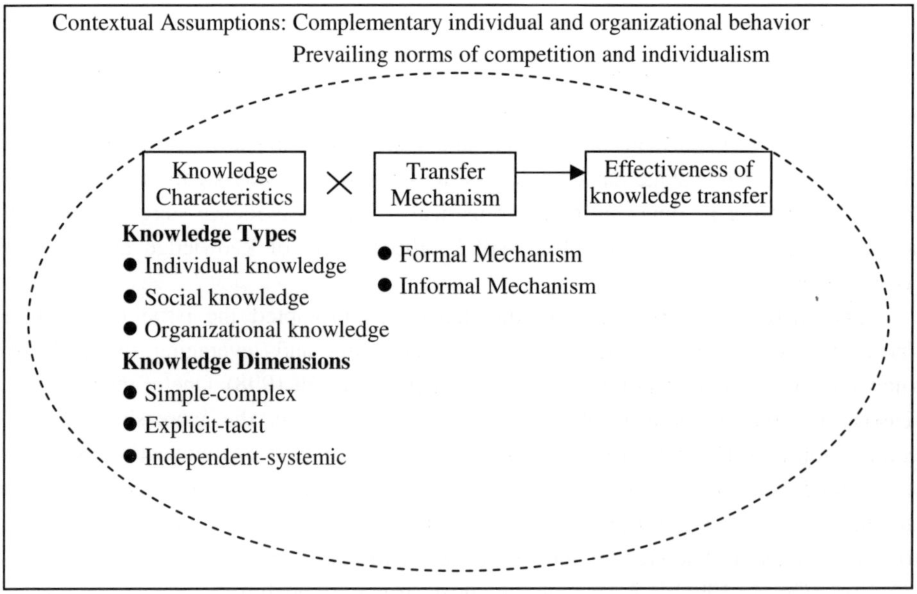

Fig. 1. Contingency between knowledge characteristics and transfer mechanism

2.1. *Knowledge and Knowledge Characteristics: Theoretical Consideration*

2.1.1. *Knowledge Types*

We adopt the typology of Griffith and his colleagues (2003) in constructing our theory, which focuses on the distinction between individual and social knowledge. They note that a major source of confusion about knowledge and knowledge management can be resolved if we recognize that there are at least three distinct types of knowledge: individual knowledge, social knowledge, and organizational knowledge. Individual knowledge is composed of the psychological components that reside within the individual, and usually comprises both explicit (e.g., architectural drawing) and tacit knowledge (e.g., insights gained from completed project, and individual's belief on cause-effect relationships). Social knowledge is a collective type of knowledge that is publicly available or embedded within the routines, culture, or norms of the team (Spender, 1996). Organizational knowledge is captured through the organization's technologies, structures, and routines (Leonard and Sensiper, 1998), and provides a basis and context for the development and transfer of individual and social knowledge. In the rest part of this paper, we shall detail the components of such knowledge to focus on how knowledge transfers among individuals and becomes available to the organization.

2.1.2. *Knowledge Dimensions*

Drawing on the work of Garud and Nayyar (1994), we suggest analyzing knowledge in terms of three dimensions of knowledge: simple versus complex, explicit versus tacit, and independent versus systemic. These dimensions, some researchers argued (Winter, 1987; Garud and Nayyar, 1994), are directly related to the ease of transfer of the knowledge asset in question: some knowledge are highly complex, tacit, and system dependent, therefore, is difficult to transfer; other knowledge is simple, explicit, and independent, and is relatively easy to transfer.

Using these dimensions, we can analyze these three types of knowledge in terms of the three dimensions. Individual knowledge can be conceptualized as either simple or complex, as tacit or explicit (or both), and, generally, as more independent or systemic. Social knowledge can be either simple or complex and is largely tacit and systemic in character (Bhaga et al., 2002). Organizational knowledge is either explicit or tacit, is usually more complex than simple, and is largely systemic in character. Garud and Nayyar (1994) note that the position of knowledge along each of the three dimensions affects the amount of information required to describe it and the amount of effort needed to transfer it. Therefore, if the type of knowledge (individual, social, or organizational) being transferred is complex, tacit, and systemic, then it is more difficult to transfer and to absorb.

2.2. *Formal Transfer Mechanisms*

2.2.1. *Direction*

Demsetz (1991) identifies direction as the principal means by which knowledge can be transferred at low cost between "specialists and the large number of other persons who either are non-specialists or who are specialists in other fields." Directions refer to the specific set of rules, standards, procedures, and instructions (Demsetz, 1991), such as directives for hazardous waste disposal or airplane safety checks and maintenance. We suggest that some knowledge (explicit, simple, and independent) can be well captured through direction, its transfer relies more on formal manners such as direction, and the performance specification for the outcome of the transfer is more stringent. A crucial characteristic of the knowledge being transferred (i.e., the directives, policies, and procedures) is that it is highly explicit, simple, and system independent that ensures its possibility of being captured through direction. In contrast, if tacit knowledge is transferred by such mechanism, in the form of rules, instructions, directives, formulae, expert systems, it will inevitably involve substantial knowledge loss (Grant, 1996a).

2.2.2. *Organization Structure*

Organization structure provides a mechanism for knowledge transfer which is dependent upon the need for communication of knowledge in explicit form. The essence of organization structure is that individuals located in different divisions (marketing, product engineering, process engineering, etc.) develop sequential patterns of interaction which permit the transfer of their specialized knowledge without the need for communicating that knowledge. These patterns of interaction appear automatic and rely heavily upon formal procedures such as document exchange among divisions, problem solve meeting, cultural and technical training, etc, as a fixed response to a defined structure arrangement (Grant, 1996a).

2.3. *Informal Transfer Mechanisms*

2.3.1. *Community of Practice*

The essence of informal mechanism is to build informal networks among people so that knowledge can be transferred internally through experience. The community of practice is an effective means of accomplishing that transfer (Birkinshaw and Sheehan, 2002). Communities of practice develop when there are ample opportunities for informal contact. As pointed out by Roberston and his colleagues (1996), distant, informal, spontaneous contact between different organizational sub-units might be important for knowledge activities. Practically, many companies have adapted this idea by encouraging the establishment of informal communities. Computer-services company (CSC) has several hundred communities of professional employees, each one based on a particular competence or practice area. To be true communities of practice, as distinct from communities of users—informal, voluntary users' groups focus on sharing of relevant experiences that enable acquisition or transfer of tacit knowledge about technology applications (Nambisan et al. 1999), they should be kept informal and their size should be limited to a relatively small number of members who have existing expertise.

2.3.2. *Center of Excellence*

Another informal mechanism that many companies use is the center of excellence, that is, a small group of experts in a single location with a mandate to spread their knowledge throughout the company. HP Canada has centers of excellence in R&D; Sara Lee has them in manufacturing and in support activities; and 3M Europe has them in corporate marketing. In the case of 3M Europe, the center for key account management was based in Stockholm, and the manager in charge of the group would travel to other 3M businesses in Europe to explain the center's recent work and how its new knowledge could be spread throughout the company.

2.3.3. *Social Interaction*

Social interactions are effective in fostering informal knowledge transfer within an organization. Social interaction allows individual units to accumulate social capital that can help them gain access to new knowledge. The flows of knowledge through interunit networks require social interaction to promote trust and to reduce perceived uncertainty about providing new knowledge to other units (or acquiring new knowledge from other units). Knowledge transfer involves a complex social process that demands collaborative efforts. Social interaction is indispensable in this process as it can create trust and foster cooperation.

2.3.4. *Corporate Socialization*

Socialization is important as a way of enhancing the organization's information-processing capacity (Etzioni, 1961; Hedlund, 1986) and for building an underlying set of norms and values that can facilitate knowledge transfer. Van Maanen and Schein (1979) defined organizational socialization as the process by which "an individual is taught what behaviors and perspectives are customary and desirable within the work setting." As Buchanan (1974), Edstrom and Galbraith (1977), and Ouchi (1979) argued, socialization can be a powerful mechanism for building identification with and commitment to the organization as a whole. Some of the key processes through which such socialization occurs are job rotation across units and management development programs involving participants from several units (Edstrom & Galbraith, 1977). In the context of this article, corporate socialization for knowledge transfer can be defined as the processes through which a common set of values, norms, and beliefs among a group of individuals is developed to provide the preconditions for a management system in which employees' willingness to share and transfer knowledge is high. Expressed in terms of knowledge transfer, we can argue that individuals will only participate willingly in knowledge exchange once they share a sense of identity or belonging with their colleagues (Bresman et al., 1999). A summary of different organizational mechanisms of knowledge transfer is provided in Table 1.

Table 1. Comparison of Knowledge Transfer Mechanism: Formal Mechanism vs Informal Mechanism

	Formal Mechanism	Informal Mechanism
Specific contents	Management policies and systems such as direction; organization structure; organizational design; IT support	Social arrangements that aim to create an environment to encourage knowledge transfer, such as community of practice; center of excellence; social interaction; corporate socialization
Management processes	Top management acts as monitor and allocator; leaders as commanders, dependent on information processing; chaos not allowed; emphasis on division and permanent structures	Top management acts as catalyst, architect, protector; leaders as catalysts and sponsors; emphasis on combination and temporary constellations
Knowledge being transferred	Knowledge residing in various component forms, including written documentation, structured information stored in electronic databases, codified human knowledge stored in expert systems, documented organizational procedures and processes explicit, computerized/documented knowledge	Knowledge embedded in organizational culture, transformations (production processes and work procedures), tacit knowledge in diverse forms

Adopted from Nonaka, 1994; Tan et al. 1999; Hedlund, 1994

3. Propositions Development

3.1. *Transfer Individual Knowledge*

In the second section, it is recognized that knowledge exists in individuals, social context, and the organization. Individual knowledge is conceptualized as a continuum from explicit to tacit (Griffith et al., 2003). Explicit individual knowledge may include explicit facts, axiomatic propositions, and symbols, can be codified or articulated in manuals, computer programs, training tools, etc., relatively simple and independent, and is proved to be transmittable in formal, systematic language (Kogut and Zander 1992). Tacit individual knowledge is highly context specific and has a personal quality, complex and systemic, which makes it more challenging to transfer (Nonaka 1991), difficult to formalize and communicate (Nonaka 1994). Formal mechanism like structured processes fail to transfer the tangible elements of tacit knowledge (Pfeffer and Sutton 1999) and significant information loss can be experienced when trying to use such mechanism, especially for some experientially derived forms of tacit knowledge. Consequently, tacit individual knowledge is best transferred by informal mechanisms that can provide rich communication media and a way in that tacit knowledge could be well captured. The above discussion leads to following propositions:

Proposition 1a: *The effectiveness of knowledge transfer will be more likely to achieve when transfer individual knowledge that has an explicit quality by formal mechanism.*

Proposition 1b: *The effectiveness of knowledge transfer will be more likely to achieve when transfer individual knowledge that has a tacit quality by informal mechanism.*

3.2. *Transfer Social Knowledge*

Social knowledge can be either explicit or tacit and is mostly complex and systemic in character, composed of cultural norms that exist as a result of working together, and its salience is reflected in our ability to collaborate and develop transactional relationships. Nonaka (1994) suggested a "spiral of knowledge" in which individuals' explicit and tacit knowledge transform and build upon one another to form social and organizational knowledge. Explicit individual knowledge becomes objectified knowledge while tacit knowledge becomes collective knowledge at the social level of analysis (Spender 1996).

Objectified knowledge (e.g., the due date for a particular task) is highly observable and rule based, can exist independently of the individual knowers. The core argument here is that this kind of knowledge is explicit and independent, can be easily transferred or disseminated to another location by formal mechanisms (e.g., utilization of information technology), because when tacitness and system dependence is low, knowledge transfer is achieved more quickly, the level of interpersonal interaction between units can be much lower.

Proposition 2a: *The effectiveness of knowledge transfer will be more likely to achieve when transfer objectified knowledge that is explicit and independent in nature by formal mechanism.*

Collective knowledge is embedded in the team's routines, norms, and culture. Because mutual interaction is necessary for the combination of various elements of tacit individual knowledge into collective knowledge, anything that reduces the level of social interaction may impede the transfer of collective knowledge. Thus, collective knowledge has a tacit quality and requires informal mechanisms to facilitate its transfer.

Proposition 2b: *The effectiveness of knowledge transfer will be more likely to achieve when transfer collective knowledge that is tacit in nature by informal mechanism.*

The third type of social knowledge is shared understanding among team members (e.g., the identity of the emergent leader). Similar to the process whereby individuals form new tacit knowledge through experience, teams may form new tacit knowledge through collective action. This tacit knowledge forms the basis of shared understanding (Leonard and Sensiper 1998). Shared understanding is associated with high level of interdependence (Janz et al. 1997), systemic and complex in nature. Interdependence requires a high level of communication (Tschan and von Cranach 1996), while formal mechanism constrains the richness of communication (Griffith et al., 2003). Therefore, this kind of knowledge is best transferred through informal mechanisms that can provide enriched forms of media and communication. Taken together, social knowledge may be considered a continuum from objectified knowledge, through collective knowledge, to shared understanding in a manner similar to the continuum of individual knowledge, which suggests a formal-informal way to manage its transfer.

Proposition 2c: *The effectiveness of knowledge transfer will be more likely to achieve when transfer shared understanding that is systemic and complex in nature by informal mechanism.*

3.3. *Transfer Organizational Knowledge*

Organizational knowledge is captured through the organization's technologies, structures, and routines (Leonard and Sensiper, 1998). Technological knowledge, including such information as product specifications and safety guidelines, is found to be the least problematic to transfer and share (Child and Faulkner, 1998), because this kind of knowledge is explicit, independent, and relatively simple, can be codified and acquired with relative ease. The transfer of technological knowledge is normally less socially sensitive and formal transfer mechanisms will be appropriate (Child and Faulkner, 1998), because this solution supports the declarative nature of technological knowledge.

Proposition 3a: *The effectiveness of knowledge transfer will be more likely to achieve when transfer technological knowledge that is simple, explicit, and independent by formal mechanism.*

Knowledge embedded in organization structure(e.g., expertise pertaining to a firm's logistics, IT design and processes, knowledge of major customers in a region, business frameworks, project experiences, engineering drawings, market reports) is mostly explicit and system dependent, that is, closely related to organizational systems, process, and rules, having dedicated physical infrastructure, and all relevant functional activities involved (i.e., research, development, engineering, manufacturing, etc.). Transfer of structure-embedded knowledge needs richer context and media, because such knowledge requires more than just codification. Even formal mechanisms with the most advanced technical support can dramatically fail to transfer the structure-embedded knowledge if those mechanisms are founded on a misunderstanding of the underlying system of such knowledge. Thus, we contend that transfer of structure-embedded knowledge will rely more on informal mechanisms such as through a small number of centers of excellence, each based on a history of success within a given technological area and each with a relatively high level of autonomy to develop that knowledge as it sees fit.

Proposition 3b: *The effectiveness of knowledge transfer will be more likely to achieve when transfer structure-embedded knowledge that is explicit and system dependent by informal mechanism.*

Organizational routines—multi-actor, interlocking, reciprocally-triggered sequences of actions (Cohen and Bacdayan, 1994)—are another major repository of organizational knowledge. Routine-based knowledge, including the processes for integrating across business units, is mainly tacit and complex, because routines themselves are hard to observe, analyze, and describe, and there are considerable causal ambiguity surrounding it. As proposed by Cohen and Bacdayan (1994), a pivotal characteristic of routines is that the underlying knowledge of the parts of routines is often partially inarticulate. Consequently, transfer of routine-based knowledge requires a process of informal mechanisms, i.e., the development of coordination patterns, social interaction, informal communication, learning by doing which typically involves considerable face-to-face interaction between the two parties to the transfer, so as to allow individuals to transfer and integrate their specialized knowledge without the need to articulate what they know to others.

Proposition 3c: *The effectiveness of knowledge transfer will be more likely to achieve when transfer routine-based knowledge that is tacit and complex by informal mechanism.*

4. Conclusions

In this paper, we began with the perspective that knowledge transfer is crucial to organizations' competitive advantage, and have presented a discussion of knowledge types, dimensions, and characteristics, and transfer mechanisms based on a review, interpretation, and synthesis of a broad range of relevant literature. Two common modes of transfer mechanisms are identified to seek synergies by structuring dynamics of knowledge transfer in organizations, and to be more efficient in the transfer of different knowledge. Several general conclusions may be drawn from our work.

1. The literature review revealed the complexity and multi-faceted nature of knowledge and knowledge transfer. Different perspectives and taxonomies of knowledge were reviewed and discussed. For example, knowledge may be tacit or explicit; it may reside in individuals, groups, social systems or documents, computer repositories, physical settings, policies, and processes. Thus, no single or optimum approach to knowledge transfer and knowledge management can be developed. Various knowledge management approaches and systems are required to deal with the diversity of knowledge types and dimensions effectively (Alavi and Leidner, 2001).

2. Knowledge transfer involves distinct but interdependent processes of transfer activities. At any point in time, an organization and its members can be involved in multiple knowledge transfer activities. As such, knowledge transfer is not a monolithic but a dynamic and continuous organizational phenomenon. Furthermore, the complexity, resource requirements, and underlying tools and approaches of knowledge transfer vary according to the type, dimensions, and characteristics of knowledge being transferred.

3. Knowledge transfer can be formal or informal. Formal transfer mechanisms, such as direction, organization structure, organizational design, may ensure greater distribution of knowledge and legitimacy of the transfer but may inhibit initiative. Informal mechanisms, such as community of practice, center of excellence, social interaction, corporate socialization, may be effective in promoting socialization but may preclude wide dissemination.

The most interesting finding in this study is that the separation of organizational mechanisms on knowledge transfer has great importance both in reality and research ease. Drawing on knowledge management literature, we identified two different types of knowledge transfer mechanisms, formal and informal mechanisms, viz. those focused on structural arrangement, normalization, and control, and those focused on the social process of knowledge transfer. Each is important in affecting knowledge transfer outcomes. The central issue of formal mechanism is 'calculative' design and control, which is defined as "regulating the transfer activities within an organization so that they are in accord with the expectations established in policies, plans and targets" (Child, 1973). Under the formal mechanism, control is primarily 'bureaucratic' and 'normative' (Baliga and Jaeger, 1984), individuals' performance and behavior is monitored to preclude opportunistic behavior. The informal mechanism proposes a system of primarily 'social' or cultural connection, whereby individuals are imbued with the values and goals of the organization and thus act in accordance with them (Hedlund, 1986; White and Poynter, 1990).

At the same time, we get to a contribution of knowledge approaches to organizational theories by providing a new "contingency" factor (contingency between knowledge characteristics and transfer approaches) for understanding organizational mechanisms. As indicated earlier, the nature of the knowledge being transferred will have an important impact on the transfer process. If the relevant knowledge is tacit, complex, and system dependent, it is a continuous activity of knowing and thus not readily communicated in written or symbolic form. Such transfers can be facilitated by informal mechanisms, through high level of communication, social interaction, and corporate socialization. By contrast, explicit, simple, and independent knowledge is discrete or "digital", usually captured in records of the past such as libraries, archives, patents, blueprints, and databases. This kind of knowledge can be effectively transferred by formal mechanisms, because it does not rely on a strong social bond between the parties (Bresman et al., 1999). Establishing tight links to knowledge characteristics and transfer mechanisms should help us to unlock the dynamics of knowledge transfer. This will shed new light on the interactions with organizational mechanism and knowledge transfer.

5. Acknowledgments

We gratefully acknowledge the financial support from the National Nature Science Foundation of China under the grant number 70121001 & 70571062.

References

Alavi, M., and Leidner, D. E. (2001) "Review: Knowledge Management and Knowledge Management Systems: Conceptual Foundations and Research Issues", *MIS Quarterly*, 25(1): 107-136.

Baliga, B.R., and Alfred M. J. (1984) "Multinational corporations: Control systems and delegation issues". *Journal of International Business Studies*, 15(2): 25-39.

Bartlett, C. A., and Ghoshal, S. (1989) *Managing across borders: The transnational solution.* Boston: Harvard Business School Press.

Bhagat, R.S., Kedia, B.L., Harveston, P.D., and Triandis, H.C. (2002) "Cultural Variations in the Cross-Border Transfer of Organizational Knowledge: An Integrative Framework", *The Academy of Management Review*, 27(2): 204-221.

Birkinshaw, J. (2001) "Why is Knowledge Management So Difficult?" Preview By Birkinshaw, J. *Business Strategy Review*, 12: 11-18.

Birkinshaw, J., and Sheehan, T. (2002) "Managing the Knowledge Life Cycle" *MIT Sloan Management Review*, 44(1): 75-84.

Bresman, H., Birkinshaw, J.M., and Nobel, R. (1999) "Knowledge transfer in international acquisitions". *Journal of International Business Studies, 30*(3): 439-462.

Buchanan, B. (1974) "Building organizational commitment: The socialization of managers in work organizations". *Administrative Science Quarterly*. 19: 533-546.

Child, J. (1973) "Strategies of control and organizational behavior". *Administrative Science Quarterly*, 3: 1-17.

Child, J., and Faulkner, D. (1998) *Strategies of cooperation: Managing alliances, networks, and joint ventures*, New York: Oxford University Press.

Cohen, M. D., and Bacdayan, P. (1994) "Organizational Routines Are Stored As Procedural Memory: Evidence from a Laboratory Study", *Organization Science*, 5(4): 554-568.

Demsetz, H. (1991) "The Theory of the Firm Revisited", in O. E. Williamson and S. Winter (Eds.), *The Nature of the Firm*, New York: Oxford University Press, 159-178.

Dixon, N.M. (2000) *Common Knowledge: How Companies Thrive by Sharing What They Know,* Boston, MA: Harvard Business School Press.

Doz, Y. L., and Prahalad, C. K. (1981) "Headquarters' influence and strategic control in MNCs". *Sloan Management Review,* 23(1): 15-29.

Edstrom, A., and Galbraith, J. R. (1977) "Transfer of managers as a coordination and control strategy in multinational organizations". *Administrative Science Quarterly,* 22: 248-263.

Etzioni, A. (1961) *A Comparative Analysis of complex Organizations*. Free Press, New York.

Hedlund, G. (1986) "The hypermodern MNC-A heterarchy?" *Human Resource Management*, 25(1): 9-35.

Hedlund, G. (1994) "A model of knowledge management and the N-form corporation". *Strategic Management Journal, 15*: 73-90.

Janz, B, D., Colquitt, J. A., and Noe, R. A, (1997) "Knowledge Worker Team Effectiveness: The Role of Autonomy, Interdependence, Team Development and Contextual Support Variables," *Personnel Psychology,* 50(4): 877-904.

Kogut, B., and Zander, U. (1992) "Knowledge of the firm, combinative capabilities, and the replication of technology". *Organization Science, 4*: 383-397.

Gakbraith, C. S. (1990) "Transferring Core Manufacturing Technologies in High Technology Firms", *California Management Review*, 32(4): 56-70.

Garud, R. and Nayyar, P.R (1994) "Transformative capacity: continual structuring by intertemporal technology transfer". *Strategic Management Journal,* 15:, 365-385.

Grant, R.M. (1996a). "Prospering in dynamically-competitive environments: Organizational capability as knowledge integration". *Organization Science, 7(4)*: 375-387.

Grant, R.M. (1996b). "Toward a knowledge-based theory of the firm". *Strategic Management Journal, 17 Special Issue: Knowledge and the Firm (Winter, 1996)*: 109-122.

Griffith, T.L., Sawyer, J.E., Neale, M.A. (2003) "Virtualness and knowledge in teams: managing the love triangle of organizations, individuals, and information technology". *MIS Quarterly,* 27(2): 265-287.

Gupta, A.K. and Govindarajan, V. (1991) "Knowledge flows and the structure of control within multinational corporations". *Academy of Management Review*, 16(4):, 768-792.

Leonard, D., and Sensiper, S. (1998). "The Role of Tacit Knowledge in Group Innovation". *California Management Review,* 40(3): 112-132.

Nambisan, S., Agarwal, R,, and Tanniru, M. (1999) "Organizational Mechanisms for Enhancing User Innovativeness in Information Technology," *MIS Ouarterly* 2(3): 365-395.

Nonaka, I. (1991) "The knowledge-creating company". *Harvard Bus.Rev*. 69: 96-104.

Nonaka, I. (1994). "A dynamic theory of organizational knowledge creation". *Organization Science, 5*(1): 14-37.

Nonaka, I., and Takeuchi, H. (1995). *The knowledge-creating company.* Oxford University Press, New York.

Ouchi, W. G. (1979) "A conceptual framework for the design of organizational control mechanisms". *Management Science*. 25: 833-848.

Pfeffer, J., and Sutton, R. I. (1999) "The Smart-Talk Trap," *Harvard Business Review* 77(3): 143-142.

Prahalad, C. K, and Doz, Y. L. (1981). "An approach to strategic control in MNCs". *Sloan Management Review.* 22(4): 5-13.

Robertson. M,, Swan, J., and Newell, S. (1996) "The Role of Networks in the Diffusion of Technological Innovation," *Journal of Management Studies* (33): 335-361.

Spender, J.C. 1996. "Making knowledge the basis of a dynamic theory of the firm". *Strategic Management Journal, 17* (Special Issue): 45-62.

Teece, D.J., Pisano, G., and Shuen, A. (1997) "Dynamic capabilities and strategic management". *Strategic Management Journal, 18*(7): 509-533.

Tschan, F., and von Cranach, M, (1996) "Group Structure, Process and Outcome," in *Handbook of Work Group Psychology*, M, E, West (ed.), John Wiiey & Sons, New York: 95-121.Sons.

White, R. E., and Poynter, T. A.. (1984) "Strategies for foreign-owned subsidiaries in Canada". *Business Quarterly*, Summer: 59-69.

Winter, S.G. (1987). Knowledge and competence as strategic assets. D. Teece, ed. *The competitive challenge: Strategies for industrial innovation and renewal.* Ballinger, Cambridge, MA, 159-184.

Van Maanen, J., and Schein, E. H. (1979) "Toward a theory of organizational socialization". In B. M. Staw (Ed.), *Research in Organizational Behavior*, 1: 209-264. Greenwich, CT: JAI Press.

von Krogh. G. (1998) "Care in Knowledge Creation", *California Management Review,* 40(3): 133-153.

EMOTIONALLY INTELLIGENT KNOWLEDGE SHARING BEHAVIOUR MODEL FOR CONSTRUCTING PSYCHOLOGICALLY AND EMOTIONALLY FIT RESEARCH TEAMS

R. KHOSLA and M. HEDJVANI
Research Centre for Computers, Communication and Social Innovation
School of Management, La Trobe University,
Melbourne, Vic 3086, Australia
E-mail: r.khosla@latrobe.eud.au

K.G. YAMADA, K. KUNEIDA and S. OGA
C&C Innovation Res. Labs. NEC Corporation
8916-47 Takayama-cho, Ikoma-Shi, Nara, 630-0101, Japan
E-mail: kg-yamada@cp.jp.nec.com

Knowledge sharing is an important driver for innovation in research teams and organizations. This paper views knowledge sharing as occurring in a quasi knowledge market of buyers and sellers. It makes unique contributions in terms of i) constructing a knowledge sharing behavior model based on different categories of knowledge sellers/buyers; ii) outlines application of non-invasive method for measuring the transient emotional state changes of a knowledge worker while they are being evaluated on their knowledge sharing behavior, iii) describes novel method for determining psychological and emotional fitness of knowledge workers to facilitate team or organization innovation and iv) design of emotionally intelligent knowledge management systems involving cognitive & non-verbal or emotional information.

Keywords: Knowledge sharing behavior model, Innovation, Knowledge market, Emotional states

1. Introduction

Innovation is the primary enabler for the organizations or teams to succeed in present competitive era (Davila, Epstein and Shelton 2006). Knowledge sharing is a vehicle for nurturing innovation and knowledge creation in teams and organizations (Nonaka & Takeuchi, 1995). In order to facilitate effective group innovation in organizations among knowledge workers it is important to analyze their knowledge sharing behavior and determine their psychological and emotional fitness in a team/organization. Researchers in the knowledge management community (Davenport & Prusak, 1998) have established that knowledge sharing occurs in a quasi knowledge market of buyers and sellers. This research models the knowledge sharing behavior of knowledge workers or researchers based on this well established perspective. A unique aspect of this research is that it considers psychological as well as emotional components of knowledge sharing.

Psychological and emotion profiling components of an Emotionally Intelligent Knowledge Sharing Behavior Modeling System (EIKSBMS) are described. A two dimension four category based knowledge sharing behavior model is developed. It is underpinned in constructs of a quasi knowledge market, namely, knowledge buying and selling. Fourteen areas are used to evaluate the knowledge sharing behavior of a knowledge worker or a researcher. The evaluation of knowledge workers using this model enables development of team or organization specific benchmarks for comparing knowledge sharing behavior profiles of two or more knowledge workers. The two dimensional, four category knowledge sharing behavior model based on existing work in the selling and buying behavior reported in (Davenport & Prusak, 1998; Buzzotte, Lefton & Sherberg, 1981). This model is in contrast to other studies which have examined the effect of personality traits on the knowledge sharing behavior (Hsu, Wu & Yeh, 2007; Matzler et al., 2008). This includes Big-5 personality model, the concept which was originally triggered by Thurstone (1934). Most of these studies have analyzed personality traits in a generic manner rather than in a direct manner in the context of quasi knowledge market (as reported in this paper). In the context of knowledge sharing behavior researchers have looked at use of Theory of Reasoned Action (TRA) Theory of Planned Behavior (TPB) for modeling knowledge sharing intent rather than developing distinct categories of knowledge sharing behavior types. Thus it is difficult to use their work for developing organization specific knowledge sharing behavior profile benchmarks for mixing and matching people in constructing psychologically compatible research teams. In the absence of behavior categories it may also be difficult to determine other psychological information like their motivation needs from a management perspective. Secondly, existing TRA and TPB related studies are not underpinned in a quasi knowledge market of knowledge buyers and sellers developed by Davenport and Prusak (1998), which is also the focus of this paper. Thirdly, existing TRA and TPB related studies have examined knowledge sharing intent in limited contexts and corpus of questions (e.g. 20 questions used by Ryu et al. (2003)). The limited corpus of questions can be ineffective because the human subjects or knowledge workers can get away with masked behavior in responding to the questions. One requires a much larger corpus of constructs and questions to get a reliable pattern of behavioral commitment of the knowledge workers. Additionally, studies with limited corpus or contexts do not facilitate adequate benchmarking or comparison of knowledge sharing behavior in different contexts. This is important in terms of identifying the training needs of knowledge workers in different contexts once they become part of a new team.

In terms of emotional component, non-verbal data forms an important component of human communication and behavior (Mehrabian, 1972; Picard, 1997). 55% of our communication is said to be through facial expressions and body gestures (Mehrabian, 1972). The second part of this paper involves modeling of non-verbal emotional responses of knowledge workers using a web camera while they are being evaluated on their knowledge sharing behavior. This enables comparison of emotional profiles of two or more knowledge workers for determining emotional fitness or cohesiveness in a research team based on their knowledge sharing behavior. It also enables correlation of emotional responses with cognitive responses provided by the knowledge worker while being evaluated on their knowledge sharing behavior using the four category behavioral model. Among other aspects, the correlation improves the information quality for distinguishing between knowledge workers in terms of their emotional drive and motivation. The paper is structured as follows: Section 2 discusses the theoretical underpinnings related to psychological component of knowledge sharing behavior. Section 3 outlines the psychology based knowledge sharing behavior model. Section 4 discusses the theoretical underpinnings related to emotion profiling component of knowledge sharing behavior. Section 5 briefly outlines the approach and methodology for design of emotionally intelligent knowledge sharing behavior model for constructing psychologically and emotionally fit research teams. Section 6 describes some interesting implementation aspects related to benchmarking, psychological and emotional fitness. Section 7 concludes the paper.

2. Knowledge Sharing Behavior Psychological Component - Theoretical Underpinnings

This section describes the relationship between knowledge sharing and innovation as the prime driver for constructing the knowledge sharing behavior model and the grounding of the knowledge sharing behavior model in quasi knowledge market of knowledge buyers and sellers.

2.1 Knowledge Sharing and Innovation

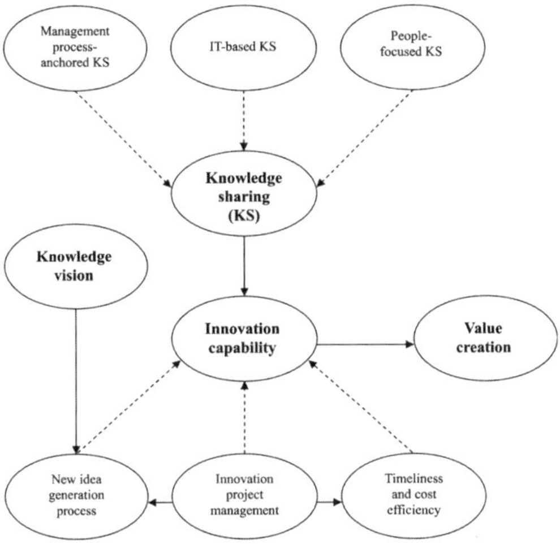

Figure 1: The linkage betweens KS, Innovation and Value creation (Saenz, Aramburu & Rivera, 2009)

Innovation can be defined from variety of perspectives (Gopalakrishnan & Damanpour, 1997; Herkema, 2003; Abou-Zeid & Cheng, 2004; Plessis, 2007). This research investigates and models relationship between knowledge sharing (an element of knowledge management) and innovation (Darroch & McNaughton, 2002; Hong, Hwang & Lin, 2003; Saenz, Aramburu & Rivera, 2009). Since our study is on research teams, and the final product of research teams would be primarily innovation, we define innovation as the radical or incremental process of sharing and acquiring knowledge, transferring and transforming it to form new ideas or breakthroughs. Saenz et al (2009) stated that there is a link between knowledge sharing (KS) mechanisms and the firms' innovation capability. They considered three main mechanisms for knowledge sharing which are "people-focused KS", "IT based KS" and "management process-anchored KS" as shown in Figure 1. They divided the innovation capability constructs into three items including "new idea", "innovation project management" and "time and cost efficiency". The reason for this was to look further into the innovation implementation and the value which is resulted from that. Having a knowledge vision is valuable for supporting the "ideation" (Davila, Epstein and Shelton 2006) according to this study. In this work we aim to further examine the people focused knowledge sharing mechanisms and particularly psychological motivation theory.

2.2 Knowledge Market of Buyers and Sellers: a quasi market

Knowledge market is the place, in which knowledge is being exchanged, bought, found and generated. The main actors of knowledge market are buyers (knowledge seekers, users), sellers (knowledge providers), brokers and even sometimes entrepreneurs who take the advantage of the knowledge as the source of power and value across the firm. In knowledge market, the pricing system is to an extent determined by participants gaining the utility and value for themselves and their team or organization (Davenport & Prusak, 1998; Cross & Prusak, 2003). According to Davenport and Prusak (1998), the knowledge market in organization is highly dynamic and is known to be a kind of "quasi market", a market in which exchange of goods can't be forced by agreements and formal contracts. Although in knowledge market we observe both the actors buyer and seller, there is a fundamental difference compared to the conventional market. In knowledge market the buyer is more eager to buy the product (i.e. knowledge) whereas in conventional market seller is generally more willing to sell their product. Another difference is changing nature of the role of sellers and buyers in the knowledge market through the time. Considering the research team, one person can be the knowledge seller at one time and knowledge buyer at another time.

3. Knowledge Sharing Behavior Model

In this research the focus is how to construct psychologically fit and emotionally cohesive research teams based on people focused knowledge sharing behavior model as against IT focused agent mediated knowledge market modeling (Zmud, 1984). The knowledge sharing behavior model shown in Figure 2 is conceptually underpinned in two concepts, a quasi market of knowledge buyers and sellers discussed in the last section and psychological factors or personal drives or need/s which motivate different types of knowledge sharing behaviors in a quasi market of knowledge.

The concept of knowledge buyers and sellers is analogous to interaction based selling and buying of a product with the difference that the product here is knowledge. So in this research the authors have built upon the work in behavioral psychology in studying need driven psychological factors which govern selling and buying behavior (Buzzotte, Lefton & Sherberg, 1981; Khosla, Goonesekera & Chu, 2008) and developed a model for knowledge sharing behavior. The knowledge sharing behavior model is shown in Figure 2 and consists of two dimensions and four behavior categories. These two dimensions are "warm-hostile," and submissive-dominant." The two dimensions "Submissive------ Dominant" and "Warm-----Hostile" are the two most significant dimensions in which knowledge selling and buying behavior is expressed. These two dimensions give rise to four broad groups of knowledge workers, i.e., Dominant-Hostile (DH), Submissive-Hostile (SH), Submissive-Warm (SW), and Dominant-Warm (DW).The description for each category for the knowledge sellers is summarized in Figure 2.

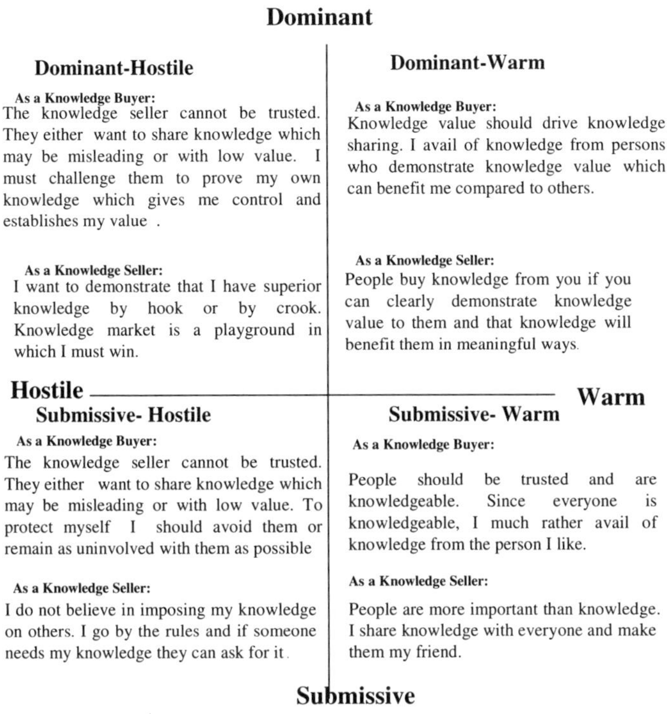
Dominant
Dominant-Hostile
As a Knowledge Buyer:
The knowledge seller cannot be trusted. They either want to share knowledge which may be misleading or with low value. I must challenge them to prove my own knowledge which gives me control and establishes my value .
As a Knowledge Seller:
I want to demonstrate that I have superior knowledge by hook or by crook. Knowledge market is a playground in which I must win.
Dominant-Warm
As a Knowledge Buyer:
Knowledge value should drive knowledge sharing. I avail of knowledge from persons who demonstrate knowledge value which can benefit me compared to others.
As a Knowledge Seller:
People buy knowledge from you if you can clearly demonstrate knowledge value to them and that knowledge will benefit them in meaningful ways.
Hostile
Warm
Submissive- Hostile
As a Knowledge Buyer:
The knowledge seller cannot be trusted. They either want to share knowledge which may be misleading or with low value. To protect myself I should avoid them or remain as uninvolved with them as possible
As a Knowledge Seller:
I do not believe in imposing my knowledge on others. I go by the rules and if someone needs my knowledge they can ask for it.
Submissive- Warm
As a Knowledge Buyer:
People should be trusted and are knowledgeable. Since everyone is knowledgeable, I much rather avail of knowledge from the person I like.
As a Knowledge Seller:
People are more important than knowledge. I share knowledge with everyone and make them my friend.
Submissive

Figure 2: Knowledge Sharing Behavior Model

Warmth is regard for others. A warm person is optimistic and willing to place confidence in others. Hostility is lack of regard for others, the attitude that other people matter less than oneself. A hostile person rarely trusts others. Submission is the disposition to let others take the lead in personal encounters. It includes traits like dependence, unassertiveness, and passiveness. Dominance is the drive to take control in face-to-face situations. It includes a cluster of traits like initiative, forcefulness, and independence. The reasons for using this particular model are a) the domain experts found it less complex, b) they found it easy to relate with as it mimicked their way thinking for typifying/categorizing inter-personal behavior among knowledge workers and, c) they found this model close to inter-personal behavior training programs they had undergone.

One could use more dimensions like IQ, temperament, etc which could be associated with the model. However, it was felt a) it would make the model more complex, b) marginalize distinctions between knowledge workers and make documenting the knowledge more difficult, and c) it would be better develop a subsystem, with only these additional dimensions and put the conclusions of the two systems together.

The behavioral descriptions of the four categories are shown in Figure 2. These descriptions are shown from knowledge buyer as well as knowledge seller perspective. The behavioral model and four categories are also related to Abraham Maslow's model of hierarchy of human (personal) needs which determine the motivating needs or personal drives of knowledge workers. For example, a SH knowledge worker is driven by security and biological needs which form the lowest level of unfilled need. A SW knowledge worker is driven more by social needs and less by security needs. They believe all knowledge workers are well meaning and their needs to socialize and befriend people prevent them from discriminating among knowledge workers on the basis knowledge value or benefit. On the other hand, a DH knowledge worker is driven by independence and control needs. The common hostile dimension in both SH and DH leads them not to trust other fellow knowledge workers. However, both adopt different strategies to deal with their lack of trust of others. A SH knowledge worker avoids getting involved in knowledge sharing with other, whereas, DH knowledge worker's control needs drive them to demonstrate their superiority over other knowledge workers. Finally, as per the model the DW knowledge worker represents the ideal knowledge sharing behavior, wherein they engage in knowledge sharing with other knowledge workers based on knowledge value and mutual benefit. The pursuit of knowledge value is their mean of satisfying their high level need for self-realization.

The behavioral categories and their needs can also be understood and correlated in the context of the pricing system elements of the knowledge market defined by Davenport and Prusak (1998) and psychology driven motive system defined by McClelland (1985). The pricing system for knowledge market described by emphasized that in knowledge market participants are concerned about the expected utility rather than just money. There are four constructs introduced as the possible forces which shape the knowledge market pricing system: reciprocity, reputation, altruism and trust. The psychology driven motive system identifies the possible sources of motivation in human being. These sources or categories are "achievement, power, and affiliation (i.e. love) and avoidance (i.e. fear) related motives (McClelland, 1985). There is a clear match between this categorization and the knowledge market pricing system constructs. Table 1 shows the correlation between four behavior categories, the four pricing system elements of knowledge market as well as the four psychological motive groups based on the motive system theory. A SH knowledge worker's behavior is underpinned in lack of trust of other workers resulting in avoidance and lack of involvement in knowledge sharing. On the other hand, a SW person is driven by need to socialization and intimacy which are reflected in altruism and affiliation. They believe that altruism can't exist without love among people and the need for trust in the environment can clearly solve problems which are connected to avoidance related issues. The DH knowledge worker is motivated by needs of independence and control which are satisfied through power and reputation as a proof of superiority of knowledge. Finally, DW knowledge worker is motivated by need for self-realization which is reflected through sense of achievement and reciprocity in terms of mutual benefit of knowledge. DW category is mostly searching for gaining tangible benefits from knowledge sharing .Reciprocity can be seen as a form of achievement related motive for enhancing mutual benefit and knowledge value

4. Knowledge Sharing Emotion Profiling Component - Theoretical Underpinnings

It is useful to understand the possible link between cognitive responses of a user and their emotions from the perspective human communication, human behavior and correlation between cognitive and emotional responses. Several models of human emotions have been devised by researchers (Sloman, 1987; Ortony, Clore & Collins, 1994; Izard, 1990; Roseman, Antoniou & Jose, 1996). The model which compares favorably with findings in psychological, cognitive science and neurobiological communities is the Sloman's three layer information processing architecture (Picard, 1997).

Table 1: Correspondence between Knowledge sharing Behavior category, knowledge market pricing system and motive system

Behavior Category of Knowledge Sharing Model	Knowledge Market Pricing Element (Davenport and Prusak [8])	Motive System Category (McClelland [23])
Dominant-Hostile (DH) (independence and control)	Reputation	Power
Dominant Warm (DW) (self-realization)	Reciprocity	Achievement
Submissive-Hostile (SH) (security)	(lack of) Trust	Avoidance
Submissive Warm (SW) (socialization)	Altruism	Affiliation (love)

Table 2: Affect Space Model with +ive and -ive emotional state quadrants I, IV, II and III respectively

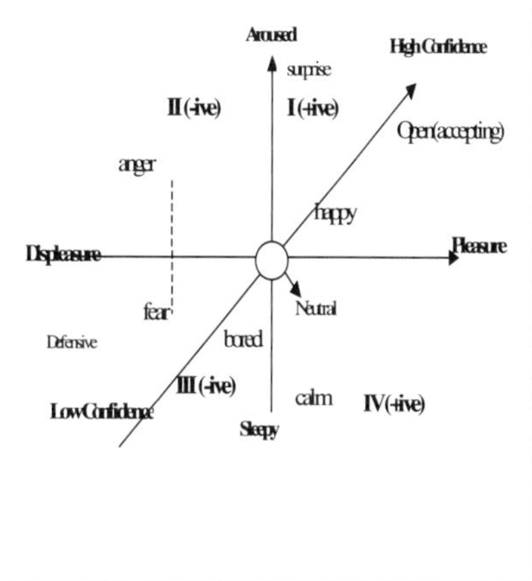

In Sloman's architecture, as the first layer, the reactive Layer detects thing in its environment, and executes fairly automatic processes to determine how to react. The deliberative Layer is capable of planning, evaluating options, making decisions, and allocating resources. The emotions involved in goal-success or goal-failure, i.e., those which are cognitively assessed, are also found in this layer. The third layer, Self-Monitoring Meta-Management Layer, prevents certain goal from interfering with each other, and can look for more efficient ways for the deliberative layer to operate, choose strategies and allocate its resources. In particular, it illustrates the need for a higher "self-monitoring" process for management of emotions. The latter is a crucial piece of a system if it is to develop the skills of emotional intelligence for regulating and wisely using its emotions (Picard, 1997).

The EIKSBMS described in this paper evaluates a knowledge worker in terms of their notion of self in context of their knowledge sharing behavior. That is, it evaluates their disposition, attitude or beliefs towards fourteen different areas related to research, peers, etc. There are 60 selling behavioral questions in all and at least 4 questions in each area (related to 4 selling behavior categories). Some areas have two sets of 4 questions. The questions in each area are deliberately designed to contradict each other in order to facilitate a pattern of commitment in the responses. Based on the nature of the application and evaluation, the emotions are triggered by the self-monitoring layer (as it is challenged by the contradictory nature of attitude/belief based questions) and expressed through physiological indicators like facial expressions. An affect space model developed by psychologists (Lang, 1995) and employed for facial expression analysis (Picard, 1997; Cohn & Kanade, 2006) is shown in Table 2. The model involves three dimensions, namely, Valance (measured on a scale of pleasure (+) to displeasure (-)), Arousal (measured on scale of excited/aroused (+) to sleepy (-)) and Stance (measured on a scale of high confidence (+) and low confidence (-)). Facial expressions correspond to affect states like happy, surprise and tired. Figure 3 shows the affect space model with several labeled emotional states. Like in everyday life, in human-computer interaction people's emotions are characterized more by subtle variations or transient changes in facial/emotional expressions (during the interaction) rather than as prototypical emotional expressions (Edwardson, 2000). It can be noted from Table 2 that emotional state like anger, sadness and fear are not being specifically measured. In other words, subtle variations or changes are modeled using positive, negative and neutral (no change) states. The positive state is represented by positive emotional state quadrant of the affect face model shown in Table 2. The negative state is represented by negative emotional state quadrant in Table 2. The neutral state shown in Table 2 represents the area which is enclosed by the original face model of a human subject. The model can thus be divided into quadrants, each quadrant being considered to represent positive or negative emotional states. Note that what we are modeling here is change in emotional state with time and whether this change is in a direction towards a positive or negative quadrant of the affect space model.

5. Approach and Methodology

This research has been conducted along three dimensions, namely, field studies, generalizability and modeling precision. The field studies involve analysis of actual knowledge sharing behavior and emotional profile of knowledge workers in research institutions and ICT industry using the knowledge sharing behavior model (Figure 2) and affect space model (Table 2) and facial action coding system respectively. The generalizability dimension involves a random survey of knowledge workers in ICT industry. The primary purpose of the random survey is to establish the reliability of the 60 measured items (i.e., knowledge sharing behavior questions in the survey). The field studies and random survey are in process at the time of writing this paper.

The third dimension involves development of knowledge sharing behavior model shown in Figure 2 and emotional state and intensity profile of knowledge workers (based on affect space model in figure 3 and Facial Action coding systems (Ekman & Friesen, 1978)) for measurement of 14 independent variables associated with knowledge sharing behavior and 4 dependent variables related to knowledge behavior categories, and 36 independent variables associated with facial features (or facial action units) and 4 dependent variables (emotional state changes (+ive, -ive, neutral) and intensity). The rest of this section outlines briefly the methodology for the design and analysis of these independent and dependent variables

5.1 Knowledge Sharing Behavior Psychological Component Analysis Phase

Very few knowledge workers in the real world could be expected to be perfect fits in any category. In fact the behavioral profile of most of them will have parts in each category. Thus although the behavioral model can provide us some basis for distinction, it cannot be used as a conclusive proof of a knowledge workers primary selling knowledge sharing behavior It is here that the role of the domain experts becomes extremely important. How do they use this knowledge in a manner which helps them to deal effectively with knowledge workers? What areas they feel are important for gauging knowledge sharing behavior? What areas are overlooked or considered unimportant?

Answers to these questions would provide us the basis for evaluating and determining a knowledge worker's primary or predominant knowledge sharing behavior category. The primary or predominant behavior category is the category which determines a knowledge worker's interactions with other knowledge worker's in knowledge selling and buying scenarios. It further establishes their corresponding unfilled personal or motivating need related to the predominant behavior category.

The areas for evaluation of a knowledge workers' knowledge sharing behavior are shown in Figure 3

Questions	Behavior Category
1. You treat knowledge sharing with every peer as a challenge which must be met successfully.	DH
2. You determine who are best peers for knowledge sharing and devote your time and energy on them only.	DW
3. You do your job. You do not significantly interact with your peers	SH
4. You believe knowledge sharing follows from friendship. Since one person's vote is as good as another's, you do not discriminate among peers	SW

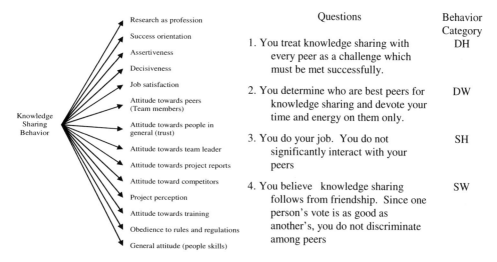

Figure 3: 14 Areas for Gauging Knowledge Sharing Behavior and Sample Questions Related to Attitude Towards Peers or Team Members

These areas have been identified after several discussions with research team leaders and areas like trust and job satisfaction identified by other researchers (Ryu, Ho & Han, 2003; Kuoa & Young, 2008). After determining the different areas and their weights, attributes related to each of these areas with respect to different behavioral categories have been determined. The attributes of each of these areas have been designed in the form of questions. At least four questions have been designed for each area (one belonging to each behavior category) based on the knowledge sharing behavior model. The other parameters that have been kept in view while designing the questions are tone, length, total number, ordering and the pattern of questions. A sample set of four questions related to the area of competition is shown in Figure 4 and each question is related to one of the four behavioral categories. In order to quantify the varying degree of importance attached to the different areas of selling behavior by the domain experts (research managers), weights have been assigned to them on a scale of 1 to 10 using AHP technique. In order to determine the primary behavioral category of the knowledge worker the accumulated answer score in each behavioral category on all the questions is calculated using the formula:

$$\sum_{i=1}^{i=14} = \text{[Area Weight \_i]*[Answering Option Percentage Weight]}$$

5.2 Knowledge Sharing Behavior Emotion Component Analysis Phase

A standard webcam has been used to assist in pupil tracking and normalization of facial images. Gabor wavelets has been used among several facial expression modeling techniques for tracking the changes in the facial action units (Akamatsu et al., 1998; Calder et al., 2001; Lee, 1996). Fuzzy rules have been used for inferencing neutral, +ive and –ive states and emotional state intensity based on facial action parameters involving angle and magnitude of movement of facial features like eye brows, cheeks and lips.

6. Implementation – Benchmarking, Psychological and Emotional Fitness

This section is divided into two parts, namely, Benchmarking and Psychological Fitness, and emotional fitness and correlation of psychological and emotional profiles.

6.1 Benchmarking and Psychological Fitness

Figure 4(i) shows a sample comparison of pruned scores of two subjects in four behaviour categories (SH, SW, DH and DW). The comparison can be used for organisation or team specific benchmarking (or determining psychological fitness of a new knowledge workers' in context of knowledge sharing behaviour profile against an existing knowledge worker (or research team member shown as benchmark profile in Figure 4(i) who represents the desired knowledge sharing behavioural attributes). The comparison indicates a high degree of correlation or fitness between the benchmark profile and new knowledge worker (candidate profile in Figure 4(i)). In other words, the candidate will have less training needs if included in the team and represents a high level of psychological fitness in terms of knowledge sharing behaviour and consequently can contribute effectively towards group or organisational innovation.

6.2 Emotional Fitness and Correlation of Emotional and Psychological Profiles

In order to determine emotional fitness and correlation between cognitive and emotional responses in context of knowledge sharing behaviour, a high resolution web based camera is used to capture the video sequence of a candidate answering the questions.

The expressions presented are not contrived, that is, the expressions are genuine responses to the questions being presented. Figure 4 (ii) also shows the difference images and visualizations of the neural network classification. The sequence shown is taken at a time between a new question being presented to the candidate and the candidate answering that question. Gabor wavelet and neural network classifier are used for processing and classifying the negative, positive and neutral emotional state of the sales candidate (Abou-Zeid & Cheng, 2004). The expression in Figure 14 (ii) (a) was classified as a +ive emotional response with low emotional intensity as it represents a mix of roughly equal proportions of neutral and positive as indicated by the blue and green respectively and absence of red (which represents negative emotion change). The expression in Figure 14 (ii) (b) was classified as primarily neutral indicated by the diminished green in (b) and the shift from cyan to a more blue colour in the top half of the classification image with respect to (a). The expression in Figure 14 (ii) (c) classification indicates a dominance of red and is classifies as –ive emotional state change with high emotional intensity because of absence of any other colour representing +ive or neutral states. These +ive, -ive emotional state changes are used to construct emotional profile of the candidate for all the questions. The emotional profile is then compared with emotional profiles of other team members in order to determine whether the new team member or candidate lies within highest and lowest emotional band based on emotional profiles of other team members.

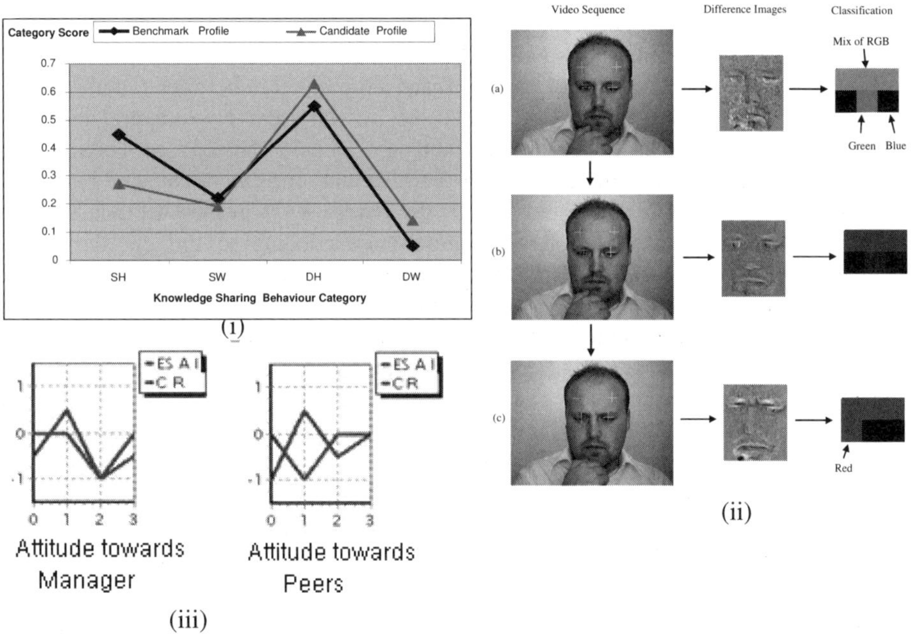

Figure 14: (i) Comparison of Candidate's profile with Benchmark profile based on cognitive responses (answers to questions), (ii) Classification of +ive, neutral and –ive Emotional State Changes Based on Sequence of Images from Video. (iii) Correlation of Emotional (**ES A I – Emotional State And Intensity**) with Cognitive Responses (CR) in Context of Attitude Towards Peers and Manager (team leader) respectively

Experiments both in the field and in laboratory have confirmed that either input (i.e., cognitive/keyboard or emotional) provides incomplete and inaccurate information for knowledge computation and interpretation. The correlation of the emotional state profile and knowledge sharing behavior profile is done at 3 levels. Level 1 correlation involves correlating the emotional state profile with knowledge sharing behavior profile of the candidate in each area of knowledge sharing behavior evaluation (shown in Figure 3). As mentioned in section 2 each area the candidate is evaluated based on 4 questions related to DH, SW, SH, and DW knowledge sharing behavior categories respectively. The correlation at level 1, among other aspects, provides insight into which knowledge sharing behavior dimension is more prevalent in the candidate in one or more areas. For example, if emotional states positive (with high intensity) and positive (med) are related to affirmative answers to DH and SH questions in Figure 3 then they indicate that the Hostile (H) dimension is more emphasized in the candidate than the Dominant (D) dimension in the area of attitude towards peers. Level 2 correlations involve correlating the emotional state and behavior profiles based on each behavioral category. Level 3, firstly, involves fine grain correlation related to all the 60 questions. Secondly and finally, it involves emotional profile and selling behavior profile correlation and comparison with organization specific or organization defined benchmark/s.

The level 1 correlation is shown in Figure 14 (iii). They are used to determine good and less good correlations between cognitive and emotional responses in 14 areas of evaluation. The numbers (0, 1, 2 and 3) on X-axis represent the four questions (corresponding to four behavioral categories, DW, DH, SH, SW) in each area (e.g. attitude towards manager). The numbers (1, 0, -1) on Y-axis represent 'Yes', 'Not Sure' and 'No' answer or Cognitive Response (CR) to a question. Cognitive responses "To a Large Extent Yes' and 'To a Large Extent No' are represented in between 0 and 1, and 0 and -1 respectively. The numbers 1, 0 and -1 also represent +ive, neutral and –ive Emotional State (ES) responses are corresponding to a cognitive response. The ranges 0 to 1 and 0 to -1 also captures the intensity of the +ive and –ive emotional state responses respectively. For example, in Figure 14 (iii) the point (-1, 2) in the 'Attitude towards Manager' graph represents a good correlation corresponding to the question "You welcome criticism from your boss…" That is, it shows to a negative cognitive response and a negative emotional state response. On the other hand, a positive cognitive response (point (1, 0.5) in the 'Attitude towards Peers' graph) and a negative emotional response (point (1,-1) the 'Attitude towards Peers' graph) indicate a less good correlation. The comparison between two candidates can be done based on number of similar or dissimilar good and less good correlations and also in terms of similar or dissimilar emotional state intensity. The good and less good correlations can also be used to customize the interview of a candidate. For example, good correlation tends to confirm that a candidate firmly believes in the scenario portrayed by a question corresponding to a particular area and behavioral category. A less good correlation means the candidate may be probed on the particular question during the interview.

7. Conclusion

Knowledge sharing is a vehicle for nurturing innovation and knowledge creation in teams and organizations. Knowledge sharing occurs between knowledge buyers and knowledge sellers in a knowledge market. Measurement of knowledge sharing behavior involves both rational and affective or emotional characteristics of knowledge workers. The rational characteristics are influenced by psychologically driven personal needs and subjective norms or culture of an organization. This paper describes a unique and novel method for modeling psychological and emotional fitness of a knowledge worker in a research team environment. These two parameters can be used to construct research teams to enhance team and organizational innovation and developing team or organization specific psychological and emotional fitness benchmarks. In the process it develops a two dimension four category knowledge sharing behavior model of knowledge buyers and sellers. This paper also heralds a new way of designing emotionally intelligent knowledge management systems which involve analysis and correlation of cognitive and non-verbal or emotional data where ever people are involved.

References

Abou-Zeid, E., & Cheng, Q. (2004). The effectiveness of innovation: a knowledge management approach, *International Journal of Innovation Management*, 8*(3)*, pp. 261–274

Akamatsu, S., Gyoba, J., Kamachi, M., & Lyons, M. (1998). Coding facial expressions with Gabor wavelets", Automatic Face and Gesture Recognition, Proceedings of Third IEEE International Conference, pp: 200 – 205, 4-16 April 1998.

Buzzotte, V. R., Lefton, R. E., & Sherberg, M. (1981). *Effective Selling Through Psychology*, Psychological Associates New York

Calder, A. J., Burton, A. M., Miller, P., Young, A. W., &Akamatsu, S. (2001). A principal component analysis of facial expressions. *Vision Research*, 41, pp. 1179-1208

Cohn, J. and Kanade, T. (2006). Use of Automated Facial Image Analysis for Measurement of Emotion Expression, *The Handbook of Emotion Elicitation and Assessment.* Oxford University Press Series in Affective Science, J. A. Coan & J. B. Allen, ed., 2006

Cross, R., & Prusak, L. (2003) The political economy of knowledge market, in Easterby-Smith, Mark and Marjorie A. Lyles, eds. Handbook of Organizational Learning and Knowledge Management. Oxford: Blackwell Publishing, pp. 454-72

Darroch, J, R, McNaughton (2002) Examining the link between knowledge management practices and types of innovation, *Journal of Intellectual Capital*; 3*(3)* ABI/INFORM Global, pg. 210

Davenport, T.H., Prusak, L. (1998). Working knowledge: How organizations manage what they know, Harvard Business School Press, Boston, Massachusetts, USA

Davila, T., Epstein, MJ., & Shelton, R (2006). Making Innovation Work: How to Manage it, Measure it, and Profit from it, Pearson Education, Upper Saddle River, NJ., USA

Edwardson, M. (2000). Emotion Profiles of customers and their impact on marketing strategy, *Customer Loyalty*, May 2000, Sydney.

Ekman, P., & Friesen, W. (1978). *Facial Action Cording System: A Technique for the Measurement of Facial Movement*, Consulting Psychologists Press, Palo Alto, CA

Gopalakrishnan, S., & Damanpour, F. (1997). A review of innovation research in economics, sociology and technology management, Omega: *The International Journal of Management Science*, 25*(1)*, 15–28

Herkema, S. (2003) A complex adaptive perspective on learning within innovation projects, *The Learning Organization*, 10*(6)*, pp. 340-346.

Hong, JC., Hwang, MY., & CL, Lin. (2003). Chi and Organizational Creativity: A Case Study of Three Taiwanese Computer Firms, *Creativity and innovation management*, 10*(4)*, pp. 202-210

Hsu, BF., Wu, WL., & Yeh, RS. (2007). Personality Composition, Affective Tie and Knowledge Sharing: A Team Level Analysis, PICMET 2007 Proceedings, 5-9 August, Portland, Oregon – USA

Izard, C. E. (1990). Facial Expressions and the Regulation of Emotions, *Journal of Personality and Social Psychology*, 58 *(3)*, pp. 487-498

Khosla, R., Goonesekera, T., & Chu, M. (2008). Separating the wheat from the chaff: An intelligent sales recruitment and benchmarking system, *Expert Systems with Applications*, 36, pp.3017–3027

Kuoa, F.Y., & Young, M.L. (2008). Predicting knowledge sharing practices through intention: A test of competing models, *Computers in Human Behavior*, 24*(6),* pp. 2697-2722

Lang, P.J. (1995). The Emotion Probe: Studies of Motivation and Attention, *American Psychologist*, 50*(5),* pp. 372-385

Lee, T. (1996). Image Representation Using 2D Gabor Wavelets, IEEE Transactions on Pattern Analysis and Machine Intelligence, 18(10):9590971, Oct. 1996.

Matzler, K., Renzl, B., Müller, J., Herting, S., & Mooradian, T.A. (2008). Personality traits and knowledge sharing, *Journal of Economic Psychology*, 29, pp. 301–313

McClelland, DC. (1985). *Human Motivation*, Scott: Freshman and Company, USA

Mehrabian, A. (1972). *Nonverbal communication,* Aldine Transactions, USA

Nonaka, I., & Takeuchi, H. (1995). The Knowledge-Creating Company, Oxford University Press, Oxford

Ortony, A., Clore, G. L., & Collins, A. (1994) *The Cognitive Structure of Emotions*, Cambridge University Press.

Picard, R.A., (1997). *Affective computing*, MIT Press

Plessis, M D. (2007). The role of knowledge management in Innovation, *Journal of knowledge management*, 11*(4),* pp. 20-29

Roseman, I. J., Antoniou, A. A., & Jose, P. E. (1996). Appraisal determinants of emotions: Constructing a more accurate and comprehensive theory. *Cognition and Emotion*, 10, 241-277.

Ryu, S., Ho, S. H., & Han, I. (2003). Knowledge sharing behavior of physicians in hospitals, *Expert Systems with Applications*, 25 *(1),* pp. 113-122.

Saenz, J., Aramburu, N., & Rivera, O. (2009). Knowledge sharing and innovation performance: A comparison between high-tech and low-tech Companies, *Journal of Intellectual Capital*, 10*(1),* pp. 22-36

Sloman, A. (1987). Motives, Mechanisms, and Emotions. *Cognition and Emotion*, 1, 3: 217-33.

Thurstone, LL. (1934). The vector of the mind, *Psychological Review*, 41*(1)*

Zmud, RW. (1984). An Examination of 'Push-Pull' Theory Applied to Process Innovation in Knowledge Work, *Management Science*, 30 *(6),* pp. 727-738

FUNDAMENTALS FOR AN IT-STRATEGY TOWARDS MANAGING VIABLE KNOWLEDGE-INTENSIVE RESEARCH PROJECTS

PAUL PÖLTNER

Vienna University of Technology; Institute of Computer-Aided Automation
Research Group for Industrial Software (INSO); Wiedner Hauptstraße 76/2, 2nd Floor
Vienna, 1040 Vienna, Austria
E-mail: paul.poeltner@inso.tuwien.ac.at

THOMAS GRECHENIG

Vienna University of Technology; Institute of Computer Aided Automation
Research Group for Industrial Software (INSO); Wiedner Hauptstraße 76/2, 2nd Floor
Vienna, 1040 Vienna, Austria
E-mail: thomas.grechenig@inso.tuwien.ac.at

Based on existing research in the field of viable system modelling, social systems and the corporate genome, this paper presents a framework for the modelling and managing of viable knowledge-intensive research projects, which require the generation of new knowledge within a dynamic and complex world. This framework presents an overall look at the different levels which need to be established in order to implement a new, self-organised and viable system able to realise the defined aims of research projects.

1. Introduction

Current economic developments are driven by two major forces: information and communication. In our so-called information economy, which has existed as such for roughly a century, information is the driving force. Recent developments in internet technology are leading society in a new direction, that of the "networked economy," where communication is a second major driving force (Benkler, 2006). The implied capitalistic development of this new economy is referred to by (Boltanski & Chiapello, 2006) as networked capitalism; the dominant values in this system are activity, flexibility, communication, creativity and autonomy. In order to cope with these developments, organisations must open their borders and connect with different partners within the value chain (Reichwald & Piller, 2006). As value chains have increased in complexity and flexibility over the last century, current research and development activities are no longer undertaken by a single organisation, but rather by teams of different partners from different organisations.

Interlinked with technological developments in the internet sphere are the new free software (Raymond, 2001) and open source software movements started in the 1990s (Stallman, Lessig, & Gay, 2002). These developments marked the opening of the frontier for universal participation in the creation of competitive software products. Recent technological developments, most notably that of Web 2.0, have established a new force for creating content (O'Reilly, 2005). (Howe, 2008) describes this amateur-created content as "crowdsourcing." These new technologies allow new kinds of group-forming, where everybody can help in solving bigger problems (Shirky, 2008). These new communities become collectively intelligent and are able to solve complex problems no single individual could cope with. In this sense, collective intelligence is the phenomenon whereby connected people and computers can act more intelligently than a group of experts (Atlee u. a., 2008).

Confronted with these developments, organisations need to adjust their corporate cultures. They must shift from acting as closed source innovation teams to pursuing a so-called open innovation philosophy (Chesbrough, 2005). Ideas for new products and services need not only to come from inside the company but also from the "crowd" outside.

In order to cope with these new developments, organisations need to devise new forms of cooperation and collaboration. In the case of value chains, these new forms are known as collaborative network organisations (or virtual organisations, smart organisations, etc) (Camarinha-Matos & Afsarmanesh, 2004). Collaboration networks can be as simple as the digitisation of some sort of information (e.g. Amazon), whereby physical processes are substituted by ICT, or as complex as phenomena like virtual organisations, collaboration networks and innovation networks, in which agile networks of partners cooperate in innovative ways. These new forms of collaboration save money and time, reduce the number of steps of interaction, prevent mistakes due to lack of information,and enhance knowledge and trust (Nagel, Walters, Gurevich, & Schmid, 2005).

The first part of Section Two of this article presents the theoretical basis for the model, which will be described in Section Three. Guidelines for the design of a research project will be discussed in Section Four.

2. Literature

2.1. *System theory and social systems*

The basis of system theory was defined by Bertalanffy and Wiener. Bertalanffy, a biologist, was searching for a way to describe the relationships between different parts of a body. According to him, a system is considered to be open if it interacts with its environment (Heylighen & Joslyn, 1992). Cybernetics, defined by Ashby, provides a model to describe the behaviour of a machine. His Law of Requisite Variety states that "only variety in R can force down the variety due to D; variety can destroy variety" (Ashby, 1957).

Systems generally consist of two parts: an element (or node) and a relation (the node can also be a system in and of itself). Variety in a social system describes the system's complexity, which encompasses its connectivity and dynamic (Schuh, Friedli, & Kurr, 2005). In order to control such a system, the variety must be changed, because according to Ashby's Law of Requisite Variety, the variety of the control system must match the variety of the system (Masak, 2007).

The social system was first defined by Luhmann. He defines a system as a difference within the environment; the differentiation in a social system is made through communication. One of his key points is that social systems are self-referential: they can observe themselves as a system and define what it is that differentiates them from the environment. He calls this phenomenon "re-entry". In his model, he differentiates between social systems. Society is a special social system which encompasses all other social systems and does not know any social system out of its borders. Society consists in this context only of communication. Luhmann defines an organisation as a social system which controls access to work. Developments such as education (school and university levels) as well as monetary and law systems prepare the environment for organisations. He notes that entry and acceptance to an organisation is a sort of membership, whereby one must agree to follow its rules and guidelines for observation of and communication with the environment. In other words, the organisation defines one's worldview (Luhmann, 2009).

2.2. *Management cybernetics*

The founder of management cybernetics was Stafford Beer, who researched in the field of living systems and defined the Viable System Model (VSM). In this model, a system is viable if its identity is sustainable. In order to be viable according to the VSM, a system needs to have five subsystems: System 1 is the operative element, which is responsible for daily business interactions with the environment. System 1 can consist recursively of subsystems, which need to have the same structure as the upper system (p.e. business unit, subsidiary, etc,). System 2 is responsible for coordination between the different subsystems of System 1; following the guidelines of Ashby's system theory, it balances complexity through variety management. System 3 controls and regulates the whole system, and tries to optimise resources. System 4 interconnects with the environment, defines the overall vision, and models the system's organisation and environment. Finally, System 5 defines the identity of the system (Masak, 2007).

In order for an organisation to cope with complexity, Beer suggests variety engineering (management), which assumes that a system is self-organised and therefore has the ability to control and regulate itself. Any business activity can be split into three systems: the management, the organisation and the environment. The management reduces or increases the organisation's complexity according to the needs dictated by its environment. The management of the system receives data from the environment and, using a model, evaluates their potential for viability of the organisation. Therefore, a management process cannot be better than that model it is based upon. The management process itself is split into three parts: the operative level, which guarantees efficiency (productivity and quality), the strategic level, which guarantees effectiveness, and the normative level, which guarantees that all stakeholders' requirements are fulfilled. Intelligent organisations fulfil all these management requirements recursively at every level, which implicates that they are also self-organised at every level (Schwaninger, 1999).

According to Kruse, the problem with self-organised systems is that people have the tendency to stick with a certain strategy and try to optimise this (Theory of Best Practice). This theory of self-organised systems can be applied to organisation forms in environments which are unstable (dynamic) and complex, where at some point in time best practice has stopped working (Kruse, 2004). At some point of instability, known as a bifurcation point, self-organised systems have the ability to reach a new, unpredicted level of stability. This can only be realised in an unstable environment (Heylighen, 1999). In order to cope with a dynamic market, the management needs to find a balance between stability and instability.

One of the central elements of self-organised systems is the theory of iterations, which states that complex systems can be built up by means of several recursive iterations. In a social system, simple rules and stable corporate cultures are the mechanisms necessary to build complex systems. These rules create a reality which limits the complexity of the problem space. Thus, the corporate culture defines the set of rules for a complex, self-organised system to evolve (Kruse, 2004).

2.3. *(Knowledge) Management model*

Any self-organised system needs a model to proof its concepts. The definition of the corporate strategy necessary for the model's development hinges on a specific view the environment. Porter's "The Five Competitive Forces That Shape Strategy" is useful for defining this strategy and orienting companies on the market (Porter, 2008). Porter's so-called market-based view presents different strategic business units, which are in compliance with the requirements of the segmented markets.

Another approach is the resource-based view (Grant, 1991), which concentrates on the strengths and weaknesses of the company's resources and capabilities. A strategy based on this view identifies resource gaps in order to fulfil customer requirements more effectively than competitors do. Grant views resources and capabilities as the primary sources of profit for a firm. Resources are the basic units, and can be seen as the input to processes (capital equipment, skills, employees, etc.). Capabilities are the result of a sum of resources; they can be described as complex patterns of coordination between people and between people and other resources.

In the information economy, knowledge can be seen as the most important strategic resource (Zack, 1999). Zack therefore suggests linking knowledge of strategic opportunity with the SWOT (strength, weakness, opportunities, and threats) analysis. He separates the knowledge resource into core knowledge, advanced knowledge and innovative knowledge. Innovative knowledge is the knowledge required to lead the industry. The knowledge-based view can be seen as the link between strategic management and knowledge management.

Maier presents an integrated concept of a process-oriented knowledge management strategy, which focuses on the market and on internal resources (Maier, 2007). The first step in this strategy should be the identification of resources related to knowledge management. The second step evaluates these resources against the market. Next, the resources deemed to be strategically relevant are combined to form capabilities. Finally, looking to the market, strategic business fields are defined. Knowledge management in this context supports the integration of resources into capabilities. Dynamic capabilities are comprised here of organisational and managerial processes (Teece, Gary Pisano, & Amy Shuen, 1997). With his process-oriented view, Maier integrates the resource-based and market-based views into one framework. Business processes are defined in accordance with customer requirements along a value chain, while the knowledge management process helps to evolve new core competences to implement business processes (Maier, 2007).

Knowledge management itself is an interdisciplinary field, which can be divided into many layers, each of which can be isolated and studied independently. At the heart of knowledge management is a core theory, which incorporates a specific knowledge process and organisational, social and managerial elements (Schwartz, 2007). The bare minimum necessary for an efficient knowledge management strategy is a technical system. Knowledge networks provide an efficient means to manage knowledge sharing and creation. In order for these networks to evolve, they again need facilitating conditions, a knowledge process and an architecture (Back, Enkel, & Krogh, 2006).

This article will draw on the theories of Scharmer (Scharmer, 2007), which will be discussed in Chapter 4. One of Scharmer's key concepts is that of a five-movement process to collectively generate new knowledge. The first movement, called co-initialing, involves forming a group (project team) and creating a common sense of purpose for the upcoming project. The second movement, called co-sensing, entails the observation of the environment and the collective gauging of its potential. In the third movement, co-presencing, everything is let go and is opened up to a possible future and defined goal. In the fourth movement, this goal is prototyped, and in the fifth and final movement it is implemented in an evolving ecosystem. Open innovation can help to create such a future in a larger environment within the internet.

2.4. *The capability-driven organisation*

(Aurik, Jonk, & Willen, 2002) present the concept of the capability-driven organisation, which goes a step further than Meier's knowledge management strategy. At the core of this concept is the idea that the company consists of a sum of capabilities. Each capability is represented as a gene of the company, and the sum of an organisation's capabilities is represented as the corporate DNA. (Aurik u. a., 2002) write: "Just as each human gene is a piece of DNA working as an instruction manual for a particular human characteristic, each business capability is a component of the value chain that makes a unique contribution to a company's output." The sum of all corporate DNAs is the corporate genome. A capability is an element of a value chain and consists of a set of activities and assets. Capabilities on which the company has some edge will help business excel. These capabilities can be capitalised on through coordination with other organisations in the creation of agile value chains. At the same time, capabilities with low business value can be bought in. In the end, every value chain will be separated into a sum of capabilities, with each organisation responsible for one capability, and one organisation responsible for the orchestration of all the different capabilities. A value chain can be broken up into three layers of chains: the physical value chain, which can be seen as the real production chain, the transaction value chain, which defines the transaction and control processes, and the knowledge value chain, the highest layer (Aurik u. a., 2002).

3. A model for self-organised viable collaborative networked organisations

As previously discussed, collaborative networked organisations (CNO) will become more and more relevant in the near future. Companies need to cooperate with different partners, both internal and external, in order to work agilely in accordance with market requirements. The model to be presented provides a means to manage such a structure.

3.1. *The model*

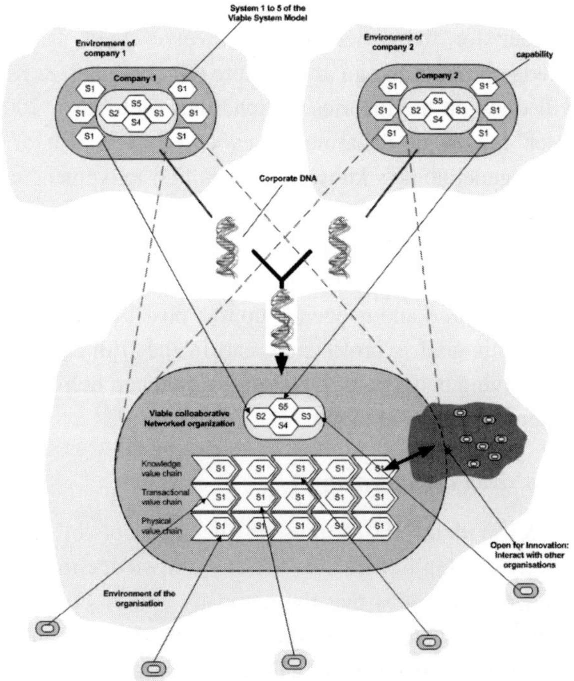

Fig. 1: Viable collaborative networked organisation

Figure 1 represents the whole model. At its core, every organisation consists of a corporate DNA. This corporate DNA is the sum of the organisation's capabilities, or "genes" (e.g. forecasting, manufacturing, accounting). For this model, a capability is considered to be a combination of different resources (Grant, 1991), which are the result of a process of organisational learning (Maier, 2007) and produce some business value.

Every company is viable in the sense of the viable system model and therefore consists of five subsystems (as described in Chapter 2.2) (Masak, 2007). Following the theory of Luhmann, every organisation is a social system which differentiates itself by communication from its environment (as presented by the bubble in Figure 1). Knowledge management (itself another capability of the organization) is responsible for the development and enhancement of these capabilities. The model assumes an organisation which is viable and self-organised. Therefore, the viable organisation contains a management level, which is responsible for the normative and strategic management of the system itself (Schwaninger, 1999).

It is crucial to define the rules and the vision of the company from the outset in order for the whole system to be manageable in dynamic and unstable environments. Depending on the complexity and strategy of the organisation, Subsystems 1 to 5 may comprise one or more capabilities (described as S1 to S5 in Figure 1), with several Systems 1 for different operational activities. Using the theory of the corporate genome, the whole corporation can be described both in terms of capabilities and in terms of resources. Resources can include processes, learning cycles, management methods, know-how, skills, etc.

After defining company vision and taking stock of resources, the next step is to create a viable collaboratively networked organisation. (Aurik u. a., 2002) emphasise that there are two kinds of strategies: those focused on single capabilities, and those focused on capabilities along a value-chain. The organisations in this model are single capability-focused, and therefore provide only for some specific parts of a value chain. When two or more separate companies agree on forming a collaborative organisation, however, each organisation can provide for some specific part of that newly formed organisation with its own capabilities. In other words, the DNA of the different organisations will be mixed, creating a value chain to realise defined customer requirements at the market level. Ultimately, a new system, which is a subsystem the other companies will be created. This system is able to recreate itself if necessary and is responsible for the implementation of a specific value chain. This value chain can be separated into three different layers: the knowledge value chain, the transactional value chain and the physical value chain (as described in Chapter 2.4). Furthermore, the newly created viable organisation must be able to communicate with the crowd and therefore open its borders for new innovations.

3.2. *Strategic management*

The strategic management process itself must be performed recursively at every level in the system (System 4 in the VSM and S4 in Figure 1). The management process is again based on the rules and policy (the identity and corporate culture) of the system, which must once again be defined (System 5 and S5 in Figure 1). On a strategic level, the first step is an identification of the company resources and an analysis of the completive environment with a SWOT analysis. In the next step, the capabilities are crystallised (Maier, 2007) and the core strategic products and services of the organisation are defined.

This type of forming leads to a sort of matrix organisation. This is differentiated by the fact that capabilities themselves are customer-focused, since every capability can be integrated into another value chain. Additionally, if the capability of one organisation is not strong enough, it can be replaced by the capability of another organisation (Aurik u. a., 2002). The value chain, defined by the market manager in System 4, will lead the strategic orientation, thus focusing on customer requirements and combining the different capabilities into value chains.

In order to create a viable collaboratively networked organisation, System 4, or the market manager, starts with a SWOT analysis, evaluating strengths, weaknesses, opportunities and threats. Next, the network can be initiated through an analysis of its market possibilities and an identification of possible partners. The next step involves the planning of the new system itself: the different corporate DNAs are brought together and combined along the three value chain layers to form a new, stronger value chain. During the creation of the organisation, the system is self-optimised through the five systems of the viable system model. In the initiation phase, the identity and corporate culture of the different organisations are combined and implemented in System 5. As this newly formed organisation is part of the other systems as well, it will also be coordinated and controlled by Systems 2 and 3 (Schubert, 2008).

4. Implementation of a collaboratively networked organisation for research projects

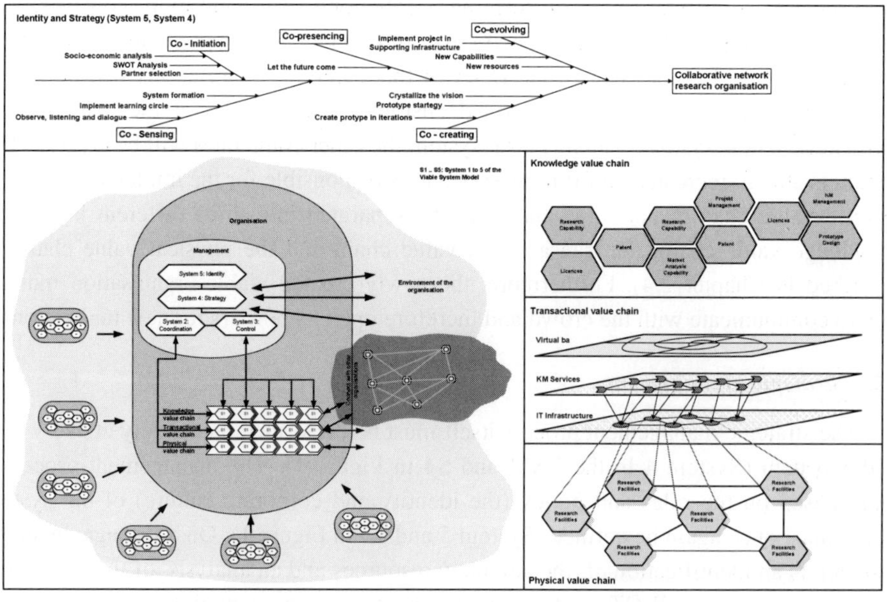

Fig. 2: Viable collaborative networked research organisation

The requirements for the implementation of research projects in the European environment are particularly high, as public research organizations are unable to fulfil all the needed capabilities themselves. David and Metcalfe note that "knowledge of markets and organisations and factor input availability are key aspects for innovation and not the specialisation of public research organisations. So a division of labour exists between public research organisations and companies." (European Communities, 2008) In the following, a viable collaboratively networked organization will be developed in accordance with the five steps of Theory U (Scharmer, 2007).

4.1. *Co-initiation*

The first phase for the implementation of a new complex research project is the formation of the new system. The lead partner, who takes the initial steps, needs to define a starting vision for the new project.

Once the first idea has been defined for the project, a socioeconomic analysis will define the baseline for further investigations (European Chemicals Agency, 2008). This socioeconomic analysis investigates the society, the culture and the people that the new project might have an impact on. Next, the lead partner must undertake a SWOT analysis to investigate its own capabilities in relation to the identified environment (Schubert, 2008).

Following this analysis, possible partners with specific capabilities need to be identified. In this phase, it is important to evaluate a core group of people (organisations) who share a common (Scharmer, 2007). At this stage, the research proposal should be created and the general conditions (in terms of intellectual property, time and money) defined. If this step goes wrong, the whole new system cannot evolve.

4.2. *Co-sensing*

In the second phase, the new viable collaboratively networked research organization will be born. In this step, the corporate DNA (the sum of capabilities) of the different participating partners will be brought together and orchestrated into a new organisation. The value chain for this research model will be defined according to the Theory U process. The new system identity and strategy must be defined based on the genes of some partners in Systems 4 and 5 (Schwaninger, 1999) of the viable system. The rules and the vision for the system will help the system to be self-organised so that every participating party can work independently toward the overall aim of the project.

In the next step, a chain of "Systems 1 – 2 – 3" will be created in order to bring the system to life. Starting with the physical value chain, the different partners will provide different research facilities with different capabilities. In the second layer, a integrated knowledge management process needs to put into action. Based on the concepts of service-oriented architecture, this layer can be divided into different levels. The lowest level is the IT Infrastructure of the different partners. Within these IT Systems, different knowledge services are provided, which can be orchestrated to form an overall virtual ba

(Pulier, 2005) (Krafzig, Banke, & Slama, 2004) (Maier, 2007). In the knowledge value chain, different capabilities like patents, licenses, developing methods, sharing experiences and the embedding of the crowd will be implemented in the overall system. The described system must be open to its environment in order to communicate and exchange information. This will lead to higher viability, which will in turn help to solve more complex socioeconomic problems.

In the next step, the system will be able to start to operate. In this step, observation, listening, and dialogue are crucial to gain a sense of the problem space (Scharmer, 2007).

4.3. *Co-presencing*

The creative part of the process takes part in the co-presencing phase. At this point, the system needs to investigate possible future outcomes, and open its heart, its mind and its will. At this stage, after several rounds of observation, listening and dialogue, the system is ready to greet the new possible future (Scharmer, 2007).

4.4. *Co-creating*

After the future has come (Scharmer, 2007), the precise project vision must be defined and the strategic steps distributed to the different participating partners in the project. The coordination of activities will be led by System 2 in accordance with the overall rules and culture of the system. Starting with a core team and an open policy, the new project can evolve in an open ecosystem. The aim is to develop a prototype of the possible future. This needs to be done in several iterations and must incorporate feedback from the stakeholders (Scharmer, 2007). The viable organisation must support this process by through self-organisation and open exchange with its environment. New technologies from different fields of research can also support this process, depending on the required complexity.

4.5. *Co-evolving*

The last step of the viable collaborative network research organisation is to implement the newly created reality into a supporting infrastructure (Scharmer, 2007). At this point, the viable system can launch its newly created capabilities into an evolving ecosystem by creating new subsystems which will keep on working. In addition to capabilities, the viable system will have also created resources (artefacts), which can flow back to the different mother systems and be used to realise new capabilities beneficial to the system's overall aim, identity and strategy.

5. Conclusion and outlook

The theoretical framework presented here is a starting point for further discussions in the field of management of collaboratively networked organizations. Many different disciplines factor into the setting up of such a system; knowledge management (which again depends on a wide variety of scientific fields) is just one of these important fields.

Technology is also crucial, and a great deal of emphasis must be placed on the technological implementation of such an agile system. The flexible combination of different capabilities in the technological layer requires a high level of standardisation and interoperability, for which service-oriented architecture is just one starting point for further investigation.

On a management level, the theories of Stafford and the Corporate Genome Theory present yet another perspective on the corporate structure. As in other modern management theories, companies need to be flat and flexible and focus on their core capabilities.

References

Ashby, W. R. (1957). An introduction to cybernetics. London: Chapman & Hall Ltd.

Atlee, T., Benkler, Y., Homer-Dixon, T., Levy, P., Malone, T., Martin, R. H. P., u. a. (2008). Collective Intelligence: Creating a Prosperous World at Peace (1. Aufl.). Earth Intelligence Network.

Aurik, J. C., Jonk, G. J., & Willen, R. E. (2002). Rebuilding the Corporate Genome: Unlocking the Real Value of Your Business. Wiley.

Back, A., Enkel, E., & Krogh, G. V. (2006). Knowledge Networks for Business Growth (1. Aufl.). Springer.

Benkler, Y. (2006). The wealth of networks. Yale University Press.

Boltanski, L., & Chiapello, È. (2006). Der neue Geist des Kapitalismus (Sonderausgabe.). Uvk.

Camarinha-Matos, L., & Afsarmanesh, H. (2004). Collaborative networked oganizations. Springer.

Chesbrough, H. W. (2005). Open Innovation: The New Imperative for Creating And Profiting from Technology (1. Aufl.). Harvard Business School Press.

European Chemicals Agency. (2008). REACH Navigator - Guidance on Socio-Economic Analysis - Restrictions. Abgerufen Juni 22, 2009, von http://guidance.echa.europa.eu/docs/guidance_document/sea_restrictions_en.htm?time=1233561701.

European Communities. (2008). Knowledge for Growth: European Issues and Policy Challenges. European Communities. Abgerufen von http://ec.europa.eu/invest-in-research/pdf/download_en/knowledge_for_growth_bat.pdf.

Grant, R. M. (1991). The Resource-Based Theory of Competitive Advantae: Implications for Strategy Formulation. California Management Revew, 114-135.

Heylighen, F. (1999). The science of self-organization and adaptivity. Center "Leo Apostel", Free University of Brussels, Belgium. Abgerufen von http://pespmc1.vub.ac.be/papers/EOLSS-Self-Organiz.pdf.

Heylighen, F., & Joslyn, C. (1992). What is Systems Theory? Abgerufen Juni 21, 2009, von http://pespmc1.vub.ac.be/SYSTHEOR.html.

Howe, J. (2008). Crowdsourcing: Why the Power of the Crowd Is Driving the Future of Business (1. Aufl.). Crown Business.

Krafzig, D., Banke, K., & Slama, D. (2004). Enterprise SOA: Service Oriented Architecture Best Practices (2005undefined Aufl.). Prentice Hall International.

Kruse, P. (2004). next practice. Erfolgreiches Management von Instabilität (3undefined Aufl.). GABAL-Verlag GmbH.

Luhmann, N. (2009). Die Gesellschaft der Gesellschaft (neuauflage.). Suhrkamp Verlag.

Maier, R. (2007). Knowledge Management Systems: Information and Communication Technologies for Knowledge Management (3undefined Aufl.). Springer.

Masak, D. (2007). SOA? Springer.

Nagel, R., Walters, J., Gurevich, G., & Schmid, P. (2005). Smart Business Networks Enable Strategic Opportunities Not Found in Traditional Business Networking. In Smart Business Networks (S. 127-143). Abgerufen Juni 12, 2009, von http://dx.doi.org/10.1007/3-540-26694-1_9.

O'Reilly, T. (2005). Web 2.0: Compact Definition? - O'Reilly Radar. Abgerufen Juni 20, 2009, von http://radar.oreilly.com/archives/2005/10/web-20-compact-definition.html.

Pulier, E. (2005). Understanding Enterprise SOA (illustrated edition.). Manning.

Raymond, E. S. (2001). The cathedral and the bazaar. O'Reilly.

Reichwald, R., & Piller, F. T. (2006). Interaktive Wertschöpfung. Open Innovation, Individualisierung und neue Formen der Arbeitsteilung (1. Aufl.). Gabler, Betriebswirt.-Vlg.

Scharmer, C. O. (2007). Theory U: Leading from the Future as it Emerges (1. Aufl.). SoL, the Society for Organizational Learning.

Schubert, H. (2008). Netzwerkmanagement: Koordination von professionellen Vernetzungen - Grundlagen und Praxisbeispiele (1. Aufl.). Vs Verlag.

Schuh, G., Friedli, T., & Kurr, M. A. (2005). Kooperationsmanagement. Hanser Verlag.

Schwaninger, M. (1999). Intelligente Organisationen. Konzepte für turbulente Zeiten auf der Grundlage von Systemtheorie und Kybernetik. Wissenschaftliche Jahrestagung der ... und Systemanalyse; WS 19) (1. Aufl.). Duncker & Humblot GmbH.

Schwartz, D. G. (2007). A.Birds-Eye.View.of. Knowledge.Management: Creating.a.Disciplined.Whole.from. Many.Interdisciplinary.Parts. In Knowledge Management in Modern Organizations (S. 18-29). London: Idea Group Inc.

Shirky, C. (2008). Here Comes Everybody: The Power of Organizing Without Organizations. Penguin Press HC, The.

Stallman, R. M., Lessig, L., & Gay, J. (2002). Free Software, Free Society: Selected Essays of Richard M. Stallman (First Printing, First Edition.). Free Software Foundation.

Teece, D. J., Gary Pisano, & Amy Shuen. (1997). Dynamic capabilities and strategic management. Strategic Management Journal, 18(7), 509-533. doi: 10.1002/(SICI)1097-0266(199708)18:7<509::AID-SMJ882>3.0.CO;2-Z.

Zack, M. (1999). Developing a Knowledge Strategy, (California Management Review), 125-145.

A NEW FRAMEWORK OF KNOWLEDGE MANAGEMENT BASED ON THE INTERACTION BETWEEN HUMAN CAPITAL AND ORGANIZATIONAL CAPITAL

ZHENG FAN*

College of International Business, Shanghai International Studies University,
DaLian Road (W), Shanghai, 200083, China
E-mail: fanzh280@shisu.edu.cn

SHUJING CAO, FENGHUA WANG

College of International Business, Shanghai International Studies University,
DaLian Road (W), Shanghai, 200083, China
E-mail: cao_shujing@126.com; wangfenghua@shisu.edu.cn

This paper starts with an analysis of the interaction between human capital and organizational capital. It continues to explore a core-competence-based knowledge management mechanism, by which a new framework of management can therefore be constructed. It provides solid theoretical foundation and rich practical implications for business to accomplish independent innovation in management as it unveils the intrinsic law governing the nurturing of corporate intelligence.

1. Research Background

Economists and managerialists have always been probing into the core elements of enterprise competitiveness. Among those, Prahalad's theory of core competence (Prahalad 1990) has received heightened attention. Although they are not quite uniform on the definition, content, and extension of the concept core competence, almost all of scholars mention the concept of knowledge capital in their theories (Fan 2002).

Human capital is the foremost carrier of knowledge capital of firms. However, in a free society, human capital cannot be possessed but rented (Wiig 1997). In a competitive firm, people and knowledge should be separated. Firms are not only economic entities but also knowledge entities. The concept of structural capital or organizational capital is thus proposed. It is defined as those that are left to the firm after the employees go back from work in the evening, or the company's asset that remains in the firm after their 8 hours' working time (Edvinsson). It is also the infrastructure that gives support to human capital to create fortune. It is termed as the Corporate IQ by Bill Gates and is considered the genuine competence of firms (Gates, 1999).

However, it is not necessarily to the best of a firm to have the most organizational capital. Some certain degree of rigidity might appear in the process of organizational capital accumulation, which might result in negative effects on the exertion and

* This research is a part of the research project "Corporate Knowledge Capital Management: from the Perspective of the Interaction between Human Capital and Organizational Capital" funded by the National Social Science Foundation.

development of human capital. Therefore it is to the core of corporate competence research to study the mechanism of a positive interaction between human capital and organizational capital.

In this way, the fundamental goal of knowledge capital management is consistent with the goal of overall management (Bukowitz 1999), which can be stated as "to form the organization's ability to survive for a prolonged time period by continuously developing values for stakeholders". Knowledge management offers a new perspective to observe an organization and its managerial process.

2. Literature Review

The exploration of the core-competence-based positive interaction mechanism between human capital and organizational capital shall borrow from such managerial and economic disciplines as strategic management, knowledge management, etc. The following are some relevant conclusions in these fields.

- Recently the research on core competence in the field strategic management has further embedded the concept of knowledge capital (Broking, 1996). Based on this, Fan constructed a theoretical system of knowledge-capital-based core competence (Fan 2002). This research on the interaction between human capital and organizational capital will extend the above-mentioned groundwork and expand into its implications for application.
- It is not necessarily to the best of a firm to have the most knowledge capital. Only those that possess the properties of value-creating, extendable, difficult to imitate, and self-learning can be integrated to construct the core competence. Therefore, the essential issue in the research of the interaction between human capital and organizational capital is to search for the core-competence-based organizational capital that is most competitive. Research in this field is still so far unexploited.
- For the moment, researches on knowledge management are basically following the knowledge classification schema adopted by the two most influential Japanese ideologists Nonaka and Tskeuchi. According to their schema, knowledge are divided into two categories, explicit and tacit (Nonaka 1994, 1995). In fact, they admit in a later research that this is only a general classification schema (Nonaka, 2005). There is a category of indistinct knowledge in between (knowledge about process, structure, and relationship, only to name a few) that is more closely related to corporate competence. A research by Xu and Chen also mentioned this category (Xu 2002), though no systematic research conclusions have been published so far. This paper is to breakthrough the above schema and adopts a transform system consisting of id knowledge, ego knowledge and superego knowledge.
- The management function system (Planning, Organizing, Command, Coordinating and Controlling) by Koontz (1985) and the management application system (organization, people, and operation) by Donnelly (1995) are playing a

dominant role in constructing the knowledge framework for the management descipline. These old structures are no longer fit for newest situations. Thereupon, Chinese and Foreign management scholars start to research on it. For example, Management: Modern Views, wrote by Mingjie Rui (Rui 1999), integrates many new studies in management. Magretta's what is management (Magretta 2002) also breaks through this structure and brings management into two concepts of designing and executing. However, there haven't appeared any research achievements to restructure management on the core of management, i.e. the interaction between human capital and organizational capital.

Based on this, this paper would begin with the interaction of human capital and organizational capital, and explore a core-competence-based knowledge management mechanism, by which a new framework of management can therefore be constructed. It provides solid theoretical foundation and rich practical implications for businesses to accomplish independent innovation in management as it unveils the intrinsic law governing the nurturing of corporate intelligence.

3. Management Matrix of Human-to-Organizational Capital and its Implementation Method

Knowledge refers to those intelligent products that can be learned and are related to work activities. It includes work output, experience summarization, theoretical achievements, time planning skills and tactics, communication skills, management skills, thinking set, mental experience and so on. It is the resource database of corporate core competence. Basically, knowledge could be classified by the following two dimensions:

3.1 From the perspective of ontology

Basically, corporate knowledge exists either at personal level or is shared between organization members. The former is referred to as personal knowledge while the latter shared knowledge. Personal knowledge exists in the mind of an individual organizational member or appears as the corporate knowledge in terms of personal skills. This kind of knowledge is individually-owed and can be used individually for solving special tasks or problems. It can be transferred. But the moving of an individual might result in potential problems in retaining and accumulating such knowledge. Shared knowledge is the method of how knowledge is distributed and shared between organization members. It is the cumulative knowledge of firms, which exists as the rules, procedures, conventions and share code of conduct. It will guide the activities to solve problems and the interactions among organization members. Shared knowledge stands for the memory of an organization. It can be either stored in the knowledge reservoir of a firm or exchanged among members through interaction. Shared knowledge doesn't equal the sum of personal knowledge. Whether it is greater or smaller than the sum of personal knowledge depends on the transform mechanism of how personal knowledge turns into shared knowledge (Glynn 1996).

In fact, knowledge does not only exist in the two forms of personal knowledge and shared knowledge. Organizations can be examined at personal level, team level, organizational level, as well as inter-organizational level. Knowledge can therefore be classified into four categories.

- Personal knowledge. Knowledge owned by individuals in the group.
- Team knowledge. Knowledge owned by a combination of individuals to achieve some task or goal.
- Organizational knowledge. Knowledge owned by a combination of individuals who has an established management system.
- Inter-organizational knowledge. Knowledge existing between an organization and its important customers, supplier and competitors.

3.2 From the perspective of epistemology

From the perspective of epistemology and based on the complexity of knowledge (Tiwana, 2001), Polanyi, a famous management master, classifies knowledge into two distinct categories of explicit knowledge and tacit knowledge. Explicit knowledge can be clearly expressed with normal language, encoded in language or by machine, compressed into several simple symbols and easily transferred between individuals. Tacit knowledge is the individual knowledge that takes root in personal experiences, including such invisible elements as beliefs, opinions, instincts and values, etc. Tacit knowledge is hard to encode. It is fit for face-to-face communications and synchronous transferring mode.

Although knowledge may be classified into explicit and tacit conceptually, it is difficult to separate them in practice. Nonaka (2005) defined tacit knowledge as analog knowledge and explicit knowledge as digital symbols. He also pointed out there are two levels of tacit knowledge. The first level is the technical level involving those hard-to-define informal skills, which is usually referred to as know how. The other level is the cognitive level. It involves beliefs, comprehensions, ideals, values, emotions and mindsets. This level of knowledge always affects the way we feel about the world around us. It is usually considered to be only natural and perfectly justified.

Based on former researches, this paper further supplements the classification schema. Borrowing from Freud (Freud 1958), the author proposes that three forms of knowledge, namely id, ego and superego knowledge, exist respectively at the four level, i.e. individual level, team level, organizational level, and inter-organizational level (Fan 2007).

- Id knowledge. It is equivalent to explicit knowledge, which is independent of the knowledge subject. Id knowledge is the knowledge that is easiest to transfer and share. It is both easy to encode and formalize and convenient for learning and imitating.

- Ego knowledge. It is the technical or indistinct part of tacit knowledge. It is the experience and skills that are accumulated by individuals or organizations in their learning and working process. Proper channels and methods should be selected transfer such knowledge. It can't exist independent of the subject and is hard to encode or imitate.
- Superego knowledge. It is deeper than ego knowledge and is equivalent to the cognitive level of tacit knowledge. Knowledge subjects form this kind of potential knowledge in the long-term learning and working process. It can only be acquired through reading between lines. It might be an inborn talent that is hard to imitate or transfer. Superego knowledge could only be transferred between knowledge subjects through a long-term learning without learning process.

The final goal of human-to-organizational capital is to accomplish the transference from personal, team and inter-organizational knowledge into organizational knowledge, by which an organization improves its intelligence quotient and enhances its sustainable competence. Exhibit 1 shows the transference between three forms of knowledge, namely id, ego and superego knowledge, at four organizational level, i.e. personal, team, organizational and inter-organizational.

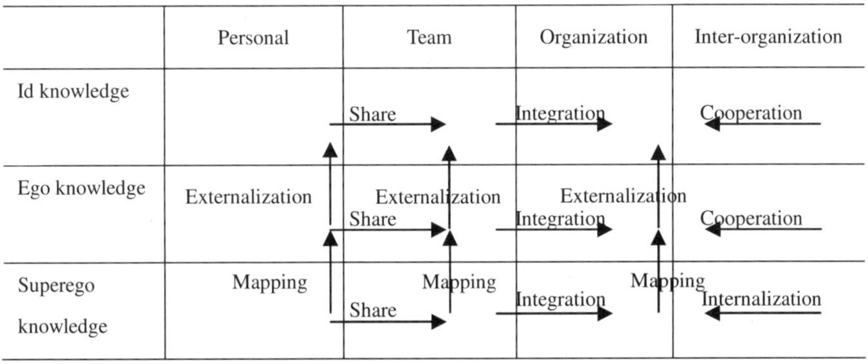

Exhibit 1: Knowledge Transfer Matrix in an Organization

The knowledge possessed by knowledge subjects, either at personal, team, organizational or inter-organizational level, can also be divided into id, ego and superego knowledge categories. And these three kinds of knowledge are able to transform into each other. The final goal is to accomplish the transformation of id and ego knowledge into superego knowledge to improve the efficiency of knowledge utilization. Two transformation processes are involved: ① the mapping process, from which id knowledge is transformed into ego knowledge. Through this process, a knowledge subject turns his potential ability into practical skills. ② the externalization process, from which ego knowledge is transformed into superego knowledge. It is the process to formalize and encode knowledge, which is similar to the explicitization of tacit knowledge. Exhibit 2 shows the transformation processes and detailed implementation method.

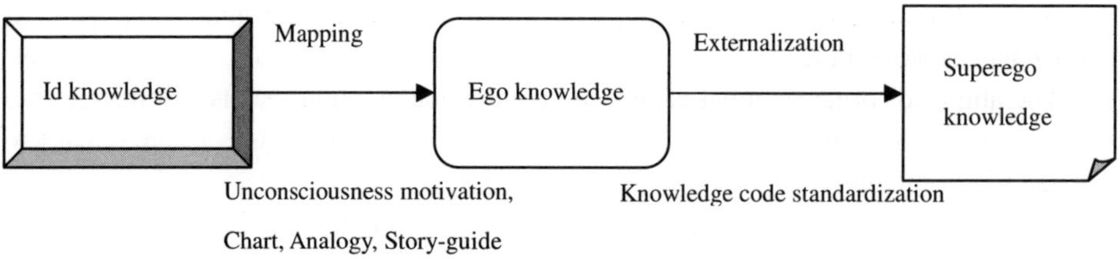

Exhibit 2: Transformation between Superego, Ego and Id Knowledge

4. Organization-to-Human Capital Leadership Style and Guiding Compass

Core competence shall possess four necessary properties: value creating, extendable, hard to imitate, and self-learning (Fan 2002). The core-competence-based interaction between human capital and organizational capital involves four aspects (see Exhibit 3): ① id knowledge transformation: the mechanism to create value for customers. ② ego knowledge transformation: the mechanism to become hard to imitate by competitors. ③ superego knowledge transformation: the mechanism to extend in the future. ④ human-organization capital transformation: the mechanism to learn from the past self.

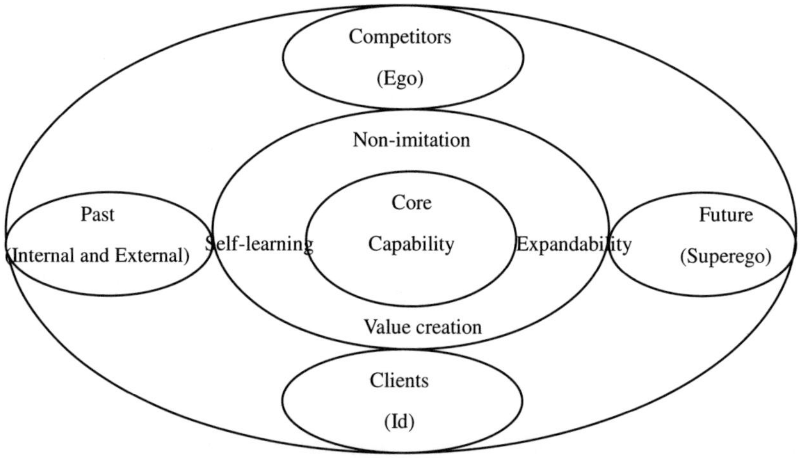

Exhibit 3: Core Competence: the Four Feature Parameters Compass

4.1 Id-knowledge-based value creation: management philosophy + business model

Knowledge capital usually brings value to firms in two ways: strategic positioning and financial / economic value. The former is measured in qualitative terms (such as image, evolvement gesture) while the latter in quantitative terms (such as sales revenue, stock price, cash flow, etc.). This paper is based on the former one. According to Freud's theory, innovation and innovative thinking are generated unconsciously, or from id knowledge, as we term it.

The ability of organizational capital to create value creation mainly originates from such two aspects as management philosophy and business model, both of which are dependent upon the id-knowledge-based creation and innovation. Management philosophy involves forming in mind the awareness to create value, promoting the concept of value creation by reshaping people's mode of thinking, and accomplishing the goal of value creation. Business model offers material support and structural as well as system guarantee for its operation. If we can say that management philosophy provides is the headspring to tempt people, we can also say that business model would be the sacrifice to motivate people to act.

4.2 Ego-knowledge-based non-imitation: structural capital + process knowledge

Non-imitation or uniqueness equals societal complexity and causal fuzziness (Nelson 1982). It means the uniqueness of corporate core competence is usually caused by a complicated society and some coincidence, which makes it hard to imitate or copy. Once a firm possesses the competence, it is difficult for its competitors to imitate in a short time. When a firm's competitive advantage does not come from one single value activity but from a unique process resulted from a combination and integration of several value activities, it is even harder to imitate. Because the effective combination and integration of different value activities would involve both a large amount of detailed work and a long-term commitment to cooperate with each other, the firm's tacit knowledge (ego-knowledge, as we term it) is particularly relevant. Therefore it is not easy to be possessed, transferred or imitated.

Ego-knowledge-based non-imitation mainly originates from such two aspects as structural capital and process knowledge, both of which are included in the concept of ego-knowledge. Organizational structure and structural capital means the firm's internal organizing method, appearing as the static form of organization. Process knowledge means the method to connect different internal departments in an organization, appearing as the dynamic form.

4.3 Superego-knowledge-based extendibility: product platform + information platform

Extendibility examines the future growth of a firm. It refers to the ability to realize economies of scale or economies of scope on a structural knowledge platform in the future. In fact, the determiner core in the phrase core competence implies the extendibility of core competencies, i.e., the extent to which economies of scale and economies of scope are accomplished. Core competence is likes a source of skills. With the radiating effect of such knowledge and information platform as structural network and framework, core competence extends energy to final products. Innovative products are then offered to consumers to satisfy consumer needs. In order to make it happen, knowledge about products needs to be digitalized, or explictized. Information technology can be employed to model the causal relations in a firm, making use of a relevant database. This database can be understood with the technical skills and final products produced with the competence, which reveals that extendibility comes from superego knowledge.

Superego-knowledge-based extendibility mainly originates from two aspects: product platform and information platform. Firms can extend their technical capital and innovative ability by making use of the product platform and information platform which are based on technical value chain, Product platform contains the designing ideas and elements embodied in a combination of products. Information platform shared by a firm is the infrastructure for creation and innovation.

4.4 Id-ego-superego-transformation-based self-learning: personal learning + organization learning

Self-learning examines the past of a firm. It refers to a firm's ability to learn organically, to memorize and to accumulate knowledge as a real person can do. Core competence is the comprehensive learning ability of a firm since it is learned and accumulated gradually in the past. It usually embodies the accumulation and transformations between id, ego and superego knowledge of the firm. It is the quintessence of learning-by-doing by a group of people and will be enhanced and refined in the process of applying and sharing continuously. Continuous learning is an endless circulative process involving learning → accepting new challenge → accumulating relevant experience → learning ……. This process helps a firm to acquire sustainable competitive advantage.

Id-ego-superego-transformation-based self-learning mainly originates from two aspects: personal learning and organization learning. Personal learning follows the path of individual to organization to individual while organization learning follows the path of organization to individual to organization. A firm's core competence is the comprehensive learning ability of that firm. It is accumulated gradually from learning in the past. Peter Senge quotes the marketing director SHELL in his book the Fifth Discipline: "the only sustaining competitive advantage of a firm is the ability to learn faster than your competitors" (Senge 1990). The essence of a learning organization is for it to act like a real person, learning continuously to find and solve problems.

5. Conclusion: A New Framework of Management Based on the Interaction between Human Capital and Organizational Capital

The fundamental goal of knowledge management is consistent with the goal of overall management (Bukowitz 1999), which can be stated as "to form the organization's ability to survive for a prolonged time period by continuously developing values for stakeholders". Knowledge management offers a new perspective to observe an organization and its managerial process.

In the past, management is usually considered as "planning, organizing, leading and controlling". This traditional definition needs to be changed. The complexity of competitive environments demands a new way to think about the responsibilities of managers. Therefore some scholars proposed a new definition of management: "Management is to lead an organization to study, innovate and implement" (Underwood 2006). Here, we define management as the searching for a positive interaction mechanism between human capital and organizational capital. The new definition is also related to the traditional management functions (see to Exhibit 4).

<table>
<tr><th>Traditional management function</th><th colspan="2">Knowledge-based new management system</th></tr>
<tr><td>Planning</td><td>the transformation of id knowledge:
value creativity mechanism for clients</td><td rowspan="3">Management:
Human-to-organizational</td></tr>
<tr><td>Organizing</td><td>the transformation of ego knowledge:
non-imitate mechanism for competitors</td></tr>
<tr><td>Controlling</td><td>the transformations of superego knowledge:
expandability mechanism for the future tense</td></tr>
<tr><td>Leading</td><td>the transformation from human to organizational capital:
self-learning mechanism for the past tense</td><td>Leading:
Organizational-to-human</td></tr>
</table>

Exhibit 4: A New Framework of Management from the Perspective of Knowledge Management

- The core of the planning function is to search for the mechanism to create value for customers, which involves id knowledge transformation.
- The core of organizing is to search for the mechanism to become hard to imitate by competitors, which involves ego knowledge transformation.
- The core of controlling is to search for the mechanism to extend in the future, which involves superego knowledge transformation.
- The core of leading is to search for the mechanism to learn from the past self, which involves the accumulation and transformations between id, ego and superego knowledge. It is especially reflected in the aspect of how an organization activates human capital. On the other hand, the transforming of human capital into organizational capital can be summarized as the management activities, which appears to be an integration of the traditional management functions of planning, organizing and controlling.

References

Brooking (1996), Intellectual Capital. International Thomson Business Press.

Bukowitz/ Willams (1999), The Knowledge Management Fieldbook. Parson Education Limited.

Donnelly (1995), Fundamentals of Management. IRWIN.

Edvinsson (1997), Developing Intellectual Capital at Skandia, LRP, 130.

Fan, Zheng (2002), Core Competence: Knowledge-capital-based core competence, Shanghai: Shanghai Jiao Tong University Press.

Fan, Zheng (2002), The integration of knowledge capital and core competence, Beijing: Economic Management, 11.

Fan, Zheng (2007), Management: interaction between human capital and organizational capital, Shanghai: Foreign Language Education Press.

Freud (1958), On Creativity and the Unconscious. Harper Row Publisher Inc..

Gates (1999), Business @ The Speed of Thought using a Digital Nervous Eyetem, Beijing: Beijing University Press.

Glynn, MaryAnn (1996), A framework for relating individual and organizational intelligence to innovation. Academy of Management Review, 21: 1081-1111.

Koontz, H (1985), Management. McGraw-Hill.

Magretta (2002), What Management Is. The Sagalyn Literary Agency.

Nelson, Winter (1982), An Evolutionary Theory of Economic Change. Cambridge:Belknap,.

Nonaka,I (1994), A Dynamic Theory of Organizational Knowledge Creation. Organization Science.

Nonaka,I./ Takeuchi,H (1995), The Knowledge-creating Company: How Japanese Companies Create the Dynamics of Innovation, New York: Oxford University Press.

Nonaka /Tskeuchi (2005), Helix of Creating knowledge, Beijing: Intellectual Property Press.

Polanyi, M (1966), The Tacit Dimension. routledge & kegan paul..

Prahalad, C. K. / Hamel (1990), G.The Core Competence of the Corporate, Harvard Business Review. 5-6.

Rui, Mingjie (1999), Management: Modern Views, Shanghai: Fudan University Press.

Senge, Peter M (1990), The Fifth Discipline: The Art & Practice of the Learning Organization, New York: Currency Doubleday.

Tiwana, Amrit (2001), the Essential Guide to Knowledge Management, Pearson Education Inc.

Xu, Qingrui (2002), Organization-learning-based transformation from human capital to organizational capital, Economic Management, 6.

Underwood, Jim (2006), What Your IQ? . The Sagalyn Literary Agency.

Wiig,K.M (1997), Integrating Intellectual Capital and Knowledge Management, Long Rang Planning, 3.

KNOWLEDGE MANAGEMENT OF HEALTHCARE BY CLINICAL-PATHWAYS

TOMOYOSHI YAMAZAKI

School of Knowledge Science, Japan Advanced Institute of Science and Technology, Ishikawa Prefecture, Japan
E-mail: yamazaki-cp@jaist.ac.jp

KATSUHIRO UMEMOTO

School of Knowledge Science, Japan Advanced Institute of Science and Technology, Ishikawa Prefecture, Japan
†E-mail: ume@jaist.ac.jp

Healthcare is a knowledge-intensive service provided by professionals, such as medical doctors, nurses, and pharmacists. Clinical pathways are used by many healthcare organizations (HCOs) as a tool for performing the healthcare process, sharing and utilizing knowledge from different professionals. In this paper, case studies were performed at two HCOs that use clinical pathways actively in the healthcare process. Theoretical model construction, sharing, utilization, and creation of the knowledge by different professionals, were tested by the case study of two HCOs which use clinical pathways actively. The theoretical model was a knowledge creation model which creates new knowledge continuously. In this theoretical model, clinical pathways are suggested to be an effective tool for knowledge management in healthcare.

1. Introduction

The current healthcare is asked to lower costs, and simultaneously is also required to improve the quality of continuous care. Furthermore, healthcare is a knowledge intensive service provided by professionals, such as medical doctors, nurses, and pharmacists. Therefore, in many HCOs, management based on knowledge management used in the industrial world is being carried out (Bose, 2003).

From the latter half of the 90s, clinical pathways began to be used as a tool for performing optimization of healthcare resources and enhancement of care quality by HCOs (Every, 2000). Now, clinical pathways are used as a tool for carrying out knowledge management in many HCOs. However, knowledge management used in many HCOs only shares and utilizes different professionals' knowledge through information technology (IT). No concrete theoretical model of creation of new knowledge by health-care professionals using clinical pathways has been built. New knowledge needs to be created for continuous enhancement of quality of healthcare treatment, and a theoretical model for this is required. (Vanhaecht, 2006).

The aim of this research is filling in current gaps in this knowledge, through construction of a theoretical model of systematic knowledge creation in the healthcare process according to professionals' collaboration using clinical pathways.

2. Clinical pathways

Clinical pathway applies critical-path idea methods (used in process control in industry) to the healthcare process as a management tool, and was developed in the

United States in 1985 (Zander, 1988). Clinical pathways have been designed as an approach to improve the quality of healthcare.

Such clinical pathways are structured instruments which lead to optimal interdisciplinary patient care. Practice of clinical pathways involves all healthcare professionals, physicians, nurse staff, physiotherapists, social workers, etc. Clinical pathways can offer everyday standard diagnosis and healthcare treatment. It can be thought of as a visualization of the patient healthcare process. The development and implementation of clinical pathways are multi-faceted and resource-intensive processes involving all concerned parties. Clinical pathways are used in healthcare in many countries (Campbell, 1998; Zander, 2002).

Sharing and integration of the knowledge of diverse professionals are important for implementation of a successful healthcare process using clinical pathways. Clinical pathways establish optimal resource utilization and improve communication among doctors, nurses, and other staff (Coffey, 2005). However, in the healthcare process using clinical pathways, it is difficult to respond to patients' individuality (Kwan, 2003; Shi, 2008).

3. Knowledge management

Knowledge management is a business concept. The scope of knowledge management encompasses individual competence and organizational memory, knowledge creation from tacit to explicit knowledge, and includes the role of organizations in facilitating the creation of knowledge. New knowledge is created by the interaction of tacit knowledge and explicit knowledge. The interaction of different knowledge is performed "Ba." The setting of "Ba" is very important in knowledge management (Nonaka, 1995).

Another theory of knowledge-management is the "communities of practice." "Communities of practice" are phenomena said to: galvanize knowledge-sharing knowledge and change". They are defined as, "groups of people bound together by shared experience and passion for joint enterprise." This can be described as cross-functional terms-brought together to capture and spread ideas and know-how (Etienne, 2000). However, the disadvantageous of the "communities of practice" model is its informal nature.

4. Healthcare knowledge

Within modern healthcare discipline, emphasis was placed on formalized. Evidence based medicine (EBM) provide a tool for communicating the relative effectiveness of health interventions where quantitative data exists. Many regard the evidence-base as not really telling the whole story. Many Healthcare professionals can not manage their patients simply as biomedical models, and that there is often another dimension to disease and management of patient-care. The failure to recognize the limitations of EBM leads to tension being created when can not be implemented. Healthcare professionals often lack a language with which to communicate important knowledge for patient, by which there is no evidence base. The recognition of this limit is important for many healthcare professionals (Simon, 2002).

Clinical guidelines have been defined as "systematically developed statements to assist practitioner and patient decisions about appropriate healthcare for specific clinical circumstances." Clinical guidelines are created based on EBM (Schneider, 2006).

5. Knowledge management in healthcare

Knowledge management is used in many HCOs, because, healthcare is a knowledge intensive service provided by professionals. When healthcare organization (HCO) introduces knowledge management into their process management, it is important to take into consideration the culture inherent to each expertise (Russ, 2005).

In knowledge management, sharing and utilizing scientific evidence of explicit knowledge is required for implementation of evidence based medicine (EBM). However, there is no combination with a scientific basis about explicit knowledge acquired by clinical experience which each professional has accumulated, so, carrying out effective clinical practices is difficult. Therefore, knowledge management which can share and utilize, both explicit and tacit knowledge is required by HCO (Sandars, 2006).

In modern health care systems, healthcare providers face ever new challenges with regard to quality and cost of care, as well as to satisfaction and training of professionals. In order to solve these challenges, the introduction of knowledge management in healthcare process management is effective (Kitchiner, 1996).

The core of a team working in modern healthcare is changing from the doctor to the patient. Accordingly, within a team, knowledge management which can create the optimal healthcare process for the patient by various professionals will be required (Metaxiotis, 2006).

Knowledge management of HCO must provide (Wahle, 2008).

(i) Framing of the standardized healthcare process, and support of the optimized clinical practice.
(ii) Effective and efficient management of health-care professional employment.
(iii) Better quality care offered to the patient, and related provision of information.

6. Knowledge management by clinical pathways in healthcare

Clinical pathways are developed through collaborative efforts of doctors, nurses, pharmacists, and others to improve the quality and value of patient care. Clinical pathways are prepared using clinical guidelines' based on EBM of the visualized knowledge. But, healthcare professionals' context knowledge is essential in using a clinical guideline. The production process of a clinical guideline is based on agreement formed by this discussion, so, the care team can provide optimal healthcare treatment. Clinical pathways are a tool for utilizing diverse knowledge (Mitton, 2007).

A typical healthcare process can be managed by clinical pathway. However, clinical pathway is not suitable in some complicated cases. (Cardoen, 2008).

7. Research approach

We carried out the case studies in two hospitals, Saiseikai Kumamoto Hospital and Fukui General Hospital, which use clinical pathways activity for healthcare process management.

Case studies were performed from May-06 to October-07. Methods of research included analysis of documents relevant to clinical pathways activity, and interviews with clinical pathways administrators. The purpose of the interviews was to obtain information about the intentions and interpretations of clinical pathways activity which was not obtained from document analysis. By analysis of the data obtained from our investigation, it is possible to observe the healthcare process using clinical pathways common to two hospitals. The extraction of the knowledge process from these clinical pathways is our main goal.

8. Research result

8.1 Case 1: The clinical pathway activity of Saiseikai Kumamoto Hospital

8.1.1 The background and the characteristics of Clinical pathway activity

In 1996, clinical pathways were introduced at this hospital. The main reason for introducing it was for patients to understand the outline of healthcare contents by clinical pathway. The introduced clinical pathway was a tool which promoted communication between healthcare professionals and patients. The administrators of this hospital considered the new use of clinical pathway. The chief hospital administrator understood that clinical pathway was an improvement tool of healthcare quality after participating in a clinical pathway seminar held in 1998 in Boston. Especially, the chief hospital administrator noted that clinical pathways were effective in the collaborative work in healthcare by professionals. As a result, clinical pathway activity rule of this hospital is that all the staff members participate.

8.1.2 Details of Clinical pathway activity

Clinical pathway activity is a healthcare process constituted of production, implementation, and improvement process.

(i) Production process;

Clinical pathways are produced in workshops (WS) in which all professionals related to a specific disease participate. In WS, the healthcare target "outcome" is set up as a milestone of the patients' condition. Accordingly, in the WS, discussions by diverse healthcare professionals to agree about the formation regarding "outcome." The expression of diverse ideas from many participants is important in clinical pathways production. In addition, guidelines and the medical records are referred to in clinical pathway production.

(ii) Implementation process;

Many clinical business routines using clinical pathways are assessed by healthcare professionals for "outcome." The objective assessment of "outcome" is important in the implementation process of clinical pathways. The condition of a patient whose "outcome" assessment is different from the usual case is called "variance." In using clinical pathways, response of "variance" by healthcare professionals adapts for a patient's individuality. It is important to necessarily write down the medical records of a patient's condition which cannot be assessed by "outcome." The intuition obtained by observation by professionals is also recorded.

(iii) Improvement process;

All the related professionals gathered as in the production process, and used statistical analysis of "variance" to improve the clinical pathways. Based on the analysis of "variance" the diverse healthcare professionals involved discussed the issues. The responses led to setup of new "outcome." Clinical pathways administrator said that the healthcare process using clinical pathways verifies healthcare contents. Setup of the subjective hypotheses by specialists was effective for the creation of new "outcome." Professionals' new knowledge is required for creation of new "outcome."

8.2 Case 2: The clinical pathway activity of Fukui General Hospital

8.2.1 The background and the characteristics of Clinical pathway activity

In 1999, the healthcare professionals of ophthalmology referred to clinical pathways of other hospitals, and produced their own. In 2000, the chief hospital administrator, who considered standardization of services for patients, determined to make clinical pathway activity into a tool of the healthcare process management at the hospital.

The concept of clinical pathway activity is a tool which makes possible the sharing of medical records among patients and healthcare professionals.

8.2.2 Detail of Clinical pathway activity

Clinical pathway activity is a healthcare process consisting of production, implementation, and improvement process. And so, a system which decreases the user load in all the processes was built.

(i) Production process;

Although the related professionals produced the clinical pathway using collaboration, it was carried out based on the clinical pathway production manual. The method of setting concrete "outcome" was written down in the manual. The agreement formation by discussion of diverse professionals was essential to setting the "outcome." Clinical pathways administrator said, "different professionals' diverse knowledge is visualized in setting "outcome" by free discussion, the environment for this is important." In addition, guidelines and medical records are referred to in clinical pathways production.

(ii) Implementation process;

Assessment of "outcome" was considered to be important in the implementation process. Furthermore, response and record when "variance" occurs in the condition of patients were also considered to be important. The healthcare professional needs observation of a patient's new condition which could not be assessed by "outcome." The professional necessarily writes down new patient information in medical records. And, the professional's subjective judgment using patient's medical record is also important.

(iii) Improvement process;

"Variance" was totaled and statistical analysis conducted. The improvement of "outcome" was made from analysis of data using "variance" analysis table. However, the agreement formation by discussion of the related professionals was necessary for the improvement of "outcome." The clinical pathway administrator said, "By conducting factor analysis using "variance," the quality of the healthcare treatment offered to a patient can be improved." In addition, setting a new "outcome" of a patient's new condition which could not be assessed by "outcome" is important in this process. Setting a new "outcome" needs a lot of patient information which was written down the medical records. Therefore, patient information was collected in the process of implementation.

8.3 The healthcare process in common clinical pathways activity

The outline of the research result is shown in Table 1.

The clinical pathways activities of two hospitals consisted of processes of "production," "implementation," and "improvement." And each process was connected to the next continuously.

Table 1: Research result of Cases study

	Case 1	Case 2
Production Process	All the related professionals' participation were indispensable	Although a setup of "outcome" was the purpose, the production manual existed.
	The Purpose of this process is the setup of "outcome"	The related professionals' participation were desired
	The environmental setting which extracts diverse knowledge was important.	Most important was expressing diverse ideas
	The guidelines and medical records were referred for	The guidelines and medical records were referred for
Implementation process	Clinical business routine was the assessment of "outcome"	Assessment of "outcome" based on a manual was clinical routine
	The responses and records of "variance" were important	The responses and records of "variance" were important
	Subjective records were also important.	The intuition of professional wrote down medical records
Improvement process	Improvement of "outcome" based on "variance"	Improvement of "outcome" based on "variance" analysis table produced by the total of "variance
	This process should be essential to enhancement in quality	This process should be essential to enhancement in quality

The common elements acquired from the contents of each process are as follows.

(i) Production process;

a) In this process, setup of "outcome" was important.

b) In setup of "outcome", participation was required of all related professionals.

c) The environment for discussion of professionals in setting the "outcome," for agreement formation is important.

d) The guidelines and medical records are referred to in production.

(ii) Implementation process;

a) The objective healthcare process (by assessment of "outcome") was recorded.

b) The response and record of "variance" showed the response of the patient individually to the health care process.

c) Record of the condition of patients could not reach desired "outcome" was also considered as important.
d) Subjective judgment of professionals is also considered as important.
(iii) Improvement process;
a) "Outcome" was improved using statistical analysis of "variance" obtained in the implementation process.
b) In the improvement process, participation was required of all related professionals, as in the production process.
c) The quality of the healthcare treatment offered was upgraded by improvement of "outcome."
d) Setting a new "outcome" by hypothesis based on observation of new patient's condition is recommended.

9. Research findings

From the research result, a theoretical model which shows the knowledge process of clinical pathway activity using the concept of "outcome" and "variance" was built (Fig. 1). The theoretical model shows the interaction in the healthcare process of clinical pathways, tacit knowledge, and explicit knowledge. The tacit knowledge used in the healthcare process is context knowledge which each professional has, such as know-how and skill. The explicit knowledge used in the healthcare process is objective knowledge, such as the guidelines and the contents of medical records.

The characteristics of the theoretical model, including the interaction of tacit knowledge and explicit knowledge, include:

(i) Each healthcare process is shown "Ba" of Knowledge process which carries out the interaction of different knowledge,
(ii) Each "Ba" are "Accept", "Integrate", and "Practice" and connected spirally,
(iii) "Accept" exists in the production process, and discussion is needed to set an "outcome" by accepting the knowledge from different participant,
(iv) A contradiction model which can create new knowledge continuously was built from case studies of two hospitals.
(v) "Integrate" exists in the processes of production and implementation, and through participants' discussion, integrates expertise into optimal whole knowledge, and sets up "outcome.
(vi) "Practice" exists in the processes of implementation and improvement, and practicing leads to optimal knowledge on the clinical side, and the professionals acquire new knowledge.
(vii) Spiral risen "Accept" exists in the improvement process, the new knowledge acquired by practice, and the result of "variance" analysis, setting a new "outcome" by hypothesis is accepted, and the clinical pathway is improved.

In this model, if the process of improvement did not exist, dynamic knowledge creation difficult. Clinical pathway administrators also consider the process of improvement as very important.

10. Discussion

"Ba" of this theoretical model has the interaction of tacit knowledge and explicit knowledge. This differs a little from the "SECI" model (Umemoto, 2004). Using guidelines and medical records of explicit knowledge is essential for production of clinical pathway. Clinical pathway activity was no interaction between the tacit knowledge which exists in the "SECI" model, on these case studies. On healthcare process, explicit knowledge was suggested that it is an interface among the professionals from whom formal knowledge differs.

Sharing of different knowledge is important for continuous implementation of knowledge management. Accordingly, environmental structure of "Ba" which accepts different knowledge is knowledge management administrator's essential condition. The creation of new knowledge is possible because diverse knowledge is shared (Nomura, 2002). Clinical pathway administrators were doing their best to the environmental setting which diverse knowledge expresses for setup of "outcome." Environmental setting of "Ba" is suggested that it is required for knowledge management of clinical pathway activity.

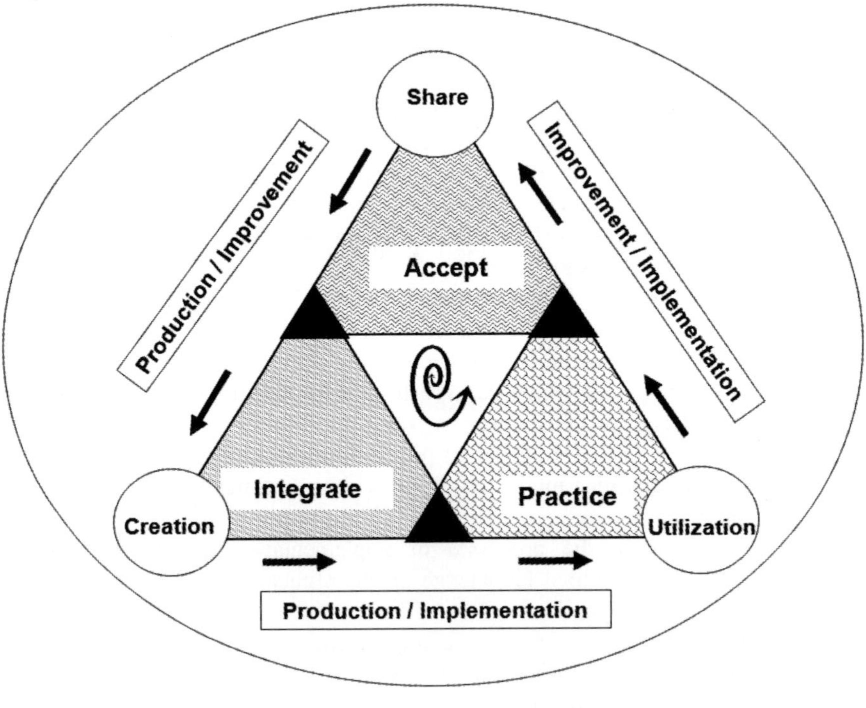

Fig 1. Theoretical Model

11. Conclusion

The theoretical model which can create new knowledge continuously was built from case studies of two hospitals.

This study's implications are as follows:

(i) Not only the healthcare work process, but, the knowledge processes are included in clinical pathways.
(ii) "Ba" of this knowledge process consists of "Accept", "Integrate", and "Practice."
(iii) Each "Ba" is carrying out the interaction of different knowledge.
(iv) These "Ba" are organizational knowledge creation models connected spirally.
(v) However, if the process of improvement does not exist in clinical pathways, this model does not function.

In future study, we will create a system to observe the process of Knowledge sharing. We plan to produce a system that supports clinical pathway activity.

References

Bose, R., (2003) "Knowledge management-enabled health care management systems: capabilities, infrastructure, and decision-support", *Expert systems with Applications*, 24: 59-71.

Campbell, H. Hotchkiss, R. Bradshaw, N. (1998) "Integrated Care Pathways", *British Medical Journal*, 316: 133-137.

Cardoen, B., Demenlemeewster, E., (2008) "Capacity of Clinical Pathways: A Strategic Multi-level Evaluation Tool", *Journal of Med Syst*, Vol. 32, pp. 443-452.

Coffey, R. Richards, J. Remmert, C., (2005) "An Introduction to Critical Paths", *Quality Management in Health Care*, 14: 46-55.

Etienne, W., William, S., (2000),"Communities of Practice. The Organizational Frontier", *Harv Bus Rev*, R001100: 1-20.

Every, N., Becker, R., Kopecky, S., (2000) "Critical Pathways A Review", *Circulation*, 101: 461-465.

Kitchiner, D., Davidson, C., Bundred, P., (1996) "Integrated Care Pathways: Effective tools for continuous evaluation of clinical practice", *Journal of Evaluation in Clinical Practice*, 2: 65-69.

Kwan, J., Sandercock, P., (2003) "In-Hospital Care Pathways for Stroke: A Cochrane Systematic Review", *Stroke*, 34: 587-588.

Metaxiotis, Kostas., (2006), "Healthcare Knowledge Management", In: Schwartz, D. (Ed.) *Encyclopedia of Knowledge Management*: 204-210, London: IDEA GROUP REFERENCE.

Mitton, C., Adair, C., Mckenzie, E., (2007) "Knowledge Transfer and Exchange: Review and Synthesis of the Literature", *Milbank Quarterly*, 85: 729-768.

Nomura, T., (2002) "Design of "Ba" for Successful Knowledge management", *Journal of Network and Computer Applications*, 25: 263-278.

Nonaka, I., Takeuchi, H., (1995) *The Knowledge-Creating Company: How Japanese Companies Create the Dynamics of Innovation*, New York: Oxford University Press.

Russ, M., Jones, J., (2005) "A typology of knowledge management strategies for hospital preparedness: what lesson can be learned?", *International Journal of Emergency Management*, 2: 319-342.

Sandars, J., Heller, R., (2006) "Improving the Implementation of Evidence-Based Practice: A knowledge management perspective," *Journal of Evaluation in Clinical Practice*, 12: 342-346.

Schneider, J., Peterson, A., Vaughn, T. (2006) "Clinical Practice Guidelines and Organizational Adaptation", *International Journal of Technology Assessment in Health Care*, 22:58-66.

Shi, J., Su, Q., Zhao, Z., (2008) "Critical Factors for the Effectiveness of Clinical Pathway in Improving Care Outcomes", *Service Systems and Service Management,* 2008 International Conference on: 1-6.

Simon, de L., (2002) "A Knowledge-management Model for Clinical Practice", *Journal of Postgraduate Medicine*, 48: 297-303.

Vanhaecht, K., Witte, K., Depreitere, R., (2006) "Clinical Pathway Audit Tool: Systematic review", *Journal of Nursing Management*, 14: 529-537.

Umemoto, K., Endo, A., Machado, M., (2004) "From Sashimi to Zen-in: Evolution of Concurrent Engineering at Fuji Xerox", *Journal of Knowledge Management*, 8:89-99.

Wahle, E., (2008)"How to handle Knowledge Management in Healthcare: A Description of Model to Deal with the Current and Ideal solution" , In: Jennex, E. (Ed.) *Knowledge Management concepts, Methodologies, Tools, and Applications*: 1881-1893, New York: INFORMATION SCIENCE REFERENCE.

Zander, K. (1988) "Nursing Case Management: Strategic Management of Cost and Quality Outcomes", *Journal of Nursing Administration*, 18: 23-30.

Zander, K. (2002) "Integrated care pathways: eleven international trends", *Journal of INTEGRATED CARE PATHWAYS*, 6: 101-107.

FACTORS AFFECTING KNOWLEDGE MANAGEMENT AT A PUBLIC HEALTH INSTITUTE IN THAILAND

VALLERUT POBKEEREE*
Department of Public Health Administration
Faculty of Public Health, Mahidol University, Bangkok, Thailand
E-mail: vallerut@gmail.com

PATHOM SAWANPANYALERT
National Institute of Health, Department of Medical Sciences
Ministry of Public Health, Nonthaburi, Thailand
E-mail: pathoms@dmsc.moph.go.th

NIRAT SIRICHOTIRATANA
Department of Public Health Administration
Faculty of Public Health, Mahidol University, Bangkok, Thailand
E-mail: nithats@gmail.com

This knowledge management (KM) study focuses on factors affecting KM at a Ministry of Public Health institute. The developed questionnaires were distributed to all institute staff. Four major factors were investigated in the survey: Organizational Culture, Information and Technology, KM Content, and Administration and Management. Statistical analysis was used to calculate the relationships among factors and KM according to the KM model from the Thai Knowledge Management Institute. There was a 78.8% response rate. Organizational Culture, Information and Technology, and Administration and Management were found to be significant factors associated with KM. In addition, other elements within these factors had a significant relationship with KM. However, KM content, organizational structure, and conflict did not have a significant relationship with KM. The authors found quality management systems i.e. ISO 9001, ISO 17025 or ISO 15189 played an important role in KM at the institute. The authors also found drawbacks and room for KM improvement in the institute. The results in this paper can be used as knowledge-based evidence to enhance and improve the institute's routine operation and its performance.
Keywords *Public health, Knowledge management, Thailand*

1. Introduction

Any organization that would like to be a learning one needs to accept changes and learn to keep vital knowledge within its personnel as a living information network (Buckman, 2004). Knowledge is identified as power and provides a competitive resource for any organization that wants to be successful in their goals and functions. Building a knowledge-driven organization is therefore a milestone of any ministry in the country.

As a national public health laboratory providing services for the whole country, becoming a learning organization is also a goal of the Thai National Institute of Health (NIH). In order to become a learning organization, KM needs to be initiated.

The NIH is an important institute located in the Department of Medical Sciences, Ministry of Public Health (MOPH). Crucial functions of the institute are to carry out important medical science research for the Ministry, to provide day-to-day services on diagnostic testing for confirmation laboratory tests and to serve as a national reference laboratory for other ministry departments/divisions.

* Corresponding author: Vallerut Pobkeeree; contact: vallerut@gmail.com; Tel: +6687-512-8644

2. Research Objectives

This study looks at four major factors; Organizational Culture, Information and Technology, KM Content, and Administration and Management that can be significantly related to KM in the NIH. The objective is to find which factors and their internal elements affect KM at the institute. Moreover, the authors have attempted to make staff opinions known in order to provide evidence-based information to improve KM activities in the future.

2.1 The defined terms of independent and dependent variables

The independent variables are the following four major factors and their elements:

- Organizational Culture refers to any element which could affect the culture of the organization and reflect the institute's approach to KM work. In this study, they are trust among colleagues, participation, motivation or incentives, leadership, organizational structure, communication, organizational climate and personal attitude.
- Information and Technology (IT) refers to infrastructure, IT management, and accessibility of data, information and knowledge within the institute.
- KM Content refers to the selected topic to which will be used to carry out KM activities.
- Administration and Management refers to the policy on KM or plan to implement or create a KM position at the institute, information on KM evaluation to personnel in the institute and staff evaluations.

These major factors have been previously formulated and mentioned in a few studies (Syed-lkhsan and Rowland, 2004, Chua and Lam, 2005, and Oliver and Kandadi, 2006). For some, organizational culture is the most important factor affecting how KM will proceed (Ardichvili et al., 2006 and Al-Alawi et al., 2007). Slagter (2007) found that elements of organizational culture i.e. trust, leadership style, structure and motivation were critical success factors in KM in senior employees of the studied company. Kulkarni et al. (2007) determined that organizational support structure was also a contributing factor to the success of KM. Since there are many elements affecting organizational culture that impact KM in organizations, these elements were put into the study questionnaire.

IT is another crucial factor for public health organizations but Slagter (2007) did not find technology was important to KM among her older subjects. The Association of State and Territorial Health Office in the US (ASTHO, 2005) found many challenges with this factor. For example, no verification process for public health records, obsolete hardware, incompatible software, inadequate training etc.

The two other factors are KM Content and Administration and Management. Choosing relevant, useful and up-to-date content for the KM project is as important as dealing with other factors. Evaluation of work is also an attribute in the factor of Administration and Management. If an organization does not make a systemic effort to evaluate its own tasks, it is unlikely to succeed with its KM project.

The dependent variable in this research refers to the tuna (fish) model of KM from the Knowledge Management Institute (KMI) of Thailand (Phasukyud, 2004). The tuna or KM model comprises three components: the head of the fish is Knowledge Vision (KV), the body is Knowledge Sharing (KS) and the rear part is Knowledge Asset (KA). KM is structured and shown in the right hand box (Figure 1) in the conceptual framework.

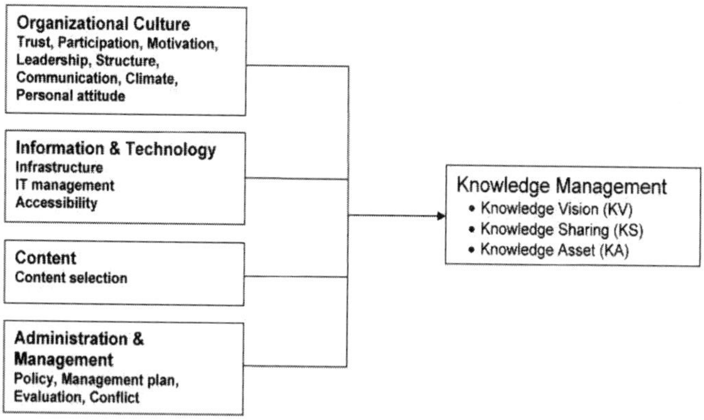

Figure 1 Conceptual framework of the study

KV is defined as the organization's goal of implementing and proceeding with KM. The organization needs to have a reason to implement KM and decide if the goal is in the common interest of its staff. Initiatives from top management are also considered as a vision of the organization.

KS is the largest and the most difficult part of the model. Each individual has to feel that he/she would like to share and when he/she shares, they will learn. The key of KM is this KS (Phasukyud, 2004 and Al-Alawi et al., 2007).

KA is the knowledge repository of an organization. It is generally referred to as either IT or each individual who has embedded intelligence in him/her (Ichijo and Nonaka, 2007 and Phasukyud, 2004) as an intangible asset. This study emphasizes the tangible knowledge handled by IT as KA which would be ready for use in the organization. The study does not focus on the intangible or non-IT asset because the research questionnaire does not cover and measure intangible knowledge.

3. Research Methodology and Design

The hypotheses of the study were designed with regard to the four major factors and their elements.

H_A: There is a significant relationship between Organizational Culture and KM

H_B: There is a significant relationship between Information Technology and KM.

H_C: There is a significant relationship between Content and KM

H_D: There is a significant relationship between Administration and Management and KM.

To test these hypotheses, the authors created an appropriate questionnaire which consisted of the factors, elements and KM components of the KM model. (Phasukyud, 2004). Moreover, the Knowledge-Based View (KBV) theory suggested that obtaining and using appropriate knowledge is important to comprehending organization performance. (Morgan, et al. 2003) The theory highlighted the two types of knowledge, tacit and explicit knowledge, which interact with each other. Both types of knowledge were elaborated in this study's discussion on how knowledge flows in the institution along with the KM model of Takeuchi and Nonaka (2004).

The developed KM questionnaire was designed to acquire staff opinion on factors and elements affecting KM and was distributed to all NIH staff. A range of agreement from a Likert scale was employed from strongly agree (5 points) to strongly disagree (1 point). Two items were provided for each model construct and an average was calculated.. The content validity of the questionnaire was investigated by three KM experts. The reliability test was calculated using Cronbach's coefficient alpha (Crawford, 2005) and the alpha was 0.88.

4. Data Analysis and Results

Although the respondents belonged to the same organization (NIH), they were distinct by the fact that they were divided into 34 sections, each with a different task within the organization. 386 out of 490 questionnaires were returned, which was a response rate of 78.8%. Interviews occurred with only some staff or section chiefs who were available and who volunteered because of time constraints. Twenty individuals were interviewed and provided their opinions, comments and suggestions. The data was analyzed by SPSS version 11.5 for Windows. Personal characteristics are shown in Table 1. Pearson correlation (r) was used to compute relationships among the major factors and their elements and KM. Other major factors affecting KM and its components (KV, KS and KA) were analyzed using bivariate correlation. Elements of major factors were analyzed using the same statistics. The arithmetic mean ($\overline{X}$) and standard deviation (SD.) of these factors and elements were also employed to assess the participants' opinions.

Summaries of responses to the factors and their respective elements that affect KM are shown in Table 2. 40 % (data not shown here) of participants were not sure if the current Organizational Structure could support the institute's KM activity; the mean of this element was the lowest ($\overline{X}$ = 2.92) and the SD. was the highest (SD.= 0.93). The high SD. could indicate low accuracy of the data. The same was true for Conflict where 44 % of respondents were not sure whether conflict among staff could affect KM.

Table 1. Personal Characteristics

Personal characteristics	Result (%)
Gender:	
Male	27.2
Female	72.8
Age (years)	
21-30	49.7
31-40	25.4
41-50	18.2
51-60	6.7
Education	
Lower than bachelors	26.7
Bachelors	56.2
Masters and higher	17.1
Work experience at the institute (years)	
< 1	11.7
1-5	42.5
6-10	15.0
>10	30.8
Job characteristics	
Administration & Management	17.8
Academic development	10.9
Laboratory (routine & research)	63.5
Other services	7.8

Table 2. Mean and Standard Deviation of Participants' Opinion Level

Factors Affecting KM	$\overline{X}$	SD.	Interpretation
Organizational Culture			
Participation	3.69	0.58	Agree
Trust	4.32	0.60	Strongly agree
Motivation	3.87	0.82	Agree
Leadership	4.00	0.63	Agree
Organizational structure	2.92	0.93	Somewhat agree
Communication	4.29	0.61	Strongly agree
Organizational climate	3.71	0.84	Agree
Personal attitude	3.73	0.74	Agree
Information Technology			
Infrastructure	3.85	0.72	Agree
IT admin. & management	3.67	0.78	Agree
Accessibility	3.80	0.70	Agree
Content			
Content selection	3.56	0.83	Agree
Administration and Management			
Policy	3.44	0.81	Agree
Management aspect	3.93	0.66	Agree
Evaluation	3.80	0.65	Agree
Conflict	3.07	0.88	Somewhat agree

Table 3. Pearson Correlations between KM and its Components

	KS		KA		KM	
	r	Sig.	r	Sig.	r	Sig.
Knowledge Vision (KV)	0.603	0.000	0.590	0.000	0.845	0.000
Knowledge Sharing (KS)	--	--	0.662	0.000	0.879	0.000
Knowledge Asset (KA)	--	--	--	--	0.871	0.000

Table 3 shows that all KM components are significantly related on their own and also among each other.

Table 4 summarizes the four major factors and their respective elements that affect KM. The authors found there were significant relationships between KM and three factors; Organizational Culture, Information Technology, and Administration and Management. Therefore, hypotheses H_A , H_B and H_D are accepted ($p < 0.001$). But H_C is rejected which means there was no significant relationship between KM and Content (Content selection). In addition, there were some elements within the major factors that had no significant relationship to KM (namely organizational structure and conflict) as shown in the same table. The remaining elements had a significant relationship to KM ($p < 0.001$).

In addition, it was also found that there were significant relationships between the KM components (KV, KS, and KA) and the three factors - Organizational Culture, Information Technology, and Administration and Management - (data not shown here). These results could infer that most organizational factors have positive relationships to KV, KS, and KA, which means if there are any changes in the factors this could result in a similar change to KV, KS and KA. However, the study could not determine the magnitude of the change.

Table 4. Summary of factors and their elements affecting KM

Factors Affecting KM	Knowledge Management (KM)	
	Pearson Correlation	Sig.
Organizational Culture	**0.375**	**0.000**
Participation	0.103	0.045
Trust	0.227	0.000
Motivation	0.201	0.000
Leadership	0.273	0.000
Organizational structure	-0.069	0.175
Communication	0.234	0.000
Organizational climate	0.298	0.000
Personal attitude	0.278	0.000
Information Technology	**0.378**	**0.000**
Infrastructure	0.200	0.000
IT admin. & management	0.376	0.000
Accessibility	0.277	0.000
Content	**-0.043**	**0.404**
Content selection	-0.043	0.404
Administration and Management	**0.368**	**0.000**
Policy	0.340	0.000
Management aspect	0.217	0.000
Evaluation	0.429	0.000
Conflict	-0.085	0.098

5. Discussion

5.1 Knowledge management through the KM model

Knowledge Vision: This is usually initiated by senior or top management of the institute. Their vision corresponds to the department's or ministry's strategy to make the institute become a learning organization. Kreitner and Kinicki (2005) mentioned that a learning organization has various attributes i.e. innovative, knowledge acquisition, or knowledge transfer. If the behavior of people in the organization adheres to these attributes then the organization could overcome barriers to accomplishing its goals. Knowledge vision also includes an organization's mission. An organization should know its direction and mission in order to generate knowledge (Ichijo and Nonaka, 2007). It should also know its strengths and weaknesses and even if the situation changes, the knowledge vision usually does not change. This is because it is created as a result of meetings and discussions and senior management have invested significant amounts of thought, time and effort. The NIH has its own regular clients from both the public and private sectors and attempts to satisfy them through a quality management system (QMS) which will be mentioned below in the section on KA.

Knowledge Sharing: Knowledge sharing is knowledge transfer (Al-Alawi et al., 2007) and the authors investigated how knowledge was transferred and how some individuals learned. When a new test was performed in a particular laboratory and when someone from that laboratory had learned through training from outside their lab, that person would perform or demonstrate the test for their colleagues who had not attended training or did not know the test method. Laboratory personnel learn from a tacit to tacit knowledge connection as a socialization step, as highlighted in the SECI model (Takeuchi and Nonaka, 2004). The model of knowledge is created through tacit and explicit knowledge interaction. After each individual had learned, their embedded tacit knowledge was formulated as documents or records as explicit knowledge in order to allow others to study or learn from them. This corresponds to externalization (from tacit to explicit knowledge). When lab personnel learn concepts and express them as report documents, manuals or other forms of explicit knowledge such as meetings, usual conversation, or a conference, this process is considered to be what Takeuchi and Nonaka (2004) called combination (explicit to explicit knowledge) in their model. After lab personnel have learned through all three processes they develop more technical know-how, absorb and internalize explicit into tacit knowledge within individuals and become more valuable to the laboratory. This last process is called internalization (explicit to tacit knowledge) and the conversion between tacit and explicit knowledge has then formed a spiral of knowledge creation through those four processes. The institute can therefore obtain practical and new knowledge to turn into new routines by knowledge conversion (Takeuchi and Nonaka, 2004).

Knowledge Asset: Knowledge asset of the institute is both tangible and explicit knowledge e.g. Standard Operating Procedure (SOP), Work Instruction (WI), paper documents or documents from artificial intelligence (Metaxiotis et al., 2003), and intangible, as tacit knowledge e.g. real intelligence of human resources of the institute. Bowditch and Buono (2001) noted that more than half of the knowledge in an organization is in tacit form. Explicit knowledge needs to be expressed as a knowledge asset through active commitment of staff and their chiefs. Interestingly, each laboratory section conforms to requirements of the QMS prior to KM implementation and those requirements have an important role and add outstanding value to knowledge asset as well as KM. The system adheres to the requirements of the International Organization for Standardization (ISO). The authors found various sections had implemented ISO 9001 (Quality Management Systems - Requirements) or ISO 17025 (General Requirement for the Competence of Testing and Calibration Laboratories) or ISO 15189 (Medical Laboratory - Particular Requirements for Quality and Competence) in their laboratories. This system is an institute policy that has been implemented across sections. Generally each section has adhered to one of these standards in setting up its laboratory. Therefore, many processes and activities have a strengthened knowledge management program within the section. These ISO requirements have been taken seriously and facilitated knowledge flows and developed best possible practice in the institute.

5.2 Organizational factors and their elements

There were one factor and two elements (Table 4) that did not have a significant relationship to KM ($p > 0.05$): organizational structure (in Organizational Culture), content selection (in KM Content); and conflict (in Administration and Management).

Organizational structure: The institute's structure is a hierarchy structure and this attribute could constrain knowledge sharing (Riege, 2005). However, our study found that the structure did not have a significant relationship to KM (Table 4, $p = 0.175$). The institute has two committees involved in KM: one is a steering committee as its members are from top management; the other is a working group committee. The staff in both committees who are assigned to work on this KM also have their routine functions. Oliver and Kandadi (2006) called this kind of structure a hybrid KM structure. They did not find any specific type of structure that could be best for KM activity. From Table 2, the organizational structure scored the lowest mean which could be interpreted as staff did not know how the structure is relevant to KM.

Content: It is known that tacit knowledge is context-specific (Takeuchi and Nonaka, 2004) and difficult to formulize and transfer. Both tacit and explicit knowledge are found in individual laboratories at the institute. Each laboratory has its own specific tests to perform and some of them are quite complicated. The authors found that it was hard to implement KM or select a KM topic applicable across the whole institute. Therefore, the content had no significant relationship to KM. However, this factor might not be accurate since it only contained one element (Table 4, content selection).

Conflict: Conflict could have positive or negative outcomes depending on its intensity and how it was solved (Kreitner and Kinicki, 2004). If working groups have little conflict their performance or outcomes would not be productive or creative. On the other hand, if there is too much conflict, it could destroy performance. Staff at the institute agreed that conflict occurred and 30% of the staff thought there were people who had too many things to do in their daily tasks and felt indifferent to KM activity. Many did not realize they had implemented KM many times as part of their routine job. No matter what conflict happens among staff, KM activity will carry on. It is quite beneficial to the institute that conflict does not have any significant relationship with KM since conflict is quite common among sections or staff. It has helped them find new approaches to working together without too much tension or effect on KM activities.

Factors and elements that have a significant relationship to KM ($p < 0.05$) are described below.

Participation: Even though participation had a significant relationship to KM, some section chiefs believed that staff did not sincerely agree to participate in KM activities across the institute but had politically agreed to participate since they were expected to and were persuaded that KM could benefit their routine. Explicit knowledge as a result of KM activity was included in departments' websites as well as the ministry's website. One interviewee mentioned that she did not know if staff from other sections would access the websites and make use of the information and knowledge.

Trust: When people trust they tend to open their minds and accept other people's thoughts, opinions and information (Bowditch and Buono, 2001). The respondents in this study trusted their colleagues especially when they had trouble relating to their jobs, but the level of trust was not measured. Ichijo and Nonaka (2007) wrote that the more people trust each other the more knowledge would be transferred, and trust is directly associated with successful organizational innovation. This is compatible with Rhodes et al. (2008) findings that trust among staff had increased tacit knowledge transfer.

Motivation: In the private sector, bonuses and pay incentives usually motivate staff. In the public sector, non-financial awards or recognition programs are generally used. Nevertheless, one interviewee said he did not believe that the top management of the institute or the ministry had provided sufficient motivation. Difficult tasks by some staff did not even get verbal recognition, which could cause low job creativity or poor performance. Some staff perceived this as insincerity of top management.

Leadership: We found top management across the institute supported KM activities in terms of providing time and budget across the institute. Singh (2008) found that certain leadership styles had a significant relationship to KM of an organization. Bryant (2003) and Crawford (2005) also stated there was an apparent relationship among transformational leadership and KM. Additionally, a leader can maintain an organizational culture in order to help facilitate knowledge transfer in an organization. Janson and McQueen (2007) wrote about interviews with 31 leaders who innovatively succeeded in their jobs. The leaders used tacit knowledge, collected from their routine practice and experience, to facilitate conversations with their staff, an action which cannot be explained in explicit knowledge.

Communication: Formal and top-down (vertical) communications are usually practiced in the institute among top management and sections. Informal and horizontal communication occurs within laboratory sections by verbal communication. The communication within the institute normally used hardcopy letter, internet, intranet and e-mail for information and knowledge. These approaches of communication are also true in Plessis (2007) study. Effectiveness and efficiency of communication within the institute were not been investigated. Many staff mentioned they usually do not know details of other laboratory sections. Despite this, they at least know who can be contacted when knowledge is needed through informal conversation. A more structured or formal communication should be conducted to gain a significant impact of KM in the institute.

Climate: The climate is a measurement of staff's expectations on what the organization should be in terms of supporting knowledge sharing. The study showed the institute's climate has provided sufficient physical space and an appropriate psychological environment for staff to interact with each other. This climate can be referred to as "Ba" in this study. Nonaka and Toyama (Ichijo and Nonaka, 2007) defined 'Ba' as not only space for knowledge sharing, but also as the context where knowledge is created, transferred and utilized. Ba emerged through interactions between staff in the organization. Staff can see other staff physically interact with other staff in projects and meetings.

Attitude: Personal attitude is important to organizational performance for quality and quantity of outcomes. It can influence individuals to behave in a particular way instead of another (Bowditch and Buono, 2001). Having knowledge does not help a person get promoted at the institute. It is individual competency related to his/her publication and seniority regarding hierarchy in the organization chart that would be considered in getting a higher position. Liebowitz and Chen (2003) found people in a public organization usually kept knowledge for their own personal career path. Another study (Sun and Scott, 2005) found that 71 % respondents fear to lose ownership or fear to lose control of knowledge.

Information and Technology: This factor and its elements were significantly related to KM as consistent with a previous study (Rhodes et al., 2008). The institute has sufficient IT infrastructure and web connection is available, but most staff usually use the internet rather than intranet. This is especially true since when a particular task is complete, staff put their explicit knowledge on the department website rather than the intranet. When asked one interviewee said "Some people believe that some staff or section chiefs intend not to put details of their work on the website or intranet and use computer storage limitation as an excuse. It seems that knowledge put on a department website is more appropriate and useful to the public rather than to staff in the institute". Another statement: "I think the hardware of the institute should be upgraded and more e-mail account space should be provided according to staff position". Another statement was "Staff use of the department e-mail account is compulsory but space is very limited. Top management and clerks have the same account size". IT is an aspect of KA and forms a tool to store the institute's explicit knowledge especially data and information as part of the document control, which requires incorporated electronic and hardcopy documents. The quality management system of ISO requires a great focus on documents as well as KM, in order to transform tacit to explicit knowledge so that staff can learn. However, the documentation for ISO requirements is sometime laborious and a drawback to KM. Staff found they have to spend time on records and documents rather than actual testing itself.

Policy: KM policy was put in writing and a steering committee was formed to develop approaches for KM implementation. The committee consists of middle managers who are usually section chiefs. The group functions are to develop and manage a variety of KM activities e.g. selecting a KM topic that can be implemented across the institute; for example, laboratory safety. The staff need training on the issue and the working group needs to find particular trainers from within and outside the institute. The KM working group committee tries to encourage lab personnel and other staff to learn about the topic and apply it to day-to-day tasks. Not all staff have a chance to participate in every selected KM topic. In addition, knowledge transfer from experienced or highly skilled staff and from personnel about to retire should be accounted for with a clear policy.

Administration and Management: The administration and management section's work is generally reactive to internally oriented tasks rather than proactive. One interviewee said "Many times, work at the institute is on an ad-hoc basis". This is typical of any public institute in a developing country. Staff have to obey the department's or the ministry's top management. Another one said "There should be management directions with regard to a clear approach to KM practices in the section".

Evaluation: The questionnaires mentioned personal performance evaluation and work evaluation in general. The personal performance evaluation was usually led by each section chief who asked each staff member to evaluate themselves first, after which the section chief evaluated them. They discussed strengths and weaknesses in relation to work performance as well as completing an evaluation form. Furthermore, staff competency is included in the performance evaluation in order to ensure that staff are actively involved in understanding all test processes. In addition, the work evaluation is done according to the institute's key performance indicators and the Office of the Public Sector' development indicators as well as the requirements of ISO 9001 (very general management), ISO 17025 (specific to the laboratory field) and ISO 15189 (very specific to medical laboratories).

6. Conclusions and Recommendations

There is a significant relationship between KM and three major factors and some, but not all, of their elements;

- Organizational Culture: participation; trust; motivation; leadership; communication; organizational climate; and personal attitude.
- Information and Technology: infrastructure; IT administration and management; and accessibility.
- Administration and Management: policy; management aspect; and evaluation.

To serve the rapid changes occurring in the public health sector and assist the institute in becoming a true learning organization, the institute should provide in-depth understanding of KM to its staff to help facilitate managing knowledge in practice and document any best possible practice. The institute has a unique feature in its ISO certified laboratories which has contributed significantly with KM activity. The research was conducted on staff perceptions and individual perspectives. Further study could involve clients of the institute or other organizational factors that could impact KM. The findings do not represent other public health institutes and they may not be extrapolated to other public sectors in the country. However, the results could encourage further KM activities and future surveys.

Acknowledgements: The authors thank Assoc. Prof. D. Sujirarat, Assoc. Prof. P. Luksamijarulkul, Dr. B. Sriwanthana for their suggestions and special thanks to all interviewees and respondents of Thai National Institute of Health for their collaboration.

References

Ardichvili, A., Maurer, M., Li,W., Wentling, T. and Stuedemann, R. (2006) "Cultural influences on knowledge sharing through online communities of practice", *Journal of Knowledge Management*, 10 (1): 94-107.

Association of State and Territorial Health Official (ASTHO). (2005) *Knowledge Management for Public Health Professional*, Washington, DC: ASTHO.

Bowditch, J.L. and Buono, A.F. (2001) *A Primer on Organizational Behavior 5th edition*, John Wiley & Sons, Inc. New York, USA.

Bryant, S. E. (2003) "The role of transformational and transactional leadership in creating, sharing and exploiting organizational knowledge", *Journal of Leadership and Organizational Studies*, 9 (4): 32-44.

Buckman, R.H. (2004) *Building Knowledge Driven Organization*, McGraw-Hill, New York.

Chua, A. and Lam, W. (2005) "Why KM project fail: a multi-case analysis", *Journal of Knowledge Management*, 9 (3): 6-17.

Crawford, C.B. (2005) "Effects of transformational leadership and organizational position on knowledge management", *Journal of Knowledge Management*, 9 (6): 6-16.

Ichijo, K. and Nonaka, I. (2007) *Knowledge Creation and Management*, Oxford University Press, New York.

Ismail Al-Alawi, A., Yousif, N. and Mohammed, Y. (2007) "Organizational culture and knowledge sharing: critical success factors", *Journal of Knowledge Management*, 11 (2): 22-42.SO (2007)

Janson, A. and Mcqueen, J.R. (2007) "Capturing leadership tacit knowledge in conversions with leaders", *Leadership and Organization Development Journal*, 28 (7): 646-663.

Kreitner, R. and Kinicki, A. (2004) *Organizational Behavior 6th edition*, The McGraw-Hill companies, Inc. New York, USA.

Kulkarni, U.R.., Ravindran, S., and Freeze, R. (2007). "A knowledge management success model: theoretical development and empirical validation", *Journal of Management Information Systems,* 23 (3): 309 - 47

Lamproulis, D. (2007) "Cultural space and technology enhance the knowledge process", *Journal of Knowledge Management*, 11 (4): 30-44.

Leshabari, M.T., Muhondwa, E.P., Mwangu, M.A. and Mbembati, N.A. (2008) "Motivation of health care workers in Tanzania: a case study of Muhimbili National Hospital", *East Afr J Public Health*, 5(1): 32-7.

Liebowitz, J. and Chen, Y. (2003). "Knowledge sharing proficiencies: the key to knowledge management in Holapple, C.W. (Ed.)", *Handbook on Knowledge Management 1: knowledge Matters*, Berlin: Springer-Vertag.

Manolopoulos, D. (2008) "An evaluation of employee motivation in the extended public sector in Greece Employee", *Relations*, 30 (1): 63-85.

Metaxiotis, K., Ergazakis, K., Samouilidis, E. and Psarras, J. (2003) "Decision support through knowledge management: the role of the artificial intelligence", *Information Management & Computer Security*, 11 (5): 216-221.

Morgan, N.A., Zou,S., Vorhies, D.W. and Katsikeas, C. S. (2003) "Experiential and Informational Knowledge, Architectural Marketing Capabilities, and the Adaptive Performance of Export Ventures", *Decision Science*, 34 (2), 287-320.

Oliver, S. and Kandadi, K.R. (2006) "How to Develop Knowledge Culture in Organizations? A Multiple Case Study of Large Distributed Organizations", *Journal of Knowledge Management*, 10 (4): 6-24.

Phasukyud, P. (2004) *Knowledge management for beginner*, Yaimai, Bangkok (in Thai).

Plessis DM, (2007) "Knowledge Management: what makes complex implementations successful? ", *Journal of Knowledge Management*, 11 (2): 91-101.

Rhodes, J., Hung, R., Lok, P., Lien, Y.H.B. and Wu, C.H. (2008) "Factors influencing organizational knowledge transfer: implication for corporate performance", *Journal of Knowledge Management*, 12 (3): 84-100.

Riege, A. (2005) "Three-dozen knowledge-sharing barriers managers must consider", *Journal of Knowledge Management*, 9 (3): 18-35.

Singh, S.K. (2008) "Role of leadership in knowledge management: a study", *Journal of Knowledge Management*, 12 (4): 3-15.

Slagter, F. (2007) "Knowledge management among the older workforce", *Journal of Knowledge Management*, 11 (4): 82-96.

Sun, P.Y.T. and Scott, J.L. (2005) "An investigation of barriers to knowledge transfer", *Journal of Knowledge Management*, 9 (2): 75-90.

Syed-lkhsan, S.O.S. and Rowland, F. (2004) "Benchmarking knowledge management in a public organization in Malaysia", *Benchmarking: An International Journal*, 11 (3): 238-266.

Syed-lkhsan, S.O.S. and Rowland, F. (2004) "Knowledge Management in a Public Organization: a study on the relationship between organizational elements and the performance of knowledge transfer", *Journal of Knowledge Management*, 8 (2): 95-111.

Takeuchi, H. and Nonaka, I. (2004) *Hitotsubashi on Knowledge Management,* Singapore: Saik Wah Press Pte.

THE INFLUENCE OF KNOWLEDGE MANAGEMENT CAPABILITY AND KNOWLEDGE MANAGEMENT INFRASTRUCTURE ON MARKET-INTERRELATIONSHIP PERFORMANCE: AN EMPIRICAL STUDY ON HOSPITALS

WEN-TING LI
Department of Information Management, National Chung Cheng University, Minhsiung, Chia-Yi, 62100 Taiwan
E-mail: peggywendy@gmail.com

SHIN-YUAN HUNG
Department of Information Management, National Chung Cheng University, Minhsiung, Chia-Yi, 62100 Taiwan
E-mail: syhung@mis.ccu.edu.tw

The fierceness of competition and the barriers to knowledge management has embraced the healthcare industry. In this study the benefits of knowledge management capability and infrastructure are examined to resolve these problems, based on the resource-based view. In addition, based on the process-oriented perspective, the innovation on business process will be used as a mediator to improve specific business value in the healthcare industry. From the empirical data, this study finds knowledge management capability and technical context of knowledge infrastructure benefit market-interrelationship performance through the innovation on business process. Especially, cultural knowledge infrastructure is beneficial to market-interrelationship performance directly and indirectly. Surprisingly, structural knowledge management infrastructure falls to affect innovation on business process. The reason might be the high degree in centralization within the hospital. However, this study also generally demonstrates the proposed model. The findings illustrate the significance of the perspective of practice and provide guidance for further research. Finally, the inherent limitations are also mentioned.

1. Introduction

The trend of healthcare industry faces the depressed financial environment. This condition is not only happened in OECD (Organization for Economic Cooperation and Development) countries, but also happened in Taiwan. Information technology within healthcare organizations has rapidly changed. From the healthcare environment, the financial motivation and patient leverage in motivation of the medical service activities are changing (Wilson and Lankton 2004). Before the 1995, the competition among hospitals was not significant in Taiwan. Since 1990, "the Executive Yuan charged the Department of Health actively to promote the National Health Insurance (NHI) Program" (Chang 1998, p.308). In 1995 the program of fix reimbursement for health care benefit to hospitals was promoted continuously in Taiwan (Chang et al. 2006). These policies exerted fierce financial pressure on hospitals in Taiwan. In order to face the competitive environment, hospitals not only adopted information technology (e.g. Picture Archiving and Communication System, PACS), but also provided additional services and built brand image (e.g. promoting the healthcare quality). But the technology adoption is not a necessity for generation of the superior performance in the same industry (Chang et al. 2006).

From the resource-based view, the intangible resource is superior to the tangible (Ray et al. 2004), especially in those hospitals which are knowledge-based organizations (Lin et al. 2008). However, the prior researches of the profit of knowledge management have founded the different outcome. Gold et al. (2001) knowledge management capability has impact on the organizational effectiveness. Lee and Choi (2003) points out that the knowledge management architecture has impact on the organization creativity through knowledge creation, which in turn improves organizational performance. But the other study found no relationship between knowledge creation and organizational performance (Droge et al. 2003). The knowledge resource has no specific value before knowledge application (Drew 1997; Droge et al. 2003). The various way of application of knowledge is the determinant whether that knowledge is helpful or detrimental (Brockman and Morgan 2003). Therefore, the appropriate infrastructure and application can help knowledge resources to result in generating the value in place, which in turn can improve the business value. Despite the architecture of knowledge contexts has been pointed out (e.g. Zack 1999; Alavi and Leidner 1999; Gold et al. 2001; Lee and Choi 2003), but little research has investigated the intermediated value of knowledge management resource. Additionally, the value of the resources has considered the business process capability, which in turn can provide the business value of knowledge resource (Radhakrishnan et al. 2008). In hospitals, the business process improvement is the essence for the bottom line for operational cost (Devaraj and Kohli 2000).

However, the knowledge management within the hospitals in Taiwan has the barriers of knowledge flows, including knowledge source, knowledge receiver, knowledge transferring, and organizational context (Lin et al. 2008). To resolve the barriers of knowledge management in healthcare industry, this study not only investigates the way to deploy and exploit knowledge resource effectively but also appraises the knowledge benefits. Based on the process-oriented perspective, this study investigates the knowledge resource and knowledge context of organizational infrastructure applied to the business processes. In addition, the culture within the hospital is also the interesting issue while the leverage of patients is increasing. In summary, based on the resource-based view and process-oriented perspective, this research investigates four key questions:

(i) Does the value of knowledge management capability lead to the innovation on business process?
(ii) How does the value of knowledge management infrastructure enjoy the innovation on business process?
(iii) Does the innovation on business process lead to the metrics within the market-interrelationship performance?
(iv) Does the cultural knowledge context directly lead to the market-interrelationship performance?

2. Theoretical Background

From the broader view of knowledge-based, knowledge management capability subsumes the information-based, the technology-based and the managerial perspective from the execution opinion (Alavi and Leinder 1999). Based on the synergies of knowledge management, knowledge management capability includes product knowledge, customer knowledge, and managerial knowledge which is related to the governing business units (Tanriverdi 2005). Based on the resource-based view, the knowledge management resources should subsume knowledge management infrastructure and knowledge management capability. The knowledge management infrastructure is the basic infrastructure to support the knowledge management activities in the firms. The knowledge management capability is involved in the primary knowledge management activities and practices in the firms.

2.1. *Knowledge management capability*

Knowledge management capability is the organizational capability which in dynamic hypercompetitive environments, which capability creates the valuable business activities. From the theoretical insights of the resource-based view (RBV) within strategic management (Barney 1991), the knowledge capability is not only the strategic resource, but also the development and distribution knowledge resource as well. The firm posses the varied knowledge resource, but the most-strategic knowledge management resources are the product, customer, and managerial relatedness knowledge (Tanriverdi 2005). The interrelationship between the resource and capability is complex, and the capability refers to the coordination of resource and the people who exploit the resources (Grant 1991).

The knowledge management capability includes the three perspectives which are related to the product, customer and management. The complementarities among the product, customer and managerial knowledge can generate the super-additive value synergies (Tanriverdi and Venkatraman 2005). In order to gain the value, these three knowledge resources may need to exist simultaneously. Through coexistence of those knowledge relatedness resources can attach inimitable value in the same industry (Tanriverdi and Venkatraman 2005).

2.2. *Knowledge management infrastructure*

The separated embeddedness of knowledge management (KM) infrastructure was comparatively more valuable and inimitable, which can represent the more comprehensive concept (Sambamurthy et al. 2003). Based on the concepts of maximum social capital, the critical elements of the knowledge management infrastructure are technology, structure and culture (Gold et al. 2001). The context of knowledge management architecture refers to the strategic context, knowledge context, organizational context, and technology context (Zack 1999). The Knowledge management infrastructure is the basis for the knowledge management application. In order to support knowledge management activities and manage knowledge resources, the

KM infrastructure has the three contexts which is technical, structural, and cultural knowledge management. The technological context is capable of supporting knowledge sharing, storage, and management (Alavi and Leidner 2001). The structure refers to the support of the knowledge management activities and motivation for the knowledge sharing (O'Dell and Grayson 1998; Zack 1999). The cultural context is the knowledge management behaviors and the organizational vision (Gold et al. 2001; Alavi et al. 2006).

2.3. *The innovation on business process*

The definition of the innovation on business process is the combination of "the adoption of a process view of the business with the application of innovation to the key processes" (Davenport 1993, p. 1). Business process is defined by the activities underlying value generating processes (Melville et al. 2004). Business process is a set of interdependent activities and tasks undertaken to achieve business goals (Raghu and Vinze 2007). From the perspective of resource-based, business process is related the resource exploitation in organizations (Melville et al. 2004). The exploitation of knowledge resources is the most-strategic resource within multiple business firms (Tanriverdi 2005). However, exploitation is about reusing and sharing the existing resources, and exploration is related to the knowledge creation (Gray 2001). Therefore, based on the resource-based view, the business process outcomes come from the advantage of the knowledge resource exploitation.

2.4. *Market-interrelationship performance in healthcare organization*

The organizational overall performance is revealed after by aggregating each business value within the value chain (Ray et al. 2004). The business value in the value chain subsumes the production interrelationships and the market interrelationships (Porter 1985). The production interrelationships include the inbound logistics (e.g. Supplier relations) and operations, the market interrelationships associate the outbound logistics (e.g. customer relations), marketing and sales, and service (Porter 1985; Tallon 2000). The market interrelationship involves the value of the sharing in reaching and interacting with the consumer to enhance the opportunities and sharing market-related activities (Porter 1985). The specified business value chains reflect the business value superior than the other firms within the same industry, and then have the impact on the specified organizational performance (Melville et al. 2004). While the prior research indicated IT can support to generate improved performance in hospitals as knowledge intensive organizations (Devraj and Kohli 2000), knowledge management practices may not directly impact on financial performance, but through effect on the product leadership, customer intimacy, and operational excellence, then reach the financial performance (Mckeen et al. 2006). Therefore, the metrics of the market-interrelationship performance is preferred to measure the knowledge management investment. The three metrics of market-interrelationship performance are customer relations, marketing and sales, and service (Porter 1985; Tallon 2000).

3. Research Model and Hypotheses Development

3.1. *Research model*

The proposed model is depicted in Figure 1. Based on the resource-based view and process-oriented perspective, this research model suggests knowledge management capability and knowledge management infrastructure are hypothesized to positively influence organizational market-interrelationship performance through the innovation on business process. The market-interrelationship performance metrics include service enhancement, sales and marketing support, and patient relations.

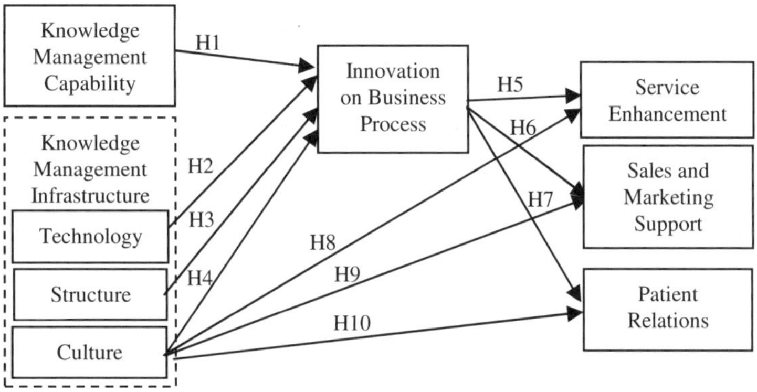

Figure1. Research Model

3.2. *Hypotheses development*

According to the resource-based view, the knowledge resource exploitation and the application of kernel knowledge resource will result in the underlying the innovation on business processes (Melville et al. 2004; Raghu and Vinze 2007). The effective management of knowledge resource could not create unnecessary redundant knowledge, but create the necessary redundant knowledge which improves the innovation on business process (Nonaka 1990). The capability of knowledge management seems as the essence related to the innovation and improvement of process (Earl 2001). Based on the KM infrastructure, the organization can achieve the maximum value of knowledge resources. The value of knowledge management underlies the generation of value of the business processes (Raghu and Vinze 2007). Additionally, the value of knowledge management resources could create the innovation (Nonaka 1994; Fichman 2004). The effectiveness of knowledge resource deployment has influence on the innovation (Nonaka 1990). Thus, these observations lead to the following hypotheses:

Hypothesis 1. *Knowledge management capability will be positively related to the innovation on business process.*

Hypothesis 2. *Technological knowledge management infrastructure capability will be positively related to the innovation on business process.*

Hypothesis 3. *Structural knowledge management infrastructure will be positively related to the innovation on business process.*

Hypothesis 4. *Cultural knowledge management infrastructure will be positively related to the innovation on business process.*

Business process outcome has the profit for the organization, and the innovation on business processes is related to the operational efficiency, effectiveness, and flexibility (Karimi et al. 2007). The innovation on business process also includes improved productivity, increased responsiveness, and reduced waste (Karimi et al. 2007). Business process is a set of interdependent activities and tasks, which is made to achieve business goals (Raghu and Vinze 2007). The strategic business goals of the service-oriented industry are regarding the market interrelationship performance. The market interrelationship performance includes service enhancement, marketing support, and patient relations (Porter 1985). Therefore, these observations suggest the following hypotheses:

Hypothesis 5. *The innovation on business process will be positively related to service enhancement.*

Hypothesis 6. *The innovation on business process will be positively related to sales and marketing support.*

Hypothesis 7. *The innovation on business process will be positively related to patient relations.*

The literature investigates the relationship between the organizational culture and the organizational performance (Barney 1986; Hult et al. 2003; Ray et al. 2004). Culture is an organizational tacit that is measured by the firm's actions (Brockman and Morgan 2003). Additionally, the knowledge-centered culture (Janz and Prasarnphanich 2003), entrepreneurship and cohesiveness culture (Brockman and Morgan 2003), and a clear corporate vision culture (Gold et al. 2001) positively affect improved organizational outcome. A clear corporate vision culture emphasizes entrepreneurship and creativity in finding new market and direction of growth (Brockman and Morgan 2003). The cultural knowledge management infrastructure is a strategic resource which may directly influence the superior performance (Baer and Frese 2003; Hult et al. 2003). The superior cultural knowledge management is knowledge sharing and contribution to achieve the valuable outcomes (Alavi et al. 2006). These observations suggest the following hypotheses:

Hypothesis 8. *Cultural knowledge management infrastructure will be positively related to service enhancement.*

Hypothesis 9. *Cultural knowledge management infrastructure will be positively related to sales and marketing support.*

Hypothesis 10. *Cultural knowledge management infrastructure will be positively related to patient relations.*

4. Research Methodology

4.1. *Measures*

All of the variables are operationalized by multiple items. First, knowledge management capability was measured with 12 survey items adapted from the Tanriverdi (2005) the previously validated instrument. Second, knowledge management (KM) infrastructure consists of technological, structural, and cultural KM infrastructure. The measurement scales of the technological, structural, and cultural KM infrastructure were measured by seven-point Likert scales and adapted form Gold et al. (2001) previously developed and validated instrument. The innovation on business process was measured using the previous validated instrument from Karimi et al. (2007). Then, the innovation on business process examined the operations improvement and the change of business process, which posited resulting in the profit outcome (Clark and Stoddard 1996; Fichman 2004; Karimi et al. 2007). Finally, market-interrelationship performance was measured by the impact of the innovation on business process leading to competitive advantage within the same industry. Moreover, the valuable business activity of market-interrelationship consist of three constructs, which is service enhancement, sales and marketing support, and patient relations (Porter 1985; Tallon et al. 2000). Service enhancement, sales and marketing support, and patient relations measured by seven-point Likert scales and adapted from Tallon et al. (2000). Additionally, the pretest and the pilot test are used to check the content validity.

4.2. *Data collection and analysis*

The sample list is obtained from the database of Bureau of National Health Insurance in Taiwan. The data was collected for the year 2007. The sample in this study includes 25 medical centers, 72 regional hospitals and 401 distinct hospitals. According to the resources of the hospitals (e.g. numbers of the beds, number of the physicians), the department of health of government group hospitals into medical centers, regional hospitals, and distinct hospitals in Taiwan. Hence, this study investigates the proposed model through a mail survey targeting 497 hospitals in Taiwan. Data was collected from the chief information officer (CIO) in sampled hospitals. In total, 170 questionnaires were obtained from 497 hospitals. Of these 129 questionnaires was usable, after excluding incomplete questionnaires and non-implementation of knowledge management. Consequently, the effective response rate is about 26 percent. The response rate of the medical centers is 96 percent, and the response rate of regional hospitals is 82 percent.

4.2.1. *Reliability and validity analysis*

For the internal consistency reliability was tested by the Cronbach's alpha. All of the Cronbach's alpha values of the variables are higher than 0.86, which were above the recommend value of 0.70. Convergent validity test assess the different measures gathered indicating the same concept (Kerlinger and Lee 2000).

The convergent validity test uses the correlation of items with total-score. All the items with item-to-total correlation scores are higher than recommend value of 0.50, ranging from 0.52 to 0.90. For discriminant validity test, the factor analysis is used. (Kerlinger and Lee 2000). Factor analysis adopts the principal factor analysis and varimax rotation grouping the items representing each construct. Therefore, the factor analysis is used to check undimensionality among items. Items with factor loading values less than cutoff value of 0.5 are deleted. From correlations among constructs, the cultural knowledge management infrastructure is more strongly correlated to the market-interrelationship performance than technological and structural knowledge management infrastructure. The pairs of correlations are below the recommend cutoff value of 0.9 (Hair et al. 2006), which shows no multicollinearity problem. The lower of the correlation metric indicates the conditions that free of the multicollinearity. Additionally, the result of the collinearity test of the dependent variable also suggests no multicollinearity problem. The variance inflation factors were less than the threshold value of 10, ranging from 1.73 to 2.70 (Hair et al. 2006). In addition, in order to satisfy the normality of the variables in the survey, the better method is the use of normal probability plots (Hair et al. 2006). All of the normal probability plots represent almost straight diagonal line. There is no normality of the variables problems.

4.3. *Hypotheses testing*

From the previous mention that research model and the hypotheses, the hypotheses were analyzed using structural equation modeling based path analysis. The structural equation modeling use AMOS 7.0. The SEM can provide various causal links and are useful for explaining multiple observable variables (Joreskog and Sorbom 1982). The SEM based path analysis also estimates the variances and covariances of independent variables in contrast to the multiple regression testing. In addition, the SEM is related to the multivariate technique, which is the multiple regression to examine the relationship among the variables. The overall validity of the model is measured by the goodness of fit indices. Specifically, the fit indices are used to access the rational acceptable model, which including the absolute, incremental, and badness of fit index (Hair et al. 2006). The model fit measures is shown in Table 1.

Table 1. The Model Fit Statistics

Indices	Recommendation Value	Value
p-value	> 0.05	0.097
χ^2/df	< 3.00	1.642
GFI	> 0.90	0.973
AGFI	< 0.90	0.891
RMSR	< 0.08	0.023
CFI	> 0.90	0.992
NFI	> 0.90	0.979
RMSEA	< 0.08	0.071

The results of the hypotheses tested by structural equations modeling are shown in Figure 2. Additionally, the standardized parameter estimates and statistical significance of all hypotheses are shown in Figure 2. Overall, nine of ten hypotheses are supported in the proposed model. The result indicated knowledge management capability is positively associated with innovative business process at the 0.001 level, which support hypothesis 1. In addition, the standardized coefficient score of 0.44 shows that knowledge management capability would significant influence the innovation on business process. Hypothesis 2 is supported by the relationship between technological KM infrastructure and the innovation on business process has weak statistical significance at the 0.1 level. However, hypothesis 3 which proposes structural KM infrastructure has positive influence the innovation on business process is not supported. As for cultural KM infrastructure, the results indicate cultural KM infrastructure would positively influence the innovation on business process, service enhancement, sales and marketing support, and patient relations. Hence, hypothesis 4, 8, 9 and 10 are statistically supported at the 0.001 level.

The relationship between the innovation on business process and market-interrelationship outcomes has positive association. The results of the relationship between the innovation on business process and service enhancement has statistically significant influence at the 0.001 level, which support hypothesis 5. Hypothesis 6 is also supported at the 0.001 level, which demonstrates that the innovation on business process positively influence on sales and marketing support. Lastly, business process would positively impact on patient relations, supporting hypothesis 7 at the 0.1 level. Additionally, the four antecedents (knowledge management capability, technology, structure, and culture) explain 62.9% of the variance in the innovation on business process. Moreover, the innovation on business process in conjunction with the four antecedent variables and cultural knowledge management infrastructure explains 42.6% of the variance in service enhancement, 38.3% of variance in sales and marketing support, and 65.8% of variance in patient relations.

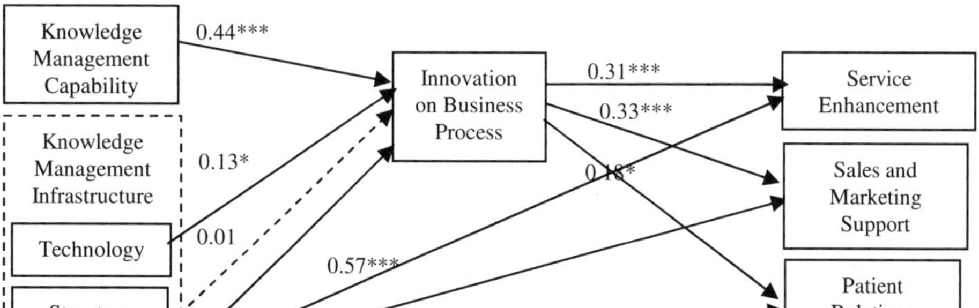

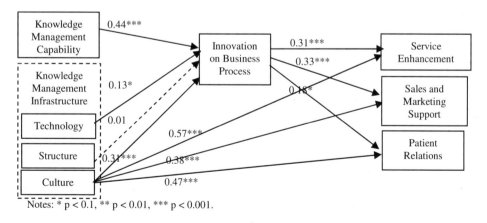

Notes: * $p < 0.1$, ** $p < 0.01$, *** $p < 0.001$.

Figure 2. The Path Model Results

5. Discussion

This study started with the objective of addressing the research question, which is related to the source of value of knowledge management. In addition, the value of knowledge management impacts hospitals primary value activities, which in turn leads to the superior competitive advantage within the same industry. Therefore, the major research questions include: (1) does the value of knowledge management capability lead to the innovation on business process, (2) how does the values of knowledge management infrastructure enjoy the innovation on business process, (3) does the innovation on business process lead to the metrics within the market-interrelationship performance, and (4) does the culture of knowledge context lead to the market-interrelationship performance directly? In order to explore these questions, resource-based view and process-oriented perspective are taken as the theoretical bases in this study. Based on resource-based view, the knowledge resources of knowledge management capability and infrastructure are postulated to create the valuable and inimitable knowledge resource, which in turn affects innovation (Nonaka 1994). The value of knowledge-related valuable activities is related to the business process change positively. The business process change achieves the process efficiency, process flexibility and process effectiveness (Karimi 2007). The business process positive is related to the innovation on business process (Davenport 1993). Therefore, this study proposed ten hypotheses related to the previous four questions.

The empirical findings of this paper suggest that knowledge management capability is positively associated with the market-interrelationship performance through the innovation on business process. The valuable resource of the knowledge management capability creates the valuable resources delivered by the innovation on business process. This result is in line with Raghu and Vinze (2007) and Radhakrishnan et al. (2008). In addition, the findings reveal that technological and cultural KM infrastructure has significant and positive effects the innovation on business process, and also that cultural KM infrastructure is beneficial to market-interrelationship performance.

These findings confirm the IT and non-IT resource implementation of the previous study, and these resources effected to relative business process and specify value chains (Ray et al. 2005; Radhakrishnan et al. (2008). Additionally, the inimitable and rare cultural KM infrastructure has the significant influence the three metrics of market-interrelationship performance. The three metrics of market-interrelationship performance are the service enhancement, sales and marketing support, and patient relations.

Thus, the findings generally support to the proposed hypotheses, except for structural KM infrastructure is not significant association with the innovation on business process. This result is in line with the report of hospital structure of the previous empirical study which pointed out high degree of hospital centralization (Chang et al. 2006). The centralization is the hamper of the valuable knowledge resource creation (Lee and Choi 2003). Therefore, the structural KM infrastructure has no significant influence on the innovation on business process. Based on the process-oriented perspective, the result also demonstrates positive association between the innovation on business process and market-interrelationship performance. One of the most valuable chains of business value within the healthcare industry is the market-interrelationship performance. Knowledge management capability, technological and cultural KM infrastructure enables this business value to be achieved through the innovation on business process.

6. Conclusion

In line with Ray et al. (2005), this study contributes to integrate the resource-based view and process-oriented perspective. Based on the resource-based view, the valuable resource of the KM capability and the context of KM infrastructure accrued the innovation on the business process. Consequently, the process-oriented perspective is the mediation to deliver the value of knowledge capability, which is beneficial to the market-interrelationship performance. As such, this study concentrates on the mediation of the innovation on business process as a critical value, reflecting the valuable KM capability and context of KM infrastructure. Additionally, cultural KM infrastructure is one of the critical resources in healthcare organizations within the service-based industry.

The innovation on business process is effected by the knowledge deployment and resources. The dynamic capability of knowledge management infrastructure is capable of improvement absorbing, exploiting and transfer of the valuable knowledge to generate innovative business processes. The results of this research could help hospital managers to reach strategic knowledge management related decisions. The decision is related to the type of knowledge management infrastructure and capability deployment. In addition, it allows effective deployment of strategic knowledge resources.

Longitudinal study is needed to further explore these issues. The longitudinal study provides the insight of knowledge resource accumulation accrued and the innovation within the business process. Based on stages of innovation diffusion, the different stages achieve different valuable business value chains. Furthermore, from the circle of resource-based view, the innovation on business process could generate resources and capability for the organizations (Porter 1991).

Although the findings of this study had found some interesting results, the necessary of consideration of the inherent limitations. One limitation is that the data focuses on relatively large hospitals. The results may not be the same in the small hospitals. Another limitation is that the empirical analysis was conducted in the healthcare industry. The generalizability of the results may be limited.

References

Alavi, M., Kayworth, T.R., and Leidner, D.E. (2005) "An empirical examination of the influence of organizational culture on knowledge management practices", *Journal of Management Information Systems*, 22(3): 191–224.

Baer, M., and Frese, M. (2003) "Innovation is not enough: climates for initiative and psychological safety, process innovations, and firm performance", *Journal of Organizational Behavior*, 24(1): 45–68.

Barney, J. (1991) "Firm resources and sustained competitive advantage", *Journal of Management*, 17(1): 99–120.

Barney, J.B. (1986) "Organizational culture: can it be a source of sustained competitive advantage", *Academy of Management Review*, 11(3): 656–665.

Chang, H. H. (1998) "Determinants of Hospital Efficiency: The Case of Central Government-Owned Hospitals in Taiwan", *Omega*, 26(2): 307–317.

Chang, I. C., Hwang, H. G., Yen, D. C., and Lian, J. W. (2003) "Critical factors for adopting PACS in Taiwan: view of radiology department directors", *Decision Support Systems*, 42(4): 1042–1053.

Devaraj, S., and Kohli, R. (2000) "Information technology payoff in the health-care industry: a longitudinal study", *Journal of Management Information Systems*, 16(4): 41–67.

Droge, C., Claycomb, C., and Germain, R. (2003) "Does knowledge mediate the effect of context on performance? some initial evidence", *Decision Sciences*, 34(3): 541–568.

Gold, A.H., Malhotra, A., and Segars, A.H. (2001) "Knowledge management: an organizational capabilities perspective", *Journal of Management Information Systems*, 18(1): 185–214.

Grant, R.M. (1996) "Prospering in dynamically-competitive environments: organizational capability as knowledge integration", *Organization Science*, 7(4): 375–387.

Karimi, J., Somers, T.M., and Bhattacherjee, A. (2007) "The impact of ERP implementation on business process outcomes: a factor-based study," *Journal of Management Information Systems*, 24(1): 101–134.

Lee, H., and Choi, B. (2003) "Knowledge management enablers, processes, and organizational performance: an integrative view and empirical examination", *Journal Management Information Systems*, 20(1): 179–228.

Lin, C., Tan, B., and Chang, S. (2008) "An exploratory model of knowledge flow barriers within healthcare organizations", *Information & Management*, 45(4): 331–339.

Melville, N., Kraemer, K., and Gurbaxani, V. (2004) "Review: information technology and organizational performance: an integrative model of it business value", *MIS Quarterly*, 28(2): 283–322.

Radhakrishnan, A., Zu, X., and Grover, V. (2008) "A process-oriented perspective on different business value creation by information technology: a empirical investigation", *Omega*, 36(6): 1105–1125.

Raghu, T.S., and Vinze, A. (2007) "A business process context for knowledge management", *Decision Support Systems*, 43(3): 1062–1079.

Ray, G., Barney, J.B., and Muhanna, W.A. (2004) "Capabilities, business processes, and competitive advantage: choosing the dependent variable in empirical tests of the resource-based view", *Strategic Management Journal*, 25(1): 23–37.

Tallon, P.P., Kraemer, K.L., and Gurbaxani, V. (2000) "Executives' perceptions of the business value of information technology: a process-oriented approach", *Journal of Management Information Systems*, 16(4): 145-173.

Tanriverdi, H. (2005) "Information Technology Relatedness Knowledge Management Capability, and Performance of Multibusiness Firms", *MIS Quarterly*, 29(2): 311–334.

Wilson, E.V., and Lankton, N.K. (2004) "Interdisciplinary research and publication opportunities in information systems and healthcare", *Communications of the Association for Information Systems*, 14: 332–343.

Zack, M.H. (1999) "Managing codified knowledge", *Sloan Management Review*, 40(4): 45–57.

Due to the space of a printed page, all reference is not listed in the list of references. Please contact the authors if you need the further information.

FUNCTIONAL DYNAMICS IN SYSTEM OF INNOVATION: A GENERAL MODEL OF SYSTEM INNOVATION METAPHORIC FROM TRADITIONAL CHINESE MEDICINE

XI SUN and XIN TIAN

School of Management, Graduate University of Chinese Academy of Sciences
Beijing, 100190, China
E-mail: sunxi-b08@mails.gucas.ac.cn; tianxin05@ mails.gucas.ac.cn

XINGMAI DENG

School of Management and Economic, Beijing Institute of Technology
Beijing, 100081, China
E-mail: dxingmai@gmail.com

Based on a comparison between two strands in SI and an analysis on the notion of "ideal model," this paper builds a general model of SI through the metaphor form function-defined ideal model in Traditional Chinese Medicine (TCM). This general dynamic model metaphoric from TCM is built on the base of Yin-Yang-Five-Phases theory. It is made up of five sub-systems and the supporting networks of innovation. Both static descriptions and evolutional dynamics of SI are discussed. Policy implications are given based on the basic features of SI as a complex adaptive system.

1. Introduction

The concept of "systems of innovation" (SI) is still in the state of art because of conceptual diffuseness and strands of methodologies. This restricts its effect in policy making. This paper tries to develop a model to study SI in a systematic manner. Although path-dependence is important in SI, we argue there is rationality to develop an ideal model of SI because of the convergent global competition and common features of innovation. The ideal model introduces the systematic thought of Traditional Chinese Medicine (TCM) by metaphor based on the function-defined approach. The archetype in TCM is an ideal model of human body, so the SI model here is also ideal to manifest what SIs should be, as complex adaptive systems (CAS). That needs a description of dynamics among sub-systems of SI. The central topic of both models is harmonies among all function-defined sub-systems. Disharmony would be adjusted by self-organization or outside interventions. Human body is intervened by therapy, while SI by policy.

This paper is organized as follows. Section 2 will present the two main strands in SI research, i.e. the actor-defined and function-defined approach and analyze the rationality to develop an ideal model of SI. Section 3 will give an introduction to the systematic thought in TCM, which are mainly the Yin-Yang thought and the Five Phases theory. The metaphorical model will be developed in Section 4. Modeling is conducted by the basic logic of TCM: to identify Yin and Yang in SI firstly, then to metaphorize different functions of SI into different functional sub-systems in human body. Analyses on systematic dynamics are possible when the fundamental metaphors are established.

Section 5 discusses policy implications of the metaphorical model with some examples in China. The last part concludes this paper from the perspective of methodology.

2. Divergent Systems of Innovation (SI) Approach in the Past Two Decades

The SI approach emerged in the 1980s when the systemic nature of innovation was increasingly realized. Currently, SI is still the most attractive realm in innovation research. However it is not a formal theory, but an approach or conceptual framework.

2.1. *Origins of SI and the Actor-defined Systems of Innovation*

All the earliest researches on national innovation systems (NIS) could be classified into two strands. Freeman (1987) and Nelson (1993) could be seen as the springs of SI in macro-level that emphasizes the arrangement of institutions and the role of R&D. While Lundvall (1992) highlighted the theoretical analysis on interactions between producers and users, what he called the micro-foundation is NIS. These two strands get no agreement on the key issues in NIS: Nelson (1993) stresses the balance between public and private technology, while Lundvall (1992) put learning in the core of NIS. This reflects the lack of a general definition of NIS (Edquist, 2007).

But there are some similarities between them, one of which is that they defined NIS by actors and relations among actors, which are partly influenced by institutions (Freeman, 1992; Lundvall, 1992). This has deep influence on the SI approach. From then on, Patel and Pavitt (1994), Metcalfe (1995) and OECD (1997) define NIS as actors-based innovation networks regulated by institutions. Because of relative success on the research of the systemic nature of innovation, the SI approach developed several other specifications. The notion of sectoral systems of innovation (SSI) focuses on the innovative and production processes in a border defined by sectors (Breschi and Malerba, 1997); regional innovation systems focus on interactive learning embedded in region (Cooke et al., 1997); technological systems focus on the generation, diffusion and utilization of specific technologies in technology networks (Carlsson and Stankiewitz, 1995). All these SIs are defined and analyzed by institutions and actors, or agents.

We label all researches stated above as actor-defined SI approach. It considers actors and institutions as the main components of SI. It has obvious shortcomings: (1) actors in SI tend to play multiple roles, this will make the inter-relations complex (Galli and Teubal, 1997); (2) the difficulty in description of system's dynamics makes this approach lack a system-level explanatory factor (Liu & White, 2001); (3) the border of system is set a priori to nation, region or technology, while actors are hybrid of innovation functions and unrelated ones, thus the presupposed border is illogical (Johnson, 2001). Thus, a new approach emerged, which define and analyze SI by functions.

2.2. *Function-defined System of Innovation*

In the retrospect of SI research, Edquist (2005) compares function-defined and actor-defined approaches. He admitted the importance to study functions in SI in a systematic manner. Actually, the function-defined approach in SI emerged in late 1990s.

Galli and Teubal(1997) is the earliest paper that gives attention to functions in SI. They emphasized the role functions played in SI research and developed a function-based componential approach. They categorized functions into hard and soft functions and different linkages link all components in SI. Liu & White (2001) inherited this approach, constructed a framework including 5 fundamental activities— R&D, end-use, education, implementation, linkage—and focused on the performance implications of a system's structure and dynamics. This model focused more on system-level characteristics, but little on inter-functional relations and dynamics in SI.

Johnson (2001) sorted functions in SI to basic and supporting ones. Basic functions affect the innovation process directly, supporting ones indirectly. In the following empirical work, the list is modified to 5 functions (Jacobson et al., 2004): to create new knowledge, to guide the direction of search processes, to supply resources, to facilitate the creation of positive external economies and to facilitate the formation of markets.

Hekkert et al. (2007) focuses on the processes important for well performing SIs. The authors depict three motors of change in SI in terms of processes and functions, which are demonstrated as A, B, C in Fig.1. Bergek et al. (2008) added insights from political science, sociology of technology and organization theory to describe a systematic approach. 6 steps constitute the scheme (Fig.2). They clarified each functions in step3a. In their latest research on functional dynamic of TIS, Suurs and Hekkert (2009) identified 7 functions in technological innovation systems. Interactions between functions result in cumulative causation in the formation of TIS. The authors acknowledge that complex interactions may lead to complex development process.

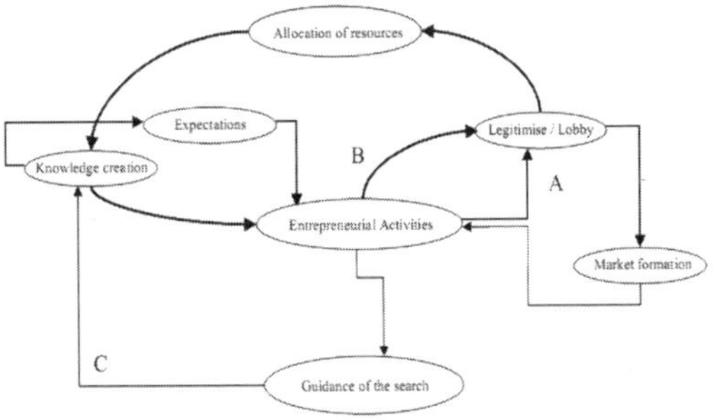

Fig. 1. Functional dynamics in Hekkert et al. (2007)

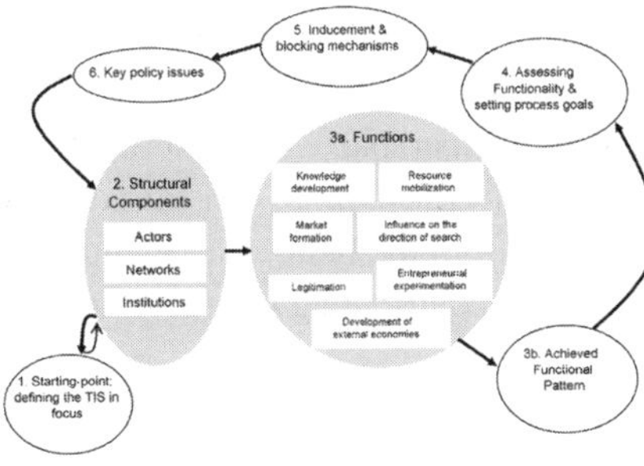

Fig. 2. Policy schemes in Bergek et al. (2008)

We can conclude that functional dynamics approach (FDA) calls for not only the classification of functions, but also the inter-functional dynamics in SI. A clear landscape of functional dynamics derives from a clear definition of innovation process and corresponding functions. Dynamic relations among functions are complex, this is one of the difficulties to build FDA. But we are sure that all functions should not be inter-reinforcing ones as there are not only positive feedbacks but also negative.

The two main approaches are both in dilemmas: the actor-defined approach is weak to explain systematic performance in innovation, while the function-defined one is still deficient to manifest fundamental rules and mechanisms of innovation system. Simply, the *systems of innovation* approach have paid most attention on the nature of *innovation*, but few on the *systematic methodology* that is important to model *system.*

Then, another question comes forth: is there any "ideal model?" In terms of Todtling and Trippl (2005), does one size fit all? They think there should be no highly specific general system model in SI because of different development paths. But some theoretical argument at micro-level may give us some new insights in this problem. Just as Eisenhardt et al. (2001) states, dynamic capabilities of firms are "idiosyncratic in their details and path dependent in their emergence, they have significant commonalities across firms (popularly termed 'best practice')." Commonalities are determined by the interaction between fundamental nature of activities and competition. Different SIs have different actors and relations among them, international competition environment and fundamental nature of innovation are alike more or less. It is possible to develop a model to manifest the commonalities among systems based on a proper methodology of system. Summarily, heterogeneities of SI are largely related to the specific forms of actors and institutions, while functions of SI are similar. Thus, we may find an ideal model of SI by FDA under the help of a suitable systematic methodology.

3. Traditional Chinese Medicine: the Potential Proper Methodology of System

TCM may be the methodology we need. It is a philosophical thinking of ancient China. It is holistic to build a functional model embedded in the environment rather than to open the black box of human body reductively.[*] Human organism was seemed "not a machina with a single deux", and "for any recognizable continuance of identity its parts were not separable."[†] Chinese doctors give every patient a unique treatment based on specific diagnosis and constitutions. Such "philosophy of organism" is a world-view "derived from the biological, evolutionary and holistic facets of natural science which ... have been contributing to 'a rectification of the mechanical Newtonian universe.'"[‡]

3.1. *Yin-Yang Theory in Traditional Chinese Medicine*

TCM begins and ends with Yin and Yang and never goes outside Yin and Yang. Yin and Yang are a general term for two opposites to describe how things function in relation to each other and to the universe. All things have both a Yin and Yang aspect. The Yin aspect is associated with such qualities as cold, rest, constringency and downwardness.

[*] Obviously, the difference between TCM and Western ones to identify subsystems in human body is similar with the difference between functions-defined approach and actors-defined approach in SI. The most important monographs in Chinese medicine in English is Needham et al. (2000) and Kaptchuk (2000) , some expressions on Chinese medicine in this section refer to the two books.

[†] Needham, J.,(1974), "Science and civilization in China,vol.5, part 2",Cambridge University Press:p92.

[‡] Peterson, W. J.(1980),"'Chinese scientific philosophy' and some Chinese attitudes towards knowledge about the realm of heaven-and-earth", Past & Present 87(1):20-30.

The Yang aspect is associated with heat, stimulation, radiation and upwardness. They contain within themselves the possibility of opposition and change and depend on each other for definition, mutually creating and controlling each other. Furthermore, they transform into each other. It is only through this kind of mutual creation and restriction that dynamic equilibrium can be established. Harmony means that Yin and Yang are relatively balanced; disharmony means that the proportions are unequal.

TCM believes that normal physiological functions of human body result from unified and opposite relation between Yin and Yang and the internal viscera, both functional and corporeal are of the two counter-reacted aspects which are interdependent, inter-supporting and inter-consuming in harmony. Disharmony would result in disease. Both of them are always in dynamic balance in which one waxes while the other wanes. Even under normal conditions though, Yin and Yang cannot be in absolute balance.

The basic Yin and Yang substances of the body include Qi, Blood, Essence, etc. Qi could be seemed as matter on the verge of becoming energy, or energy at the point of materializing. It promotes all organic activities, thus is the source of transformation in the body. Blood in TCM is not same to "blood" in West. The major activity of Blood is to circulate continuously through the body, nourishing, maintaining, and moistening its various parts. Essence is the Substances that underlie all organic life. It is the source of organic change. It is supportive, is the basis of reproduction and development.

3.2. *The Theory of Five Phases (Wu Xing) and its Applications in Medicine*

The Five Phases theory is to classify phenomena in terms of 5 processes, represented by wood, fire, earth, metal, and water. It is a system of correspondences and patterns that subsume events and things, especially in relation to their dynamics.

Each Phase is an emblem that denotes a category of functions and qualities. Wood is associated with active functions that are growing. Fire designates functions that have reached the most active state and are about to decline or rest. Metal represents functions in declining. Water represents functions that have reached a maximal state of rest and are about to start a new cycle. Earth designates balance or neutrality and is a buffer among other Phases. In terms of Yin-Yang theory, Wood is the Yang in Yin, Fire is the Yang in Yang, Metal is the Yin in Yang, Water is the Yin in Yin and Earth is the buffer between Yin and Yang. The Five Phases can also be used to describe annual cycle in terms of biological growth. Wood corresponds to spring and is associated with birth, Fire corresponds to summer and growth, Metal corresponds to autumn and is associated with harvest, Water corresponds to winter and is associated with storage, Earth corresponds to the change from one season to the next and the activity of transformation.

The Five Phases generate sequences and movement, as well as qualities which are important in TCM. These correlations (solid lines in Fig.3a), are known as the Mutual Production order. They represent the way in which the Five Phases interact and arise out of one another. Production implies that one activity can promote or bring forth another. Another sequence is known as the Mutual Checking or Mutual Control order. In this sequence, each phase is to control or restrict the corresponding Phase (broken lines in

Fig.3a). Production and Control have inseparable correlations in the Five Phases. They oppose each other and yet also complement each other. Production leads to growth and development while Control balance and coordination during development and change. However, once any one of the Five Phases becomes excessive or insufficient, there would appear abnormal counter-control known as insult and humiliation. By insult is meant that one of the Five Phases over-controls upon another one when the latter is weak. Humiliation means that the strong bullies the weak. It is also a morbid condition in which one phase fails to control the other in the regular order, but in reverse order. It is clear that the order of humiliation is just the opposite to that of insult.

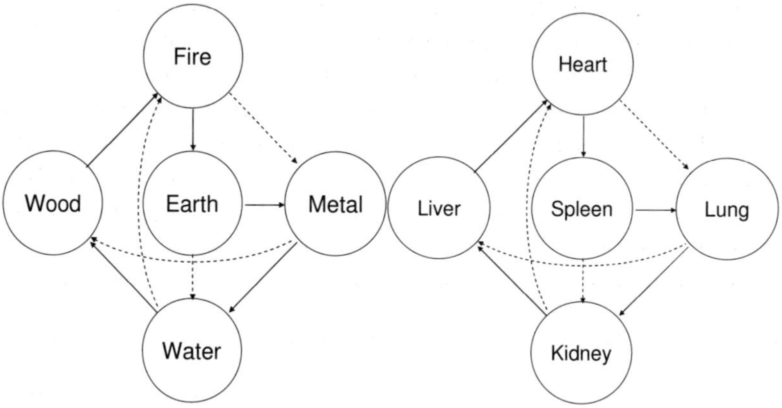

Fig. 3a. Inter-dynamics of Five Phases Fig. 3b. Inter-dynamics of Five Yin Organs

In TCM, the Five Phases Theory is used to explain different kinds of medical problems by analogizing and deducing their properties and interrelations. In the sense that the Phases correlate observable phenomena of human life into images derived from macrocosm, they serve a similar function as that of elements in other medical systems. TCM recognizes five Yin Organs (*wu-zang*) and six Yang Organs (*liu-fu*), all are defined by function but remote to the anatomic reality. The Yin Organs are Liver, Heart, Spleen, Lungs and Kidneys, by sequence which corresponds to Wood, Fire, Earth, Metal and Water in the Five Phases (Fig 3b). Because the Yin Organs are generally more important in medical theory and practice, thus we only give further illuminations to them.

-Liver rules flowing and spreading. Liver or Liver Qi moves the Qi and Blood in all directions, sending them to every part of the body.

-Heart dominate Blood and Vessels. It propels and regulates the circulation of Blood. Under the impulse of Heart-Qi, Blood is transported to all parts of the body.

-Spleen rules the transformation and transportation. It is the primary organ of digestion and is the crucial link in the process by which food is transformed into Qi and Blood, thus it is viewed as the source for the production and transformation of Qi and Blood. Aside from this, Spleen governs Blood. It keeps Blood flowing in its proper paths.

-Lungs dominate Qi and respiration. They are the place of exchange between the gases inside and outside the body. They regulate Water channels, govern dispersing and descending, and communicate with numerous vessels to coordinate functional activities of the whole body, assisting Heart to adjust normal circulation of Qi and blood.

-Kidneys store the Essence and are seemed as the "foundation of prenatal life". They are the foundation of the entire process of Water movement and transformation, they rule Water through their Yang aspect.

The Mutual Production order of the Five Phases in five Yin Organs describe normal generative functions, that is the different phases of Qi's movement, i.e. birth, growth, transformation, harvest and storage. The producer here is called Mother and the produced, Child. Some patterns of disharmony can be explained by reference to the Mutual Production order, especially patterns of Deficiency. And a disharmony within the Control order might mean that an Organ controls excessively over the Organ it regulates (insult), then it would lead to a Deficiency in the regulated Organ. Or the Organ that should be regulated may become the regulator, such conditions usually happen when the former regulator is deficient (humiliation), while the regulated one excites excessively.

3.3. *Meridian in Traditional Chinese Medicine*

Meridian comprises an invisible network that links together all the Substances and Organs. These networks are unseen but important: the Substances Qi and Blood move along them, carrying nourishment and strength. Because Meridian makes all tissues and organs in the body an organic whole, it is essential for maintenance of harmonious balance. Furthermore, the Meridian connects the interior of the body with the exterior. Thus we can say the Meridian is the interface of human body which is a dissipative structure. Meridian theory assumes that disorder within a Meridian generates derangement in the pathway and creates disharmony along the Meridian, or that such derangement is a result of a disharmony of the Meridian's connecting Organs.

In TCM, the human body is in dynamic balance of Yin and Yang in both the whole system and its function-defined sub-systems. All sub-systems, especially the Five Yin Organs interact with each others through Meridian to seek a relative balance among different functions at the system level. Health is the result of harmony between Yin and Yang and among different functional sub-systems. Thus, there exists an ideal model of human body which is in the dynamic harmony in TCM. All diseases are resulted in the deviation from the ideal model. Slight deviation could be self-adjusted by internal systemic dynamics, while serious ones need therapy as an intervention.

4. A Metaphorical Model of SI Based on Traditional Chinese Medicine

This section tries to build a ideal model of SI derived from TCM. Because the archetype is used to describe the ideal state of human body as a CAS, the ideal model of SI also describes a self-organized process of innovation in nation, region or sector. The metaphorical model following will take TCM as an archetype and a reference in methodology. But does not have to correspond to the archetype strictly. It is necessary to declare that the main purpose of this paper is to introduce the fundamental methodology in TCM which is in a systematic manner into the SI research. So this paper only gives a conceptual framework and some tentative explanation of system dynamics in SI which are analyzed qualitatively without any numeric experiment or simulation.

4.1. *Description of Basic Static Features of Sub-systems*

It is important to make proper metaphors of Yin and Yang in SI. Because Yin is usually associated with functions that tend to form concrete bodies, we can link it with finance-related functions in SI that usually resulted in the formation of capital goods. Another support to this metaphor is that the Essence stored in Kidneys is considered as money that can finance any Organs to function normally. Yang is typically related with stimulation, radiation and increase. In knowledge economy, the most critical engine of economic growth and commercial success is knowledge. Thus it is reasonable to link Yang with the movement of knowledge. There needs a network to link all functional modules together like Meridian in human body so that different functions could interact with each other. Here we call it the Supporting Networks of Innovation.

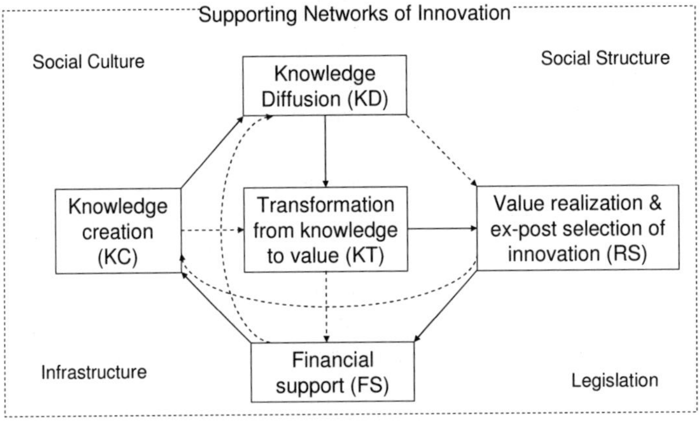

Fig. 4. Metaphorical model of System of Innovation

Based on the definitions of Yin and Yang in SI, the metaphorical model corresponding to the Five Phase theory has five sub-systems defined by functions linked by the supporting networks. Functions are assorted into knowledge creation, knowledge diffusion, transformation from knowledge to value, value realization and ex-post selection of innovation and financial support. They correspond to Liver (Wood/birth), Heart (Fire/growth), Spleen (Earth/transformation), Lungs (Metal/harvest) and Kidneys (Water/storage) respectively. It has to note that the sequence is just a logical path to describe innovation, but not innovation process in reality. Supporting networks of innovation comprise social culture, social structure, infrastructure and legislation (Fig. 4). Although the model is not suitable to enterprises, some micro-dynamics will be discussed in view of their importance as micro-foundation in the holistic mechanism.

- Knowledge creation (KC). R&D has an increasing importance today among the various ways to create knowledge. It is the main part in KC dynamics. R&D also relates to knowledge assimilation, which is significant for followers to create knowledge. Knowledge base embodied on capital goods and talents is necessary for and restricts knowledge creation. Comparatively, the input of knowledge base is the Yin aspect in KC, while the emergence of new knowledge is the Yang one. The Yin aspect links KC with FS, that is to say capital support will come true when the capitalists believe the knowledge base may be enough to innovate. At the micro-level, new knowledge concludes tacit knowledge which is personal techniques derived from recursive practices (Ziman, 2000). At the macro-level, knowledge is mostly created by public research institutions and enterprises. The most important issue here is to keep the balance between public knowledge and private ones (Nelson, 1988).

- Knowledge diffusion (KD). Education and training, personal transfer among universities and industries, information exchange through social networks, licenses of patents under IPR protect and other non-market approaches, e.g. imitation, are the main approaches to diffuse knowledge at macro-level (Freeman, 1987; Morone and Taylor, 2004). Those approaches constitute a knowledge diffusion network. The nucleus of KD is to govern and utilize this network suitably, just as the Heart rules Blood and the Vessels. "To govern" may be the Yin aspect of KD, while "to utilize" the Yang one. The paths of diffusion are context-specific. The structure of interaction is determined by the relation between knowledge suppliers and users, which is affected by the supporting network, including IPR legislation and technological infrastructure. Efficiency of KD is influenced by various factors, from spontaneous reform on routines to legislation, the former of which may be initiated by competition. Knowledge itself would make no sense for innovation until it transforms into product what is valuable for the customers.

- Transformation from knowledge to value (KT). Enterprises are the main actors to transform knowledge into value. They "digest" resources obtained outside of the SI under the help of knowledge and capital in SI, transform them into a new kind of knowledge carrier. Knowledge embodied in processes and routines are the most important determinant in this period. There are two aspects of this kind of knowledge: to govern or to integrate all resources into the transformation process and to create something valuable. Efficient routines in knowledge transformation improve productivity. KT is greatly related to entrepreneurial activities. Entrepreneurs organize resources and find a solution to satisfy customers' needs. The solution is an integration of capital goods and knowledge. The accesses to resources, such as market information, customers and skilled workers decide the specific model of entrepreneurial activities. Transaction structure that associated with the supporting networks determines business model. Entrepreneurship and competition are the most important dynamics in this module.

- Value realization and ex-post selection of innovation (RS). Entrepreneurs realize the value of their solutions in market. Market is a vital mechanism of ex-post selection of innovations (Ziman, 2000). When innovation realizes its value, it would be imitated by competitors, thus effective competition in SI assists KD module to adjust knowledge circulation. Access to market is determined by the bargain among innovators, competitors, users and dealers, which is affected by the supporting network. Integration of useful solution and proper access leads profit and competitive advantage.

- Financial support to other parts of the SI (FS). Investment is indispensable in every function module in SI. This sub-system are the foundation upon which the entire process of capital movement in SI. Knowledge to govern the portfolio of innovation investments is one of the most important knowledge in SI. So, this sub-system also promotes the KT sub-system to transform knowledge to value. Comparatively, to get more capital to finance innovation is another aspect of this module. Access and amount of financial support to innovation determine innovation behavior of the system as a whole.

4.2. *System Dynamics: Sub-dynamics and Inter-functional Dynamics*

System dynamics in the metaphorical model of SI include both micro-level and macro-level. Sub-dynamics enable modules to generate and reinforce itself to be competent to internal coordination and outside competition. They are the foundation of SI, while the inter-functional dynamics link the system as a whole. It should be noted that this list of functions and tentative explanations on system mechanism in SI require further revisions as and when research on SI dynamics provides new insights.

4.2.1. *Sub-dynamics in sub-systems*

Just as the whole system is in a harmonious matching process, every part of the system dynamics should be in an evolutionary balance. Thus it is significant to describe these micro-dynamics of the system clearly and roundly.

The most important issue to incent KC module is to keep the balance between the creation of public and private knowledge. Government has to keep a suitable scale of public knowledge creators for two purposes. On one hand, to continuously supply public knowledge which market is failed to incent private ones to do; on the other hand, to prevent private ones from depending on public supply of competitive knowledge.

Knowledge diffuses through market and non-market approaches. It also changes the balance between public and private knowledge bases. A proper legitimation on IPR protection could incent the innovators to create more knowledge and facilitate knowledge diffusion. Orientation of education also affects knowledge diffusion. Continual reforms on education system are key constituents of sub-dynamics in KD module.

To keep a sustainable transforming capability of SI, it is remarkable to cultivate an entrepreneur-friendly environment. Emerging enterprises are less inertial to keep old routines which are based on outdated knowledge, thus the main drivers for the emergence of new routines and models in transformation. The successful ones introduce new routines into the whole economy. Thus, to keep multiple springs of competing transforming routines by encouraging entrepreneurship is in the core of the KT module.

Competition is a crucial part of evolutionary dynamics in the RS module, but not the only driver of this sub-system. In an effective market, interactions between producers and users are co-evolutionary process. The co-evolution results in mutual enlightenments about customers' needs, by which transformation is oriented. Customers' cognition about their needs is sometimes the outcome of a recursive explanatory process, which adjusts the ex-post selection and is determinant to the uncertainty in innovation.

Commitment is determined by strategic intent and resources. Contradictions between financial needs and existing resources cause the introduction of external resources and the knowledge about efficiency of innovation investment. The former leads to strategic alliances and utilization of capital market. Permanent improvement on the latter causes dynamic optimization of innovation investment portfolio and capital sources portfolio.

4.2.2. *Inter-functional dynamics in ideal state*

Harmony emerges when competent sub-systems match with each other closely by interactions. Tentative clarifications of harmonious Mutual Control Cycle in the metaphoric model are given as following.

KC controlling KT: Application of new knowledge in transformation could prevent KT from rigidity which is the byproduct of increasing returns of knowledge bases.

KD controlling RS: diffusion of knowledge erodes the appropriablity of innovators.' Thus, followers' imitations incent innovation by less lucre and more furious competition.

KT controlling FS: competent routines in transformation utilize resources properly, and have decisive effect to prevent excessive thirst in investment and overflow of capital.

RS controlling KC: enterprises try their best to exploit the potential of existing knowledge bases. Market propels knowledge in the orientation decided by customers' need to restrain the Yang aspect of KC from ascending excessively.

FS controlling KD: the development of FS sub-system is part of the solution to excessive imitation by those SMEs who are short of capital to innovate indigenously.

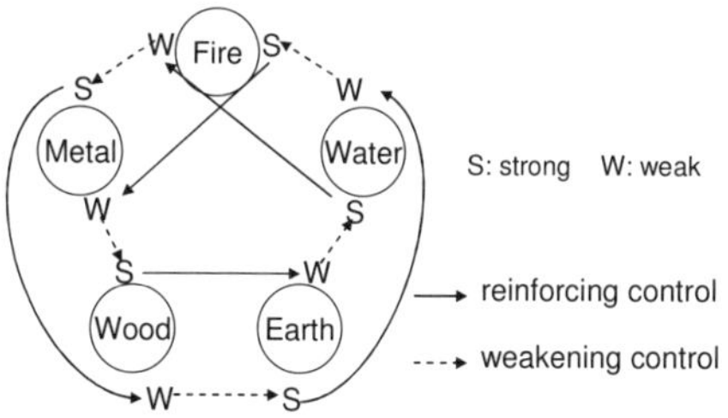

Fig. 5. Sequence of self-coordination by mutual control in Five Phases system

Any problem will lead to disharmony. If changes are moderate, SI can adjust by self-coordination. Otherwise, it could not be adjusted spontaneously and result in disharmonies. Fig.5 is the general sequence of self-coordination by mutual control.

4.2.3. *Inter-functional dynamics in disharmonious systems*

Harmony would be destroyed when balances among functional modules are broken or the supporting networks are not expedite. Concretely as following: ① KC not producing KD: supporting networks are insufficient to deliver knowledge to the diffusion network. ②Fire not producing Earth: 1) KD diffuse improper knowledge to KT, e.g. students could not learn the knowledge they will need in their occupation; and 2) the FS Yang could not help KT utilizes investment appropriately, which causes waste even disorder in KT. ③KT not producing RS: access for innovation to market would be severed for many reasons. In developing countries, a large broker and symptom of "foreign is better"(FIB) may be blocks for entrepreneurs. ④RS not producing FS: producers not entrepreneurs invest their profit to innovation-unrelated realms. ⑤FS not producing KC: once both capital and knowledge base are insufficient, it is difficult to create knowledge especially in those emerging areas which have a high threshold in scientific infrastructure. Above five items are the disharmonies in Mutual Producing Cycle. There also exist disharmonies in Mutual Controlling Cycle, while we do not discuss these here because of length limitation.

Obviously, disharmonies here are similar to "system failure" in evolutionary economics. It is necessary to clarify that situations described above are just basic forms of disharmonies of the system. Realities of deviated SI are usually a certain combination of basic forms. Thus some more analyses are needed to develop proper innovation policy.

5. Policy Implications of Metaphorical Model: Some Issues about China's NIS

Because the introduction of methodology in TCM which originated more than two thousand years ago to research CAS of human body, the metaphorical model may seem to be complex and remote to common SI research. Thus, it is useful to discuss its policy implications. Some issues analyzed following are related to the situation of NIS in China.

(1) Is the idea of general model inconsistent with the common sense in SI research? Traditional SI research emphasize the path-dependence, thus it seems popular that there is no ideal model in SI. This argument can be discussed from two perspectives. On one hand, harmony is realized through dynamic balances between knowledge and capital, and among sub-systems what are linked by supporting networks. So the structure of SI is changing all the time motivated by internal self-adjustment. Thus the ideal model corresponds to a set of states but not an isolated point. That means the model is so robust that it has many specific forms in reality which are highly related to environment and initial conditions. On the other hand, those failed systems which could not incent innovations properly are deviated from the ideal model. Any deviation is determined by path-dependence, thus deviation is highly specific bases on history. Remedies to the deviations should be corresponding to the heterogeneous disharmonies. So there could exist a framework of anticipatory institutional changes (AIC, Galli and Teubal, 1997) in the transition of SIs, but this framework should not be a simple graft of "best practices," reversely a treatment derived from specific deviation.

(2) A holistic and generative view on policy-making is very important to SIs in transition. The ideal model surveys SI in a holistic to reflect the systemic nature of innovation. It tells the policy makers that a proper AIC should take all aspects into consideration. Innovation policies in developing countries like China are usually

developed without anticipatory design on system level. For example, one defect in the evolution of China's SI is the separate reform courses on enterprises and S&T system since 1980s. No coordination exists between these two reforms, so both the reform on S&T system and the reform on enterprises always get half the result with twice the effort (Lu, 2006). Furthermore, the ideal model holds a generative perspective on SI. System dynamics determine the transferring order and corresponding results of deviation among sub-systems. It implies that sequence of policy implementation is so important that it shapes new path-dependence of system in future. Once there is some disarrangement in policy sequence, the efficiency of system transition would be debased and paths of transition in next phase would be altered. In the reform of S&T system in China in 1990s, lots of public research institutes were reformed into S&T enterprises. This changed the transaction structure between knowledge suppliers and users. While most of the enterprises which have limited absorptive capabilities and inefficient competition, have not realized the significance of knowledge and innovation. Furthermore, the old institutional junctions of both sides are destroyed with the repeal of industrial ministries in earlier time. Thus, this reform was not effective as expected.

(3) Multi-causation or one-to-one relationship? Dynamics in the CAS deny the one-to-one relations between phenomena and essence. There exist multiple causations in SI. Therefore, policy makers have to make sure the essence of disharmonies in SI. A false judgment may leads to inefficient, even opposite outcome. For example, Chinese government is glad to see the surge of R&D expenditure in enterprises. But there are several possibilities for a surge in enterprises R&D. It can be resulted in the shortage of knowledge on governing innovation investment portfolio (Deficiency in FS Yang). It also can be derived from the incompetence of enterprises to integrate resources in the process of transformation (KT is humiliated by FS.). It is also related to the lack of knowledge bases (to prevent FS not producing KC) and inadequacy in education to play its role in KD module (FS insults KD). Thus, a proper investment arrangement on R&D should be shaped based on a clear understanding of multiple causations in the whole system.

6. Conclusion

The paper has carried out an experiment to build an ideal model of systems of innovation based on a selection of basic approach in the research of SI and the help of the basic thought of TCM. Although some concrete explanations to system dynamics are still not supported by existing research, such as the situation of FS humiliated by KD, this paper analyzes SI with some unique methodologies. The main conclusions of this paper on the methodology in SI research can be summarized as follow:

(1) Compared to the actor-defined approach, FDA may be more helpful to future research in SI in a systemic manner. This is decided by the inconsistency between the systemic nature of innovation and the component-based reductionism.

(2) As a CAS, dynamic mechanism in SI should be analyzed from both the micro and macro levels. This is the most crucial suggestion from TCM. In FDA model, evolution of SI is seemed as the synthetic outcome of both sub-dynamics and inter-module dynamics.

(3) Innovation policies intervened to the CAS have to be developed on the basis of a thorough consideration. Therefore, a holistic and generative policy framework should be formed in view of systemic heterogeneity and multi-causations among sub-systems.

References

Bergek, A., Jacobsson, S., Carlsson, B., Lindmark, S., and Rickne, A. (2008), "Analyzing the functional dynamics of technological innovation systems: A scheme of analysis", *Research Policy* 37:407–429.

Breschi, S., and Malerba, F. (1997), *Sectoral innovation systems: technological regimes, Schumpeterian dynamics, and spatial boundaries*, in Edquist 1997a: 130-156;

Carlsson, B., and Stankiewitz, R. (1995), *On the nature, function and composition of technological systems*, in Calsson 1995: 21-56.

Cooke, P., Gomez, M.U. and Etxebarria, G. (1997), "Regional innovation systems: Institutional and organisational dimensions", *Research Policy* 26(4/5): 475-491.

Dosi, G., Freeman,C., Nelson, R. G. and Silverberg, L. S. (1988), *Technical change and economic theory*, London: Pinter.

Edquist, C. (1997a), *System of innovation: technologies, institutions and organizations*, London: Printer.

Edquist, C. (1997b), *System of innovation approaches-their emergence and characteristics*, in Edquist 1997a: 1-35.

Edquist, C. (2005), *System of innovation: perspectives and challenges*, in Fagerberg et al. 2005: 181-208.

Eisenhardt, K. M. and Martin, J. (2000), "Dynamic Capabilities: what are they", *Strategic Management Journal* 21(Special issue):1105-1121.

Fagerberg, J., Mowery, D. C., Nelson, R. (2005), *The Oxford handbook of innovation*, Oxford: OUP.

Freeman, Christopher (1987), *Technology, institution and economic performance: lessons from Japan*, London: Pinter.

Galli, R. and Teubal, M.(1997), *Paradigmatic Shifts in National Innovation Systems*, in Edquist 1997a: 342-70.

Hekkert, M.P., Suurs, R.A.A., Negro, S.O., Kuhlmann, S. and Smits, R.E.H.M. (2007), "Functions of innovation systems: A new approach for analyzing technological change", *Technological Forecasting & Social Change* 74:413–32.

Jacobsson, S., and Bergek, A. (2004), "Transforming the energy sector: the evolution of technological systems in renewable energy technology". *Industrial and Corporate Change* 13: 815–849.

Johnson, A. (2001), *Functions in innovation system approaches*, DRUID's Nelson-Winter Conference, Aalborg, Denmark.

Kaptchuk, T. J. (2000), *The web that has no weaver: understanding Chinese medicine*, New York: McGraw-Hill.

Liu, X. and White, S. (2001),"Comparing innovation systems: a framework and application to China's transitional context", *Research Policy*30(7):1091–1114.

Lu, Feng (2006), *The paths to indigenous innovation*, Guilin: Guangxi Normal University Press.

Lundvall, B. A. (1992), *National systems of innovation: towards a theory of innovation and interactive learning*, London: Pinter.

Morone1, P. and Taylor, R. (2004), "Knowledge diffusion dynamics and network properties of face-to-face interactions", *J Evol Econ* 14:327-351.

Needham, Joseph, Lu, Gwei-djen and Sivin, N. (2000), *Science and civilization in China*, Volume VI, Part VI :Medicine, CUP.

Nelson, R.(1988), "Institutions supporting technical change in the United States", in Dosi, G. et al. (1988):.

Nelson, R.(1993),*National innovation systems: a comparative analysis*, New York: OUP.

OECD (1997). *National innovation systems* [EB/OL]. www.oecd.org.

Sorenson, O. and Stuart, T. E. (2001), "Syndication networks and the spatial distribution of venture capital investments", *American Journal of Sociology* 106 (6): 1546-1588.

Suurs, R. A. A., Marko P. Hekkert (2009), "Cumulative causation in the formation of a technological innovation system: The case of biofuels in the Netherlands", *Technological Forecasting & Social Change*: 2-38.

Todtling, F., and Trippl, M. (2005), "One size fits all? Towards a differentiated regional innovation policy approach", *Research Policy* 34:1203–1219.

Ziman, J. (2000), Technological innovation as an evolutionary process, New York: CUP.

COLLABORATIVE WRITING WITH A WIKI IN A PRIMARY FIVE ENGLISH CLASSROOM

MATSUKO WOO, SAMUEL CHU, ANDREW HO and XUANXI LI
Faculty of Education, The University of Hong Kong
E-mail: matmuku@hku.hk, SAMCHU@HKU.HK, a_ho_1@yahoo.com, xuanxi6@hku.hk

Many studies have been conducted on the application of Web 2.0 technologies (e.g., wikis) in an educational environment including: exploring the potential of their use, the effects they have on student learning and their effectiveness when combined with appropriate instructional practices. However, whether or not these findings at the tertiary and high school levels are applicable to young learners at the primary level, have yet to be determined. Through case study design, this small-scale study explored the challenges and potential benefits that a wiki may bring to students and teachers in a Primary five English class. The study examined the wiki's key affordances for collaboration that may have an impact on students' writing abilities, through the analysis of collaborative writing projects. To understand human activity in a complex classroom environment, Activity Theory was used as an analytical lens to help examine students' learning processes and outcomes. The study found that the use of a wiki in a class of primary five students in a Hong Kong Chinese primary school was perceived positively. Students enjoyed using the wiki, and the overall perception was that it helped foster teamwork and improved writing. The tracking functionality of the wiki gave in-depth information about the types of edits the students were making and helped the teachers to assess students' collaboration and development. Findings from this study may help provide practical recommendations for primary school English language teachers and help illustrate the potential that Web 2.0, specifically wikis, can bring to influence young language learners.

1. Introduction

The current educational setting emphasizes the integration of Web 2.0 technology in language teaching and learning (Education Bureau, 2007; Richardson, 2009) and teachers in this current technology-driven climate are being pressured to integrate technology into their teaching. This study aims to address research problems at both a theoretical and a practical level. At the practical level, how can we integrate Web 2.0 technology, (e.g., wikis) into daily English language writing lessons with primary school students? What are the benefits and potential of this technology for teachers and students in Hong Kong where English is taught as a second language (L2)? Does wiki technology enhance students' writing and in what way? How can we harness the power of collaborative technology into an effective teaching tool?

At the theoretical level, many studies have started to appear on the application of Web 2.0 in education involving collaborative tools called wikis. These studies focus on the application of wikis and explore their usage potential, the effects they have on student learning, and their effectiveness when used with appropriate instructional practices. They occur across different subject disciplines, including English language, geography, engineering, and library and information science, at both the tertiary and the secondary level (Chu, 2008; Engstrom & Jewett, 2005; Mak & Coniam, 2008; Nicol, Littlejohn, & Grierson, 2005). However, whether or not these findings are applicable to young learners at the primary school level and whether they are transferable to L2 learning for young learners needs further investigation. Wiki's tracking system provides teachers with information on how students collaborate within their group, which is difficult to assess in a traditional classroom environment. Peer feedback has been found to help improve L2 students' writing (Yang, Badger, & Yu, 2006). Providing a genuine audience enhances learner motivation, which helps L2 students become more engaged writers (Lo & Hyland, 2007). If implemented properly, these are some of the factors that a wiki technology may help enhance through a platform of sharing, peer commenting, and co-constructing (Richardson, 2009).

This study intends to investigate the relatively less visited area of primary schools to examine whether or not the findings of other researchers are applicable to young learners of English as a second language. The study used a case study approach to explore the challenges and potential benefits that a wiki may bring to students and their teacher in a local Hong Kong upper primary English language class. Through collaborative writing, the study examined how a wiki's collaborative affordances may have an impact on students' writing outcomes. The findings may illuminate the potential that Web 2.0, specifically wikis, can bring to influence young learners, and help provide practical recommendations for primary school English language teachers.

2. Literature Review

Literature on collaborative learning in second language (L2) acquisition strongly supports the importance of social interaction and collaboration in L2 learning (Saville-Troike, 2006) and writing (Hyland, 2003). Most of the literature views technology supported collaborative learning using computer-mediated communication in L2 learning in a positive light (Jones, Garralda, Li, & Lock, 2006). New technologies have had a tremendous impact on the teaching and learning of writing in the last few decades (Goldberg, Russell, & Cook, 2003; Hyland, 2003), and there are both advantages and disadvantages for L2 writing. Although, some researchers have been critical of computer aided/assisted instruction in language learning (Angrist & Lavy, 2002; Hyland, 2003), generally, the literature seems to point to web-based collaborative learning as potentially promising technology in L2 learning as well as L2 writing (Goodwin-Jones, 2003).

Many studies have shown that: (a) the easy accessibility, simplicity, openness and transparency of wiki pages helps learners share information and resources across the groups and among their group members, and makes it easier for students to work at their own pace (Nicol, et al., 2005); (b) students have positive perceptions about how wikis can improve collaborative group work and the quality of their work (Chu, 2008); (c) the effectiveness of wiki application in learning and teaching depends on careful planning and training of both students and instructors to familiarize them with the technology, on class size, and on motivating students to learn from one another based on discovery or project learning principles (Engstrom & Jewett, 2005; Raman, Ryan, & Olfman, 2005); and (d) affordances provided by a wiki and affordances required by a learning task need to match for technology implementation to be effective (Bower, 2008). Researchers (Hazari, North,

& Moreland, 2009) found that university male students tend to have higher satisfaction with wiki technology than their female counterparts. However, whether or not gender plays any role with young L2 writers using a wiki technology is yet to be examined.

Wikis have been used across different subject disciplines, as mentioned in the Introduction at both the tertiary and the secondary level, but a research gap exists in that it is not clear whether or not these findings can be applied to young learners at the primary level and are transferable to L2 learning for young learners.

3. Conceptual Framework

The literature in the three broad areas of: (1) collaborative and cooperative learning, (2) L2 learning and writing, and (3) computer-supported collaborative learning (CSCL) and online collaboration seems to indicate that the common prevailing learning theories in these paradigms tend to be mainly from constructivism (Parker & & Chao, 2007) and from a socio-cultural perspective (Hyland, 2003; Lantolf, 2000). Specific learning theories developed from them include: knowledge creation (Lipponen, Hakkarainen, & Paavola, 2004), knowledge building (Scardamalia & Bereiter, 2006), the process-oriented method (Strijbos, Martens, & Jochems, 2004), and expansive learning based on activity theory (Engestrom, 2001). One of the underlying theories in L2 writing is from a socio-cultural perspective (Hyland, 2003), which is also prevalent in CSCL and online collaboration (Crook, 1994). The literature also shows that activity theory with its socio-cultural perspective seems to be applicable to all these paradigms on which this study is based: collaborative learning, L2 writing, and CSCL with online collaboration.

As a result, a theoretical framework of the activity system was chosen for this case study to help interpret how a tool, a wiki technology, mediated students' activity in a collaborative environment, where the objective of the task was to create a piece of writing, with the ultimate goal being to improve students' writing abilities and the whole learning outcome. Activity theory, which has its roots in the works of Vygotsky and his protégée Leont'ev (1978), consists of three components: *mediating artifacts or tools* (e.g., instruments, signs, procedures, machines, and methods), the *subject* of the activity (e.g., individuals or groups), and the *object* (e.g., the subject's purpose of the activity), which leads to the ultimate *goal or outcome* of the activity. Engestrom (1987) expanded this triadic model further into a more complex model of an activity system by adding three other dimensions: *rules* of conduct within the social context of the activity, the *community* of participants involved in the activity, and a *division of labour* that imparts roles to the participants within the social context of the activity.

4. Methodology

To explore how collaborative writing using wiki technology influences the development of students' L2 writing abilities in the complex and continuously changing dynamics of a classroom environment, a case study design was chosen using both quantitative and qualitative data. Activity theory was used as the conceptual framework.

Based on the research gap identified in the literature review, an overarching research question was proposed: How does collaborative writing involving the use of the wikis influence the development of students' writing abilities in upper primary English language classrooms? The following four sub-questions were formulated to guide in data collection: (1) What are the perceived benefits and challenges for students and teachers using wikis in a collaborative writing environment? (2) What are the key affordances in the use of wikis that encourage and support students in collaborating actively in the co-construction of their writing assignments? (3) How might the learning outcome of students' writing using wikis differ from that of the normal collaborative writing without wikis? (4) Does gender influence the student learning outcomes when using a wiki technology?

4.1. *Participants and Intervention Programme*

A class of 38 primary five students and their English subject teacher were selected for this case study by the purposeful sampling method. The school was selected from Chinese primary schools of mid to high level in terms of students' ability to write in the English language. This was to ensure that the primary five students of ages 10 to 11 years were able to write a minimum of 100 words in English so that a sufficient quantity of writing could be produced to examine the effect of the collaboration using the technology.

The students and their teachers participated in an intervention programme for approximately six weeks, only during their English writing lessons. The intervention programme was based on the integration of a wiki in their existing English language curriculum (HKCECES, 2008) in collaborative writing within project-based learning. The teacher chose for its user friendliness, one of the wiki tools available from various vendors called PBwiki at the time, but now renamed PBworks. During the project, students were asked to co-construct their writing on PBworks pages created for each group, and exchange their comments through its platform. The students worked collaboratively in mixed ability and gender groups of four to six to produce a general description on a topic of their choice from different animals. The lessons were planned for both face-to-face learning situations in the classroom or the computer laboratory, and online learning outside their normal classroom. The writing process lessons were planned collaboratively with the teacher and the researcher during the study to ensure the wiki technology implementation. Although the study focused on just one classroom, for ethical reasons, the intervention programme was offered to other classes and their English teachers on a voluntary base.

4.2. *Data Collection and Analysis*

The data was collected and examined through a triangulation method using multiple sources of evidence, such as student and teacher questionnaires given after the intervention programme, a semi-structured interview with the teacher, focus group discussions with selected students, and editing information recorded in the wiki system.

The teacher questionnaire consisted of open-ended questions, while the student questionnaire consisted of both open-ended and closed-ended questions. Responses to the closed-ended questions were given according to a five point Likert scale to examine the participants' perceptions, the wiki's collaborative affordances, and the learning outcomes. The interview and group discussions were conducted after the questionnaires to clarify the respondents' answers, or to probe further to understand better the learning phenomenon.

Editing information generated by different groups was collected automatically online through the wiki system, and analyzed and sorted by type of revision or contribution. The types of revision were categorized using an adapted version of Mak and Coniam's (2008) four identifiers. The four identifiers from their study with secondary students were: (1) adding ideas, (2) expanding ideas, (3) reorganizing ideas, and (4) correcting errors (e.g., grammar, spelling and punctuation). Group writings were analyzed using a score sheet adapted from Lo and Hyland's (2007) study on Hong Kong primary five students composition writing. To verify the accuracy of coding by categories and evaluation of the group writing, two raters double coded and marked independently, and discussed the results for a consensus. Tests scores from pre and post-tests and school writing exams assessing writing skills were given before and after the intervention programme to examine any significant improvement in the quality of the students' writing. Pre and post-tests were adapted from the Territory Wide System Assessment for Primary 6 English Language Reading and Writing (Education Bureau, 2008). Activity theory was used as an analytical lens to interpret the data for final analysis from a broader picture within the social cultural context of the study.

5. Findings and Discussion

5.1. *Student and Teacher Perceptions*

Data from student questionnaires indicate that students generally perceived the use of a wiki in their group writing positively, addressing the sub-research questions (1) - (3). This is supported by Chu's (2009) findings that primary four students regarded the use of information technology (IT) positively in their inquiry project-based learning. In the questionnaires, the students were asked whether they enjoyed using the wiki (Q1), whether the wiki helped them work better as a team (Q2), whether the wiki helped them write better (Q3), whether commenting on the wiki helped in improving their writing (Q6), and whether the wiki was useful for group work online (Q7). Table 1 shows the responses to these closed-ended questions, to which students indicated their responses using a five point Likert scale. All the questions had ratings over 3 from the lowest of 3.5 (Q2) to the highest of 3.8 (Q6 and Q7). One of the highest positive responses concerned how comments from peers posted on the wiki platform helped in improving the students' writing (Q6). This was also echoed in the students' answers to the open-ended questions:

"We can share our comments and teach other." (Student=S27)

"We write comments to correct our mistakes." (S15)

"Others can give comment to me and help me make it better." (S18)

"They give me some message and I feel so happy." (S24)
"When I don't know how to write, somebody can comment on your work." (S39)

Table 1. Descriptive Statistics: Students' Perception of a Wiki

Question Items	Mean /SD	Median	N	Frequency Not at all (1)	(2)	(3)	(4)	Very much so (5)
Q1: Enjoy using PBwiki	3.6(.75)	4.00	38	0	2	14	18	4
Q2: Work better as a team	3.5(.80)	3.00	38	0	4	16	15	3
Q3: Write better in groups	3.6(.88)	4.00	38	0	5	9	19	5
Q6: Commenting on PBwiki improves writing	3.8(.72)	4.00	38	0	1	10	21	6
Q7: Useful for group work on-line	3.8(.73)	4.00	37	0	1	10	20	6

Note 1: Rating based on a 5 point Likert scale from 1, 'not at all' to 5, 'very much so', where 3 is the mid-point.

The teacher's perceived benefits from the open-ended questionnaires provide some answers to the sub-research question (1): "... students will be more motivated to find the information they look for from the Internet" and "They will exchange their ideas via the platform as well as it is more efficient and convenient". Table 2 shows how actively the students exchanged their ideas on a wiki platform as observed through its tracking system. The frequency of comments during the study period ranged from a high of 28 to a low of nil. Comments varied from: (a) simple positive and negative feedback to full elaborated feedback, (b) simple suggestions of form and content in providing ideas, and (c) miscellaneous responses to the above (a)/(b), or commenting on issues irrelevant to the writing topic.

Table 2. Activities Recorded in Wiki's Tracking System

Group	A	B	C	D	E	F	G	H	Total
No of posted edits	14	10	10	27	13	4	1	3	82
No of posted comments	28	14	9	4	11	0	16	0	82
Total activities	42	24	19	31	24	4	17	3	164
Duration in days	28	17	35	34	23	4	8	14	
Evaluation of group writing	47	42	43	48	20	23	29	26	
Word count	207	123	325	171	562	244	593	353	

Note 1: Evaluation of writing rated by 2 markers, based on accumulative score for content, organization, language, and graphics or pictures with a maximum of 65 points.
Note 2: Word count denotes the number of words in the group writing.

Responses to open-ended questions in student questionnaire concerning problems and challenges showed some technical problems that students encountered while using a wiki during their project. For example, they cited the computer being slow, not being able to edit at the same time, having difficulty in creating pages, or taking a long time in loading information. This is not surprising when a new technology is introduced into classrooms. Other challenges were on collaborative perspectives and some may not be specific to wiki technology, but the technology afforded an environment that encouraged students to engage in collaborative behaviour as illustrated below, where, whatever challenges the students encountered, they solved their problems in their own ways:

"Someone will change our work and we talked to the teacher and the teacher to cancel this problem. Sometime the computer isn't working so we call each other." (S3)

"Our ideas may be different, but we use 投票[votes] to choose the title." (S35)

Some of the problems and challenges that the teacher reported were: (1) uneven gender distribution of this class (13 boys and 27 girls) created conflict in gender grouping; (2) job distribution among group members; (3) technical problems such as slow loading time when students were using PBworks simultaneously; (4) some students had restricted or no access to computer or Internet at home; and (5) inadequate training of skills, such as scanning and skimming, note-taking, and translation of information, all of which are necessary to handle the large amount of information from the internet to accomplish the tasks. Her solutions to these challenges were reported in the order mentioned above: (1) she created a student preference table to facilitate even gender distribution and foster better understanding of gender differences within the groups, thus enhancing effective peer learning; (2) each group chose a member in their group to write and collate information while the other members collected new information and commented on the writing; (3) students saved their findings and comments in their personal USB as a back-up, or e-mailed them to the members in charge of collating and organizing the ideas; (4) those having problems accessing computers at home were encouraged to use computers at school, in the public library, or at other members' homes; (5) skills were taught after the problem had been identified (e.g., the use of the online dictionary for translation).

Focus group discussion was conducted with eight students and their English subject teacher. Eight students were selected, as evenly as possible, to represent both genders as well as positive and negative respondents. Although the students in the focus group discussion mentioned the difficulties and challenges that they faced, overall, they were positive about their experience with the wiki technology. This is in line with the findings from the student questionnaires. Similarly, teacher's comments recorded in the open-ended questionnaire reflected what the students had reported. She felt that the students had improved their writing skills, as she commented: "Students read more and they learnt and used some new vocabulary and language forms". Other skills that she observed were, "Improvement in reading, IT, collaboration skills and subject knowledge was observed". This teacher perceived her primary five students using a wiki technology in a collaborative writing to improve in skills involving writing, reading, IT, collaboration and subject knowledge, which were also supported in the findings from a study with primary four students in Chinese writing project using IT (Chu, 2009).

5.2. *Analysis of Revisions*

Wiki's tracking system provided information that helped understand in depth what kind of editing was taking place and how that would affect student collaboration and writing skills, addressing sub-research questions (2) and (3). Table 2 shows the number of activities recorded in the tracking system varying from 1 - 27 for the number of edits posted and 0 - 28 for the comments posted during the first edits on Jan 22nd to the last edits on March 14th, 2009. Most groups from A - E were actively involved in either editing or commenting as seen from the table of recorded activities in wiki's tracking system. Some groups posted more comments than editing to accomplish their group writing, while others frequently edited through the platform rather than commenting, as in the case of group F and H, which had no comments recorded. Group G actively contributed to the group writing through comments, but constructed their group writing on Microsoft word before pasting onto a wiki, thus showing a low frequency count on the editing record. The active groups spent more days working on their group work as seen from the number of days counted from the first edits to the last edits. Those groups that spent more days on their work tended to have higher evaluation on their written work based on a scoring method adapted from Lo and Hyland (2008).

A detailed analysis of the edits shows that most concern content, such as the adding; reorganizing; replacing; and elaborating of ideas, rather than form, such as syntax; spelling; punctuation; and formatting. Table 3 shows the types of editing done by eight different groups as recorded in wiki's tracking system, categorized according to Mak and Coniam's (2008) adapted version of identifiers. The fact that there were more edits on the content of ideas may be due to the spell checks that are built into PBworks system and the access to the internet. The spell checks helped students ease their cognitive load, thus allowing them to concentrate on the content. Similarly, a host of ideas and information was made available through the internet, freeing the students to focus on analyzing and evaluating the content and extract the main points for their own writing. Other reasons might be that the students tended to feel at ease communicating through their familiar domain of technology, as was found in a study with peer tutoring for L2 writers using ICQ (Jones, et al., 2006). The local study found that online interaction tended to produce more discussions concerning content and process, while face-to-face peer tutoring focused on forms such as syntax, vocabulary, and style. Although the study was conducted with university students, the results may be applicable to primary students who are familiar with MSN technology. As one student wrote on an open-ended questionnaire: "We can use the Wiki like an MSN to talk"(S14). Another reason might be that students are more actively involved in the self-correction process when they have doubts or reservations about the feedback from their peers, while feedback from teachers is believed to be correct and will not lead to further self-initiated correction, as was reported in a study of L2 writers' peer-feedback (Yang, et al., 2006).

Since the text type for this group writing was a general description, most of the first and second edits show new ideas being added, with the new ideas not being students' original ideas, but new information from the internet. While exploring the use of the wiki platform, students frequently visited to change their spacing, fonts, and other formats for pictures as recorded under the formatting. Surprisingly, common edits concerned other content such as elaborating, reorganizing and replacing ideas. This is a good sign in encouraging good writing skills, especially in L2 writing, where many students tend to focus on form rather than content (Hyland, 2003). Those groups that edited frequently tended to revise more, as in Group D, which recorded 27 visits and had 65 revisions on their work. On the other hand, frequent visits did not mean that quality revisions were taking place, as in the case of Group B, who had 10 visits but recorded 12 content revisions. This compared to Group F, who had only 4 visits, but also had a greater number of content revisions, 16. Here, we are assuming that quality revisions mean content revisions rather than changes in forms. Table 3 shows that Groups A, B, C and D, with a higher number of revisions, tended to have better writing scores compared to the other groups, who had a lower number of revisions.

Table 3. Types pf Revision by Groups

Group	A	B	C	D	E	F	G	H	Total by Types
Content edits:									
Adding new ideas	12	10	17	21	13	6			79
Elaborating on existing ideas	2		1	6					9
Reorganizing existing ideas		2	1	3	2	4			12
Replacing existing ideas	5		3	5	3	6		6	28
Sub-total	19	12	23	35	18	16	0	6	136
Form edits:									
Grammar	1		1	4		1			7
Spelling		2		1					3
Punctuation		1		2		1			4
Formatting	14	11	10	23	7	4		1	70
Sub-total	15	14	11	30	7	6	0	1	84
Total revision by Groups	34	26	34	65	25	22	0	7	
No of posted edits	14	10	10	27	13	4	1	3	
Evaluation of group writing	47	42	43	48	20	23	29	26	

Note: Due to difficulty in deciphering individual efforts, two students without the consent forms in Group A and D were not singled out from their group work, thus N= 40.

All the groups were able to write 309.8 words on average, with the lowest word count being 123 and the highest count, 593. With these students, length was not a problem, especially when they reported that with access to the Internet, they were able to produce so much information. As stated by their teacher: "... with the use of Internet resources, students tend to write more than they used to on paper." They needed to exercise their critical thinking skills to choose the appropriate information for their writing, as one student commented, "It was too difficult to group too much information when we were doing the work. We chose the main point in each information"(S29). Another skill they needed was to paraphrase the information in their own words to avoid plagiarism, which the teacher realized as the project progressed. During the teacher interview, the teacher mentioned that she had noticed students cutting and pasting the information straight from the internet. Subsequently, the teacher gave a mini-lesson on how to paraphrase information taken from other sources in their own words and to acknowledge the source of information.

Although a wiki platform seems to provide affordances for writers to focus on content, this doesn't necessarily happen automatically, as shown by differences in the quality of revision for Groups B and F. Quality content still needs to be encouraged and enforced through teacher instruction, and some groups may need more support in content revision than others. The tracking system provides teachers with windows of information on what is happening in each group's editing process. The teacher in this study was beginning to realize the usefulness of the tracking system, as she commented: "I could easily know and check who worked and edited on their work as there were email notifications to remind me of every change my students made in their work in PBwiki", and "I usually give them general comments on their work in lesson, orally".

5.3. *Gender Differences*

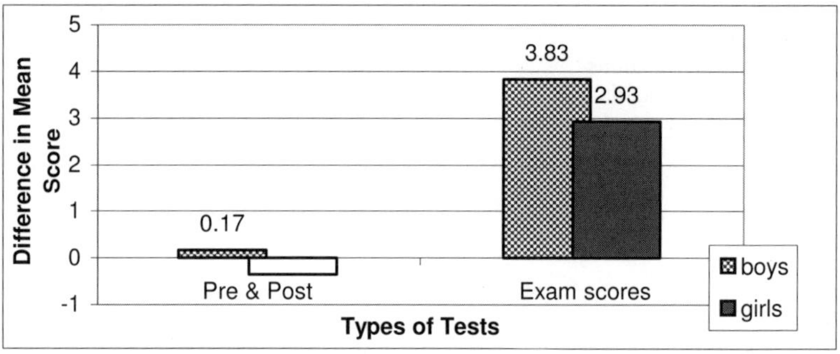

Note 1: Pre and post test scale ranging from 0 to 7 and exam score scale from 0 to 60.
Note 2: A blank bar indicates negative value of –0.35.

Fig. 1: Graph Showing Difference in Mean Score by Test Types and Gender

Fig. 1 shows both the difference of mean scores between pre and post-tests assessing the students' writing skills (boys' mean difference =0.17 and girls' mean difference =-0.35 in a scale of 0 to 7) and school writing exams given before and after a wiki intervention (boys' mean difference=3.83 and girls' mean difference=2.93 in a scale of 0 to 60). In both instances, the scores were higher for boys than for girls. However, paired t-test by statistical software SPSS showed that boy's pre and post test scores did not show any significant difference while the girls' decrease was significant with p=0.023 where p< 0.05. Similarly, paired t-test on boys' school exam scores before and after the intervention was not significant while the girls' increase was significant with p=0.002 where p< 0.05. Some girls tend to shy away from a new technology and this may hamper their writing. This came to light during the focus group discussion as a girl commented that she is not good at IT skills and thus it takes her a long time to type and that she prefers paper and pencil. This sentiment was echoed by few other girls in the group. Boys, on the other hand, have shown positive perception towards a wiki as seen from some of their written comments in student questionnaires. When asked if PBworks helped them to write better in their own writing, few boys responded: "Yes, because I love using computer to do writing" (S14), " I can be faster with internet than writing on paper" (S13). The boys' mean rating on the Likert scale, ranging from 1 to 5 described in section 5.1, was higher than the girls in all the closed-ended questions from the questionnaires, though an independent t-test for each question showed no significant difference between boys and girls. These findings are inconclusive due to the limitations of the study involving short time frame. An unbalanced gender distribution in the class, where less than one third of the class is boys (12 out of 38) may have also influenced the outcome. Whether there is any gender factor for teaching implication using a wiki may need further investigation.

5.4. *Comparison Using Activity Theory*

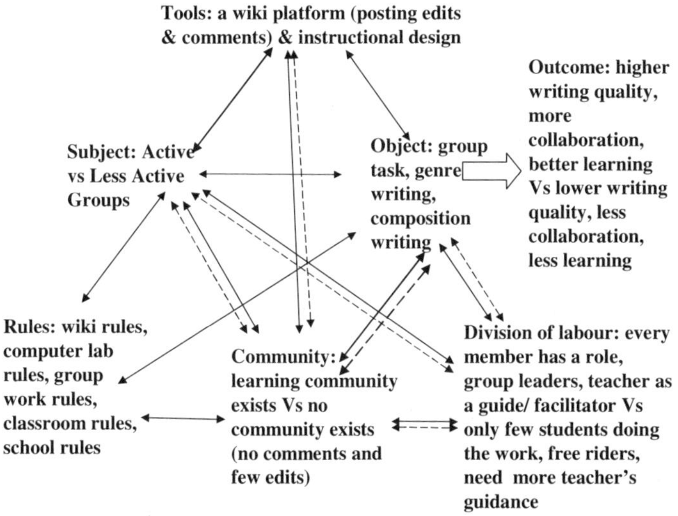

Fig. 2: Comparison of Active and Less Active Groups Based on Activity Theory (Engestrom, 1987)

From the activity theory perspective, all six elements of the activity system: tools, subject, task objective, community, division of labour and rules need to be in place for any successful learning outcomes to occur. This was seen in the active groups (Group A, B, C & D), where a wiki platform promoted collaboration through its affordances provided by posting edits and comments during the course of group writing to co-construct a general description of their own chosen topic. Rules for wikis and group work set up by the teacher for students to follow, existence of learning communities with the members willing to share and support each other, and roles that each group member are willing to take up, all facilitate the collaborative activity leading to a productive outcome. Any one of these elements may break down, such as with the less active groups (Group F & H), who posted nil comments or only few edits indicating low collaboration level. This may mean that there is no learning community among the group members, and that members are not actively carrying out their roles. A common scenario is that a few members are doing all the work, and the rest are free riders. This signals that teachers may need to provide more guidance to these groups to help create a learning community by assigning roles or encouraging sharing among the members. Once one of the six elements ceases to operate, the other elements may start to break down, creating internal contradictions or tension (Engestrom, 2001) between the elements. This chain reaction may also include the complete abandonment of the tool and the total cessation of peer-to-peer comments, as in the case of group F and H. Fig. 2 shows a detailed comparison of the active and the less active groups within their activity systems, and the dotted lines indicate the tension between the elements.

6. Conclusion and Teaching Implications

The study found that a class of primary five students in a Hong Kong Chinese primary school were positive in their perceptions of using a wiki. The students enjoyed using the wiki and commented how it helped them to work better as a team and write better, encouraged peer-to-peer interaction, and facilitated online group work. Both the students and their teacher perceived the exchange of comments through a wiki platform as beneficial to their collaboration and construction of their group writing. Among the eight groups observed in this primary five class, those active groups that spent more time working on their group work tended to produce better quality writing.

A detailed analysis of the types of revisions in the wiki's tracking system indicates that the content of ideas, for example, the adding; reorganizing; replacing; and elaborating of ideas was being revised rather than forms, such as syntax; spelling; punctuation; and formatting. This may be due not only to PBworks' affordances in providing writers with spell checks to lessen their cognitive loads, but also to the ease with which the internet allows a host of ideas and information to be made available, freeing writers to focus on analyzing and evaluating the content to extract main points for their own writing. Other reasons considered are that students feel at ease with communicating through technology, which tends to produce more content and process discussions (Jones, et al., 2006), and that peer feedback activates self-corrections (Yang, et al., 2006). Among this class of primary five students, those groups revising idea changes more than forms seemed to produce higher quality writing. Although the wiki technology affordances may provide the opportunity for writers to focus on content, it will not happen automatically, and a teacher's role becomes ever more important in directing students to the right skills. Wiki's tracking system gives in-depth information about the types of edits the students are making and helps teachers assess their collaboration and development of their group writing process, a task that maybe difficult to monitor in traditional group work. This can help teachers decide on the kind of support to be given, and provide feedback when necessary during the course of writing and not at the end when the product is finished.

The general findings from the active groups and the less active groups were compared using the theoretical framework of the activity theory. The active groups' involvement in comments and edits in the wiki's tracking system indicates that all six elements of activity systems are necessary and important for a group to collaborate actively in a writing project. On the other hand, a low frequency of comments and edits posted on the wiki platform indicates a warning signal that collaboration is not working. The activity theory points to the elements of community of learning and division of labour that may need to be re-examined. For example, teachers need to assist group members in sharing and helping each other to create a learning community, or to assign roles so that each member has a role to play. All six elements of the activity system: tools, subject, task objective, community, division of labour, and rules need to be in place for an effective implementation of a computer supported collaborative learning environment.

7. Limitations of the Study

The intervention programme in this study may not be long enough for participants to fully acquire and internalize the skills needed to produce a significant effect in the improvement of the quality of their writing. These skills include both wiki technology and information literacy skills such as information searching on the internet, scanning, skimming and critically reviewing information, and note taking skills involved in project-based learning. Since using a wiki technology was a new experience for both the teacher and the students in this study, a "Hawthorn effect" in terms of novelty may have affected their enthusiasm and overall outcomes. This was a small-scale case study involving one class with one subject teacher and the subjective perspective associated with the questionnaires cannot be generalized beyond this study. A lack of data and information on why some groups have high or low collaboration, points to the need for further research on in-depth analysis of collaborative process within the groups.

References

Angrist, J., & Lavy, V. (2002). New evidence on classroom computers and pupil learning. *Economic Journal, 112*, 735-765.

Bower, M. (2008). Affordance analysis-mathching learning tasks with learning technologies. *Educational Media International, 45*(1), 3-15.

Chu, S. K. W. (2008). TWiki for knowledge building and management. *Online Information Review, 32*(6), 745-758.

Chu, S. K. W. (2009). Inquiry project-based learning with a partnership of three types of teachers and the school librarian. *Journal of The American Society for Information Science and Technology, 60*(8), 1671-1686.

Crook, C. (1994). *Computers and the collaborative experience of learning*. London: Routledge.

Education Bureau (2007). *Consultation document on the third strategy on information technology in education: Right technology at the right time for right task.* Hong Kong: Government of HKSAR.

Education Bureau (2008). Territory-wide System Assessment 2007 (Primary Schools) Quick Guide Retrieved Feb 26, 2009, from http://www.systemassessment.edu.hk/pri/eng/index_eng.htm

Engestrom, Y. (1987). Learning by expanding. http://communication.ucsd.edu/MCA/Paper/Engestrom/expanding/toc.htm

Engestrom, Y. (2001). Expansive learning at work: Toward an activity theoretical reconceptualization. *Journal of Education and Work, 14*(1), 133-156.

Engstrom, M. E., & Jewett, D. (2005). Collaborative learning the Wiki way. *TechTrends, 49*(6), 12.

Goldberg, A., Russell, M., & Cook, A. (2003). The Effect of Computers on Student Writing: A Meta-Analysis of Studies from 1992 to 2002. *The Journal of Technology, Learning, and Assessment, 2*(1).

Goodwin-Jones, B. (2003). Blogs and wikis: Environments for on-line collaboration. *Language Learning & Technology, 7*(2), 12.

Hazari, S., North, A., & Moreland, D. (2009). Investigating Pedagogical Value of Wiki Technology. *Journal of Information Systems Education, 20*(2), 187.

HKCECES (2008). *Specific Guidelines for English Language Primary 4-5 Levels.*

Hyland, K. (2003). *Second language writing*. Cambridge: Cambridge University Press.

Jones, R. H., Garralda, A., Li, C. S. D., & Lock, G. (2006). Interactional dynamics in on-line and face-to face peer-tutoring sessions for second language writers. *Journal of Second Language Writing, 15*, 1-23.

Lantolf, J. P. (2000). Intorducing sociocultural theory. In J. P. Lantolf (Ed.), *Sociocultural theory and second language learning* (pp. 1-26). Oxford, U.K.: Oxford University Press.

Leont'ev, A. N. (1978). *Activity, consciousness, and personality*. Englewood Cliffs, N.J.: Prentice-Hall.

Lipponen, L., Hakkarainen, K., & Paavola, S. (2004). Practices and Orientations of CSCL. In J.-W. Strijbos, P. A. Kirschner & R. Martens (Eds.), *What we know about CSCL and implementing it in higher education* (pp. 31-50). Boston, Mass.: Kluwer Academic Punlishers.

Lo, J., & Hyland, F. (2007). Enhancing students' engagement and motivation in writing: The case of primary students in Hong Kong. *Journal of Second Language Writing, 16*, 219-237.

Mak, B., & Coniam, D. (2008). Using wikis to enhance and develop writing skills among secondary school students in Hong Kong. *System, 36*, 437-455.

Nicol, D., Littlejohn, A., & Grierson, H. (2005). The importance of structuring information and resources within shared workspaces during collaborative design learning. *Open Learning, 20*(1), 31-49.

Parker, K. R., & & Chao, J. T. (2007). Wiki as a teaching tool. *Interdisciplinary Journal of Knowledge and Learning Objects, 3*, 57-72.

Raman, M., Ryan, T., & Olfman, L. (2005). Designing knowledge management systems for teaching and learning with wiki technology. *Journal of Information Systems Education, 16*(3), 311-320.

Richardson, W. (2009). *Blogs, wikis, podcasts, and other powerful web tools for classrooms* (2nd ed. ed.). Thousand Oaks, Calif.: Corwin Press.

Saville-Troike, M. (2006). *Introducing second language acquisition*. Cambridge : New York: Cambridge University Press.

Scardamalia, M., & Bereiter, C. (2006). Knowledge Building: Theory, Pedagogy, and Technology. In R. K. Sawyer (Ed.), *The Cambridge handbook of the learning sciences* (pp. 97-115). New York: Cambridge University Press.

Strijbos, J. W., Martens, R. L., & Jochems, W. M. G. (2004). Designing for interaction: Six steps to designing computer-supported group-based learning. *Computers & Education, 42*(4), 403-424.

Yang, M., Badger, R., & Yu, Z. (2006). A comparative study of peer and teacher feedback in a Chinese EFL writing class. *Journal of Second Language Writing, 15*, 179-200.

CROSS-LANGUAGE KNOWLEDGE SHARING MODEL BASED ON ONTOLOGIES AND LOGICAL INFERENCE

WEISEN GUO

Science Integration Program (Human), Department of Frontier Sciences and Science Integration, Division of Project Coordination, The University of Tokyo, 5-1-5 Kashiwa-No-Ha Kashiwa-Shi, Chiba-Ken 277-8568, Japan
E-mail: gws@scint.dpc.u-tokyo.ac.jp

STEVEN B. KRAINES[†]

Science Integration Program (Human), Department of Frontier Sciences and Science Integration, Division of Project Coordination, The University of Tokyo, 5-1-5 Kashiwa-No-Ha Kashiwa-Shi, Chiba-Ken 277-8568, Japan
[†]E-mail: sk@scint.dpc.u-tokyo.ac.jp

Vast amounts of new knowledge are created on the Internet in many different languages every day. How to share and search this knowledge across different languages efficiently is a critical problem for information science and knowledge management. Conventional cross-language knowledge sharing models are based on natural language processing (NLP) technologies. However, natural language ambiguity, which is a problem even for single language NLP, is exacerbated when dealing with multiple languages. Semantic web technologies can circumvent the problem of natural language ambiguity by enabling human authors to specify meaning in a computer-interpretable form. In particular, description logics ontologies provide a way for authors to describe specific relationships between conceptual entities in a way that computers can process to infer implied meaning. This paper presents a new cross-language knowledge sharing model, SEMCL, which uses semantic web technologies to provide a potential solution to the problem of ambiguity. We first describe the methods used to support searches at the semantic predicate level in our model. Next, we describe how our model realizes a cross-language approach. We present an implementation of the model for the general engineering domain and give a scenario describing how the model implementation handles semantic cross-language knowledge sharing. We conclude with a discussion of related work.

1. Introduction

We live in an age of knowledge explosion. Knowledge sharing can significantly increase social capital (Widen-Wulff et al., 2004). But much of knowledge on the Internet is represented in diverse languages, which limits our ability to share and search knowledge globally. The traditional approach to share knowledge across diverse languages by manually translating each knowledge resource from the original language to all of the other languages is too slow and costly for tasks such as sharing scientific findings between researchers.

Automated cross-language technologies have been developed that use natural language processing (NLP) technologies to extract keywords for matching knowledge resources between different languages. However, NLP-based approaches cannot produce accurate matching results because of the ambiguity of natural language (Hunter and Cohen, 2006). Even thesauri or classification schemata are insufficient (Goldschmidt and Krishnamoorthy, 2008) because they do not support expressions of semantic relationships between keywords or named entities in text. Furthermore, the need to handle multiple languages in cross-language knowledge sharing models exacerbates the problem of natural language ambiguity. Some approaches to decrease the ambiguity have been reported in the literature. For example, Littman et al. (1998) used a latent semantic indexing technique to implement cross-language information retrieval. However, even these sophisticated NLP technologies do not address the fundamental issue of ambiguity in representing knowledge with natural language, an issue that is particularly problematic in a multilingual knowledge sharing situation.

Semantic Web technologies can be used to express knowledge in a computer-interpretable enable matching at a semantic predicate level, e.g. matching of both named entities and predicates stating the semantic relationships between them. Specifically, ontologies constructed in a language such as OWL-DL can represent domain knowledge within a description logic (DL) formalism (www.w3.org/TR/2004/REC-owl-features-20040210). Then DL-based inference can be used in knowledge search to find more useful matching results (Guo and Kraines, 2008).

We present a cross-language knowledge sharing model in this paper that is based on ontologies and logical inference. Using this model, knowledge providers can publish knowledge resources in their native languages, and knowledge seekers can search for knowledge in different languages, thereby enabling cross-language knowledge sharing. Furthermore, both the descriptors of the knowledge resources and the search queries are represented in a form that can be interpreted semantically by a computer, which enables the computer to infer embedded meaning that is implied but not explicitly expressed. Therefore, the knowledge system implementing this model returns matching results represented in diverse languages that should be more accurate than those of conventional keyword based systems because matching is done at the semantic predicate level.

The rest of the paper is organized as follows. In section 2, we review the state of the art of knowledge sharing on the Internet. In section 3, we present the cross-language knowledge sharing model and describe the cross-language method that we have developed to implement the model. We discuss the related work in Section 4 and conclude this paper in Section 5.

2. Knowledge Sharing using Information Retrieval and Semantic Web Technologies

Knowledge sharing is an activity through which knowledge is exchanged among people and/or organizations (Lin, 2007). In this paper, we focus on knowledge existing in explicit digital form on the Internet. A knowledge sharing community consists of two main types of the knowledge users: knowledge providers and knowledge seekers. Community members can be both types: each knowledge user may both provide knowledge resources and seek knowledge resources. The goal of a knowledge sharing system is to return the correct knowledge resources to the knowledge seeker. A global-scale knowledge sharing community will invariably include knowledge users from different countries speaking different languages.

Information Retrieval (IR) technologies can quickly find matching results by matching keywords provided by knowledge seekers with knowledge resources that are represented in natural language. In this approach, the matching system uses automatic techniques such as Natural Language Processing to determine which knowledge resources match the keywords based on the natural language representations of those resources. Conventional cross-language knowledge sharing models are based on these IR technologies. However, the problems of natural language ambiguity and grammatical complexity, which already make it difficult to determine matches with free-text in a single language, become even more serious when dealing with different languages, which results in a rapid decrease in matching precision and recall.

The problem of natural language ambiguity can be addressed by enabling people to create descriptions of knowledge resources in a computer-understandable format. For example, accuracy of matching knowledge resources can be increased by considering predicate-level semantics (Hunter et al., 2008). In particular, Semantic Web technologies, such as ontologies and logical inference, can be used to implement knowledge sharing systems that can match knowledge resources with search descriptions at the level of a grammatical sentence. These systems, such as EKOSS (Kraines et al., 2006) and Annotea (Kahan et al., 2001), are based on a semantic model for matching knowledge resources, which we call Model SEM. In this model, the knowledge providers describe their knowledge resources using computer-interpretable semantic statements instead of natural language. The knowledge seekers also input their queries in a semantic way, rather than just listing keywords. For example, the EKOSS system uses semantic matching methods based on description logics (Kraines et al., 2006; Guo and Kraines, 2008) to match the descriptions of knowledge resources and the search queries. Because the EKOSS implementation of Model SEM supports semantic matching, it can help the knowledge seekers find more correct matching results by reducing the ambiguity in both descriptions of knowledge resources and search queries.

We suggest that the use of Semantic Web technologies to enable people to create computer-interpretable semantic statements describing knowledge resources and requirements could address the issues of ambiguity and grammatical complexity in cross-language knowledge sharing. Based on Model SEM, this paper presents a new model for cross-language knowledge sharing, which we call Model SEMCL. In this model, the knowledge providers describe their knowledge resources by creating computer-interpretable semantic statements using their preferred language. In the same way, the knowledge seekers use their preferred language to describe their queries. The system is able to infer semantic matches between the descriptions and the queries, and it then displays the matching results in the preferred language of the knowledge seeker (Fig. 1).

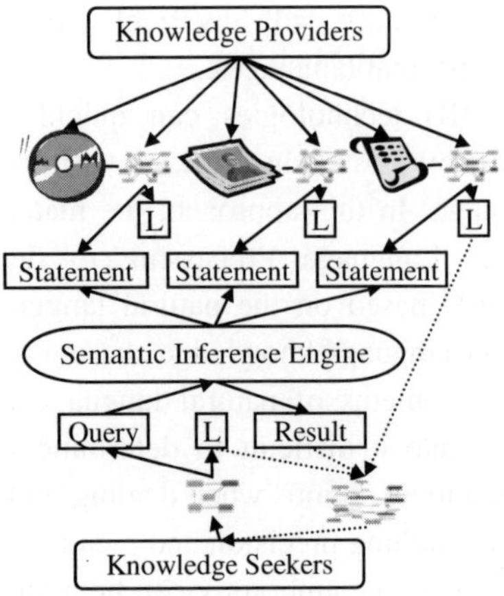

Fig. 1. Model SEMCL. "Statement" denotes semantic statement information. "L" denotes language information. "Query" denotes semantic query information. "Result" denotes matching result information.

The following section gives the details of our proposed Model SEMCL.

3. The Cross-Language Knowledge Sharing Model SEMCL

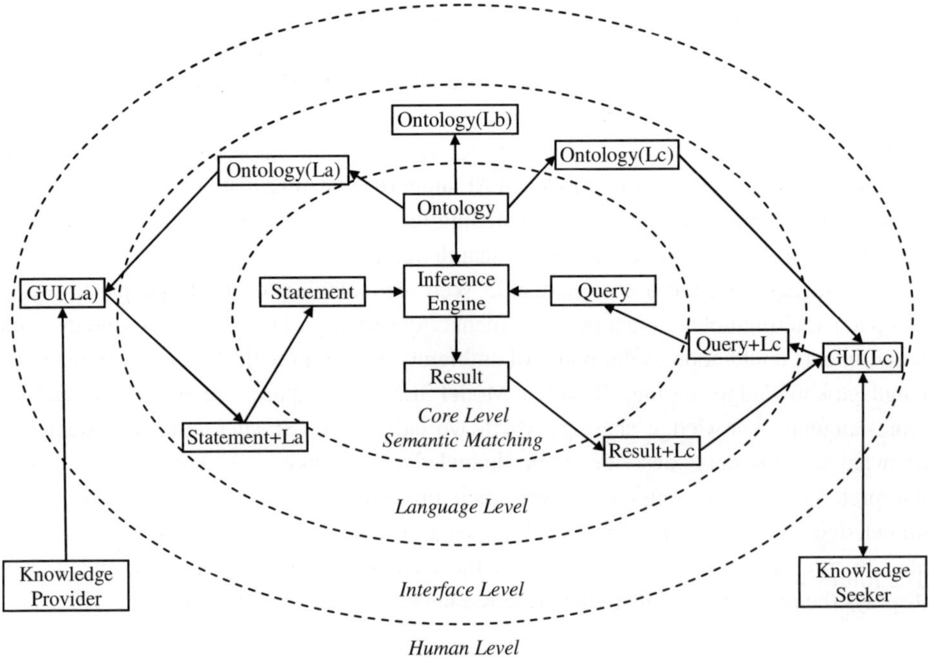

Fig. 2. The framework of Model SEMCL.

Fig. 2 shows the framework of Model SEMCL supporting three hypothetical languages: La, Lb, and Lc. Model SEMCL has four levels: the core semantic matching level, the language level, the user interface level, and the human level. At the center of Model SEMCL is the domain ontology, which is comprised of classes and properties together with labels in plain text. Translations of the class and property labels in the domain ontology to the other languages (Ontology(La), Ontology(Lb), and Ontology(Lc)) are made by a human or machine translator before running the knowledge sharing system.

At the human level, there are two types of users: Knowledge Providers and Knowledge Seekers. Knowledge Providers use the domain ontology to create computer-interpretable semantic descriptions of their knowledge resources, descriptions that are populated by instances of the ontology classes together with properties that describe specific relationships between those instances. Because these descriptions are free from the ambiguity of natural language and grounded in the logic supported by the ontology, they can be used by computers for inference (Guo and Kraines, 2008). The language level of Model SEMCL supports the cross-language sharing and searching. The user interface level of Model SEMCL provides multi-language graphic user interfaces (GUIs), which users can use to provide or seek knowledge in their preferred language.

In Fig. 2, a Knowledge Provider, who prefers to use language La, uses the GUI in language La (GUI(La)) to create a semantic description (Statement + La) of her/his knowledge resource in language La. A Knowledge Seeker, who prefers to use language Lc, uses the GUI in language Lc (GUI(Lc)) to create a semantic query (Query + Lc) in language Lc. The matching results produced by the Inference Engine at the core semantic matching level (Result) are augmented with the language information for Lc to create (Result + Lc), which is shown to the Knowledge Seeker in GUI(Lc).

To make this kind of cross-language searching possible, each knowledge description has two parts: semantic statement (Statement) and language information. Each search query also has two parts: semantic query (Query) and language information. The language information is maintained in the language level. The semantic statement and semantic query go into the core level to be matched by the Inference Engine, which uses reasoning in the supported logic as well as optional rule-based reasoning to match all the available semantic statements with each semantic query. When the Inference Engine finds some matching results (Result), it returns them to the Knowledge Seeker. Language information is added to the matching results when it goes through the language level to the user interface of the Knowledge Seeker. In summary, Model SEMCL uses ontologies to handle the ambiguity of natural language, logical inference for semantic matching, and the method of separating language from semantics to handle the cross-language issue. The following subsections give the details for each of these techniques.

3.1. *Knowledge representation and search*

In Model SEMCL, there are two kinds of knowledge. The first kind is the domain knowledge: the basic concepts and their relationships in the targeted knowledge domain. The second kind is the knowledge that the Knowledge Providers want to share, which is described using the first kind of knowledge. In Model SEMCL, the first kind of knowledge must be created prior to the operation of the knowledge sharing system and kept relatively stable. It should also have sufficient detail to represent the second kind of knowledge, which makes up the contents of the knowledge base in Model SEMCL.

We have created an implementation of Model SEMCL for the domain of engineering knowledge. In our implementation, the first kind of knowledge is represented by using an OWL-DL ontology that we have created for that domain. There are five main classes in the ontology – substances, activities, physical objects, events, and classes of activities (actors and spatial locations are special kinds of physical objects) – as well as several properties that can be used to specify relationships between the classes or instances of the classes (Fig. 3). For example, an instance of the class "activity" can have a relationship with an instance of the class "class of activity" using the property "has activity class". Each main class is divided into subclasses to represent more specific concepts from the engineering domain.

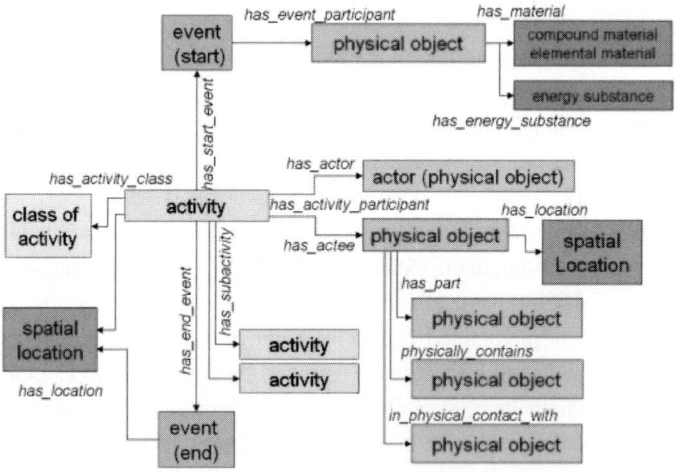

Fig. 3. The main classes and properties of the general engineering domain. Major classes are shown in boxes colored according to class type, and properties are shown as directed arrows.

The second kind of knowledge, knowledge shared by the Knowledge Providers, is represented using the classes and properties provided in the first kind of knowledge. Specifically, the entities described by each piece of shared knowledge are represented as instances of ontology classes, and the specific relationships that are described between those entities are represented using ontology properties. For example, consider the following accident report:

"The central region of Seongsu Bridge, which was built in the capital city Seoul city in Korea, suddenly collapsed on October 21, 1994. A diesel bus fell, and several people were killed. According to the investigation after the accident, the collapse was caused by fractures in the steel girders of the bridge."

The knowledge that is expressed in this report can be represented using the domain ontology as shown in Fig. 4.

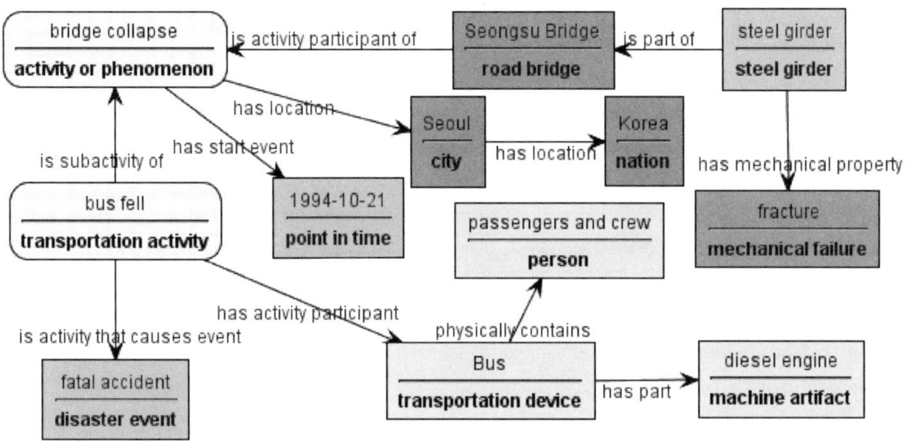

Fig. 4. The knowledge description of "Collapse of the Korea Seoul Seongsu Bridge." Boxes show instances of classes from the domain ontology, colored according to the major upper class as shown in Fig. 3. The text above the line in a box is the instance label. The text below the line in a box is the class name of that instance. Arrows show properties expressing the asserted relationships between instances.

In Model SEMCL, all knowledge resources are represented as knowledge descriptions in this way. When the Knowledge Seekers want to find knowledge resources, they create semantic queries, also based on the domain ontology, and send them to the Inference Engine (an example is given in section 3.3).

Upon receiving a semantic query, the Inference Engine matches it with all the available semantic statements using a DL reasoner. First, the Inference Engine loads the domain ontology to the knowledge base. Then it loads the semantic statement for one knowledge resource. Finally, it evaluates the semantic query against the knowledge base that now contains the ontology and the statement. If each ontology class in the query can be mapped to an instance in the knowledge base subject to the properties specified for that class in the query, then the semantic statement that was loaded to the knowledge base is said to match with the query (an example is given in section 3.3).

3.2. *Cross-language knowledge sharing*

Model SEMCL handles the cross-language issue by separating the language information from the semantic statement in the knowledge description that is created by the Knowledge Provider. Only the semantic statement is used to obtain the matching result. The language information is added to the semantic statement of the matching results before showing them to the Knowledge Seeker. Because Model SEMCL uses a domain ontology instead of natural language to represent the knowledge, it is easy to separate the language information from the semantic statement.

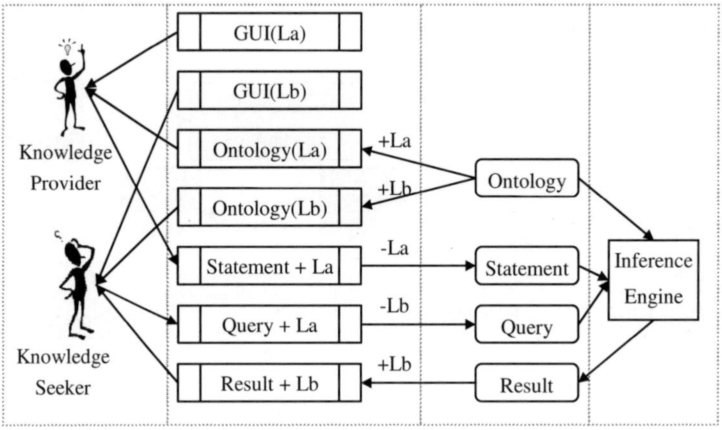

Fig. 5. The Model SEMCL cross-language mechanism.

Fig. 5 shows the overall Model SEMCL cross-language mechanism for two languages (La and Lb). In a real application, the number of languages can be more. The domain ontology and the user interface are created to form the infrastructure level and translated into each of the supported languages before running the knowledge sharing system. The interface language and ontology language are paired. In other words, if the interface language is changed to La, then the ontology language is changed to La automatically.

The Knowledge Provider uses the interface and ontology in her/his preferred language to create her/his knowledge descriptions. For example, if the preferred language is La, then "GUI(La)" and "Ontology(La)" are used, and the knowledge description "Statement + La" is created. The "Statement" is just the semantic information that remains when the language information in language La is removed. In the same way, the Knowledge Seeker uses the interface and ontology in her/his preferred language to create her/his search query. For example, if the preferred language is Lb, then "GUI(Lb)" and "Ontology(Lb)" are used, and "Query + Lb" is created. The "Query" is the part that remains when the language information in language Lb is removed. The Inference Engine evaluates matches between the Statements and Queries using the ontology. If "Query" matches with "Statement", then the matching result "Result" is created by the Inference Engine. Because the preferred language of the Knowledge Seeker is Lb, the language information for Lb is added to create "Result + Lb", which is displayed to the Knowledge Seeker.

3.3. *Scenario*

Here, we illustrate how Model SEMCL works by using a scenario involving three Knowledge Providers – Jane, Hideo, and Zhang – who are sharing knowledge on a knowledge sharing system that supports three languages: English, Japanese and Chinese.

In our scenario, Jane is the person who provided the knowledge for the article about the accident described in section 3.1, and she prefers using English. She accesses the Model SEMCL knowledge sharing system and selects the English user interface to create a description for this knowledge resource (see Fig. 4). She adds the URL of the original news report to the description so that anyone finding this description to be of interest can access the knowledge resource (the news report) for details.

Hideo is a scientist studying failure knowledge who prefers using Japanese. He created a video to explain the failure mechanism behind an airplane accident in Israel that he wants to share. He selects the Japanese user interface to create a description for this video, linked to the URL of the video. The corresponding English description is:

"On October 4, 1992, soon after the take-off of a Boeing 747 cargo air transport of El-Al Israel Airlines, the two engines on the right wing dropped off, and the air transport went out of control, finally colliding into the apartment building. Thirty-nine apartment habitants were killed in this accident. The cause of engine separation during take-off phase was fatigue failure of the pylon fuse pin."

Zhang is a vehicle engineer and a fan of car racing who prefers using Chinese. After learning of the failure of the China A1 Racing Team vehicle in the Indonesian A1 Grand Prix finals station, he created some illustrations to show the reason of transmission failure from his professional perspective that he wants to share. He selects the Chinese user interface to create a description for these illustrations and links the description to the URL of the illustrations. His description of the content of the illustrations in Chinese is as follows:

"中国A1赛车队于2006年2月12日参加了A1大奖赛印尼站决赛。其间，江腾一驾驶的赛车失去控制停在了赛道上。事故原因被认为是经过长期超强度运转的引擎老化引起的。"

The corresponding English translation is:

"The China A1 racing team participated in the Indonesian A1 Grand Prix finals station on February 12, 2006. The vehicle of Jiang Tengyi stopped on the track. The cause of the malfunction was considered to be the aging of the engine after a long time of highly intense use."

The description created by Zhang is shown in Fig. 6.

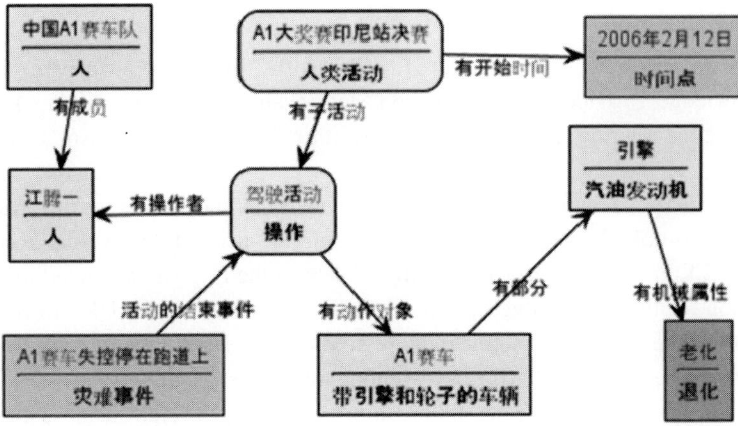

Fig. 6. The knowledge description created by Zhang in Chinese. Boxes and arrows have the same meanings as in Fig. 4.

A Knowledge Seeker named Helen, who prefers using English, is composing her thesis about mechanical failures of transportation machines. In order to find some more knowledge, she wants to utilize the knowledge sharing system. She selects the English user interface to create her query for "a disaster caused by the mechanical failure of a machine artifact that is part of a transportation device" (see Fig. 7).

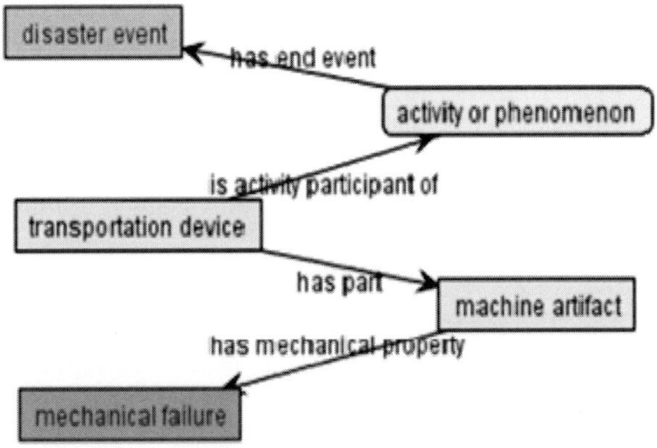

Fig. 7. The search query created by Helen in English. Boxes and arrows have the same meanings as in Fig. 4.

Helen sends her query to the Inference Engine of the Model SEMCL knowledge sharing system and waits for search results. The Inference Engine compares the semantic part of the query with the semantic statement part of Jane's description, Hideo's description and Zhang's description. Hideo's description and Zhang's description match with Helen's query (Fig. 8). However, Jane's description does not match. Even though her description does mention a disaster event, an activity, a transportation device, a machine artifact, and a mechanical failure, the object with the mechanical failure is a part

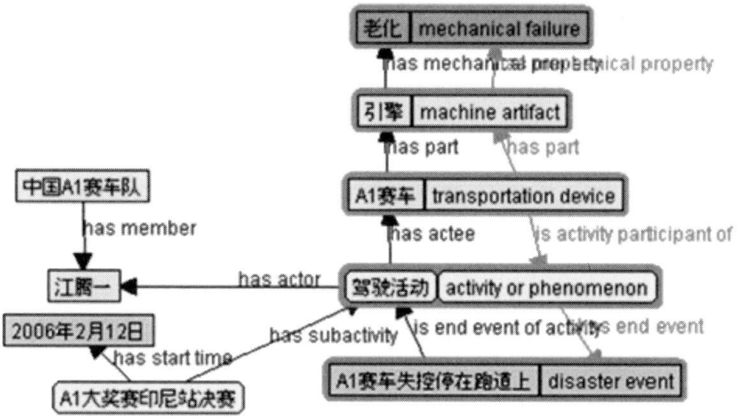

Fig. 8. Matching results of Helen's query with Zhang's description. Boxes showing the instances in the description and query only show instance labels for brevity. Boxes with thick red borders show the mappings of instances in the description (left side) with entities in the query (right side). Arrows in black with blue labels show the properties between instances in the matching description. Arrows in red with red labels show the properties between the classes in the query.

of the road bridge, not a transportation device. This example demonstrates how Model SEMCL supports cross-language knowledge sharing based on matching at the semantic predicate level.

4. Related Work

In section 2, we considered some other models for knowledge sharing. In this section, we compare Model SEMCL with some closely related work from the literature.

Littman et al., (1998) used Latent Semantic Indexing (LSI) to retrieve cross-language documents automatically. They treated a set of dual-language documents as training documents to create a dual-language semantic space in which terms from both languages are represented. Standard mono-lingual documents are represented as language-independent numerical vectors in this semantic space, so queries in either language can retrieve documents in either language without the need to translate the query. The LSI method is based on keywords. The semantic space contains the dual-language terms that form an index for speeding up the retrieval. However, the semantic space does not support classifications and relationships, so the LSI method cannot support retrieval based on matching at the semantic predicate level.

Diaz-Galiano et al., (2008) used the Medical Subject Headings (MeSH) to expand queries in the task of multilingual image retrieval. The expansion consists of searching for terms from the topic query in the MeSH vocabulary and adding similar terms. MeSH has a hierarchical structure that provides a consistent way to retrieve information using different terms for the same concepts. However, the MeSH structure does not contain typed relationships. So, the MeSH-based method also does not support retrieval at the semantic predicate level.

Wang et al., (2004) used a Publish/Subscribe system to share the knowledge. In their system, the knowledge descriptions, which they call Events, are represented with RDF. They also used a domain ontology as the domain basic knowledge which specifies the concepts involved in the Events, the relations between them, and the constraints on them. Their knowledge sharing model can be considered as an example of Model SEM.

Kraines et al., (2006) used semantic web technologies to share expert knowledge. The basic knowledge of the domain is presented to knowledge users as domain ontologies. The Knowledge Providers create knowledge descriptions for their knowledge resources, and the Knowledge Seekers create queries to search for knowledge of interest to them. Therefore, this system is also an implementation of Model SEM.

In summary, while the first two related research works support cross-language knowledge sharing, because they do not handle semantics directly, the accuracy of the matching results is limited. The last two related research works support the semantic predicate level search but do not handle the cross-language issue. Model SEMCL is a new contribution that uses the Model SEM approach to support cross-language knowledge sharing at the semantic predicate level.

5. Discussions and Conclusion

In today's age of information explosion, vast amounts of new knowledge are generated every day in a diversity of languages. How to share and search this knowledge efficiently is one of the most important problems in the information science community. Conventional cross-language knowledge sharing models that are based on natural language processing technologies suffer from the exacerbated effect of ambiguity and grammatical complexity over multiple languages. This paper began with an analysis of the task of knowledge sharing in the Internet environment. An approach to matching knowledge resources using Semantic Web Technologies, called Model SEM, was identified. A new model based on Model SEM, SEMCL, was then proposed for cross-language semantic sharing and searching of knowledge resources. We introduced the framework of our proposal for Model SEMCL, focusing on the knowledge representation and search aspects. We then used a scenario based on an implementation of Model SEMCL for general engineering knowledge to demonstrate how Model SEMCL supports disambiguation, semantic predicate level matching, and cross-language sharing. The original contribution of this work is the creation of a cross-language knowledge sharing model that uses Semantic Web technologies to enable searches across multiple languages at a semantic predicate level.

Our implementation of Model SEMCL is accessible on the EKOSS website (www.ekoss.org). Currently, the EKOSS knowledge sharing system supports three languages: English, Japanese and Chinese. To date, a number of different users of EKOSS have used their preferred languages to create semantic statements to describe their knowledge resources.

Acknowledgments

The authors thank the President's Office of the University of Tokyo for funding support.

References

Diaz-Galiano, M.C., Garcia-Cumbreras, M.A., Martin-Valdivia, M.T., Montejo-Raez, A., and Urena-Lopez, A. (2008). "Integrating MeSH Ontology to Improve Medical Information Retrieval", In Peters, C., et al. (Eds.): *CLEF 2007, LNCS* 5152, 601-606.

Goldschmidt, D.E., and Krishnamoorthy, M. (2008). "Comparing keyword search to semantic search: a case study in solving crossword puzzles using the GoogleTM API", *Software-Practice & Experience*, 38(4), 417-445.

Guo, W., and Kraines, S. (2008). "Explicit Scientific Knowledge Comparison Based on Semantic Description Matching", *American Society for Information Science and Technology 2008 Annual Meeting*, Columbus, Ohio.

Hunter, L., and Cohen, K.B. (2006). "Biomedical Language Processing: What's Beyond PubMed?", *Molecular Cell*, 21, 589-594.

Hunter, L., Lu, Z., Firby, J., Baumgartner Jr, W.A., Johnson, H.L., Ogren, P.V., and Cohen, K.B. (2008). "OpenDMAP: An open source, ontology-driven concept analysis engine, with applications to capturing knowledge regarding protein transport, protein interactions and cell-type-specific gene expression", *BMC Bioinformatics*, 9:78, doi:10.1186/1471-2105-9-78.

Kahan, J., Koivunen, M.R., Prud'Hommeaux, E., and Swick, R.R. (2001). "Annotea: An Open RDF Infrastructure for Shared Web Annotations", *Proceedings of the WWW10 International Conference*, Hong Kong, 623-632.

Kraines, S., Guo, W., Kemper, B., and Nakamura, Y. (2006). "EKOSS: A Knowledge-User Centered Approach to Knowledge Sharing, Discovery, and Integration on the Semantic Web", *ISWC 2006, 5th International Semantic Web Conference, LNCS* 4273, 833-846.

Lin, H.F. (2007). "Effects of extrinsic and intrinsic motivation on employee knowledge sharing intentions", *Journal of Information Science*, 33(2) 2007, 135-149.

Littman, M.L., Dumais, S.T., and Landauer, T.K. (1998). "Automatic cross-language information retrieval using latent semantic indexing", In Grefenstette, G., editor, *Cross-Language Information Retrieval,* chapter 5. Kluwer Academic Publishers, Boston.

Wang, J., Jin, B., and Li, J. (2004). "An Ontology-based Publish/Subscribe System", In Jacobsen, H.A., (Ed.): *Middleware* 2004, *LNCS* 3231, 232-253.

Widen-Wulff, G., and Ginman, M. (2004). "Explaining knowledge sharing in organizations through the dimensions of social capital", *Journal of Information Science*, 30(5) 2004, 448-458.

A STUDY OF EVALUATING THE VALUE OF SOCIAL TAGS AS INDEXING TERMS

KWAN YI
School of Library & Information Science, University of Kentucky
Email: kyi2@email.uky.edu

Regardless of their inherent drawbacks as indexing terms, such as semantic ambiguity and the lack of synonymy and polysemy control, the use of social tags is widespread in information organization, filtering, and discovery through social tagging information systems. There are few empirical studies that have evaluated the value of social tags as indexing terms in an operational and experimental setting. The objective of this study is to assess the indexing value of social tags in a context of an information retrieval model using the Latent Semantic Indexing (LSI) method. Socially tagged resources were classified into ten Dewey Decimal Classification (DDC) main classes. Social tags assigned to the resources were used to represent them in LSI. Similarities between resources were measured, and the aggregated similarities according to the ten DDC main classes were compared. Twenty-four different experiments were attempted for optimal results. The empirical data of this study positively demonstrates the value of social tags as indexing term.

1. Introduction

The widespread use of social tagging information systems has resulted in the important role of social tags in organizing, filtering, and discovering information on the Web. The concept of social tagging and social sharing is viewed as a new paradigm in Web information collection, organization, and retrieval. Examples of some popular social tagging applications include Delicious (http://delicious.com), Flickr (http://flickr.com), YouTube (http://youtube.com), Furl (http://www.furl.net; now acquired by Diigo), and Connotea (http://www.connotea.org), just to name a few. In these systems, any participant is allowed to select online resources, to store the selected resources into the systems by assigning tags (words), and to share the tagged resources with others, mainly through the added tags. A collective set of tags is produced as a result of the collaborative tagging process, and the outcome is called social tags. From the perspective of indexing, the social tagging (collaborative tagging) approach that yields uncontrolled user vocabularies (social tags) can be contrasted with a conventional professionals-driven indexing approach that is based on controlled vocabularies such as subject headings and thesauri. Thus, the social tagging approach can be seen as a free-style of indexing by any voluntary participants without any formal guidelines or standard rules.

Regardless of their rapidly growing popularity, social tags appear to have inherent drawbacks for indexing in that they are semantically ambiguous and lack synonymy and polysemy control (Mathes, 2004). The apparent contradiction between the popularity and the limitations of social tagging is an interesting issue to explore in information organization and discovery. There are few empirical studies that have evaluated the value of social tags as indexing terms in an operational and experimental setting. The objective of this study is to assess the indexing value of social tags in a context of an information retrieval model using the latent semantic indexing method.

2. Related Studies

2.1. *Nature of Social Tags*

The functional and linguistic aspects of social tags were examined through a number of studies using various tagging applications. Spiteri (2007) analyzed social tags collected from Delicious, Furl, and Technorati and reported the prevalent use of single-word tags over multiword tags and the predominant use of noun tags over other grammatical forms. Kipp and Campbell (2006) reported the inconsistent use of synonyms, acronyms, and spelling variations from Delicious social tags. Heckner *et al.* (2007) analyzed social tags collected from Connotea for bibliographic data and reported that 72 percent of single-word tags were nouns, 15 percent were acronyms, 12 percent were adjectives, and 1 percent were numbers.

2.2. *Tags as Indexing Terms*

Heckner *et al.* (2007) reported that the average number of social tags per bibliographic item was 2.2, and only 54 percent of social tags were found in the bibliographic metadata associated with the items. They observed that social tags are more general or more specific than author-assigned keywords. In a study of comparing user-driven tagging practices and professional-driven indexing practices, Kipp and Campbell (2006) noted the presence of time-related tags that hardly appear in traditional controlled vocabularies. Also, as for the comparison to conventional indexing method, they concluded: "tagging practices to some extent work in ways that are continuous with conventional indexing." Also, two previous studies of Heckner *et al.* (2007) and Kipp (2007) arrived at a common conclusion that social tags are quite distinct from author or professionally assigned indexing terms. In all previous studies, tags were examined and analyzed in function and form, but not in an operational indexing and retrieval mode.

2.3. *Tags vs. Controlled Vocabularies*

Spiteri (2007) examined whether social tags conform to the National Information Standards Organization (NISO) guidelines of a controlled vocabulary. She reported that the tags appeared to be aligned with the NISO guidelines in terms of the predominant use of single terms and nouns, as well as the use of valid spelling. However, she found the inconsistent use of "countable nouns" and the occurrence of ambiguous tags due to homographs, abbreviations, and acronyms. Yi and Chan (in press) investigated the feasibility of linking of social tags to Library of Congress

Subject Heading (LCSH). The study reported that two-thirds of the involved social tags were word-matched with LCSH, with an additional 10 percent of the remaining tags having potential matches.

2.4. *Latent Semantic Indexing in Indexing and Retrieval*

Latent Semantic Indexing (LSI) is an indexing and retrieval model based on Salton's vector space model (Landauer *et al.*, 1998). LSI is strong in filtering noisy and non-semantic terms from text and in discovering semantically related terms and documents. LSI has been used in a variety of information retrieval and text processing applications (Bassu and Behrens, 2003), automated document categorization (Dumais *et al.*, 1998), document clustering (Homayouni *et al.*, 2005), etc. Only a few studies have applied LSI to social tags and their related application: Choy and Lui (2006) introduced the use of LSI to measure the similarity between social tags from Delicious, and Levy and Sandler (2008) built a music information retrieval system using LSI that was based on the social tags collected from Last.fm (http://www.last.fm) and MyStrands (http://www.mystrands.com) web services.

3. Collaborative Tagging in LibraryThing

LibraryThing is an online service to help people catalog their books and access/share their catalogs, and to connect people with the same books (http://www.librarything.com/about). Figures 1 and 2 show a real example extracted from the LibraryThing service. Figure 1 shows the data associated with a specific book tagged in LibraryThing. The book's title ("Computer Science: An Overview") and author ("J. Glenn Brookshear") are displayed at the top of the middle column. At the center, a collection of social tags assigned to the book are listed in alphabetical order along with their frequency. At the top portion of the third column, external resources are listed, including "WorldCat," an online bibliographic database from OCLC (Online Computer Library Center). The link to the "WorldCat" database allows people to directly connect to the bibliographic record for the book in the database.

Figure 2 shows a collection of book titles that were classified under the 'Science' subject (not tag) and listed according to the number of people who tagged them in decreasing order. At the top of the middle column, a search box is given to search for a subject. Under the search box, a set of tags is listed, which is associated with the books under the subject. Below that, subjects related to the "Science" subject are displayed.

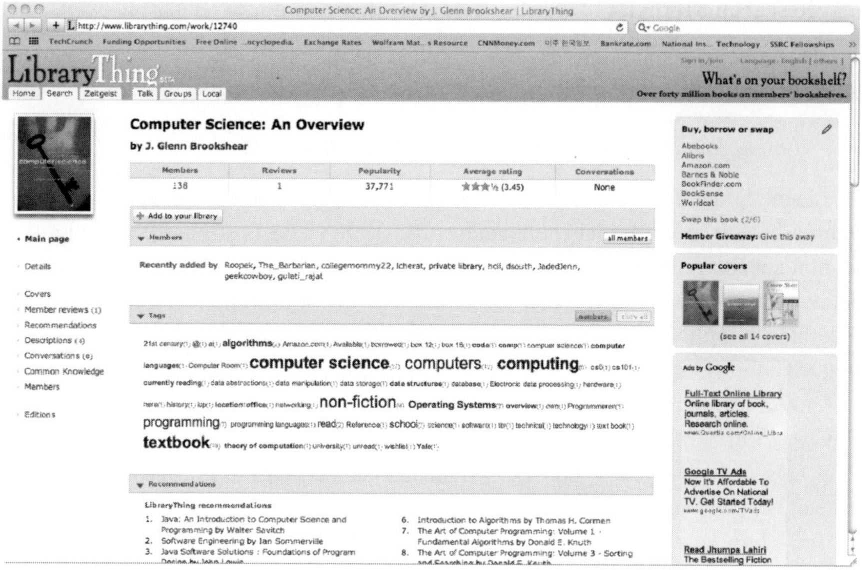

Fig. 1. A LibraryThing space for the resource (book) titled "Computer Science: An Overview" (Source: http://www.librarything.com/work/12740)

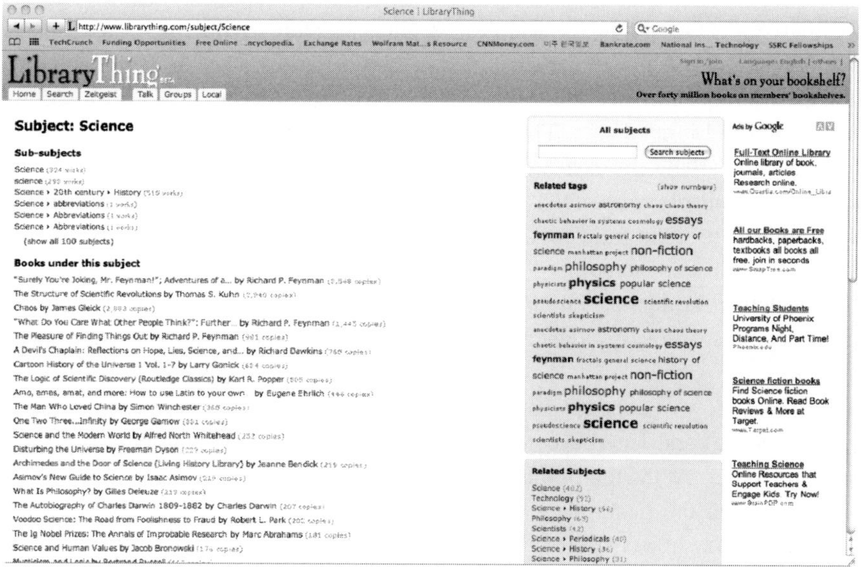

Fig. 2. A list of resources tagged under the subject of 'Science' (Source: http://www.librarything.com/subject/Science)

4. Research Methods

This experimental study aims at assessing the indexing value of social tags in an indexing and retrieval environment. Resources are indexed using the associated social tags on the basis of the Latent Semantic Indexing model, and the similarities between resources are assessed on the basis of cosine angle. Dewey Decimal Classification (DDC) (http://www.oclc.org/dewey/) is a standard library classification scheme in the U.S. For the evaluation of the social tags-based indexing, the LSI-based similarities between resources are clustered according to the same DDC main classes, and the clustered similarities for different DDC main classes are compared to each other.

4.1. *Data Collection*

For the experiment, we collected two datasets: dataset A for indexing and B for evaluation. Dataset A is a collection of social tags for fifty resources tagged in the LibraryThing social cataloging application (http://www.librarything.com). Dataset B consists of DDC numbers assigned to the fifty resources collected for social tags from LibraryThing. We want to intentionally have five resources in each of the ten DDC main classes so that there are fifty resources, equal to five resources multiplied by ten DDC main classes in total.

Fifty LibraryThing-tagged resources with five in each DDC main class were identified and collected in the following steps: (1) a list of potential resources was obtained from the 'subject' search in LibraryThing with the input of the DDC main class description. For example, we tried 'religion' as a search term for the 'subject' search to collect resources for the DDC main class of 200 (Religion). (2) The corresponding DDC number was obtained using OCLC Connexion (http://connexion.oclc.org). The selected fifty resources along with the associated DDC numbers are shown in Appendix A.

4.2. *LSI as an Indexing and Retrieval Model*

The LSI model is an extended version of the popular vector space model. That is, it is a vector space IR model mapping a high-dimensional space into a low-dimensional space by using Singular Value Decomposition (SVD). In LSI, a collection of documents are initially represented by a term (row)-document (column) matrix. It is usually a very high-dimensional and sparse matrix, with a high number of different terms (rows) and relatively few non-zero entries. The way in LSI to reduce the high dimension of the matrix is using SVD. That is, the original matrix X is projected to a new, low-dimensional space obtained by SVD, X'. The LSI model has the advantage of discovering the hidden semantic structure in the association of the high order structure of term-document matrix. More details on LSI can be read at (Deerwester *et al.*, 1990).

4.3. *Evaluation Measure*

In general, ranking can be evaluated using measures similar to the traditional measures for evaluating ranking-based information retrieval systems: recall, precision, or/and other standard metrics such as 11-point average precision and F_1. However, the popular 11-point average precision and F_1 are not suitable for the evaluation of this experiment, as a query in our experiment has only one relevant item. Instead, Mean Average Precision (MAP), another popular standard metric, is employed for the performance of this experiment (Baeza-Yates and Ribeiro-Neto, 1999). In MAP, precision is obtained at the point that the relevant item is observed in the ranking list. Then, the obtained precision values are arithmetically averaged for a set of queries. MAP yields a single positive value as the outcome of the evaluation. As the MAP single value is closer to 1, it turns out to be better.

4.4. *Experimental Design*

A conventional text pre-processing was applied to the collected social tags: removing unnecessary symbols applying a stopword list, and stemming. Salton's 571 stopword list was employed as it is one of the most comprehensive lists, and the popular Porter's stemming algorithm was applied. Stemming appears to be necessary because the occurrence of various forms of the same tag is commonly reported in almost all social tag studies.

Similarities between social tag-indexed resources were tested and measured in 24 different experimental settings with two variables *N* and *D*. All the social tags collected were not used in the indexing of the resources; only *N* most frequently occurring tags for each resource were used. To examine the effect of the variances on the performance, four different numbers of *N* (*N*=5, 10, 15, and 20) were adopted. In *N* tags, there must be *t* terms (*t* is always greater than or equal to *N*) as a tag consists of one or more than one terms. A *t*-term (equivalent to the row of the matrix) by *r*-resource (equivalent to the column of the matrix) matrix is created. As 50 resources were collected for the indexing, the value of *r* is 50. Depending on a specific value for the variable *N*, however, the value of *t* varies: 93, 197, 283, and 394, when *N* is equal to 5, 10, 15, and 20, respectively.

The LSI model takes as input a *t*-term by *r*-resource matrix (corresponding to *X* in the section of 3.2; the original dimension of the matrix is equal to *t*), and yields a matrix of the similarity between resources in a lower-dimensional space (corresponding to X' in the section of 3.2) rather than in the dimensional space of the original input matrix. The choice of the dimension of the reduced space (i.e., the number of the largest singular values of the matrix *X*; *rank* of the term-resource matrix) is an open question. As in other studies using LSI, an operational criterion was chosen for the decision, i.e., a value of dimension yielding good performance. Thus, various dimensions of the reduced space (*D*) were attempted at 5, 10, 20, 30, 40, and 50.

In an experiment situation, the LSI-based index and retrieval model results in an r-resource by r-resource matrix (resource similarity matrix). Each cell value of the matrix indicates the similarity between two resources associated with the cell in row and column. The calculation of the similarity is on the basis of the cosine angle. The resource-resource matrix is transformed to a class-class matrix (class similarity matrix), i.e., a matrix for the similarity between DDC main classes to which the resources belong. A value of the cell, *i* and *j*, in the class similarity matrix is obtained by the average of the summation of all the similarities between a resource in the class *i* and a resource in the class *j*. In the calculation, the cases in which the two involved resources are identical are not included for the following reasons: (1) the resource similarity between two identical resources is always 1 (the highest similarity); and (2) a cell on the diagonal line of the class similarity matrix contains five identical cases, but any cell out of the diagonal line does not contain such a case, so that the average similarity can be skewed if they are not eliminated. Based on the class similarity matrix, we can easily construct a ranking of all classes for a given specific class, according to the similarity value (class similarity ranking). That is, the ranking for a given class *i* can be obtained by sorting all the entries on the ith row of the class similarity matrix in the decreasing order of the associated similarity values.

4.5. *Experimental Results and Analysis*

Based on the class similarity ranking, the initial task of the resource similarity in order to measure the performance of the social tag-based indexing of resources can be treated as an information retrieval task – presenting results with ranking. As a result, the performance of an experiment is indicated by a single value measured by MAP as discussed in an earlier section.

The results for the twenty-four different experiments are shown in Table 1. A MAP in a cell in Table 1 represents the entire performance of the entire fifty-by-fifty resource similarities. The higher a value is, the better its performance is. More specifically, a higher value means that a resource is more likely to be indexed and retrieved for the DDC main class to which the resource originally belongs than for the other classes.

As for the analysis, first, compare the resultant data in the Table column by column. The maximum value in each column is shaded at the corresponding cell, 0.74, 0.73, 0.73, and 0.71 for N=5, 10, 15, and 20, respectively. Across the values of the parameter *N*, the highest value is found with N=5, and the value is slightly decreasing at higher numbers of N. Second, compare the results row by row. The maximum value in each row is marked by the asterisk symbol (*) next to the value. The maximum values are relatively evenly distributed across N=5, 10, and 15. But it is never found at the case of N=20. The values including the maximum tend to increase as the higher rank of the original matrix (increasing value of D) is employed until it reaches to D=30 for N=10 and N=20 and D=40 for N=5 and N=15. After that, it decreases. A common pattern across different N values is that the MAP values sharply drop at D=50.

An interesting finding is that the performance with N=5 is comparable to other cases in all different levels of ranks except D=50. This implies that social tags out of the top five frequently occurring tags do not help much improve the performance of indexing the tagged resources.

Table 1. Overall performance for 10 DDC main classes

		Number of social tags involved			
		N=5	**N=10**	**N=15**	**N=20**
Rank of the original matrix	**D=5**	0.46	0.55*	0.39	0.51
	D=10	0.59	0.59	0.64*	0.61
	D=20	0.7*	0.63	0.68	0.63
	D=30	0.7	0.73*	0.7	0.71
	D=40	0.74*	0.69	0.73	0.64
	D=50	0.28	0.51*	0.47	0.49
	Average	0.58	0.62	0.6	0.6

Performance results for each DDC main classes are plotted in Figure 3. For a DDC main class, four average values for N=5, 10, 15, and 20 are obtained and drawn. When N=5, the ranking of the main classes decreases from DDC-200 (Religion), DDC-400 (Language), DDC-000 (Computer Science, information & general works), DDC-600 (Technology), etc. When N=10, the ranking is DDC-000 (Computer Science, information & general works), DDC-600 (Technology), DDC-400 (Language), DDC-200 (Religion), etc. When N=15, the ranking is DDC-000 (Computer Science, information & general works), DDC-400 (Language), DDC-600 (Technology), DDC-200 (Religion), etc. When N=20, the ranking is DDC-600 (Technology), DDC-400 (Language), DDC-000 (Computer Science, information & general works), DDC-300 (Social science), etc. In any case of N, DDC-000, DDC-200, DDC-400, and DDC-600 appear at the top four rankings, except DDC-300 at N=20.

The last row of Table 1 displays the averages of all the main classes for different N values. Figure 3 indicates that there are four main classes in which the similarity value is below the average for all values of N: DDC-100 (Philosophy & psychology), DDC-500 (Science), DDC-800 (Literature), and DDC-900 (History & geography).

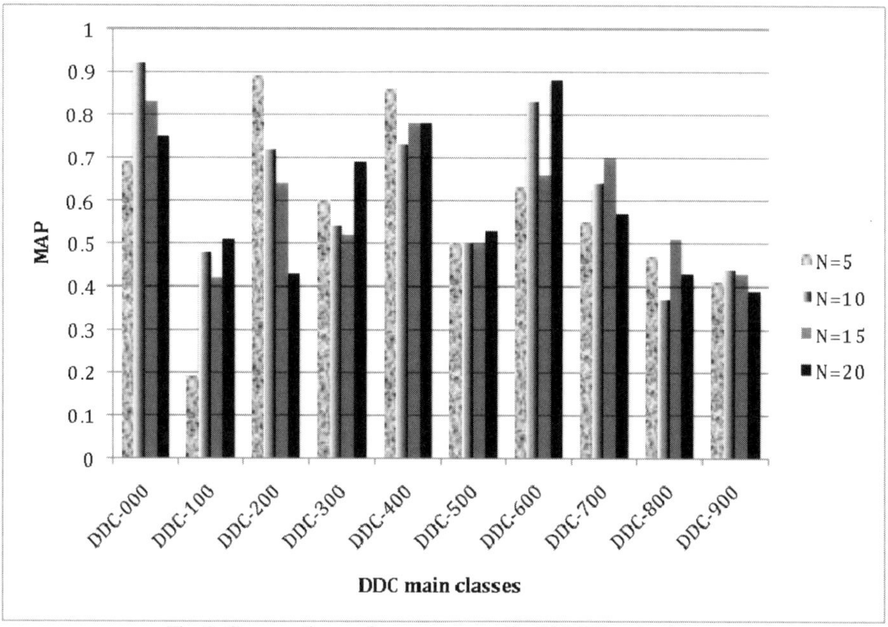

Fig. 3. Comparative performance across the 10 DDC main classes

5. Conclusions

We have conducted experiments to assess the effectiveness of social tag-based indexing in the context of information retrieval using the latent semantic indexing method. The empirical data of this study positively demonstrates the value of social tags as indexing terms. This study reaches the following empirical conclusions:

1. With D=30 (the number of dimensions in the LSI model), the social tags-based indexing performs best on average evenly in any cases of N.

2. Indexing with the top 5 most frequent social tags yields a comparable performance to indexing with the top 10, 15, or 20 tags.

3. The choice of rank in LSI is sensitive to the performance. The choice must be carefully made.

4. Resources in the following main classes tend to perform better than those in the other classes: DDC-000 (Computer Science, information & general works), DDC-200 (Religion), DDC-400 (Language), and DDC-600 (Technology).

5. Resources in the following main classes tend to perform worse than those in the other classes: DDC-100 (Philosophy & psychology), DDC-500 (Science), DDC-800 (Literature), and DDC-900 (History & geography).

A limitation of this study is that it assumes that the retrieval process uses the social tags used in indexing. That is, it is not based on real queries from real users which can more precisely measure the real power of social tag-based indexing.

Acknowledgments

The author would like to thank anonymous reviewers for their valuable comments.

Appendix

DDC main classes (Description for DDC main classes)		
	Resource URL	DDC assigned to resource
000 (Computer science, information & general works)		
	http://www.librarything.com/work/12740	004
	http://www.librarything.com/work/379191	004
	http://www.librarything.com/work/135613	004
	http://www.librarything.com/work/336884	005.1/17
	http://www.librarything.com/work/24201	004
100 (Philosophy & psychology)		
	http://www.librarything.com/work/35566	193.9
	http://www.librarything.com/work/8330	193
	http://www.librarything.com/work/15945	188
	http://www.librarything.com/work/46716	109
	http://www.librarything.com/work/9869	184
200 (Religion)		
	http://www.librarything.com/work/1429542	211.8
	http://www.librarything.com/work/2482940	200
	http://www.librarything.com/work/34883	200
	http://www.librarything.com/work/1539	242.4
	http://www.librarything.com/work/30996	291.4/2
300 (Social sciences)		
	http://www.librarything.com/work/3496	301
	http://www.librarything.com/work/637387	320.01
	http://www.librarything.com/work/71694	301
	http://www.librarything.com/work/113789	303.4/83
	http://www.librarything.com/work/851980	301.2/1
400 (Language)		
	http://www.librarything.com/work/3585	400
	http://www.librarything.com/work/3005635	401
	http://www.librarything.com/work/46108	401.9
	http://www.librarything.com/work/9844	401.3
	http://www.librarything.com/work/85655	427.994
500 (Science)		
	http://www.librarything.com/work/5655	530.092
	http://www.librarything.com/work/1669269	501
	http://www.librarything.com/work/12727	530.092
	http://www.librarything.com/work/28124	500
	http://www.librarything.com/work/170253	500

600 (Technology)		
	http://www.librarything.com/work/63548	600
	http://www.librarything.com/work/28719	600
	http://www.librarything.com/work/329572	600
	http://www.librarything.com/work/31051	600
	http://www.librarything.com/work/246181	609.51
700 (Arts & recreation)		
	http://www.librarything.com/work/315071	700/.1
	http://www.librarything.com/work/109470	700
	http://www.librarything.com/work/161742	700
	http://www.librarything.com/work/107149	700.103
	http://www.librarything.com/work/58933	704.9/424
800 (Literature)		
	http://www.librarything.com/work/2199	822.33
	http://www.librarything.com/work/7856	891.73/3
	http://www.librarything.com/work/25918	851/.1
	http://www.librarything.com/work/2236	813/.4
	http://www.librarything.com/work/10151	891.73/42
900 (History & geography)		
	http://www.librarything.com/work/15101	909.08
	http://www.librarything.com/work/49654	909
	http://www.librarything.com/work/5328305	901
	http://www.librarything.com/work/19972	901
	http://www.librarything.com/work/9810	901

References

Bassu, D., & Behrens, C. (2003). Distributed LSI: Scalable Concept-based Information Retrieval with High Semantic Resolution. In *Text Mining Workshop of the Proceedings of the 3rd SIAM International Conference on Data Mining*.

Choy, S.O. and Lui, A.K. (2006) "Web information retrieval in collaborative tagging systems", In J. Liu, & B. W. Wah (Eds.), *Proceedings of the 2006 IEEE/WIC/ACM International Conference on Web Intelligence* (pp. 352-355). Los Alamitos, CA: IEEE Computer Society.

Deerwester, S., Dumais, S., Furnas, G.W., Landauer, T. K., & Harshman, R. (1990). Indexing by latent semantic analyses. *Journal of the American Society for Information Science*, 41(6), 391-407.

Dumais, S., Platt, J., Heckerman, D., & Sahami, M. (1998) Inductive learning algorithms and representations for text categorization. In K. Makki, & L. Bouganim (Eds.), *Proceedings of the 7th International Conference on Information and Knowledge Management* (pp. 148-155). New York: ACM.

Heckner, M., Muhlbacher, S., & Wolff, C. (2007) Tagging tagging: a classification model for user keywords in scientific bibliography management systems. In *Proceedings of the 6th European Networked Knowledge Organization Systems*

(NKOS) Workshop at the 11th ECDL Conference, Budapest, Hungary. Retrieved June 2, 2009, from http://www.comp.glam.ac.uk/pages/research/hypermedia/nkos/nkos2007/papers/heckner.pdf

Homayouni, R., Heinrich, K., Wei, L., & Berry, M. W. (2005). Gene Clustering by Latent Semantic Indexing of MEDLINE Abstracts. *Bioinformatics*, 21(1), 104-115.

Kipp, M.E.I., & Campbell, D.G. (2006) Patterns and inconsistencies in collaborative tagging systems: An examination of tagging practices. In *Proceedings of American Society for Information Science and Technology*, (Vol. 43, Issue 1, pp. 1-18). Retrieved 25 June 2009 from http://dlist.sir.arizona.edu/1704/01/KippCampbellASIST.pdf

Kipp, M.E.I. (2007) Tagging Practices on Research Oriented Social Bookmarking Sites. In *Proceeding of Canadian Association for Information Science*, Montreal, Quebec, Canada. Retrieved June 1, 2009, from http://www.cais-acsi.ca/proceedings/2007/kipp_2007.pdf

Landauer, T.K., Laham, D., & Foltz, P.W. (1998) "Learning human-like knowledge by singular value decomposition: a progress report. In M. I. Jordan, M. J. Kearns, and S. A. Solla (Eds.), Advanced in neural information processing systems (Vol. 10) (pp. 45-51). Cambridge: MIT Press.

Levy, M., & Sandler, M. (2008). Learning Latent Semantic Models for Music from Social Tags. *Journal of New Music Research*, 37(2), 137-150.

Mathes, A. (2004, December) Folksonomies – Cooperative Classification and Communication through Shared Metadata. In *Academic Works*. Retrieved May 6, 2009, from http://www.adammathes.com/academic/computer-mediated-communication/folksonomies.html

Spiteri, L.F. (2007). The structure and form of folksonomy tags: The road to the public library catalog. *Information Technology and Libraries*, 26(3), 13-24.

Yi, K., & Chan, L.M. (in press) Linking Folksonomy to Library of Congress Subject Headings: An Exploratory Study. *Journal of Documentation*.

LEADERSHIP 2.0 AND WEB2.0 AT ERM: A JOURNEY FROM KNOWLEDGE MANAGEMENT TO "KNOWLEDGING"

CHEUK WAI-YI BONNIE

Environmental Resources Management (ERM),
Global Knowledge Sharing & Communication Program
2/F Exchequer Court, 33 St. Mary Axe, London, EC3A 8AA, United Kingdom
E-mail: bonnie.cheuk@gmail.com

BRENDA DERVIN

School of Communication, The Ohio State University, Columbus, Ohio 43210
E-mail: dervin.1@osu.edu

This paper introduces Dervin's Sense-Making Methodology (SMM) as an approach to KM system design using Web2.0. SMM is a philosophically derived approach which allows knowledge management (KM) researchers and practitioners to more fully understand and listen to user's needs so as to inform the design of dialogic KM practices and systems to promote knowledge sharing. Increasingly, KM systems are incorporating Web2.0 features which allow user-generated content and have a stronger emphasis on collaboration and interaction amongst users. This paper presents a "Safety Moment" project to illustrate how SMM has been applied to inform the design of a Web2.0 enabled 'knowledging' application in Environmental Resources Management (ERM), the world's largest all-environmental consulting firm. The project discussed has been implemented since January 2008 as part of ERM's commitment to improve Health & Safety Performance to ensure all ERM employees, contractors and clients are safe at work. Use of the SMM informed Web2.0 application has correlated with increased staff satisfaction, increased company reputation and reduced risks. Much is said about the need for a Leadership 2.0 to implement Web2.0. The authors argue that this project exemplar illustrates how to make Web2.0 work, we need to define Leadership 2.0 as a set of alternative management values and practices driven by a set of coherent assumptions about the nature of human communication.

1. Introduction: Leadership 2.0, Web2.0, Intranet 2.0 and Enterprise 2.0

Knowledge Management (KM) in the enterprise setting has increasingly been associated with the use of collaboration technologies, social computing and interactive online communities to leverage collective insights of all staff to inform decision making and promote innovation. Many KM practitioners argue that finally the right technologies are available at an affordable cost to make knowledge sharing happen.

Some common themes have emerged in recent KM and social computing conferences: (a) KM practitioners are trying to understand how to use blogs, wikis and social computing tools, (b) they want to understand what benefits these new tools can offer, (c) they want to figure out the best approach to encourage user adoption; and (d) they want to choose the best tools to add the most value to their companies, to help employees to grow their careers and to make it enjoyable for staff to come to work everyday.

On Wikipedia, Web 2.0 is defined as a second generation of web development and design that facilitates communication, secure information sharing, interoperability, and collaboration on the World Wide Web. Web 2.0 concepts have led to the development and evolution of web-based communities, hosted services, and applications such as social networking sites, video sharing sites, wikis, blogs, mashup and folksonomies.

McAfee (2006) introduced the term Enterprise 2.0 as shorthand for the use of Web2.0 by businesses and especially on organizations' intranets and extranets in pursuit of their goals. In ERM -- Web2.0 has been introduced using what ERM labels as LANES principles (Cheuk, 2007):

- **L**ateral Communication, i.e. supports top-down, bottom-up and lateral communications
- **A**ll staff can participate if they want to, i.e. no specialized IT skills are required
- **N**etworking, i.e. building of business and social networking across teams and geographies
- **E**xpertise visualization, i.e. visualize the expertise that staff do not know exist
- **S**elfishness yet helping others, i.e. focusing on satisfying the 'selfish' immediate needs of a user and the by-product by highlighting the collective intelligence which creates more value to all staff

These principles are typical of those guiding most Web 2.0 applications to organizational environments. Despite high enthusiasm and great expectations, the literature is replete with examples of failures in virtually every organizational context (Stephens, 2009), In the KM context, let us take two examples that the senior author has encountered.

- A senior leader set up a blog post hoping to engage in dialogue with all staff, but only a few staff commented or asked questions.
- A product development team set up a forum to invite all staff to share clients' insights, but only one or two people shared insights that were in actuality already known to the team

In both cases above, staff members didn't trust senior leaders or the product development team to hear their input. There were power issues because some junior members of staff did not feel comfortable in sharing their ideas with experts or senior staff. Few Web2.0 tools have been consciously designed to demonstrate that experts are actively listening and actively taking input seriously. Nor have design tools been applied to develop systematically constructive ways of encouraging input by those who have felt unheard and disempowered. Yet, organizational research (e.g. Putman & Kline, 2006; Weick & Browning, 1986; Weick & Sutcliffe, 2001) has repeatedly shown that it is sometimes these very voices that have the clearest visions of what may be going organizationally. Bottom line, too often Web2.0 and other online dialogue applications are still designed with top-down communication implicitly assumed as outcome. From a communication perspective, this fails because genuine dialogic communication requires a two-way quid pro quo.

In the context of repeated online communication failures, there are some typical questions that KM practitioners ask: What are the secret recipes for making Web2.0 work, or fail to work? Web2.0 appears to be low cost and easy to use, so why don't Wed2.0 applications take off in the workplace? Why are Web2.0 applications too often seen as social and informal but not performance and satisfaction critical?

What are the missing pieces? We argue here that the missing pieces involve a reconceptualization of what KM is about as well as the design of KM procedures. As a KM practitioner, the senior author of this paper has gained the following insights when introducing Web 2.0 in the workplace:

1. To make Web2.0 works, we need Leadership 2.0. However, while many uses of the term Leadership 2.0 are evident in practical and research oriented literatures, our use here goes far beyond the usual emphasis on knowledge sharing as if this is somehow a magical outcome of facilitating more message sharing.
2. Thus, Leadership 2.0, as discussed in this paper, requires a different way of thinking about 'knowledge management' and 'knowledge transfer'. It requires leaders, managers and employees redefine knowledge transfer not as a thing called 'information' to be transferred from one bucket to another, but as a process of meaningful and evolving knowledge exchange. In this paper, this process is referred to as 'knowledging' and the 'information' involved is referred to as 'knowledgings' as participants make and unmake their understandings as they move through changing and often elusive situations, as they reflect on their own understandings, as they hear and apply the understandings of others, as they struggle together to bridge knowledging gaps. When emphasis moves from 'knowledge' to 'knowledging', genuine dialogue and communication can begin to take place. As a result, both senders and recipients are facilitated in gaining new insights, and learning and/or unlearning as circumstances demand. The lines between senders and recipients become blurred. They become co-participants. In short, the transmission model of knowledge management does not apply even when seemingly made more participatory by an emphasis on creating more message exchange. Increasing the volume of messages exchange in the absence of the use of meaningful communicating procedures ends up being noise-sharing rather than knowledging-sharing.
3. Leadership 2.0, as we think about it, also redefines information literacy in the workplace. It takes information literacy to a strategic level (Cheuk, 2008). Leadership 2.0 trusts that employees will find and use information to help them get on with their work at the time they need to. Staff do not need to be spoon fed with information, and research shows spoon-feeding rarely is effective, The focus of information literacy in the workplace places less emphasis on Web2.0 tools training but more on guidance to adopt good two-way communication procedures, such as listening, evaluating, presenting and visualizing ideas with the audience's needs in mind.
4. Leadership 2.0, again as we use the term, redefines what learning in the workplace means. Learning goes beyond formal training, structured staff appraisal and staff development programs. Employees learn through self-reflection of good practices and mistakes, as well as listening to how other employees (both experts and novices) look at issues in same or different ways. Mistakes are tolerated. Hunches are invited.

> Through the learning process, the experts, the novices, the senior executives and the front line staff learn and unlearn. All learners are empowered to become more self-reflective, and experts and authorities lower their egos to listen and to learn from others.

Many KM practitioners have commented that Leadership 2.0 of the kind described above is not easily found in corporations. Since the early 20th century, most industrialized countries have implemented a set of management disciplines that have focused almost exclusively on top-down command-and-control strategies (Putnam & Krone, 2006). Although it remains a much contested issue in organizational communication research, these command-and-control strategies have proved effective when organizations have focused primarily on efficiency outcomes in assembly line production and other seemingly straightforward manufacturing and production environments. Unfortunately, command-and-control procedures have been shown to have decided limits even in these presumably routinized contexts and even more so in complex organizations whose core purposes involve knowledge sharing and meeting the demands of changing, sometimes chaotic environments. In short, what has been formalized in the literature as the top-down traditional management approach is being challenged by organizational experts who focus particularly on managing living, breathing human beings who must somehow change, refine, share and co-create their knowledgings.

For our purposes here, then, Leadership 2.0 refers to a set of alternative management values and practices designed to allow organizations and their workers to move from command-and-control structures to genuinely collaborative ways of working. While many have called the move to Leadership 2.0 a "cultural change", in this paper we focus on it as a change in the very way we think about communication. The purpose of Leadership 2.0, as we define it, is to promote "knowledging" -- in essence the using of systematic communication practices that enable participants to make and unmake, refine and expand, exemplify and abstract their "knowledging" by using systematically designed processes of self-reflection and shared communicating.

2. Literature Review: KM Philosophies

It is useful to review the literature of knowledge management and its development overtime to understand the changing philosophical assumptions which guide the development of KM practices/systems including Web2.0 tools.

Many definitions of knowledge exist. The definitional differences arise from competing, ontological and epistemological assumptions. A review of these differences is beyond purposes here. In the context of knowledge management, a number of useful overviews and critiques exist (e.g. Brown & Duguid, 2000; Dervin, 1998, 1999; Hildreth and Kimble, 2002; Nonaka and Peltokorpi, 2006; Snowden & Stanbridge, 2004; Souto, Dervin & Savolainen, 2008; Wenger, 1998; Wilson, 2002).

Informed by these reviews, we concluded that first generation KM practices/systems have been informed primarily by the positivist philosophical assumption that "knowledge" is an object which is external to human beings and can be managed by making ‘tacit’ knowledge explicit by investing in KM systems which 'capture' the knowledge of experts in databases, manuals, books and reports, and then sharing it in a hard form. It is assumed that increasing the available quantity of ‘codified’ knowledge will have a positive linear impact on operational costs and avoid reinventing the wheel. A fundamental difficulty with this view, of course, is that as social scientists have well documented, there are numerous processes that intervene between external evidences of codified knowledge and internal knowings. This is why some argue (e.g. Wilson, 2002) that knowledge cannot be managed. The KM mandate is further muddied by the realities of our increasingly complex organizational climates and the often incomplete and elusive character of that "stuff" we humans call "data" or "information" or "knowledge."

Informed by these arguments, there are scholars and practitioners who recognize the limits of the positivist philosophical assumptions and propose alternative views that differ from those applies to first generation KM systems and practices. The various authors proposing these alternatives converge on essentially four conceptualizations all of which mandate in one way or another a more communicative or dialogue-based view of KM specifically in applications labeled as KM but also in other organizational contexts where "knowledge management" is a primary focus. See for example (Brown & Duguid, 2000; Browning & Boudes, 2005; Dervin, 1998, 1999; Fairhurst & Putnam, 2004; Hildreth and Kimble, 2002; Nonaka and Peltokorpi, 2006; Snowden & Stanbridge, 2004; Souto, Dervin & Savolainen, 2008; Weick & Browning, 1986; Weick & Sutcliffe, 2001; Wenger, 1998):

1. focussing on the need to allow communicative interrogation and interpretation of knowledge as seen from recipients’ perspectives
2. cultivating knowledge workers by facilitating their learning through self-descriptive awareness
3. redefining knowledge as not just about ‘facts’ but also direction, ideas, support, confirmation and connection with other people etc. Knowledge can also sometimes be ‘objective’ and sometimes be ‘subjective’ and ‘emotional’. Sometimes, as well, knowledge can be confusions and muddles which when shared clarify what's going amiss.
4. recognizing that knowledge -- is embedded in a social context and is at least in part defined by power and in part defined by status. Knowledge sharing can be more or less effective depending how power is acknowledged.

This understanding of knowledge – through the eyes of the knowledge user – provides an alternative perspective and foundation to design KM practices/systems that:

1. look beyond information itself and promote knowledge sharing in the context in which people work
2. put more emphasis on narratives and story-telling which share knowledge that is rich in context.

Web2.0 technologies seem to allow ready implementation of these assumptions and when they become available in the enterprise setting, a typical KM application is often defined as supporting members of a community of practice to quickly exchange conversations online in an affordable way to support decision making and to innovate.

There are however issues which need to be addressed when Web2.0 and is gaining popularity because it is easy and low cost to set up:

1. It becomes very easy for a community of practice to be set up to allow members to exchange ideas. However, the result can be the reinforcing of silos that resemble current organizational structures and hierarchies rather than promoting cross-silo conversation. Because of this, old assumptions (and their related mistakes) get reified.
2. It becomes very easy for a sub-group of like-minded colleagues to dominant the communicating space in online discussions by, for example, commenting on each other's blogs or being the ones to dominant conversations in a wiki. While the quantity of user-generated content may have increased, the cross-fertilization of ideas does not necessarily improve.
3. While it becomes very easy to publish more content, this does not mean that the knowledge offered will necessarily be attended to or utilized to inform decision making. Research in communication clearly shows that an increase in talk that leads to no acknowledgment, action or improved decision-making can disappoint employees and lead to job alienation.
4. It becomes very easy to assume that power differentials do not exist in online environments when in fact they do so as much as in face-to-face meetings. An inclination to increase user adoption of Web2.0 tools needs to be balanced by providing safe, constructive and sometimes anonymous spaces for exchanging ideas (online or offline).

The difficulty we have when focusing on these new technologies that are so conducive to people speaking at each other is that they are based on a communication logic that Dervin (in press) suggests proceeds without genuine communication and exchange. In her extensive reviews, Dervin has documented how communication logics have moved from an emphasis on top-down transmission to efforts to pigeonhole people into demographic, personality, and cultural boxes in order to make transmission more effective. These approaches have not worked well and less so as our organizational climates become more complex. Now, impelled by the strengths of new technologies, we have the dominant emphasis on letting communication spontaneously flow between participants Dervin argues, however, that this logic is merely the opposite side of the same coin. Top-down transmission attempts to control messages so only the right ones flow. Uncontrolled lateral transmission too often merely increased the number of messages flowing. This, Dervin charges, merely introduces a communication logic that easily becomes a "Tower of Babel". What is needed is a logic that enables participants to come to understand each other's meanings and the grounds (experiential, cognitive, emotional, and even sometimes physical and spiritual) that human beings move from when knowledging. Dervin says this new kind of communication logic requires that we systematically apply into KM designs the kinds of communication actions that people require if they are to understand each other across organizational silos and forge effective collaborations informed by each others knowledgings.

Thus, we argue here that while Web2.0 opens up new opportunities to share ideas, the design of Web2.0 applications becomes critical for these designs must promote 'knowledging' rather than knowledge transmission. Web2.0 applications give the impression that it is easy to set up and to participate. However, the design of Web2.0 applications (or for that matter any online or offline communication application, requires attention to the disciplining of communication procedures in order for organizations, and the human beings who work in them, to reap benefits (Dervin, 2008).

The most disciplined and methodological approach to promote 'knowledging' which is the result of genuine two-way dialogue (conducted offline and/or online) is found in the discourse community focussing on communication led by Dervin. Since 1972 Dervin has systematically developed and continued to refine Sense-Making Methodology as a methodology 'between the cracks'. It should be noted that a variety of approaches focusing on sense-making (sometimes spelled as sensemaking) have emerged in recent literatures in numerous fields, primarily: knowledge management, human computer intersection, organizational communication, and communication. Recent papers provide comparisons (Dervin & Naumer, in press; Dervin & Reinhard, in press). The next section of this paper will present Sense-Making Methodology in detail.

3. An Overview of Sense-Making Methodology

Dervin began to develop Sense-Making Methodology (SMM) in the late 1960s as an alternative approach to understanding human communication. As a line of work, it fits within a communication tradition that assumes that communication must be studied communicatively -- a on-going practices in which people make and unmake sense of their changing and sometimes elusive worlds through internal and external communicatings.

The approach has always been associated with a set of metatheorectical assumptions that methodologically inform specific methods. One useful example for illustrating this point is the SMM Micro-Moment Time-Line interviewing approach (Dervin, 1983, 2008). The approach was widely adopted by Library and Information Science researchers to study information seeking and using behaviour in the 1980s and became main stream in 1990s in a variety of research contexts, e.g. the study of communication campaign and media audiences; the study of information seeking and use; the study of patients as recipients of health messages. SMM's applicability to design knowledge management practice was introduced by Dervin in 1998 when she called for alternative KM practices (Dervin, 1998). Dervin suggested that KM practitioners (as well as many other categories of system practitioners) continued to struggle with issues which she and colleagues have been zeroing in on since 1972 (Dervin and Foreman-Wernet, 2003). Those issues result from our organizations continuing to use transmission communication logics that are simply not communicative.

Dervin's Sense-Making Methodology is defined as a set of meta-theoretic assumptions, a foundation for methodological guidance, specific research methods (both for data collection and for question framing and analysis), and a set of communication and design practices. All of these elements are generated from a philosophical perspective that regards information or knowledge as a human tool designed for making and unmaking sense of a reality that is simultaneously both chaotic and orderly (Dervin, 1992; Dervin, 2008)

Sense-Making makes no distinction between data, information, knowledge and wisdom. Knowledge is the sense made at a particular point in time-space by an individual. As Dervin says, sometimes it is shared and codified; sometimes a number of people agree upon it; sometimes it is entered into a formalized discourse and gets published; sometimes it gets tested in other times and spaces and takes on the status of facts; sometimes it is fleeting and unexpressed; sometimes it is hidden and suppressed; sometimes it gets imprimatured and becomes unjust law; sometimes it takes on the status of dogma; sometimes it is besieged and surrounded by confusions and angst.

In this paper, the authors use the label 'knowledging' to refer to the gaining of new knowledge through the users' eyes in order to serve users' needs. This is informed by Dervin's (1998, 2003) call for understanding knowledge management as communication; and communication as communicatings, as verbings. Thus, knowledge management becomes the designing of 'sense-making' and 'sense-unmaking' (or 'knowledging') practices and systems to allow users to self-reflect as well as to gain multiple perspectives from listening to what others can offer, taking into account the power issues which can constraint what users are able to ask for, and ultimately to address sense-making needs at specific moments in time-space.

In order to design KM practices and systems to understand 'knowledging' processes, Dervin argues that KM practitioners and researchers have to take into account first and foremost an understanding that most of the things that organizations have tried to use to "predict" communication behavior (e.g. attending to messages, thinking about them, using them) simply have not predicted well. While some variance is accounted for it is usually very modest and further does not help us in communicating well with specific individuals. Thus, the entire roster of things about people that have been assumed to be constant attributes that predict don't work when we think communicatively. This includes age, gender, geography, work role, generation Y, department, function, service area, industry group, client team, task, lifestyle etc. Further, even outsider assessments of situational conditions do not predict well because situations are seen differently by different observers. Not only do these assumed "constancies" not predict well at one time, even more difficult is that people are constantly changing their sense-makings so what might have "predicted" modestly well yesterday will not do so for the same individuals tomorrow.

Thus, Dervin is asking KM researchers and practitioners to focus on studying and helping users-in-situations moving through time-space. For Dervin, this mandate not only informs user studies but informs the design and implementation of systems and practice. Bottom line, Dervin calls for the application of communicative procedures -- procedures that are informed by an understanding of how communication can work well -- to every aspect of research, design, and practice because these activities are all fundamentally driven by communication. The difficulty with merely inviting more message flow, Dervin challenges, is that there are yawnings gaps between what people think about and make sense of internally and what our systems and societal conventions allow them to talk about. Take, for example, the organizational emphasis on best practices which defies the realities that people learn the most from their struggles and failures and those of others.

Further, best practices are usually offered as solutions out of context when in actuality they have themselves have arisen out of struggles.

Thus, what happens when we give people access to use the new ITs (such as Web2.0 tools) to access or contribute ideas, information, content or knowledge is that messages flow without opportunities for sense-making -- for knowledging to happen. Dervin argues that most often what happens can be seen as kinds of "spontaneous talking shop" events that do not well serve the communicative design of KM systems and practices. Spontaneous communication, too often, reinforces current habits and cower structures. As a result, the communication flows miss the vital but hidden understandings that users have locked within them and do not readily share.

Evidence to date about what is happening with online communication is that these communication failures become even more exaggerated as spontaneous messages flow in forums, blogs and tweets without genuine listening and dialogue with one another. While clearly these new tools are seen as liberating by many users, evidence shows that mostly people who already agree with each other attend to each other. In short, all this increasing communication activity is not facilitating what we think of as knowledging -- where people share and hear across their different perspectives; where they share their understandings of the different pieces of sometimes complex organizational puzzles; where they reflect on their own sense-makings, where they come from and how they have helped and hindered; where they share their muddles and hunches and work together to come up with new understandings despite the reality that some understandings will remain incomplete.

Based on these arguments, we propose that the explicit design of communication procedures is critical to facilitate ‘knowledging’ and cannot be left to chance. This means that in designing Web2.0 tools, one needs to allow learning to be shared in a way that welcomes both majority and minority voices and allows users to connect internally within themselves across time-space as well as with each other. Ultimately, Web2.0 enabled KM practices/systems should allow users to be able to move forward on what they need to make sense of at the time they need to do so. Web2.0 tools are generally seen as ‘easy to use’ and users can be self-organized without the need to moderate and facilitate the dialogue. We propose that KM practitioners need to think otherwise.

Sense-Making Methodology is not about persuasion or dictating the outcomes on behalf of users (e.g. deciding what users choose to do and think as a result of having access to knowledge residing in KM systems). Companies designing Web2.0 enabled KM systems with the sole purpose of indoctrinating employees to adopt best practice policies, methodologies (as defined by experts) or to conform to senior managers’ wish will not find SMM useful. Dervin, in fact, assumes that KM systems that make these assumptions may, under some circumstances, get obedience without understanding and, thus, impede long-term organizational growth. SMM focuses on communication processes rather than outcomes. Accepting that SMM might be seen as utopian in its vision, Dervin believes that by introducing disciplined and dialogic communication practices, the methodology helps surface multiple perspectives, and open up dialogue and possibilities. Further, while applying SMM may increase uncertainty in some ways, it allows users to 'learn from within' and reflect deeply to understand and address their own needs as well as the needs of others and their organizations.

In introducing Sense-Making Methodology, Dervin has stated clearly that "the bottom-line goal of SMM from its inception has been to find out what users – audiences, customers, patients, clients, patrons, employees – 'really' think, feel, want, dream" (Dervin, 1998, pp.39). Dervin always places the term "really" in quotes because she assumes that the best we can do is surround that which we cannot touch and cannot freeze or bend to our wills.

She has elaborated that "Sense-Making uses a central metaphor – the metaphor of human beings traveling through time-space, coming out of situations with history and partial instructions, arriving at new situations, facing gaps, building bridges across those gaps, evaluating outcomes and moving on. This does not imply that all sense-making is purposive. Rather, it suggests that gap-bridging is mandated by the human condition. SMM's central meta-theoretic concepts include: time, space, horizon, movement, gap and power. Its central operational concepts include: situation, history, gap, barrier, constraint, force, bridge, sense-making strategies, outcomes, helps and hurts. These concepts are illustrated in Diagram 1, what Dervin calls the "Sense-Making Methodology Metaphor."

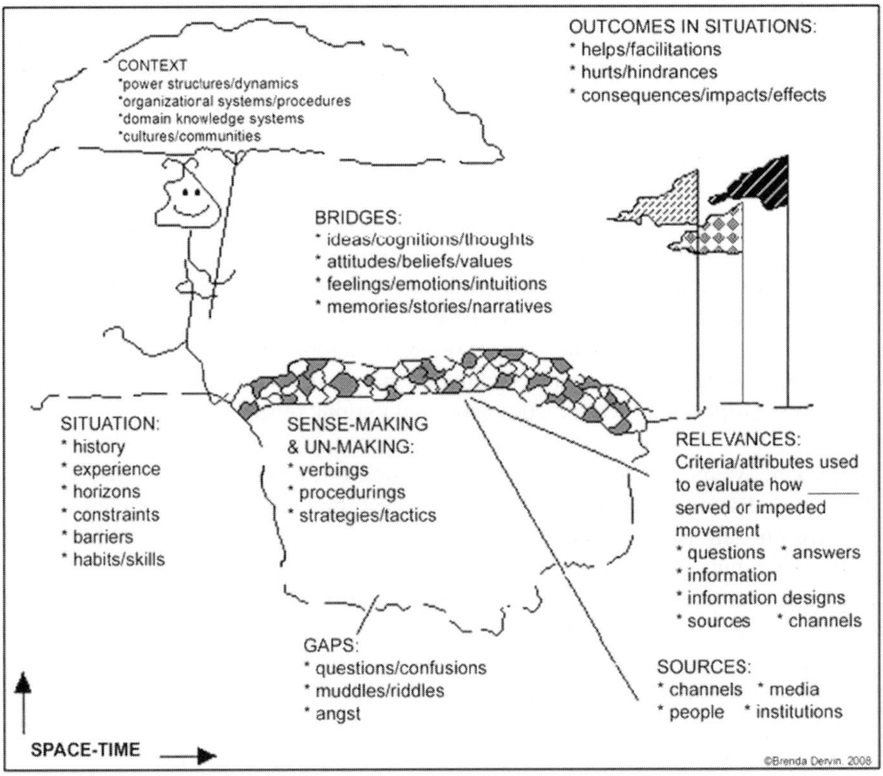

Diagram 1: Dervin's Sense-Making Metaphor (Dervin, 2008)

"This metaphor provides guidance for thinking about people, talking to them, asking questions of them and designing systems to serve them. In capsule it says, look to the gap: this is where you will find the action in sense-making and sense-unmaking; in communicating; and, in the creating, seeking, using and rejecting of information and knowledge". Earlier versions of the metaphor exists (e.g. Dervin & Foreman-Wernet, 2003), this 2008 version introduced a recent refinement showing a person carrying an umbrella moving across time-space to better reflect how SMM defines context. It also shows gaps all over the picture to reflect the meta-theoretical assumption that 'gappiness' is a fundamental human experience which is at the core of SMM. (Dervin, 2008).

The SMM metaphor asks researchers to understand users' needs by looking at the SMM triangle of 'situation', 'gaps' and 'help', and by asking these questions: (Dervin, 1992):

- What led you to this situation?
- Where did you want to get to?
- What gaps did you see?
- What got in the way?
- What help did you get along the way?
- What emotions/feelings did you experience?
- If you had a magic wand, what would you like to happen?

SMM applies this metaphor in different ways depending on research and practice purposes and to different ranges of time-space. For example, in some applications attentions are focused on entire situations; in others, on micro-moments of time-space within situations. Further, the depth of attentions to either situations or specific micro-moments in situations vary from purposively more shallow to purposively very intensive and deep. This choice depends on purposes and the extent to which stereotyped understandings dominate the social context shielding from view how individuals struggle to make sense of their relationships with themselves, with others, and with their organizational/social contexts.

In implementing methodologically this continual struggle of humans to navigate between their inner and outer worlds, their own senses of self and the demands of organizations and communities, Dervin is emphasizing that we must address issues relating to how power (internal and external) both can enable and/or constrain human sense-making and human knowledge sharing. Therefore, in designing Web2.0 enabled KM practices and systems, she stresses that:

1. We must provide safe spaces for people to attend to power issues so that they are willing to tell us things that ordinary interviewing practices miss entirely. If this cannot be done in public arenas, then anonymity structures need to be added.
2. We need to be cautious of one-way knowledge transfer from experts to novices. We must be aware of power issues and consciously promote disciplined communications procedures to invite two-way sharing and negotiating of meanings (Dervin, 1989).
3. We must be careful not to design KM systems/processes from the experts' perspectives. Instead, we must look for differences in how people see their worlds (e.g. information that is presented to them), and also the differences in how they 'make their worlds' (i.e. construct a sense of their worlds in their subject domains

and how things works). Years of SMM research has shown that if we conceptualize the human condition as a struggle through an incomplete reality, then the similar struggles of others become more informative to individual and collective sense-making, and, thus, to knowledging.

4. Designing Online 'Safety Zone' at ERM: Informed by Sense-Making Methodology

Environmental Resources Management (ERM) is the world's largest all-environmental consultancy firm which provides environmental, health and safety, risk, and social consulting services. ERM delivers innovative solutions for business and government clients, helping them understand and manage their impacts on the environment around them. ERM has 137 offices in 39 countries and employs over 3,300 staff. More information is available on www.erm.com

One of ERM's core services is to help industrial clients around the world achieve their environmental, health and safety compliance obligations, reduce accident and injury rates, and minimize impacts on the environment. While many companies have Safety Programs in place, they can become dry, corporate and unimaginative over time. While compliance-driven Safety processes are a critical part of any Safety program, they can be seen as top-down, bureaucratic and lack imagination. Many EHS directors ask: How can we add a human touch to the Safety program? How can I better engage and communicate with employees to change people's behaviors and understand the importance of Safety at work? Can Web2.0 open up new possibilities?

ERM cares about its own Health & Safety Performance and is committed to ensuring ERM is a safe place to work for employees, contractors and clients. ERM faces the same challenge that its clients do and has asked the same questions. In 2008, ERM began to implement its next generation Safety program and has fully embraced its award winning intranet named 'Minerva' and utilized Web2.0 to share knowledge on Safety related issues and policies as a strand of work to improve ERM's safety culture (Cheuk, 2009). This section draws on ERM's own experience adopting Web2.0 features on Minerva and discusses how Dervin's Sense-Making Methodology has contributed to the art of designing Web2.0 enabled 'Safety Zone' to promote the 'knowledging' of Safety topics.

4.1. *Level 1: The Web2.0 Beginning - Putting in Place a Blog*

Prior to the introduction of Minerva, employee communications about the Safety program had only been one-way. Regular headline News items would appear in the company newsletter to inform staff of Safety policies and procedures. The Safety intranet site was centrally managed by the Environmental Health & Safety (EHS) Director where all safety policies and documentations were stored. Although face-to-face meetings and training were organized in selected offices, the director was not able to easily engage with all employees worldwide. The knowledge management model then was a transmission model where best practices were defined and transferred from the EHS director (and his team of experts) to all employees with a focus on compliance.

In January 2008, ERM began its journey to fully leverage the power of a Web2.0 enabled 'Minerva' intranet to explore new ways of involving all staff in Safety dialogue and to co-create the next generation safety culture together.

The first initiative was to bring our face-to-face Safety ritual online. In ERM, all face-to-face meetings start with a Safety Moment when a member of staff will stand up and share a recent safety issue and the learning points. This ritual has been taken online by establishing a 'Safety Zone' on the Minerva homepage, which is automatically launched whenever employees log on to their computers. The 'Safety Zone' provides a virtual common room for all ERM employees to experience the weekly safety moment together.

The Safety Zone is designed using a blog feature. On clicking on the Safety Zone as shown in Diagram 2, users can access the weekly blog posts - some posts embed video or podcasts - that every staff can comment on to share their experiences on a safety topic and how to prevent similar accidents from reoccurring. Each week, a colleague from a different part of the world will contribute a Safety Moment. The blog talks about real life safety incidents ranging from near miss situations at natural gas facilities and how good communication can help avoid accidents from driving in bad weather and checking for insects that bite before embarking on certain tasks. The discussions entail lessons learnt and how such situations can be avoided.

Diagram 2: Minerva homepage showing Safety Zone

4.2. *Level 2: Not a 'Spontaneous' Blog*

ERM has taken a more disciplined approach to structure the dialogue which happens on the 'Safety Zone' blog. Unlike a free form blog where staff can post any questions and answers around any Safety issues, some communication procedures are put in place in facilitating more in-depth conversation. SMM alerted us that spontaneous dialogue can reinforce old stereotypes and patterns and existing power structures. To attend to this issue, when the safety Zone was first rolled out, a communication procedure was put in place to guide the sharing of any Safety Moments. Whether the participants were ERM employees or the EHS Director, they had to follow a structured template to invite the sharing of deeper thoughts:

- Describe a situation when you faced a Safety issue at work (e.g. 'An ERM subcontractor was drilling soil borings when they struck an underground electrical line. The electric company had removed at least on electric line but was no longer aware of the remaining line. Although no injuries were sustained, one service line was completely severed, with a second line partially severed').
- What confusion / questions / muddle did you have at that time? (e.g. 'I wonder what policies I should follow? What should I have done to prevent this from happening?')
- What helped? What hurt? (e.g. 'I remember the slogan 'I see it, I own it', I know I need to do something to avoid my staff and contractors from getting into this situation')
- Did you see that there are forces which you cannot control? (e.g. 'I felt that as the subcontractor was not an ERM employee, should I raise this issue with them')
- If you had a magic wand, what could have helped to prevent this from happening? (e.g. 'I would ensure that we insist our subcontractors also have to carry out all the required checks before we start any drilling work')
- At the end of the blog post, the contributor has to post this question to all staff 'Does anyone have a similar Safety situation that you would like to mention for our benefit?'

We are aware of power issues and that some staff may not be willing to voice their opinion or associate their names with a safety issue. The EHS Director welcomes colleagues who are hesitant about sharing their voice on the blog to send their thoughts by email to him. He will then anonymize the contribution and post it on behalf of the colleague. For example, a local Safety leader was not sure if he should be sharing a Safety Moment because he thought it could be a very local issue. He hesitated at first, the advice he was given was that the EHS Director welcomed all Safety Moments, and if he did not want to submit the local issue under his own name, he could send it to the EHS Director to be posted up on his behalf. Another participant was concerned that his comment on a Safety policy would offend a senior colleague, so his comment was sent to EHS Director and posted up as an anonymous comment.

4.3. *Level 3: Beyond Knowledge Transfer - Learning from Oneself and from Others*

The thinking behind asking employees to write a Safety Moment down on a blog (or an email sent to EHS Director) or to share a similar situation one has experienced, is that self-reflection is a learning and 'knowledging' exercise. Self-reflection (i.e. transferring knowledge from self to self) does not traditionally fall into the KM agenda as source and senders are usually seen as two different parties. Allowing other staff to reflect on experience shared by others, and then relating others' experience with self is another way of gaining deep insight or learning. Inviting all staff to share similar situations at the end of each Safety Moment aims to achieve this goal.

This new way of thinking about 'knowledging' as learning from oneself, and learning from others through self-reflection has not been explicit in KM practices when the focus is on corporate information management, information architecture or taxonomy management, with the aim to transfer information from the source to the recipients. Although KM and learning should be closely linked, in practice, corporate KM function tends to align closely with IT or strategic planning or communication (defined as marketing and advertising) department. The alignment between KM and organizational development and learning functions is rare.

Informed by SMM, in this ERM example 'knowledging' and learning becomes inseparable, as we move away from managing knowledge as 'thing' (e.g. Safety document repository, Safety news alerts) to focus on the 'flow' of knowledgings -- (i.e. the moments when people make sense of Safety Moments that others have experienced, allowing them time to reflect and do some self sense making). In this approach, knowledge management is redefined as 'knowledging' and communicating and learning become central and integrated part of knowledging processes.

4.4. *Level 4: From Top-Down Communication to Promoting Genuine Two-Way Safety Dialogue*

From the onset it is made clear that the ground rule is to allow employees to listen and learn from one another, rather than debating and arguing whose best practices are the best. All staff are asked to share their comments in a non-accusatory style. It is made clear that the Safety Zone is a space for all staff to talk about Safety issues with the Safety leader leads by example. It is expected that all staff treat one another with respect, and are not there to attack and promote one's ego.

The coaching sessions with the EHS Director were important. At one point, he raised concern with regard to a colleague posting an 'inappropriate' suggestion on the blog and was asking the intranet team to help delete the comment. The EHS Director eventually learned that he has to let go of his own expert status and ego, and step back and listen to what other employees have to say. Instead of going in and offering the best practice expert's advice, he has learned to clarify misunderstanding, point to useful documents which help users to address a Safety issue. Instead of being the know-it-all, he becomes the facilitator. The post was not taken down. Rather, the Director went in to explain how the situation has been/could be handled in other ways.

In another example, when the EHS Director spotted a trend that there were 9 near misses related to Sub-Surface Clearance (SCC) within 2 months, he organised a global one hour Safety Stand Down to ask colleagues to reflect on what went wrong and how to avoid serious injuries. After he posted the SCC Safety Moment on the blog, a sceptical comment titled 'Thanks for nothing' came in, the contributor challenged EHS Director that ERM carried out many SCC jobs in a year, and there were many which we did very well, why did we only look at the problems but did not celebrate our success. EHS Director then calmed himself down, and posted a comment acknowledging this concern, took the opportunity to explain why it was important to identity trends to avoid major injuries, and admitted that future Safety communication should place additional emphasis on successful examples. This exchange has helped all employees to better understand the importance of Safety as the EHS Director shared his thought process and struggles he faced leading to the Stand Down exercise.

When the blog was first launched, the former EHS Director was so committed and enthusiastic that he replied immediately to any comments posted up, and was seen as dominating the discussion. He was immediately coached to understand his role has changed from the expert to a facilitator to provide space for staff to exchange ideas. He eventually took up a moderator role and he would offer his own insights towards the end of the weekly dialogue.

In another example, an employee has shared a Safety Moment pointing out that the colour of a yellow Safety Jacket can attract insects in the forest during summer time. The feedback, which was a surprise to the Safety team as they had not considered this in the past, was taken seriously and led to a change in Safety guidelines. The suggestion to change the guidelines was made publicly by a senior executive leader as a blog comment. This sends a strong message that the voice of our employees is being heard, valued and utilized to inform decisions. It also sends a clear message that the leaders and experts are learning from ERM employees. And, it is an excellent example of how organizations need the knowledging inputs of their workers because, as SMM fundamentally assumes, no expert can possibly surveill all relevant inputs.

Previously, Safety News Alerts came from the EHS Director (i.e. the expert) whose role it is to inform/educate/download and ultimately ensure compliance. Currently, our Behavioural-Based Safety Program becomes a learning experience for all staff to make sense of the importance of Safety, using a combination of Web2.0 tools and blending 'knowledging' procedures that integrate 'communicating' and 'learning' to allow our staff to draw on their own experience and build commitments to Safety from within.

4.5. *Level 6: Rich Dialogue Provides Rich Context and Gives Meaning to Faceless Safety Procedures*

At the end of each Safety Moment, there is a formal reminder that there is a Safety intranet to download safety guidance/procedures and to access to the Safety Management Systems. The stories shared online create the rich context to help staff to be more motivated to use the Safety systems, forms and policies. When an employee suggests a safety procedure should be followed, the document is introduced in the context of a real situation. This gives more personal meaning to the documents as staff have the chance to reflect on their own experience before they are directed to these documents. The interaction and the conversation have given 'life' to the documents and best practices sitting on the Safety Intranet Document Repository.

The blog compliments rather than replaces the traditional intranet which provides Safety information. The Safety intranet site comes with a document repository. In order to provide an update on Swine Flu, for example, a Swine Flu Channel has been set up and uses RSS feeds to ensure that the latest information from official sources get published immediately. A monthly alert summarizing all the Safety highlights is delivered to all employees via our ERM's internal monthly newsletter.

In addition, the newly launched safety intranet comes with multimedia channels to deliver regular podcasts and video casts. For a two month period, the intranet hosted an interactive forum which supported a global consultation exercise discussing how ERM should implement our next generation Safety management and reporting system. The forum supplemented face-to-face consultation meetings and gave voice to any employee who has not had the chance to participate in face-to-face meetings. Employees were encouraged to talk about what they liked and do not like, what they found helpful or what did not help.

4.6. *Level 7: The Art of Web2.0 and Leadership 2.0 in Action*

With Web2.0, the EHS Director is no longer the only person who can share best practices on Safety issues. He is not the only expert who can publish Safety content on the intranet. All employees can now submit a Safety moment online and share their best practices from their own experience. The EHS Director becomes a coach, a facilitator to help people to make sense of Safety systems and policies. He helps to clarify misunderstandings. In the process, he comes to understand why staff do not practice Safety act as expected. By opening up the dialogue and allowing staff to voice dissent and alternative views, the Safety Program becomes more robust, human and less seen as merely a compliance and bureaucratic exercise. The ultimate goal is the same: to achieve a zero tolerance Safety Culture. It is the pathway to get there that has changed.

This example shows that the art of Web2.0 design is about blending stories, self-reflection, communication, information, knowledge and documents by design. This disciplined approach to design Web2.0 applications, informed by SMM, rests on an alternative set of assumptions about 'knowledge' that zero in on the central SMM assumptions about gappiness in terms of how human beings make and unmake sense of their realities. With this approach, knowledge management focuses on the process of knowing, learning, unlearning or simply speaking -- all seen as 'knowledging'. We propose leaders who take on board this alternative set of values and assumptions have the secret ingredients to a new kind of Leadership 2.0 – to reap the benefits of Web2.0.

In his evaluation of these efforts, Mark Clark, ERM's EHS Director said, "Companies can reap the benefits of Web2.0 only if there is a willingness to establish a genuine two-way dialogue with all staff. While Web2.0 allow users to generate content, my team and I need to constantly listen, read suggestions, stories and ideas submitted by staff and provide feedback and guidance to the employees based on their needs."

5. Conclusion

In this paper, Dervin's Sense-Making Methodology is introduced and a practical example is provided to demonstrate a discipline approached to design Web2.0 applications at ERM. The design of knowledge management practices based on an explicit set of meta-theoretical assumptions about how communication can work better is critical for developing common understandings, allowing meaningful and constructive debates, and ultimately advancing the knowledge management discipline (Dervin, 2003).

Web2.0 is generally regarded as easy because any users can generate any content at anytime they wish. There is a danger that KM practitioners assume that the application of Web2.0 does not require any design effort, whereas in fact, it requires our closest attention to communication procedures. There is a common saying that 'put the wiki or blog in place, let people run with it, and it will catch fire'. The author argues that the design of Web2.0 applications must be rigorous and well thought through. This example we have provided here suggests that a well-developed (which takes a lot of hard work), allows users to feel it is a breeze to use the tool for having meaningful dialogue.

This paper highlights an example of designing a 'Safety Moment' project informed by Sense-Making Methodology. SMM does not provide a recipe to design a one-size-fits-all solution. Rather, it provides a framework of assumptions and a set of values that leaders/designers can draw upon in their designs. In the project that serves as exemplar here, SMM allowed leaders/designers to consider six aspects of 'knowledging' when introducing a blog:

1. A conscious decision to use a blog functionality to promote genuine two-way dialogue instead of a transmission-based top-down communication approach
2. Using SMM informed questions to discipline the blog posts and the blog comments
3. Using the blog to facilitate lateral discussion rather than top-down communication. This means that the EHS director had to lower his ego to consciously ask for dissent, tolerate alternative views and learn from staff.
4. Valuing every employee's input by ensuring that the blog design did not silence certain voices. This included allowing anonymous posting to address power issues or to help colleagues who are less technically savvy be comfortable participating.

5. Using blog writing as a learning tool to promote self-reflective learning. This means expanding the scope of knowledge sharing to sharing with oneself and blending learning with knowledging.
6. Welcoming the surprises that come when you open genuine online dialogue. Some of the surprises are hard to hear; some are immediately useful innovations.

Too often, KM practitioners bemoan -- how can we get employees to be willing to share their knowledge and adopt best practices. How can we use Web2.0 to do this. We propose that these questions miss the point. We propose that knowledging must rest on sound principles of communication. We believe SMM provides an avenue that permits the conscious design of tools that are genuinely communicative and dialogic so they can address the needs of living, breathing human beings. We propose that there needs to be a new kind of Leadership 2.0 that does more than call for dialogue but implements in ways that permit us to see how knowledging is communication-based and how it involves more than sharing but reflecting and muddling and learning as well. We submit that this is the secret ingredient that will allow us to fully reap the benefits from Web2.0 for knowledge management. While the project described here is only a beginning and there is much still to learn about designing KM systems as knowledging systems, we judge this beginning as fruitful.

References

Brown, J. S. & Duguid, P. (2000). *The social life of information*. Boston, Massachusetts: Harvard Business School Press.

Browning, L & Boudes, T. (2005). The use of narrative to understand and respond to complexity: A comparative analysis of the Cynefin and Weickian models. E:CO 7 (3–4), 32–39.

Cheuk, Bonnie (2009). *Bringing Health & Safety to Life*. Inside Knowledge Magazine. June 2009 Vol 10 No 9.

Cheuk, Bonnie (2008). Delivering business value through Information Literacy in the workplace. Libri 57(3).

Cheuk, Bonnie (2007). It's more than technology: How ERM has embraced web2.0 to address environmental issues. Paper presented at the Online Information Conference 2007, London.

Denning, S. (2000). *The Springboard: How Storytelling ignites action in knowledge-era organizations*. KMCI Press.

Dervin, B. (1989). "Audience as listener and learner, teacher and confidante: The Sense-Making approach." In R. E. Rice & C. K. Atkin (Eds.), *Public communication campaigns* (2nd ed., pp. 67-86). Newbury Park, CA: Sage. Reprinted in: B. Dervin &

L. Foreman-Wernet (with E. Lauterbach) (Eds.). (2003). *Sense-Making Methodology reader: Selected writings of Brenda Dervin* (pp. 215-232). Cresskill, NJ: Hampton Press.

Dervin, B. & Naumer, C. (in press). Sense-Making. In Bates, M. J. & Maack, M.N. Encyclopedia of Library and Information Science. Taylor and Francis.

Dervin, B. & Reinhard, C. (in press). Communication and communication studies. In Bates, M. J. & Maack, M.N. Encyclopedia of Library and Information Science. Taylor and Francis.

Dervin, B. (1992) "From the mind's eye of the user: The Sense-Making qualitative-quantitative methodology." In J. D. Glazier & R. R. Powell (Eds.), *Qualitative research in information management*: 61-84. Englewood, CO: Libraries Unlimited.

Dervin, B. (1998), "Sense-making theory and practice: an overview of user interests in knowledge seeking and use", Journal of Knowledge Management, Vol 2 No 2 Dec 1998, pp.36-46.

Dervin, B. (1999) "Chaos, order and Sense-Making: A proposed theory for information design". In R. Jacobson (Ed.), *Information design*: 35-57. Cambridge, MA: MIT Press.

Interviewing Dervin, B. (2008) Interviewing as dialectical practice: Sense-Making Methodology as exemplar. Presented at International Association of Media and Communication Research (IAMCR) Meeting, Stockholm, Sweden: July 20-25.

Dervin, B., Foreman-Wernet, L. (2003) *Sense-Making Methodology Reader: selected writings of Brenda Dervin*. Cresskill, New Jersey: Hampton Press.

Dervin, B. (in press). *Hidden passions, burning questions. The other side of so-called mass audiences.* In: Foreman-Wernet, L. and Dervin, B..Audiences and the Arts: Communication Perspectives. Creskill, NJ: Hampton Press.

Dervin, B. (2003). Human studies and user studies: a call for methodological inter-disciplinarity. *Information Research*, Vol. 9 No. 1. http://InformationR.net/ir/9-1/paper166.html

Dervin, B. (2003). Verbing communication: Mandate for disciplinary invention. In B. Dervin & L. Foreman-Wernet (with E. Lauterbach) (Eds.). *Sense-Making Methodology reader: Selected writings of Brenda Dervin* (pp. 101-110). Cresskill, NJ: Hampton Press.

Fairhurst, G. T., & Putnam, L. L. (2004). "Organizations as Discursive Constructions." *Communication Theory*, 14(1), 5-26.

Hildreth, Paul M. & Kimble, Chris (2002). The duality of knowledge. *Information Research*, Vol. 8 No. 1, October 2002. http://informationr.net/ir/8-1/paper142.html

McAfee, Andrew (2006). Enterprise2.0: The dawn of emergent collaboration. S*loan Management Review, Vol 47 No 3, reprint no 47306.*

Nonaka, I., & Takeuchi, H. (1995). *The knowledge-creating company*. New York: Oxford University Press.

Nonaka, I. & Peltokorpi, V. (2006) "Objective and subjectivity in knowledge management: a review of 20 top articles" *Knowledge and Process Management*, 13(2), Apr/June, 73-82.

Putnam, L. L., & Krone, K. J. (Eds.). (2006). Organizational Communication (5 volume set). London: Sage

Snowden, D. (2002) "Complex acts of knowing: paradox and descriptive self-awareness." *Journal of Knowledge Management*, 66(2), 100-111.

Snowden, D. & Stanbridge, P. (2004). "The landscape of management: creating the context for understanding social complexity." *E:CO Special double issue*, 6(1-2), 140-148.

Souto, P. C., Dervin & Savolainen, R. (2008). Designing for knowledge worker informings: An exemplar application of Sense-Making Methodology. Presented at American Society for Information Science and Technology, Columbus, Ohio, October 24-29.

Stephens, R. (2009). Blog: http://www.collaborage.com/ (dated 22 July 2009)

Wilson, Tom. (2002) The nonsense of 'knowledge management' *Information Research*, Vol. 8 No. 1, October 2002. http://informationr.net/ir/8-1/paper144.html#sch67 Retrieved on 8 July 2006.

Weick, K.E. & Browning, L.D. (1986). Argument and narration in organizational communication. *Journal of Management*. 12(2), 243–259.

Weick, K.E. & Sutcliffe, K.M. Managing the Unexpected: Assuring High Performance in an Age of Complexity; Jossey-Bass: San Francisco, CA, 2001.

Wenger, Etienne. (1998). *Communities of Practice: learning, meaning and identity*. New York: Cambridge University Press.

MOTIVATION, IDENTITY, AND AUTHORING OF THE WIKIPEDIAN

JOSEPH C. SHIH
Department of Information Management, Lunghwa University of Science and Technology, Taoyuan County, Taiwan, (R.O.C.)
Email: joseph@mail.lhu.edu.tw

C. K. FARN
Department of Information Management, National Central University, Taoyuan County, Taiwan, (R.O.C.)
Email: ckfarn@mgt.ncu.edu.tw

Wikipedia is an online free encyclopedia which is edit by million people spontaneously. This article aims at how Wikipedians' intrinsic and extrinsic motivations influence their volitional authoring. Research model posits that altruism, expected reputation, and expected money reward affect authoring behavior. More specific, this relationship is also mediated by both attitude and identity. We also regard perceived behavioral control as a critical role for fostering volitional authoring. Sample data were from "Wikipedian Discussion Board" of a famous BBS in Taiwan. All respondents (156 samples) had posted articles in the BBS, but not all had experienced authoring in Wikipedia. Structural equation modeling was used to test the research model. According to the result, we have insight into the motivation of Wikpedian's volitional authoring.

1. Introduction

Wikipedia, a free online encyclopedia that anyone can edit, has a tremendous impact on how a great many writers gather information about the world (http://www.widipedia.org/). With no paid editors and written by numerous volunteers, Wikipedia is now emerged as the No. 1 go-to information source in the world. Wikipedia also now ranks eighth (July 2009) on the list of most visited sites on the Internet (http://alexa.com/), containing over 2.9 million articles in the English version (July 2009).

However, there are still a few people detracting the value of content (Badke, 2008), but the Wikipedian have persisted in pouring more and more items into the online encyclopedia. The phenomenon is interesting that there are still thousands of people participating in authoring items spontaneously, disregarding the controversial open source project being discredited by non-supporters. Furthermore, the economic exchange perspective posits that an individual's decision making was found upon rational rule, as benefit surpassing cost. It looks as if the Wikipedian are not consistent with this tenet obviously. This paper, accordingly, is to understand how the Wikipedian's motivation links to their volitional authoring, more specific, to examine their authoring behavior through the lens of attitude and virtual community identity.

2. Conceptual Background

2.1 Motivations for Participating in Open Source Project

Motivations are commonly categorized into extrinsic and intrinsic by researchers. Intrinsic motivations contain inherent satisfactions rather than their substantive consequence, such as volunteering and enjoying helping others which are congruent with one's value system, (Kankanhalli et al., 2005; Ryan and Deci, 2000; Wasko and Faraj, 2005). On the other hand, extrinsic motivations means a focus on expected benefits of donating, where the extrinsic rewards are believed to exceed the contribution's costs (Kankanhalli et al., 2005; Lerner and Tirole, 2002). Motivations of volunteering behavior have noticed in previous research (Clary et al., 1998), for example, Clary et al. (1998) classified six motivational categories for the volunteer. The categories include values, social, understanding, career, protective, and enhancement, and, contrasting with the functions, we describe the Wikipedian's conceivable motivation in Table 1.

Table 1 Descriptions of Volunteer's Motivations

Function	Conceptual definition	Description for Wikipedian
Values	The individual volunteers in order to express or act on important values like humanitarianism.	The Wikipedian feel it is important to help other by means of authoring.
Understanding	The volunteer is seeking to learn more about the world or exercise skills that are often unused.	Authoring lets the Wikipedian learn through direct and hands-on activities.
Enhancement	One can grow and develop psychologically through volunteer activities.	Authoring makes the Wikipedian feel better about themselves.
Career	The volunteer has the goal of gaining career-related experience through volunteering.	Authoring can help the Wikipedian to get experience related to current job.
Social	Volunteering allows an individual to strengthen his or her social relationships.	The Wikipedian identify to Wikipedia community.
Protective	The individual uses volunteering to reduce negative feelings, such as guilt, or to address personal problems.	Authoring is a good escape from day-to-day worry.

2.2 Attitude and Behavioral Control and Online Authoring

Theory of Planned Behavior (TPB) hypothesized that intention to perform a behavior is based on: attitudes, subjective norms and perceived behavioral control (Ajzen, 1991). Attitude towards performing the behavior is defined as a person's general feeling of performing that behavior if a favorable or unfavorable action. Perceived behavioral control is assumed to reflect past experience as well as anticipated obstacles. The more opportunities and resource that individuals think they possess and the fewer obstacles they anticipate, the greater their perceived control over the behavior. Participating in online activities may be determined by attitude toward and perceived controllability over target behavior, such as blogging, using instant message software, or sharing knowledge in virtual community (Hsu and Chiu, 2008; Kuo and Young, 2008).

2.3 *Social Identity and Online Prosocial Behavior*

Social identity (SI) captures the main aspects of the individual's identification with the group in the sense that a participant comes to view himself or herself as "belonging" to a certain group. A person professes "belonging" to a specific group is a psychological state, distinct from being a unique and distinct individual, conferring a collective representation of who one is (Hogg and Abrams, 1988). Many of previous studies related to online volitional behavior have emphasized the significance of virtual community identity. That participants consider themselves as parts of the target online group may strengthen the self-defining relation to the virtual community as well as foster prosocial behavior such like donating knowledge (Chiu et al., 2006; Jian and Jeffres, 2006; Ma and Agarwal, 2007).

3. Research Model and Hypotheses

3.1 *Research Model*

The present study posits intrinsic and extrinsic motivation associate with both attitude and virtual community identity (VC identity); and attitude, VC identity, and perceived behavior control (PBC) jointly affect authoring behavior. Beside, we also posits that PBC moderates both relationship of attitude-authoring and VC identity-authoring.

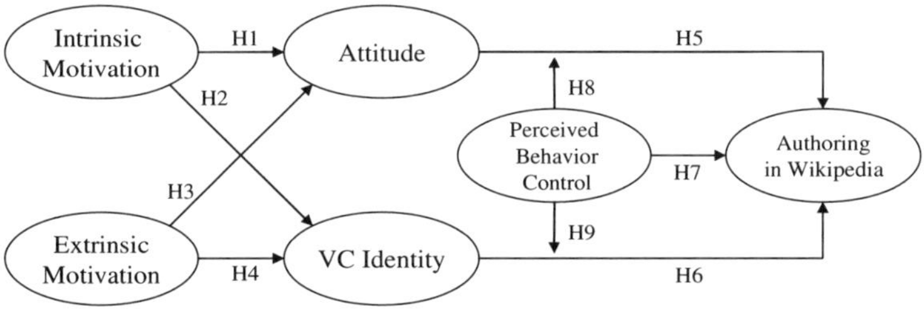

Fig. 1. Research Model.

3.2 *Research Hypotheses*

Expressing or acting on important values like humanitarianism (Clary et al., 1998), it may be the most critical motivation of the Wikipedian. People engage in contribution of open content for their own sakes rather than for some external consequences (Hars and Ou, 2002). Positive relation between intrinsic motivation and authoring in Wikipedia was reported in previous study (Nov and Kuk, 2008). Altruism is a variant of intrinsic motivation in which a Wikipedia seeks to increase the welfare of others. Furthermore, altruism have widely held to be associated with positive attitude toward on-line helping behaviors, such as authoring in blog and participating in open source project (Hars and Ou, 2002; Hsu and Lin, 2008). For example, value of altruism, to which the volunteer may reflect their willingness to help people, is the primary function of the Wikipedian's motivation (Clary and Snyder, 1999). Although Nov and Kuk (2008) proposed general intrinsic motivation in their study, more specific, we argue that altruism influences one's attitude toward authoring in Wikipedia.

H1: Altruism positively associates with attitude toward authoring.

According to social categorization, people use demographic differences or distinguishable characteristic to categorize one another (Chatman and Spataro, 2005). Wikipedians, obviously different from non-participator, are willing to self-identify themselves as a specific collective, so that those in-group members emerge virtual community identity. We have two reasons to infer the relationship. One reason is that the value system of those who are higher extent of altruism may be more possible to align with the mission of Wikipedia. Altruistic people conceive the principle of unselfish concern for or devotion to the welfare of others, whereas writing items in Wikipedia premises on participant's volitional behavior. This logic was also argued by Van Dick et al. (2006) that social identification is positively related to prosocial behavior. Another reason is that professional identity is an individual's self-definition as a member of profession collective (Chreim et al., 2007). They emphasized "role identity" which can make that a professional conducts his or her work look more like professional. Therefore, those high altruistic people are happy to profess themselves as members of Wikipedian. Depending on the virtual community identity, not only a Wikipedian's professional identity is acknowledged but also his or her altruistic authoring is encouraged. Thus, we propose the following hypothesis.

H2: Altruism positively associates with VC identity.

As economic considerations still critical to the volunteer, helper's behaviors in cyberspace are as well, Donath (1999) remarked altruism is insufficient to explain helper's motivation. This viewpoint is even more assertive by Kollock (1999) observing that motivation to contribute to online communities could spring from a variety of sources but none of them depended on altruism. In terms of their viewpoints, the volitional behaviors of the Wikipedian may be influenced by some economic considerations.

Earning reputation is regarded as an extrinsic motivation for a Wikipedian. Reputation is still an important asset, not only in real world but also in cyberspace (Wasko and Faraj, 2005), whereby an individual can leverage to achieve and maintain status within a collective. For the rank of Wikipedian growing with the number of articles edited and accumulated fame as a source of authority, cyberspatial reputation can be a strong incentive to engage authoring activities (Ciffolilli, 2003).

Next, we hypothesize the relationship between money reward and authoring behavior. According to economic exchange theory, one will make decisions by rational self-interest. Thus, prosocial behaviors such as knowledge sharing will occur if its rewards exceed its costs (Bock and Kim, 2002). In light of the rationale, the Wikipedian should have expected money reward while contributing knowledge to Wikipedia.

Obviously, the Wikipedian did not conform to the rule. That the Wikipedian plainly understand no money reward but continually author leads to hypothesize the negative relation between money reward and attitude toward authoring. However, it doesn't mean that Wikipedians hate money but merely they do not expect this extrinsic reward-in terms of money return-while authoring in Wikipedia.

H3: Extrinsic rewards associate with attitude toward authoring

H3a: Expected reputation positively associates with attitude toward authoring.

H3b: Expected money rewards negatively associates with attitude toward authoring.

For earning future reputation in virtual community, a Wikipedian regards social interaction with other aficionados as critical as authoring in virtual community. In additional to engage in authoring and contributing knowledge, the Wikipedian have to maintain a positive social relationship with other Wikipedians. The rationales are that a Wikipedian identifies to his or her community may satisfy the member's need of self-defining and manifest the status of referent power (Bagozzi and Dholakia, 2002). Earning reputation not only is an antecedent for virtual community identity but also a driven force for authoring. Again, no money return is supposed to authoring in Wikipedia that obtaining identity from the community may, so that we hypothesize a negative relationship between expected money rewards and virtual community identity.

H4: Extrinsic rewards associate with VC identity.

H4a: Expect reputation positively associates with VC identity.

H4b: Expected money rewards negatively associates with VC identity.

Spending time and effort to complete articles, the Wikipedian consider authoring is consistent with their values and positive for online readers. Theory of Reasoned Action posits that behavioral formation is determined by attitude toward the behavior and subject norms of that behavior. The Wikipedian are inducing the authoring behavior while they have a positive attitude toward authoring. Previous studies related to online knowledge sharing have shown the consistent argument (Bock et al., 2005). For example, Kuo and Young (2008) found that the more favorable the individual's attitude toward knowledge sharing practices, the stronger his/her intention to share knowledge in a teacher's virtual community.

H5: Attitude toward authoring positively associates with authoring in Wikipedia.

Social identity model of deindividuation effects (SIDE) can demonstrate the relationship between Wikipedian's community identity and authoring behavior. Volunteering allows an individual to strengthen his or her social relationships (Clay et al., 1998). In light of the rationale, community identity is useful in explaining individuals' willingness to maintain committed relationship with the group (Nahapiet and Ghoshal,

1998), such as through sharing knowledge within the virtual community (Chiu et al., 2006). Empirical studies have reported that sense of belonging is important and has been used as a test for the presence of an online community. Jian and Jeffres (2006) argues that people are motivated to contribute to shared electronic databases because by doing so they will maintain and affirm relevant identities. Hsu and Lin (2008) argued the influence of social identification for blog users needs the perception of belonging to the virtual community. Likewise, the Wikipedian will present themselves as belonging to the community through continual authoring. Once being in Wikipedian community that suppresses individual differences and emphasizes a common Wikipedian membership, individuals have a high level of group identity and act according to the objective set up by the group (Kim, 2009). Herein, the objective set by Wikipedian community is contributing knowledge, i.e. authoring in Wikipedia.

H6: VC identity positively associates with authoring in Wikipedia.

As a Wikipedian believes himself or herself having sufficient resources to author in the community, the Wikipedian can complete the authoring behavior. Some obstacles such as no available time or incapable of computer skill make authoring impossible. Perceived behavioral control is an important antecedent of behavior theoretically (Ajzen, 1991) that the belief is a form of self-evaluation which influences decisions about what behaviors to undertake (Bandura, 1977). Previous empirical studies of online behavior also have confirmed the notion (Hsu and Chiu, 2004; Kuo and Young, 2008). Accordingly, we propose the following hypothesis.

H7: Perceived behavioral control positively associates with authoring in Wikipedia.

When the Wikipedian are highly perceived control over getting through with new items for Wikipedia, the positive attitude may foster the Wikipedian more authoring behavior. In term of contrast viewpoint-low perceived behavioral control, if a person thinks it good to author in Wikipedia but he does not have time to do this or he does not have enough computer skill to fill out the job, the person will decline the extent of attitude and then impede the authoring behavior. Likewise, when high perceived behavioral control, people with high VC identity will more possibly engaged in authoring in Wikipedia. Thus, we propose the hypothesis of moderating effect.

H8: The relationship between attitude and authoring in Wikipedia is moderated by perceived behavioral control (PBC). More specific, the relationship between attitude and authoring in Wikipedia is stronger when PBC is high than low.

H9: The relationship between VC identity and authoring in Wikipedia is moderated by perceived behavioral control (PBC). More specific, the relationship between VC identity and authoring in Wikipedia is stronger when PBC is high than low.

4. Research Methodology

A questionnaire was deployed on a web site in which allows respondents to answer the questionnaire. Structural equation modeling (SEM) technique was employed to test research model as well as H1 to H7; H8 and H9, the moderating effect of perceived behavioral control on attitude and identity to authoring behavior, were tested by hierarchical regression analysis. Followings are details of the current research methodology.

4.1 Scale Development

The survey questionnaire was designed on the basis of a comprehensive literature review and was refined via several runs of pretests and revisions.

Altruism was measured by a seven-point scale adopted from Chattopadhyay (1999), developed to capture a respondent's seeking to increase the welfare of others. A sample item is "I will help co-worker (or classmate) who overloads with job (or school-homework)." Expected reputation was measure by a seven-point scale adopted from Constant et al. (1994). Attitude was measured by a seven-point scale adopted from Bock et al. (2005). Virtual community identity was measured by a seven-point scale adopted from Ellemers et al. (1999), developed to capture a respondent's identification with the virtual community in the sense that the one comes to view himself or herself as a member of Wikipedia community. Perceived behavioral control was measured by a seven-point scale adopted from Armitage et al. (1999), developed to capture a respondent's ease or difficulty of authoring in Wikipedia. After examining the nature of this scale, we regarded PBC as a formative construct that we would aggregate the score at consequent stage. In order to measure the extent in which the authors contribute to Wikipedia, we operationalized authoring in Wikipedia with two items, one is time consuming per week and another is the frequency of authoring per week. Detail items are omitted due to the limit of space in conference version.

4.2 Data Collection

A web-based site was deployed that respondents could visit to answer the questionnaire which was designed for collecting empirical data of the current study. To have a broad representation of both Wikipedian-authors and non-Wikipedian authors, participants were invited from the Wikipedian's discussion board of PTT forum which is a famous bulletin board system in Taiwan. We invited them to participate in the survey via an email, in which attaching the web-site's hyperlink, so that they could visit our web page to answer survey questions. They were also informed that we would donate 5 dollars to Wikipedian Foundation while a questionnaire was finished.

There were totally 181 respondents participating in the survey that the valid responding rate is 86% (156 valid) due to dropping 25 invalid questionnaires. Of 156 samples, the characteristics are demonstrated in Table 2

Table 2 Characteristics of Sample

Gender			Education		
Male	123	79%	Under high school	13	8%
Female	33	21%	High school	25	16%
			University	80	51%
Authoring experience			Graduated school	37	24%
Yes	107	69%	PhD	1	1%
No	49	31%			
			Age		
Years of using Wikipedia			Under 15	7	5%
Under 1	37	24%	15 to 19	14	9%
1	73	47%	20 to 24	77	49%
2	32	21%	25 to 29	40	26%
3	9	6%	30 to 34	13	8%
4	4	3%	35 to 40	3	2%
5 and above	1	1%	40 above	2	1%

5. Data Analysis

5.1 Test of Measurement Model

Initial results of the CFA indicates that model were not fit the data well. A careful and iterative inspection of LISREL output revealed that some items did not load on the designated latent factors appropriately, such as standardized loading < 0.6 or associated with high modification indices. All indices are above cut-off value except GFI is slightly lower. The detail results are demonstrated in Table 3.

Before testing the structural model, it is also necessary to examine whether the measurement model had a satisfactory level of validity and reliability. While CR is greater than 0.7 and AVE is greater than 0.5, it implies that the variance captured by the latent construct is more than that by error component (Bagozzi et al., 1991). That is, each measure is accounting for 50 percent or more of the variance of the underlying latent variable (Chin, 1998). As the reports in Table 3, CRs and AVEs are all above recommended cut-off values that the scale is of internal consistency reliability.

Convergent validity ensures that all items measure a single latent construct, and it is established if all item loadings are greater than or equal to the recommended cut-off level of 0.70 (Bassellier et al., 2003). Our results showed that almost loadings of each latent variable are above the cut-off value that only two items' are slightly lower. The details are also exhibited in Table 3.

Discriminant validity reflects the level to which the measures for each dimension are distinctively different from each other. We applied the chi-square difference test to assess the discriminant validity of the measurement model (Bassellier et al., 2003). Accordingly, we conducted 15 pair-wise tests (six constructs) that the results are reported in Table 4. All $\Delta\chi 2$ differences are significant above the level of $Pr[\chi 2(1) \geq 3.84]=0.05$, indicating strong support for discriminant validity (Bassellier et al., 2003; Venkatraman, 1989). Additionally, the correlation matrixes are reported in Table 5.

Table 3 Results of Measurement Model Test

Factor	Composition Reliability	AVE	Items	Loading	t-value	Error
Altruism	.84	.57	AL1	.63	8.67	.60
			AL2	.71	10.17	.49
			AL3	.92	14.28	.16
			AL4	.73	10.43	.47
Expected Reputation	.88	.64	ER1	.76	11.26	.43
			ER2	.91	14.86	.17
			ER3	.88	14.01	.23
			ER4	.63	8.92	.60
Expected Money Reward	---	---	EMR	---	---	---
Attitude	.91	.71	AT1	.78	11.92	.39
			AT2	.83	12.89	.32
			AT3	.89	14.39	.22
			AT4	.87	13.87	.25
Virtual Community Identity	.83	.55	CI1	.72	10.09	.49
			CI2	.74	10.58	.45
			CI3	.74	10.60	.45
			CI4	.76	11.00	.42
Perceived Behavioral Control	---	---	PBC	---	---	---
Authoring in Wikipedia	.85	.73	BE1	.83	12.91	.31
			BE2	.88	14.32	.22

Note: χ^2=229.27, df=152, χ^2/df=1.51, RMSEA=.055, NFI=.91, NNFI=.94, CFI=.96, GFI=.88, AGFI=.84.

Table 4 Test of Discriminant Validity

Test #	Construct	Constrained model $\chi^2(df)$	Unconstrained model $\chi^2(df)$	Difference $\Delta\chi^2$
Altruism with				
1	Expected Reputation	331.37(20)	29.02(19)	302.35(1)
2	Expected Money Reward	320.48(6)	3.06(5)	317.42(1)
3	Attitude	331.31(20)	34.74(19)	296.57(1)
4	Perceived Behavioral Control	315.44(6)	3.07(5)	312.37(1)
5	VC Identity	346.62(20)	28.49(19)	318.13(1)
6	Authoring in Wikipedia	99.38(10)	5.37(9)	94.01(1)
Expected Reputation with				
7	Expected Money Reward	368.39(6)	14.92(5)	242.47(1)
8	Attitude	546.85(20)	40.07(19)	506.78(1)
9	Perceived Behavioral Control	415.48(6)	13.41(5)	402.07(1)
10	VC Identity	347.16(20)	54.01(19)	293.15(1)
11	Authoring in Wikipedia	109.47(10)	14.81(9)	94.66(1)
Expected Money Reward with				
12	Attitude	507.98(6)	4.93(5)	503.05(1)
13	Perceived Behavioral Control	---	---	---
14	VC Identity	282.10(6)	9.68(5)	272.42(1)
15	Authoring in Wikipedia	91.44(2)	0.58(1)	90.86(1)
Attitude with				
16	Perceived Behavioral Control	483.40(6)	4.92(5)	478.48(1)
17	VC Identity	222.34(20)	31.27(19)	191.07(1)
18	Authoring in Wikipedia	98.00(10)	5.93(9)	92.07(1)
Perceived Behavioral Control				
19	VC Identity	289.07(6)	10.73(5)	278.34(1)
20	Authoring in Wikipedia	90.93(2)	1.77(1)	89.16(1)
VC Identity with				
21	Authoring in Wikipedia	124.20(10)	28.46(9)	95.74(1)

Table 5 Correlation Matrix

	Variables	Mean	Std.	1	2	3	4	5	6	7
1	Altruism	5.05	.94	**.73**						
2	Expected Reputation	4.82	1.15	.21	**.80**					
3	Expected Money Reward	3.21	1.68	.10	.37	---				
4	Attitude	5.89	.80	.27	.31	-.13	**.84**			
5	Perceived Behavioral Control	2.67	.87	.16	.01	-.01	.32	---		
6	VC Identity	4.39	.58	.10	.19	-.32	.58	.28	**.74**	
7	Authoring	1.16	1.12	-.05	-.09	-.23	.16	.45	.27	**.85**

5.2 Test of Structural Model and Hypotheses

The results of structural model are demonstrated in Figure 2 that all indices show a good fit between model and data. All paths coefficients and t values are also reported in Figure 2 that H1, H3, H4, H6 and H7 are supported, whereas H2 and H5 are not. Additionally, H8 and H9 were tested by means of HRA, hierarchical regression analysis. In the procedure of HRA, attitude and identity, perceived behavioral control, and the interaction items entered the model sequentially, mapping to model 1, 2, and 3. The overall model fit, path coefficients, and difference of R square of each model and its significance are reported in Table 5. The results show that H9 is supported whereas H8 is not. To have the insight of the interaction role-perceived behavioral control (PBC), a plot is exhibited in Figure 3 showing that high PBC has a stronger effect of VC identity on authoring in Wikipedia than low PBC.

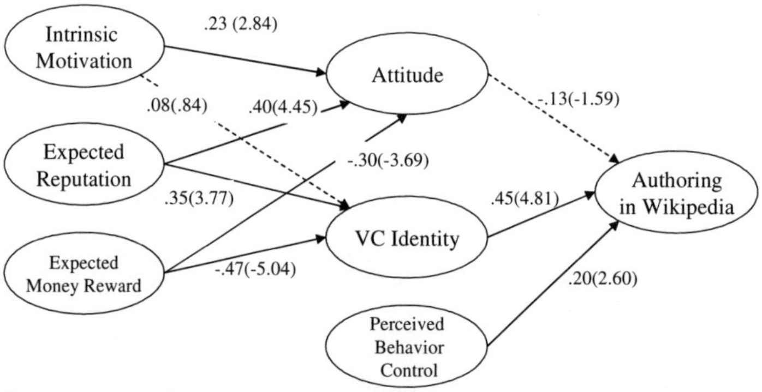

χ^2=287.37, *df*=158, χ^2/*df*=1. 81, RMSEA=.069, NFI=.90, NNFI=.94, CFI=.95, GFI=.86, AGFI=.81

Fig. 2. Results of Structural Model.

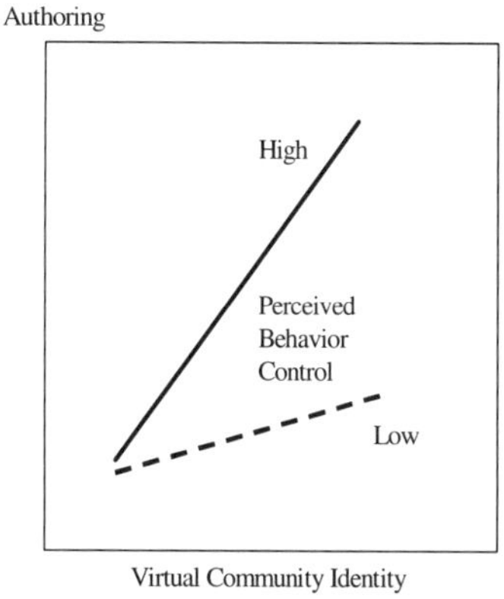

Fig. 3. Moderating Effect of PBC with VC Identity on Authoring.

Table 6 Results of Hierarchical Regression Analysis for Testing H8 and H9

Variables	Model 1	Model 2	Model 3	Note
Attitude	-.01(-.11)	-.05(-.58)	-.02(-.21)	
VC Identity	.31(3.66)	.28(3.23)	.25(2.87)	
Perceived Behavioral Control		.19(2.45)	.15(1.88)	
PBC×Attitude			-.06(-.68)	H8 is not supported
PBC×VC Identity			.22(2.30)	H9 is supported
ΔR^2	.09	.04	.03	
F change	8.61***	6.23**	3.00*	
R^2	.09	.13	.16	
Overall F-Value	8.61***	8.00***	6.11***	

6. Conclusion

Based on the results of the current research, we find out the relationship between altruism, expected reputation, and expected money reward and both attitude and identity. We also can say that virtual community identity is a more important predictor of authoring than attitude is. It is not sufficient to take action when people think "authoring in Wikipedia is good," but they praise themselves as a part of the collective, i.e. a member of Wikipedia. Identity to the community is the just force to instigate authoring in Wikipeia.This article explores the motivations determining the volitional authoring of the Wikipedian. Altruism and expected future reputation affect attitude and identity positively, but the relationship between expected money reward and its consequences is negative. We explain the latter that the Wikipedian realize the fact of no money return while they devote themselves to volitional authoring. We also find that the virtual community identity of Wikipedia is more significant to predict volitional authoring than attitude. Besides, the perceived behavioral control, an estimative competence on authoring by author himself, is an accelerator for motivating authoring. Finally, virtual community identity may foster more volitional authoring when the Wikipedian are of higher perception of perceived behavioral control than lower.

References

Ajzen, I. (1991), "The theory of planned behavior", *Organizational Behavior and Human Decision Processes*, 50(2): 179-211.

Badke, W. (2008), "What to Do with Wikipedia", *http://www.infotoday.com/online/mar08/Badke.shtml.*

Bandura, A. (1977), "Self-efficacy: Toward a unifying theory of behavioral change", *Psychological Review*, 84(2): 191-215.

Bagozzi, R.P. and Dholakia, U.M. (2002), "Intentional social Action in virtual communities", *Journal of Interactive Marketing*, 16(2): 2-21.

Bassellier, G., Benbasat, I. and Reich, B.H. (2003), "The influence of business managers IT competence on championing IT", *Information System Research*, 14(4): 317-336.

Bock, G.W., Zmud, R.W., Kim, Y.G. and Lee, J.N. (2005), "Behavioral intention formation in knowledge sharing: Examining the roles of extrinsic motivators", *MIS Quarterly*, 29(1): 87-111.

Bock, G.W. and Kim, Y.G. (2002), "Breaking the Myths of Rewards: An Exploratory Study of Attitudes about Knowledge Sharing", *Information Resource Management Journal*, 15(2): 14-21.

Chatman, J.A. and Spataro, S.E. (2005), "Using self-categorization theory to understand relational demography-based variations in people's responsiveness to organizational culture", *Academy of Management Journal*, 48(2): 321-331.

Chattopadhyay, P. (1999), "Beyond direct and symmetrical effects: The influence of demographic dissimilarity on organizational citizenship behavior", *Academy of Management Journal*, 42(3): 273-287.

Chiu, C.M., Hsu, M.H., and Wang, E.T.G. (2006), "Understanding knowledge sharing in virtual communities: An integration of social capital and social cognitive theories", *Decision Support System*, 42(3): 1872-1888.

Ciffolilli, A. (2003), "Phantom authority, self-selective recruitment and retention of members in virtual communities: The case of Wikipedia", *FirstMonday*, 8(12), *http://firstmonday.org/htbin/cgiwrap/bin/ojs/index.php/fm/article/view/1108*

Constant, D.K. and Sproull, L. (1994), "What's mine is ours, or is it? A study of attitudes about information sharing", *Information Systems Research*, 5(4): 400-421.

Donath, J. (1999), "Identity and deception in the virtual community", In *Communities in Cyberspace*, Routledge.

Ellemers, N., Kortekaas, P. and Ouwerkerk, J.W. (1999), "Self-categorization, commitment to the group and group self-esteem as related but distinct aspects of social identity", *European Journal of Social Psychology*, 29(2-3): 371-389.

Hars, A. and Ou, S. (2002), "Working for free? Motivations for participating in open-source projects", *International Journal of Electronic Commerce*, 6(3): 25-39.

Hogg, M.A. and Abrams, D. (1988), *Social identifications-A social Psychology of Intergroup Relations and Group Processes*, Routledge.

Hsu, C.L. and Chiu, C.M. (2004), "Predicting electronic service continuance with a decomposed theory of planned behaviour", *Behaviour and Information Technology*, 23(5): 359-373.

Hsu, C.L. and Lin, J.C.C. (2008), "Acceptance of blog usage: The roles of technology acceptance, social influence and knowledge sharing motivation", *Information and Management*, 45(1): 65-74.

Jian, G. and Jeffres, L.W. (2006), "Understanding employees' willingness to contribute to shared electronic databases", *Communication Research*, 33(4): 242-261.

Kankanhalli, A., Tan, B.C.Y. and Wei, K.K. (2005), "Contributing knowledge to electronic knowledge repositories: An empirical investigation", *MIS Quarterly*, 29(1): 113-143.

Kim, J. (2009), "I want to be different from others in cyberspace-The role of visual similarity in virtual group identity", *Computers in Human Behavior*, 25(1): 88-95.

Kollock, P. (1999), "The economies of online cooperation: Gifts and public goods in cyberspace", in *Communities in Cyberspace*, Routledge.

Kuo, F.Y. and Young, M.L. (2008), "A study of the intention-action gap in knowledge sharing practices", *Journal of the American Society for Information Science and Technology*, 59(8): 1224-1237.

Lerner, J. and Tirole, J. (2002), "Some simple economics of open source", *Journal of Industrial Economics*, 50(2): 197-234.

Ma, M. and Agarwal, R. (2007), "Through a glass darkly: Information technology design, identity verification, and knowledge contribution in online communities", *Information Systems Research*, 18(1): 42-67.

Nahapiet, J. and Ghoshal, S. (1998), "Social capital, intellectual capital, and the organizational advantage", *Academy of Management Review*, 23(2): 242–266.

Nov, O. (2007), "What motivates Wikipedians?" *Communications of the ACM*, 50(11): 60-64.

Ryan, R.M. and Deci, E.L. (2000), "Intrinsic and extrinsic motivations: Classic definitions and new directions", *Contemporary Educational Psychology*, 25(1): 54-67.

Van Dick, R., Grojean, M.W., Christ, O. and Wieseke, J. (2006), "Identity and the extra mile: Relationships between organizational identification and organizational citizenship behaviour", *British Journal of Management*, 17(4): 283-301.

Venkatraman, N. (1989), "Strategic orientation of business enterprises: The construct, dimensionality, and measurement", *Management Science*, 35(8): 942-962.

Wasko, M.M. and Faraj, S. (2005), "Why should I share? Examining social capital and knowledge contribution in electronic networks of practice", *MIS Quarterly*, 29(1): 35-57.

INTELLECTUAL CAPITAL AND PERFORMANCE: AN EMPIRICAL STUDY ON THE RELATIONSHIP BETWEEN SOCIAL CAPITAL AND R&D PERFORMANCE IN HIGHER EDUCATION

MOHD ISKANDAR BIN ILLYAS and ROSE ALINDA ALIAS

Faculty of Computer Science and Information Systems, Universiti Teknologi Malaysia, 81300 UTM Skudai, Johor, Malaysia

E-mail: *iskandar@fsksm.utm.my* & *alinda@utm.my*

LEELA DAMODARAN

Information Science Department, Loughborough University, Leicestershire, LE11 3U, United Kingdom

E-mail: *l.damodaran@lboro.ac.uk*

Based on the analysis of research groups in higher education in the UK, this paper investigated the relationship between social capital and the performance of those research groups. The study produced a model that considered the different dimensions of social capital and how these dimensions might have an impact on the performance of R&D in the HEI in the UK. The result from the regression analysis shows that trust has the strongest influence towards explaining the R&D performance.

1. Introduction

Social capital is a valuable and inimitable resource that leads to competitive advantage in research and development (R&D) groups. Previous studies have shown that social capital can improve organisational performance through effective networks, higher level of trust, and shared vision and understanding. Although several studies have measured the effects of social capital, there are no studies investigating the impact of social capital on research and development at a group level in Higher Education (HE). The aim of this study was to understand the effects of social capital on R&D performance in higher education. In order to achieve the aim, two objectives were identified, including the examination of different social capital dimensions on R&D performance, and the development of a social capital and R&D performance model.

2. Literature Review

In the following section we define social capital in some depth and then extend the concept to explain how social capital affects innovation in higher education. We look into the relationship between social capital and R&D processes within higher education and how it might affect its performance. We put forward several proposition to support our arguments based upon our conceptual model. Finally, we provide the findings from the analysis of data and outline some recommendation from the findings.

2.1. *Social Capital*

Social capital is the sum of the actual and potential resources embedded within, available through, and derived from the network of relationships possessed by an individual or social unit (Nahapiet & Ghoshal, 1998). It comprises the assets that may be mobilized through a network. It makes an organization, or any cooperative group, more than a collection of individuals intent on achieving their own private purposes. Its characteristic elements include high levels of trust, robust personal networks and vibrant communities, shared understandings, and a sense of equitable participation in a joint enterprise. These kinds of relationships support collaboration, commitment, ready access to knowledge and talent, and achievement of organizational goals. Social capital requires appropriate organizational investments – providing people space and time to connect, developing trust, effectively communicating aims and beliefs, and offering the equitable opportunities and rewards that invite genuine participation, not mere presence. But even when social capital investments are made solely by individuals who develop ties with one another, many real advantages accrue to the organization as a whole.

Researchers have used the social capital construct to explain different dimensions of human capital that span multiple levels of analysis from organizational learning (Huber, 1991) to a resource-based view of the firm (Barney, 2001). Theoretical advances in this field have forwarded the structural, relational and cognitive dimensions but these have not been equally balanced in empirical studies. Like "physical capital and human capital-tools and training that enhance individual productivity—'social capital' refers to features of social organization, such as networks, norms, and trust, that facilitate coordination and cooperation for mutual benefit (Putnam, 1993)."

Social capital, like other forms of capital, accumulates when used productively. Traditional economic perspectives that focus on short-term self interest and individual transactions ignore the accretion, or growth, opportunities of cooperation (Ostrom, 1990). Closely related to accretion is the self-reinforcing cyclic nature of social relations. Trustful relations tend to be self-reinforcing in the positive direction. Mistrust tends to cycle in the negative direction.

Nahapiet and Ghoshal (1998) present a theoretical model of social capital and propose three dimensions – structural, cognitive, and relational in order to facilitate the various combinations and exchange of resources within firms. However, the model doesn't consider the deeper cultural aspects, which are intrinsic in developing strong social relationships among members of organizations. Although the relational and cognitive dimensions have some connection with organizational climate, these tend to focus on superficial manifestations of organizational culture.

3. Social Capital and R&D Performance: A Research Model

Investments in human and social capital are widely believed to improve the organizational performance (M. K. Ahuja, Galletta, & Carley, 2003; Annen, 2003; Bosma, Praag, Thurik, & Wit, 2004; Dess & Shaw, 2001; Knack, 2001; Knack & Keefer,

1997; Koka & Prescott, 2002; Lesser & Storck 2001; Tsai, 2003). However, there also has been recognition of the potential risks and pitfalls inherent in utilizing social capital (G. Ahuja, 2000; Brass, Butterfield, & Skaggs, 1998; Shaul M. Gabbay & Leenders, 2001; S. M. Gabbay & Zuckerman, 1998; Hansen, 1999; Leana & Van Buren, 1999; Edwin A. Locke, 1999; Portes, 1998). Nevertheless, the notion of social capital has been moved beyond general or specific literature on concepts as trust and networks to explore concepts which help the development of a dynamic rather than a static concept of social capital (Edelman, Bresnen, Newell, Scarbrough, & Swan, 2004).

Here we advance a model that connects the independent and dependent variables of this construct. The model, shown in Figure 1, suggests that the R&D performance in higher education is influence by the pattern of social capital among the member of the academics.

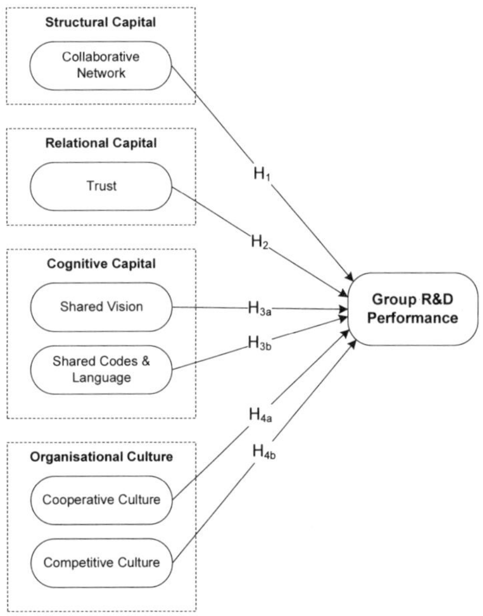

Fig. 1 Social Capital and R&D Performance

3.1. *Structural Dimension – Collaborative Network*

The studies on organizational social network were perhaps the most studied area among the different dimensions of social capital (Burt, 2000; Coleman, 1990; Granovetter, 1973; Hansen, 1998; Nohria & Eccles, 1992). However, there is a lack of agreement regarding how these dimension influence the organizational outcome. Empirical findings range from the degree of network centrality and its effect on levels of perceived trustworthiness (Tsai & Ghoshal, 1998), new linkage creation (Tsai, 2000), levels of innovation (Tsai, 2001), and levels of intra-organizational knowledge sharing (Tsai, 2002).

Harvey et al. (2002), in their research indicates that high-achieving research groups are aware and adept at leveraging this 'network advantage'. Similarly, the new production of knowledge conceptualizes knowledge as deriving not merely from individual thought but from collective processes of networking, negotiation, inter-personal communication and influence. The network of contacts sustains the group as a whole. It aids competition, strategic sense-making, collaboration and staff recruitment. It is central to exploiting existing internal and external competencies to respond appropriately to a changing environment by configuring and reconfiguring the internal and external organizational skills, resources and competencies to align with the changing environmental contingencies. Collaborative working is intimately related to networking; it represents ultimately a networking of resources: social, intellectual and infrastructural. Network connectedness is a crucial component of high-achieving research groups (Harvey et al., 2002). Therefore, we posit the following:

Hypotheses 1: The existence of collaborative networks among group members will have a positive effect on their R&D performance.

3.2. *Relational Dimension – Trust*

The notion of trust within the organisation arises as an important dimension for scholars of social capital (Coleman, 1990; Fukuyama, 1995: Putman, 1995). Several researchers have studied the relationship between trust and performance. However, the outcome of the above research has given varying results, whereby performance of a group or individual may or may not have been affected by the level of trust among the individual or group members. Among the research that established a positive relation between trust and performance are the studies of McAllister (1995) and Barclay (1997), while Dirk's (1999) study shows that trust doesn't have any significance on team performance. One of the main reasons for the variations between the results is the type of constructs used to measure the level of trust,. While some of the research used a single dimension (attitude, belief) to measure trust, other researchers explore trust from multidimensional perspectives (Costas, 2003). Hence:

Hypotheses 2: High level of trust among group members will have a positive effect on their R&D performance.

3.3. *Cognitive Dimension – Shared Visions*

Past studies have found that setting specific goals facilitates overall performance (Edwin A Locke & Latham, 1984). However, McComb *et al.* (1999) advanced the idea beyond goal setting to suggest that individuals involved in R&D activities need to have a shared understanding of the requirements in innovation activities so that they can have a common foundation or understanding upon which to act. For example, when individuals involved in R&D activities have a common or overlapping understanding of the organisation's innovation objectives, their responsibilities toward these objectives and the procedures they use to attain these objectives will be more coordinated as they share compatible knowledge. This shared mental framework (Janis A Cannon-Bowers, Salas, & Converse, 1993) facilitates decision-making and coordination so that individuals can conduct their tasks without a continuous process of interpreting and reinterpreting the meanings and expectations of the innovation process (Lynn, Reilly, & Akgun, 2000). Klimstra and Potts (1988) reported that by aligning everyone's views toward a common framework based on shared expectations and agreement, higher levels of project success occurred. Shared visions affect task performance in the sense that when team members have similar attitudes/ beliefs, "they arrive at compatible interpretations of the environment, which enable them to reach better decisions" (J. A. Cannon-Bowers & Salas, 2001). Therefore, it is hypothesised that:

H_{3a}: The group's level of shared vision is positively related to their R&D performance

3.4. *Cognitive Dimension – Shared Language*

Language is the means by which individuals engage in communication. It provides a frame of reference for interpreting the environment and its mastery is typically indicated by an individual's level of expertise (Wasko & Faraj, 2005, p. 41). Nahapiet and Ghoshal (1998) argue that to the extent that people share a common language, this facilitates their ability to gain access to people and their information. To the extent that their language and codes are different, this keeps people apart and restricts their access. Since R&D work often involves novel tasks that are inherently ambiguous and complex (Janz, Colquitt, & Noe, 1997), individuals who have a shared mental model with others can share ideas and information more efficiently and effectively (Levesque, Wilson, & Wholey, 2001). As a result of having greater shared expectations and understanding, improved coordination, communication, and better R&D performance occurred(Klimstra & Potts, 1988; Pan & Scarbrough, 1999; Rouse, Cannon-Bowers, & Salas, 1992). Hence, group members who shared the same codes and language with each other will demonstrate higher levels of R&D performance. These observations suggest the following:

H_{3b}: The group's level of shared codes and language is positively related to their R&D performance.

3.5. *Cultural Dimension – Cooperative Culture*

According to goal interdependence theory (Deutsch, 1949), cooperatively structured situations create perceptions of shared fate and promote supportive behaviour, whereby each group member looks out for the interests of the others. In addition, insights and lessons learned by one member are shared so that all can benefit vicariously from others' experiences. Therefore, it is hypothesized that:

H_{4a}: The group's cooperative culture is positively related to their R&D performance.

3.6. *Cultural Dimension – Competitive Culture*

Typically, people placed in competitive structures tend to keep valuable information proprietary - rather than share information and experience. Moreover, rather than supporting each other, people placed in competitive reward structures may be motivated to impair the progress of others in an effort to gain positive advantage (Beersma *et al.*, 2003). This discussion suggests the following proposition:

H_{4b}: *The group's competitive culture is negatively related to their R&D performance.*

3.7. *R&D Performance – Research Assessment Exercise (RAE)*

The UK higher education system has developed a range of statistics in an attempt to measure its performance. Nevertheless, the UK Research Assessment Exercise (RAE) is widely accepted as the most rigorous measure of research output available in the UK. Therefore, the data source of the academic researcher submission for the 2001 UK RAE was used as the indicators of R&D performance (dependent variable) in this study.

4. Research Methodology

The research design followed a mixed method approach. This involved a set of semi-structured interviews that informed the formulation of appropriate research hypotheses, and a questionnaire survey, that facilitated the statistical testing of these hypotheses. A total of six academic researchers from Loughborough University participated in the semi-structured interviews. During the interviews participants were asked a set of 13 questions about the effects of structural, relational, cognitive and cultural dimensions of social capital on the performance of their research groups within the university. The results of the interviews revealed that six main factors affected group performance. These were: the presence of structural dimensions (*collaborative networks*), relational dimensions (*trust*), cognitive dimensions (*shared vision* and *shared codes and language*), and cultural dimensions (*cooperative* and *competitive culture*).

4.1. *Questionnaire Development*

The primary aim of the pilot study questionnaire was to develop a reliable instrument for organizational social capital and the R&D performance that could be tested effectively in the main study. The principal construct of organizational social capital was developed comprising four sub-constructs: structural dimension, relational dimension, cognitive dimension and cultural dimension. An outline of the questionnaire is shown in Table 1. Each of the four sub-constructs of organizational social capital were developed using 7 items: collaboration cosmopolitan pattern, collaboration strategies, trust, shared vision, shared language, internal forces of cooperation and internal forces of competition.

Table 1. Outline of the Questionnaire

Construct	Sub-construct	References	Items	Total
Personal Information			12	12
Structural	Collaboration Cosmopolitan Pattern	(Bozeman & Corley, 2004)	6	18
	Collaboration Strategies	(Bozeman & Corley, 2004; Melin, 2000)	12	
Relational	Trust	(Huff & Kelley, 2003; Politis, 2003; Zaheer, McEvily, & Perrone, 1998)	10	10
Cognitive	Shared Vision	(Tsai & Ghoshal, 1998)	2	8
	Shared Language	New	6	
Cultural	Internal Forces of Cooperation	(Jashapara, 2003; Mintzberg, 1991)	5	10
	Internal Forces of Competition	(Jashapara, 2003; Mintzberg, 1991)	5	
Social Desirability Scale		(Ballard, 1992)	13	13
2001 RAE Rating			1	1
Total				72

4.2. *Sampling*

The data source of the academic researcher submission for the 2001 UK Research Assessment Exercise (RAE) was used as an effective sampling frame in this study. The RAE was a UK-wide undertaking, whereby each publicly funded university and higher education college in the UK was invited to submit information about their research activity for assessment. Information provided was assessed and quality ratings were awarded for all subjects in which research was submitted. These data were collected by the Higher Education Funding Council for England (HEFCE) on behalf of the four UK funding bodies. The information largely relates to a five-year period, running from the last RAE in 1996. The data can be searched on-line or sections downloaded from http://www.hero.ac.uk/rae/index.htm. The theoretical sample size for this study were determined from the formula given by Tull and Hawkins (1993) for a stratified sample:

$$n = \frac{\dfrac{4N(\sigma^2 T)}{\overline{x}^2}}{4\left(\dfrac{\sigma^2 T}{\overline{x}^2}\right) + Nr^2}$$

Given these parameters, the estimated stratified sample size for this study is:

$$n = \frac{\dfrac{4 * 60685(2.25)}{4^2}}{4\left(\dfrac{2.25}{4^2}\right) + 60685(0.05)^2} = 224.19$$

The stratified random sample using the 2001 RAE submission data for the pilot and main study was determined as shown in Table 2.

Table 2. Stratified Sample of Pilot and Main Study

RAE Rating	No. of RAE 2001 Submission	Pilot Study Sample	Main Study Sample
5*	11767	58	582
5	21850	108	1080
4	14879	74	736
3a	7528	37	372
3b	3174	16	157
2	1368	7	68
1	119	1	6
Total	60685	300	3000

4.3. *Main Survey*

The data for the pilot and main study were collected using an online questionnaire. The main reason for choosing the online method of data collection is it offers some advantages over the traditional postal approach from an efficiency and cost effectiveness viewpoint. One of the major assumptions for the data collection process is that most of the academic researchers in the UK have access to the Internet in order to participate in this research. The development of the online questionnaire was done using the HTML editor and the layout was design to be as simple as possible to avoid any technical complications to access the questionnaire. The questionnaire for this research can be access at http://www-staff.lboro.ac.uk/~lsmii/start.htm.

The data collected from the online questionnaire survey were used to test the hypotheses. The questionnaire included items related to the six main factors affecting group performance. Each item was measured through a 7-point scale, which 1 represents Strongly Disagree and 7 represents Strongly Agree. The questionnaire was piloted and then distributed to a sample population of 3000 academic researchers from various UK HE institutions. A total of 311 (response rate = 10.37%) researchers provided input to the questionnaire. To ensure that the research instrument measured the right elements consistently, each construct was also tested for reliability and validity. The reliability of the construct was confirmed by computing the value of Cronbach's alpha. Table 3 shows the results of the reliability and validity analysis for each of the constructs. The results demonstrated that the measurement of the research constructs were reliable (the value of Cronbach's alpha ranging from 0.72 to 0.94) and hence, suitable for further validation testing. The evidence of construct validity, which consists of convergent, discriminant and nomological validity, were provided using different correlational analyses and multi-method matrix. Factor analysis was also used to test the construct validity of each dimension. All the constructs pass the convergent validity test, but the collaboration strategies construct failed the discriminant and nomological test. With this failure in mind, the collaboration strategies construct was excluded from further hypotheses testing and does not appear in the following section.

Table 3. Reliability and Validity Test Results

Dimensions	Constructs	Reliability	Validity		
		Alpha Cronbach	Convergent	Discriminant	Nomological
Structural	Collaboration Strategies	0.72	√	Fail	Fail
Relational	Trust	0.94	√	√	√
Cognitive	Shared Vision	0.89	√	√	√
	Shared Language	0.79	√	√	√
Cultural	Cooperative Culture	0.85	√	√	√
	Competitive Culture	0.80	√	√	√

5. Results

This section presents the analysis on the relationships between the constructs. It tries to achieve the objective of the research: 1) To test the research hypothesis and 2) To evaluate the proposed model of social capital and R&D performance.

The hypotheses proposed were based on the relationship between the independent variables and the dependent variable as identified and discussed earlier. The hypotheses are evaluated by doing an analysis of correlation coefficients between each of the independent variables and the dependent variables. The results of the correlation between each of the independent variables represented by Trust, Shared Vision, Shared Codes and Language, Cooperative Culture and Competitive Culture and the dependent variables represented by the outcome of the 2001 RAE (RAE) of the test are shown in Table 4.

Table 4. Correlation Matrix of the Research Model

	Correlation Coefficients					
	RAE	Trust	Shared Vision	Shared Language	Cooperative Culture	Competitive Culture
RAE	1					
Trust	.776**	1				
Shared Vision	.590**	.666**	1			
Shared Language	.505**	.586**	.584**	1		
Cooperative Culture	.680**	.728**	.696**	.599**	1	
Competitive Culture	-.405**	-.493**	-.521**	-.495**	-.495**	1

** - Signif. LE .01

The associations between constructs were investigated by examining the correlation coefficients between the constructs. The analysis supported all the hypotheses proposed in the study. The results showed that five out of the six dimensions of social capital had an effect on the performance of research groups. These were trust (H2), shared vision (H3a), shared codes and language (H3b), cooperative culture (H4a), and competitive culture (H4b).

The second research objectives, which tries to evaluate the proposed model of social capital and R&D performance in Section 3 was tested using the multiple regression analysis technique. This analysis shows how well a set of variables (the different dimension of social capital) is able to predict a particular outcome (R&D performance). The results of regressing the five independent variables against R&D performance (RAE) can be seen in Table 5. The indicator that is important here is the value of R Square. It indicates how much of the variance in the dependent variable is explained by the model (Pallant, 2005). Table 5 shows that the value of R square is 0.632, indicates that the model (Trust, Shared Vision, Shared Codes and Language, Internal Forces of Cooperation and Internal Forces of Competition) explains 63.2 per cent of the variance in R&D performance.

Table 5. Research Model Summaries

Model	R	R Square	Adjusted R Square	Std. Error of the Estimate
	.795	.632	.625	.906

The next step is to investigate which of the variables from the model contributes more to the prediction of the dependent variable (R&D performance – RAE). The results in Table 6 show that the highest beta coefficient is 0.585 ($p<.0005$), which is for Trust. This means that this variable makes the strongest unique contribution to explaining the R&D performance (RAE), when the variance explained by all other variables in the model is controlled for. The beta value for Internal Forces of Cooperation was slightly lower (.224) ($p<.0005$), indicating that it may also contribute to the prediction of the R&D performance but at a lower level.

Table 6. Coefficients for the Variables

Model	Unstandardised Coefficients		Standardised Coefficients
	B	Std. Error	Beta
Constant	.125	.440	
Trust	.071	.007	.585
Cooperative Culture	.052	.014	.224
Shared Vision	.013	.013	.053
Competitive Culture	.007	.011	.028
Shared Language	.004	.021	.011

6. Conclusions

In conclusion, this study provides important empirical evidence on the relationship between social capital and R&D performance in higher education in the UK. Furthermore, the study reveals the variables that have a significant positive relationship with the performance of R&D are trust, shared vision, shared codes and language and internal forces of cooperation. The internal forces of competition however, have a significant but negative influence on the R&D performance.

The study also produced a model that considered the different dimensions of social capital and how these dimensions might have an impact on the performance of R&D in the HEI in the UK. The result from the regression analysis shows that trust, an element of relational dimension of social capital, has the strongest influence towards explaining the R&D performance. The study also reveals that the proposed social capital model, which consists of relational dimension (Trust), cognitive dimension (Shared Vision and Shared Codes and Language) and the Internal Forces of Cooperation and Competition explains 63.2 per cent of the variance in R&D performance.

The study makes a substantial methodological contribution for investigating social capital by offering a validated tool for measuring key constructs related to social capital in organisations. Most of the constructs have demonstrated a high level of reliability and validity in their development. Therefore, the methodological implications of this research are twofold. Firstly, by carefully defining the constructs of the different dimensions of social capital, it helps the researcher to design the instrument in a systematic way and therefore helps to develop more valid and grounded indicators. Secondly, since most of the constructs to measure the social capital were carefully selected and adopted from the previous studies, it helps the researcher to compare and evaluate its suitability and reliability to this research. The results show that all of the constructs adopted are well suited to the HE environment and this provides the evidence of construct reliability across different sector.

The findings also give rise to a range of recommendations to enhance the performance of R&D within research groups. These include provision of social space for discussion and informal communication, nurturing of a culture conducive of trust and cooperation, knowledge sharing, shared vision and shared codes and language. At the strategic level, consideration should be given to developing and implementing initiatives, based upon the findings reported in this report, that can be carried out by the university to improve research group performance. Ways of countering the negative effects of a competitive culture that might weaken R&D performance within research groups should also be explored.

Acknowledgments

This research was funded by the Ministry of Science, Technology and Innovation (MOSTI), Malaysia and Universiti Teknologi Malaysia.

References

Ahuja, G. (2000). Collaboration networks, structural holes, and innovation: A longitudinal study. *Administrative Science Quarterly, 45*(3), 425-455.

Ahuja, M. K., Galletta, D. F., & Carley, K. M. (2003). Individual centrality and performance in virtual R&D groups: An empirical study. *Management Science, 49*(1), 21-38.

Annen, K. (2003). Social capital, inclusive networks, and economic performance. *Journal of Economic Behavior & Organization, 50*, 449-463.

Ballard, R. (1992). Short forms of the Marlowe-Crowne social desirability scale. *Psychological Reports, 71*, 1155-1160.

Beersma, B., Hollenbeck, J. R., Humphrey, S. E., Moon, H., Conlon, D. E., & Ilgen, D. R. (2003). Cooperation, competition, and team performance: Toward a contingency approach. *Academy of Management Journal, 46*(5), 572-590.

Bosma, N., Praag, M. v., Thurik, R., & Wit, G. d. (2004). The value of human and social capital investments for the business performance of startups. *Small Business Economics, 23*(3), 227-236.

Bozeman, B., & Corley, E. (2004). Scientists' collaboration strategies: Implications for scientific and technical human capital. *Research Policy, 33*(4), 599-616.

Brass, D. J., Butterfield, K. D., & Skaggs, B. C. (1998). Relationships and unethical behavior: A social network perspective. *Academy of Management Review, 23*, 14-31.

Burt, R. S. (2000). The network structure of social capital. Retrieved 1 March 2003, 2003, from http://gsbwww.uchicago.edu/fac/ronald.burt/research/

Cannon-Bowers, J. A., & Salas, E. (2001). Reflections on shared cognition. *Journal of Organizational Behavior, 22*(2), 195-202.

Cannon-Bowers, J. A., Salas, E., & Converse, S. (1993). Shared mental models in expert team decision making. In N. J. Castellan Jr. (Ed.), *Individual and Group Decision Making: Current Issues* (pp. 221-246): Lawrence Erlbaum Association.

Coleman, J. S. (1990). *Foundations of social theory*. Cambridge, MA: Harvard University Press.

Dess, G., & Shaw, J. (2001). Voluntary turnover, social capital, and organizational performance. *Academy of Management Review, 26*(3), 446-456.

Deutsch, M. (1949). A theory of cooperation and competition. *Human Relations, 2*, 129-152.

Edelman, L., Bresnen, M., Newell, S., Scarbrough, H., & Swan, J. (2004). The benefits and pitfalls of social capital: Empirical evidence from two organisations in the UK. *British Journal of Management, 15*(S1), S59-s69.

Gabbay, S. M., & Leenders, R. T. A. J. (2001). *Social capital in organizations* (Vol. 18): JAI Press.

Gabbay, S. M., & Zuckerman, E. W. (1998). Social capital and opportunity in corporate R&D: The contingent effect of contact density on mobility expectations. *Social Science Research, 27*(2), 189-217.

Granovetter, M. S. (1973). The strength of weak ties. *American Journal of Sociology, 78*, 1360-1380.

Hansen, M. T. (1998). *Combining network centrality and related knowledge: Explaining effective knowledge sharing in multiunit firms* (Working paper). Boston: Harvard Business Schoolo. Document Number)

Hansen, M. T. (1999). The search transfer problem: The role of weak ties in sharing knowledge across organizational sub-units. *Administrative Science Quarterly, 44*, 82-111.

Harvey, J., Pettigrew, A., & Ferlie, E. (2002). The determinants of research group performance: Towards Mode 2? *Journal of Management Studies, 39*(6), 747-774.

Huff, L., & Kelley, L. (2003). Levels of organizational trust in individualist versus collectivist societies: A seven-nation study. *Organization Science, 14*(1), 81-90.

Janz, B. D., Colquitt, J. A., & Noe, R. A. (1997). Knowledge worker team effectiveness: The role of autonomy, interdependence, team development, and contextual support variables. *Personnel Psychology, 50*(4), 877-904.

Jashapara, A. (2003). Cognition, culture and competition: An empirical test of the learning organization. *The Learning Organization, 10*(1), 31-50.

Klimstra, P. D., & Potts, J. (1988). What we've learned managing R&D projects. *Research Technology Management, 31*(3), 23-39.

Knack, S. (2001). Trust, associational life and economic performance. In J. F. Helliwell (Ed.), *The contribution of human and social capital to sustained economic growth and well-being: International symposium report*: Human Resources Development Canada and OECD.

Knack, S., & Keefer, P. (1997). Does social capital have an economic payoff? A cross-country investigation. *Quarterly Journal of Economics, 112*(4), 1251-1288.

Koka, B. R., & Prescott, J. E. (2002). Strategic alliances as social capital: A multidimensional view. *Strategic Management Journal, 23*(9), 795-816.

Leana, C. R., & Van Buren, H. J. (1999). Organizational social capital and employment practices. *Academy of Management Review, 24*(3), 538-555.

Lesser, E. L., & Storck , J. (2001). Communities of practice and organizational performance. *IBM Systems Journal, 40*(4), 831-841.

Levesque, L. L., Wilson, J. M., & Wholey, D. R. (2001). Cognitive divergence and shared mental models in software development project teams. *Journal of Organizational Behavior, 22*(2), 135-144.

Locke, E. A. (1999). Some reservations about social capital. *Academy of Management Review, 24*(1), 8-11.

Locke, E. A., & Latham, G. P. (1984). *Goal setting: A motivational technique that works.* Englewood Cliffs, NJ: Prentice-Hall.

Lynn, G. S., Reilly, R. R., & Akgun, A. E. (2000). Knowledge management in new product teams: Practices and outcomes. *IEEE Transactions on Engineering Management, 47*(2), 221-231.

McComb, S. A., Green, S. G., & Compton, W. D. (1999). Project goals, team performance, and shared understanding. *Engineering Management Journal, 11*, 7-12.

Melin, G. (2000). Pragmatism and self-organization - Research collaboration on the individual level. *Research Policy, 29*(1), 31-40.

Mintzberg, H. (1991). The effective organization: Forces and forms. *Sloan Management Review*(Winter), 54-67.

Nahapiet, J., & Ghoshal, S. (1998). Social capital, intellectual capital and the organizational advantage. *Academy of Management Review, 23*(2), 242-266.

Nohria, N., & Eccles, R. G. (1992). *Networks and organizations: Structure, form, and action*. Boston, MA: Harvard Business School Press.

Ostrom, E. (1990). *Governing the commons: The evolution of institutions for collective action*. New York: Cambridge University Press.

Pallant, J. (2005). *SPSS survival manual: A step-by-step guide to data analysis using SPSS for Windows (Version 12)* (2nd ed.). Berkshire: Open University Press.

Pan, S. L., & Scarbrough, H. (1999). Knowledge Management in Practice: An Exploratory Case Study. *Technology Analysis and Strategic Management, 11*(3), 359-374.

Politis, J. D. (2003). The connection between trust and knowledge management: What are its implications for team performance. *Journal of Knowledge Management, 7*(5), 55-66.

Portes, A. (1998). Social capital: Its origins and applications in modern sociology. *Annual Review of Sociology, 24*, 1-24.

Putnam, R. (1993). The prosperous community: Social capital and public life. *American Prospect, 13*, 35-42.

Rouse, W. B., Cannon-Bowers, J. A., & Salas, E. (1992). The role of mental models in team performance in complex systems. *IEEE Transactions on Systems, Man, and Cybernetics, 22*(6), 1296-1308.

Tsai, W. (2000). Social capital, strategic relatedness and the formation of interorganizational linkages. *Strategic Management Journal, 21*(9), 925-939.

Tsai, W. (2001). Knowledge transfer in intraorganizational networks: Effects of network position and absorptive capacity on business unit innovation. *Academy of Management Journal, 44*(5), 996-1004.

Tsai, W. (2002). Social structure of "Coopetition" within a multiunit organization: Coordination, competition, and intra-organizational knowledge sharing. *Organization Science, 13*(2), 179–190.

Tsai, W. (2003). Corporate picnics may enhance innovation between units more than R&D. Retrieved 26 July 2003, 2003, from http://www.smeal.psu.edu/news/releases/jan01/picnics.html

Tsai, W., & Ghoshal, S. (1998). Social capital and value creation: An empirical study of intra-firm networks. *Academy of Management Journal, 41*(4), 464-476.

Tull, D. S., & Hawkins, D. I. (1993). *Marketing research: Measurement and method - A text with cases* (6th ed.). New Jersey: Prentice Hall.

Wasko, M. M., & Faraj, S. (2005). Why should I share? Examining Social Capital and Knowledge Contribution in Electronic Networks of Practice 1. *MIS Quarterly, 29*(1), 35.

Zaheer, A., McEvily, B., & Perrone, V. (1998). Does trust matter? Exploring the effects of interorganizational and interpersonal trust on performance. *Organization Science, 9*(2), 141-159.

MANAGING KNOWLEDGE IN A VOLUNTEER-BASED COMMUNITY

JOHN S. HUCK
School of Library and Information Studies, University of Alberta,
3-20 Rutherford South, Edmonton, AB, T6G 2J4, Canada
E-mail: johnscotthuck@yahoo.ca

RODNEY AL[†] and DINESH RATHI*
School of Library and Information Studies, University of Alberta,
3-20 Rutherford South, Edmonton, AB, T6G 2J4, Canada
[†]*E-mail: canada_rodneymbal@yahoo.ca *E-mail: drathi@ualberta.ca*

The study explores the current state of knowledge management (KM) in a volunteer-based community. A knowledge audit was conducted at a volunteer-based community workshop to identify knowledge needs, gaps, sources, sinks and pools. While the study identified several knowledge needs, the study found that the personal motivation of volunteers is tied to their personal knowledge needs. Addressing the personal knowledge needs of volunteers may help develop a strong pool of volunteers and help sustain the organization. A strong KM system would address current problems and facilitate the process of building the community of volunteers. The study recommendations include both technological and non-technological methods to address identified problems and to manage the knowledge in the volunteer-based community.

1. Introduction

Knowledge Management (KM) has been an area of research for some years now, and its theoretical foundations as well as importance are considerably established in the literature (Nonaka, 1994; Cook and Brown, 1999; Baskerville and Dulipovici, 2006). KM has found strong application and use in For-Profit Organizations (FPOs), primarily in large organizations that require large scale application, but there has been limited focus on issues related to KM in a small Non-Profit Organizations (NPOs) or Non-Government Organizations (NGOs) and even less in the area of volunteer communities. Communities of practice (CoP) has been a much discussed topic in FPOs as a way of sharing and disseminating knowledge among the members of the community in the FPOs, but it is a lesser explored concept in voluntary organizations from a KM perspective. Management of knowledge has been a challenge in FPOs and it seems also to be the case in a community with a charter of volunteerism, but KM's significance in any domain cannot be underestimated. There are many issues that deserve exploration concerning KM in volunteer communities. For example, what are current KM practices, what are knowledge needs, how can KM benefit them, what are the technological barriers to adopting KM systems, what is the perception of KM among volunteers, etc.

This paper explores the current state of KM and the knowledge needs of volunteers in a volunteer-based community. A knowledge audit was used to identify needs, sources, gaps, channels, sinks and pools in the knowledge management of the community. The paper presents a KM framework which includes both technological and non-technological solutions to potentially fill the identified gaps, streamline the channels, augment the sources of knowledge, and increase knowledge sharing in the community.

2. Literature Overview

2.1. *Community Bicycle Workshop: An Introduction*

Community bicycle workshops provide communal space and equipment where urban cyclists can do their own bike repairs and learn how to do bike repairs. Most of these workshops are operated by volunteers. Primary services are bike repair and maintenance, but additional services may be provided, such as: bike education; "Earn-a-Bike" programs for youth (Programs, 2008; Ledlie, 2008); donation of bikes to developing countries (About Bikes Not Bombs, 2008); bike rentals (Bikestation Santa Barbara, 2008); bike parking; and even showers, lockers and change rooms. An emerging "Bicycle Collective Network" focuses on community bicycle workshops providing a directory of workshops across North America and tools for establishing new workshops. These community bicycle workshops provide common ground for this face-to-face interaction among bicycle enthusiasts. However, emerging Web 2.0 technologies are also often used to exchange information, maintain contact, share stories, and participate in bicycle culture.

2.2. *Communities of Practice (CoP)*

The group examined in this study has its own, unique, organizational structure. A distinct volunteer community, centered around a community bicycle workshop, it demonstrates characteristics of a community of practice (Kolbotn, 2004), which has been defined as "*a group whose members regularly engage in learning and sharing similar goals, based on their shared mutual common interest*" (Evans, 2005). CoP members "*share a passion for something ... and who interact regularly in order to learn*" (Wenger, 2004). The members of this group share a common interest in using bicycles for transportation. The workshop community is embedded in a broader community of cyclists who use the workshop. These clients are ultimately the workshop's source of volunteers, and so the boundary between the community and the volunteers is permeable.

CoP theory is particularly applicable in this setting because it recognizes social structure and social participation (Lavé and Wenger, 1991) as a basis for developing shared meaning and engaging in knowledge building (Hara and Kling, 2005). Wenger (2000) has identified three basic elements of CoPs. First, members of the community share "joint enterprise" in an area, in this case a bicycle workshop for the bicycle community. This brings members together towards a common cause, namely, promoting bicycle culture in society. Second, members share mutual forms of engagement and create consistent interaction. Finally, the community shares a common repertoire of language, routines, tools, events, and resources around bicycles, an artifact of 'mutual common interest' for this community. A CoP generates an atmosphere of learning and sharing in a community and has been used in FPOs to foster knowledge sharing both in tacit and explicit form (Duguid, 2005). The literature identifies the power of CoPs to weave an organization, specifically FPOs, around knowledge needs, steward specific competencies, and provide a home for diverse identities (Wenger, 2000). CoPs provide support for social structure and participation in managing knowledge in an organization (Lavé and Wenger, 1991; Wenger, 2000), and volunteer in CoPs *"hold valuable experience and knowledge"* (Kolbotn, 2004). CoPs are trusted forums for communication using various media (Hanley, 1999) which could include technology-based communications to supplement face-to-face CoPs (Hara and Kling, 2005). Gongla and Rizzuto (2001) present an interesting case of development and use of CoPs in FPOs to create and share knowledge, and the adoption of technologies for advancement of CoPs goals.

2.3. *KM in NPOs/NGOs*

KM has its roots in the domain of business, and so its theory and early developments focused on the needs of large corporations and international businesses (Blair, 2002; Nonaka, 1994; Prusak, 2001). More recently, the discussion of KM in NPOs/NGOs has gained momentum, primarily focusing on large NGOs/ NPOs (Gilmour and Stancliffe, 2004; Larson et al., 2005; Lettieri *et al.*, 2004). There is a new shift toward understanding the KM needs of smaller NPOs/NGOs and volunteer communities (Lemieux and Dalkir, 2006; Gregory and Rathi, 2008). The literature discussing KM in small NGOs/NPOs is very limited, and deserves substantially more research to understand the issues, needs and challenges of adopting KM in small NGOs/NPOs and volunteer-based communities.

NPOs have needs similar to FPOs, such as efficient operations, human resources (i.e., volunteers), IT resources, and customer service (i.e., community members). Thus KM is important for NPOs/NGOs (as for FPOs) to meet such challenges as competition for sponsors, effective and efficient operations, and public promotion (Lettieri *et al.*, 2004; Kipley *et al.*, 2008; Helmig *et al.*, 2004; Kong and Prior, 2008). Drawing on the small business literature, Hume and Hume (2008) argued that a small scale NPO, such as a community organization, has fewer resources to implement large scale KM systems, such as intranets and portals as deployed in large FPOs, but just as much to gain from them, as KM in FPOs can "*enhance product development and/or service delivery*".

Matzkin (2008) suggested that resource poor NPOs that lack technological capability or familiarity should look to non technological solutions, such as reducing employee turnover, as a way of retaining implicit knowledge in the organization. Hume and Hume (2008) proposed that the best way to advance knowledge sharing among members is to exploit the strengths of the small NPO, with its "*stronger informal network*", start small, build incrementally and mimic expensive KM functionality with cheaper, more common technologies, such as email. Others have also argued for a *"technical robust communications exchange network"* (Kipley *et al.*, 2008). Although Hume and Hume (2008) did not suggest free webware or open source products (OSS), these are possible options for small volunteer-based communities and NPOs that would fit into their framework.

3. The Study

A knowledge audit of the chosen community was conducted to understand how the community manages and shares knowledge, identify their knowledge needs, and examine ways that current theories, tools and technologies can augment or enhance the current state of knowledge sharing within the community.

The study was conducted at the workshop of a bicycle community in a major Canadian city. The workshop operates from an industrial garage in the city where bicyclists can use workspace, equipment, and bike tools to do repairs or maintenance on their own bicycles. The workshop is operated by a bicycle advocacy society whose Board of Directors (Board) funds, directs, and oversees the workshop. The workshop is staffed with 'mechanics,' primarily volunteers, to advise and guide clients on bike maintenance and repairs. The workshop regularly receives donations of used bikes and bike parts. Used bikes are checked, repaired, and then resold to support the bicycle society. The physical space of the community bicycle workshop includes the workshop floor, a small office area (for volunteers and staff), a showroom (to show bicycles that are for sale), a parts room (containing used bike parts), and a yard (filled with used bikes). The community bicycle workshop is operated primarily by volunteer bike mechanics throughout the year. During their 'winter season' (September to May), the facility is open two or three days per week. This varies from year to year, depending on volunteer commitment and involvement. During the summer months, the workshop is able to open six days per week because paid staff is hired. This study was conducted during the winter, and so did not concern itself with the paid mechanics. At the time of this study, the volunteer core for the workshop included approximately eleven members, mostly male.

The team of volunteers included both senior volunteers, with significant experience and time spent volunteering at the workshop, and casual volunteers. All volunteers provided assistance to clients ranging from greeting clients, answering questions about using the workshop, finding tools, and suggestions on how clients can repair their bicycles. The senior volunteers provided a supervisory role, including opening and closing the workshop, coordinating volunteers, and pricing bicycles for sale.

3.1. *Knowledge Audit for Data Collection*

A knowledge audit is a process to create a map of an organization's knowledge assets and needs. It "*plays a key role in identifying a knowledge management strategy*" and the current state of KM in an organization (Liebowitz *et al.*, 2000). Thus a knowledge audit, based on the framework proposed by Burnett *et al.* (2004) and Liebowitz *et al.* (2000), was conducted at the volunteer-based community to understand the sources, flows, pools, gaps and channels related to its KM, the types of knowledge needed to support the community, and the goals and motivations of volunteers which would impact the knowledge sharing within the community.

The data for the audit was collected from three primary sources. First, one-on-one semi-structured interviews were conducted using prepared questions to facilitate discussion with five current volunteers, all male. These interviews ranged from 30 to 45 minutes and were recorded and transcribed for analysis. Three participants were ‘casual’ volunteers, who had no supervision duties, and two were ‘senior’ volunteers, who were supervisors and had been with workshop for over two years. Second, photographs were taken of the entire workshop, including the shop floor, parts room, office, showroom, and outside yard. Third, current and archival content was collected from the group's website.

4. Findings

The interviews (after transcription) and data collected from other sources were analyzed to identify knowledge needs, sources, channels, gaps, sinks and pools. The details of which are presented in the following sub-sections.

4.1. *Knowledge Needs*

The knowledge needs can be broadly divided into three categories, with some amount of overlap. These are *technical, operational* and *personal knowledge needs*. The *personal knowledge needs* of volunteers are central to their motivation as volunteers; these include socializing with other cyclists and bicycle experts, identifying people with specialized knowledge or other resources, expanding their bicycle skills, and sharing their knowledge. *Operational knowledge needs* include basic operations of the workshop, such as social skills to work with people; fixing the heating system; familiarity with the protocols, policies and precedents at the workshop; tracking sales; workshop safety; and determining prices to resell used bicycles. *Technical knowledge needs* include basic repairs such as flat tires, or adjusting brakes and gears; customizing or modifying bikes; specialized repair, such as racing bikes or tandem bikes; and knowledge of specialized bikes tools, such as the headset press. However, a key finding is that most technical bicycle problems were basic and could be solved easily by the volunteers. The most important feature of these knowledge needs is that the need arises almost always when the problem is at hand. In other words, the knowledge need must be solved immediately. If a knowledge source is not immediately available, then it cannot satisfy the knowledge need.

4.2. *Knowledge Source*

The *internal sources* were primarily people themselves or documentary information. Other internal sources of knowledge include formal courses run at the workshop, books in the workshop, and signage on the walls. The findings indicate that people are, by far, the most important internal source of knowledge, such as other volunteers, readily available experts, or even other clients in the workshop. This finding is in line with the immediacy of knowledge articulated regarding KM in the business domain (Kersten, 1993). The *external sources* included: people, such as experts who are not part of the workshop community or bicycle sales agents; two specific websites (Sheldon Brown's website and the Park Tools website); and referring clients to commercial bicycle shops.

4.3. *Knowledge Channels*

There are both formal and informal channels of sharing knowledge. Like many small NPOs, the knowledge sharing in the community occurs mainly through informal channels (Gregory and Rathi, 2008). Currently, the primary channel for all knowledge sharing and dissemination is face-to-face communication, which simulates an apprenticeship model. A large number of volunteers learn new skills or solve problems by observing other volunteers in action, asking questions, trial and error on their own, or execution with the guidance of another volunteer. Interestingly, the workshop layout deliberately encourages volunteers and clients to interact and share knowledge. Bicycle repair stands are arranged in a circle so that the users can see what others are working on, and help each other. From time to time, training courses are offered by volunteers about bicycle repair – other volunteers are invited to attend. A phone in the workshop is used to find answers to operational questions (but rarely to solve repair questions). The website of the parent society solicits repair questions and posts answers – it appears that this channel is underutilized. Email and a listserv are used to communicate between the Board and volunteers, though the volunteers themselves rarely use email/listserv to communicate amongst themselves. The channels for communication from the Board include in-person contact (some volunteers are members of the Board), email and messages posted on the parent society website, etc. Finally, referrals are another type of knowledge channel, such as referring one volunteer to another volunteer for advice.

4.4. *Knowledge Gaps*

As other studies in human computer interaction (HCI) and information seeking have found, the participants hesitated to explicitly identify and articulate their needs. The participants felt that the current operations worked well enough; however, they did point out several weaknesses in the systems. Through their comments several implicit gaps were identified in knowledge sharing. A few of those gaps are presented here.

First, the findings suggest that communication within the community (among volunteers) is low. Outside of their volunteer hours, the volunteers have minimal interaction. A few reasons for low communication include volunteers guarding their personal time from onerous volunteer obligations, as well as keeping communication simple and not time consuming. *Second*, there is a gap in exchanging knowledge related to policy and operational needs of the volunteers. This has emerged due to a communication gap between the Board and the volunteers. The lack of clear policies and procedures creates problems, such as conflicting interpretations of policies and inconsistent practices. Other examples are inconsistent or improper labeling of bicycles that are for sale, inability of volunteers to answer questions raised by clients about programs of the bicycle society, and no formalized training of volunteers (especially regarding safety procedures, first aid, and customer relations). These gaps, in particular, have led to a certain level of disorganization in the workshop. *Third*, there is no mechanism to communicate and verify referrals of a client by a volunteer on one night to a volunteer on another night. Such communication would allow volunteers to prepare in advance to serve clients when they arrive for help. This existing knowledge gap can create poor service for clients and information lost in the client interaction. *Fourth*, there exists a knowledge gap in identifying experts to provide knowledge for solutions. There is no system to solve the perennial question: "*who knows who knows who*" (Contractor, 2007). This is a big issue identified even in KM for FPOs. While the senior volunteers have developed their own knowledge networks, new volunteers can only access these knowledge networks through senior volunteers or by "*asking around*". Identifying experts is occasionally important for resolving *technical knowledge needs* but it also relates to volunteers' *personal knowledge needs.*

4.5. *Knowledge Sinks*

Knowledge sinks are often created by broken communication systems, lack of policy and procedure, etc. Thus email seems to have created the conditions for knowledge sinks, where the information does not reach its intended recipients. For instance, requests from the Board for input or feedback often receive no reply; therefore, it is difficult to verify how widely the information was dispersed. One participant indicated he was not on the email list until recently. Participants believe that a set of policies for the workshop exist, but these policies are mostly unwritten. Changes to these policies sometimes become lost in communication. Understanding how to fix the heating system is an excellent example. The heating system suffers recurring failures, but the knowledge on how to fix the heating is only shared with a few volunteers. Failure to retain this knowledge creates a knowledge sink – and sometimes cold volunteers.

4.6. *Knowledge Pools*

Several untapped or underutilized sources of knowledge were identified. The most significant one is the people whose expertise or skills go unrecognized. Volunteers tend to approach the same people for answers to particular topics. This means that other volunteers might have the same or better knowledge about the particular topic but their expertise goes unrecognized because other volunteers are not aware of this expertise. Another important source is undocumented history or previous solutions to previous problems. The books and manuals, especially on new bike technologies, were identified as an important source for knowledge, but volunteers rarely took information from books. This was either because books were poorly located or volunteers preferred a social explanation of a solution over reading the information. Similarly, tools such as blackboards and whiteboards are available in the workshop, but they are not fully used (often remain blank). These tools, for example, could be used to leave messages for other volunteers who work other shifts. Community members might not be fully aware of existing knowledge sources on the internet from other community bicycle workshops that could help address operational or technical issues. In addition, there is very rich pool of ex-volunteers or members who have left the group but no system to tap into this vast pool of knowledge. Thus this knowledge of ex-volunteers, gained through years of experience working at the workshop and with other community members, is lost. Serendipitous discoveries made by members of the community can be a good knowledge resource but unfortunately cannot be shared with other members due to lack of well organized system which could support sharing of such discoveries.

5. Discussion and Recommendations

The surprise and key finding that emerged from the knowledge audit was that, of the three types of knowledge identified, *personal knowledge needs* i.e., knowledge needs of the volunteers, is potentially far more important than *operational* or *technical knowledge needs*. It was found that a motivated and dedicated volunteer is far more valuable to the workshop than a technical guru. While the majority of clients needed help only with basic repairs (easy for most volunteers) and specialized repair problems were comparatively rare, opening hours depended on the commitment of volunteers. Therefore, workshop operations rely on volunteer participation, which depends on volunteer motivation, which is connected to a set of *personal knowledge needs*. Attracting new volunteers and keeping existing volunteers motivated, then, becomes key to determining the scope of services that the workshop can offer. New volunteers could be casual users of the workshop drawn from the periphery of the CoP into core participants. Addressing these volunteer motivations may help address the longevity and sustainability of the community. A CoP in a volunteer community needs to sustain the altruism of its members and aid the establishment of trust throughout the community (Kolbotn, 2004). Thus any proposed KM for a volunteer community should focus on meeting *personal knowledge needs* of the volunteers, rather than on solving efficiency problems, a key consideration in FPOs.

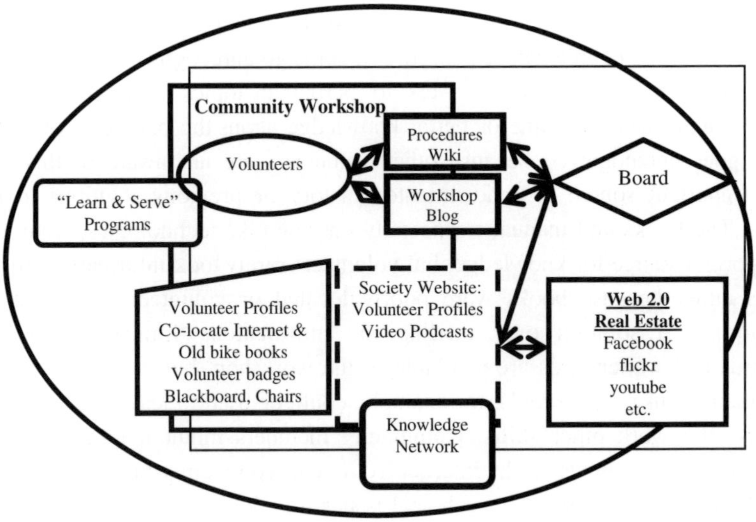

Fig. 1: Proposed Technological Framework of KM for the Volunteer-Based Community

Based on the findings, including the unexpected finding, the researchers recommended both technological and non-technological solutions to manage knowledge in the community. The technological solution (Figure 1) includes the development of a multi-faceted KM system assembled from commonly available web 2.0 technologies, which have been identified as flexible and empowering user-centered tools for KM purposes (Avram, 2006), and which are commonly used by a majority of individuals in their personal life. The various facets of the proposed KM system will address different aspects of the *technical, operational* and *personal knowledge needs*, streamline the current knowledge sources and identified pools, remove knowledge gaps and sinks, and augment the existing knowledge channels.

The technological system includes four components. First, a wiki is proposed for collaborative authoring of policies and procedures documents. This addresses the gap between Board and volunteers that relates to oversight and training, as well as the gap between volunteers who develop responses to emerging operational challenges. Second, a private blog is proposed as a record of events, to aid sharing of new knowledge or serendipitous discoveries and as a stable communications channel amongst the Board and volunteers. This addresses the knowledge sink of operational knowledge coming from the Board via the email list, where universal receipt of messages cannot be assured, and calls from the Board for volunteer input often go unanswered. The blog space can be used to share and exchange knowledge and post new information or serendipitous discoveries for the benefit of other volunteers. It also addresses the communications gap between volunteers working on different nights of the week that results in lack of coordination on policies and projects or the incomplete referral of clients to an expert volunteer working on a different day. Third, a knowledge network using a social network application is recommended. This will facilitate communication among volunteers, address the gap between specialized technical knowledge needs and identification of experts in the volunteer community, tap into knowledge pools of unrecognized expertise and peripheral and former volunteers, and aid in making successful referrals. As a supplement to this network, profiles of the volunteers could be made public on the society's website. The ability to locate expertise is relevant both to *technical* and *personal knowledge needs*. Finally, additional channels are proposed to aid passive and active sharing between volunteers and the wider workshop community. Passive sharing could include posting videos, pictures and stories on the society's website, on a public blog, or on photo and video sharing sites with a link on the society's website. Active sharing could include expanded offerings of formal repair courses ("learn and serve programs"). These measures augment the existing knowledge channels within the community and help leverage the pool of underutilized expertise.

The non-technological measures include organization of knowledge elements within the physical space of the workshop and use of available whiteboards and spaces as knowledge sharing and dissemination space. Non-technological components accomplish some of the same tasks mentioned above, but have the advantage of quick implementation and can help pave the way for acceptance of the technological measures within the culture of the workshop. For example, as an extension of the volunteer profiles on the website, photos and profiles could also be posted on the walls of the workshop; the existing whiteboard and chalkboard could be better located and used as a communications channel; a means could be provided for clients to identify volunteers when they are on duty (e.g., badges, labels, aprons); repair books and other information resources currently dispersed throughout the workshop could be co-located, organized, and labeled; and the computer could be moved out of the office area onto the shop floor to help integrate the technological solutions into the workflow of the space.

All of the components of the proposed KM exploit the capacity of social media for efficient communication and collaboration. Face-to-face communication in the workshop space remains the primary channel. However the social media, as proposed in the framework, would supplement and enhance the current KM and encourage knowledge sharing "*within*", by removing spatial and temporal barriers to communication between volunteers, and "*between*" (Hurley and Green, 2005), by facilitating communication and linkage with other geographically distributed communities.

6. Conclusion and Future Work

The proposed KM framework is ideally suited to support volunteer motivations that include the passion for learning, sharing knowledge with others, socialization and meeting new people, and pursuing bicycle customization projects that require the kind of specialized knowledge waiting to be tapped with the community. The KM system proposed here will support these *personal knowledge needs*, in addition to meeting some of the other *operational knowledge needs* already identified. It improves internal communication channels and is directed both internally and externally to peripheral members of the workshop community. Furthermore, it is muti-faceted, allowing volunteers to choose their level of participation, fits the budgetary constraints of the organization, and respects the culture of the community, as identified by one of the participants, who said "*we're kind of anti-technology nerds*", explaining, "*we like new when it's cheap and efficient*" [Nov 8, 2008, Interview C].

In the future we would like to explore other volunteer-based communities to confirm whether the *personal knowledge needs* related to volunteer motivation and dedication, as identified in this community, are indeed more important than other knowledge needs for a volunteer community to achieve its mission and goals.

Acknowledgments

We thank the volunteer community for participating in the study. The study would not have been successful without their help, support and commitment to this project.

References

"About Bikes Not Bombs", (2008) *Bikes Not Bombs,* Retrieved December 2, 2008, from http://www.bikesnotbombs.org/about

Avram, G. (2006) "At the crossroads of knowledge management and social software", *The Electronic Journal of Knowledge Management,* 4(1): 1-10.

Baskerville, R. and Dulipovici, A. (2006) "The theoretical foundations of knowledge management", *Knowledge Management Research & Practice*, 4: 83-105.

"Bikestation Santa Barbara", (2008) *Bikestation,* Retrieved December 2, 2008, from http://www.bikestation.org/santabarbara/index.asp

Blair, D. C. (2002) "Knowledge management: Hype, hope, or help?", *Journal of the American Society for Information Science and Technology* , 53: 1019-1028.

Burnett, S., Illingworth, L. and Webster, L. (2004) "Knowledge auditing and mapping: A pragmatic approach", *Knowledge and Process Management*, 11(1): 25-37.

Contractor, N. (2007) *From Disaster to WoW: Enabling Communities with Cyberinfrastructure*, Retrieved June 25, 2009, from http://dspace.anu.edu.au/bitstream/1885/46949/1/noshir.pdf.

Cook, S. D. N. and Brown, J. S. (1999) "Bridging epistemologies: The generative dance between organizational knowledge and organizational knowing", *Organization Science*, 10: 381-400.

Duguid, P. (2005) "The art of knowing: Social and tacit dimensions of knowledge and the limits of the community of practice", *Information Society*, 21(2): 109-18.

Evans, J. (2005) "A common goal", *Information Scotland,* 3(6), Retrieved Nov. 2, 2008, from www.slainte.org.uk/publications/serials/infoscot/vol3(6)/ vol3(6)article2.htm.

Gilmour, J. and Stancliffe, M. (2004) "Managing knowledge in a international organization: The work of Voluntary Service Overseas (VSO)", *Records Management Journal*, 14(3): 124-128.

Gongla, P. and Rizzuto, C. R. (2001) "Evolving communities of practice: IBM global services experience", *IBM Systems Journal*, 40(4): 842-862.

Gregory, A. and Rathi, D. (2008) "Open source tools for managing knowledge in a small non-profit organization", International Conference on Knowledge Management (ICKM), October 2008.

Hanley, S. S. (1999) "Communities of practice: A culture built on sharing", *Informationweek*, 731 (26 April, 1999), 16ER-17ER.

Hara, N. and Kling, R. (2005) "Communities of practice with and without information technology", *Proceedings of the ASIST*, 39: 338-49.

Helmig, B., Jegers, M. and Lapsley, I. (2004) "Challenges in managing nonprofit organizations: A research overview", *Voluntas: International Journal of Voluntary and Nonprofit Organizations,* 15(2): 101-16.

Hume, C. and Hume, M. (2008) "The strategic role of knowledge management in nonprofit organisations", *International Journal of Nonprofit and Voluntary Sector Marketing*, 13(2): 129-40.

Hurley, T. A. and Green, C. W. (2005) "Knowledge management and the nonprofit industry: A within and between approach", *Journal of Knowledge Management Practice*, 6. Retrieved June 25, 2009, from http://www.tlainc.com/articl79.htm

Kersten, G. E. (1993) "Negotiation support: Development of representations and reasoning", *Theory and Decision*, 34: 293–311.

Kipley, D. H., Lewis, A. O. and Helm, R. (2008) "Achieving strategic advantage and organizational legitimacy for small and medium sized NFPs through the implementation of knowledge management", *Business Renaissance Quarterly,* 3(3): 21-42.

Kolbotn, R. (2004) "Communities of practice in the Royal National Lifeboat Institution", In: P. Hildreth & C. Kimble (Eds.), *Knowledge networks: Innovation through communities of practice* : 70-78, Hershey, PA: Idea Group.

Kong, E. and Prior, D. (2008) "An intellectual capital perspective of competitive advantage in nonprofit organisations", *International Journal of Nonprofit and Voluntary Sector Marketing,* 13(2): 119-28.

Lavé, J. and Wenger, E. (1991) *Situated Learning: Legitimate Peripheral Participation*, New York: Cambridge University Press.

Larson, P., Levy, J. and Schmitz, M. (2005) "The nonprofit world in California: knowledge management on a shoestring", *Information Outlook*, 9(11): 38-41.

Ledlie, T. (2008) "Classes & programs", The Bike Kitchen. 8 Nov. 2008. Retrieved December 2, 2008 from http://www.bikekitchen.org/programs.htm

Lemieux, S. A. and Dalkir, K. (2006) "The case of a nonprofit artistic organization", *Information Outlook*, 10(1): 13-16.

Lettieri, E., Borga, F. and Savoldelli, A. (2004) "Knowledge management in non-profit organizations", *Journal of Knowledge Management,* 8(6): 16-30.

Liebowitz, J., Rubenstein-Montano, B., McCaw, D., Buchwalter, J., Browning, C., Newman, B. and Rebeck, K. (2000) "The knowledge audit", *Knowledge and Process Management,* 7(1): 3-10.

Matzkin, D. S. (2008) "Knowledge management in the Peruvian non-profit sector", *Journal of Knowledge Management* , 12(4): 147-59.

Nonaka, I. (1994) "A dynamic theory of organizational knowledge creation", *Organization Science*, 5(1): 5-37.

"Programs", (2008) *PEDAL: Pedal Energy Development Alternatives*, Retrieved December 2, 2008, from http://www.pedalpower.org/?q=education

Prusak, L. (2001) "Where did knowledge management come from?", *IBM Systems Journal,* 40(4): 1002-07.

Wenger, E. (2000) "Communities of practice: The structure of knowledge stewarding", In: Despres, C. and Chauvel, D. (Eds.) *Knowledge Horizons: The Present and the Promise of Knowledge Management*, Woburn, MA: Butterworth Heinemann.

Wenger, E. (2004) "Knowledge management as a doughnut: Shaping your knowledge strategy through communities of practice", *Ivey Business Journal*, 68(3): 1-8.

KNOWLEDGE MANAGEMENT PRACTICES IN A NOT FOR PROFIT ORGANIZATIONS: A CASE STUDY OF I2E

MATTHEW BROADDUS and SULIMAN HAWAMDEH

School of Library and Information Studies
College of Arts and Sciences
University of Oklahoma
Tulsa, OK, 74135
Email: Suliman@ou.edu

This paper studies knowledge management practices of i2E, Inc. (innovation 2 Enterprise), a nonprofit organization which focuses on expanding Oklahoma's technology-based entrepreneurial economy. i2E serves as a knowledge repository of resources for individuals who have ideas and want to develop those ideas into an enterprise. They developed a program that educates would-be entrepreneurs on how to navigate the waters of developing a business, where to find resources, and how to be successful. Educating the entrepreneurs is done through i2E's ability to manage knowledge and provide knowledge resources to their clients. This study examines the extent by which i2E uses knowledge management tools to help their clients be successful.

1. Introduction

Ideas are conceived and lost on a daily basis. Products, technology, medicines and a plethora of other innovations are born in the minds of inventors and vanish just as quickly, never coming to fruition. Many times this loss happens because an anomalous state of knowledge exists and the inventor does not have the knowledge necessary to move forward in their endeavor (Case 2007, 74). Inadequacies in information can be lacks, gaps, uncertainty, misunderstanding or any general wrongness concerning information (Belkin 1980, 137). Through a process of knowledge management, i2E provides entrepreneurs with the knowledge of how to move forward with their innovation, such as filling in the gaps, uncertainties and misunderstandings that occur in the early stages of entrepreneurial endeavors. The knowledge i2E manages and shares with entrepreneurs includes the commercial life cycle, where to find resources and how to develop business plans. i2E's ability to manage and disseminate knowledge to and from diverse sources is an example of what Wulff (2007) sees as a prerequisite for success in information intense industries. While i2E is not a typical venture capital company, their ultimate goal is the same – the creation of new enterprise. In this case study, we explore the underlying success factor of i2E and the knowledge management practices and tools that i2E uses to serve their clients.

1.1. *I2E and Oklahoma*

The Oklahoma Center for the Advancement of Science and Technology (OCAST) was created in 1987 with the purpose of fostering innovation in businesses by supporting applied research, facilitating technology transfer, providing seed-capital and fostering competitiveness in Oklahoma firms. In 1998, OCAST launched an initiative to foster the creation and long-term growth of advance technology firms in Oklahoma. i2E grew from that initiative. i2E is a private, non-profit organization focused on wealth creation and reinforcing the technology-based entrepreneurial economy in Oklahoma. Originally chartered as the Oklahoma Technology Development Corporation in 1997, i2E assumed its current name in 2004, to better reflect its high-tech vision and mission. i2E's vision is to, "facilitate the growth of high performance, advanced technology companies in the state, which will increase Oklahoma's global competitiveness, per capita income, and quality of life" (i2e.org, 2008). Their mission supports this vision through economic development, fostering the birth and nurturing the growth of advanced technology companies in Oklahoma. "This mission is accomplished through a well-designed strategy that includes: providing technology development knowledge and know-how; delivering comprehensive enterprise development services; providing access to capital, and ensuring a quality enterprise" (i2e.org, 2008). Oklahoma is lagging behind other states in technology development and the funding needed to promote such endeavors (Dobberstein, 2006). In 2006, Kansas spent four times what Oklahoma spent in innovation investment and committed to spending $500 million over the next eight years. Oklahoma only spends $10 million per year investing in innovation. In 2006, despite the low state investment, OCAST (in part through i2E) had leveraged every state dollar spent on innovation into fifteen dollars (Dobberstein, 2006).

i2E's commercialization process provides entrepreneurs with the knowledge to take a new technology through inception, validation, and commercialization by providing: hands-on marketing and business knowledge; investment resources and expertise in risk capital; and by promoting a local, innovation-based economy, (i2E.org 2008). i2E's strategy for educating entrepreneurs and providing them with resources to develop advance technology firms is based on knowledge management practices, particularly, knowledge sharing and collaboration.

2. KM Practices

Knowledge management is a new and emerging discipline that should be utilized in every organization to provide employees with the best opportunities to succeed. It is the process of identifying, organizing and managing knowledge resources, including information, learning capacity and other resources (Al-Hawamdeh, 2004). Knowledge management practices and processes include areas such as knowledge sharing and transfer, knowledge creation and discovery, communities of practice, best practices, learning organization and so on. The advancements in business and the growth in global competition demand proactive knowledge management practices as well as the deployment of knowledge management tools and technologies (Bergman, *et al.* 2004). Knowledge resides in the minds of people and therefore knowledge management is the practice of supporting individuals to share and utilize the knowledge they have (Widen-Wulff, 2007). An individual's knowledge is of no value to anyone else if it is not shared or turned into some sort of product or service. Effective knowledge sharing involves transmission and absorption of knowledge. The outcome of knowledge sharing should be the creation of new knowledge and innovation that will significantly improve organizational performance.

One of the key elements that make i2E effective at fortifying entrepreneurs is the ability to provide a learning environment in which new ideas are encouraged and fostered. Businesses that exhibit a learning culture tend to be more successful in leveraging knowledge (Widen-Wulff, 2007). Smith (1999) sees such an environment as a "rapid and continuous exchange between explicit and tacit… knowledge" that leaves little time for participants to get stuck in a negative learning pattern. i2E invests heavily in knowledge and knowledge resources in the hope of turning ideas and innovation into products and services. One way to advance innovation is through promoting best practices and communities of practice. "Communities of practice provide the platform needed for the exchange of ideas and discussions about similar problems and like solutions" (Al-Hawamdeh 2003, 130). Participants in a community of practice share their understanding about what they know and do (Lave and Wenger 1991). External communities of practice happen outside of a single organization and can include anyone with an interest in the communities focus, (Erat, *et al.* 2006, 513). "A community of practice is a group of people who share a common concern, a set of problems or a passion about a topic, who deepen their knowledge and expertise in this area by interacting on an ongoing basis," (Al-Hawamdeh 2003, 121). i2E not only employs individuals who are experts in their field, but the organization also act as a communities of practice through holding meetings, networking and collaboration. They hold regular events such as Tech Night Out and i2E luncheons in an effort to develop communities of practice. These are events where entrepreneurs, inventors, investors and others who are interested in the growth of the technology industry in Oklahoma come together as a community of practice.

In the ever changing business climate, companies are finding it more difficult to take on all of the tasks required to be successful. Therefore, many organizations are turning to collaborative practices with outside partners to help carry the burden and risks of business. Collaboration provides the opportunity for an organization to minimize risk, share knowledge, and share in the development of new ideas (Horton 1998, 4-12). i2E has leveraged this collaborative environment into a powerful network of resource development. Resource development is i2E's ability to link their clients with financial, business and technical resources, furthering their goal of expanding the growth of technology-based businesses in Oklahoma.

3. Methodology

A case study methodology is normally adopted when a holistic and an in-depth investigation is needed. Data analysis in a case study consists of examining, categorizing, tabulating, or otherwise recombining the evidence to address the initial propositions of a study (Yin, 1994). A content analysis of material relating to i2E was conducted to determine the extent by which i2E utilizes knowledge management practices, particularly knowledge sharing and collaboration. Content analysis is the classification and evaluation of documents (i.e. book, newspaper article, video, Websites, or any other media used). Content analysis is a formal, systematic method of evaluating text, giving the evaluator the opportunity to draw inferences about the information, (Webber 1990, 12). It is an attempt to characterize the meaning in a given body of discourse in a systematic and quantitative fashion (Kaplan, 1943). Information is coded in a format which represents the original intent of the author. Drawing conclusions based on the frequency of a code is the simplest and most useful way to conduct content analysis.

3.1. *Coding Procedure and Reliability Testing*

Seven areas of knowledge management were identified and each item that shows knowledge management traits was coded accordingly. For example, if a document discussed the organization participation in a forum, then the story can be coded as knowledge sharing or knowledge transfer activity. If the forum was specifically about how to raise seed money for startup companies, the story could have also been coded as resource development. The knowledge management areas used to analyze i2E include collaboration, communities of practice, innovation, knowledge creation, knowledge sharing and transfer, learning organization and resource development. To ensure consistency and reliability in the results, the researchers carried out coding independently. Disagreements in coding were resolved by jointly discussing and reviewing the articles. Reliability was also strengthened by the use of multiple data sources (Patton, 2001).

4. Findings

The findings from the content analysis of i2E support the assumption that i2E utilizes knowledge management practices in general and knowledge sharing and collaboration in particular to serve their clients. The content analyses of the documents used in this study, including newspaper articles about i2E, provided the most data. Content analysis include data was collected from Oklahoma's three leading newspapers since 2004, when i2E began operating under that name. The newspaper articles were searched using terms such as i2E, innovations, research funding, OCAST and so on. The content of each article was then evaluated based on the knowledge management element discussed above and each article was assigned codes based on the matching content.

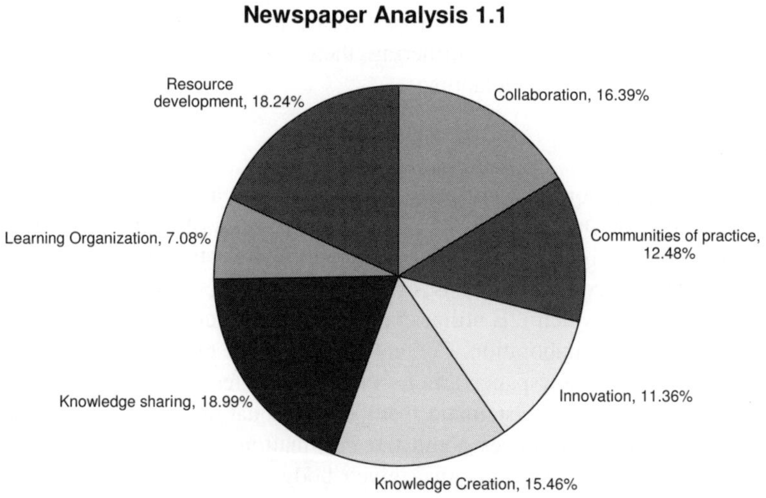

Figure 1: Newspaper Analysis

It is clear from Figure 1 that knowledge sharing is the most visible knowledge management practice. Nearly 19 percent of the newspaper articles studied dealt with i2E's knowledge sharing practices. Out of the 1,100 companies that submitted ideas to i2E for consideration, nearly 600 were brought on as clients to utilize their services. By sharing knowledge about the commercialization process and how to build a successful enterprise, i2E was successful in attracting that many ideas. Resource development and resource sharing was the subject of 18.24 percent of the newspaper articles. Again, this is not a normal function of knowledge management, but it is an important part of i2E's knowledge sharing practices. In fact, the newspaper content analysis shows that nearly half of i2E's knowledge sharing is focused on resource development. Resource development and resource sharing is true knowledge management activity, since i2E does not provide resources but rather assists clients by arming them with the knowledge needed of where to find, apply for and get those resources. According to several newspaper articles, OCAST's return on investment is 27 to 1, with much of that funding being identified through the resource development of i2E. The funding that i2E guides its clients to is different from that developed by most venture capital organizations. While many for profit venture capital groups focus on multi-million dollar investments, i2E helps provide funding for smaller startup firms. For example, in July 2006, i2E provided 10 high-tech startup firms with $100,000 each in OCAST funding. This funding provided pre-seed money which was used to stimulate additional private investment. These firms are required to raise an additional $3 for every dollar of OCAST funding they receive. i2E also provides access to angel investment funding. These are investors who help fill the financial gap between seed funding and full venture capital funding. i2E has also developed a community of practice to help develop a pool of ready angel investors.

Nearly 12.5 percent of the document content analysis showed development of, or participation in, communities of practice such as the angel investor community, Tech Night Out events and other networking opportunities. Not only does i2E develop communities of practice for their clients, but they also represent Oklahoma by participating in other out of state communities and forums. For example, i2E participates in several national technology and enterprise forums. They do this to glean knowledge for their clients and to share knowledge about technology developments in Oklahoma. Many times, collaborative practices grow from these communities of practice. The results show 16.39 percent of i2E's knowledge management activities were dedicated to building collaborations. In 2006, i2E took over operation of the dormant Oklahoma Investment Services forum. Part of the revival of this forum was designed to create communities of practice where mentoring would occur. From this mentoring, fledgling companies and inventors can develop a collaborative network of people who will invest funds, provide knowledge and share other burdens of the startup. i2E actually serves as a collaborative partner to inventors since they are taking on the burden of providing marketing and development services, another function that most venture capital firms do not perform.

From both communities of practice and collaboration, new ideas grow. While the overarching goal of i2E is to develop and innovate, only 11.36 percent of their knowledge management practices are focused on innovation. This shows that i2E takes a balanced approach to knowledge management, integrating several elements of the discipline to achieve the ultimate goal of modernization. In 2006, i2E received the 2006 Innovator Award for their role of innovation in Oklahoma. i2E's ability to utilize knowledge management practices has not only led to growth but offers more evidence of a strong knowledge management culture which includes the elements that make a learning organization. 7.08 percent of the newspaper content analysis focused on i2E's knowledge management practices involving a learning organization. While a learning organization is normally an internal function that is not always visible, i2E's learning culture can be seen in the way they learn from and teach their clients. i2E learns from its client's past successes and failures and passes improved practices to new clients. i2E stays relevant to their client's success by constantly learning, growing and adapting.

The final knowledge management category used to evaluate i2E was knowledge creation, which made up 15.46 percent of the newspaper content analysis. While i2E offers several educational programs and works to further knowledge, it does not create knowledge. The reason this category was so high was due to the Donald W. Reynolds Governor's Cup, a competition for Oklahoma college students. The Governor's Cup encourages college students to come up with or act upon existing ideas which might grow into future innovations. A $20,000 cash prize is given to both graduate and undergraduate winners. A team from Cameron University won the 2006 Governor's Cup for a business plan they developed to market a cancer drug. While the Governor's Cup does inspire the creation of knowledge, it is inaccurate to say i2E spends 15.46 percent of their knowledge management resources creating knowledge. The Governor's Cup received a higher percentage of coverage in all three newspapers due to the public nature of the competition. Each year, all three newspapers cover several stories on the competition, the teams and the innovations. However, this publicity does create and share knowledge about i2E and its endeavors in Oklahoma, knowledge that might not otherwise be known by the general public.

While the newspaper content analysis showed a wide spread variety of knowledge management activities, with somewhat equal distribution, the internal documents analysis and the Web site analysis showed a more concentrated focus on resource development and knowledge sharing. This is due to the types of material which was analyzed. Newspaper articles were written for the general public and focused on informing readers of activities, events and newsworthy happenings occurring with i2E. The Web page analysis consisted of mainly official i2E Web sites and links, which are designed to educate and inform potential and existing clients of knowledge and resources i2E offers. i2E's publicly available internal documents serve the same purpose as the Web sites, but also showcase success.

For the content analysis of web pages, each of i2E's pages where evaluated for elements of knowledge management. Those elements where then coded and compiled in the same way as the newspaper articles. The web page analysis again showed knowledge sharing (48.15 percent) as the most robust knowledge management practice at i2E (Figure 2). Resource development and resource sharing was again the second most practiced knowledge management element at 37.05 percent. If you view resource development as part of knowledge sharing, more than 85 percent of the web page analysis of i2E exhibits knowledge-sharing activities. The other five knowledge management practices were much less prevalent in web page material. Collaboration, communities of practice, innovation and knowledge creation were each represented with 3.70 percent of the web analysis. Learning organization practices were not present on the website. While i2E shows strong characteristics of being a learning organization, these traits were not evident through the web page analysis. Again, this can be explained by the focus of external knowledge sharing, rather than internal, as the web pages are designed to provide.

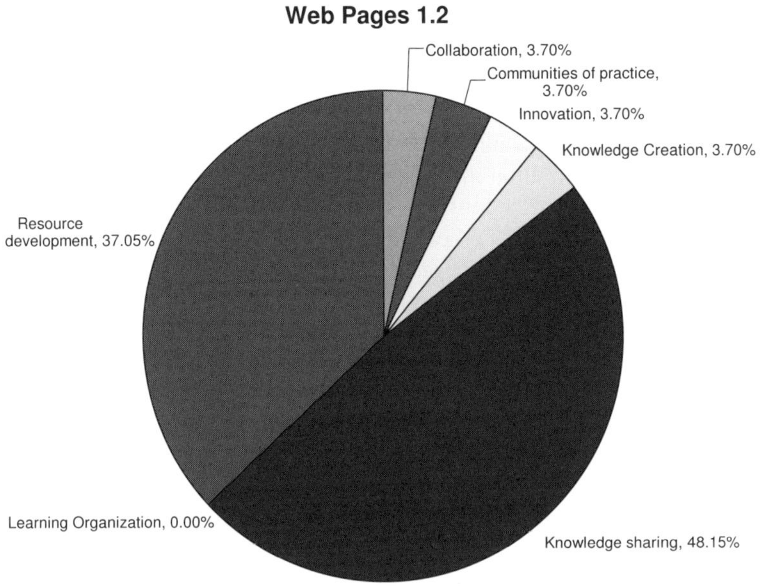

Figure 2: Web Page Analysis

The analysis of the i2E documents was conducted using their annual impact reports, biannual *Innovation and Enterprise* newsletter and their prospective client material.

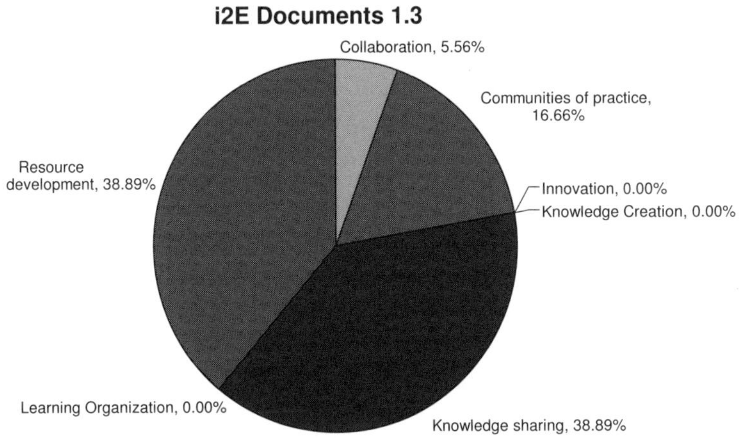

Figure 3: Internal Documents Analysis

Knowledge sharing (38.89 percent) and knowledge resource development (38.89 percent) were again the largest categories of knowledge management practices found, totaling 77.78 percent. I2E's client material showed the strongest knowledge sharing and resource development activities. The content analysis of the newsletter also showed substantial information on communities (16.66 percent) and collaborative practices (5.56 percent).

The overall analysis from the three different types of material analyzed indicates that i2E is doing well in knowledge sharing and knowledge resource development. It also shows that i2E is within the stated purpose of fostering innovation in businesses by providing the needed knowledge infrastructure for its clients. This is probably one of the most important intangible performance measures for i2E, provided beside the monetary return on investment. In 2007 and in an annual performance survey carried out by i2E, participating companies reported a $33 million in gross pay to Oklahoma's economy, with an average salary of $50,000 per year after four years in business. These companies also reported $99 million in sales revenue, 211 new jobs created, 629 jobs retained and 318 new products created for FY 2007. Of the new jobs created, 76 percent required a bachelor degree or higher. OCAST provides a technology business financing program (TBFP) which i2E administrates. Of the 102 clients surveyed for the FY 2007 report, the TBFP impact report showed the program provided 68 new jobs, retained 301 jobs and aided in the creation of 65 new products. Since the inception of TBFP, 65 companies have been funded, $7.2 million in funding has been provided, $174 million more in investments have been made and there has been a 70 percent survival rate for companies. It is also reported that since 1998, i2E clients have raised $294 million in funding. These growth patterns remain consistent through all available impact reports.

5. Conclusion

I2E's vision is to grow technology-based businesses in Oklahoma through fostering innovation in businesses. It is clear that knowledge sharing is the chief export of i2E. They provide knowledge to their clients on a vast number of topics, ranging from how to start a business to how to raise funds, as well as facilitating interaction among clients. The study of i2E through content analysis of documented information only provides a window into their knowledge management practices. While it was not fully supported by the content analysis, i2E has an interesting learning culture that should be studied further. i2E's success in comparison to traditional venture capital firms could also serve as a study in itself. While i2E provides knowledge sharing to their clients, they also have a program dedicated to education and knowledge creation, such as the Governors Cup. The successes stemming from the Governors Cup could provide a rich ground of studies to pursue.

It is important to point out some of the limitations and shortcoming of this study. The study was limited to documented information and did not include interviewing or surveying people from i2E or their clients. The other limitation and inherit weakness of the methodology used is that content analysis based on documented information is susceptible to the effect of the researcher bias in turn might affect the collection, analysis and interpretation of data. A triangulation method that combines multiple sources of data as well as qualitative and quantitative techniques can be used to enhance the content analysis technique.

References

Al-Hawamdeh, S. (2003). *Knowledge Management: Cultivating knowledge professionals*. Oxford: Chandos Publishing.

Belkin, N. (1980). Anomalous state of knowledge as a basis for information retrieval. *The Canadian Journal of Information Science* (5): 133-143.

Bergman, J., Jantunen, A., and Saksa, J. M. (2004). Managing knowledge creation and sharing: Scenarios and dynamic capabilities in inter-industrial knowledge networks. *Journal of Knowledge Management*. 8 (6): 63-76.

Case, D. (2007). *Looking for information: A survey of research on information seeking, needs, and behaviors.* 2d ed. Boston: Academic Press.

Devanport, T.H. and Prusak, (2000), Working knowledge: How organizations manage what they know, Boston, Massachusetts: Harvard Business school Press.

Dobberstein, J. 2006). Money for start-ups pushed, *The Tulsa World,* May 4, 2006.

Erat, P. et al. (2006). Business customer communities and knowledge sharing: Exploratory study of critical issues. *European Journal of Information Systems* 15 (1): 511-524.

Kaplan, A. (1943) Content analysis and the theory of signs. *Philosophy of Science*, 10: 230-247.

Kline, P. and Sanders, B. (1998). *Ten steps to a learning organization* 2d ed. Salt Lake City: Great River Books.

Lave J. and Wenger E. 1991. *Situated learning: Legitimate peripheral participation*. New York: Cambridge University Press.

Patton, M. Q. (2001). *Qualitative evaluation and research methods (3rd ed.).* Thousand Oaks, CA: Sage Publications, Inc.

Senge, P. M. 2006. *The fifth discipline: The art and practice of the learning organization.* New York: Doubleday.

Smith, P. (1999). The learning organization ten years on: A case study. *The Learning Organization* 12: 217-223.

United State General Accounting Office. 1996 *Content analysis: A methodology for structuring and analyzing written material.* Washington D.C.: United States general accounting office.

Webber, R. (1990). *Basic content analysis.* 2d ed. California: Sage University Papers.

Widen-Wulff, G. (2007) *Utilization of information resources for business success: The knowledge sharing model* 15 (1): 46-67.

Yin, R. (1994). *Case study research: Design and methods* (2nd ed.). Thousand Oaks, CA: Sage Publishing.

PERSONAL INFORMATION MANAGEMENT TOOLS REVISITED

YUN-KE CHANG[1]
Wee Kim Wee School of Communication and Information, Nanyang Technological University,
31 Nanyang Link
Singapore, 637718, Singapore
E-mail: ykchang@ntu.edu.sg

MIGUEL A. MORALES-ARROYO[†], CHAN-CHOY CHUM, TIN-SENG LIM,
and KOK-YUIN YUEN
WKWSCI, Nanyang Technological University, 31 Nanyang Link
Singapore, 637718, Singapore
[†]E-mail: mangel@ntu.edu.sg

Facing a rapidly growing collection of digital resources, users are challenged to organize their personal digital resources in such a way that they can be re-accessed and re-used when they are needed in the future. Personal Information Management (PIM) tools are designed to help users to achieve that. However, questions remain whether these tools are able to meet users' requirements and expectations. Survey questionnaire was used with 119 participants. The results suggest that most respondents are comfortable with the existing PIM tools, and they are capable of managing digital resources of different characteristics and shelf life. This paper reports the results of a study in how users manage their personal digital resources in terms of types of digital resources, memory and cue functions, and effectiveness of existing PIM tools and usefulness of certain information structures. Our findings reveal that users actually prefer to have PIM tools that are able to handle multi-format digital resources. These findings may provide valuable insight into how PIM tools can be made more versatile and usable for organization of personal digital resources.

1. Introduction

Personal digital resources (e.g. emails, audio and video files, digital photographs, word documents, etc.) have been increasing rapidly due to the recent advancement of technology and user's growing reliance on various types of digital information (Lyman & Varian, 2003). The management of these resources is largely referred to as Personal Information Management (PIM) and is practiced by all computer users.

The exponential growth of digital resources means that PIM has become increasingly difficult and time consuming (Barreau, 1995). Digital resources may be generated by the users as the result of their professional and personal activities. Some of those digital results, and sometimes several copies, may be stored in personal computers, handheld devices, and/or on Internet repositories to which the user has access. However, human capabilities to organize and retrieve personal information may be limited due to time restrictions, fallibility of human memory, confusing the sequence the timing of events, and cognitive overload, among others.

The advent of information and multimedia technology has also changed the landscape of personal digital resources. These resources are becoming indispensable, both for work and leisure purposes. Research has found that users spend huge amount of time and work to storage and retrieval their personal information (Dumais et al., 2003;

Freeman & Gelernter, 1996), which could potentially affect productivity as precious time and energy are wasted in organizing and retrieving needed information. As a result, improving PIM capabilities would be an important issue for all users.

Ideal PIM tools should improve users' access to the complete and quality information in the right form to perform desirable tasks when and where they are needed (Bergman, Boardman, Gwizdka, & Jones, 2004). They would also provide flexibility for users to manipulate the resources by organizing, annotating, grouping, or providing links to information to improve the searching and retrieval process. In other words, better PIM will allow us to improve employee productivity, which may in turn lead to better teamwork. However, there are few researches reported on improving PIM, and tools that support PIM have changed little over the years (Whittaker et al., 2004).

As digital information resources can manifest in different formats, it can be challenging for users to organize those items in such a way that they can be re-accessed and re-used when they are needed in the future (Fertig, Freeman, & Gelernter, 1996; Kelly, 2006). Currently existing PIM tools seem able to help users to meet some of the challenges. However, with the growth and the increasing complexity of digital resources, these tools may not be able meet the users' expectations in the future. This research attempts to understand how users currently organize their information basing on file attributes. Our main objective is to explore how users manage their personal digital resources, particularly the relationships and underlying structures between PIM tools and file attributes when users organize their knowledge and information to serve as base to develop their organizational strategies.

2. Literature Review

Some PIM tools can easily be found in a personal computer to help us manage the vast amount of information we collected. PIM tools in the personal computer can generally be classified into two types which are multiple and specific (Bergman, Boardman, Gwizdka & Jones, 2004; Malone, 1983), classified by types and formats digital information. The iFinder from the Mac Operating System (OS) and the Windows Explorer from the Windows OS are examples of multiple PIM tools. These tools allow users to search or browse all the directories and files of different formats stored in a computer. Some examples of specific PIM tools include iCal, iMail, QuickTime and iTunes found in the Mac OS or Address Book, Microsoft Outlook, Windows Media Player and Windows Slideshows found in the Windows OS. Unlike multiple PIM tools, specific tools focus on PIM in the context of specific digital resources such as emails, textual-based documents, audio, photos and movie files. However, as some resources overlapped in terms of its format (e.g. multimedia resources), most of the media-based PIM tools such as QuickTime, RealPlayer and Windows Media Player usually allows users to perform multiple tasks such as playing a movie file or listening to an audio file.

Besides those in the personal computer, there are also PIM tools that are provided by manufacturers of digital devices such as digital cameras or mp3 players. These tools can be referred to as Original Equipment Manufacturer (OEM) software. Some of the examples are photo organizer software provided by digital cameras or media organizers provided by mp3 players. Similar to specific PIM tools, the focus of OEM software is in managing and organizing specific digital resources such as photos and music files. But with the increase usage of multimedia resources, some OEM software can support resources with different formats. Nonetheless, their function is still restricted.

PIM tools can also be found on the Web and the most common ones are webmail services such as Gmail, Yahoo! Mail and Hotmail. These services allow users to manage emails, calendar and contacts. Other services such as Flickr, MySpace and Facebook not only allow users to manage blogs, emails, photos, videos and music, but also share the resources among their friends and communities. As these PIM tools are based on the Web, they do not need to be installed in the personal computer. This means that storage space may not be an issue but accessibility is dependent on whether the user is connected to the Internet.

Some research has been done with software prototypes that help to understand how to handle personal information in a better way. Specifically, these prototypes have used ontology, task management, and task inference. The use of ontology to understand user's personal interests has been employed in different applications such as search engines (Gauch, Speretta, Chandramouli, & Micarelli, 2007; Kim & Chan, 2008). The majority of these methods utilize linguistic structures as hierarchies, lacking of deep understanding of user needs. Ontology was reported to be used on systems such as OntoPIM (Lepouras et al., 2006) and Gnowsis (Sauermann, 2005). Both systems were designed for PC environment, and evaluation has been conducted to study how well user's tasks were handled.

Another prototype that used an Activity-Centered Task Assistant (ACTA) has been put into operation as an add-in for Outlook in Microsoft. It has a container with a set of pre-delineated elements named components, which contains frequent used elements and come into view as sub-folders, and create an email hierarchy (Bellotti & Thornton, 2006). Research into task inference in human-computer interaction has been profuse for many years (Diaper & Stanton, 2004). Explicit examples of task detection and prediction could be found in search engines when they offer suggestions at the time the user is typing her query. However, when the task detection is incorrect, some of the applications could annoy the users.

Other research was in the area known as knowledge organization systems, which includes classification algorithms, vocabulary databases, thesauri, and ontology, and taxonomies (Tudhope & Nielsen, 2006). The main objective was to model the fundamental semantic composition of a specific domain with the intention of retrieval digital resources.

Attributes or memory cues are also important for the retrieval process and their selection may vary according to the retrieval method (browse or search). For textual-based resources such as emails, social and temporal attributes such as sender, recipient or dates are mostly used for the retrieval process using the browse method, while the contents (e.g. title, subject) are associated with searching (Whittaker, Bellotti, & Gwizdka, 2006). Likewise, for image or media-related resources, visual attributes are used when browsing for the resources while contents such as titles are the preferred attributes for searching (Rodden & Wood, 2003).

Despite the wide range of PIM tools available, they all serve a unilateral purpose of helping users to complete a task by providing a platform for users to search and retrieve resources that are stored in different locations (work, home), devices (laptop, mobile phone, PDA) or applications (calendar, word files, emails, contacts, favorites) (Bergman, Boardman, Gwizdka & Jones, 2004). Most PIM tools provided a range of features to help enhance their performance. Normally, these features are catered for different resource types. For instance, if users want to manage their photos or movie files, the PIM tools allow them to rename each file. The tools may provide a list of functions such as arranging the files according to their creation date. Some PIM tools such as Microsoft Windows Media Player even help users to organize the resources according to their format type or through information that are tagged with the files such as author and title. This automated function is often restricted and at times inefficient, and sometimes users still need to organize the resources manually.

3. Methodology

A survey questionnaire was used to investigate how users manage their personal digital resources. The questions were designed to understand how users handle digital resources from the instance they receive them, followed by organizing the information, before storing away for future retrieval. The analysis of statistical trends and relationships between PIM tools and information recourse attributes was conducted to understand how people choose to manage digital information in a particular way.

3.1. *Respondents*

The survey was conducted on students and working professionals with tertiary educational background. Convenient sampling was used. It was expected that this group of people is more likely to be computer literate and have experience managing digital resources like text, audio, image and video contents. It is assumed that this combination of participants would generate a good mix of information contents and information management styles.

There were 118 responses for this survey, and all of them have at least high school level of education. The breakdown of the age group is 88% of them belong to 20-40 years group, and 12% belong to older than 40-age group. The sample consists of 23% students, 35% technical professionals, 16% R&D staff, and 26% others. 94% of them have at least five years of experience of using computers.

3.2. *Data collection*

To undertake the objectives of this research, a questionnaire was created and administered to the sample as depicted previously. It included items associated to PIM applications and how they handle digital resources, and what file attributes are the most important to use when organizing certain types of digital resources. Data was collected in September 2008. Among other questions, types of investigated information resources include *Text, Email, Photo, Audio, Video, Animation, Graphical drawing, and* Games; PIM attributes are *Date, Author, Format, File name, and File size;* types of PIM applications were divided into *OS file manager, Media organizer, OEM software, Web-based organizer, and Email organizer*. Information retrieval issues considered were: usefulness of prompts, retrieval process easy to use, accuracy of the retrieved information, and fast retrieval time.

3.3. *Data analysis*

In this research, correspondence analysis was first performed on contingency tables, which were formed by tabulating applications vs. attributes used to organize personal information. The software used was SPSS 14.0, and specific details about the results are presented in the *Result* section.

Correspondence analysis is an exploratory data reduction method to represents relationships between two or more categorical variables by using cross tabulation and more frequently two-way tables. Correspondence analysis is often applied as a feature-based procedure in which participants are requested to select attributes for specific products and services (Hair, Anderson, Tatham, & Black, 2009). The results of this method could be represented graphically in a low-dimensional map, usually two dimensions in which similar items are drawn closer and vice versa. The low-dimensional map of columns and rows in the same graphical representation is helpful in uncovering the character of the relationships. These relationships among variables are exposed by fragmenting categorical data into a lower set of dimensions (Clausen, 1998; Greenacre, 1984).

As a data reduction procedure, correspondence analysis presents no least than four advantages. First, it is a practical way to recognize underlying structures in contingency tables. In other words, it identifies the relationships between variables in a low dimensional space. Second, it is extremely adaptable in relation to data prerequisites since it can use binary data. Third, the outcomes obtained from this analysis reveal participant predilections in a graphical representation when using customary use or self-reported data. Finally, this procedure is a nonparametric and is not restricted by distributional assumptions. Nevertheless, a disadvantage of this method is the difficulty to interpret the dimensions generated c.f. (Clausen, 1998; Greenacre, 1984; Carroll, Green & Schaffer, 1987).

4. Results

4.1. *Specific applications or Multiple PIM tools?*

Based on the survey conducted, all of the respondents indicated that they used PIM tools to manage their digital resources. Most respondents used specific PIM applications to manage text-based, song/music and email contents. These applications allow the respondents to perform specific tasks which multi-purpose PIM applications are not able to do, or because the former ones perform the task better than the latter ones. For audio content, respondents would consider the issue of portability of transferring the contents from different platforms. Portable media devices, such as MP3 player and mobile phone's media functions, have more powerful features to organize, retrieve, and play these types of contents, and thus are more favorable among respondents than other applications.

The results also shows that the respondents preferred using operation system's file manager to organize their photos, videos, flash animation, graphical drawing, games and to a large extent, audio files. This result was interesting, as one would expect the respondents to rely on media organizers or OEM software to manage these resources as these applications are specially designed to handle this range of resource types.

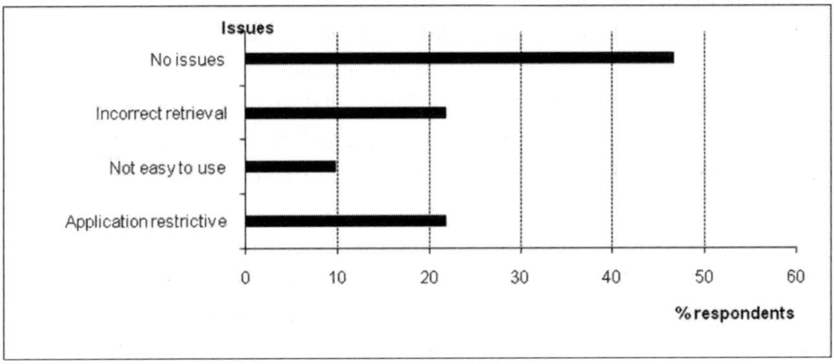

Fig. 1. Chart showing the breakdown of the retrieval issues faced by respondents

Fig. 1 shows the breakdown of the different retrieval issues faced by respondents. More than fifty percent of the respondents felt that they did not encounter any major issue with the retrieval process when using different types of PIM tools.

4.2. *Correspondent analysis*

It is desirable to outline contingency tables in a low-dimensional map for effortless construal of any relationship between rows and columns. In this case, the use of correspondence analysis explores potential relationships between software applications and their attributes for the management of digital information. The Chi-square test of independence is employed to decide the statistical significance dependency between columns and rows, which is the first step in the understanding of this analysis.

In the summary table (see Table 1), we have to check the chi-square value and verify how significant is to validate the supposition rows and columns are related. In this case four dimensions are significant (the eigenvalues called inertia), but essentially one dimension carries highest value of *inertia* (dimension 1), which represent the percent of variance explained in this instance 37.5%, and the four dimensions together explain 43.6% of the variance. This reflects the fact that the relationship between software applications and their attributes for the management of digital information, whereas significant, is moderate.

Table 1. Summary

Dim.	Singular Value	Inertia	Chi Square	Sig.	Proportion of Inertia: Accounted for	Proportion of Inertia: Cumulative	Confidence Singular Value: Standard Deviation	Confidence Singular Value: Correlation 2
1	.612	.375			.860	.860	.031	-.026
2	.218	.048			.109	.969	.039	
3	.103	.011			.024	.994		
4	.053	.003			.006	1.000		
Total		.436	371.532	.0(a)	1.000	1.000		

a. 28 degrees of freedom

The eigenvalues (*Inertia*) stand for the significance of each dimension, and singular values are the square roots of the eigenvalues. *Proportion of Inertia* columns in table 1 represent percent of variance each dimension explains of the variance explained. Singular values explain the maximum canonical correlation between the categories of software applications and document attributes for the management of digital information for each dimension. In this study, two dimensions are able to explain 96.9 % of the 43.6% variance, with the first dimension describes 86%. Therefore, two dimensions were chosen for further analysis.

Table 2. Overview Row Points(a), PIM Applications

Application	Mass	Score in Dimension 1	Score in Dimension 2	Inertia	Of Point to Inertia of Dimension 1	Of Point to Inertia of Dimension 2	Of Dimension to Inertia of Point 1	Of Dimension to Inertia of Point 2	Of Dimension to Inertia of Point Total
1 Text	.134	-.486	.027	.027	.052	.000	.724	.001	.725
2 Email	.135	1.925	.080	.306	.817	.004	.999	.001	1.000
3 Photo	.132	-.054	-1.138	.038	.001	.787	.006	.992	.999
4 Audio	.135	.038	.492	.008	.000	.150	.016	.934	.950
5 Video	.127	-.444	.211	.018	.041	.026	.856	.069	.925
6 Animation	.114	-.385	.032	.011	.028	.001	.982	.002	.985
7 Graphical drawing	.113	-.417	.176	.014	.032	.016	.866	.055	.921
8 Games	.111	-.410	.178	.015	.031	.016	.753	.050	.803
Active Total	1.000			.436	1.000	1.000			

a. Symmetrical normalization

The Overview Row Points output (see table 2) displays several features relevant in the analysis of row points. The Mass column indicates how one unit of mass is spread over the cells on the original contingency table. Scores in dimension represent the coordinates used to plot the correspondence graphic. The term inertia in correspondence analysis is used to stands as measure of variance. Contribution of points to dimensions is useful to discern the meaning of each dimension. Finally, contribution of dimensions to points gives an idea of the quality of representation of each row. In our case, all applications are well represented, and the one with the lowest quality of representation is text.

The Overview Column Points, as shown in Table 3, is similar to the previous table with the exception that it represents the column variable in the correspondence table.

Table 3. Table Overview Column Points(a), PIM Attributes

		Score in Dimension			Contribution				
					Of Point to Inertia of Dimension		Of Dimension to Inertia of Point		
Attribute	Mass	1	2	Inertia	1	2	1	2	Total
1 Date	.108	.789	-1.243	.078	.110	.765	.529	.468	.998
2 Author	.143	1.669	.521	.253	.651	.178	.965	.033	.999
3 Format	.093	-.275	.267	.010	.011	.030	.412	.137	.549
4 File name	.583	-.482	.025	.085	.221	.002	.975	.001	.976
5 File size	.074	-.235	.274	.010	.007	.026	.252	.123	.375
Active Total	1.000			.436	1.000	1.000			

a. Symmetrical normalization

A graphical low-dimensional map was developed to determine a complete image of the relationships between applications and file attributes when users organize their knowledge and information. The most remarkable advantage of this graphical representation is the recognition of applications in which the file attributes relationships are stronger. The overall map is displayed in Figure 2. The Chi-square showed that the relationship between applications and file attributes was relevant ($\chi^2 = 371.53$, df = 28, $\alpha < .000$). The eigenvalues for the first two dimensions described an accumulated of inertia equal to 42.3%. In the positive site of dimension 1, the most relevant application is email, and the most significant attribute is author. In the negative side of dimension 1, the notable applications are text, video, drawing, animation, and games, and the meaningful attribute is file name. In the positive site of dimension 2, the relevant application is audio, and the meaningful attribute is author. In the negative side of dimension 2, the important application is photo, and the significant attribute is date.

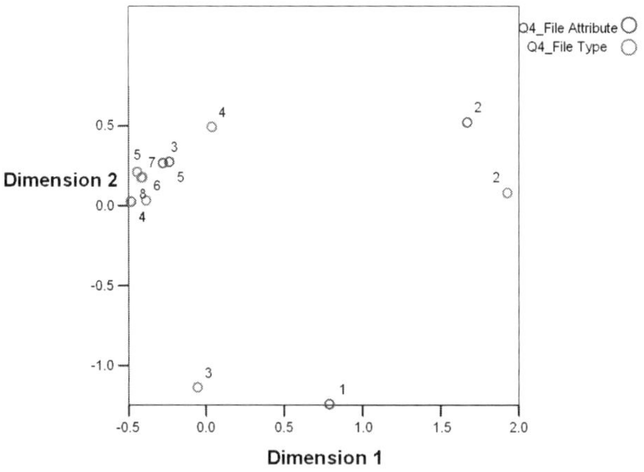

Fig. 2. Figure caption should be centered to the page. Longer captions should be justified to the full text width

Dimension 1 is dominated by email/author relationship and text and multimedia application/file name. It is apparent that users organize their email by author and text and multimedia files by file name. In dimension 2, there is a relationship between photos and date. In general, the organization of multimedia files is dictated file name, date, and format attributes. Actually, there are no strong relationships in the positive section of dimension 2. In fact, the strongest relationship between application and attribute, when it comes to organize information, is email/author.

5. Discussion

The findings did provide some answers for our research objective. One of the main purposes of PIM tools is to help users to manage their resources in a way that help them to complete a task which basically can be defined as finding the right resource at the right time and place when an information need arises (Bergman et al., 2004). This will in turn facilitate the completion of an outstanding task or meeting the knowledge and information needs. Besides, PIM tools can generally be classified into two types which are multiple and specific. Our findings reveal that users actually prefer to have PIM tools that are able to handle multi-format digital resources.

Organizational strategy and choosing the right attributes to manage resources could be a difficult task. Our findings, however, revealed the interesting fact that most respondents do not face any issues when they organised their different types of digital resources. Apparently, this may indicate that the current PIM tools can satisfy their needs in managing the digital resources, or perhaps, the amount of digital resources is still manageable and most respondents may have certain discipline in their management of digital resources. However, our results do not indicate how efficient retrieval process is or the user satisfaction with the tools.

In addition, the findings also revealed that users rely on textual attributes (filenames) when they search for the resources. Perhaps the key explanation is textual attributes could serve as keywords which users can use to perform the search function.

As different set of attributes are related to different retrieval methods, we believe that users may face difficulties in the retrieval process. The respondents claimed that they do not have any difficulty in retrieving the digital resources. A plausible reason is perhaps users may not be too worried about finding the right resources at the right time. Interestingly, most of them prefer speed. One explanation could be the manageable size of the collection of personal digital. This allows users to scan through the result list to identify the required resources. Furthermore, the user already knows the document does exist, so naturally precision is not the highest priority. The user would rather want to retrieve that piece of information quickly instead.

This research has some drawbacks that are imperative to emphasize. First, the data is self-reported. Although, these data are helpful and facile to gather, they could be lack of accuracy. Second, the study was limited to specific population. The results could have been different with other population who are less ICT literacy. Finally, the analysis ignored the dynamic nature of the information retrieval process. Future research should try to focus on these issues.

6. Conclusions

While the rapid of growth and increase complexity of digital resources has fuelled advance of searching and retrieval technology in commercial databases, it is surprising to find out that Personal Information Management (PIM) tools have changed little over the years. Nonetheless, this research supplied an exploration of the relationship and underlying structures between specific applications and file attributes when users organize their knowledge and information to serve as base to develop their organizational strategies. Correspondence analysis pointed out a moderate relationship between applications and file attributes.

References

Barreau, D. (1995). Context as a factor in personal information management systems. Journal of the American Society for Information Science. *Journal of the American Society for Information Science, 46*(5), 327–339.

Bellotti, V., & Thornton, J. (2006). *Managing Activities with TV-Acta: TaskVista and Activity-Centered Task Assistant.* Paper presented at the In Proceedings of the Second SIGIR Workshop on Personal Information Management Seattle.

Bergman, O., Boardman, R., Gwizdka, J., & Jones, W. (2004). *Personal Information Management.* Paper presented at the Proceedings CHI '04 Conference on Human Factors in Computing Systems.

Clausen, S-E. (1998). *Applied Correspondence Analysis.* Thousand Oaks, CA: Sage Publications.

Diaper, D., & Stanton, N. (2004). *The handbook of task analysis for human-computer interaction.* Mahwah, NJ: Erlbaum.

Dumais, S., Cutrell, E., Cadiz, J., Jancke, G., Sarin, R., & Robbins, D. (2003). *Stuff I've seen: a system for personal information retrieval and re-use.* Paper presented at the In Proceedings of the 26th annual international ACM SIGIR conference on Research and development in informaion retrieval Toronto, Canada.

Fertig, S., Freeman, E., & Gelernter, D. (1996). *Lifestreams: An Alternative to the Desktop Metaphor.* Paper presented at the Proceedings of the CHI '96 conference companion on Human factors in computing systems: common ground, Vancouver, British Columbia, Canada.

Freeman, E., & Gelernter, D. (1996). Lifestreams: a storage model for personal data. *ACM SIGMOD Record, 25*(1), 80 - 86.

Gauch, S., Speretta, M., Chandramouli, A., & Micarelli, A. (2007). User Profiles for Personalized Information Access. In P. Brusilovsky, A. Kobsa & W. Nejdl (Eds.), *The Adaptive Web* (pp. 54-89). Berlin: Springer.

Greenacre, M. (1984). *Theory and Application of Correspondence Analysis.* London: Academic Press.

Hair, J., Anderson, R., Tatham, R., & Black, W. (2009). *Multivariate data analysis* (7th ed.). Upper Saddle River, NJ: Prentice Hall.

Carroll, J., Green, P., & Schaffer, C. (1987). Comparing interpoint distances in correspondence analysis: A clarification. *Journal of Marketing Research, 24*(4), 445–450.

Kelly, D. (2006). Evaluating personal information management behaviors and tools. *Communications of the ACM, 49*(1), 84-86.

Kim, H.-R., & Chan, P-K. (2008). Learning implicit user interest hierarchy for context in personalization. *Applied Intelligence, 28*(2), 153-166.

Lepouras, G., Dix, A., Katifori, A., Catarci, T., Habegger, B., Poggi, A., et al. (2006). *OntoPIM: From Personal Information Management to Task Information Management.* Paper presented at the In Proceedings of the Second SIGIR Workshop on Personal Information Management, Seattle.

Lyman, P., & Varian, H. (2003). How Much Information. Retrieved February 13, 2009, from http://www.sims.berkeley.edu/how-much-info-2003

Malone, T. (1983). How Do People Organize Their Desks? Implications for the Design of Office Information Systems. *ACM Transactions on Office Information Systems, 1*(1), 99-112.

Rodden, K., & Wood, K. R. (2003). *How Do People Manage Their Digital Photographs?* Paper presented at the Proceedings of the SIGCHI conference on Human factors in computing systems, Ft. Lauderdale, Florida.

Sauermann, L. (2005). *The Gnowsis Semantic Desktop for Information Integration.* Paper presented at the In Experiences and Visions Proceedings of the 3 rd Conference Professional Knowledge Management, , Kaiserslautern, Germany.

Tudhope, D., & Nielsen, M. (2006). Introduction to Knowledge Organization Systems and Services. *New Review of Hypermedia and Multimedia, 12*(1), 3-9.

Whittaker, S., Bellotti, V., & Gwizdka, J. (2006). Email in personal information management. *Communications of the ACM, 49*(1), 68 - 73.

Whittaker, S., Jones, Q., Nardi, B., Creech, M., Terveen, L., Isaacs, E., et al. (2004). ContactMap: Organizing communication in a social desktop. ACM Transactions on Computer Human Interaction 11, pp.445–471. *ACM Transactions on Computer Human Interaction, 11*(4), 445-471.

COMPETENCIES SOUGHT BY KNOWLEDGE MANAGEMENT EMPLOYERS: CONTENT ANALYSIS OF ONLINE JOB ADVERTISEMENTS

SHAHEEN MAJID

School of Communication & Information,
Nanyang Technological University, Singapore
asmajid@ntu.edu.sg

RIANTO MULIA

Nanyang Technological University, Singapore
riantomulia@gmail.com

Content analysis of job advertisements is considered a reliable method for determining the demands of job market. The aim of this study was to identify competencies required by knowledge management (KM) employers through analyzing job advertisements appeared in selected job portals. The study used 110 English language job advertisements from China, Hong Kong, India, Malaysia, the Philippines, and Singapore. It was found that a majority of the advertisements did not ask for knowledge management qualifications rather a general degree or a qualification in computing, business or library and information studies was preferred. It was also noted that almost all job advertisements put more emphasis on personality traits than other competencies, namely KM core processes, KM technologies, and human capital management. The highly sought after personality-related competencies were communication skills, analytical thinking skills, and leadership skills. The top three competencies related to KM core processes were knowledge transfer and sharing, knowledge discovery and acquisition, and knowledge organization. The top three IT and infrastructure related competencies were familiarity with content management systems, knowledge portals, and development and maintenance of knowledge repositories. This paper suggests that KM academic programs should regularly review their curricula to incorporate new trends and competencies required by the KM job market.

1. Introduction

Organizations need well-educated and competent knowledge professionals for successfully implementing their knowledge management (KM) initiatives and strategies. Inadvertently, it is causing an upsurge in demand for knowledge professionals possessing a desired set of knowledge, skills and attitudes. As knowledge management is an emerging discipline, currently no standard and widely accepted competency framework for KM professionals is available (Luthra, 2008). However, KM academic programs have been trying to design such curricula which can provide a wide range of desired competencies to their graduates. Some KM professional associations, such as Information and Knowledge Management Society (iKMS), have proposed a competency framework for knowledge professionals (iKMS, 2008). Based on two web surveys, Hazeri, Sarrafzadeh and Martin (2007) reported that communication and networking skills were the most desired competencies for information and knowledge professionals, closely followed by teamwork skills, creative thinking skills, decision-making skills, and document management skills.

Gutsche (2009) argued that across industries, competencies provide a foundation for building coherent efforts to improve knowledge, skills and attitudes of employees. Recently, WebJunction (http://www.webjunction.org/1) with help from OCLC (http://www.oclc.org/asiapacific/en/ global/default.htm) have compiled a competency index for library and information professionals. In this index competencies are presented in three broad categories of library and information management, information technology, and personal/interpersonal competencies.

Due to multi-disciplinarily nature and diversity in knowledge management activities, recruitment of KM professionals with an appropriate set of competencies is becoming a challenge for employers. They use a variety of techniques such as job application forms, curricula vitae, individual and panel interviews, psychometric testing, assessment centres, motivation testing, job trials, graphology, job-specific aptitude tests, group-based activities and references for selecting suitable individuals (El-Kot and Leat, 2008). Each of these methods tries to measure different aspects of applicants to ensure that the selected individuals possess appropriate qualifications, personality traits, and professional competencies. That is why, nowadays the competency-based approach to recruitment is considered crucial in achieving organizational excellence (Hogg, 2008).

Various techniques, such as questionnaires, observations, case studies, interviews, job analysis, and competency profiling can be used to understand the needs of job market. The content analysis of job advertisements is considered part of the competency profiling technique and has been used by many studies. Majid and Bee (2003) noted that job advertisements can be used to identify gaps between knowledge and skills provided by academic programs and the competencies sought by potential employers. Thompson, Martens & Hawamdeh (2008) studied the roles and responsibilities of knowledge management professionals outlined by hiring organizations through content analysis of their job advertisements. The data was collected from 1200 job postings containing information about the recruiting organizations, the location of position, the main requirements and skills desired in the applicant, the qualifications needed, and the offered salary. The content analysis of the job postings were used to identify major areas and trends in the information and knowledge profession.

Kennan, et al. (2007) used job advertisements to compare market expectations of information professionals in Australia and the USA. They found a higher emphasis on behavioural and interpersonal skills in both countries. Promis (2008) used job advertisements to study soft skills sought by library and information employers and concluded that creative thinking, critical and analytical thinking, data manipulation skills and decision-making skills were required by all levels of professionals. Ferguson, Hider, and Lloyd (2008) analyzed KM job advertisements and found some overlap between competencies required by KM and Library and Information Studies (LIS) employers.

Several recent studies have used online job portals for profiling competencies sought by employers from different industries. Online job advertisements are becoming popular as many employers feel advertising through such portals is more effective, economical, and less time consuming, with the additional advantage of reaching out to a higher number of potential applicants. This approach was proven effective for Dell which recruited 50 per cent of its employees through online applications (Ismail, 2008). The popularity of online job portals can be seen from a substantial increase in the number of visitors to these websites (Pathak, 2005). As a result, job portals are becoming more efficient, using sophisticated recruitment systems.

As it is obvious from the above discussion that knowledge management is an emerging discipline, it is desirable to identify a standard competency set for KM professionals. Different methods can be used to identify competencies sought by employers and content analysis of job advertisements is one of the reliable techniques for this purpose. Although this method has been widely used in other disciplines, it is not extensively used in knowledge management sector. The purpose of this study was to identify competencies sought by employers through analyzing KM job advertisements, appearing in different job websites. The findings of this study will help understand demands of the KM job market and academic programs can utilize this knowledge to reorient their curricula for meeting the needs of KM employers.

2. Method

For this study job advertisements appearing in different online job websites were identified, collected and analyzed. As knowledge management is a multi-disciplinary domain, its professionals are expected to performance a wide range of tasks. Certain common tasks undertaken in many organizations, such as developing organizational repositories, the Internet applications and technologies, content management, infra-structure development and maintenance, and human resource management might be performed by other individuals not directly involved in knowledge management activities. It was, therefore, decided to only include those English language advertisements that exclusively deal with knowledge management operations. The criterion used for the selection of online advertisements was that either the word 'knowledge management' should appear in the job title or at least one of the job descriptions should mention it. In addition, those job advertisements which listed 'knowledge management' as one of the desired qualifications were also included in this analysis. In total, 110 job advertisements from China, Hong Kong, India, Malaysia, Singapore and the Philippines, were retrieved from 20 job portals (Table 1). The data was collected during the first half of the year 2008.

Table 1. List of Online Job Portals (N=110)

Job Portal	No. of Advertisements	%
Naukri.com	31	28.2%
JobStreet.com	26	23.6%
51Job.com	8	7.3%
Recruit.net	7	6.4%
Monster.com	6	5.5%
ChinaHR.com	5	4.6%
JobsDB.com	4	3.6%
ZhaoPin.com	4	3.6%
JobsAhead.com	3	2.7%
FundooDataJobs.com	2	1.8%
JobsViewer.com	2	1.8%
KMTalk.net	2	1.8%
Other job portals	10	9.1%

Data cleaning was considered desirable as some job advertisements appeared on multiple job portals or advertised through independent job recruitment agencies which may hide the identity of the advertising company. Advertisements with similar job titles, job descriptions, qualifications and work experiences were identified and carefully examined to remove duplication. Job advertisements with very brief job descriptions were removed as it was difficult to determine their suitability for this analysis.

The collected job advertisements were analysed to derive a list of required competencies as well as other job requirements. The collected data was grouped under four major categories: *Core KM processes* – 22 competencies were identified related to certain specific KM operations and processes; *ICT applications and infrastructure* – 21 ICT related competencies were identified; *Personality traits* - 65 qualities related to behaviour, attitude and personality traits were collected; and finally *Qualification* – academic and professional qualifications mentioned in job advertisements.

3. Findings

3.1 *Job Advertisements from Different Countries*

It was found that India had the highest number of job advertisements posted on online job portals compared to rest of the countries in Asia (Table 2). Since the job advertisements were extracted from those online job portals which only supported the English language, this could be one of the reasons why China, Malaysia and Hong Kong - which have a fairly vibrant knowledge management sectors - did not appear to post many knowledge management jobs. These countries might have posted more advertisements in non-English job portals or preferred advertising in local newspapers and magazines.

Table 2. Job Advertisements by Country

Country	No. of Jobs	%
India	46	41.8
Singapore	22	20.0
China	16	14.6
Malaysia	12	10.9
Hong Kong	9	8.2
Philippines	5	4.5
Total	110	100

3.2 *Number of Positions by Job Level*

The collected job advertisements, based on the length of required work expereince, were grouped under entry-, middle- and senior-level positions. Jobs requiring up to two years' of work experience were categorized as entry-level jobs, jobs requiring 2 to 5 years' of experience as middle-level positions while advertisements asking for more than 5 years' of experience were categorized as senior-level positions. Many of the entry-level positions, using different job titles, were lumped together under the title Executive or Knowledge Officer. Moreover, in order to avoid redundancy, the word knowledge management was removed from all job titles. For example, the job title 'Manager (Knowledge Management)' was replaced with 'Manager'.

It was found that one-half of the advertised jobs were for entry-level positions (Table 3). Forty-one (37.3%) of the advertisements were for middle-level positions while only 14 (12.7%) were for senior-level knowledge management positions.

Table 3. Breakdown of Advertisements by Job Positions

Job Level	Job Titles	No. of Jobs	%
Entry-level Positions	Executive/ Knowledge Officer	50	45.5%
	Assistant Manager	5	4.5%
Middle-level Positions	Manager	24	21.8%
	Assistant Director	8	7.3%
	Senior Manager	8	7.3%
	Assistant Vice President	1	0.9%
Senior-level Positions	Head	5	4.5%
	Chief	2	1.8%
	Director	2	1.8%
	General Manager	1	0.9%
	Team Leader	3	2.7%
	Vice President	1	0.9%

Further data analysis revealed that out of 46 advertisements from India, 63.1% were for the entry-level jobs, 23.9% for middle-level and 13% for senior-level positions (Table 4). A majority (54.6%) of the KM job advertisements from Singapore was for middle-level positions, followed by entry-level positions (40.9%). A somewhat similar pattern was observed for China and Hong Kong where a majority of the KM advertisements was for middle- and entry-level positions. It was, however, interesting to note that one-third of the advertisements from Malaysia and 60% from the Philippines were for senior-level positions.

Table 4. Level of KM Job Advertisements form Different Countries

Job Level	India	Singapore	China	Malaysia	Hong Kong	Philippines
Entry level	29 (63.1%)	9 (40.9%)	5 (31.3%)	6 (50.0%)	4 (44.4%)	2 (40.0%)
Middle level	11 (23.9%)	12 (54.6%)	11 (68.7%)	2 (16.7%)	5 (55.6%)	-
Senior level	6 (13.0%	1 (4.5%)	-	4 (33.3%)	-	3 (60.0%)
Total	46 (100%)	22 (100%)	16 (100%)	12 (100%)	9 (100%)	5 (100%)

3.3 *Competencies Sought by Employers*

For the purpose of data analysis, the competencies desired by KM employers were divided into three major categories: KM core processes, KM technologies, and personality-related competencies. The KM core processes included those competencies that were required for identifying, capturing, organizing, disseminating and using knowledge in an organization. The technology competencies included those KM technologies and tools that could help improve the effectiveness and efficiency of KM operations and processes. Finally, the personality competencies included personality-related skills, attitudes, traits, and other characteristics of potential KM professionals.

3.3.1 KM Core Processes Competencies

Competencies related to KM core processes were edited and categorized under 22 broad categories, with some degree of overlap. The top five competencies in this group (Table 5) were knowledge transfer, dissemination and sharing (40.9% advertisements); knowledge creation, sourcing and discovery (37.3%); knowledge organization and classification (25.5%); knowledge access and retrieval (23.6%); and knowledge capturing and retention (21.8%). The most frequently mentioned KM core competency from India, Hong Kong and China was knowledge transfer, dissemination and sharing. The competency related to knowledge creation, sourcing and discovery was most frequently sought by employers from Singapore, Malaysia, and Hong Kong. The ability to champion, drive and manage knowledge management initiatives was indicated by a majority of advertisements from the Philippines.

Table 5. Top Five Competencies Related to KM Core Processes
(Multiple responses)

Rank	Competency Understanding of:	No. of Advertisements (N=110)
1	Knowledge transfer, dissemination and sharing	45 (40.9%)
2	Knowledge creation, sourcing and discovery	41 (37.3%)
3	Knowledge organization and classification, including metadata and taxonomies	28 (25.5%)
4	Knowledge access and retrieval	26 (23.6%)
5	Knowledge capturing and retention (i.e. codification)	24 (21.8%)

It was worth noting that certain other important KM competencies such as understanding of Return-on-Investment (ROI), knowledge measurement, and knowledge audit were not mentioned by many advertisements.

3.3.2 KM Technologies Competencies

The KM technologies related competencies were also edited and categorized under 21 broad categories. The top ICT related competencies (Table 6) included: the knowledge of content and document management systems (25.5%), and knowledge portal and knowledge flow systems (18.2%). The next top three technology-related competencies, mentioned by 13.6% of the advertisements each, were development and/or maintenance of KM infrastructure and applications; development and/or maintenance of knowledge-bases and KM repositories; and the knowledge of Microsoft Office application suite.

Table 6. Top Five KM Technologies Related Competencies
(Multiple responses)

Rank	Competency Knowledge of:	No. of Advertisements (N=110)
1	Content and document management systems	28 (25.5%)
2	Knowledge portal and knowledge flow systems	20 (18.2%)
3	Development and/ or maintenance of KM infrastructure and applications	15 (13.6%)
4	Knowledge-base and KM repositories	15 (13.6%)
5	Microsoft Office application suite	15 (13.6%)

3.3.2 Personality-related Competencies

A big diversity was observed for personality-related competencies. Altogether 65 such competencies were sought by KM employers. These competencies were edited and grouped under their broader categories. Among the top five personality-related competencies were (Table 7): ability to communicate effectively (63.9%); analytical and decision-making ability (47.2%); writing skills (38.0%); leadership skills (30.6%); and instructional skills (27.8%).

Table 7. Top Five Personality Related Competencies (Multiple responses)

Rank	Competency	Percentage of Advertisements (N=110)
1	Ability to communicate effectively	63.9%
2	Analytical and decision-making ability	47.2%
3	Effective writing skills	38.0%
4	Leadership skills	30.6%
5	Training and presentation skills	27.8%

3.4 *Qualifications Sought by Employers*

Once again a considerable diversity was observed in the type of qualifications sought by knowledge management employers. As shown in Table 8, a general bachelor's degree was the most frequently sought after qualification (38.0% advertisements). A bachelor's or postgraduate degree in computing was the next most frequently required qualification (26.9% advertisements), while a bachelor's or postgraduate degree in information management was the third most frequently mentioned qualification (14.8%).

Table 8. Top Five Qualification Sought by Employers (Multiple responses)

Rank	Qualification	Percentage of Advertisements (N=110)
1	General bachelor's degree	38.0%
2	Bachelor's or postgraduate degree in computing	26.9%
3	Bachelor's or postgraduate degree in information management	14.8%
4	Bachelor's or postgraduate degree in business and commerce	11.1%
5	Bachelor's or postgraduate degree in library	9.3%

Altogether 95 (86.4%) advertisements asked for a bachelor's degree, 41 (37.3%) a master's degree, 11 (10.0%) a diploma or a higher diploma, and 5 (4.5%) of the job advertisements asked for a professional certificate in knowledge management.

Some variations were also observed for the types of quantifications preferred by employers from different countries. Over two-thirds of the advertisements from India asked for a general degree, whereas 50% of the advertisements from Singapore and China preferred a degree in computing. Similarly, 60% of the job advertisements from the Philippines asked for a degree in business and commerce. It was, however, interesting to note that only job advertisements from Singapore (32% advertisements), Malaysia (25%) and Hong Kong (22%) asked for qualifications in knowledge management.

4. Conclusion

Knowledge management is still an evolving discipline and efforts are being made to understand the types of competencies required by its professionals. In recent years many academic programs have emerged, preparing KM professionals at different levels. However, gap between the academic curricula and the skill-set required by employers has always been one of the hot topics of discussion. One way to overcome this problem is to understand KM job market as well as the types of competencies sought by potential employers. The KM academic programs can use this knowledge to re-align their curricula to effectively meet expectations of the job market.

A noteworthy pattern observed in this study was that only a few advertisements asked for Knowledge management qualifications. One possible reason could be that in some of the surveyed countries the Knowledge Management discipline is still in its infancy and qualified KM professionals are not readily available. Another possible explanation could be that as knowledge management is a multi-disciplinary subject, many employers might be looking for those individuals who possess more generic qualifications. Nevertheless, the KM academic programs need to closely watch developments in this discipline and continue evolving their curricula.

References

El-Kot, G., and Leat, M. (2008) "A Survey of Recruitment and Selection Practices in Egypt", *Contemporary Middle Eastern Issues, 1*(3), 200-212.

Ferguson, S., Hider, P., and Lloyd, A. (2008) "Are Librarians the Ultimate Knowledge Managers? A Study of Knowledge, Skills, Practice and Mindset", *Australian Library Journal,* 57 (1): 39-62.

Gutsche, B. (2009) "Competency Index for the Library Field. WebJunction/OCLC", retrieved July 05, 2009, from http://www.webjunction.org/competencies.

Hazeri, A., Sarrafzadeh, M., and Martin, B. (2007) "Reflections of Information Professionals on Knowledge Management Competencies in the LIS Curriculum", *Journal of Education for Library and Information Science, 48*(3): 168-186.

Hogg, C. (2009) "Competency and Competency Frameworks", retrieved July 05, 2009, from http://www.cipd.co.uk/subjects/perfmangmt/competnces/comptfrmwk.htm.

iKMS. (2008) "iKMS Announcements", retrieved July 05, 2009, from http://www.ikms.org/.

Ismail, I. (2008). "Jobs Now a Click Away", retrieved July 05, 2009, from http://www.nst.com.my/Current_News/techNu/Monday/CoverStory/20080303152232/Article/index_html.

Kennan, M.A., Willard, P., Wilson, C.S., and Cole, F. (2007) "Australian and US Academic Library jobs: A comparison", *Australian Academic & Research Libraries*, 38 (2): 111-128.

Luthra, P. (2008) "Understanding the Process of Building KM Competencies", retrieved July 05, 2009, from http://papers.ssrn.com/sol3/papers.cfm? abstract_id=1126118.

Majid, S. and Bee, W.W. (2003) "Competencies Sought by Employers of Information and Knowledge Professionals: An Analysis of Job Advertisements", *Journal of Information and Knowledge Management*, 2(3): 253-260.

Pathak, S. (2005) "Job Portals Set to Expand Base in Small Towns", retrieved July 05, 2009, from http://www.tribuneindia.com/2005/20051207/jobs/main4.htm.

Promis, P. (2008) "Are Employers Asking for the Right Competencies? A Case for Emotional Intelligence", *Library Administration & Management*, 22 (1): 24-30.

Thompson, K., Martens, B.V. and Hawamdeh, S. (2008). "Knowledge Management Competencies and Emerging Trends in the KM Job Market". Knowledge Management Competencies and Professionalism, Proceedings of the 2008 International Conference. Ohio, USA, 23 - 24 October 2008.

MIGRATION OR INTEGRATION: KNOWLEDGE MANAGEMENT IN LIBRARY AND INFORMATION SCIENCE PROFESSION

MANIR ABDULLAHI KAMBA*

Department of library and Information Science
Bayero University, Kano 234/Northwestern zone, Nigeria
E-mail: manirungr@yahoo.com

ROSLINA OTHMAN

Department of library and Information Science
International Islamic University Malaysia. Gombak, Kuala Lumpur Malaysia
†*E-mail: roslina@iiu.edu.my*

Knowledge management (KM) today has become a diversified field of study and practice, which attract different disciplines and background to be co-opted or absorbed without boarder-line. Most of the academic articles that deal with Knowledge Management (KM) in some way always start by trying to define it. The fact is that, there is no standard or stable definition of the concept because most of the writers failure to look back to the history. After all, library and information science profession have been the custodians of documented knowledge since time immemorial. This paper portrayed that Knowledge management (KM) is an extension of librarianship that focuses on both the external and internal information resources (knowledge) management with the integration of technologies, directed towards the successful achievement and success of organisations in general. The paper also highlighted the major barriers to LIS engagement in the knowledge management; it further explains that integrating knowledge management in the LIS profession is a future not a barrier. The paper concludes with some suggested directions for LIS schools, practitioners, educators and researchers.

1. Introduction

Prior to the widespread and the use of ICTs in the like of computers, the Internet, and other related networking technologies, libraries are in existence since time immemorial and are established for the purpose of capturing, storing, and managing the knowledge acquired from individuals, organizations and the societies in general for the development of future generation. Supporting this, Manir (2007) mentioned that, historically, we have heard that, knowledge were preserve in the form of learning materials such as bones, clay tablets, papyrus etc. but with development taking place in the world, knowledge were transmuted in the form of paper specifically, books, journals and reports, etc. During renaissance period, i.e. the age of enlightenment, this was the period that the world witnessed instrumental development of knowledge production and distribution, with the advent of printing machine by Guttenberg. This clearly indicates that ever before and from the beginning of the world knowledge was managed in different formats, even before the establishment of the Libraries.

Today, generation of knowledge, management and the use of knowledge resources are becoming crucial in the creation of wealth. Knowledge is making life easier for human development around the world. Therefore effective management of knowledge resources is now playing a key role in wealth creation and successful achievement of organizations, societies and world at large.

The world's strongest economies are no more emphasizing on industrial production but rather becoming powerhouses of knowledge. Knowledge today becomes the most effective weapon to fight against enemy. In this context, a knowledge or information seeker is trying to find a connection between what already exists in his/her mind and what exists in his external environment. This however, shows that organizations, institutions and agencies in their entire ramification are dwelling into a serious competition of rat race, which is leading them to hunt for talent (knowledge) as a product of information. Omuniyi (2000) stated that, organizations today are trying very hard to employ best brains with the belief that innovations will automatically follow once the best brains are hired. This clearly indicated that managing knowledge has a direct relationship with success and achievement of individual, societies and organizations.

1.1 Transition from Scarcity of Information to Overflow of Information

The origin and development of knowledge repositories known as libraries have been traced to the early civilizations in Egypt, Greek, Rome and few others respectively. The contributions of these civilizations and as a result of time and space resulted to, or formed the bedrock of knowledge repositories on which past is being transmitted to the future. This serves as the beginning point where the model library and information system evolved to act as the hub or container of information, which transcends to knowledge.

There two movements that emanate as a result of knowledge which started from scarcity of information or knowledge to the overflow of information this movement has made it necessary for knowledge to be preserved and manage effectively for societal and organizational developments. These movements can be categorized into two (2) era that is, Pre-modern era and Modern era.

Pre-modern Era: It is the era that witnessed the scarcity of knowledge and information, in this era literacy and knowledge was not widespread in almost any culture, so there were few people capable of writing histories and production of knowledge. This era was characterized by three movements or transformation in different periods below is the graphical illustrations of these periods and movements.

Fig. 1.

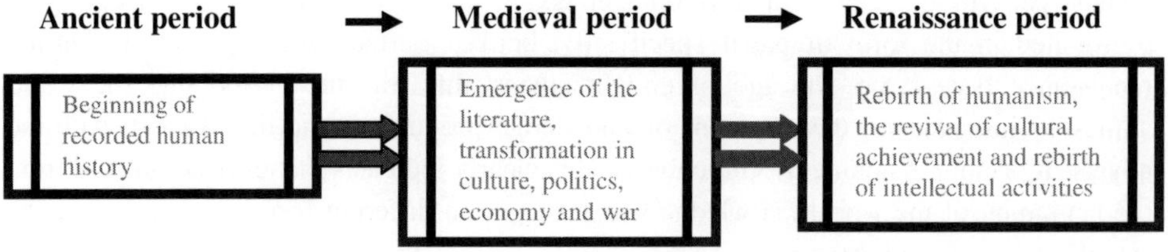

Modern Era: This era witnessed the overflow of information and knowledge through development of technologies in the production and preservation of knowledge. It is the era which witnessed rapid development in human society through industrialization and technological revolution. This has to do with a society in which the conditions for generating knowledge and processing information have been substantially changed by a technological revolution focused on information processing, knowledge generation, and information technologies. This era is characterized by two (2) movements and revolutions i.e. industrial revolution and information revolution which is further divided into two i.e. information society and knowledge society even though some scholars categorize them to be one. Graphical representation of this era is shown below:

Fig. 2.

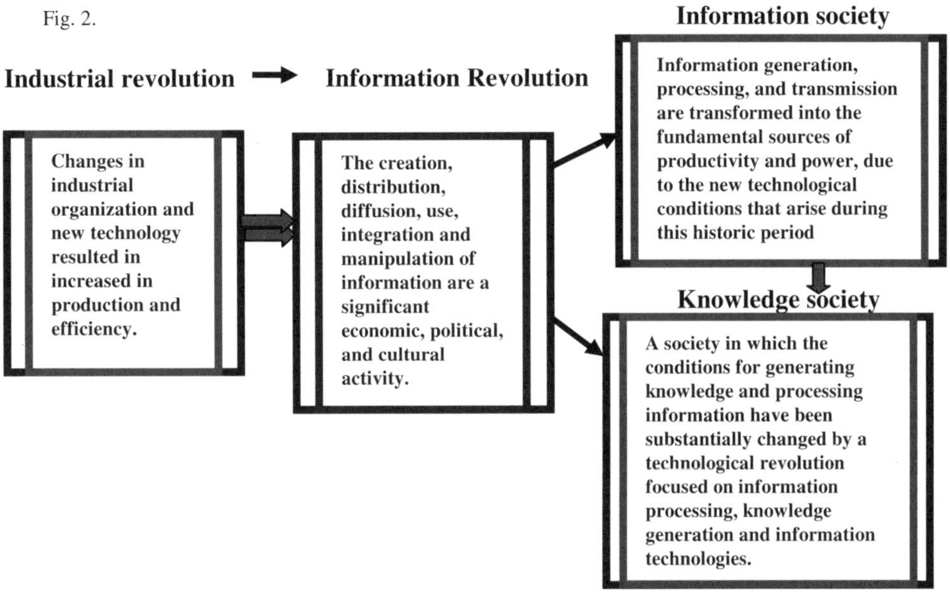

From the above movements and revolutions we can conspicuously see that, different periods of development exists which represent scarcity and overflow of information or knowledge for the development of human kind. These periods consider information and knowledge as the key to the advancement of societies; supporting this statement, Al-Hawamdeh (2002) mentioned that, "knowledge and innovation played an important role in the development of society. The transformation from an agrarian society to the information society has largely been brought about as a result of accumulation of knowledge through the centuries". Knowledge by its very nature depends on other knowledge to build on. In a similar review, Duffy, (1999) and Narayanan, (2001) all maintained that knowledge creation is, in fact, a process of value addition to previous knowledge through innovation.

This also implies that the more knowledge an individual, society or organization already possess the more they we will be in a position to create and transfer to others. Al-Hawamdeh (2002) further lamented that, the key to economic success is always linked to the advances in knowledge creation and the ability of a nation in translating knowledge into products and services. But while knowledge existed since the existence of mankind, it is only recently that it has been recognized as a factor of production. Foray & Lundvall,

(1996) stated that many people have recognized that knowledge is the only meaningful economic resource in the knowledge society. It has been now recognized that information and knowledge are the drivers propelling productivity and economic growth, leading to a new focus on the role of information, technology and learning in economic performance.

According to Drotner, (2005) since the 1980s, a number of fundamental developments have served to change a situation of scarcity into a situation of overflow. This has led to dramatical shift from industrial society to information society where information and knowledge becomes the weapons for fighting economic and other developments. As we move from a concept of the information society on to a concept of a knowledge society, the role of libraries and the information professionals must undergo similar changes of priority. These movements come, as result of impact of globalization and commodification of media from the late 1980s and emergence of computers and later the Internet and mobile technologies.

2. Library and Information Science Profession as Custodian of Knowledge

Libraries are indispensable part of societal development; this is because they serve as repositories of knowledge which further underscored by the fact that main activities of any individual, societies, organizations and educational institutions are geared towards pursuance of knowledge. As such progress in all fields of human Endeavour is limited where there are no libraries. This is why Wali (1991) stressed that, "libraries acquire various types of human communication records, published or unpublished, written or oral in recorded form and store them for later use". In this regard, Agoulu and Agoulu (2002) described libraries as the society's memory standing in the same relationship as the human memory does to an individual. The society draws upon its library in the same way an individual draw upon his memory to meet his varied needs.

It is well known fact that, libraries have developed historically in tandem with the industrial society, and their formation is mostly based on enlightenment ideals of freedom of expression and of universal access to information and works of imagination (Drotner, 2005). In addition to this, libraries are established in the industrial societies to serve as a remedy to the scarcity of information and (quality) entertainment and to secure universal access. The definition of information and fiction is clear, since these concepts have a physical materiality: they are books, journals, records and films. For this reasons, libraries becomes not only the custodian of knowledge but rather the life wire that keep knowledge alive, fresh and thus continue the process of education successfully by consulting the various sources of information to advance knowledge. Over the years libraries have supported individual, organizations and societies in knowledge provision and literacy, thereby ensuring that they do not relapse into underdevelopment and confusion. As we are witnessing the over flow of information and knowledge due to development in information technology and the Internet, library and information science profession is facing a great challenge. Librarians and the profession tend to be conservatives without showing any sign to accept changes that make the field lucrative and competitive by successfully integrating the new technologies in discharging their responsibilities.

Failure to answer the clarion call, which comes as a result of information revolution, clearly invites or gives automatic tickets to other profession to take over the management of knowledge. This integration and migration of the other disciplines into the responsibilities of librarianship has clearly indicates the ineptitude of library and information profession to meet up with the challenges of the information society. Koenig (2005) stated that, despite the obvious overlap with librarianship, our field has done comparatively poorly on capitalizing on that overlap. The KM movement has gone through a number of stages, and it is now moving into a stage of recognizing the importance of and incorporating information and knowledge external to the parent organization. Such information and knowledge has always been field of librarianship.

Basically, many disciplines see that marrying the concept of management and knowledge can provide success and efficiency in the developments of organizations. Shanhong (2000) opined that, "knowledge has become the driving force for social development, the attention of the society to information and knowledge is rising and people's demands for information and knowledge are increasing step by step. Moreover, as information and knowledge has become an important productive factor for the modern economic system, the society will inevitably require intensified management of information and knowledge which stand as a challenge to the librarians today. This challenge led to the emergence of knowledge management as discipline and profession, since it operates with out border i.e. a universal acceptor.

3.1 Knowledge Management (KM)

The concept of knowledge society or movement from information society to knowledge society marked the beginning of knowledge management as a new name but not new practice; even though there are some additional elements that made it to differ from information management or library management. Knowledge management is emerging as a key concern of organizations, particularly those who have already redesigned their business processes and embedded a total quality approach into their practices. (Drotner, (2005) reiterated that Knowledge Management further emerged as result of competition that arises between information society and knowledge society, while the term information society focuses on the raw materials so to speak ('information'), the term knowledge society serves to emphasize the various menus ('knowledge') that may result from people's handling of the raw materials.

Knowledge Management activities are replacing the work of special librarians in organizations and institutions; this is because knowledge management encompass assessing, changing and improving human individual skills and/or behaviour in the process of undertaking his daily activities and inline with the development of his organization. Shanhong (2000) indicated that, in the knowledge economy, the management refers to effectively identify, acquire, develop, resolve, use, store and share knowledge, to create an approach to transforming and sharing of tacit and explicit knowledge, and to raise the emergency and innovation capability by utilizing the wisdom of the team.

3.1 Is Knowledge Management, A Migration OR Integration into Library and Information Science?

The point of contention here is whether the emerging discipline of knowledge management is a migration of ideas or integration? Majority of writers are of the opinion that knowledge management (KM) is a new discipline separate from library and information science profession, while others maintained that it is part of or it is integrated in the library profession which gather momentum to snatch the responsibilities of special librarians or librarians in organisations. In the same vain others are with the opinion that knowledge management (KM) migrated from other fields and take over the position of library and information profession in the management of knowledge. All these arguments could sound to be true and defensive, depending on the individual understanding of the following questions, what is knowledge management? How knowledge management emerge as a new discipline? What lead to the idea of knowledge management? Is knowledge management a new field, if yes what happened with knowledge that was preserved before the industrial revolution? What does knowledge management mean to library and information service professionals? After all, don't librarians and information professionals organize and provide access to knowledge? Is knowledge management just a new income stream for consulting firms when other business words lose their cluster?

The fact is that, knowledge management is neither a migration nor integration but rather, is all encompassing dealing with library management, information management and focussing more on the success and achievement of organisation with aid of technologies. Knowledge Management is diversifying the library and information profession making it more valuable, fashionable. In fact, Knowledge management (KM) is more than managing or organizing books or journals, searching the Internet for clients or arranging for the circulation of materials. However, each of these activities can be part of the knowledge management spectrum and processes (Broadbent, 1998). Knowledge management (KM) is about enhancing the use of organizational knowledge through sound practices of information management and organizational learning. The purpose is to deliver value to the business (Broadbent, 1998).

According Koina (2002) librarians are the ultimate knowledge managers. We all know that. After all, haven't we been the custodians of documented knowledge for centuries? According to the literature, many librarians still believe that knowledge management is simply managing information and explicit or documented knowledge, which is what they have been doing for many years, and that eventually everyone else will deduce this. However, information and knowledge are not the same thing at all. Information is simply contextualized data. To become knowledge, there needs to be an added human element. Information tends to be tangible, whereas knowledge is information that is interpreted and synthesized. This according to Southon and Ross Todd (2004) "carries a key assumption that library and information professionals have an important role to play in knowledge management and, if anything, serves to 'stake a claim' in the knowledge management territory, in part, as a vehicle for enhancing the professional image and role of the information professional".

The argument between migration or integration of knowledge management into library and information science profession provide an interesting contrast in perspective. Southon and Ross Todd (2004) explain that in many respects the view of library/information management represented the traditional view - that is, that of a provider of physical artifacts of knowledge. The focus was on the technical processes of gathering and organizing information to enable access, with little engagement with what is done with that information or the overall impact of the service on the organisation. The view of knowledge management, on the other hand, involved processing of the information and adapting it to the needs of the user in the light of overall organizational objectives (Southon and Ross Todd 2004). This more strategic view is similar to that being promoted as the ideal for modern information services (Goulding et al, 1999). Thus, it is found that library/information management is seen in very narrow terms, which are consistent with the low esteem, whereas knowledge management appears to challenge many of them to think more broadly, contextually and strategically, in terms that are more likely to advance their roles in the organization, while staying within the information framework. (Southon and Ross Todd, 2004)

From the above discussions we can see categorically that knowledge management is an extension of library and information science focusing on modern information provision targeted mainly on using the tacit and explicit knowledge and information for organisational success and achievement. This has been explained further by Drucker, (1999) that "what we call the Information Revolution is actually a Knowledge Revolution. What has made it possible to routinize processes is not machinery; the computer is only the trigger. Software is the reorganization of traditional work, based on centuries of experience, through the application of knowledge and especially of systematic, logical analysis. Thus, Knowledge management is seen as the discipline within which library and information science reside, and is concept that attracts many organisations and disciplines, because it deals with organizational efficiency, maximizing organization's potential, competitive advantage, building a learning organization and managing intellectual capital.

3.2 Is Knowledge Management A Barrier OR A Future to Library and Information Profession?

The role of knowledge management in library and information profession tend to be future than barrier, this is because KM will become more and more important along with the development of knowledge economy. Southon and Ross Todd (2004) stated that, knowledge management (KM) presents a major shift in focus regarding the development and use of knowledge and information in increasing the effectiveness of any organization. It presents an opportunity for information professionals to make themselves relevant to their parent organisations in a much more vital way than has generally been the case. It also presents a major challenge to information professionals to engage with issues that have not generally been regarded as their task, either by themselves, or by those for whom they work (Southon and Ross Todd, 2004). A body of literature has emerged that explicitly addresses that, there is a future for library and information professional within the context of

Knowledge Management. For example the study of Rooi & Snyman (2006) found that, knowledge management would create an environment conducive to knowledge sharing; managing the corporate memory; transfer of information management and related skills to a new context that is linked to business processes and core operations. Furthermore, KM will develop a corporate information literacy; and finally, management of information in a digital/electronic environment

According to Schwarzwalder (1999), writing from an IT perspective, however, does outline some of the benefits of including librarians as KM players, such as their commitment to sharing information (unlike many people in organizations), their effectiveness, their customer-oriented attitude and their awareness of the ways in which people communicate information needs and of patterns of information use. Indeed, librarians determine success by the way in which people use a system, not according to the way they *could* use one if only they did things the way the system designers intended – a point of contrast, it is suggested, with the information systems and technology community (Snyman 2001, p.274). There is some evidence that KM has extended the job market of LIS professionals beyond traditional libraries and information centres.

In summary, knowledge management becomes a future to library and information profession as a result of the following benefits: It helps the library and information professionals to ensure the right information to be provided and at the right at time, based on the need of users within organisations; it helps the library and information professionals to get the right people at the right time to make the right decisions using the specific organisational information and knowledge; it helps library and information professionals to collaborate with other organisational staff to provide organizational agility. Similarly, it make the library and information professionals through organisational activities to provide operational efficiency in the organization; it make library and information professionals to be aggressive thereby providing information and knowledge that will increase innovation rate; Knowledge management creates employee growth and continuous learning of the library and information professionals; it makes library and information professionals to be integral part and parcel of the core growth and improvement of organisations.

4. Tacit Benefits

One of the greatest achievements of knowledge management to library and information professionals is on the area of tacit knowledge and information. The introduction of knowledge management has create awareness to library and information professionals, thereby making them to understand that tacit knowledge is very vital in attaining organisational success and achievements. The specific benefits are it makes library and information professionals to improved team work and communication within the organisation; it makes the library and information professionals to reduced problem solving time; it helps the library and information professionals to improve the profitability while reducing the high cost to organisation. In addition, it makes library and information professionals to have consistency in discharging their activities; it helps them to improve their project management skills; it helps them to be more on user centred by involving customer participation in the process of attaining organisational success; it makes the library and information professionals to be part of business process improvement.

4.1 Challenges for Library and Information Science Professionals

There is a general consensus by scholars and researchers within the literature of library and information science that Knowledge Management (KM) has presented exciting challenges to Library and Information Science professionals. As such their skills are regarded by some as highly relevant and they could provide useful input into what has turned out to be a multi-disciplinary approach to KM development in organizations, but, as Doug (2004) points out, this is an opportunity that requires a great deal of preparation and a new way of thinking. According to Sarrafzadeh (2004) although LIS professionals may have excellent information management skills, they need to gain additional skills and cross existing boundaries in order to become significant players in KM. The obstacles might be personal, organizational and/or professional; some may arise from the personal characteristics of LIS graduates and some from their inappropriate type of education. However, in another review Abell and Oxbrow (2001) stated that from the employer's point of view the specific challenges could be as follows: lack of business knowledge; lack of understanding of the interplay between information and organizational objectives; poor team and leadership skills Lack of management skills. In addition to this, Schwarzwalder (1999) claims that the major disadvantage of librarians as KM players is that they have little or no influence in terms of changing organizational culture. Librarians are poorly placed as change agents but as already suggested, they can expand their influence by partnering with other groups within their organizations. In our own opinion we establish that the challenges faced by library and information science professionals emanate within four perspectives i.e. individual, organisational, technological and Library and information science education.

1). **Individual:** there are serious problems among the library practitioners such as

a. Indifferent attitudes or lukewarm attitudes of the librarians towards the profession itself.
b. Conservatism, majority of the practitioners are conservative in nature, they develop phobia on any new changes into profession especially with regards to Information Technology and lack of organisational knowledge.
c. Lack of technical know how and show on integrating the new concepts into the field, and Tacit knowledge is difficult to capture and manage by individuals
d. Majority of librarians gives much concern with the external information resources rather than internal resources, and lack of required management skills
e. Lack of knowledge on business process identification and analysis
f. Lack of understanding the knowledge process within the business process
g. Lack of understanding the value, context and dynamics of knowledge and information within the organisation.
h. Lack of knowledge on mapping and flows of information in the organisation.

2). **Organisational**

a. Questioning the integrity of Library and Information science professional's capability to serve as knowledge managers, lack of acceptance by the organisations and Organisational knowledge and information politics
b. Organizational feudal or anarchist approach to information professionals, always seeing them as blood suckers.
c. Recruitment differences on employing who is capable of becoming knowledge manager.
d. Data Accuracy: Valuable raw data generated by a particular group within an organization may need to be validated before being transformed into normalized knowledge.
e. Data Interpretation: Information derived by individuals or groups in organisation may need to be mapped to a standard context in order to be meaningful to someone else in the organization.
f. Data Relevancy: The quality and value of knowledge depend on relevance. Knowledge that lacks relevance simply adds complexity, cost and risk to an organization without any compensating benefits
g. Monitoring of various departments to ensure that they take responsibility for keeping their repositories clean of redundant files.
h. Lack of adequate finance allocated to the libraries or knowledge repositories to join a network with similar institutions for effective sharing of knowledge
i. Lack of training programmes that will enhance professional development

3). **Technological**

a. Lack of knowledge and skills to use the Information technologies and frequent changes in the production of technologies, most of the technologies today become obsolete quickly.
b. Knowledge bases tend to be very complex and large: When knowledge databases become very large and complex, it puts the organization in a fix as a result of changes in technology and lack of relevant and adequate information technology facilities
c. Lack of customize software that will facilitate knowledge management activities and knowledge sharing among organisations.

4). **Library and information science schools**

a. Most of the LIS schools lacked business understanding and commitment to organizational goals.
b. Lack of awareness on the knowledge management and its importance to the profession.
c. There is no develop course or training on the technical skills required to embed knowledge processes within organisations, to promote business understanding

among information professionals, and to facilitate other key skills needed in KM environments.

d. The nomenclature of programs provided in the library schools is not adequately enough to prepare information professionals to become knowledge managers.
e. Teaching the students on how to capture and manage tacit knowledge is not so easy. It is hard to know what is in human mind. It is also difficult to capture knowledge and manage it within large organizations.
f. Lack of researches by academics on the perception of knowledge management from various angles of organisation and institutions

Often it was a mismatch between what were incorporated in LIS syllabus and acquired by librarians, and what were demanded by the industry implementing Knowledge Management. Othman et al (2008) identified the demand for data mining knowledge and skill among others which were lacking among librarians. Knowledge motivates actions and enables confident decision making, and thus business intelligence knowledge and skill is essential. Without such knowledge and skills, knowledge management is a barrier for the librarian or information professionals.

There are elements within knowledge management that called for knowledge and skills recognized as coming from LIS field, such as knowledge repository, knowledge sources for a particular domain; however, techniques and tools must be kept updated and matched with what are available today. Most LIS courses maintained the same tools and techniques without considering the latest development in related fields such as information technology and computer science (Othman et al, 2008). Serious consideration should be given on mapping the knowledge management courses deriving from LIS as having a relationship with courses from other fields, such as business and management, law, and computer science. LIS professional could offer and should acquire skills and knowledge on 'KNOWLEDGE management' rather than 'knowledge MANAGEMENT', since the former would expand the horizon of LIS by opening up more opportunities in the acquisition of latest techniques and tools and being relevantly related to computer science, law and business and management.

5. Conclusion and Way Forward

It is clearly seen that knowledge management is not a new field or discipline, neither a migration or integration but rather an extension or continuation of traditional process of library and information management, but in different format adding value to knowledge. Today, the libraries, information centres, information professionals and library and information science schools need to make a transition from being a cost dependent to value added profession i.e. from being information and service providers to fully participating as knowledge partners for the satisfaction of customer's needs and organisational success.

This provide ample opportunity for library and information professionals to redesign, reaffirm, restructure and reinvent their roles and methods by which they create new value from the organisation knowledge and attain progress and success within the organisation. To achieve this, the library and information professionals need to make a U turn, from being the custodian and hoarders of knowledge to be partners in creating a new knowledge itself and adding value to the organisational knowledge. As knowledge management emerged as a domain which attracts different disciplines, field of knowledge clearly show that collaboration is the final answer to library and information professionals otherwise they will become incompetent with several deficiencies and proficiencies as they embark to take the full advantage of the new discipline.

References

Abell, A. & Oxbrow, N. 2001, *Competing with Knowledge: The Information Professionals in the Knowledge Management Age*. London: Library Association Publishing.

Al-Hawamdeh, S. (2002) "Knowledge management: re-thinking information management and facing the challenge of managing tacit knowledge" *Information Research*, 8(1), paper no. 143 [Available at http://InformationR.net/ir/8-1/paper143.html]

Agoulu, C.C. and Agoulu, I.E. (2002) Libraries and Information management in Nigeria: seminal essays on themes and problems. Maiduguri: Edlibform. P.430-452.

Broadbent, M (1998) The Phenomenon of Knowledge Management: What Does it Mean to the Information Profession? Available online @ www.google.com. Retrieved 17/9/2009

Drotner, (2005). Library innovation for the knowledge society: Scandinavian Public Library, Quarterly Volume 38 NO. 2 2005

Drucker, P. (1999). *Beyond the information revolution*. The Atlantic Online. Available: http://www.theatlantic.com/issues/99oct/9910drucker.htm [2001, 21st May 2001]

Duffy, J. (1999). Harvesting experience: reaping the benefits of knowledge. Kansas: ARMA International

Foray, D. & B. D. Lundvall, (1996) The knowledge-based economy: from the economics of knowledge to the learning economy, in: *Employment and growth in the knowledge-based economy*, pp. 11-32 Paris: OECD

Goulding, A, Bromham, B, Hannabuss, S and Cramer, D, (1999). Supply and demand: the workforce needs of library and information services and personal qualities of new professionals. *Journal of Librarianship and Information Science* 31(4), 212.

Koenig, M.E.D (2005) KM moves beyond the organization: the opportunity for librarians. World Library and Information Congress: 71th IFLA General Conference and Council "Libraries - A voyage of discovery" Oslo, Norway *Conference Programme:* http://www.ifla.org/IV/ifla71/Programme.htm

Koina, C. (2003). Librarians are the ultimate knowledge managers? *The Australian Library Journal, 52*(3), 269-272. Available at:
http://www.alia.org.au/publishing/alj/52.3/full.text/koina.html

Manir, A. K. (2007) The role of Library to the Development of Knowledge Society. Applied Psychology Selected Readings. Vol. 4. (1).

Narayanan, V. K. (2001). *Managing technology and innovation for competitive advantage*. Englewood Cliffs, NJ: Prentice Hall

Ominuyi, O.O. and Ademoye, A.A. (2000) A role of Libraries Towards Achieving the goals of literacy for all: efforts in Nigeria. Middle Belt Journal of Library and Information Science vol. 1 (1&2).

Othman, R., Noordin, M.F. and Jarjis, J. (2008) "Structuring the Competencies for Executive Knowledge Management Program", paper presented at the *International Conference on Knowledge Management 2008*, Columbus, Ohio, USA, October 2008.

Rooi, H. V. and Snyman, R. (2006) "A Content Analysis of Literature Regarding Knowledge Management Opportunities for Librarians" *Aslib Proceedings* 58, no.3: 261 – 271.

Sarrafzadeh, M. (2004), "The Implications of Knowledge Management for Libraries and LIS Professionals", Paper Presented to RMIT Business Research Student Candidature Review Conference, Melbourne, 16- 18 August 2004

Schwarzwalder, Robert (1999) "Librarians as Knowledge Management Agents." *EContent* 22, no. 4: 63-65.

Shanhong, T (2000) Knowledge Management in Libraries in the 21st Century. Paper presented at 66th IFLA Council and General Conference Jerusalem, Israel, 13-18 August, 2000

Snyman, R.M.M. (2001) "Do employers really know what they want? An analysis of Job advertisements for information and knowledge managers", *Aslib Proceedings*, 53, 7,273- (9 pages), viewed 17 September 2009, retrieved from ProQuest database.

Southon, G. and Todd, R (2004) Library and information professionals and knowledge management: conceptions, challenges and conflicts *The Australian Library Journal* volume 50 issue 3

Wali, S.R.A. (1991) The role of Public Libraries in the provision of education for all. In kolo, I. and Indabawa, S.A. et al (ed.) Readings in Education for all.

EVALUATING INTELLECTUAL ASSETS IN UNIVERSITY LIBRARIES: A MULTI-SITE CASE STUDY FROM THAILAND

SHEILA CORRALL[†] and SOMSAK SRIBORISUTSAKUL
Department of Information Studies, University of Sheffield, Regent Court Sheffield, S1 4DP, United Kingdom
[†]*E-mail: s.m.corrall@sheffield.ac.uk*

Intellectual assets are strategic resources that libraries can use to add value to services, but their intangible attributes make them hard to evaluate. An exploratory case study used document analysis, interviews and a questionnaire to develop and test indicators of intellectual assets and related performance measures at three university libraries in Thailand. The study demonstrated the feasibility of applying an intellectual capital perspective and a scorecard process model to design a workable system for evaluating library intangibles, particularly where libraries have a pre-existing interest in knowledge management and a culture of assessment.

1. Introduction

Library evaluation cannot be separated from its context. If the operating environment changes, libraries need new measures to monitor their performance under new conditions (Rowley, 2005). For example, electronic metrics and impact indicators have been devised to measure library performance in digital environments and evaluate the customer service experience as libraries respond to advances in information technology and high expectations of users (Brophy, 2006). The knowledge-based economy is pushing organizations towards adoption of knowledge management (KM) as a means of creating organizational value, on the basis that KM initiatives can help to create benefits that customers desire. A need to assess the intellectual assets (IAs) of libraries as another bottom-line indicator is emerging from this context of value-oriented services (White, 2007).

Some writers have encouraged library practitioners to consider organizational knowledge in libraries and information services as IAs, intellectual capital (IC), or intangibles (Koenig, 1998; Huotari and Iivonem, 2005). Evaluating IAs can be seen as a stepping-stone towards managing knowledge, but it is not easy to launch this idea in academic libraries. Librarians in higher education institutions (HEIs) do not always recognize that recent developments in performance measurement (PM) have made them more accountable for the knowledge used in service delivery, in addition to their use of tangible assets, such as equipment and buildings. They are also less familiar with managing IAs than with other KM-related processes, such as work on knowledge access and repositories (Townley, 2001).

A review of library research on intangible assessment reveals that the literature has particularly grasped the importance of service quality, but given less attention to IAs. Applications of intangible measurements in libraries have concentrated on library scorecards, adopting Kaplan and Norton's (1996) Balanced Scorecard (BSC) model to group both financial and non-financial measures under four perspectives: finance, internal process, customer, and innovation and learning (Ceynowa, 2000; Cribb, 2005; Self, 2003). There have been few empirical studies in the broad area of knowledge assets assessment for academic libraries, although Barron (1995) and Dakers (1998) examined staff skills and competence to audit tacit knowledge in human resources (HR) in public and national libraries respectively, and Van Deventer (2002) implemented IC management for an information services unit in a large research organization to disclose intangible stocks and activities in an IC report.

The present multi-case study explores the feasibility of IA evaluation in academic libraries through an investigation of three universities in Thailand. The central research question was 'how do Thai university libraries, as representatives of developing-nation libraries, develop performance indicators (PIs) to evaluate their organizational IAs?' The study was guided by the following four sub-questions derived from this question:

- What are the most important IAs for Thai academic libraries?
- Why do library administrators want to evaluate library IAs?
- How do libraries choose PIs as proxies to demonstrate their IAs?
- What PIs are suitable for evaluating library IAs?

This paper argues that a specific model for evaluation of these assets can help libraries exploit them to add high value to services and bring future benefits to information supply operations. It demonstrates that library administrators are interested in intangibles; that IC theory can be adapted for identifying knowledge resources in academic libraries; and that the methodology described is appropriate for developing PIs related to library IAs. The paper presents a review of the conceptual framework, description of the research methodology, analysis of the case background and discussion of the main findings.

2. Theoretical Framework

This study utilises two paradigms to underpin identification and assessment of IAs in academic libraries: the resource-based view (RBV) and the IC perspective. First, taking the RBV, today's organizations realize that their knowledge base and intangible assets represent a strategic resource. Such resources are characterized as strategic by four distinguishing features: they are valuable, rare, inimitable and non-substitutable. In contrast, all tangible assets, such as budgets or premises, can easily be acquired by rivals. An organization can accordingly claim sustained competitive advantage over others in its domain or sector if it possesses IAs (Barney, 1991; Meso and Smith, 2000).

Secondly, using the IC perspective, organizations regard their knowledge base and intangible assets as good long-term investments, similar to other capital assets, which will enable them to create value in products and services for stakeholders. The term 'corporate memory' is often used in this context: when an organization plans to evaluate its corporate memory, it is attempting to measure its stocks of intangibles and assess its learning activities (Stewart, 1997; Marr, 2005).

2.1 Intellectual Assets

IAs have been given various names, definitions and components, because this specialist field involves several disciplines, such as strategic management, accounting and HR (Marr and Moustaghfir, 2005). In this study the terms 'intellectual assets', 'intangible assets', 'intangibles' and 'knowledge resources' are used interchangeably to denote knowledge-based items, or manifestations of the existence of knowledge, owned (or held) by an organization, whose value can be extracted and used to increase organizational effectiveness in accordance with its strategy (Green, 2007).

IAs can be distinguished from 'intellectual capital': Bukowitz and Williams (2000), describing practice in PricewaterhouseCoopers, explain that IC resembles 'raw knowledge', which is not yet articulated and converted into IAs; thus, tacit knowledge belongs to each employee and may not serve any purpose for the organization. In other words, ownership and strategic alignment differentiate organizational IAs from IC.

For corporate purposes, it is commonly accepted that there are three areas of intangible strategic resources, comprising HR, structural capital and relational capital:

- *human resources* are collective capabilities derived from individuals in firms, which include capacities, experience, motivation, and staff satisfaction;
- *structural capital* is organizational competence in the forms of databases, technology, routines and culture;
- *relational capital* signifies the networks developed by organizations with customers, suppliers, partners and stakeholders (OECD, 2006: 9).

In the library world, many academics and practitioners have classified knowledge resources into groups with a strategic management and strategic accounting lens. Kaplan and Norton's (1996; 2004) BSC and related Strategy Map is a popular reference point. Another approach is Sveiby's (2001) Dynamic Intangible Assets Monitor (IAM), which uses accounting theory for disclosing stocks of intangible assets parallel to tangible assets. Libraries seem typically to use a four-fold categorization of IAs, introducing *collection and service assets* as an additional area alongside those typically used in the corporate sector, scoping their categories as follows:

- *human assets* include expertise, core competencies and learning;
- *structural assets* embrace a diverse range of library management systems such as organizational structure, management information and work processes;
- *relationship assets* include customer relationships, reputation and image;
- *collection and service assets* emphasise unique collections of information materials, added-value services and new products (Koenig, 1998; Pierce and Snyder, 2003; White, 2004; Cribb, 2005).

2.2 *Indicator Development for Intangible Evaluation*

Contemporary academic libraries have to communicate their strategic impact to their parent institutions by maximizing appreciation of library roles. IA measurement is a potential tool which HE libraries can initiate as part of KM programmes within larger management systems (Huotari and Iivonen, 2005). White (2007) points out the benefits of intangible assessment, in that it helps libraries to:

- expand the scope of traditional evaluation towards a library's worth;
- align library management's ability with the parent organization's IC strategy;
- utlise information on IAs to make decisions about the maintenance and improvement of organizational knowledge.

Evaluation models for knowledge resources in the business context have usually begun with an extended balance-sheet approach to show value for money. However, the scorecard method tends to be the preferred approach to indicator development for reporting intellectual performance, since this model lets organizations design 'fit-for-purpose' indicators in the form of a feedback loop. Scorecard measures can be revised or changed when organizations the analyze causes and effects of previous assessments (Rylander *et al.,* 2000; Shulver *et al.,* 2000). This method also provides the foundation for well-known guidelines on disclosing intangible assets, including those of the European Union (MERITUM, 2002), the Danish Ministry of Science, Technology and Innovation (Denmark, 2003) and the Japanese Ministry of Economy, Trade and Industry (Japan, 2005). For the library sector, White (2004) has suggested that the organizational knowledge of academic libraries could be assessed by the scorecard method.

The scorecard process model for developing PIs typically has three main steps, which shaped the conceptual framework and practical design of the study:

(i) linking stakeholders' expectations to key success factors (KSFs) relying on IA components,

(ii) building PIs based on these KSFs to describe *qualitative* targets for knowledge resources,

(iii) translating each prospective indicator into *quantitative* measures of intangible stocks and learning activities (Probst *et al.,* 2000; Rylander *et al.,* 2000).

3. Research Methods

The project employed a mixed methodology, selecting the case study design as a flexible research strategy, enabling the use of varied data sources (Eisenhardt, 1989). Library practitioners have often favoured a qualitative methodology for PI projects, such as BSC implementations (Ceynowa, 2000; Cribb 2005; Self, 2003). This helps to generate indicators which meet local needs, but are less amenable to inter-institutional comparison. Others have combined qualitative and quantitative methods (Cotta-Schonberg and Line, 1994; Cullen, 2006), developing indicators that are both meaningful and robust, by adopting a 'pragmatist' philosophy (Tashakkori and Teddlie, 2003).

Mixed methods are more useful than employing only qualitative or quantitative approaches when researchers want to examine the complex results of a distinctive situation and normalize them by comparing findings with other organizations (Petty and Guthrie, 2000). A mixed methodology is also a pragmatic choice for studies with both theoretical and practical aims.

The case approach is particularly appropriate for researching areas where there have been few previous studies (Benbasat *et al.,* 1987) and was widely used to generate theories, find indicators of intellectual performance and diversify the context of measurement when the field of IC measurement emerged in the 1990s (Petty and Guthrie, 2000; Marr and Chatzkel, 2004), reinforcing its suitability for researching this area in Thai university libraries, where there has been no prior work in the field. Case studies are well suited to answering 'why' and 'how' questions, having been used in France to answer such questions in relation to intangible indicator development (MERITUM, 2002). They are also well suited to examining elaborate phenomena in natural settings (Yin, 2003), thus supporting the necessary investigation here of issues such as the institutional context of libraries and the opinions of different stakeholders.

4. Data Collection and Analysis

Fieldwork was carried out in two stages over five months. The first stage (July to August 2007) was used to test and refine the methodology by conducting a single-case pilot at a Thai university library chosen as a representative site, using Yin's (2003) criteria of convenience, ease of access, proximity to the field researcher's normal workplace and the availability of experts willing to make suggestions about the research design.

The second stage (June to August 2008) collected data for the main multiple-case study involving three Thai university libraries. Selection of sites for the main study was informed by prior research on IC measurement and Yin's (2003) replication logic. The first criterion was library size, cited by Pors *et al.* (2004) as a significant determinant of the number of management tools deployed, with implementation of IC measurement tending to be associated with large numbers of staff (Wang, 2006). Another criterion was readiness for intangible assessment, indicated by adoption of management models such as BSC, Total Quality Management and benchmarking tools, such schemes being thought to aid understanding of IC measurement (Roberts, 2003). The final criterion was an active interest in intangibles or KM. Case sites were selected after browsing the websites of 39 libraries as potential participants.

Data for the pilot were derived from three sequential methods: document analysis, semi-structured interviews and a self-administered questionnaire survey. In the main study, the self-administered questionnaire was replaced by the researcher administering the survey instrument to groups of staff collectively, as a result of participant feedback about difficulties in interpreting some questions. Purposive sampling was used to select interview participants.

Both quantitative and qualitative content analysis have been used in business studies of IC measurement (OECD, 1999; MERITUM, 2002). A qualitative approach was used here to examine strategy, policy and other administrative documentation as a pre-interview procedure in the qualitative phase of the study. Document analysis was used to familiarize the researcher with the sites, to capture official requirements for evaluating strategic resources and to compare existing elements of PM with the language of the IC movement, thus facilitating communication with library personnel.

Semi-structured interviews have been widely used in empirical IC research, typically with the other modes of data-gathering used here (OECD, 1999; MERITUM, 2002). The semi-structured interviews were conducted with senior managers/associate directors at each site to verify the categorization of intangibles and framework for evaluation proposed in the conceptual model; to explore administrators' attitudes towards their libraries' IAs; and to identify KSFs as a basis for formulating draft indicators of intellectual performance, thereby linking organizational strategy to knowledge assets measures (Bontis *et al.,* 1999).

Self-administered questionnaires and interviews have both been used in library settings to test developed measures (King Research, 1990; Cotta-Schonberg and Line, 1994; Lithgow and Hepworth, 1993), along with other techniques, such as Delphi panels (Harer and Cole, 2005) and focus groups (Cullen, 2006). The structured questionnaire-based group interviews formed the quantitative phase of the study here and were used to test the relevance and transparency of the proposed indicators and sample measures with middle managers and specialist staff as potential users of the indicators at the operational level. Senior managers previously interviewed were asked to review the questions derived from the qualitative phase and to suggest additions or changes.

Qualitative data from the library documentation and in-depth interviews were analysed line-by-line and coded using specialist software (NVivo7) to generate themes and compare categories. Quantitative data were analysed using a spreadsheet (Excel) to generate descriptive statistics, such as the mean values for respondents' ratings of the understandability and importance of the proposed indicators. The data from each site were analysed and written-up as individual case reports in a standard format, first describing the contextual influences on PM, represented by each library's strategy, organizational structure and institutional model for service evaluation; second, presenting the findings from documentary sources and key informants on library IAs, in terms of their identification and classification, and the motives and criteria for their evaluation; and, third, reporting the results of the user acceptance tests for the proposed indicators and measures, conducted via structured interviews. Finally, evidence from the three cases was systematically compared to identify similarities and differences in relation to the four themes of the research questions, prior to synthesising the findings from the cross-case analysis for comparison with the related literature to support formulation of theoretical propositions from the cases.

5. Case Background

The formal strategies, governance structures and steering models for service evaluation of the case libraries are important contextual dimensions underlying the process of developing PIs for their IAs. Table 1 summarizes and compares key elements of the organizational context explored at the three sites.

Table 1. Organizational contexts of the case libraries

Dimensions	Elements	Case library sites K	SW	T
Strategy	Mission contents			
	• Contributions to institutional goals (teaching, study and research)	✓	✓	✓
	• Provision of information resources and services	✓	✓	✓
	• Interventions on lifelong learning/information literacy		✓	✓
	• Library staff, technology and administration	✓		
	• User focus		✓	
	• Information access			✓
	Objectives contents			
	• Supply electronic resources and provide users with remote access	✓	✓	✓
	• Develop and train library staff	✓	✓	✓
	• Improve library premises/facilities	✓	✓	
	• Manage library operations and evaluate its performance	✓		✓
	• Sustain relationships with other organizations	✓		✓
	• Know users and respond to their needs		✓	✓
	• Ensure that library collections meet the university curricula		✓	
Organization structure	Bureaucratic hierarchy	✓	✓	✓
	Library director sharing authority through a standing advisory committee	✓	✓	✓
Steering model of library evaluation	Use the QA system and standards required by the parent organization	✓	✓	✓
	Service quality evaluation elements			
	• Strategic and operational planning	✓	✓	✓
	• The effectiveness of learning support services	✓	✓	✓
	• Administration/management responsibilities	✓	✓	✓
	• Finance and budgeting	✓	✓	✓
	• The mechanism for auditing internal QA	✓	✓	✓
	• Continuous improvement and organizational development	✓		✓
	• Preservation of art and culture		✓	
	• Organizational information systems			✓
	Number of QA measures	35	30	18
	Evaluation criteria			
	• Measuring the library's QA progress based on the PDCA cycle	✓	✓	✓
	• Overall library performance determined by the examiners' judgements	✓	✓	✓

5.1 Library Strategies

The three strategies had many common elements. Their mission statements all acknowledged their contributions to institutional goals, in addition to the provision of information resources and services. Two libraries also highlighted their roles in lifelong learning/information literacy, but there were some elements mentioned at only one site (e.g. the SW mission specifically mentioned user focus). Similarly, their strategic objectives all emphasized delivery of electronic resources and the development and training of library staff, but other issues, such as library premises and collections, did not feature in all cases.

5.2 Management Structures

The organization structures of the libraries are quite similar, reflecting their shared institutional status as public universities. They all work within a governance structure characterized by institutional rules and regulations, standardized procedures for library staff and a hierarchy of authority, with co-ordination and delegation of work by senior staff to lower levels. However, although decision-making is centralized, they all have a standing committee that enables library managers to participate in administration and in addition they use project teams with membership drawn from different divisions to implement action plans and encourage co-operation among groups.

5.3 Performance Evaluation

All universities in Thailand are obliged to meet standards specified by the Office for National Educational Standards and Quality Assessment and the three case libraries accordingly each work within a formal institutional quality assurance (QA) framework that has a strong influence on their approach to performance evaluation.

The libraries' information supply or service delivery chains are identified as a sub-system in the monitoring of university performance, which is based on the input–process–output–outcome model, shown in the following examples:

- *Inputs* — annual budget, workforce, office equipment, leadership, plans;
- *Processes* — management processes, work processes for producing information products, procedures for delivering services;
- *Outputs* — the quantity and quality of library collections and services;
- *Outcome* — user satisfaction.

Interestingly, library K differs slightly in its definition of inputs, separating intangible inputs (e.g. strategies, plans and leadership) from tangible inputs (e.g. finance and workforce) and then categorizing its intangibles as the managerial context that precedes the tangible inputs.

The libraries undertake internal quality audits of their operations in accordance with their institutional QA standards for learning support systems, which define specific evaluation elements (as shown in Table 1) and also specify the QA measures to be used for evaluation, which are of four types, reflecting the input–process–output–outcome model. The evaluation elements are similar across the cases, but there is significant variation in the number and nature of the measures used, with library T having only 18, compared to 30 and 35 for the other two libraries. Examples of measures include size of professional staff (input), throughput for library activities (process) and use of library collections (output). Only library T claims to measure outcomes, via the results of its user satisfaction surveys.

The evaluation process involves producing a self-assessment report, incorporating documentation and performance data; hosting a visit by university auditors, gathering direct evidence to substantiate the report; and then receiving and responding to the audit findings. The auditors are all formally trained in the use of the Plan–Do–Check–Act (PDCA) cycle, underlining the formality and rigour of the process.

6. Case Findings

Qualitative data from the document review and semi-structured interviews with a total of 12 library administrators across the three sites were analysed to identify the core IAs of the three libraries, classify these assets into the four predefined categories identified above (in section 2.1), explore the administrators' motives for intangible evaluation and then develop a draft set of PIs.

6.1 Core Intellectual Assets

Documentation associated with the libraries' QA systems was used to explore existing service quality evaluation elements and related performance measures relevant to assessment of intangible aspects of library performance, such as measures used to evaluate the effectiveness of their administration, their services and their strategic and operational planning. The assumption here was that IAs were already included in the current evaluation process, but not recognized as such, because they were hidden behind the measured QA elements; so the aim was to identify these hidden assets and map them onto the four-fold framework described. Thus, user satisfaction surveys conducted by the SW library provided staff with knowledge of user experiences, which could be categorized as a relationship asset.

Library T's strategy documentation was a particularly fruitful source for identifying potential intangible assets, as it had adopted Kaplan and Norton's (2004) Strategy Map tool as a means of depicting its vision, mission, strategic priorities, desired outcomes and key PIs from the four BSC perspectives (external stakeholder, innovation and learning, financial and internal). So this library had already identified crucial intangible resources alongside tangible resources; for example, in addition to specifying 'first-class facilities' (a tangible asset) as a desired outcome, it specified 'effective teams' (an intangible human asset) as a desired outcome associated with the learning and growth perspective.

Although the QA and strategy documentation was valuable in the initial identification of IAs, some examples of assets essential to quality service delivery could only be specified in detail after the interviews with library administrators. Table 2 shows the range of IAs identified at the case sites, arranged in the four categories. Many examples conform to the broad IC taxonomy found in national guidelines (e.g. Denmark, 2003; Japan, 2005) and business literature reporting companies' IC, which classify the concept into three categories: human capital, structural capital and relational capital (OECD, 2006). However, the fourth category of collection and service assets is library-specific and distinctive in the way that it combines assets from the other categories.

Table 2. Intellectual assets of the case libraries

Category	Library K	Library SW	Library T
Human assets	• Service mindset • Mental agility • Expertise • Skills • Team spirit • Commitment to library goals	• Adaptability skills • Group participation/ teamwork • Commitment to library strategy	• Education and training • Competence development
Structural assets	• Minutes of knowledge sharing meetings • Reports of working groups • Quality control records • Management information system	• Quality assurance documentation, e.g. handbooks, self-assessment reports and work procedures	• Output from knowledge management projects, e.g. best practices, success stories and lessons learned
Relationship assets	• Relationships with key stakeholders • Users' feedback	• Relationships with university executives • Public image of the library • Marketing communications	• Interaction between library workers and users
Collection and service assets	• Frequently used services • Users' praise at service points • Information resources frequently requested • Digital collections • In-house databases	• Core course materials • New search tools • Electronic archives • New/value-added services • Collections and services that satisfy users	• Information resources requested by target users • Top-ranking services • New services • Digital collections

Previous work on intangible assets in the library sector has restricted the identification and classification of IC in academic libraries to the three recognized categories of the IC taxonomy (Van Deventer, 2002; Pierce and Snyder, 2003; Iivonen and Huotari, 2007). However, the results here suggest that it is necessary for academic libraries to add the 'collection and service assets' category to the classification of library IAs. Collection and service assets are the end-products of core knowledge-based processes in libraries, such as collection development, service enhancement and innovations in library and information work. They form a distinct fourth category in being essentially derived from a combination of human, structural and relationship assets. Identification of this additional category contributes to our further understanding of library services and information resources as library assets not wholly embraced in the broad IC taxonomy.

Human, structural and relationship assets are crucial to the internal procedures of library operations, but such procedures are less important strategically in shaping users' perceptions of the value of information services, as users only perceive and take interest in the resources and services that are the end-products of library operations (Saracevic and Kantor, 1997). Consequently, library stakeholders' perceptions of value are essentially connected with collection and services assets, rather than with other categories of library IAs, with this fourth category reflecting the distinctive identity of academic libraries, whose mission is to provide library services and information resources to users in support of teaching, learning and research in HEIs (Brophy, 1991). Moreover, these distinctive assets are directly relevant to the working practices of staff at all levels of library organizations, in addition to being experienced, recognized and appreciated by library stakeholders, which underlines their significance as a strategic resource.

6.2 Motives for Evaluation

The interviews with administrators also explored their motives for evaluating the libraries' IAs, in terms of the incentives for gathering information on their knowledge resources and reasons for identifying them specifically. All the libraries had established KM projects and although their programmes were at different stages of development, the administrators all recognized a need to monitor and measure their progress. Libraries K and T wanted to demonstrate the effects of their KM projects, which had been initiated a few years ago; the SW library was at an earlier stage of KM development, but also recognized information about its KM activities had potential value in getting messages across to university executives.

Similarly, all the libraries saw the evaluation of intangibles as complementing their existing QA procedures, going beyond operational performance to more strategic concerns. Libraries SW and T both mentioned the need for library-specific measures that went beyond the standard university performance evaluation; one SW administrator wanted to differentiate the library and position it ahead of other university support services, 'Every support unit uses the same list of mandatory QA measures. If we have new performance indicators to augment our QA measures, we may show our distinctive quality that causes us to be in front when compared with other subsidiaries in the university community'.

The director of library T made a similar point, linking this to use of the BSC, 'the existing QA measures used in the Office produce the management data that reflects the overall performance of the University rather than the specific results of the library operations... We want a particular type of measure chosen from the BSC framework to prove the value of our library and information work contributing to the University's academic excellence'.

The administrators identified several different stakeholder groups they wanted to target with information about their IAs. The director of library T suggested that the development of such measures could raise awareness of important intangibles among library staff, 'Intangibles such as proactive services, value added collections and staff commitment to organizational change are very important to the whole organization… In our current evaluation of library services, it's hard to make the library personnel become aware of these intangibles if we don't have any new indicators for assessing them'.

The interviews thus identified two main motives for evaluating intangibles, namely to monitor the effectiveness of the libraries' KM activities and to communicate the libraries' value to stakeholders. The libraries' KM-related motives are in line with findings from other sectors: Mouritsen *et al.*'s (2004) survey of Danish companies found 85 per cent of respondents had used IC statements to underpin KM implementation and other sources confirm this association of IA evaluation with KM processes (Marr *et al.*, 2002; Denmark, 2003; Thorleifsdottir and Claessen, 2006). The library respondents' desire to find new ways to communicate their contributions to their universities similarly reflects other commentators' recognition of the need to go beyond tangible assessment to demonstrate library impact (Abels *et al.*, 2004; White, 2007). The link between surfacing information on IAs and reporting performance via BSCs has also been acknowledged previously (Koenig, 1998; Kaplan and Norton, 2004).

6.3 Indicator Development Process

The interviews also established the framework for assessment of the libraries' knowledge assets by exploring the administrators' measurement viewpoints and evaluation criteria. At each site, existing QA standards and processes were seen as the starting-point for measuring intangibles. Essentially, they all wanted to integrate new PIs for intangible assets into their existing QA measures, offering both conceptual and practical reasons; for example, to build on staff familiarity with the QA system and harmonize with existing measures to avoid perceptions of increased workload, as well as the logic of treating intellectual resources in the same way as other library resources. But they also wanted to advance their assessment activity strategically: for example, an associate director at library K argued that their existing audit only helped them "Plan" and "Do" operational tasks, whereas using the BSC could help them 'to "Check" and "Act" strategically'; library T was already using the scorecard approach to relate evaluation to its strategic objectives (via its Strategy Map) and welcomed the opportunity simply to extend this with new intangible measures.

On evaluation criteria, as intangible evaluation was a novel idea for them, all three groups of administrators emphasized *simplicity* as an essential criterion to facilitate widespread introduction and willing participation. In addition, they again wanted to harmonize with the existing evaluation criteria of their QA systems, by using the input–

process–output model. Library T's use of the BSC meant that it was already linking its measures to its mission, strategic priorities and desired outcomes, and the director gave examples of relevant measures already used (e.g. percentage of clients satisfied with services and numbers of best-practice documents created).

Development of initial PIs for the three libraries was guided by the three-step process model outlined above: defining KSFs, identifying PIs and choosing measures (quantifiable inputs, processes and outputs) associated with library IAs. The documented strategic objectives of the libraries were used to identify possible KSFs related to intangibles, which were then analyzed to identify the types of measures (efficiency, effectiveness, etc.) required to assess the library's performance.

One of the investigators acted as facilitator during the indicator development process. Within each library, the process facilitator interpreted the library administrators' interview data, which yielded further insights into their strategic objectives to supplement the data extracted from strategy documents. He next designed the PIs as broad statements articulating expectations for intellectual performance and converted the libraries' existing QA measures to surrogate measures for quantifying their intellectual assets and activities. He then asked the library administrators responsible for overseeing the formal evaluation of library operations and services to review the initial PIs and measures, to determine whether they fitted the library contexts. After the reviews, the facilitator incorporated the proposed indicators and measures in questionnaires for acceptance testing with users through small-scale surveys, as described in the next section (6.4).

Table 3. Comparative classification of key success factors

Asset type	**Factor category**		**Key success factors**		**Evaluation aspect**
		Library K	Library SW	Library T	
Human assets	Human	Competent and ambitious workers	Library staff training and development	HR linked to value-based management	*Efficiency and effectiveness*
Structural assets	Managerial	Managing and directing the library systematically		Enhanced enterprise in managing library operations	*Efficiency and effectiveness*
	Technological		Effective use of information systems and technology in library work		
Relationship assets	Social	Enduring collaborations with other institutions	Understanding of the community served	Sustainable partnership	*Sustainability*
Collection and service assets	Marketing	Quality of collections and efficiency of services	Library services that meet users' needs	User-oriented provision of collections and services	*Quality*

Table 3 shows that each library placed considerable emphasis on human, social and marketing factors, with similarities evident in the human, relationship and collection/service assets, but striking differences in their structural assets, where libraries K and T stressed different aspects of management, while the SW library identified usage of information systems and technology as key to successful strategy implementation. Table 3 also shows that in each library the complete set of KSFs covered four aspects of evaluation, although there were some variations in both the types of assets and specific examples identified in each case.

The administrators all agreed that the indicators should take the form of statements articulating an expected level of intellectual performance, composed mainly of action verbs and key activities.

Table 4. Proposed performance indicators for evaluating intellectual assets

Asset type	**Performance indicators** Library K	Library SW	Library T
Human assets	• Develop personal competencies and skills suitable for modernized work in a learning centre • Build up staff loyalty, motivation and team morale	• Encourage library personnel regularly to develop their job skills and capabilities • Support exchange of personal knowledge among library workers • Give library and information professionals a chance to demonstrate competencies outside the workplace	• Enhance staff expertise in library and information work • Foster loyalty and increase teamwork skills of staff members
Structural assets	• Enable a learning environment through managerial systems	• Establish efficient processes and procedures for managing library operations • Use practical knowledge recorded in QA documents to improve supply of information products and services • Apply information technology in harness with information access improvement and service quality enhancement	• Implement KM activities to promote knowledge sharing through daily work • Have success in disseminating collective knowledge to library staff and sharing it with other organizations
Relationship assets	• Promote sustainable cooperation by dealing with other organizations in a win-win situation	• Give priority to user satisfaction • Initiate culture preservation projects as a part of social responsibility	• Promote library programmes/events to increase client awareness and secure adequate funding
Collection and service assets	• Put a high value on core collections in response to readers' needs • Place a high value on core services in response to users' needs	• Deal with users promptly on the service counters • Improve the quality of learning space for users in the library premises	• Provide library collections and services that users need • Increase user satisfaction by improving the service delivery process

Table 4 shows the number of indicators suggested ranged from six to ten, with staff development emerging as the most prominent shared concern. As it was difficult to find *direct* input, process and output measures of the four abstract areas of evaluation (efficiency, effectiveness, sustainability and quality), surrogate or proxy measures that *indirectly* demonstrated the growth or decline of IAs were identified. The surrogate measures most often selected by the three libraries were:

Input measures

- Total costs of staff development, education and training
- Investments in knowledge-based infrastructure (e.g. database systems)

Process measures

- Number of team meetings arranged to enable knowledge exchange
- Frequency of staff satisfaction surveys
- Frequency of user satisfaction surveys and focus groups

Output measures

- Level of staff satisfaction
- Number of new quality management documents produced (e.g. best practices)
- Number of visits to the library and its website
- Number of suggestions from users

The use of Kaplan and Norton's (1996) BSC framework for the indicator development process is significant here as although a growing number of libraries are now adopting this approach, designing scorecards for their particular circumstances is still seen as a new challenge (Matthews, 2008) as library practitioners have not generally been good at developing indicators that connect their activities with organizational strategies (Ford, 2002). The internal focus of the libraries' approach to measurement, shown by their concentration on inputs, throughputs and outputs (but not outcomes or impacts) is consistent with the focus of the MERITUM (2002) and Danish guidelines (Denmark, 2003) on IC reporting, which are also based on scorecard methods.

The libraries' selection of efficiency, effectiveness and quality as key dimensions for monitoring and evaluation is in line with established practice in the sector. However, the Thai cases also emphasise sustainability or stability as a fourth key dimension, which arguably reflects the bureaucratic culture and hierarchical structure of the Thai HE sector and supports Kaarst-Brown *et al.*'s (2004) and Pors's (2008) claims that the stability associated with hierarchical cultures in libraries enables them to have efficient operations, easy control of daily tasks and secure financial support from their parent organizations.

6.4 Practicality of Indicators

The quantitative survey tested acceptability of the proposed indicators and measures with staff who would be expected to use them. Respondents were asked to rate the indicators and sample measures proposed for their particular library for understandability and importance, using a four-point Likert scale in each case (where 4 meant very easy to understand and 1 meant very difficult).

Overall, the indicators related to human assets were seen as easiest to understand and indicators relating to relationship assets ("sustainable cooperation", "social responsibility" and "promotion and marketing of library programmes") were among the lowest ratings; but none of the indicators was judged as difficult to understand, with only two out of the total set of 23 having mean scores below 3 (2.80 and 2.89).

The importance ratings also recorded high mean scores, with only one value below 3 ("social responsibility", recorded as 2.67 at the SW library). However, the ranking of similar indicators varied slightly across the sites, with staff loyalty and teamwork gaining the highest score (a maximum rating of 4.0) at library T and being ranked equal top at library K, while user satisfaction and prompt service were ranked above the staff-oriented indicators at SW library; but it must be noted that the differences here were minimal.

These findings need to be related to their organizational and operational context. Although the concept of IA evaluation was new to all the libraries, they all had established systems for evaluating library performance and the survey respondents had all been involved in this process. Harer and Cole (2005) emphasise the significance of library professionals' previous knowledge of PM in reaching a comprehensible set of indicators. The libraries thus had a 'culture of assessment', which encouraged staff to pay attention to the results they produced and how these would be perceived by stakeholders (Lakos and Phipps, 2004).

Another key factor which probably helped to make the indicators easy to understand was the deliberate use of words and phrases found in the libraries' existing strategy and quality documents or of terms used by the administrators in their interviews (such as 'user satisfaction surveys', 'staff development' and 'knowledge-sharing activities'). The importance of relating and mapping institutional use of language to the terms and categories of IA evaluation practice is stressed in published guidelines (MERITUM, 2002; Roberts, 2003; Thorleifsdottir and Claessen, 2006). Bukowitz and Williams (2003) argue that establishing these links helps to create a shared understanding and avoid confusion over meaning and nomenclature.

The nature of the survey sample is also significant here. The participants were all staff with operational line management roles, responsible for ensuring the quality of t services delivered in their areas, attending to the development of their team members' abilities as needed, but with little stakeholder interaction beyond their immediate clients. This may explain why indicators for evaluating human assets had high mean scores, while indicators designed to assess longer-term relationship assets (e.g. sustained collaboration, social responsibility) had lower scores.

Finally, the high importance ratings show that when indicators are directly tied to a library or other organisation's strategic intent they can be made more relevant to participants, as asserted by Franceschini *et al.* (2007: 8-9), 'Indicators and strategies are tightly and inevitably linked to each other. A strategy without indicators is useless; indicators without a strategy are meaningless.'

7. Conclusion

In a knowledge-based economy, libraries should consider the value of their knowledge resources as organizational assets enabling the development and provision of value-added products and services. Library practitioners need to extend their existing measurement systems to cover intangible resources, but they should move beyond the assessment of service quality to the evaluation of IAs.

The case study presented describes the successful application of intangible asset measurement using a mixed-methods approach in a real-world context. Models and tools devised by strategists and accountants for the corporate world offer a viable framework for developing IA indicators and corresponding performance measures related to the KSFs of library and information services. However, for this sector, the standard IC taxonomy needs to be expanded beyond human, structural and relationship assets to reflect the distinctive contribution of library collection and service assets and thus communicate their value to stakeholders.

The evidence from the case suggests that the proposed developmental model of IA indicators is compatible with the quality management systems operated by many library and information services and that there are broad similarities between the assets of different libraries, but with variations in the details and types of assets. The findings also suggest that identification of intangible resources may be facilitated by prior experience of service assessment and engagement with KM, and in addition that institutional culture and terminology have an influence on the implementation of PM. More generally, the investigation affirmed the importance of explicitly linking the evaluation of intangible knowledge resources to institutional strategic objectives.

Acknowledgements

The authors gratefully acknowledge the cooperation and contribution of the library staff at the universities that participated in this study. They are particularly indebted to the directors of the libraries for giving permission to conduct the fieldwork.

References

Abels, E.G, Cogdill, K.W and Zach, L. (2004) "Identifying and communicating the contributions of library and information services in hospitals and academic health sciences centers", *Journal of the Medical Library Association,* 92(1): 46–55.

Barney, J. (1991). "Firm resources and sustained competitive advantage". *Journal of Management,* 17(1), 99–120.

Barron, D.D. (1995) "Staffing rural public libraries: the need to invest in intellectual capital", *Library Trends* 44(1): 77–87.

Benbasat, I., Goldstein, D.K. and Mead, M. (1987) "The case research strategy in studies of information systems", *MIS Quarterly,* 11(3): 369–386.

Bontis, N., Dragonetti, N.C., Jacobsen, K. and Roos, G. (1999) "The knowledge toolbox: a review of the tools available to measure and manage intangible resources", *European Management Journal,* 17(4): 391–402.

Brophy, P. (1991) "The mission of the academic library", *British Journal of Academic Librarianship*, 6(3): 135-148.

Brophy, P. (2006) *Measuring Library Performance: Principles and Techniques.* London: Facet.

Bukowitz, W.R. and Williams, R.L. (2000). *The Knowledge Management Fieldbook.* rev. ed. London: Pearson Education.

Ceynowa, K. (2000) "Managing academic information provision with the balanced scorecard: a project of the German Research Association", *Performance Measurement and Metrics*, 1(3): 157–164.

Cotta-Schonberg, M. and Line, M.B. (1994) "Evaluation of academic libraries: with special reference to the Copenhagen Business School", *Journal of Librarianship and Information Science,* 26(2): 55–69.

Cribb, G. (2005) "Human resource development: impacting on all four perspectives of the balanced scorecard", *World Library and Information Congress: the 71th IFLA General Conference and Council, 14-18 August 2005, Oslo, Norway,* The Hague: International Federation of Library Associations and Institutions. http://www.ifla.org/IV/ifla71/papers/075e-Cribb.pdf

Cullen, R. (2006) "Operationalising the Focus/Values/Purpose Matrix: a tool for libraries to measure their ability to deliver service quality", *Performance Measurement and Metrics*, 7(2): 83–99.

Dakers, H. (1998) "Intellectual capital: auditing the people assets", *INSPEL,* 32(4): 234-242.

Denmark (2003) Ministry of Science Technology and Innovation. *Intellectual Capital Statements – The New Guideline*. Copenhagen: Danish Ministry of Science, Technology and Innovation.

Eisenhardt, K.M. (1989) "Building theories from case study research", *Academy of Management Review,* 14(4): 532–550.

Ford, G. (2002) "Strategic uses of evaluation and performance measurement", In: Stein, J., Kyrillidou, M. and Davis, D. (eds) *Proceedings of the 4th Northumbria International Conference on Performance Measurement in Libraries and Information Services, 12 to 16 August 2001, Pittsburgh, USA*, pp. 19–30. Washington, DC: Association of Research Libraries.

Franceschini, F., Galetto, M. and Maisano, D. (2007) *Management by Measurement: Designing Key Indicators and Performance Measurement Systems.* Berlin: Springer.

Green, A. (2007) "Intangible assets in plain business language", *VINE,* 37(3): 238–248.

Harer, J.B. and Cole, B.R. (2005) "The importance of the stakeholder in performance measurement: critical processes and performance measures for assessing and improving academic library services and programs", *College and Research Libraries*, 66(2): 149–170.

Huotari, M.-L. and Iivonen, M. (2005) "Knowledge processes: a strategic foundation for the partnership between the university and its library", *Library Management*, 26(6/7): 324–335.

Iivonen, M. and Huotari, M.-L. (2007) "The university library's intellectual capital", *Advances in Library Administration and Organization*, 25: 83-96.

Japan (2005) Ministry of Economy, Trade and Industry, *Guidelines for Disclosure of Intellectual Assets Based Management.* Tokyo: Japanese Ministry of Economy, Trade and Industry.

Kaarst-Brown, M.L., Nicholson, S., Stanton, H.M. and von Dran, G.M. (2004) "Organizational cultures of libraries as a strategic resource", *Library Trends,* 53(1): 33–53.

Kaplan, R.S. and Norton, D.P. (1996) *The Balanced Scorecard: Translating Strategy into Action.* Boston, MA: Harvard Business School Press.

Kaplan, R.S. and Norton, D.P. (2004) *Strategy Maps: Converting Intangible Assets into Tangible Outcomes.* Boston, MA: Harvard Business School Press.

King Research (1990) *Keys to Success: Performance Indicators for Public Libraries,* London: Office of Arts and Libraries.

Koenig, M.E.D. (1998) "From intellectual capital to knowledge management: what are they talking about?", *INSPEL,* 32(4): 222–233.

Lakos, A. and Phipps, S. (2004) "Creating a culture of assessment: a catalyst for organizational change", *Portal: Libraries and the Academy,* 4(3): 345–361.

Lithgow, S.D. and Hepworth, J.B. (1993) "Performance measurement in prison libraries: research methods, problems and perspectives", *Journal of Librarianship and Information Science,* 25(2): 61–69.

Marr, B. (2005) "Strategic management of intangible value drivers", *Handbook of Business Strategy,* 6(1): 147–154.

Marr, B. and Chatzkel, J. (2004) "Intellectual capital at the crossroads: managing, measuring, and reporting of IC", *Journal of Intellectual Capital*, 5(4): 224–229.

Marr, B. and Moustaghfir, K. (2005) "Defining intellectual capital: a three-dimensional approach", *Management Decision,* 43(9): 1114–1128.

Marr, B., Schiuma, G. and Neely, A. (2002) "Assessing strategic knowledge assets in e-business", *International Journal of Business Performance Management,* 4(2/3/4): 279–295.

Matthews, J.R. (2008) *Scorecards for Results: a Guide for Developing a Library Balanced Scorecard.* Westport, CT: Libraries Unlimited.

MERITUM (2002) *Guidelines for Managing and Reporting on Intangibles (Intellectual Capital Report).* Brussels: European Commission, Measuring Intangibles to Understand and Improve Innovation Management Project.

Meso, P. and Smith, R. (2000) "A resource-based view of organizational knowledge management systems", *Journal of Knowledge Management,* 4(3): 224–234.

Mouritsen, J., Bukh, P.N. and Marr, B. (2004) "Reporting on intellectual capital: why, what and how?", *Measuring Business Excellence*, 8(1): 46–54.

OECD (1999) *The OECD International Symposium on Measuring and Reporting Intellectual Capital: Experiences, Issues, and Prospects.* Amsterdam: Organisation for Economic Co-operation and Development.

OECD (2006) *Intellectual Assets and Value Creation: Implications for Corporate Reporting.* Paris: Organisation for Economic Co-operation and Development, Directorate for Financial and Enterprise Affairs, Corporate Affairs Division.

Petty, R. and Guthrie, J. (2000) "Intellectual capital literature review: measurement, reporting and management", *Journal of Intellectual Capital,* 1(2): 155–176.

Pierce, J.B. and Snyder, H. (2003) "Measuring intellectual capital: a valuation strategy for library and information centers", *Library Administration and Management,* 17(1): 28–32.

Pors, N.O. (2008) "Management tools, organizational culture and leadership: an explorative study", *Performance Measurement and Metrics*, 9(2): 138–152.

Pors, N.O., Dixon, P. and Robson, H. (2004) "The employment of quality measures in libraries: cultural differences, institutional imperatives and managerial profiles", *Performance Measurement and Metrics,* 5(1): 20–27.

Probst, G., Raub, S. and Romhardt, K. (2000) *Managing Knowledge: Building Blocks for Success*. Chichester: John Wiley & Sons.

Roberts, H. (2003) "Rules of thumb in building indicators for knowledge transfer and how to use these indicators", In: *How to Develop and Monitor Your Company's Intellectual Capital: Tools and Actions for the Competency-Based Organisation*, pp. 26–29. Oslo: Nordic Industrial Fund, The Frame Project.

Rowley, J. (2005) "Making sense of the quality maze: perspectives for public and academic libraries", *Library Management*, 26(8/9): 508–518.

Rylander, A., Jacobsen, K. and Roos, G. (2000) "Towards improved information disclosure on intellectual capital", *International Journal of Technology Management,* 20(5/6/7/8): 715–741.

Saracevic, T. and Kantor, P.B. (1997) "Studying the value of library and information services, Part 1: Establishing a theoretical framework", *Journal of the American Society for Information Science,* 48(6): 527–542.

Self, J. (2003) "From values to metrics: implementation of the balanced scorecard at a university library", *Performance Measurement and Metrics*, 4(2): 57–63.

Shulver, M., Lawrie, G., Andersen, H. and Cobbold, I. (2000) *The Soft Side of the Balanced Scorecard: Developing Strategically Relevant Measures of Intellectual Capital*, 2GC Working Paper. Maidenhead: 2GC Ltd.
http://www.2gc.co.uk/pdf/2GC-WP-Intellectual-Capital-090311.pdf

Stewart, T.A. (1997) *Intellectual Capital: the New Wealth of Organizations.* London: Nicholas Brealey.

Sveiby, K.E. (2001) "A knowledge-based theory of the firm to guide in strategy formulation", *Journal of Intellectual Capital,* 2(4): 344–358.

Tashakkori, A. and Teddlie, C. (2003) *Handbook of Mixed Methods in Social and Behavioral Research*, Thousand Oaks, CA: Sage.

Thorleifsdottir, A. and Claessen, E. (2006) *Nordic Harmonized Knowledge Indicators: Putting IC into Practice*. Oslo: Nordic Innovation Centre.

Townley, C.T. (2001) "Knowledge management and academic libraries", *College and Research Libraries*, 62(1): 44–55.

Van Deventer, M.J. (2002) *Introducing Intellectual Capital Management in an Information Support Services Environment*. PhD, University of Pretoria.

Wang, H. (2006) "From 'user' to 'customer': TQM in academic libraries?", *Library Management*, 27(9): 606–620.

White, L.N. (2007) "Unseen measures: the need to account for intangibles", *The Bottom Line: Managing Library Finances*, 20(2): 77–84.

White, T. (2004) "Knowledge management in an academic library case study: KM within Oxford University Library Services (OULS)", *World Library and Information Congress: the 70th IFLA General Conference and Council, 22-27 August 2004, Buenos Aires, Argentina*. The Hague: International Federation of Library Associations and Institutions. http://www.ifla.org/IV/ifla70/papers/089e-White.pdf

Yin, R.K. (2003). *Case Study Research: Design and Methods*. 3rd ed. Thousand Oaks, CA: Sage.

FROM FOR-PROFIT ORGANIZATIONS TO NON-PROFIT ORGANIZATIONS: THE DEVELOPMENT OF KNOWLEDGE MANAGEMENT IN A PUBLIC LIBRARY

KRISTEN HOLM

School of Library and Information Studies, University of Alberta,
3-20 Rutherford South, Edmonton, AB, T6G 2J4, Canada
E-mail: kristen.holm@gmail.com

KELLY KIRKPATRICK[†] and DINESH RATHI*

School of Library and Information Studies, University of Alberta,
3-20 Rutherford South, Edmonton, AB, T6G 2J4, Canada
[†]*E-mail: kellykirkpatrick_00@yahoo.ca* * *E-mail: drathi@ualberta.ca*

This paper explores the issue of managing knowledge within a medium sized public library, and how knowledge management (KM) principles, often practiced in corporate environments can be effective within non-profit organizations. The study investigates how organizational structure and culture as well as knowledge exchange strategies within a library setting promote the practice of KM. In addition, the paper also identifies a technological gap in the organization's current strategies and recommends an Intranet based solution to augment current knowledge sharing practices. This study seeks to contribute to the body of research related to the practice of KM within the library domain, identify successful knowledge sharing initiatives already in practice as well as propose a low cost IT based solution with the potential to enhance the practice of KM within libraries.

1. Introduction

Within today's competitive business environment, managing knowledge is important for both For-Profit Organizations (FPOs) and Non-Profit Organizations (NPO). To date, much of the knowledge management (KM) research has focused on FPOs and there are a limited number of studies related to NPOs, especially public libraries. This paper seeks to contribute to the advancement of research related to KM in public libraries through the presentation of formal and informal knowledge sharing strategies used in a specific library. As well, the paper endeavors to provide a deeper understanding of the current state of KM within NPOs and develop a base for other libraries to begin learning, adopting and deploying KM. Additionally this paper aims to identify Web 2.0 based tools with the potential to augment current knowledge sharing practices in NPOs.

According to Jantz (2001), there is a strong similarity between FPOs and NPOs, such as public libraries. Like FPOs which seek to disseminate their products and services to customers in an effective and efficient manner, public libraries attempt to disseminate information and knowledge to the communities that they serve. Commonalities between public libraries and FPOs include competition, operating budgets, organizational structures, strategic planning, product procurement and customer service. In order to maximize efficiency and success within the domains listed above FPOs have developed KM techniques and strategies. Large FPOs such as Dow Chemicals, Texas Instruments, Buckman Laboratories and Xerox have successfully deployed KM as a strategic tool used to maximize competitive advantage and cost savings as well as enhance productivity, staff morale and customer satisfaction (Chua and Goh, 2008).

As mentioned above, libraries strive to provide the community with as much access to information as possible. This is reflected in the International Federation of Library Associations' (IFLA) "Public Library Manifesto" (2004), which advises that libraries are to, "be organized effectively and [that] professional standards of operation must be maintained". While librarians continue to ensure that they provide exceptional service to their communities, behind the scenes KM is often neglected. To date, KM has scarcely been employed within library settings to enhance internal procedures. Considering the similarities between the day-to-day operations of NPOs and FPOs, Teng and Hawamdeh (2002) note that government organizations and libraries have the potential to benefit from a KM program as practiced in private industry. Furthermore, librarians' understanding of information systems makes them well equipped to develop effective KM strategies.

This paper explores the current state of KM and the strategies adopted to manage knowledge in a specific public library. It also examines how some of the KM concepts successfully applied within FPOs run parallel to practices occurring in NPOs. Based on the findings, this paper recommends possible tools and techniques to augment the current systems, as well as strategies for knowledge sharing.

The following section will provide a literature overview of KM within NPOs and Libraries. It will be followed by a discussion of the study's methodology, and then will present findings which lead to recommendations and a discussion. Finally this paper closes with conclusions and acknowledgements.

2. KM, Non-Profit Organizations and Libraries: An Overview

KM is "an approach to adding or creating value by more actively leveraging the know-how, experience, and judgment" that is present within an organization (Ruggles, 1998). Through KM organizations are attempting to tap into their knowledge base to "harness their internal processes and resources" (Nonaka, 1994) and create value for the organization (Dalkir, 2005). The majority of KM frameworks concentrate on the concept of knowledge as tacit and explicit (Nonaka, 1994). Today, the amount of knowledge circulating and freely available within society is growing at an unprecedented rate (Owen, 1999; Lee and Hong, 2002). Considering the complex nature and value of knowledge, KM continues to gain momentum as an important tool within modern businesses and organizations (Owen, 1999; Quaddus and Xu, 2005: Nonaka, 1994) and not surprisingly the KM literature has strong links to business and the private sector (Yi, 2008; Chua and Goh, 2008).

Recently there has been a focus on exploring the use and adoption of KM principles developed within FPOs and applying them in small NGOs (Lemieux and Dalkir, 2006; Gregory and Rathi, 2008) and NPOs including both public and academic libraries (Jantz, 2001; Teng and Hawamdeh, 2002; Mphidi and Snyman, 2004; Parirokh et al., 2008). Although many scholars have recognized the benefits of adopting KM and have highlighted the similarities between libraries and FPOs in many respects, few attempts have been made to design and implement KM in libraries (Jantz, 2001). A similar notion also emerges from the findings of a survey done by Yi (2008), which states that the practice and benefits of KM are *"...stressed more often in academia and used less often in libraries"*.

Recently, studies related to the use of KM within libraries have begun to emerge. Sarrafzadeh et al. (2006) and Yi (2008) present their survey results to gauge both librarians' and graduate students' perceptions of the practice of KM. Their studies reveal that librarians understand the concept of KM and its potential to improve processes within the library. Sarrafzadeh's et al state, *"knowledge management offers potential benefits for the development of libraries and the LIS profession itself"* (2006). Jain (2007) focuses on identifying the KM principles being adopted by employees within academic libraries in Africa. Jantz (2001) looks at the implementation of KM within reference services, and Mphidi and Snyman (2004) and Skok and Kalmanovitch, (2005) explore the use of Intranet based KM technologies in libraries and a NPO respectively. With this in mind, it becomes apparent that the potential use of KM within a library setting is beginning to be recognized by the library community.

3. The Study

This study was conducted in a medium sized public library in Alberta, Canada. For the purposes of this study a medium sized public library can be defined as being a singular organization, not part of a larger branch system, serving a population over 10,000 people. This particular library currently has one location and serves a bedroom community with a population of nearly 60,000 people. One of the biggest challenges facing this library is the community's growing population. As the population continues to grow, the library will have to start thinking about expanding their facilities.

3.1. *Knowledge Audit of the Public Library*

The first step in understanding the current state of KM within an organization is to conduct a knowledge audit (Liebowitz, et al. 2000). The knowledge audit is defined as *"a method of reviewing and mapping knowledge in an organization including an analysis of knowledge needs, resources, flows, gaps, users and uses"* (National Health Service, 2006). Different tools and techniques such as questionnaires, walkthroughs, flowcharts and interviews (Liebowitz, et al. 2000) are used to conduct knowledge audits within an organization. The knowledge audit is helpful in understanding not only the current state of KM in an organization but also employees' knowledge needs and the gaps that exist in the current system.

This particular audit was conducted through face-to-face interviews using open ended question as a guiding instrument, and a similar approach was used by Gregory and Rathi (2008) in their study of a small NGO. This study made use of email as a recruitment tool. The library director sent a message drafted by the researchers to all library staff members. The recruitment email was sent through the library director for two reasons. First, the researchers wanted to formalize the relationship with the library by involving management in the proposed research. Second, the researchers had limited access to the contact details of individual staff members. The recruitment email contained an information letter and a disclosure of voluntary participation by the staff in the proposed research. The staff recruitment criterion was open to ensure voluntary participation and the researchers choose participants from different departments and positions to ensure diverse perceptions and a well rounded picture of the organization.

The researchers completed exploratory qualitative interviews with five employees but only four were included in the analysis. The fifth one was omitted due to a technical problem. The length of the interview sessions varied between half an hour and one hour. The questions were developed as a guide for the researchers and in the interview process participants were given the freedom to direct discussion and encouraged to discuss topics in detail. This helped the participant to have "*some latitude to answer in their own way*" and gave the interviewer an opportunity to "*probe for more information in promising areas*" (Streatfield, 2000). The guiding questions were divided into four different thematic areas including: establishing an organizational overview, understanding the knowledge needs unique to the participant's role, formal knowledge sharing strategies and informal knowledge sharing strategies.

4. Findings of the Study

The data was collected and analyzed, and the findings from the study are entwined with the KM strategies and concepts reflected in the literature on KM in FPOs. Thus, manifesting the KM concepts identified and deployed within FPOs run parallel to practices occurring in a NPO. The results have been organized into four main themes. These include organizational structure and culture, formal knowledge exchange strategies, informal knowledge exchange strategies and technologies currently used to manage knowledge. Based on these emerging themes an Intranet based KM framework has been proposed to manage knowledge at all levels of the organization.

4.1. *Organizational Structure and Culture*

According to McDermott and O'Dell (2001) knowledge networks in FPOs often develop informally as people seek out the information that they need to complete their jobs. These networks become increasingly successful as people make use of the expertise of colleagues working outside of their core team (McDermott and O'Dell, 2001). The interview process revealed that the Library's employees are familiar with the organization's structure and that communication across department lines occurs. This was reflected from the fact that employees were able to identify knowledge resources in other departments. Table 1 shows an overview of the organizational structure developed by the researchers and represents different tasks carried out by each department in the library. These tasks were identified by the participants in their interviews reflecting that the employees consistently understand the responsibilities of their colleagues working in other areas.

Interviews further revealed that communication across department lines often occurs as employees become more embedded within the organization through the development of personal networks. This was exemplified in the experience of one of the interviewees who in reflecting on sharing knowledge across department lines, notes that "Sharing information in other ways has arisen more as I have gotten to know people in other departments... it is almost like if you were [isolated within your department] and that is all that you do than there is less information available." For this participant, having a deeper understanding of the context of the organization is crucial in fulfilling their information needs.

McDermott and O'Dell (2001) also note that it is critical for knowledge sharing to be supported by management and directly embedded into a FPOs corporate culture for knowledge networks to thrive and develop. Considering the nature of library work and its emphasis on making information accessible, it is no surprise that another participant identified colleagues working across department lines as a valuable source of knowledge. The participant notes that, "I don't think [sharing knowledge] happens naturally, but is instead something that has to be established within the organization first... I would want to feel free to wonder down and ask people across departments. Talk to people and ask anyone. That's why I think there is so much sharing of informal information within this particular library".

Table 1: Organization Overview

Administration: - Budget preparation - Human resources - Working with library board - Liaison work outside library - Public relations - Policy implementation - Strategic planning	**Public Services:** - Adult's and Children's services o Preference o Programming o Collection management o Customer relations o Weeding o Assistive technology - Resource center
Technical Services: - Information Technology (IT) o Implementation o Maintenance o Support - Material processing and ordering - Cataloguing	**Circulation:** - Checking material in/out - Fundraising - Re-shelving books - Memberships - Customer service - Management of volunteers

4.2. *Formal Knowledge Exchange Strategies*

Further analysis also reveals that the library has several channels that facilitate formal knowledge exchanges. Hansen et al. (1999) describe the formal exchange of knowledge within FPOs as the transfer from "people to document". Through this process Hansen et al. (1999) note that knowledge is "*...extracted from the person who developed it, made independent of that person, and reused for various purposes.*" These formal channels include meetings, knowledge exchange through training and development, documentation and conference participation and publications (Hansen et al., 1999; Earl, 2001; Spencer, 2003) and are discussed in following sub-sections.

Meetings: Within this public library meetings were frequently mentioned as an arena for formal knowledge exchanges. These meetings allowed individuals working in different roles and departments to share and acquire knowledge. Reflecting on department head meetings held every couple of weeks, one participant stated, "We meet regularly to share information and make decisions on things that have to be done." The key elements of these meetings were formally documented and the library has a policy to share both formally (in meeting minutes) and informally (email). Through the organization of these meetings, the library has developed a cross-departmental committee system, similar to cross-functional teams in FPOs (Rathi, et al, 2008) and provides an important avenue for problem solving across department lines. Once meetings are completed, the attendees share details with their colleagues and are responsible for disseminating newly acquired knowledge. The employees who were not present at the meeting can use the newly generated knowledge in guiding their professional decisions.

Training and Development: Within the library training and development is considered an important channel of formal knowledge exchange. The library encourages employees to enhance their knowledge base through training and professional development. This is accomplished through in-house and external training organized by library employees as well as vendors. Within the library, employee Web 2.0 training occurred and was well received by participants. One participant stated, "...[this was] probably [the program] that stands out the most because it was not specific to department, it was for everyone." The library encourages its staff to engage in external training such as partaking in a reference courses. One manager asserts, "We have asked that anybody who is working on the reference desk...have a library tech diploma or a library science master's degree or that they at least take [a reference course] to make sure that they have some basic knowledge when they are out there on the desk".

Conference Participation: Within this organization conferences are perceived as an important avenue for formally acquiring new knowledge and the library encourages its employees to participate. One manager noted, "I go to a few conferences a year" Another reflected, "I was sent [to a conference] and that was something that definitely enhanced my knowledge."

Documentation and Publications: In KM, both codified internal and external documents play an important role in knowledge exchange. The library encourages employees to codify both organizational and individual knowledge resources.

Formal documentation of mission statements, policies, procedures and goals of the library represent the largest and most prominent group of vital documents. The library has codified a large number of documents including library board meeting minutes, budget reports, strategic planning documents, statistical information, policy and procedures manuals, job descriptions, memos and meeting minutes. These documents work on two levels. These documents are central to running the library and maintaining a sense of credibility and accountability to stakeholders.

Less formal documents created by individual employees enable staff to effectively complete their responsibilities. Keeping a record of previously completed tasks, especially related to important projects, ensures that employees have quick access to historical data and are able to learn from the past. One of the participant said, "...I try to keep a record of every program I have ever done so I can go back and see, and find what books I used, find the author, and find the exact title. It might be something that I want to use".

External Resource Sharing: Employees often use external resources such as published works to make informed decisions. One manager claimed, "I can't make a decision in a vacuum." The participant makes extensive use of external publications and listserves to gather pertinent information. The acquired documents are then often shared and discussed with colleagues.

4.3. *Informal Knowledge Exchange Strategies*

Within FPOs informal knowledge exchanges play a crucial role in meeting the knowledge needs in an organization (McDermott and O'Dell 2001). Informal exchange strategies often focus on human interactions and tacit form of knowledge (Nonaka 1994). Some of the informal knowledge exchange strategies adopted by this library include networking, mentoring, (Hansen, 2002; Swart and Kinnie, 2003) reliance on sharing expertise and personal experience.

Networking: Networking contributes to the informal knowledge exchange process. Two interesting themes of sharing knowledge through networks emerged in the interviews. Networking at conferences provides an environment for formal knowledge exchanges among participants and an avenue for networking with colleagues working in other libraries. This was highlighted by an employee who states, "...something that definitely enhanced my knowledge was just talking to some of the people at the conference ... you just start interacting with people in an informal way." The networks created at the conferences provide an avenue for the continued sharing of ideas with the wider library community.

Mentoring: Human interaction through mentoring was effectively used in the library in knowledge exchanges. Mentoring plays a crucial role within this library because it ensures that tacit knowledge gained by senior employees through years of experience is transmitted to other employees. One of the managers endorsed this concept and said, "I am trying to train one of my staff members to be a backup to me because I feel that I have so much knowledge that is not written down that I need to show it to somebody else." At the same time employees also feel that they have much to gain from the mentorship. One participant said, "I get informal training from certain staff members in the library" and "a lot of them have been around for ten or more years, so I get such a huge base of knowledge to pick through."

Sharing Personal Experiences and Expertise: Sharing day-to-day experiences with colleagues contributes to the acquisition of job related knowledge. This is highlighted by one employee who states, "The other way I acquire [knowledge] is just through experiences I have in the library. When I am dealing with someone in a particular area, I may notice something that I had not noticed before in terms of resources that we have". The employees share their personal experiences with colleagues through free time discussion. This helps their coworkers advance their knowledge and expertise.

The use of employee expertise was found to be vital in accomplishing tasks. One of the participant stated, "I am not an expert on either [acquisition and cataloguing] so I rely on individuals in my department who have the expertise to explain that to me," and "when it comes to the technologies side I rely 90% on my technician who has the technical knowledge to keep me apprised of situations". No single person can possess all the necessary knowledge to complete their job and employees rely on the network of experts in different domains to accomplish tasks. Thus these networks facilitate pooling of critical knowledge from different domains without being part of any formal network such as committee work or membership in a cross-function team.

5. Recommendations and Discussions

The following recommendations are based on the findings from the knowledge audit process. The audit revealed that part-time employees were on the edge of the information exchange within the library. Information was shared on a day-to-day basis which often led to the exclusion of part-time employees. In addition, formal documents were not centrally stored and this created problems in accessibility. Also, email was the most prevalent mode of knowledge exchange using technology. This limited the online social discourse among employees by excluding those not directly included in the email.

Currently, the library uses technologies such as email, listservs and blogs to manage knowledge within the organization. Email was mentioned abundantly throughout all the interviews and comprised nearly half of the references made to technology use. Reliance on email was more prevalent among newer staff member who had not yet had the opportunity to forge relationships with other coworkers. One of the interviewees reflects, "...at first [communication] was through email. This is something that was standard even though I was part-time. Sharing information in other ways have risen more as I have gotten to know people in other departments". In addition to email, sporadic use of technologies such as external blogs and listservs was reported. Use of these technologies was the result of personal preference and not due to organizational support.

To date, the library employs many non technical strategies in managing their knowledge. The implementation of a technology based system could facilitate a more efficient and effective knowledge exchange process (Marwick, 2001; Alavi and Leidner, 2001). The library has Information Technology (IT) infrastructure, to support their current operations, which could be utilized to build technology based KM system.

It is therefore recommended that a low cost intranet based technological solution is proposed to the library. Mphidi and Snyman (2004) defined Intranet as "*an network that uses internet concepts and technologies within an organization in order to be accessed by employees to share knowledge*". The benefits of the implementation of an intranet-based system include consistency, centralization, interactivity and better communication (Skok and Kalmanovitch, 2005). Through the development of an Intranet-based system information can be centralized, and therefore easily accessed. Using the Intranet as a backbone, it is recommended that Web 2.0 tools are incorporated in the system. The proposed Web 2.0 tools would provide a channel for more informal knowledge exchanges (Avram, 2006) among employees, both full time and part time.

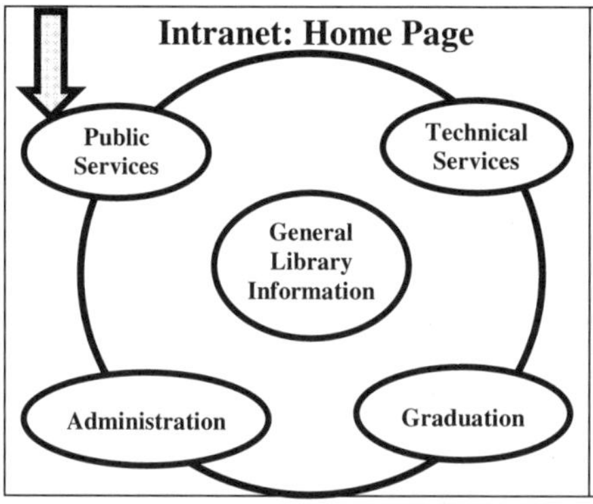

Fig. 1: Overview of Intranet-based KM

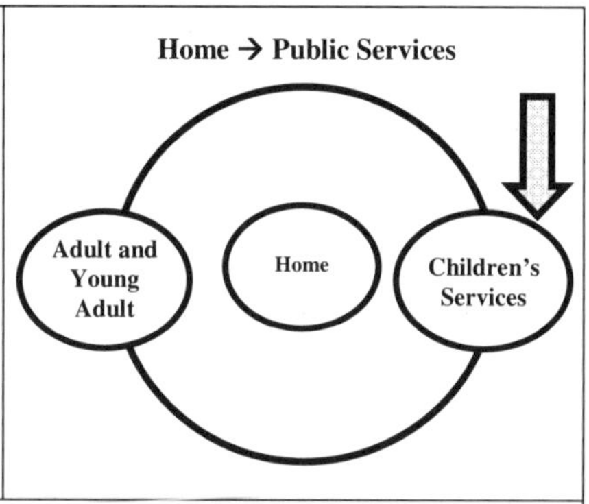

Fig. 2: Public Service Page (Second Level)

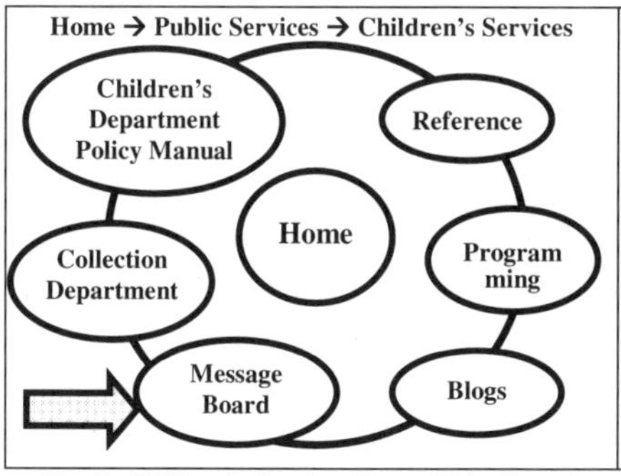

Fig. 3: Children's Services Page (Third Level)

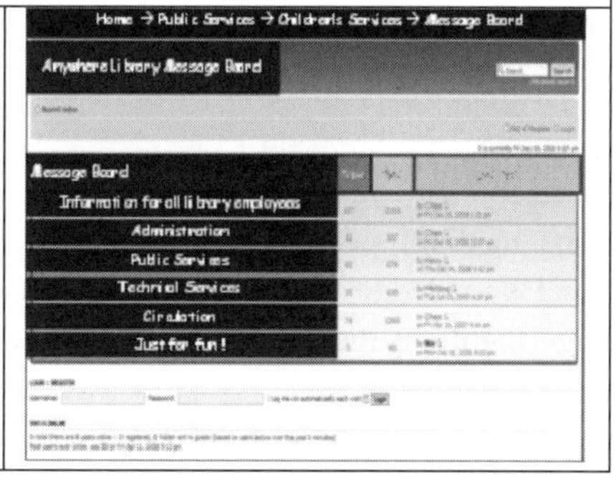

Fig. 4: Message Board

Figures 1 to 4 present screenshots of a conceptual prototype for an Intranet-based system that would address the needs of this organization. The arrow in Figure 1 to 3 symbolized the click i.e., by clicking on *Public Services* in Figure 1 will lead to screenshot as shown in Figure 2 and so on. The prototype is designed based on both the structure of the organization and the specific tasks in different departments. One of the key considerations in designing the system was to develop a usable and clean interface to ensure users do not feel overwhelmed (Nielsen, 2000). Through out the four layers the use of adequate white space, consistent page layout, a recognizable "home" button and a bread crumb trail (e.g., Home → Public Services) adheres to usability design principles. Figure 1 includes the four departments within the library and a universal space for all employees. Figure 2, shows the second level of the proposed system for "Public Services". This is divided into two categories with adult services on one side and children's services on the other. Figure 3 shows different section of the proposed KM system in Children's Services and these including Web 2.0 technologies to facilitate formal and informal knowledge sharing among employees. The Web 2.0 technologies, including a message board, a wiki and blogs, have been identified by Avram (2006) as tools for KM. Figure 4 delves deeper into the Web 2.0 message board to facilitate discussion among employees as well as with library patrons. Towards meeting these Web 2.0 requirements, specific technologies have been proposed. The following Open source software (OSS) products are recommended with library budget constraints in mind:

- Bushtail intranet software: Developed specifically for public libraries and it contains several of the features that have proposed in our prototype including room bookings, calendars, scheduling needs and message board space
- Word Press: This common blogging software is tried and tested, easy to use and secure. Highly popular, this technology can be used by people with little knowledge of html and technology in general.
- PM Wiki: Described as "one of the best wikis available" (opensourcecms.com), this tool is customizable, powerful, and easy to use.
- phpBB: According to their website "phpBB is the most widely used forum on the World Wide Web" (phpBB.com). Due to its popularity there are numerous amounts of community support available online. In addition to being well used this software also is incredible easy to install and maintain.

6. Conclusion and Future Work

The medium sized public library in this study employs a variety of formal and informal knowledge exchange strategies to meet their functional goals. However, the findings highlight the lack of a centralized technological support system. With this in mind, an Intranet based system was proposed to augment current strategies and encourage participation of both full time and part time employees. The proposed system takes into account employees' roles and responsibilities and the organizational structure and culture. An interesting finding was that many of the strategies used in FPOs to manage knowledge run parallel to strategies used within this organization. This supports Teng and Hawamdeh's (2002) argument that key KM concepts used in the private sector have the potential to benefit NPOs. The findings of this study could help a large number of NPOs, including libraries, which are in the process of planning, adopting or implementing KM in their organization.

There is much potential for further studies in this area which could include increasing the sample size within this organization for better saturation of themes, implementation and evaluation of the proposed Intranet based system, and extension of the study to more number of libraries including both public and academic libraries to generalize the identified themes and to compare the knowledge needs in different types of libraries. We believe this work would help in developing a prototype KM system for public libraries.

7. Acknowledgments

The authors would like thank the management and the employees of the public library for giving them an opportunity to carry out the study. Without their active support and contribution this study would not have been possible.

References

Alavi, A., and Leidner, D. (2001) "Review: Knowledge Management and Knowledge Management Systems: Conceptual Foundations and Research Issues", *MIS Quarterly*, 25(1): 107-136.

Avram, G. (2006) "At the crossroads of knowledge management and social software", *The Electronic Journal of Knowledge Management,* 4(1): 1-10.

Chua, A. Y. K. and Goh, D. H. (2008) "Untying the Knot of Knowledge Management Measurement: A Study of Six Public Service Agencies in Singapore", *Journal of Information Science*, 34(3):259-274.

Dalkir, K. (2005) "*Knowledge Management in Theory and Practice*", Oxford: Elsevier Butterworth-Heinemann, 2005.

Earl, M. (2001) "Knowledge Management Strategies: Toward a Taxonomy", *Journal of Management Information Systems*, 18(1): 215–223.

Gregory, A. and Rathi, D. (2008) "Open Source Tools for Managing Knowledge in a Small Non-Profit Organization", International Conference on Knowledge Management (ICKM).

Hansen, M. T. (2002) "Knowledge Networks: Explaining Effective Knowledge Sharing in Multiunit Companies", *Organization Science*, 13(3): 232-248.

Hansen, M. T., Nohria, N. and Kiemey, T. (1999) "What's Your Strategy for Managing Knowledge?", *Harvard Business Review*, 106-116.

IFLA (2004) "Public Library Manifesto", Accessed, December 6, 2008, from, http://www.ifla.org/VII/unesco/eng.htm.

Jain, P. (2007) "An Empirical Study of Knowledge Management in Academic Libraries in East and Southern Africa", *Library Review*, 56(5): 377-392.

Jantz, R. (2001) "Knowledge Management in Academic Libraries: Special Tools and Processes to Support Information Processing", *Reference Services Review*, 29(1): 33-39.

Lee, S. M. and Hong, S. (2002) "An Enterprise Wide Knowledge Management System Infrastructure", *Industrial Management and Data Systems*, 102(1): 17-25.

Liebowitz, J., Rubenstein-Montano, B., McCaw, D., Buchwalter, J., Browning, C., Newman, B., Rebeck, K. and the Knowledge Management Methodology Team (2000) "The Knowledge Audit", *Knowledge and Process Management*, 7(1): 3-10.

Lemieux, S. A. and Dalkir, K. (2006) "The Case of a Nonprofit ARTISTIC Organization", *Information Outlook*, 10(1): 13-16.

Marwick, A. D. (2001) Knowledge Management Technology, *IBM Systems Journal*, 40(4): 814-830.

McDermott, R and O'Dell, C. (2001) "Overcoming Cultural Barriers to Sharing Knowledge", *Journal of Knowledge Management*, 5(1): 76-85.

Mphidi, H. and Snyman, R.. (2004) "The Utilization of an Intranet as a Knowledge Management Tool in Academic Libraries", *The Electronic Library*, 22(5): 393-400.

Nanoka, I. A (1994) "Dynamic Theory of Organizational Knowledge Creation", *Organization Science*, 5(1): 14-37.

National Health Service, UK. (2006) "Definition of Knowledge", Accessed Nov. 7, 2008, from, www.library.nhs.uk/knowledgemanagement/Page.aspx?pagename=GLOSSARY

National Health Service, UK. (2004) "Definition of Knowledge Audit", Accessed Nov. 7, 2008, from, www.library.nhs.uk/knowledgemanagement.

Nielsen, J. (2000) "*Designing Web Usability: The Practice of Simplicity*", Indianapolis, IN: New Riders Publisher.

Owen, J. M. (1999) "Knowledge Management and the Information Professional", *Information Services and Use*, 19: 7-16.

Parirokh, M., Daneshgr, F. and Fattahi, R. (2008) "Identifying Knowledge Sharing Requirements in Academic Libraries" *Library Review*, 57(2): 107-122.

Quaddus, M. and Xu, J. (2005) "Adoption and Diffusion of Knowledge Management Systems: Field Studies of Factors and Variables", *Knowledge Based Systems*, 18:107-115.

Rathi, D., Twidale, M. B., Singh, V. and Bisen, A. (2008) "Users = Designers: A Participatory Approach in Designing Knowledge Management System", International Conference on Knowledge Management (ICKM).

Sarrafzadeh, M., Martin, B. and Hazeri, A. (2006) "LIS Professionals and Knowledge Management: Some Recent Perspectives" *Library Management*, 27 (9): 621-635.

Skok, W. and Kalmanovitch, C. (2005) "Evaluating the Role and Effectiveness of an Intranet in Facilitating Knowledge Management: A Case Study at Surrey County Council", *Information and Management*, 42(5): 731-744.

Spencer, J.W. (2003) "Firms' Knowledge-Sharing Strategies in the Global Innovation System: Empirical Evidence from the Flat Panel Display Industry", *Strategic Management Journal*, 24(3): 217–233.

Streatfield, D. (2000) "Ask if you don't know... The Research Interview", Retrieved, 25 February 2008, from, http://www.informat.org/notea04.html.

Swart, J. and Kinnie, N. (2003) "Sharing Knowledge in Knowledge-Intensive Firms, Human Resource", *Management Journal*, 13(2): 60-75.

Teng, S. and Hawamdeh, S. (2002) "Knowledge Management in Public Libraries" *Aslib Proceedings*, 54(3): 188-197.

Yi, Z. (2008) "Knowledge Management for Library Strategic Planning: Perceptions of Applications and Benefits", *Library Management*, 29(3): 229-240.

NETWORK STRUCTURE, STRUCTURAL EQUIVALENCE AND GROUP PERFORMANCE: A SIMULATION RESEARCH ON KNOWLEDGE PROCESS

HUA ZHANG*

School of Management, Xi'an Jiaotong University, 28 Xianning West Road, Xi'an, 710049, China
E-mail: zhang_hua@live.cn

YOUMIN XI

Xi'an Jiaotong-Liverpool University
Suzhou, 215123, China y
E-mail: ymxi@xjtu.edu.cn

According to the trade-off between information diffusion and diversity in an efficient network, we extend Lazer's simulation model on parallel problem solving by adding partner selection strategy: structurally equivalent imitation. In this way we can examine how the interaction of network structure with agent behavior affects the knowledge process and finally influence group performance. Our simulation experiment suggests that when agents adopt structure equivalence imitation the whole organization implicitly would be divided into independent sub-groups which converge on the different performance level and lead the whole group to a lower performance level.

Keyword: network structure, structural equivalence, agent behavior, group performance

1. Introduction

According to the different definition on social capital, there is still controversy over the optimal structure of that over the relative benefits of brokerage network and cohesive network structure. The former refers to a particular network which occupies the sole intermediate position between others who are disconnected and can interact only through the broker; the latter refers to the situation in which all the members are connected each other. Proponents of brokerage argue for the benefits of unique information which is the valuable resource of innovation; proponents of cohesive network argue for the benefits of efficient information diffusion and normal trust which promotes cooperation (Coleman 1988; Burt 2004).

Research on this social capital debate has often focused on these two types of network affects without considering the network content. Next to structure, the network literature has recently showed increased attention for the influence of the content conveyed through ties on resource acquisition (Rodan et al 2004; Fleming et al 2007) and the individual's strategic orientation (Obstfeld 2005).

Prior studies highly illuminate the passive role of network in adjusting the knowledge process in organization but neglect the active role that individual can play in keeping individual heterogeneity and linking to the different others. Without considering

* Work supported by National Nature Science Foundation of China (70121001 and 70772109)

network content variables some plausible conclusions deduced from the above studies would be argued: dose diversity can always lead to a high performance level? How the interaction of network structure with agent behavior affects group performance? To address these questions and extend what has been, until now, peripheral attention to actor's behavior strategy in exploration-exploitation literature. This paper focuses on the individual behavior, beginning with the assumption that advice network structure is a factor but not the only factor accounting for knowledge process. We contribute to a greater clarity and better understanding of how agent's partner selection affects the knowledge process and finally lead to different performance level. By considering the agent's behavior we can also explore how the interaction of network with agent behavior affects the group performance.

2. Literature review and concept model

Inherent to the social capital debate is a paradoxical trade-off between cohesive networks promoting cooperation and information diffusion efficiency and sparse networks flexible to heterogeneous knowledge and ideas. Since we cannot simultaneously maximize both facets of a network, this reflects a sharp trade-off between information diffusion and diversity in an efficient network (figure 1).

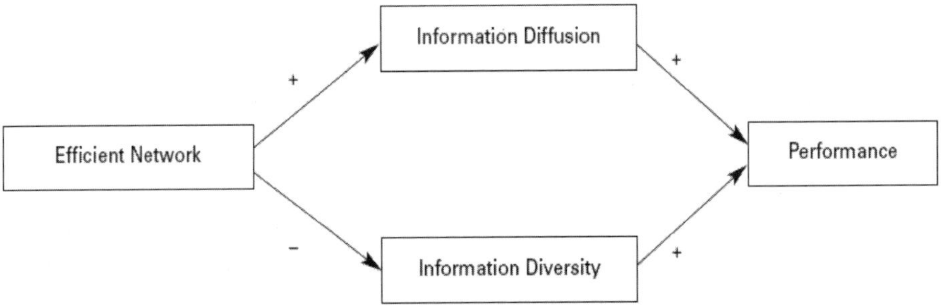

Figure 1: The trade-off between information diffusion and diversity in an efficient network.
Source: Lazer, David; Friedman, Allan. Administrative Science Quarterly. 2007

In recent years the role of network content and its interaction effect with network structure has emerged as an important area of inquiry in our understanding of innovation and group performance. It is well recognized that network content variable including the attribute of actors and actors' behavior pattern complement network structure to promote creativity and innovation on the one hand and cooperation and coordination on the other. According to their surrey research, Rodan (2004) proposed that, while network structure matters, access to heterogeneous knowledge is of equal importance for overall managerial performance and of greater importance for innovation performance. Developing a social definition of creative success and tracing the development of creative ideas, Fleming propose that interaction of structure with the personal attributes affects the brokerage on generating the initial insight and future idea development (Fleming et al 2007). Obstfeld introduced tertius iungens strategic orientation and propose that this orientation with dense social networks and diverse social knowledge predict individual involvement in innovation (Obstfeld 2005).

While prior work has demonstrated a relationship between network structure and group performance, inadequate attention has been paid to network content (Rodan, S etl, 2004). Our study draws on both structural and content perspectives in examining the way network structure affects knowledge process which contributes to group performance. Particularly, we focus on actor's partner selection. Contrasting to the 'know how' and 'know what' knowledge, 'know who' reflects another emergent important kind of knowledge in organization learning (Borgatti and Cross 2003). By considering the agent's partner selection behavior in inquiring information in their advice network, we can examine how the interaction of network structure with agent behavior affects knowledge process (figure 2).

Previous simulation research on agents' communication design almost paid all their attention on agents' neighbors (Hanaki et al 2007; David and Friedman 2007). That is, agents could only communicate with those who are directly connected with them. Although this nearby imitation pattern reflects agent's some kind of geography proximity, but this design leads to some plausible conclusions. Such as in Lazer's study, when agents only consider emulating their direct neighbors, regardless of what the network structure is, network density became the main factor affecting knowledge diffusion. Network topological structure is supposed to be an important role in information diffusion (Cowan 2004). We argue that different network structures would have different influence on coordinating exploration and exploitation even they may have the same density. Lazer.D also indicated that some different assumptions on emulate process could have significant effects on group performance (David and Friedman 2007).

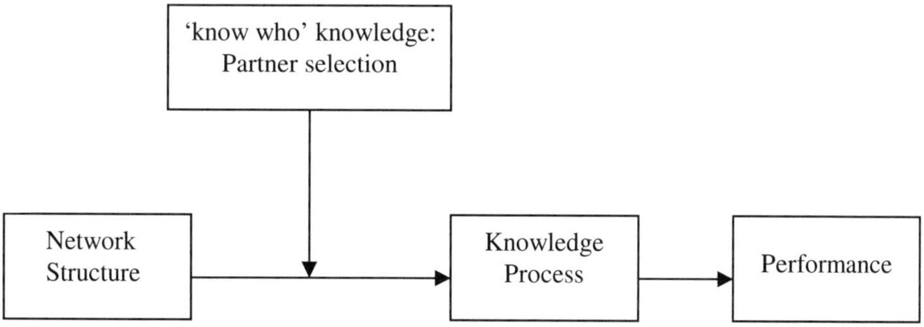

Figure 2: Concept model: how partner selection influence the relationship between network structure and knowledge process

Following the preceding discussion on the potential risks of ignoring actor's other imitation behavior, rather than assuming agent emulate the directly connected neighbors, we assume that agents will pay more attention on those who are structurally equivalent. Loosely speaking, structural equivalence refer to the extent to which two nodes are connected to the same others (Stanley and Katherine 1994). The fact that two agents are structurally equivalent indicates that they may have the same social position, same role or even completely substitutable. Based on the similarity theory agent are more likely to do the same thing as those who are similar with themselves. Structural equivalence also grasps agents' myopia perfectly. Because of myopia agents are unable to directly evaluate all the potential solutions in the whole organization, besides emulating the directly connected people, imitation pattern of structurally equivalent is another heuristic partner selection rule when agent faces complexity problem.

Drawing on the discussion above it is very reasonable to assume that structurally equivalent people are the favorite targets of imitation.

3. The model

3.1. *Problem space and NK model*

In this paper we extend Lazer's simulation model on parallel problem solving by adding the partner selection rules. The concept of parallel problem solving is first proposed in Lazer's study, which portrays a context where all the agents are engage in the same problem solving and the success of any one or subset of agents has no direct effect on other agents (David and Friedman 2007). NK model was used to portray this parallel problem solving. In NK model, K controls the degree of independence among decisions which ranges from 0 to N-1. Different values of K represent different extent in complexity of problem space (figure 3).

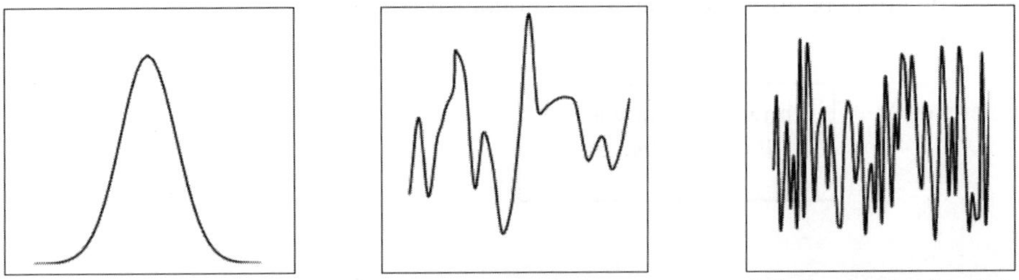

A: A simple problem space, similar to K = 0.

B: A complex rugged space with local maxima and minima, similar to 0 < K < N − 1.

C: A chaotic space in which the value of every point is independent of adjacent points, similar to K = N − 1.

Figure 3: Problem spaces represented by NK model.
Source: Lazer, David; Friedman, Allan. Administrative Science Quarterly. 2007

3.2. *Partner selection*

We assume that agent is myopic, unable to detect the best solution in group. Furthermore, there is also lacking incentive for agents to public their solutions. To improve their performance and explore at a higher level in the future agents have to interact with other agents and mimic the most successful one among the available candidates.

Besides the most adopted agent's communication pattern ---near neighbor selection we introduce another heuristic partner selection rule: structurally equivalent selection. In our model agents tend to emulate those who are structurally equivalent with them. The two agents are supposed to be exactly structurally equivalent if they have the same relationship to all other agents (Stanley and Katherine 1994). Pure structural equivalence can be quite rare in social relations but approximations to it may not be so rare. In network structure analysis researchers often are interested in the examining the degree of structural equivalence. There are many ways in which agents could be defined as approximate structural equivalence. And some algorithms have been particularly useful in applying graph theory to define the structural equivalence, such as "Euclidean Distance", "Correlation" (Stanley and Katherine 1994). Actually there are indeed a very large number of the algorithms we can use to examine group sets of agents into categories based on some commonality in their positions in network. For the sake of simplicity, we here only consider a relaxed criterion: agents will fall into the same class if they have the same sum of out-degree and in-degree. This criterion relaxes the conditions of the same agents actor connects to/with. Rather than connecting to the same agents, only the sum of degrees represent for structural equivalence.

3.3. *Network structure*

Our imitation pattern of structural equivalence is defined by the sum of a node's degree. In this case, not only network density but also network structure will affect system-level performance differently. To explore the influence of structurally equivalent imitation on system performance, we employ a regular network and an asymmetry network. The former is represented by a fixed grid to represent the advice network in which everyone has the constant number of connectors (we will call this network RU for short) and the other is a preferentially attached network (we will call this network PA for short). In a RU network, each individual is assumed to be connected by its fixed number neighbors on either side of it (see figure 4, in this paper each person has 4 neighbors).

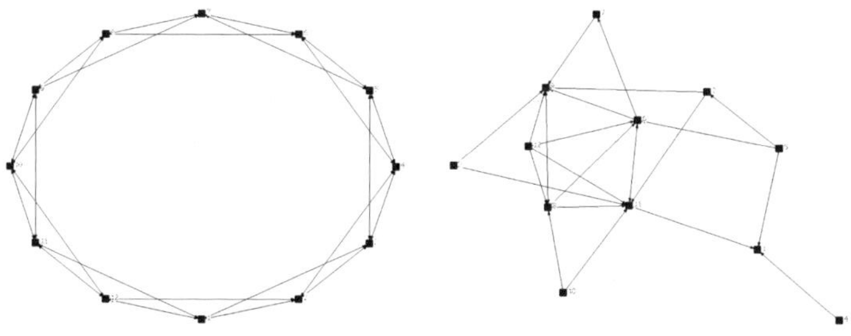

Figure 4: Preferentially attached network and regular network

We employ Jan's algorithm to create a preferentially attached network which captures a "rich-get-richer" dynamic, by which nodes that already have many interactions are more likely to add a further interaction than the nodes that have few interactions (Jan and Nicolaj 2007). Notice that, to eliminate the effect of network density, we create these two kinds of networks with the same density.

4. Results and interpretation

The simulation experiment is conducted under the following conditions: we consider a organization of 50 agents. All the organization members are engaging in solving a problem including 10 decisions. That means, we assumed N=10, and K=4 for the NK model. When N=10, there are 1,024 possible solutions for each problem space. The initial solutions of the actors are randomly generated, and those 50 agents are randomly placed in their communication networks.

Figure 5 illustrates the effect of RU network and PA network on the equilibrium performance level when agents adopt the structurally equivalent imitation strategy. As shown in Figure 5 RU network quickly finds a good solution and outperforms PA network all the time. This result can be explained by their dramatically different topological structure.

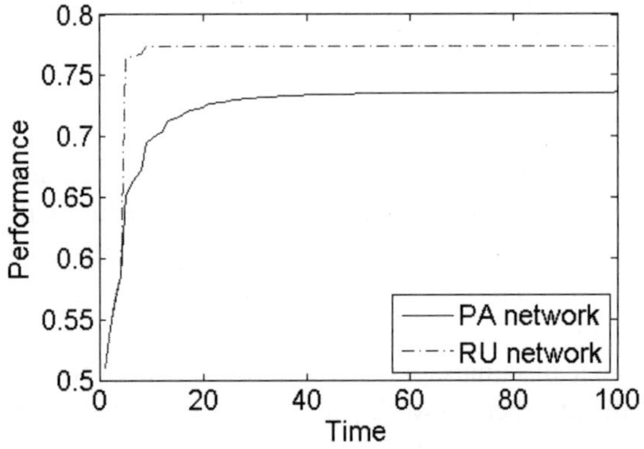

Figure 5: The organization performance change with PA network and RU network under the condition of structurally equivalent imitation

All the agents are the structural equivalent in RU network while in PA network agents belong to a few structural sub-groups because of the structurally equivalent partner selection. That is, PA network is no longer a single-component network but RU network still does. This brings both positive and negative effect on performance: on the one hand, agents only search the best solutions in the sub-group they belong to, the existence of sub-group keeps the information diversity from the whole organization's angle, which positively affects organization performance; on the other hand, there is no communication among agents belonging to different sub-group. Sub-groups in PA network are independent with each other. This structural obstacle cut off the information diffusion, which is negatively related to performance.

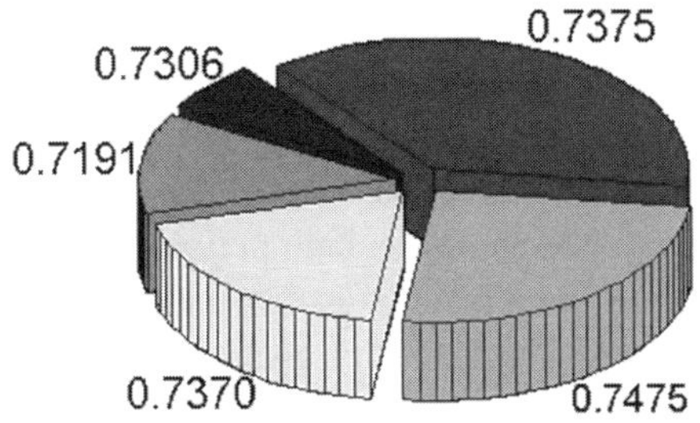

Figure 6: The ratio of sub-group in organization with final performance

When agent chooses those who are structurally equivalent to emulate, the whole organization is partitioned to several independent sub-groups and agents belonging to different sub-groups have no opportunity to communicate each other at all. Just like the local search good solutions only spread in a close circle and can not diffuse over the whole organization. Structure equivalence keeps the diversity from the system-level angle at the mean time builds the bastions which stops good solutions diffusion. In this case, each sub-group will converge on different performance level. This result is captured in Figure 6, which plot the final performance level every sub-group achieved. Furthermore, Figure 6 also shows the ratio of the number of the sub-group over the whole organization, which suggests that large sub-groups can not necessarily lead to a high performance level. This result contradicts Kent's research in which he propose that large organization have the advantage over small organization in coping with complexity (Kent et al 2006). Our experiment shows that sometimes large organization can not outperform small organization. Although these sub-groups keep diversity lack of communication among different structurally equivalent sub-group leads to a lower performance level the whole organization achieved.

5. Conclusion

According to the debate on the trade-off of information diffusion and diversity in a network, we add partner selection to the Lazer's simulation model to examine how the partner selection affects knowledge process and finally influence group performance.

Previous studies assuming that agents emulate the directly connected people get to the conclusion that network density attribute to the final organization performance regardless of what topological structure of advice network is. In our extending model we assume another heuristic partner selection rule which agents choose to emulate their structurally equivalent peer, under the condition of this agent imitation strategy network topological structure (even with the same density) plays a significant role in knowledge flow and finally influence the group convergent performance level. Agent's imitation pattern determines the direction of knowledge flow. When agents adopt the structurally equivalent imitation the whole organization no longer is a single-component network but can be seen as many independent sub-group. No communication among different sub-groups will lead the whole group to a lower performance level.

Our simulation study has much management implication for new product development team and R&D institution. In the situation of such an organization where all the engineers are solving the same complex problem which may has many plausible solutions, the challenge confronting to the manager is how to structure the advice network and induct engineers' behavior to achieve a high performance level both in the short-run and long-run. Our simulation experiment suggests that both network configuration and actor behavior can be employed to achieve this goal.

Notice that when granting more freedom to organization members they may actually choose to emulate their structurally equivalent peers. Over time, people may lock in to a limited set of people with whom they are familiar with and frequently interact, which might be efficient but yield suboptimal solution if other people are better sources. Especially when the sub-group is small, our experiment has proved this point. Give the importance of people as critical sources of knowledge, our study indicate the needs to avoid people's structurally equivalent imitation and other path dependence actions.

In this paper, we have considered only a very simple rule to judge the structural equivalence----the sum of the indegree and outdegree, and our design of imitation extent is equally simplistic, thus, many obvious extensions are easily conceivable.

6. Acknowledgments

We gratefully acknowledge the financial support from the National Nature Science Foundation of China under the grant number 70121001 & 70772109

References

Borgatti, S. P. and R. Cross (2003). "A relational view of information seeking and learning in social networks." *Management Science* 49(4): 432-445.

Burt, R. S. (2004). "Structural Holes and Good Ideas." *American Journal of Sociology* **110** (2): 349-399.

Coleman, J. S. (1988). "Social capital in the creation of human capital." American journal of sociology **94** (S1): 95-120.

Cowan, R. and N. Jonard (2004). Network structure and the diffusion of knowledge. *Journal of economic Dynamics and Control* **28** (8): 1557-1575.

Fleming, L. and S. Mingo, et al. (2007). Collaborative Brokerage, Generative Creativity, and Creative Success. *Administrative Science Quarterly* **52** (3): 443-475.

Hanaki, N. and A. Peterhansl, et al. (2007). Cooperation in evolving social networks. *Management Science* **53** (7): 1036-1050.

He, Z. L. and P. K. Wong (2004). Exploration vs. exploitation: An empirical test of the ambidexterity hypothesis. *Organization Science* **15** (4): 481-494.

Lazer, D. and A. Friedman (2007). The Network Structure of Exploration and Exploitation. *Administrative Science Quarterly* **52** (4): 667-694.

Miller, K. D. and M. Zhao, et al. (2006). Adding interpersonal learning and tacit knowledge to March's exploration-exploitation model. *The Academy of Management Journal* (AMJ) **49** (4): 709-722.

Obstfeld, D. (2005). Social Networks, the Tertius Iungens Orientation, and Involvement in Innovation. *Administrative Science Quarterly* **50** (1): 100-130.

Rivkin, J. W. and N. Siggelkow (2007). Patterned interactions in complex systems: Implications for exploration. *Management Science* **53** (7): 1068-1085.

Rodan, S. and D. C. Galunic, et al. (2004). "More than network structure: how knowledge heterogeneity influences managerial performance and innovativeness." *Strategic Management Journal* **25** : 541-556.

Wasserman, S. and K. Faust (1994). Social network analysis: Methods and applications, Cambridge Univ Pr.

EXPLORING THE KNOWLEDGE CREATING COMMUNITIES: AN ANALYSIS OF THE LINUX KERNEL DEVELOPER COMMUNITY

HAOXIANG XIA*

Institute of Systems Engineering, Dalian University of Technology, No.2, Linggong Road Dalian, 116024 China

E-mail: hxxia@dlut.edu.cn

SHUANGLING LUO and TAKETOSHI YOSHIDA

Graduate School of Knowledge Science, Japan Advanced Institute of Science and Technology Nomi, Ishikawa 923-1292, Japan

E-mails: {slluo, yoshida} @jaist.ac.jp

The knowledge creation processes and activities in online communities become prominent in our society, with the proliferation of all sorts of online communities. This phenomenon brings enormous challenging research issues. In this paper, we give an in-depth analysis on an actual case of the Linux kernel developer community, to illustrate that such community is essentially an evolutionary collective-intelligent system; and this system grows through the spontaneous self-organization processes. This work may pave the way for further theoretical exploration of the knowledge-creation processes in online communities; and on the other hand it has practical implications for developing computing technologies to facilitate the development of the "knowledge-creating communities."

1. Introduction

In the last decades, the growing significance of knowledge to the social and economic development of our society has attracted tremendous efforts in "Knowledge Management" (e.g. Nonaka & Takeuchi 1995; Alavi & Leidner 2001). These efforts generally set the focus on studying the knowledge systems inside the boundary of a formal organization like a business company, a governmental department and an academic institute. However, many knowledge activities and processes are beyond the institutional boundaries. One noteworthy phenomenon is that the online communities, which have been proliferated with the explosive development of the Internet and the Web, have become a prominent vehicle for knowledge creation, dissemination and utilization. The knowledge processes in these online communities are fundamentally different from those in a formal organization. The knowledge creation, dissemination and utilization in an online community are basically accomplished by independent contributors or participants in a self-organizing and "autopoietic" [a] fashion, while in the formal organization these knowledge processes usually take place under the centralized managerial control to achieve some well-defined organizational objectives. Therefore, the theories and models for organizational knowledge management cannot be simply transplanted to study the knowledge activities and processes in the online communities. The studies on the

* Work partially supported by National Natural Science Foundation of China under Grant No.70871016

[a] Autopoiesis is the process whereby an organization produces itself, as described in: Varela F.J. Maturana H.R. & Uribe, R. Biosystems 5:187–196, 1974

knowledge activities and processes in an online community would be a challenging issue; and at the same time they are both of theoretical value to examine a type of knowledge systems that are critically different from the firm-based knowledge systems and of practical value to enhance the knowledge production and utilization in our society.

One noteworthy knowledge-intensive online community is the Linux kernel developer community. The Linux Kernel is the operating system kernel that underpins all distributions of Linux operating systems. Linus Torvalds initiated it in 1991 as an open-source software (OSS) project. Linux is one of the most fascinating success-stories of the OSS movement. Moreover, it is fascinating that the Linux Kernel is primarily developed by thousands of part-time voluntary programmers scattered across the Internet without formal organization or centralized control. Along with the development of the Linux Kernel, an online community of the contributors (or the Linux Kernel developer community) also rapidly grows. Due to the miraculous success of Linux, it would be worthwhile to examine how the collective actions of the voluntary contributors develop such large-scaled and complex software of high quality without centralized coordination. As software development can be regarded as one form of knowledge creation, this examination is from another aspect to explore the knowledge creation in the loosely connected online communities of independent participants.

Therefore, in this paper we try to explore such "knowledge-creating" online communities by giving an analysis on the actual case of the Linux-kernel developer community (LDC for short). In an earlier effort, we suggested that many online communities manifest some degree of community intelligence (Xia et al. 2008; Luo et al 2009). Following that view of community intelligence, we try to explore the underlying dynamics for the evolution of the LDC as well as the development of this community's knowledge product, the Linux kernel.

2. A Short History of the Linux-kernel Developer Community

To facilitate further discussion, the history of Linux is shortly introduced, with the focus being placed on the growth of the developer community in which the Linux kernel is collectively created and continually updated.

Linus Torvalds initially developed Linux in 1991, when he was a student in computer science at University of Helsinki. His initial motivation was to write programs in order to use some UNIX functions in his own PC with an 80386 processor. He implemented a task-switching program, a disk driver and a small file system, which constituted Linux 0.01. On 25 August 1991, he announced this skeletal operating system in the newsgroup "comp.os.minix" and asked for suggestions for the preferable features. Then, his continuous efforts ended up to Linux 0.02, which debuted on October 5th. Together with the free release of the source code, he posted another message in the same newsgroup to seek feedbacks as well as possible contributors or co-developers. This was a critical event for Linux since it started the collective journey of Linux development. The response was instantly positive; of the first ten people to download Linux, five sent back bug fixes, code improvements, and new features. By the end of the year, when Linux finally became a stand-alone system in Version 0.11, more than a hundred people worldwide had joined the Linux newsgroup and the mailing list (Kurabawa 2000). Since then, the Linux developer community rapidly expands, together with the rapid development of the Linux operation system.

One critical measure is the development of the Linux kernel in term of the source lines of code (SLOC). The actual SLOCs in some typical versions are listed in Table 1. This table shows that the Linux kernel rapidly expands in the past 18 years.

Table 1 Growth of SLOC in Linux Kernel (Some Typical Versions)
(Data Source from: Wikipedia article on "Linux Kernel", available at:
http://simple.wikipedia.org/wiki/Linux_kernel)

Release Year	Kernel Version	Source Lines of Code
1991	Linux 0.0.1	10,239
1994	Linux 1.0.0	176,250
1996	Linux 1.2.0	310,950
1999	Linux 2.2.0	1,800,847
2001	Linux 2.4.0	2,210,149
2003	Linux 2.6.0	5,929,913
2008	Linux 2.6.25	9,232,484

Another critical measure for the growth of the LDC is to count the community size. Since its creation in 1991, this open operating system has attracted increasing numbers of developers worldwide. In the year of 1993, there were over 100 developers worked on the Linux Kernel. More recently, as reported by Koah-Hatman et al. (2008), each release since version 2.6.11 generally contains the work of nearly 1000 developers. Since 2005, about 3700 individual developers have contributed to the kernel. Their report also shows that the number of developers gradually increases from 483 in Version 2.6.11 to 1057 in Version 2.6.24.

The previous description reveals much information for the LDC. Linux had a somewhat haphazard starting-up, since Torvalds himself was not even aware that he was writing an operating system when he began programming the first task-switching system in 1991. He did not anticipate at that time that Linux would catch such persistent enthusiasms from so many developers and users, nor could he imagine that Linux would become such huge and complex software and such a successful product. From this haphazard starting-up, the community rapidly develops together with the explosion of the Linux (kernel) product. Behind the success of the Linux operating system and the growth of the Linux developer community, two questions naturally come to the fore: what are the underlying dynamics of the evolution of this Linux developer community; and why this huge and complex software product can be successfully created in this largely open community without thorough planning or centralized control.

3. Some Previous Views on the LDC

The intriguing phenomena of the Linux operating system and the corresponding developer community have attracted great attention in the last decade. Here we just give a short description on a few typical views.

One well-noted work is given by Raymond (1999), who distinguished two different styles of software development, i.e. the "cathedral" model of most of the commercial world and the "bazaar" model of the Linux world. The success of the Linux project is then attributed to the inherent openness in the bazaar model. On one hand, Raymond believes one success factor of Linux is the frequent releasing and updating so that the users can quickly detect the bugs; on the other, with a large developer base, the project leader Linus Torvalds can safely rely on others to write and test the code for him. The openness is surely an important factor for enhancing Linux development. It is, however, farfetched to use the openness to explain everything.

Kuwabara (2000), by contrast, argued that the bazaar analogy is too simplistic, and the success of the Linux project should be understood from an evolution and complex-adaptive-system (CAS) point of view. To him, behind the Linux project is a bottom-up engineering approach that effectively challenges the top-down worldview entrenched in the monolithic software engineering approach. We largely agree with his CAS view; our further argument is that the Linux developer community is not merely an evolutionary system, but also an evolutionary intelligent system. Another drawback of Kuwabara's work is that he points out that the Linux project should be considered as a CAS, but the underlying mechanisms of the formation of this CAS is not well addressed.

Iannacci (2005), in his PhD dissertation, gave a social epistemological analysis for the LDC. The major focus is on the coordination mechanisms that are emerged in the community. Three mechanisms are analyzed in his work, namely standardization, loose-coupling to form a "heterachical" structure, and partisan mutual adjustment. Lee and Cole (2003), from the knowledge-creation perspective, attempted to develop a community-based model of knowledge creation, adopting the evolutionary framework suggested by Campbell (1960) and emphasizing the role of criticism and critical evaluation as a key driver in the evolutionary processes.

The prior endeavors, among many others, contribute to enrich our understandings of the knowledge-creating online communities in general, and the Linux kernel developer community in particular. However, their work reflects the partial facts of the LDC from different facets; more inquiries are still needed to achieve a more comprehensive view.

4. The LDC as an Evolving Communal-intelligent System

Based on the prior observations of the LDC development and the current work on explaining the LDC phenomena, in this section we give our analysis on the LDC, basically regarding this community as an evolutionary collective-intelligent system in which the participants collectively create knowledge and solve problems. On one hand, the collective knowledge work around the development of the Linux operating system is the most fundamental driving-force of the community; on the other hand, the most apparent way to measure the evolution of this community is to observe the growth of its primary knowledge product (i.e. the Linux system). Thus, the development of this LDC largely reflects the phenomenon of community intelligence, as conceived in the authors' earlier work (Xia et al. 2008, Luo et al. 2009). Subsequently, we try to explain the evolution of the LDC from the aspect of community intelligence; and we hope this analysis would in turn enrich our understanding of the nature of community intelligence.

4.1. *The LDC as a Bottom-up and Evolutionary Knowledge-creating Community*

The starting point of our analysis is that the LDC is a bottom-up and evolutionary "knowledge-creating" community. This view furthermore contains two points.

First, in the LDC the knowledge-creation is the primary action that fundamentally impels the community development. Furthermore, in this community the knowledge creation is conceptually comprised of two categories of actions, namely knowledge-building and knowledge networking. The reason of the existence of the Linux developer community is that the participants collectively and collaboratively develop Linux. This is inherently a knowledge-building process and what is built is basically represented as the Linux source code and annotations, as well as the related documentations. Therefore, this knowledge-building process persists as Linux development continues and the LDC exists. At the same time, knowledge networking among the participants or contributors ubiquitously takes place throughout such knowledge building. One basic means of knowledge networking is through the instant discussions within the community. In the LDC, the contributors have dense discussions with one another, primarily via the Linux-kernel mailing list. Through such discussions, large amount of technical knowledge spreads and simultaneously, the contributors may also improve their "know-how" knowledge, together with the development of an implicit reputation system within the community. The knowledge networking can also take place in an indirect way. In this way, one may learn from other contributors' patches and bug fixes and knowledge transfer happens. In short, the knowledge building and knowledge networking generally constitute the overall process of the knowledge-system evolution in the entire community.

Second, the evolution of the communal knowledge system is not a monolithic process, corresponding to the "bottom-up" engineering of Linux development as Kuwabara contends. Linux is developed by thousands of independent programmers without complete goal setting, thorough planning, or top-down task-assignment. As stated, when Torvalds initially announced Version 0.01 in 1991, he himself had no clear intention for the future of Linux and he just asked for feedbacks and suggestions on the features that Linux should contain. During the entire process of Linux development, he also avoids imposing long-term plans and visions on the community:

"That way I can more easily deal with anything new that comes up without having pre-conceptions of how I should deal with it. My only long-range plan has been and still is just the very general plan of making Linux better." (Interview, cited from Kuwabara 2000)

Instead, the stage-goals of development usually rise from collective efforts and discussions. Unlike a formally organized software project, neither Torvalds nor any other sub-system maintainer authoritatively arranges a particular contributor to accomplish a particular task. From the very beginning, it has been left to each contributor to decide what to work on at the moment:

"In developing Linux, you have complete freedom to do whatever you feel like doing. There's no specification anywhere of what the Linux kernel has to end up doing, and as such there is no requirement for anyone to do anything they are not interested in." (Personal Interview, cited from Kuwabara 2000)

Thus, the entire project is carried out in a spontaneous mode without global coordination. In the project, nobody can anticipate what will be added or modified in the next release of the Linux kernel. Associated with this spontaneous and bottom-up development of the Linux operating system is the endogenous growth of the corresponding community of the developers. This LDC again grows from bottom up as the result of the free choices of the contributors. No one can exactly anticipate who will join the community by submitting patches and bug fixes at the next stage of work, or who will leave because of any reason. Without formal organization, this community has, up until now, somehow stabilized to be an effective community that efficiently creates complex software of high quality.

4.2. *An Exploration of the Underlying Dynamics of the LDC Evolution*

Following the previous view of the LDC, we can try to explore the underlying dynamics. The basic observation is that there are dense communications within the Linux developer community and these communications play a critical role in programming the Linux kernel and in the development of the LDC itself. The Linux-kernel mailing list is the central discussion forum for the developers. In the later 1990s, the kernel traffic has reached up to six megabytes of posts in a week, according to a report by Zack Brown, (cited from Kuwabara 2000). In another research, Lee & Cole (2003) counted the total number of emails sent to the mailing list during 1995 to 2000. They found that 14,535 people had sent at least one e-mail to the mailing list; and each person has averagely sent 14 emails over 5 years, since there were 199,374 emails archived as of August 26, 2000.

It can be argued that these communications, which are mostly localized, serve as the micro-foundation of the evolution of the entire LDC and of the creation of Linux. These localized communications activate some self-organization processes so that they eventually enable the macro-level evolution of the entire community.

Coordination is doubtlessly critical to the quality of Linux as well as to the development of the community. Without coordination, the integrity of the Linux product would not be possible, nor could the developer community grow to be a coherent or creative one. However, as the contributors have complete freedom to do whatever they like to do, the top-down coordination is generally absent in this community. Instead, coordination in the LDC is an emergent property generated from bottom up. One simplest case of coordination is the task "assignment" (tasks are unofficially assigned, as the tasks are voluntarily done). For one contributor, the good performance in his past work reinforces his reputation and trustworthiness for the quality of his other contributions. Such coordination is indeed activated by the indirect communications. The contributor transfers knowledge by submitting the patches; and other community members simultaneously get "know-how" knowledge when obtaining the technical knowledge related to the submitted patch. As a result, such indirect knowledge communication impels possible future collective and collaborative work.

More direct technical communications are also pervasive in the LDC, basically via the Linux-kernel mailing list. Randomly picking up a thread from the mailing-list archive, we often see intensive discussions on some particular technical problem. For example, Michael Zick reported a bug fix on May 22nd, 2009 by posting the following message:

> "Found in the bit-rot for 32-bit, x86, Uni-processor builds:
>
> ...
>
> Submitted: M. S. Zick" (Source: Linux-kernel mailing list, archived at: http://lkml.indiana.edu/hypermail/linux/kernel/0905.2/02562.html)

Immediately, this message causes intensive discussion. Under this thread, there were 31 postings on that same day. At least 6 persons participated. Among them, Zick posted 13 messages, Andi Klein posted 4, Ingo Molnar posted 1, Peter Anvin posted 4, Samuel Thibault posted 4, Dreier posted 2 and there are 3 other anonymous postings (probably posted by the above-listed authors too). This is a common scenario of the technical discussions in the Linux kernel developer community. It is not unusual that such technical discussions give rise to the emergent collaborations among the participants. Iannacci (2005) terms this kind of coordination as "partisan mutual adjustment" and argues that collaboration teams or "social networks" may appear from such communications. These social networks are open to contributions from everybody. However, they usually contain strong ties among a limited number of participants because of their frequent interactions and a stable core may form around the strongly tied participants.

Besides facilitating the formation and adjustments of the collaborative teams or networks, the coordination through discussions also plays a critical role in the advancement of the overall Linux kernel project. Kuwabara mentioned an example of the row I/O patch, submitted by Stephen Tweedle in 1998 and rejected by Torvalds several times before the final version was at last applied into the kernel. In the example, an iteratively improved technical solution was achieved by collective work of the involved developers coordinated through communications.

From the prior description, we can perceive that the emergent coordination is a key element that makes order grow from chaos in the LDC, as through such coordination the structuring of collaborative teams or networks takes place and the patches with good quality are often the result of the coordinated work.

Closely related to the emergent coordination is the evolution of an implicit reputation system underlying the LDC. It is the common case that the highly reputed or trusted persons play a central role in the communications and collaborations. They often become the primary coordinators (e.g. sub-system maintainers) in many collective efforts. However, their reputations are, in turn, the result of the performances of their previous contributions in submitting patches and in the discussions.

Kuwabara (2000) describes a feedback process for the self-reinforcement of the individual reputation, as shown in the following figure.

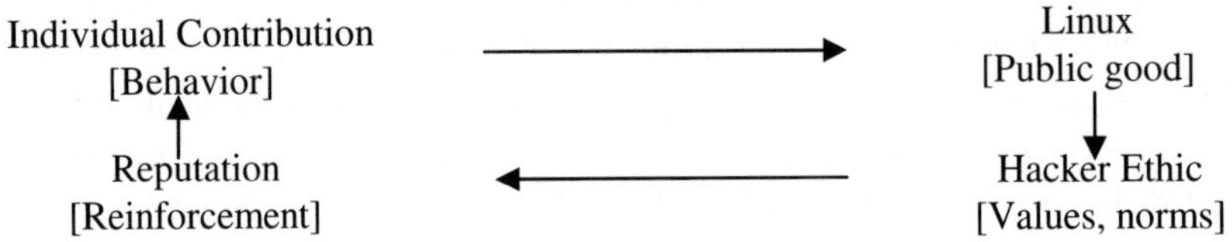

Fig. 1. The Reinforcement of the Individual Reputation in the Linux Developer Community (Source: Kuwabara 2000)

In this process, the reputation of an individual increases according to the contributions he or she makes and in turn, the increasing of his or her reputation may foster the further contributions from the same individual. Kuwabara uses such reinforcement process to explain the motivations for a community member to contribute. We argue that this process also has influences to the evolution of the community itself. With the increasing reputation, an individual may play an increasingly important role in the development actions; thus the evolution of the implicit reputation system is a critical factor for the formation and adjustment of the overall structure of the community.

From another aspect, the communications also stimulate "stigmergic" processes (Theraulaz & Bonabeau 1999). The stigmergic processes basically function through the technical building of the Linux system. As previously cited from the project leader Linus Torvalds' assertion, "my only long-range plan has been and still is just the very general plan of making Linux better", the global goal-setting and long-range planning are absent in developing Linux. Moreover, the development of Linux is the collective work of massive autonomous contributors who also lack global sight of the project. With these two essential features, the development of Linux is the collective architecting without blueprint, resembling the nest-construction activities in the insect societies such as the termite colonies. Thus, it is natural to suppose that the stigmergic processes may exist in the Linux developer community, analogous to the collective nest-construction in a termite colony. Following this analogy, the general situation of Linux development is that the contributors decide what to do in terms of what they have done. Therefore, no one, including Torvalds, knows in advance what would be added or modified in the next release; and the overall development is always open-ended. But during this open-ended process, their product is increasingly complex, increasingly powerful, and increasingly fitted to the environment (i.e. to better satisfy user needs and to cope with the technology advances outside the Linux project).

Generally, there are two sources to stimulate the stigmergic interactions. One situation is the amplification of some personal ideas and suggestions inside the community. Another situation is the adaptation to environmental or external changes, especially technological innovations outside the Linux project.

Responding to the internal and the external "stimuli", some member(s) may trigger a stigmergic process in the community, acting like a termite emits pheromones onto a site to call for other termites to continue building there. Such a stigmergic process is generally a self-reinforcement process. If one ongoing topic is active, intriguing and brings many open challenges, then many contributors would be attracted to this topic. As more progresses are made, they further the amount of open issues. Gradually, when the "constructing" on this topic is going to complete, the contributors may step away because there is not as much work left.

Bringing the previous discussions together, we can tell that the self-organizing processes around the emergent coordination, the evolving reputation system and the stigmergic interactions in constructing the software system shape the overall process of the evolution of the LDC. Thus, the emergence of the global properties can be examined in the next part of this section.

4.3. *The Overall Evolution as Emergent Global Property*

We contend that the entire Linux developer community manifests high collective intelligence. Such community intelligence is firstly and most-remarkably represented by the Linux operating system itself. Today, the Linux kernel has become an extremely complex software system containing over 9 million source lines of code. Building such a system looks like a mission impossible to a collectivity of part-time hackers without any formal organization, as it is difficult task even for the largest corporations. The efficiency and effectiveness in the building of the Linux system have unquestionably proved the high "intelligence" of this online community. Kroah-Hatman et al. (2008) showed the rate of change of Linux kernel from Version 2.6.11 to 2.6.24, as depicted below.

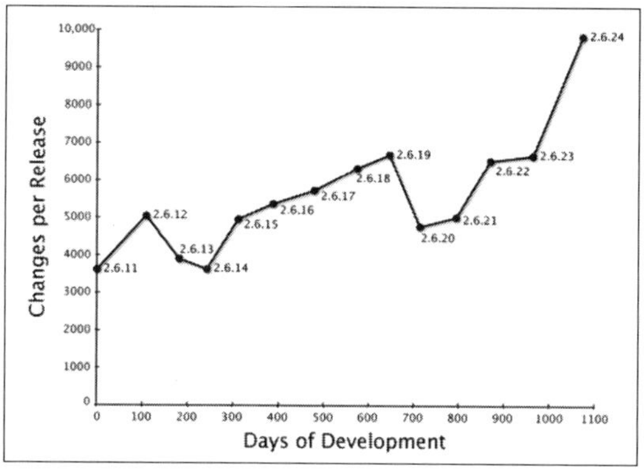

Fig. 2. Rate of Change of Linux Kernel from Version 2.6.11 -2.6.24

According to Figure 2, on average within 100 days the community announces a new stable release, which contains thousands of pieces of changes from the previous release. This figure convincingly illustrates the highly efficient work done by the Linux developer community. For the effectiveness of the Linux contributors' work, it is difficult to get direct quantitative measurement. The complexity of the system on one hand and the adoption rate[b] on the other hand have illustrated the effectiveness of their development.

In addition to the external measurement of the efficiency and effectiveness of the development work, the global regularity of the LDC can also been seen internally. As the internal measure, two properties are shortly discussed here, i.e. the global structuring of the community and the emergence of the norms of code quality and coding style.

One global consequence of the previously discussed self-organization processes is the formation and evolution of the community structure. Most remarkably, a hierarchical structure gradually forms during the evolution of the community. This structure was described by Kroah-Hatman in his 2008 presentation at Google, as shown in Figure 3.

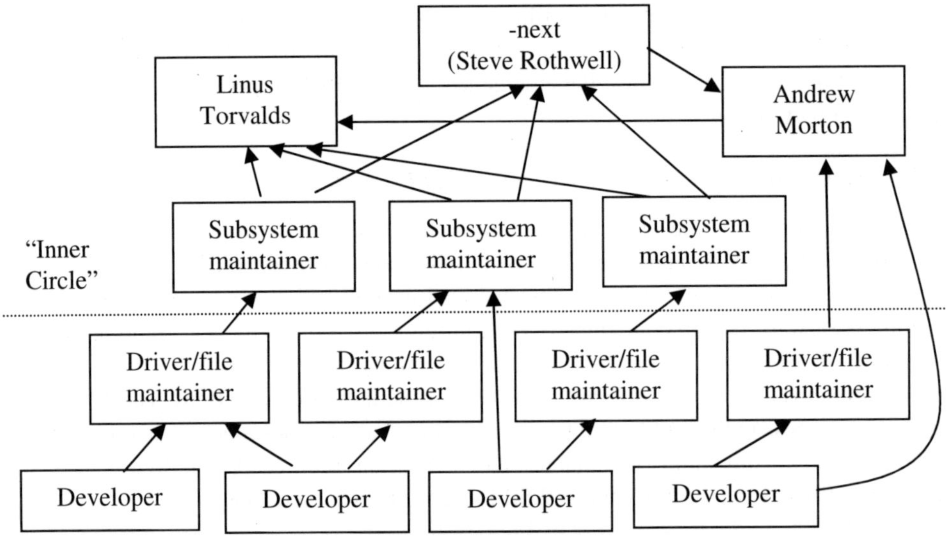

Fig. 3. The Emergent Hierarchical Structure of the LDC (Adapted from a figure in: www.kernel.org/pub/linux/kernel/people/gregkh/talks/kernel_devel-google-2008-06-05.pdf)

This hierarchical structure is actually a core-periphery structure. In this structure, the project leader Torvalds works closely with a limited number of lieutenants. They are core developers and subsystem maintainers. The peripheral participants are the *ad hoc* patch-submitters and bug-reporters. Torvalds himself explained this structure in a post:

[b] e.g. IDC's report for Q1 2007 says that Linux now holds 12.7% of the overall server market, source: Linux Watch, at http://www.linux-watch.com/news/NS5369154346.html

"The fact is, we've had "patch penguins" pretty much forever, and they are called subsystem maintainers. They maintain their own subsystem, i.e. people like David Miller (networking), Kai Germaschewski (ISDN), Greg KH (USB), Ben Collins (firewire), Al Viro (VFS), Andrew Morton (ext3), Ingo Molnar (scheduler), Jeff Garzik (network drivers) etc etc. ...
A word of warning: good maintainers are hard to find. Getting more of them helps, but at some point it can actually be more useful to help the _existing_ ones. I've got about ten-twenty people I really trust, and quite frankly, the way people work is hardcoded in our DNA. Nobody "really trusts" hundreds of people. The way to make these things scale out more is to increase the network of trust not by trying to push it on me, but by making it more of a _network_, not a star-topology around me." (Source: Linux Kernel Mailing List Archive, at:
http://lkml.indiana.edu/hypermail/linux/kernel/0201.3/1070.html)

In this post, Torvalds clearly stated that the structuring of the community relies on a "network of trust." He himself trusts a small number people in the "inner circle" or the subsystem maintainers and each maintainer trusts a small number of other developers and so on... This network of trust is in fact the implicit reputation system underlying the community. Correspondingly, the evolution of this reputation system generally directs the adjustment of this working structure of the community. In short, the overall structure of the Linux developer community is emergent instead of organized top-down; the subsystem maintainers grow, instead of being officially assigned. This structure is furthermore flexible. An active contributor who performs well in his previous contributions may play an increasingly vital role in the community; by contrast, if one contributor becomes less active, he might gradually become the peripheral participants.

Another measure is the formation of the global norms in the community. With the growth of the community, the formats of submitting patches and reporting-bugs become standardized. The standards on the code quality and the coding styles are also enforced. An example given by Kuwabara (2000) is the Italian programmer Andreas Arcangeli's patches for the printer code:

"[Arcangeli] made substantial improvements, then branched out, but tended to do some pretty sloppy things - to the point where Linus said "go away." Andreas refused to go away, and eventually had major changes to the kernel accepted. All Linus did was enforce coding standards." (Personal Interview 1999, cited from Kuwabara 2000)

At first glimpse, it looks like standardization attributes to the personal efforts of Torvalds and his close co-developers, but factually it is the result of the coordination of the entire community. Without the abundant base of contributors, this standardization is impossible. Without the adoption of the standards by the contributors, this standardization is either impossible. In turn, this standardization is a means of the emergent coordination of the whole community and the accepted norms or standards are actually become a proportion of the communal knowledge.

To sum up, according to the prior analysis we can claim that the view of evolutionary community intelligence facilitates to explain, at least partially, the development of the LDC and the success of the Linux kernel project. On the other hand, this LDC also provides an excellent actual case to enrich our understandings on the knowledge system developments in online communities.

5. Conclusion

In this work, we give an in-depth analysis on the actual case of the Linux kernel developer community, to illustrate that such community is essentially an evolutionary collective-intelligent system and this system grows through the spontaneous self-organization processes. This work may pave the way for further theoretical exploration of the knowledge-creation processes in online communities and it has practical implications for developing computing technologies to facilitate the development of the "knowledge-creating communities."

References

Alavi, M. & Leidner, D. (2001) "Knowledge Management and Knowledge Management Systems", *MIS Quarterly*, 25(1):107-136.

Campbell D. T. (1960) "Blind Variation and Selective Retention in Creative Thought as in Other Knowledge Processes", Psychology Review, 67:380-400.

Iannacci F. (2005) *The Social Epistemology of Open Source Software Development: The Linux Case Study*. Ph.D. Dissertation, University of London.

Kroah-Hatman G., Corbet J., McPherson A. (2008) "How Fast it is Going, Who is Doing It, What They are Doing, and Who is Sponsoring It", *Report at the Linux Foundation.*

Kuwabara K. (2000) "Linux: A Bazaar at the Edge of Chaos", *First Monday*, 5(3). at: http://firstmonday.org/htbin/cgiwrap/bin/ojs/index.php/fm/article/view/1482/1397

Lee G. K. & Cole R.E. (2003) "From a Firm-based to a Community-based Model of Knowledge Creation: The Case of Linux Kernel Development", *Organization Science*, 14(6): 633-649.

Luo, S., Xia H., Yoshida T. & Wang Z. (2009) "Toward Collective Intelligence of Online Communities: A Primitive Conceptual Model", *Journal of Systems Science and Systems Engineering*, 18(2): 203-221.

Nonaka, I. & Takeuchi, H. (1995) *The Knowledge Creating Company: How Japanese Companies Create the Dynamics of Innovation*. Oxford: Oxford University Press.

Raymond R. (1999). "The Cathedral and the Bazaar". *Knowledge, Technology & Policy*, 12(3): 22-49.

Theraulaz G., Bonabeau E., (1999) "A Brief History of Stigmergy", Artificial Life 5:97-116

Xia H., Wang Z., Luo S., and Yoshida T., (2008) "Toward a Concept of Community Intelligence: A View on Knowledge Sharing and Fusion in Web-mediated Communities", In: *Proceedings of the 2008 IEEE International Conference on Systems, Man, and Cybernetics*, Singapore, 2008. pp.88-93, IEEE Press.

SYSTEMIC THINKING IN KNOWLEDGE MANAGEMENT

YOSHITERU NAKAMORI

School of Knowledge Science, Japan Advanced Institute of Science and Technology
1-1 Asahidai, Nomi, Ishikawa 923-1292, Japan
E-mail: nakamori@jaist.ac.jp

This paper considers the problem of knowledge integration, and proposes a theory of knowledge construction systems, which consists of three fundamental parts: a knowledge construction system, a structure-agency-action paradigm, and evolutionally constructive objectivism. The paper starts with a brief introduction of our basic systems approach called informed systems thinking, followed by a summary of our proposal: a theory of knowledge construction systems, and then gives a detailed explanation of the theory.

1. Introduction

The main principle of *the theory of organizational knowledge creation* proposed in Nonaka and Takeuchi (1995) is that *new knowledge is created by the interaction of explicit and tacit knowledge.* Tacit knowledge refers, in the field of knowledge management, to knowledge known by an individual, which is difficult to communicate to others because it includes emotions and intuition. Therefore, socialization and externalization are emphasized in Nonaka theory to obtain group explicit knowledge from individual tacit knowledge via group tacit knowledge; the last is shared mental models, technical skills, etc.

Another important concept in Nonaka theory is *Ba* which is a Japanese word meaning place. Nonaka uses it as creative environment; actually Nonaka and Konno (1998) called *the dynamic context which is shared and redefined in the knowledge creation process Ba*, which does not refer just to a physical space, but includes virtual spaces based on the Internet, for instance; and more mental spaces which involve sharing experiences and ideas. They stated that knowledge is not something which can exist independently; it can only exist in a form embedded in *Ba*, which acts as a context that is constantly shared by people.

Similar ideas exist in systems theory: for instance, Churchman (1970) states that all knowledge is dependent on boundary judgments. This paper follows this idea in such a way that our theory chooses three important dimensions (or subsystems) from the high-dimensional *Creative Space* (Wierzbicki and Nakamori, 2006) and require actors to work well in each dimension (or subsystem) in collecting and organizing distributed, tacit knowledge. These are *Intelligence* (a subsystem or a scientific dimension), *Involvement* (a subsystem or a social dimension) and *Imagination* (a subsystem or a creative dimension). When the theory is interpreted from a viewpoint of sociology, the *Creative Space* is considered as *Social Structure* which constrains and enables human action, and consists of a *scientific-actual front*, a *social-relational front* and a *cognitive-mental front* corresponding respectively to the three dimensions or subsystems.

Our theory introduces two more dimensions or subsystems: *Intervention* and *Integration*, which correspond to *social action* and *knowledge* from a sociological point of view. This paper follows the definition of *systemic intervention* in Midgley (2000) that *systemic intervention is purposeful action by an agent to create change in relation to reflection upon boundaries.* Our actors collect knowledge on all three structural dimensions or fronts, with a certain purpose, and synthesize those distributed knowledge to construct new knowledge. In this sense, the subsystem *Intervention* together with *Integration* corresponds to Midgley's *systemic intervention.* As Wang Yang-Ming the 14th-century Confucianist contends that *knowledge and action are one, for purpose, and with consequences* (Zhu, 2000).

The theory to be presented in this paper aims at integrating *systematic approach* and *systemic (holistic) thinking*; the former is mainly used in the dimensions or subsystems *Intelligence*, *Involvement* and *Imagination*, and the latter is required in the dimensions or subsystems *Intervention* and *Integration.* Leading systems thinkers today often emphasize *holistic thinking* (Jackson, 2003; Mulej, 2007), or *meta-synthesis* (Gu and Tang, 2005). They recommend and require *systems thinking* for a holistic understanding of the emergent characteristic of a complex system, and for creating a new systemic knowledge about a difficult problem confronted. Our theory aims at synthesizing objective knowledge and subjective knowledge, which inevitably requires intuitive, holistic integration.

With a similar idea, Wierzbicki et al. (2006) proposed an informed, creative systemic approach, named *Informed Systems Thinking*, which should serve as the basic tool of knowledge integration and should support creativity. This systemic thinking emphasizes three basic principles: *the principle of cultural sovereignty*, *the principle of informed responsibility*, and *the principle of systemic integration.* If the first is a thesis, then the second is an antithesis and the third is a synthesis.

The problem here is: how are we to fulfill a systemic integration in the context of knowledge synthesis? One of the answers to this is *Theory of Knowledge Construction Systems*, the topic of this paper, which consists of three fundamental parts: *a knowledge construction system* (Nakamori, 2000, 2003), *a structure-agency-action paradigm* (Nakamori and Zhu, 2004), and *evolutionally constructive objectivism* (Wierzbicki and Nakamori, 2007). The main characteristics of this theory are: *fusion of the purposiveness paradigm and purposefulness paradigm*, *interaction of explicit knowledge and tacit knowledge*, and *requisition for knowledge coordinators.*

2. Theory of Knowledge Construction Systems

Wierzbicki et al. (2006) proposed to redefine systems science as the discipline concerned with methods for the *intercultural* and *interdisciplinary* integration of knowledge, including soft inter-subjective and hard objective approaches, *open* and, above all, *informed. Intercultural* means an explicit accounting for and analysis of national, regional, even disciplinary cultures, means trying to overcome the incommensurability of cultural perspectives by explicit debate of the different concepts and metaphors used by diverse cultures. *Interdisciplinary* approach has been a defining feature of systemic analysis since Comte (1844), but has been gradually lost in the division between soft and hard approaches. *Open* means pluralist, as stressed by soft systems approaches, not excluding by design any cultural or disciplinary perspectives (Linstone, 1984; Jackson and Key, 1984; Flood and Jackson, 1991). *Informed* means pluralist as stressed by hard systems approaches, not excluding any perspectives by ignorance or by disciplinary paradigmatic belief, and is most difficult to achieve.

A basic novel understanding related to this approach is the essential extension of the skeleton of science (Boulding 1956). Wierzbicki et al. (2006) named this approach *Informed Systems Thinking* which consists of three principles:

- *The principle of cultural sovereignty*: We can treat all separate levels of systemic complexity as independent cultures, and generalize the old basic cultural anthropology: no culture shall be judged when using concepts from a different culture.
- *The principle of informed responsibility*: No culture is justified in creating a cultural separation of its own area; it is the responsibility of each culture to inform other cultures about its own development and be informed about development of other cultures.
- *The principle of systemic integration*: Whenever needed, knowledge from diverse cultures and disciplines might be synthesized by systemic methods, be they soft or hard, without a prior prejudice against any of them, following the principle of open and informed systemic integration.

It is, however, quite difficult to perform the principle of systemic integration unless we have theories or methods for knowledge construction. We summarize here *the theory of knowledge construction systems*, the main proposal of this paper, which consists of three fundamental parts:

- *A knowledge construction system*: A basic system of the theory called the *i*-System to collect and organize a variety of knowledge, which itself is a systems methodology (Nakamori, 2000, 2003).
- *A structure-agency-action paradigm*: A sociological interpretation of the *i*-System to emphasize the necessary abilities of actors when collecting and organizing knowledge (Nakamori and Zhu, 2004).
- *Evolutionally constructive objectivism*: A new episteme to create knowledge and justify collected, organized, and created knowledge (Wierzbicki and Nakamori, 2007).

The main characteristics of this theory are:

- *Fusion of the purposiveness paradigm and purposefulness paradigm*,
- *Interaction of explicit knowledge and tacit knowledge*, and
- *Requisition for knowledge coordinators*.

With the *i*-System we always start with searching and defining the problem following to the purposiveness paradigm. Since the *i*-System is a spiral-type knowledge construction model, in the second turn we use the *i*-System to find solutions following the purposefulness paradigm. However, it is almost always the case that when we found an approximate solution we face new problems.

This paper accepts the idea of Nonaka and Takeuchi (1995) that new knowledge can be obtained by the interaction between the explicit knowledge and the tacit knowledge. The use of the *i*-System means that we have to inevitably treat the objective knowledge such as scientific theories, available technologies, social-economical trends, etc. as well as the subjective knowledge such as experience, technical skill, hidden assumptions, paradigms, etc.

The theory requires people who accomplish the knowledge synthesis. Such persons need to have the abilities of knowledge workers in a wide-ranging areas and of innovators. However they cannot achieve satisfactory results unless they possess the ability to coordinate the opinions and values of diverse knowledge and people. We should establish an educational system to train human resources who will promote knowledge synthesis in a systemic manner.

3. Knowledge Construction System

A knowledge construction system called the *i*-System was proposed in Nakamori (2000, 2003), which is a systemic and processual approach to knowledge creation. The five ontological elements or subsystems of the *i*-System are *Intervention* (the will to solve problems), *Intelligence* (existing scientific knowledge), *Involvement* (social motivation), *Imagination* (other aspects of creativity), and *Integration* (systemic knowledge), and they might correspond actually to five diverse dimensions of *Creative Space*.

These five ontological elements were originally interpreted as nodes. Because the *i*-System is intended as a synthesis of systemic approaches, *Integration* is, in a sense, its final dimension (in Figure 1 all arrows converge to *Integration* interpreted as a node; links without arrows denote the possibility of impact in both directions). The beginning node is *Intervention*, where problems or issues perceived by the individual or the group motivate their further inquiry and the entire creative process. The node *Intelligence* corresponds to various types of knowledge, the node *Involvement* represents social aspects, and the creative aspects are represented mostly in the node *Imagination*.

Observe that the node *Intelligence*, together with all existing scientific knowledge, corresponds roughly to the basic epistemological dimension (with three levels: *Emotive Knowledge - Intuitive Knowledge - Rational Knowledge*) of *Creative Space*. The node Involvement stresses the social motivation and corresponds roughly to the basic social dimension (with three levels: *Individual - Group - Humanity Heritage*) of *Creative Space*.

When analyzing these dimensions Wierzbicki and Nakamori (2006) have found that binary logic is inadequate and even rough, three-valued logic barely sufficient for a detailed analysis. For example, it is not only necessary to distinguish between the knowledge on the level of individual, group and humanity heritage; it is also important to distinguish motivation related to the interests of individual, group and humanity. While an organization operating in the commercial market rightly stresses the interests of the group of people employed by it (or of its shareholders), educational research activity at universities might be best promoted when stressing the individual interests of students and young researchers; on the other hand, the interests of humanity must be protected when facing the prospect of privatization of basic knowledge.

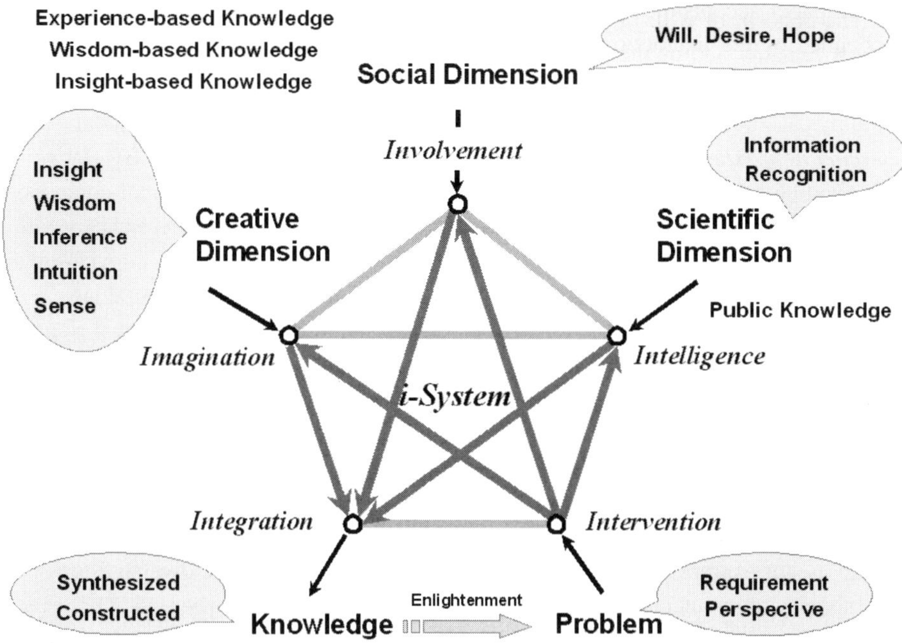

Figure 1: The *i*-System (from a systems scientific viewpoint).

Other nodes presented in Figure 1 indicate the need to consider other dimensions of *Creative Space*, and additional dimensions result in additional complexity. The node *Imagination* seems to be an essential element of only individual intuition; but it could include inter-subjective emotions and intuition. All creative processes can be related to three levels of imagination: *Routine - Diversity - Fantasy*. We utilize imagination in diverse degrees depending on the character of a creative process. The lowest level is *Routine* that involves imagination, but in a standard, well-trained fashion. We are able to use imagination more strongly, to involve an element of *Diversity*, but we must be motivated to do this by professional pride, pure curiosity, monetary rewards, etc. Finally, we have also the highest level of imagination, which might be called *Fantasy*. The 20th Century tradition of not speaking about metaphysics (started by Wittgenstein, 1922) relegated fantasy to the arts and the emotions. However, fantasy is an essential element of any highly creative process, including the construction of technological devices and systems.

The node *Intervention* is difficult to consider separately in Oriental philosophy and culture, with their concepts of unity of mind and body, and unity of man and nature: the will to do something is not considered as a separate phenomenon, it is simply a part of being, and being should be such as not to destroy the unity of man and nature. In a culture seeking consensus and harmony, such an explanation and such principles are sufficient. Western culture pays more attention to the problems related to human intervention and will. The concept of will, of freedom to act and intervene, has been for many centuries and still remains one of the central ideas of Western culture. Concerning any creative activity, it is clear that the role of motivation, of the will to create new ideas, objects of art, technological devices, etc. is a central condition of success. Without *Drive, Determination, Dedication* no creative process will be completed. By *Drive* we understand here the basic fact that creativity is one of the most fundamental components of self-realization of mankind. *Determination* is the concentrated Nietzschean will to overcome obstacles in realizing the creative process. *Dedication* is a conviction that completing a creative process is right in terms of Kantian transcendental moral law.

Integration in the original *i*-System is a node intended to represent the final stage, the systemic synthesis of the creative process. Thus, in this stage we should use all systemic knowledge; applying systemic concepts to newly created knowledge is certainly the only explicit, rational knowledge tool that can be used in order to achieve integration. Thus, any teaching of creative abilities must include a strong component of systems science. The apparently simplest is *Specialized Integration*, when the task consists of integrating several elements of knowledge in some specialized field. But even this task can be very difficult as, for example, the task of integrating knowledge about the diverse functions of contemporary computer networks. It becomes more complex when its character is *Interdisciplinary*, as in the case of the analysis of environmental policy models. However, the contemporary trends of globalization result today in new, even more complex challenges related to *Intercultural Integration*, as in the case of integration of diverse theories of knowledge and technology creation. In fact, the *Intercultural Integration* of knowledge might be considered a defining feature of a new interpretation of systems science.

4. Structure-Agent-Action Paradigm

The structure-agency-action paradigm was adopted when understanding the *i*-System from a social science viewpoint (Nakamori and Zhu, 2004). The *i*-System can be interpreted as a structurationist model for knowledge management. Viewed through the *i*-System, knowledge is constructed by actors, who are constrained and enabled by structures that consist of a *scientific-actual*, a *cognitive-mental* and a *social-relational* front, mobilize and realize the agency of themselves and of others that can be differentiated as *Intelligence, Imagination* and *Involvement* clusters, engage in r*ational-inertial, postrational-projective* and *arational-evaluative* actions in pursuing sectional interests. Note that here we identify the elements *Intelligence, Imagination* and *Involvement* with agencies of actors. See Figure 2.

The following are the working definition of some keywords that are essential to the concerned paradigm. These keywords have quite different but deeply ingrained meanings in other disciplines beyond contemporary social theories.

- *Structure*: the systemic contexts and their underlying mechanisms, which constrain and enable human action.

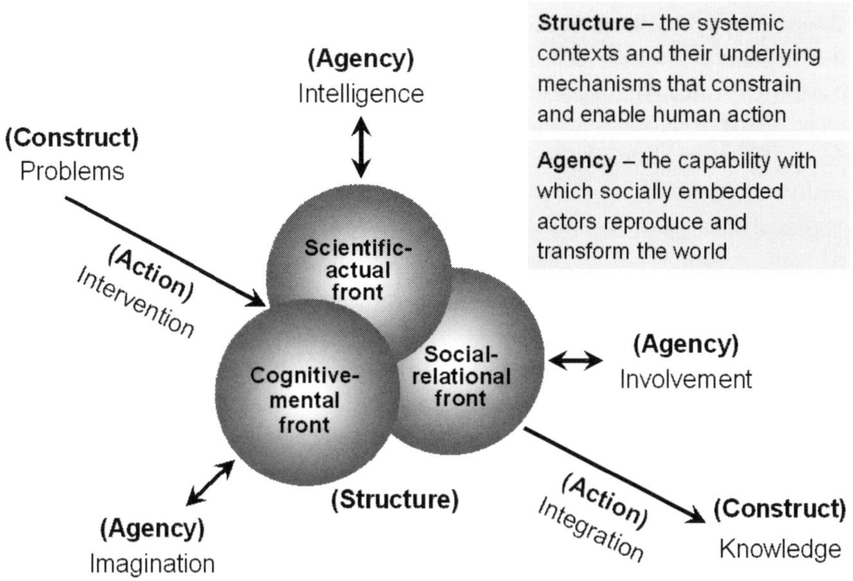

Figure 2: A sociological interpretation of the *i*-System.

- *Agency*: the capability with which actors, who are socially embedded, reproduce and transform the world.
- *Construction*: the social process during which actors create, maintain and transform the world (both the structure and actors themselves).

The exploration in Nakamori and Zhu (2004) intended particularly to unpack the structure, agency and action black boxes, investigate the complexity, ambiguity and emergent properties internal to each of them, as well as those implicated in the relationships between. While structure complexity provides possibilities for innovation, agency complexity allows actors exploit those possibilities in differing ways. Knowing (integrating or in-forming) and practice (intervening) are seen as constituting each other, from which knowledge is emerging and embodied, over time, back into structures and agency.

In this paper we focus on the agency complexity only, which is directly related to the theory of knowledge construction systems. The *i*-System differentiates human agency into *Intelligence, Imagination* and *Involvement* clusters, so that agency can be understood in an organized way, not treated as a black-box.

By *Intelligence* we mean the intellectual faculty and capability of actors: experience, technical skill, functional expertise, etc. The vocabulary related to intelligence addresses logic, rationality, objectivity, observation, monitoring and reflexivity. The accumulation and application of intelligence are mission-led and rational-focused (Chia, 2004), discipline- and paradigm-bound, confined within the boundary of normal science (Kuhn 1962), which leads to knowing the game and incremental, component improvement (Tushman and Anderson, 1986).

Seeing *Intelligence* as inertial and paradigm-bound though, the *i*-System does not regard *Intelligence* as negative per se. Rather, to the *i*-System, *Intelligence* is indispensable for creativity. As Polanyi (1958) puts it, science is operated by the skill of the scientist and it is through the exercise of this skill that he shapes his scientific knowledge. Following Sewell (1992), we see the search for intelligence as a process of transposition: actors apply and extend codified rules and procedures to a wide and not fully predictable range of unfamiliar cases outside the context in which they are initially learned. *Intelligence* becomes liability to innovation only when it blocks actors from seeing alternatives.

In the *Imagination* cluster we include intuition, innocence, ignorance, enlightenmental skill and post-rationality, which leads to a vocabulary of feeling the game, playful, fun, chaotic, illogic, forgetting, upsetting, competency-destroying, knowledge-obsoleting and risk-taking. This brings us beyond the thoroughly-knowledgeable (Archer, 1995) and over-rationalized agents (Mestrovic, 1998) that are portrayed in Giddens's structuration theory (Giddens, 1979).

Involvement is the cluster in human agency that consists of interest, faith, emotion and passion, which are intrinsically related to intentionality and habits of the heart (Bellah et al., 1985), as well as the social capital (Bourdieu, 1985), social skill and political skill (Garud et al., 2002) that make intentionality and the heart being felt. As human agency, involvement can produce managerial and institutional effects, particularly in dealing with the social-relational front, in that it helps or hampers researchers' efforts to make the game.

Note that even if the actors work well using their agencies, this does not guarantee the validity of the obtained knowledge. We need a theory for knowledge justification, which will be given later by the name of *Evolutionary Constructive Objectivis*m.

5. Evolutionary Constructive Objectivism

There is a general agreement that we are living in times of an informational revolution which leads to a new era. Knowledge in this era plays an even more important role than just information, thus the new epoch might be called Knowledge Civilization Era. Among many changes, the most important one might be the changing episteme - the way of constructing and justifying knowledge, characteristic for a given era and culture (Foucault, 1972).

The destruction of the industrial episteme and the construction of a new one started with relativism of Einstein, indeterminism of Heisenberg, with the concept of feedback and that of deterministic chaos, of order emerging out of chaos, complexity theories, finally with the emergence principle. The destruction of the industrial era episteme resulted in divergent developments of the episteme of three cultural spheres: hard and natural sciences, technology, and social sciences with humanities:

- *Paradigmatism* in hard and natural sciences (Kuhn, 1962) : Theories should fit to observations or outcomes of empirical tests, but such theories that are consistent with the paradigm are welcome, while theories that contradict the paradigm are rejected, even if they would better fit observations or empirical outcomes.

- *Falsificationism* in technology (Popper, 1934, 1972): Knowledge and theories evolve and the measure of their evolutionary fitness is the number of attempted falsification tests they have successfully passed.
- *Postmodern subjectivism* in social sciences and humanities: Knowledge is constructed by people, thus subjective, and its justification occurs only through inter-subjective discourse.

The episteme of knowledge civilization era is not formed yet, but it must include an integration, a synthesis of the divergent episteme of these three cultural spheres, as well as a synthesis of different aspects of Oriental and Western episteme. The integration must be based upon a holistic understanding of human nature; here humanity is defined not only by language and communicating, but also by tool making, and by curiosity.

This paper considers *Evolutionary Constructive Objectivism* as a possible episteme in the knowledge-based society, and adopts it as one of the elements of the theory of knowledge construction systems. It is originally considered for testing knowledge creation theories (Wierzbicki and Nakamori, 2007), consisting of three principles:

- *Evolutionary falsification principle*: Hypotheses, theories, models and tools develop evolutionarily, and the measure of their evolutionary fitness is the number of either attempted falsification tests that they have successfully passed, or of critical discussion tests leading to an inter-subjective agreement about their validity, which corresponds to the group tacit knowledge in Nonaka theory.
- *Emergence principle*: New properties of a system emerge with increased levels of complexity, and these properties are qualitatively different than and irreducible to the properties of its parts.
- *Multimedia principle*: Language is just an approximate code to describe a much more complex reality, visual and preverbal information in general is much more powerful and relates to intuitive knowledge and reasoning; the future records of the intellectual heritage of humanity will have a multi-media character, thus stimulating creativity.

Although these principles were developed with the purpose of validating knowledge creation models such as the *i*-System, this paper reuses them as principles to test the obtained knowledge. Because it usually takes time to evaluate new knowledge, the idea here is to evaluate the models, methods or processes through which the new knowledge emerges. See Figure 3.

Based on these three fundamental principles, we can give a detailed description of an epistemological position of constructive evolutionary objectivism, closer in fact to the current episteme of technology than to that of hard sciences.

- The innate curiosity of people about other people and Nature results in their constructing hypotheses about reality, thus creating a structure and diverse models of the world. Until now, all such hypotheses turned out to be only approximations; but we learn evolutionarily about their validity by following the *falsification principle*.
- Since we perceive reality as more and more complex, and thus devise concepts on higher and higher levels of complexity according to the *emergence principle*, we shall probably always work with approximate hypotheses.

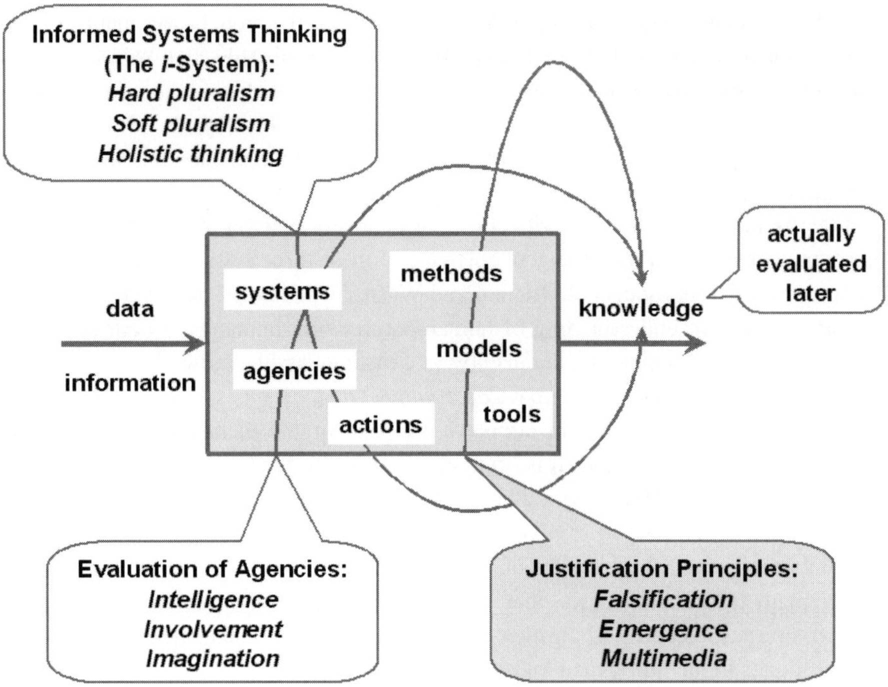

Figure 3: Justification of knowledge through evaluation of tools to get it.

- According to the *multimedia principle*, language is a simplified code used to describe a much more complex reality, while human senses (starting with vision) enable people to perceive the more complex aspects of reality. This more comprehensive perception of reality is the basis of human intuition; for example, tool making is always based on intuition and a more comprehensive perception of reality than just language.
- A prescriptive interpretation of objectivity is the *falsification principle*; when faced cognitively with increasing complexity, we apply the *emergence principle*. The sources of our cognitive power are related to the *multimedia principle*.

Figure 3 shows the concept of justification of knowledge through evaluation of models, tools, etc. to get that knowledge as well as through evaluation of attitudes and agencies of actors or analysts in collecting that knowledge.

6. Concluding Remarks

This paper proposes a theory of knowledge construction systems, which consists of three fundamental parts: the knowledge construction system, the structure-agency-action paradigm, and evolutionally constructive objectivism. The first is a model of collecting and synthesizing knowledge, the second relates to necessary abilities when collecting knowledge in individual domains, and the third comprises a set of principles to justify collected and synthesized knowledge. This paper reached a conclusion that we should nurture talented people called the knowledge coordinators. How can we nurture such people? One of the answers is that we should establish knowledge science, educate young students by this discipline, and encourage learning by doing.

However, at the present stage, knowledge science is more a theme-oriented interdisciplinary academic field than a normal science. We believe that its mission is to organize and process human-dependent information and to feed it back to society with added value. Its central guideline is the creation of new value (knowledge) - such innovation being the driving force of society, but it mainly deals with the research area involving social innovation (organizations, systems, or reorganization of the mind). However, society's progress is underpinned by technology and the joint progress of society (needs) and technology (seeds) is essential, so it also bears the duty to act as a coordinator (intermediary) in extensive technological and social innovations.

In order to fulfill the above mission, knowledge science should focus its research on observing and modeling the actual process of carrying out the mission as well as developing methods to carry out the mission. The methods can be developed mainly through the existing three fields. These are the application of information technology/artistic methods (knowledge discovery methods, ways to support creation, knowledge engineering, cognitive science, etc.), the application of business science/organizational theories (practical uses of tacit knowledge, management of technology, innovation theory, etc.) and the application of mathematical science/systems theory (systems thinking, the emergence principle, epistemology, etc.).

However, it will take some time to integrate the above three fields and establish a new academic system. We should first attempt their integration in practical use (problem-solving projects), accumulate actual results and then to establish them as a discipline in a new field. Finally we believe that the concepts and directions of knowledge science will collapse the wall between hard and soft in systems science.

References

Archer, M.S. (1995) *Realist Social Theory: The Morphogenetic Approach,* University of Cambridge Press: Cambridge.

Bellah, R.N., Madsen, R., Sullivan, M.M., Swidler, A. and Tipton, S.M. eds. (1985) *Habits of the Heard*, University of California Press: Berkeley.

Boulding, K. (1956) "General systems theory: The skeleton of science", M*anagement Science*, 2: 197-208.

Bourdieu, P. (1985) "The forms of capital", *In Handbook of Theory and Research for the Sociology of Education*, 241-258, Richardson JG. (ed.), Greenwood: New York.

Chia, R. (2004) "Strategy-as-practice: Reflections on the research agenda", *European Management Review*, 1: 29-34.

Churchman, C.W. (1970) "Operations research as a profession", *Management Science*, 17: 37-53.

Comte, A. (1844) *A General View of Positivism*, Translation in 1865, London.

Flood, R.L. and Jackson, M.C. (1991) *Creative Problem Solving: Total Systems Intervention*, John Wiley & Sons: New York.

Foucault, M. (1972) *The Order of Things: an Archeology of Human Sciences*, Routledge: New York.

Garud, R., Jain, S. and Kumaraswamy, A. (2002) "Institutional entrepreneurship in the sponsorship of common technological standards: The case of Sun Microsystems and Java", *Academy of Management Review*, 45(1): 196-214.

Giddens, A. (1979) *Central Problems in Social Theory: Action, Structure and Contradiction in Social Analysis*, Macmilian: London.

Gu, J.F. and Tang, X.J. (2005) "Meta-synthesis approach to complex system modeling", *European Journal of Operational Research*, 166(3): 597-614.

Jackson, M.C. (2003) *Systems Thinking: Creative Holism for Managers*, John Wiley & Sons: Chichester.

Jackson, M.C. and Keys, P. (1984) "Towards a system of systems methodologies", *Journal of the Operational Research Society*, 35: 473-486.

Kuhn, T.S. (1962) *The Structure of Scientific Revolutions*, (2nd ed. 1970) Chicago University Press: Chicago.

Linstone, H.A. (1984) *Multiple Perspectives for Decision Making*, North-Holland.

Mestrovic, S.G. (1998) *Anthony Giddens: The Last Modernist*, Routledge: London.

Midgley, G. (2000) *Systems Intervention: Philosophy, Methodology and Practice*, Kluwer/Plenum: New York.

Mulej, M. (2007) "Systems theory - a world view and/or a methodology aimed at requisite holism/realism of human's thinking, decisions and action", *Systems Research and Behavioral Science*, 24(3): 347-357.

Nakamori, Y. (2000) "Knowledge management system toward sustainable society", In *Proc. of the 1st International Symposium on Knowledge and System Sciences*, 57-64, September 25-27, Ishikawa, Japan.

Nakamori, Y. (2003) "Systems methodology and mathematical models for knowledge management", *Journal of Systems Science and Systems Engineering*, 12(1): 49-72.

Nakamori, Y. and Zhu, Z.C. (2004) "Exploring a sociologist understanding for the *i*-System", *International Journal of Knowledge and Systems Sciences*, 1(1): 1-8

Nonaka, I. and Takeuchi, H. (1995) *The Knowledge-Creating Company: How Japanese Companies Create the Dynamics of Innovation*, Oxford University Press: New York.

Nonaka, I. and Konno, N. (1998) "The concept of Ba: Building a foundation for knowledge creation", *California Management Review*, 40(3): 40-54.

Polanyi, M. (1958) *Personal Knowledge: Towards a Post-Critical Philosophy*, Routledge & Kegan Paul: London.

Popper, K.R. (1934) *Logik der Forschung*, Julius Springer Verlag: Vienna.

Popper, K.R. (1972) *Objective Knowledge*, Oxford University Press: Oxford.

Sewell, W.H.Jr. (1992) "A theory of structure: Duality, agency, and transformation", *American Journal of Sociology*, 98(1): 1-29.

Tushman, M.L. and Anderson, P. (1986) "Technological discontinuities and organizational environments", *Administrative Science Quarterly*, 31: 439-465.

Wierzbicki, A.P. and Nakamori, Y. (2006) *Creative Space: Models of Creative Processes for the Knowledge Civilization Age*, Springer-Verlag: Berlin-Hidelberg.

Wierzbicki, A.P. and Nakamori, Y. (2007) "Testing knowledge creation theories", Presented at *IFIP-TC7 Conference*, Cracow, Poland, July 23-27, 2007.

Wierzbicki, A.P., Zhu, Z.C. and Nakamori, Y. (2006) "A new role of systems science: informed systems approach", In *Creative Space: Models of Creative Processes for the Knowledge Civilization Age,* Wierzbicki AP., Nakamori Y. (eds.), Chapter 6, 161-215, Springer-Verlag: Berlin-Heidelberg.

Wittgenstein, L. (1922) *Tractatus Logico-Philosophicus*, Cambridge.

Zhu, Z.C. (2000) "Dealing with a differentiated whole: The philosophy of the WSR approach", *Systemic Practice and Action Research*, 13(1): 21-57.

STUDY ON THE METHODS OF IDENTIFICATION AND JUDGEMENT FOR OPINION LEADERS IN PUBLIC OPINION

LIU YIJUN*

Institute of Policy and Management, Chinese Academy of Sciences, Beijing 100190, China

Center for Interdisciplinary Studies of Natural and Social Sciences, Chinese Academy of Science, Beijing 100190, China

E-mail: yijunliu@casipm.ac.cn

TANG XIJIN GU JIFA

Academy of Mathematics and Systems Science, Chinese Academy of Sciences, Beijing 100190, China

Center for Interdisciplinary Studies of Natural and Social Sciences, Chinese Academy of Science, Beijing 100190, China

E-mail: jfgu@amss.ac.cn

During the process of opinion evolution, the individuals look for emotional support and depend on opinion leaders complying with "psychological balance" principle and "Emotional resonance" principle. That is the root cause of generation of opinion leaders. This paper adopts meta-synthetic approach (MSA) and social network analysis (SNA) to identify and judge the opinion leaders and master their behaviors and traces for further exploring the nature of opinion and then effectively controlling and guiding opinion.

1. Introduction

Opinion leaders refer to the individuals who can informally influence other people's attitudes or change their behaviors. The mass media often influence audience and then change their attitudes and behaviors through interpersonal relations. Opinion is basically transmitted from the mass media to opinion leaders, and in turn to people who the leaders want to influence, which is well-known as secondary communication theory (Chen, 1999). Opinion leaders can be treated as audience and also leaders to influence audience. The special position of opinion leaders during opinion evolution process builds their enormous force.

The main effects of opinion leaders include analysis of social problems by critical thinking mode, integration of different public awareness and the dispersive views and awaking people's consciousness. This evaluation not only pointed out the direction of ethos but also judged the different views to overcome some misconception of the public. Once the public summarized their views, they will be infected by faith and passion and become followers of a certain opinion (Liu, 2002). Therefore, opinion leader is always viewed as announcer, persuader and prover.

---

* Work partially supported by Institute of Policy and Management(CAS) Science Foundation for Youths on 2009.

In general, opinion leaders have the following characteristics, belonging to the same group as general members with many same attributes even the leaders owned the special status because of their knowledge and capacity, keeping in more touch with various sources of information and outside environment than other audiences and acting as sources of information and leading role of other members in a certain area.

Due to the "psychological balance" and "Emotional resonance" principles (Liu and Gu, 2008; Liu, Niu and Gu, 2009) in the social behavior entropy theory (Niu, 2001), the public continually look for the emotional support and depend on opinion leaders. That is the root cause of generation of opinion leaders.

Hegselmann etc al. (2002) figured out that opinion can be formed in a group as small as a few experts or as large as in the whole society. Based on this viewpoint, Section II of this paper will use meta-synthetic approach (MSA) and expert mining (EM) to identify and judge "expert leaders" during the process of experts argumentation. In section III, social network analysis (SNA) will be involved to find out the "opinion leaders" during the opinion formation and evolution over network. Conclusion and the future works will be proposed in Section IV.

2. Identify Opinion Leaders based on MSA

Social public opinion is a complex system. Identifying the opinion leaders emerged in the individuals mass behaviors during the evolution of public opinion is further a complex systems engineering. So this paper adopts meta-synthetic approach as a directional and advanced way to guide the identification of opinion leaders.

2.1. *Meta-synthetic Approach and Expert Mining*

MSA, proposed by a Chinese system scientist Qian Xuesen (Tsien HsueShen), is one of the system methodologies to tackle with open complex giant system (OCGS) problems from the view of systems in the early 1990s (Qian, Yu and Dai, 1990). Here, we regarded OCGS problems such as social public opinion as ill-structured or wicked problems. This approach expects to unite organically the expert group, data, all sorts of information, the computer technology, and even scientific theory of various disciplines and human experience and knowledge for proposing hypothesis and quantitative validating. Later it is evolved into Hall of Workshop for Meta-Synthetic Engineering (HWMSE) which emphasizes to make full use of breaking advances in information technologies (Gu and Tang, 2003; Gu and Tang, 2005).

Expert mining (EM), as a new mining method, is put forward based on the meta-synthetic approach (Gu, 2006; Gu, Song and Zhu, 2008). This method emphasizes expert experience, ideas and wisdom mining. It is not built on the basis of mass data but in a smaller group of samples based on the thinking of experts to conduct in-depth experience in mining. This method is also different from those based on artificial intelligence-based expert system because it focuses more on people - machine, human-oriented to people's wisdom and the wisdom of the main groups. Mining expert system methodology, which combines science, scientific thinking and knowledge of scientific theories and makes full use of modern computer technology, is the development of the former theory and technology.

This section tries to identify and judge expert leaders by expert leader judgment module with guidance of MSA and EM.

2.2. *Hall for Workshop of Expert Argumentation and Expert Leader Judgement Module*

Based on MSA, expert mining method and knowledge creation model, the Hall for Workshop of Expert Argumentation is to provide a distributed computer platform. On which, participants bring out new ideas and knowledge through communication and collaboration (Tang and Liu, 2004; Liu and Tang, 2005). The Hall integrates proposals and views from experts to build solution and compute quantitatively degree of centralization and consensus.

Aiming to the discussion topic, the Hall for Workshop of Expert Argumentation expresses the registered ID (shown in rectangular box) and keywords (shown in ellipse box) as a visualized two-dimensional map, as shown in Figure 1, The experts owning high degree of concerns will be centralized. This provides a new way to share knowledge and solve unstructured problems.

Discussion space is a joint thinking space for the participants. Via the 2-dimensional space, thc idea association process to stimulate participants' thinking, idea generation, tacit knowledge surfacing and even wisdom emergence is exhibited based on the utterances and keywords from participants. The global structure and relationships between participants and their utterances are shared by all participants in the session. It helps the user acquire a general impression about each participant' s contributions toward the discussing topic, and understand the relationships of each thinking structure about the topic between participants.

The expert leader judgement module of the Hall for Workshop of Expert Argumentation constructs the consistent matrix based on the sameness and difference of keywords from all participants. The largest eigenvector will be computed to achieve sort of speaker. The sort can also be used to exhibit contribution of each participant (Tang and Liu, 2004). The matrix A can be expressed as,

$$a_{ii} = |U_i| \quad \text{and} \quad a_{ij} = |U_i \cap U_j|, i \neq j. \tag{1}$$

Where, U_i represents the set of keywords from no. i participant.

After discussion, participants will be evaluated to help analyze quantitatively discussion result and try to find out key speaker based on effects on group from each participant. Those key speakers are "opinion leader".

2.3. *Example Analysis*

The Xiangshan Science Conference (XSSC, www.xssc.ac.cn), which is initiated in 1993 in similar to Gordon Research Conferences and denotes as the general designation of a series of small-scale academic meetings which bring together a group of scientists working at the frontier of research of a particular area and enable them to discuss in depth all aspects of the most recent advances in the field and to stimulate new directions for research, is a top-level science forum for interdisciplinary and cutting-edge studies and can be viewed as a platform for knowledge sharing and creation in China. Next we apply our tool to analyze Xiangshan Science Conference.

Figure 1 shows the process and result map of analyzing "the brain, consciousness and intelligence" topic with experts meeting system (Liu and Tang, 2005). Detail of design and development of the system will not be explained here. Figure 1(b) is different from Figure 1 because one new expert ("Pan") is added into the discussion. But the two maps own the same character that the expert "Wang Yunjiu" locates at the center of the discussion. That indicates that he actively involved in the "brain" research and relative meeting. This result can be verified by the record in text mode from Xiangshan Conference.

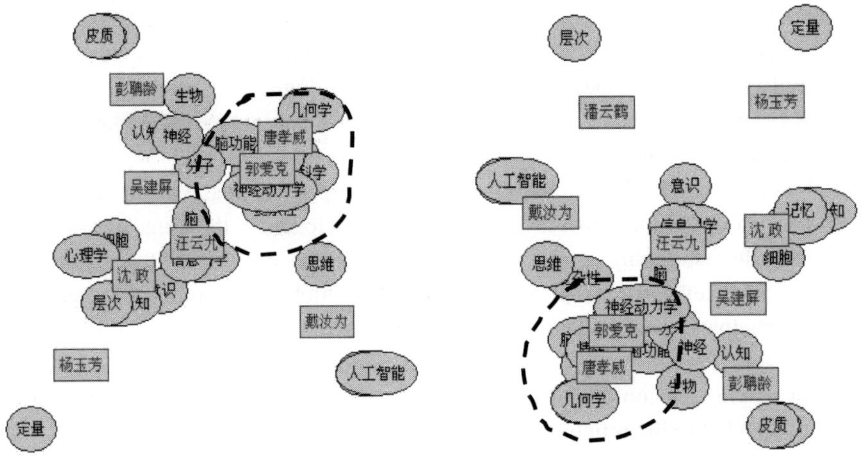

Figure 1(a)

Figure 1(b)

Figure 1. Two-dimensional Distribution of Participants and Keywords

Table 1 lists the evaluation of participation based on agreement and discrepancy matrixes. It is shown that user 郭爱克 holds highest rank based on both eigenvectors, which may be justified by his active role as one of chairpersons or plenary speech contributors among those conferences, which furthermore exposes his big influence in neuroscience field in China.

Table 1. Evaluction of 9 Participantions.

Maximum eigenvector of agreement matrix:	(0.3761, 1.0914, 0.3082, 0.6179, 0.2522, 0.3618, 0.3125, 0.1937, 0.1092)
Rank of the top five participants:	郭爱克 > 汪云九 > 唐孝威 > 彭聃龄 > 戴汝为

Due to less staff and simple content, Prof. Guo can not be defined as “opinion leader”. Instead, “leader expert” is better. However, such a new idea builds an important basis for research of identifying “opinion leader”.

The social network analysis proposed in the following section of this article can be used to identify “opinion leaders" from a large scale of participants.

3. Detect Opinion Leader based on SNA

3.1. *SNA*

Social network analysis (SNA), as a new paradigm for sociological research (Liu, 2004; Luo, 2005), is proposed in 1930s and enhanced in 1970s. This article intends to detect the “opinion leaders” by this method. In fact, the opinion leaders are those special individuals who appear during the formation of opinion from microcosmic individual actions to macroscopical group behavior.

“Social network” refers to the social actors and the collection of the relationship between different actors. That is, a social network is a collection of a number of points (social actors) and the connection between the points (the relationship between actors). “Social network” emphasizes that each actor has a certain extent relationship with other actors. Social network analysis build models for these relationships, try to describe the structure of relations between group members and study the effect on group and individual from this structure.

Social network analysis can be used to identify quantitatively the “opinion leaders” because this approach has exactly described the relationship between the subjects of opinion in a very good way. In which, the social network position refers to a series of individual actors who have the similar characters in social activities, relationship and interaction located in the same relationship network, network factor refers to combination of relations to link the social positions and mode of the relation between the actors or positions.

Some other concepts such as point, edge, degree, betweenness, cutpoint, component, subgroup and centralization and so on are involved in SNA. During the formation and evolution of opinion, this article particularly concerns the "cutpoint".

3.2. *Cutpoint*

In graph theory, the only one point connecting two sub-graphs is called as cutpoint. The cutpoint is very important because its absence will divide network into independent segments named after block. Such a point is important to not only network but also the other point That is, cutpoint plays the "opinion leaders" role among the subjects of opinion.

3.3. *Example Analysis*

A series of serious terrorist attacks occurred in the in the eastern part of United States at September 11, 2001. With this incident, World Trade Center in New York, the Pentagon where U.S. Department of Defense locates in Washington and some other important buildings had been attacked and heavy casualties were caused. By the later survey, this is an organized and purposeful terrorist activity against the interests of the people, the U.S. security and even world peace. After that, not only the United States governments but also experts around the world analyze this incident in-depth for getting more meaningful and valuable information and forecasting such terrorism. Figure 2 (http://www.orgnet.com/tnet.html) shows the social network analysis of key man of 9 • 11 terrorist events.

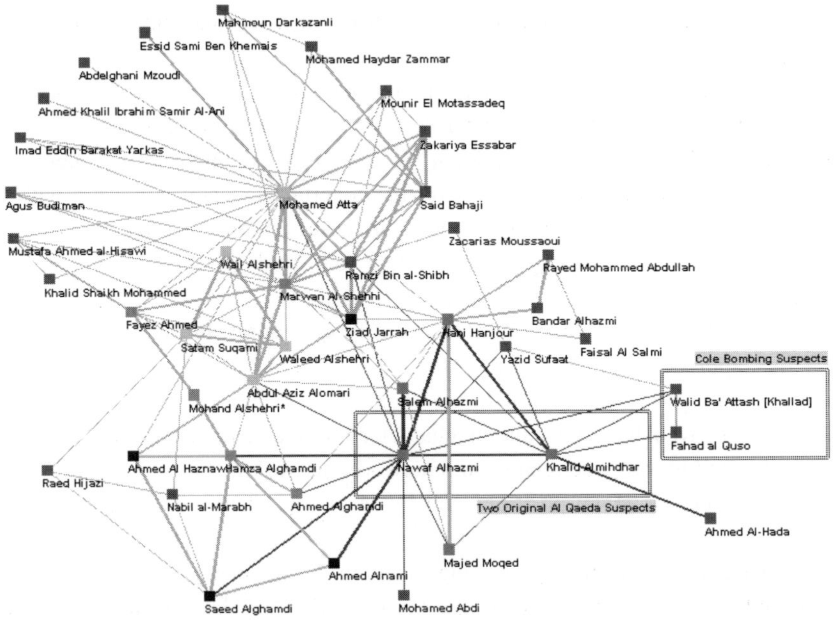

Figure 2. Social network analysis of participants of 9 • 11 terrorist events

This case is involved here to indicate that social network analysis is a good method and technique to identify the “key persons”. Analogously, opinion leader can be easily identified in a war of opinion through the "cut point" algorithm if the network topology of opinion subjects had been built out.

Nie et al (2005) have analyzed the relationship between scientific collaborators (385 articles and 192 authors produced from different NSFC major research) through social network analysis and found out the "expert leaders" of the network of scientific cooperation with cut-point algorithm.

4. Conclusions

Due to the "psychological balance" and "Emotional resonance" principles, the public continually look for the emotional support and depend on opinion leaders. That is the root cause of generation of opinion leaders. In this paper, MSA and SNA are involved to identify the opinion leaders and master their behaviors and traces for further exploring the nature of opinion and then effectively controlling and guiding opinion.

Opinion leaders play the key roles in the process of guiding opinion. Trend of opinion would be obviously affected through intervening and controlling opinion leaders. In future, intervening of opinion leaders during formation and evolution of opinion by soft control theory will be studied in-depth.

References

Chen, L. D. (1999) "Public Opinion", *Beijing: China radio and television press.* (in Chinese)

Gu, J. F. (2006) "Expert mining for discussing the social complex problems", *MCS2006*, Beijing, September 22.

Gu, J. F., Song, W. Q., Zhu, Z. X. (2008) "Expert Mining and TCM knowledge", *KSS 2008*, Guangzhou, December11-13.

Gu, J. F., Tang X. J. (2005) "Meta-synthesis approach to Complex System Modeling", *European Journal of Operational Research*, 166(33): 597-614.

Gu, J. F., Tang,X. J. (2003) "Some Developments in the Studies of Meta-Synthesis System Approach", *Journal of Systems Science and Systems Engineering*, 12(2): 171-189.

Hegselmann, R., Krause, U. (2002) "Opinion Dynamics and Bounded Confidence Models, Analysis, and Simulation", *Journal of Artifical Societies and Social Simulation*, 5(3):1-33.

http://www.orgnet.com/tnet.html

http://www.xssc.ac.cn.

Liu, J. (2004) "An Introduction to Social Network Analysis", *Beijing: Social Sciences Academic Press.*

Liu, J. M. (2002) "Principles of public opinion", *Beijing: Huaxia Publishing Co., Ltd* (in Chinese)

Liu, Y. J., Gu, J. F. (2008) "Systems Analysis and Modeling of Opinion Infection", *IEEE International Conference on Systems, Man and Cybernetics*: 484-488.

Liu, Y. J., Niu, W. Y., Gu, J. F. (2009) "Study on Public Opinion Based on Social Physics", *Proceedings of the 20th International Conference on Multiple Criteria Decision Making* : 318-324.

Liu, Y. J., Tang, X. J. (2005) "A Preliminary Analysis of Xiangshan Science Conference as Transdisciplinary Argumentation", *New Development of Management Science and Systematic Science* : 35-40.

Liu, Y. J., Tang, X. J. (2005) "The Introduction of Some Mental Models and Tools for Creativity Support", *Systems Engineering –Theory & Practice*, 5(2): 56-61.

Luo, J. D. (2005) "Social Network Analysis", *Beijing: Social Sciences Academic Press.*

Nie, K., Tang, X. J., Gu, J. F. (2005) "An Analysis of a Practical .Scientific Collaboration Network", *New Development of Management Science and Systematic Science*: 261-267.

Niu, W.Y. (2001) "Social physics: significance of the discipline's value and its application", *Science, forum*. 54(3): 32-35. (in Chinese)

Qian, X. S., Yu, J. Y., Dai, R. W. (1993) "A new Discipline of Science - the Study of Open Complex Giant Systems and its Methodology", *Chinese Journal of Systems Engineering & Electronics*, 4(2): 2-12.

Tang, X. J., Liu, Y. J. (2004) "Computerized Support for Idea Generation During Knowledge Creating Process", *Proceedings of Second International Conference on KEST*, Tsinghua University Press: 81-88.

Tang, X.J., Liu, Y.J. (2004) "Exploring Computerized Support for Group Argumentation for Idea Generation", *Proceedings of* 5th *Knowledge and System Sciences*: 296-302.